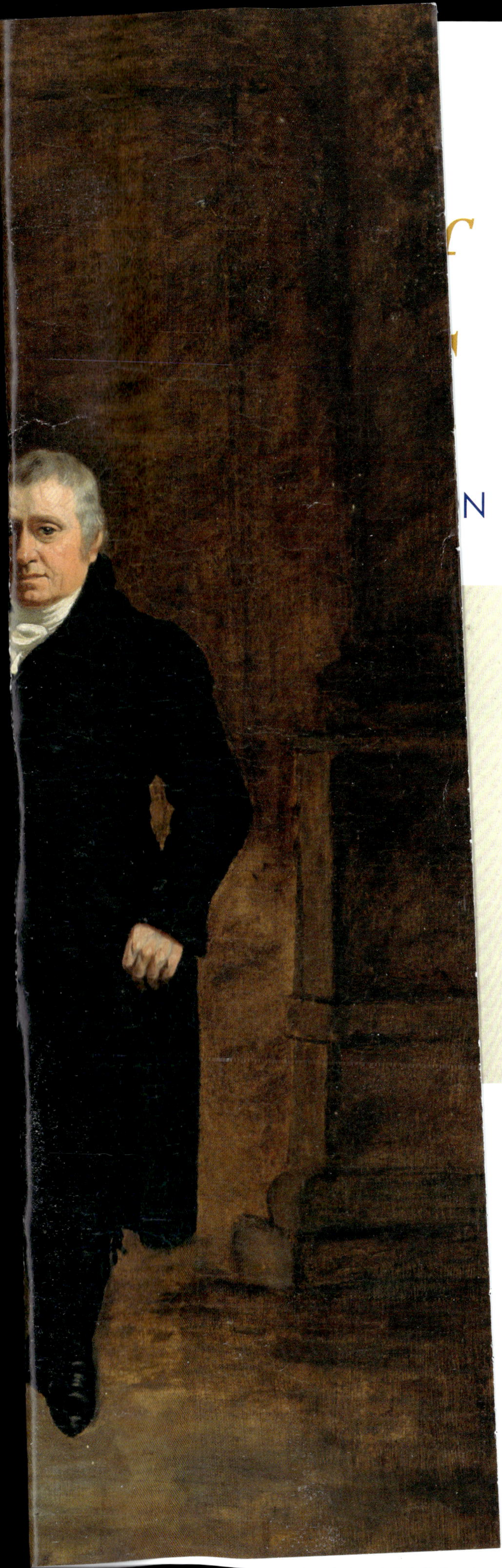

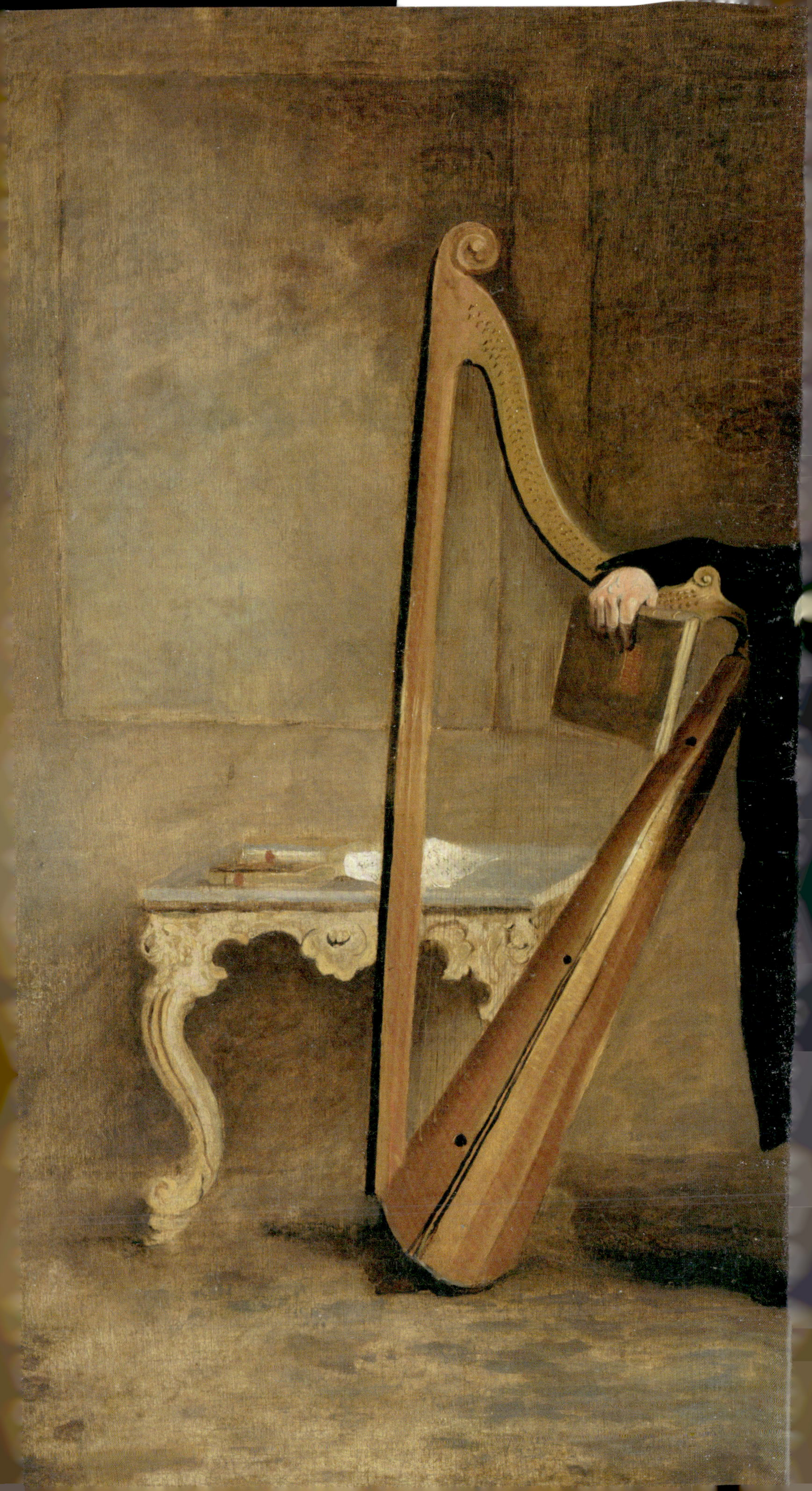

The ART of MUSIC

BRANDING the WELSH NATION

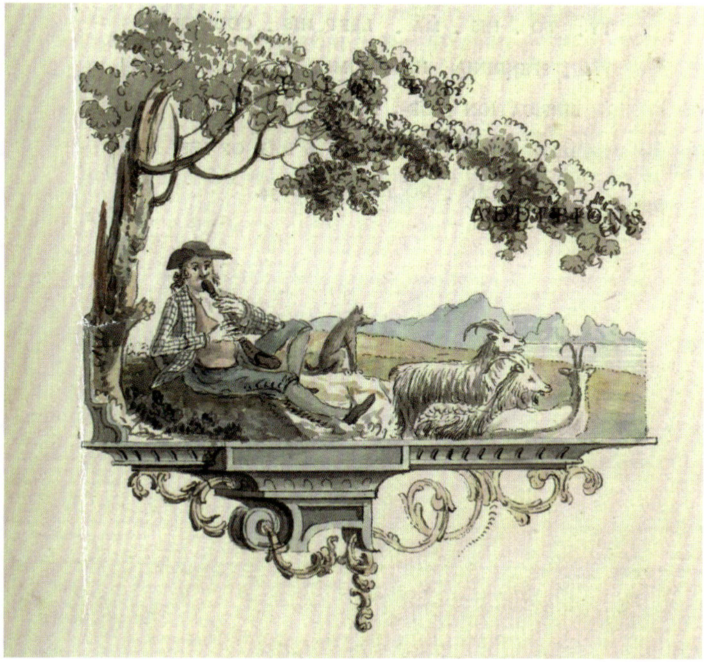

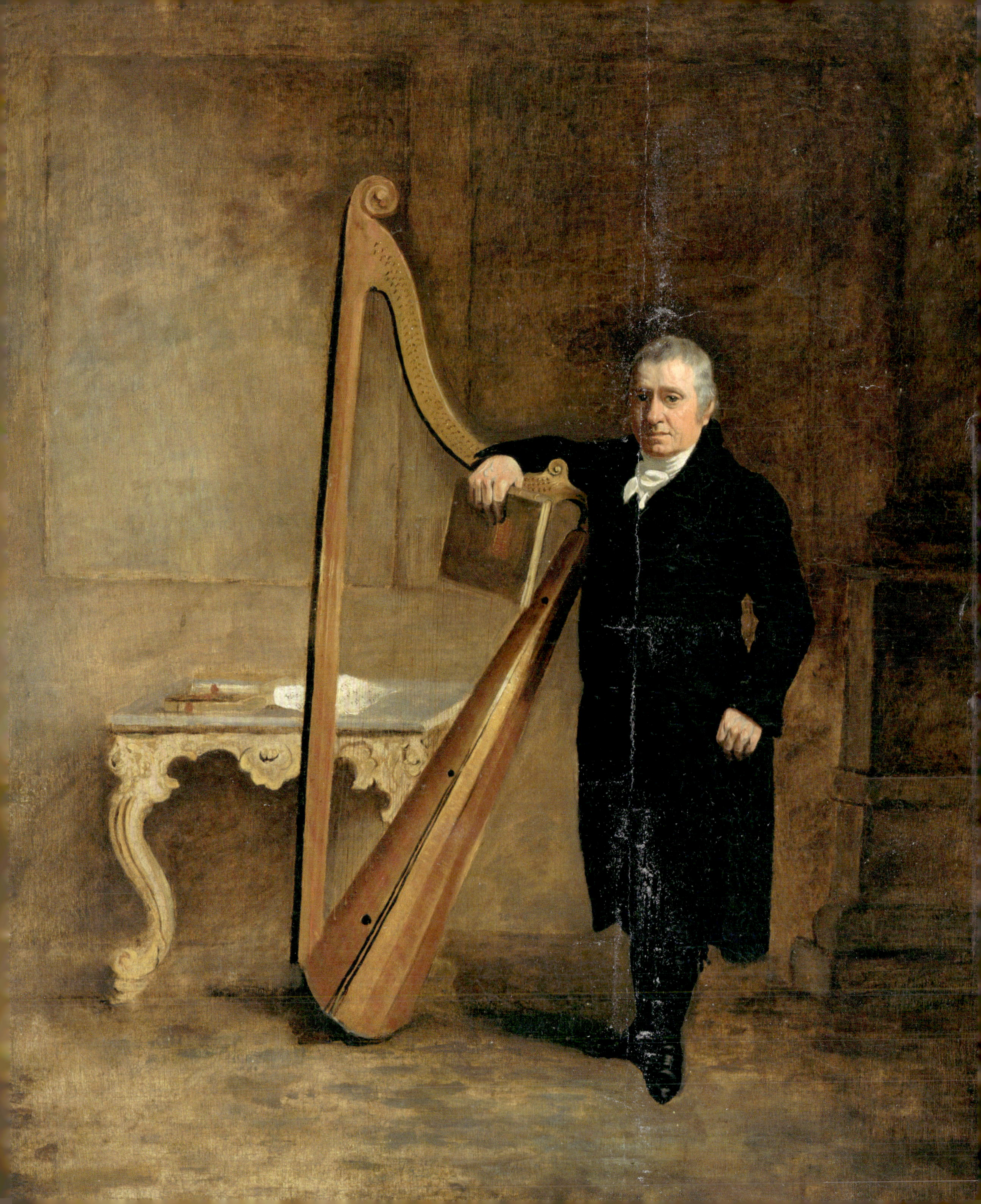

The ART of MUSIC

BRANDING the WELSH NATION

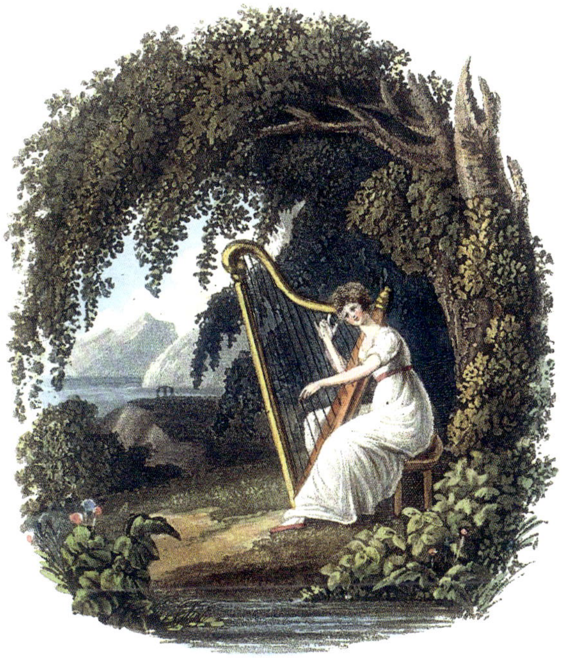

PETER LORD and RHIAN DAVIES

PARTHIAN

PARTHIAN

Parthian
The Old Surgery
Cardigan SA43 1ED
www.parthianbooks.com

The Art of Music is published with the support of:
The Honourable Society of Cymmrodorion
The Marc Fitch Fund
The Books Council of Wales
The National Library of Wales
The National Museum of Wales
The Rhys Davies Trust
The Estate of the late John D. Pickles

First published in 2022

ISBN: 978-1-914595-25-7

Index: Ceridwen Lloyd-Morgan
Design: Isobel Gillan
www.isobelgillanbookdesign.co.uk

Printed and bound by Gomer Press, Llandysul SA44 4JL

A cataloguing record for this book is available from the British Library.

MARC FITCH FUND

THE HONOURABLE SOCIETY OF CYMMRODORION

CYNGOR LLYFRAU CYMRU
BOOKS COUNCIL of WALES

LLGC NLW LLYFRGELL GENEDLAETHOL CYMRU
THE NATIONAL LIBRARY OF WALES

AMGUEDDFA CYMRU

THE RHYS DAVIES TRUST

FRONTISPIECE: Moses Griffith, *Playing the Pibgorn*, c.1778-81

RIGHT: John Downman, *Edward Randles and His Daughter Elizabeth*, 1807

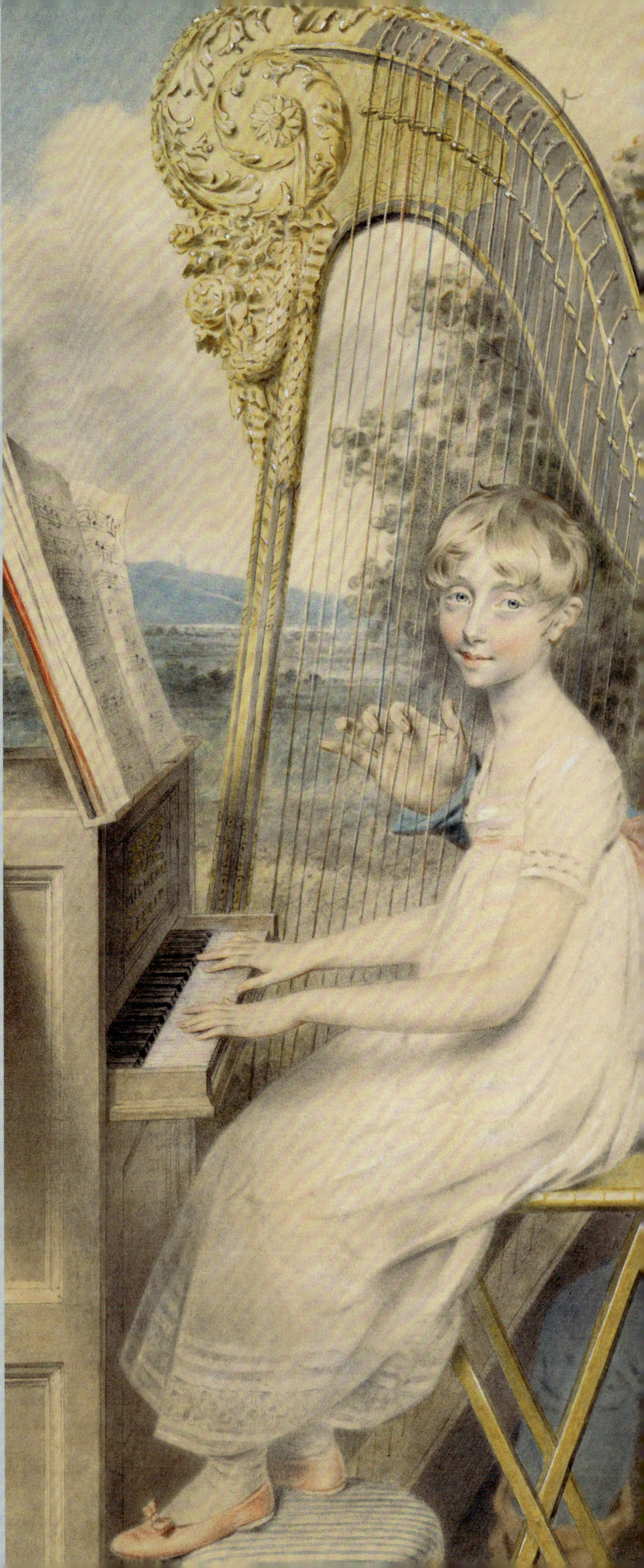

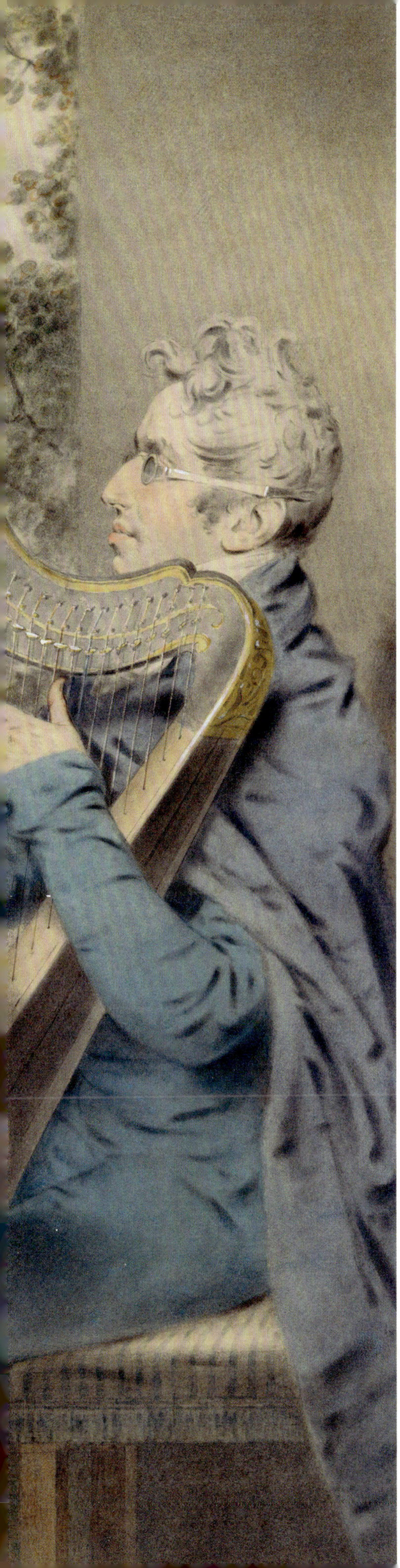

Contents

Preface

The origins of this book lie in our dissatisfaction with the constraints imposed on the understanding of cultural history by a tendency to confine commentary within traditionally defined areas of artistic practice. Musicians, visual artists and creative writers have never lived in isolation from one another, yet much academic research and writing is undertaken within frameworks that fail to explore the interactions between them.

These interactions have sometimes taken place at a personal level between contemporaries, and at other times through the influence of compositions and artworks on interdisciplinary practice. As the narrative reveals, several significant individuals have been active across both disciplines. The exploration of all these interactions has resulted in fresh insights into the development of Welsh music and Welsh visual art.

Wider perception of the nature of cultural evolution, especially when expressed within national frameworks, reflects the inclination to isolate areas of artistic practice. Wales presents an extreme example, having become strongly identified with music – and especially choral music – while at the same time marginalising the influence of visual culture. As a corrective, the book traces the history of the identification of Wales as the 'Land of Song', examining the role of pictures in the evolution of the trope and considering the imaging of musicians, their practice, and their institutions.

Crucially also, the book considers the construction of symbols – notably the Bard and the national costume – as archetypes and stereotypes that link visual and aural perception. The exploitation of the resultant branding for wider political and societal ends has had a profound influence on the state of the nation, certainly from the eighteenth century until our own time.

The authors wish to acknowledge the intellectual and practical support of the many colleagues who have made this publication possible. Significant financial assistance from the Honourable Society of Cymmrodorion, the Marc Fitch Fund and the Books Council of Wales, together with a donation from the Estate of the late John D. Pickles, have all enabled Parthian Books to proceed.

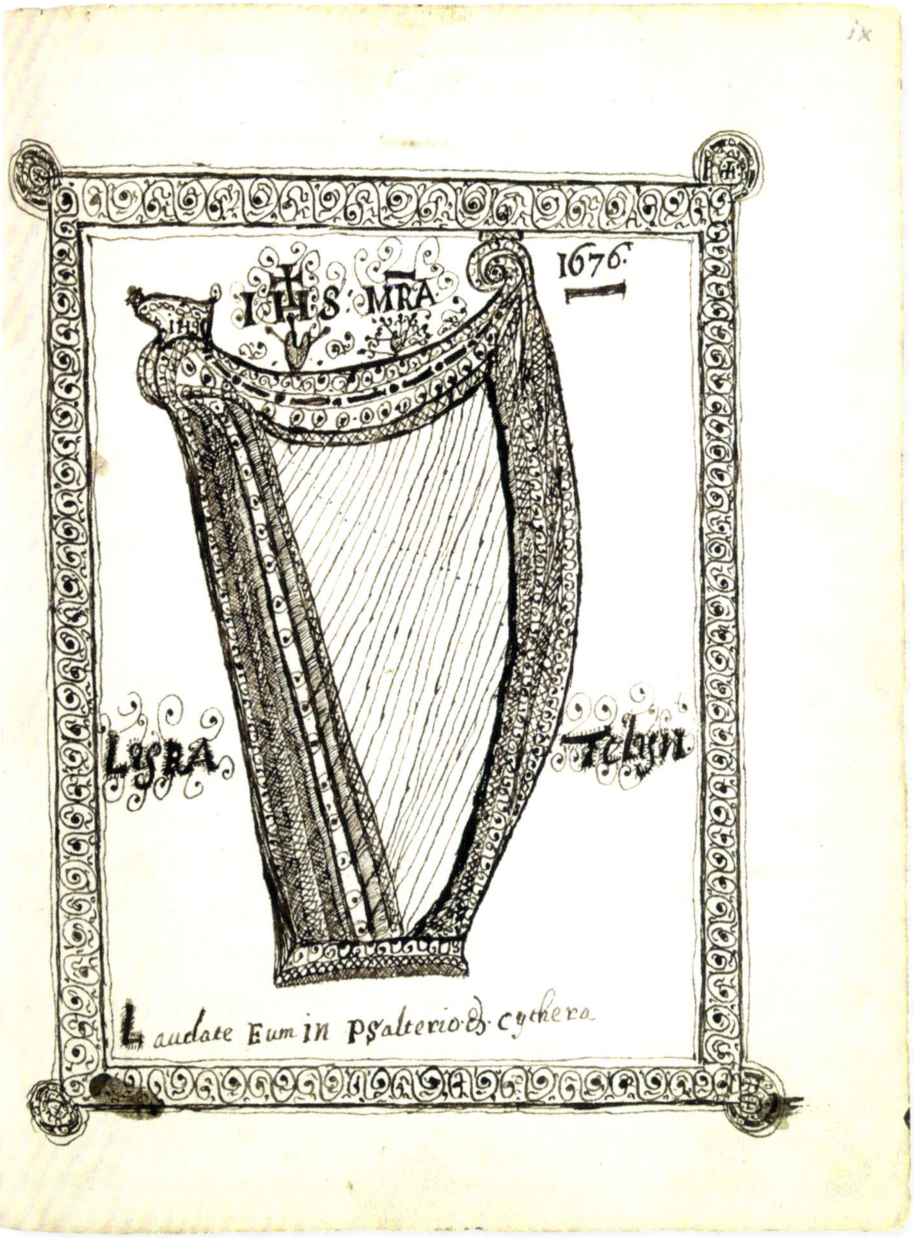

Gwilym Pue,
Lyra/Telyn, 1676

The work of the staff of the National Library of Wales and the National Museum of Wales has been essential as well as the generous support in kind provided by each institution. We thank Ceridwen Lloyd-Morgan and Isobel Gillan for their expertise and commitment to realise the book to its full potential.

Peter Lord and Rhian Davies,
November 2022

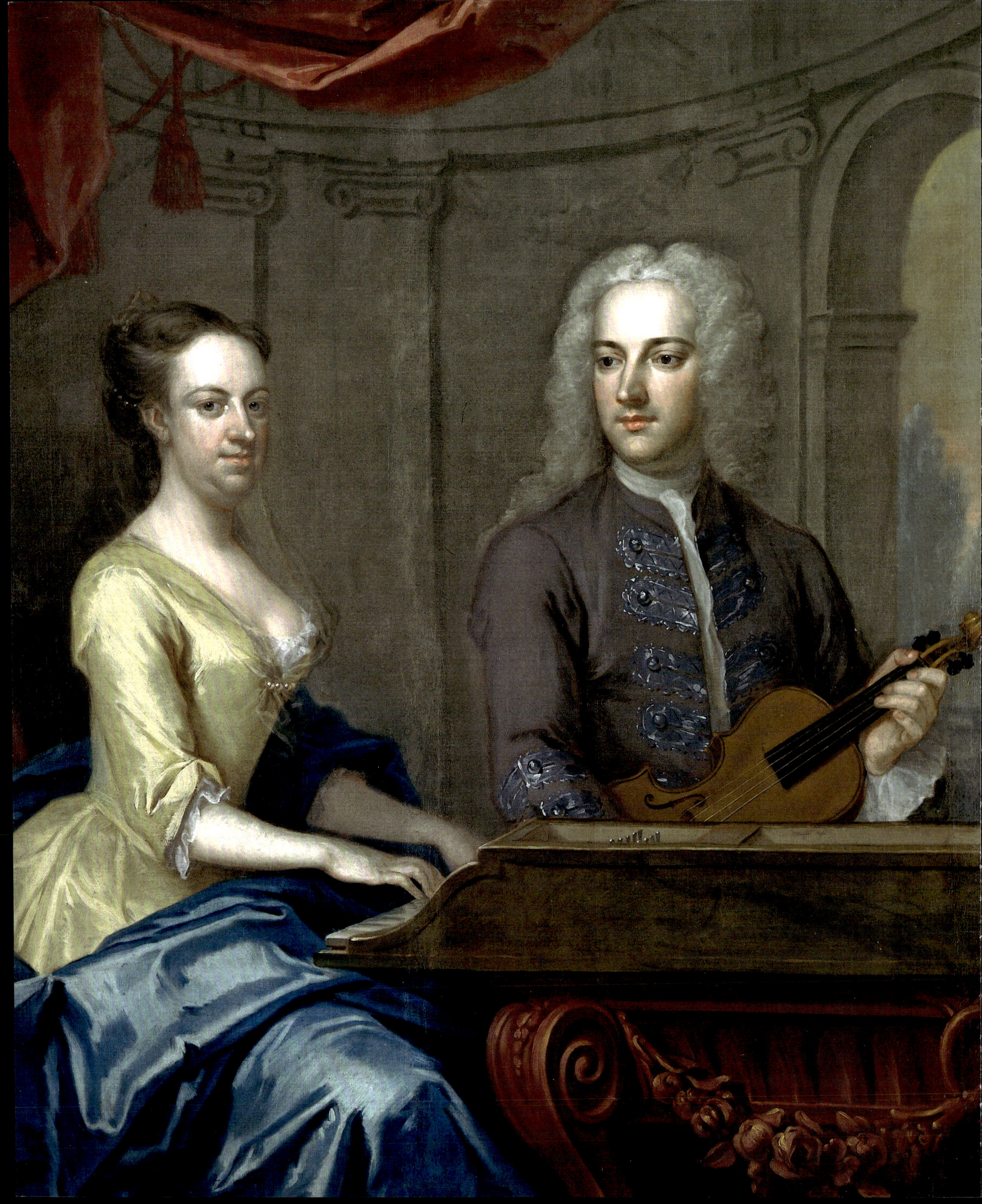

CHAPTER ONE

PRELUDE

ORIGINS

1 Unknown artist, *The natural disposicion of Welshmen*, from Andrew Boorde, *The fyrst booke of the introduction of knowledge*, c.1550

In about 1550, a helpful Englishman called Andrew Boorde published a guide and phrase book for his compatriots to use when venturing abroad, entitled *The fyrst booke of the introduction of knowledge*. With regard to travelling in Wales, Boorde advised his readers that any native person the visitor encountered was likely to demonstrate a propensity for prophecy, an addiction to alcohol, and a particular affection for music:

> And yf I haue my harpe, I care for no more;
> It is my treasure, I do keep it in store;
> For my harpe is made of good mares skyn,
> The stringes be of horse heare, it maketh a good din;
> My songe, and my voice, and my harpe doth agree,
> Muche lyke the hussyng of a bomble be ...[1]

Illustrating Boorde's text was a woodcut, depicting the author's archetypal character, dressed in everyday clothes and standing to play a small, single-strung harp. Clearly, as early as the mid-sixteenth century and toward the end of the reign of Henry VIII, an association between Welshness and musicality was well established in the mind of this particular Englishman.

Four hundred years later, in Dylan Thomas's radio drama *Under Milk Wood*, the Revd Eli Jenkins made the same association. In what would soon become a celebrated phrase, he eulogised the singing of Polly Garter with the words 'Praise the Lord! We are a musical nation'. But by that time, an outsider's perception had been transformed into an insider's cherished tradition, indeed into a badge of self-identification. The notion of Welsh musicality had become a received wisdom – a national brand, exploited abroad and scarcely ever challenged at home. Motivated by patriotisms of various hues, the transformation had been engineered by antiquarians and practising musicians, by poets, novelists and visual artists, at work from the second half of the eighteenth century until the Great War through successive waves of cultural revival.

For the antiquarians, the roots of the tradition extended back to the belief that the decayed remnants of prehistoric druidic culture had been reformed in the early twelfth century by Prince Gruffudd ap Cynan into a new bardic order, in

1 Andrew Boorde, *The fyrst booke of the introduction of knowledge* (London, c.1550, 1870 edition), p. 126. Boorde's reference to 'buzzing' indicates that the instrument with which he was familiar was the bray harp – the buzzing sound of which was produced by L-shaped wooden pegs attached to the sound board that resonated with the strings.

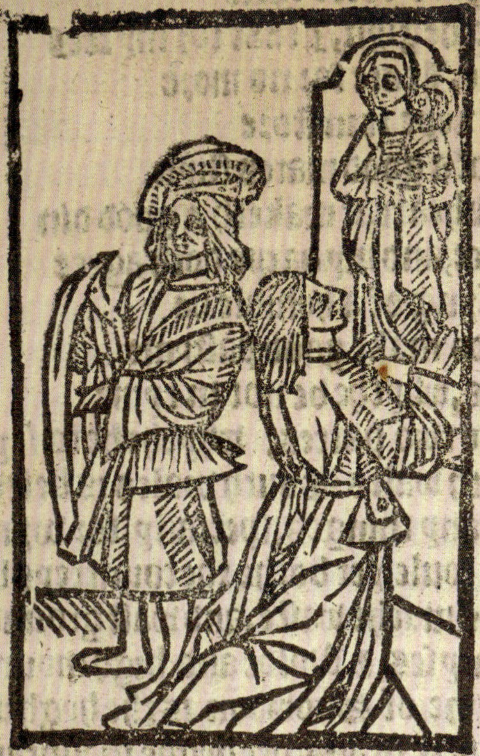

❡ The second chapytre treateth of Wales. And of the natural disposicio̅ of welshme̅. Teaching an Englyshman to speake some welsh.

I Am a welshman, and do dwel in Wales
I haue loued to serche boudgets & looke in males
I loue not to labour, nor to delue nor to dyg
My fyngers be lymed lyke a lyme twyg
And wherby ryches I do not greatly set
Syth all hys fyshe that commeth to the net
I am a gentylman and come of brutes blood
My name is, ap Ryce, ap Dauy ap Flood
I loue our Lady, for I am of hyr kynne
He that doth not loue hyr I beshrew his chynne
My kyndred is ap hoby, ap Jenkin, ap goffe
Bycause I do go barlegged, I do cach the coffe
And if I do go barlegged it is for no pryde
I haue a gray cote, my body for to hyde

I do

which music integrated with poetry played a central role. Given its importance in the constructs of the eighteenth century in particular, it is strange that *The History of Gruffudd ap Cynan*, probably written within a century of his death in 1137, makes no mention of this event.[2] Nevertheless, a fragment of contemporary documentation does survive to suggest that outside Wales a particular association was already made at this time between Welsh musical practice and two particular instruments. The Codex Calixtinus, written in about the year 1140, records that among pilgrims before the altar of St James at Santiago de Compostela, 'Some sang to the accompaniment of the … lyre, some to the timbrel, others to the flute, others to the British and Welsh harp and crwth.'[3]

The medieval harp and crwth became crucial to the tradition that the eighteenth-century antiquarians sought to construct.[4] Nevertheless, the earliest documentary invocation of the Gruffudd ap Cynan tradition had not appeared until the Caerwys Eisteddfod of 1523, and early evidence for the nature of a distinct Welsh soundworld is scanty. Indeed, much of the evidence that does survive tends to place Welsh practice firmly within a pan-European tradition, rooted in ecclesiastical patronage. Only two decorated music manuscripts remain, and their places of origin are uncertain and the names of the scribes responsible for

2 Unknown scribe, Musical notation from the Pen-pont Antiphonal, mid-14th century

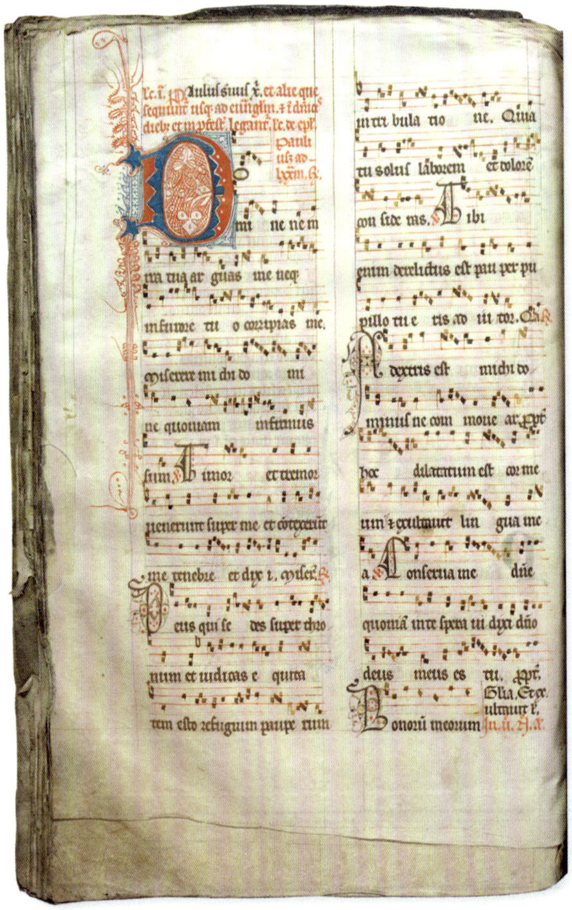

2 The history does mention the death in battle of the King's harper in 1094. See D. Simon Evans (ed.), *A Mediaeval Prince of Wales: The Life of Gruffudd ap Cynan* (Felinfach, 1990), and Paul Russell, *Vita Griffini Filii Conani: The Medieval Latin Life of Gruffudd ap Cynan* (Cardiff, 2005).

3 The text is given in G. Hartwell Jones, *Celtic Britain and the Pilgrim Movement* (London, 1912), p. 569, and attributed there to the MS of the 'Codex of Pope Calixtus II', written c.1140 and held at Santiago Cathedral. However, the English translation of the Santiago Codex given in Alison Stones, *Pilgrim's Guide to Santiago de Compostela: A Critical Edition* (London, 1998), does not contain this text. It seems most unlikely that Hartwell Jones had invented the reference, and it is presumed, therefore, that his source was an unidentified variant manuscript (of which several exist), which he inadvertently muddled with the earliest of the group, that still held at Santiago de Compostela.

4 Daines Barrington reported hearing a crwth played by John Morgan of Anglesey as late as 1770 in 'Some account of two musical instruments used in Wales', *Archaeologia*, 3 (1775), p. 32.

5 For the 'Pen-pont Antiphonal', see Owain Tudor Edwards, *Matins, Lauds and Vespers for St David's Day* (Cambridge, 1990).

6 See Sally Harper, 'The Bangor Pontifical. A Pontifical for the use of Salisbury', *Welsh Music History*, 2 (1997), pp. 65–99. Harper reviewed the evidence for the origin of the manuscript, pp. 73-4, concluding that it was likely to have been made for Bishop Anian II in East Anglia, perhaps in the workshop that also produced the 'Hours of Alice de Reydon'. See also pontifical.bangor.ac.uk/manuscript-and-commissioner.php.en.

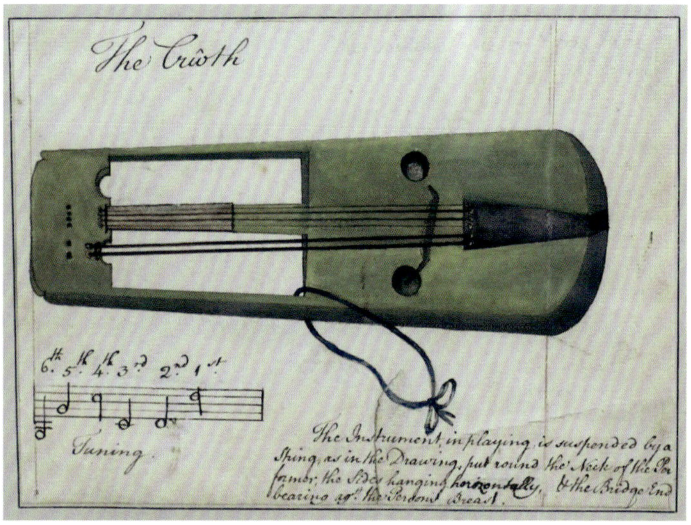

3 Probably Daines Barrington, *The Crwth*, c.1770

4 Unknown scribe and artist, musical notation and portrait of Bishop Anian II, from the Bangor Pontifical, *c.*1320–8

their production are unknown. Both manuscripts date from the fourteenth century, but the music of the Pen-pont Antiphonal, although written down later, was probably composed earlier. The offices given in the manuscript, which is associated with Pen-pont in Breconshire by later marginalia, were scored for two parts, chanting in response one to the other.[5] The Latin texts written under the notation on a four-line stave were decorated with delicate drawings of heads and architecture. Similarly, the Pontifical of Bishop Anian of Bangor includes decorated initials, and also a depiction of the Bishop himself, in the act of blessing a church with holy water. The portrait precedes the office for the consecration of an altar.[6]

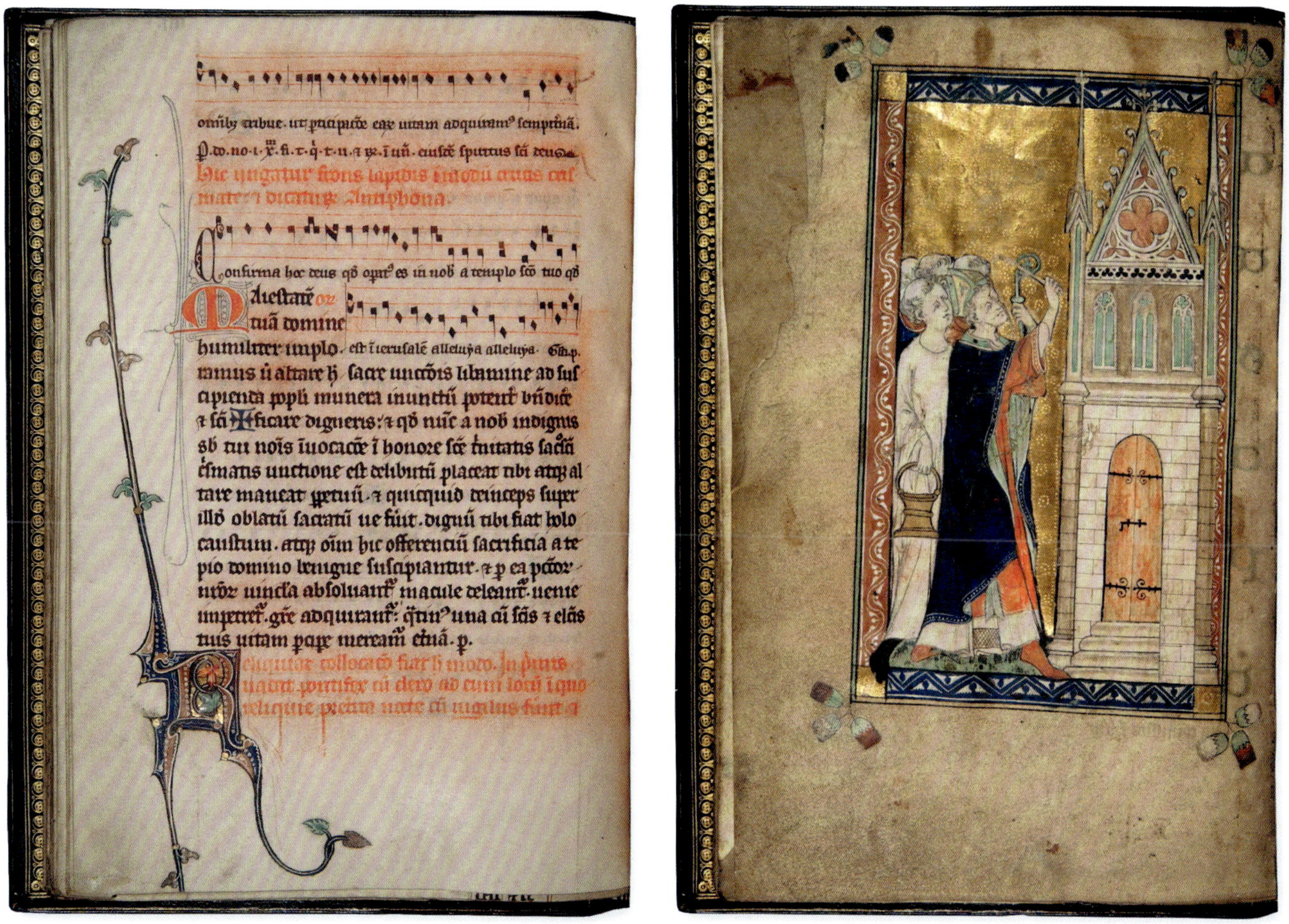

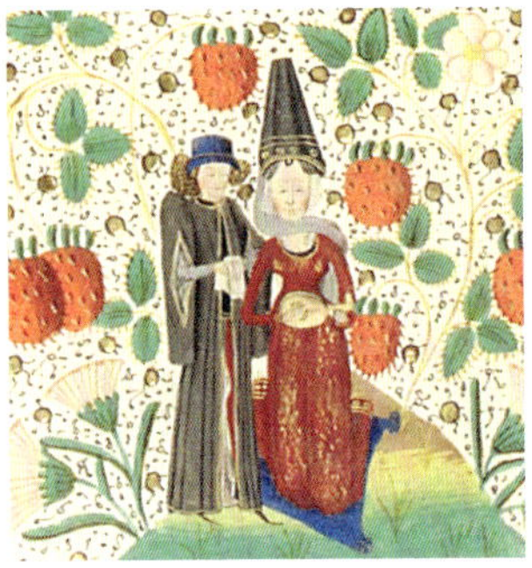

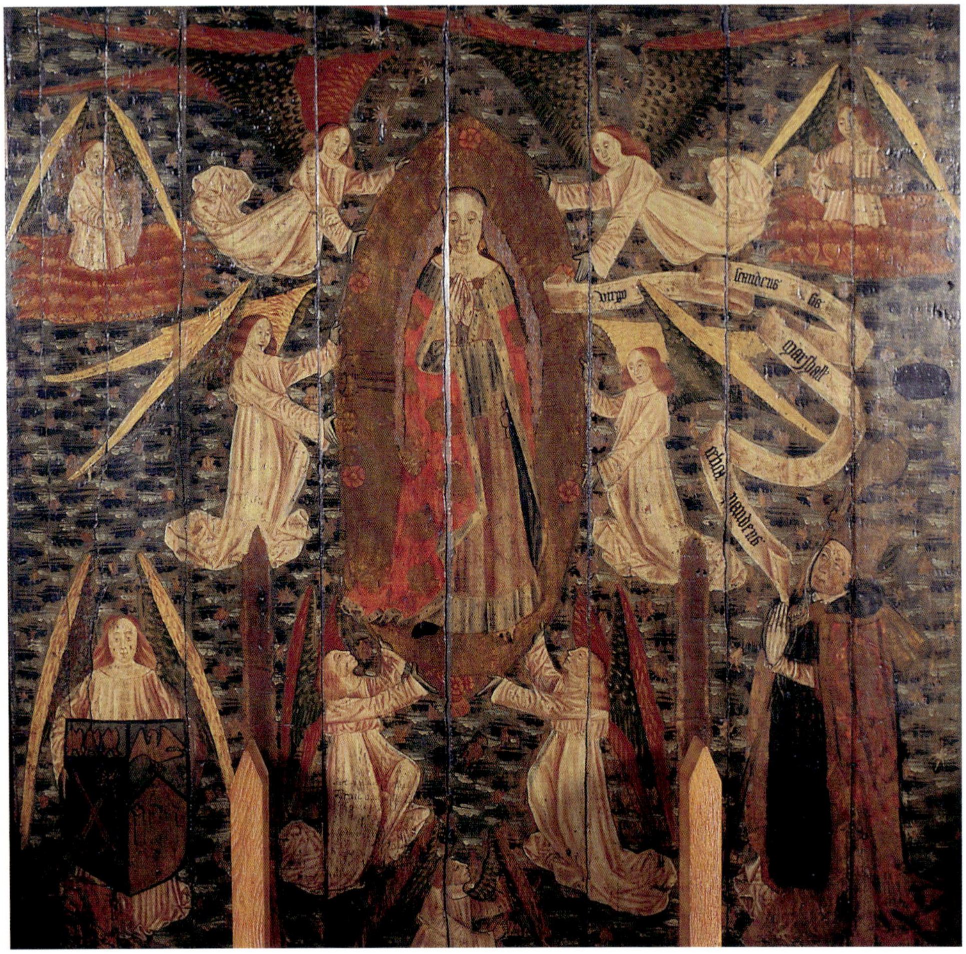

5 Unknown artist, detail from the manuscript copy of Quinte Curse Ruffe, 'Des faiz du grant Alexandre', owned by Sir John and Lady Dwnn, *c.* 1467-77

6 Unknown artist, *The Assumption of the Virgin*, from the throne of Bishop John Marshall, Llandaff Cathedral, late 15th century

Depictions of the musicians who may have played this music survive in Welsh churches, but date from the intensive spate of rebuilding in the fifteenth century which followed the severe depredations of the Glyndŵr Revolt. Perhaps the earliest surviving painted images of musicians are those that decorate the throne of Bishop John Marshall at Llandaff. They represent an angelic lutenist and a harper – though whether the application of wings to the lutenist may be taken to mean that the instrument was in fact played in church is another matter. It was certainly in use in a domestic context in the homes of the wealthy throughout western Europe. A decade or so before the commissioning of the Bishop's throne at Llandaff, Sir John Dwnn of Cydweli received a sumptuous gift in recognition of his diplomatic service to King Edward IV in Flanders. The King's sister, Margaret, Duchess of Burgundy, presented Dwnn with an elaborate copy of a history of the exploits of Alexander the Great. Underneath one of the battle scenes depicted in the manuscript stand a couple, the woman to the fore, playing a lute of identical pattern to that depicted in the Llandaff painting.[7]

7 The text was a translation of the original written by Quinte Curse Ruffe, 'Des faiz du grant Alexandre', BL Royal MS 17 F I.

8 The evidence was reviewed in Edmund A. Bowles, 'Were musical instruments used in the liturgical service during the Middle Ages?', *The Galpin Society Journal*, 10 (May 1957), pp. 40–56.

9 'Awdl foliant i'r Abad Dafydd ab Ieuan o Lyn-y-groes', see gutorglyn.net/gutorglyn/poem/?poem-selection=113. See also Sally Harper, 'Musical imagery in the poetry of Guto'r Glyn', in Dylan Foster Evans, Barry J. Lewis and Ann Parry Owen (eds.), *'Gwalch Cywyddau Gwŷr': Ysgrifau ar Guto'r Glyn a Chymru'r Bymthegfed Ganrif* (Aberystwyth, 2013), pp. 177–202.

The carved musician angels who adorn the roof of the Church of St Giles in Wrexham expand the range of instruments employed at the time, since they include also a bagpiper. He may not necessarily have been heard in church, though in the street and the marketplace a wide range of instruments was certainly used in the religious mystery plays, to the extent that throughout Europe, by the second half of the fifteenth century, traditionalists within religious communities were voicing increasing complaints about the infiltration of secular musicians into the sacred space. But notwithstanding the ecclesiastical location of the carvings and paintings of musicians, how instrumental music featured at the time in the performance of the mass and other church music, such as the singing of psalms, remains unclear.[8]

However, the poetry of the period provides some hints as to the nature of religious music in Welsh churches in the period of the surviving carvings and paintings, and a suggestion of distinct practice. It appears that (as in the rest of Europe) the organ was considered exceptional among musical instruments and was indeed played to supplement the liturgy. Its music was enjoyed by the fifteenth-century poet Guto'r Glyn on a visit to the Cistercian abbey of Valle Crucis, near Llangollen, for example, although if the wider context was ecclesiastical, the particular occasion he described does not appear to have been liturgical:

Yno ar ginio organau – a dyf,	[There over lunch the sound of organs rises,
Cerdd dafod a thannau;	Poetry and harp music;
Ac yno mae'r Guto gau	And there the Guto is sheltered
O fewn pyrth yn fanw parthau.	Within its doors as a tame piglet.][9]

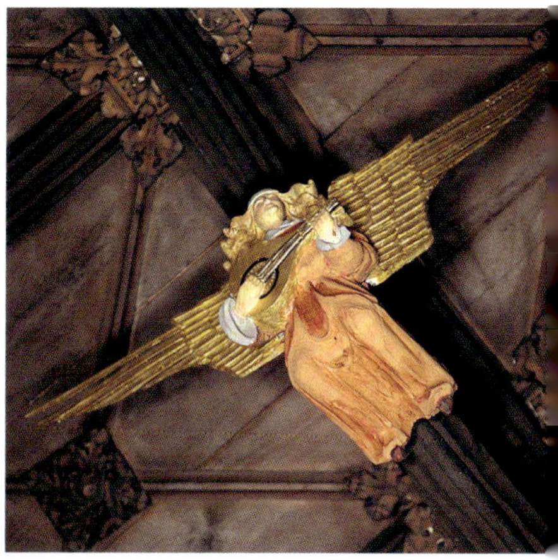
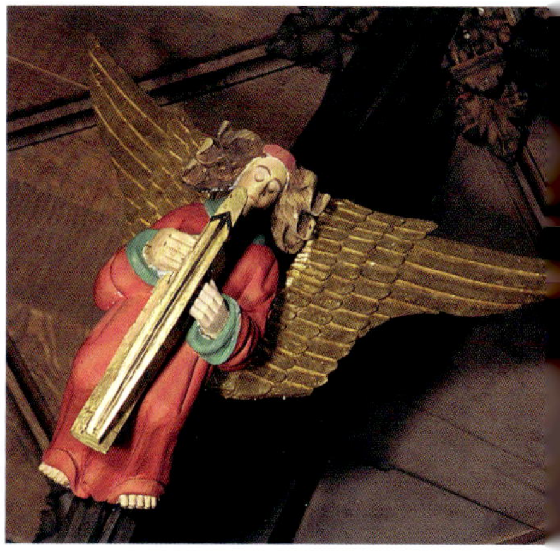
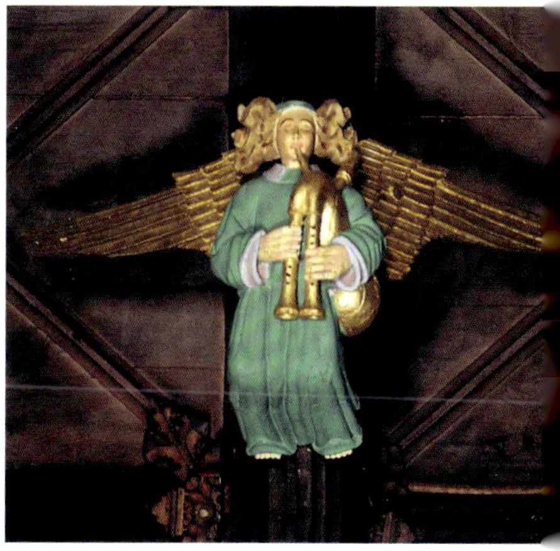

7 Unknown sculptor, *Angel Musicians from the Church of St Giles, Wrexham*, 15th century

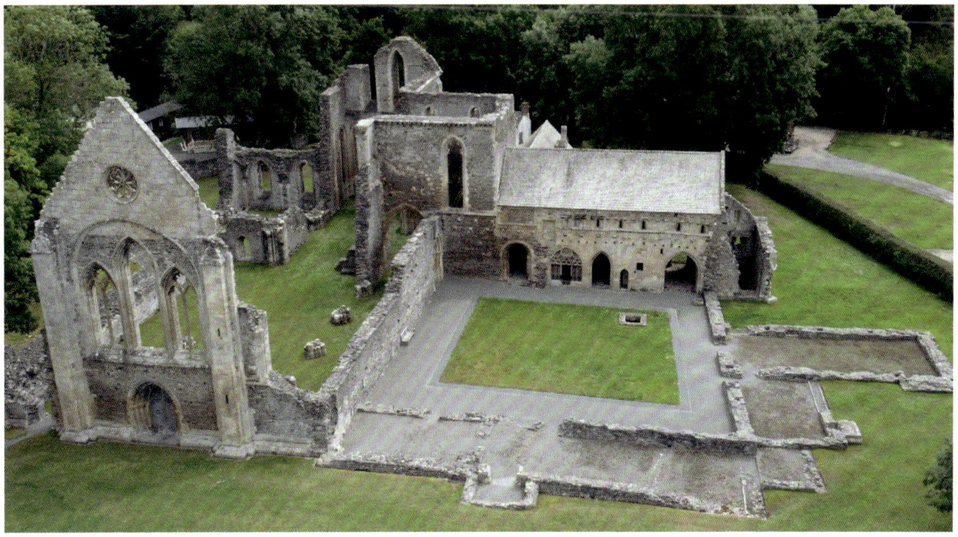

8 Valle Crucis Abbey, Llangollen

Guto'r Glyn's conjoining of 'poetry and harp music' hints at the persistence of a parallel secular musical practice with distinctly Welsh characteristics of form and patronage. His verse resonates with the *cerdd dant* tradition, operating in a grey area in which the European ecclesiastical mainstream and indigenous secular practice overlapped at a wealthy – and perhaps increasingly worldly – Cistercian abbey.

Guto'r Glyn lived long enough to experience the first consequences of the victory of Henry Tudor at the Battle of Bosworth Field in 1485, which would fundamentally and permanently change the mindset of the Welsh gentry and intelligentsia. The perception that, with the establishment of the Tudor dynasty in England, ancient prophecies had been fulfilled and the original inhabitants of the Islands of Britain were once again sovereign over all their peoples would condition Welsh consciousness through five subsequent centuries and, therefore, the context within which successive cultural revivals were manifested in music and in visual culture. The gentry would be the primary beneficiaries of the new regime. In 1506, in Pembrokeshire – the county through which Henry Tudor had marched to begin his campaign to win the English throne – Sir Rhys ap Thomas celebrated the first anniversary of his elevation to the Order of the Garter with a grand tournament at his home, Carew Castle. Gentry from all parts of Wales attended him there, including Gruffudd Dwnn, son of Sir John Dwnn, recipient of the magnificent Burgundian manuscript in which the lutenist (perhaps his mother) was depicted. Like his parent's manuscript, the courtly drama of the tournament reflected a new romanticism for an imagined past of chivalry, rather than a practical military purpose, and the ceremonial included musicians:

> Sir Rice having reserved a great companie of the better sort of his guests, he leads them to the castle, with drummes, trumpets, and other warlike musicke. Over the gate, at the entrance, was hung up a goodlie faire table, wherein was represented the species and pourtraiture of St George and St David embracing one another with this mottoe, Nodo plus quam Gordiano.[10]

The use of the Latin tag 'A knot stronger than the Gordian' represents a very early iteration of the unionist mindset, rooted in the accession of Henry Tudor to the throne, that would echo down the centuries in Welsh music, in writing about its history, and in its visualisation. Sir Rhys himself memorialised his tournament

10 Ralph A. Griffiths, *Sir Rhys ap Thomas and His Family* (Cardiff, 1993), p. 251.

11 The conventional explanation for the presence of the panel at Cotehele House in Cornwall is the marriage of Catherine St John, widow of Gruffudd ap Rhys, to Piers Edgecombe of Cotehele, see Peter Lord, *The Visual Culture of Wales: Medieval Vision* (Cardiff, 2003), pp. 268–9. Alternative interpretations are reviewed in Nicholas Riall, Rachel Hunt, Daniel Huws, Bethan Miles, Samantha Riches, Catherine Richardson, Eleanor Lowe and Dan Miles, 'A Tudor cupboard at Cotehele, Cornwall', *Archaeological Journal*, 163 (2006), pp. 147–79.

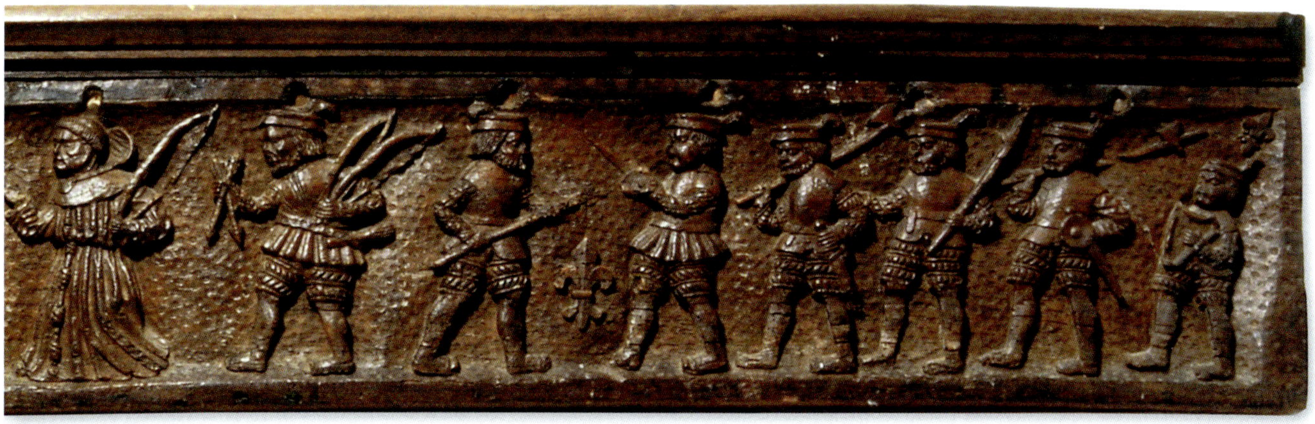

in the unusual form of a carved bedstead, illustrating the processions, the jousting and the music. A conspicuously diminutive harper was perhaps an individual of short stature known to the company, or might suggest that in the faux-military context of the tournament the harp music was provided by a child. A second carving, a panel within what is now known as the Cotehele Tester (but which probably began life as the front of a cupboard), may be by the same hand, though both the precise location of its origin in Wales and the date of its production – apparently by one Harry ap Griffith – are matters of speculation.[11] The carving is sufficiently detailed to see that the *crythor* holds the instrument with the aid of a neck strap.

9 Unknown maker, *Bedstead of Sir Rhys ap Thomas*, c.1507

10 Probably Harry ap Griffith, *The Cotehele Tester*, early 16th century

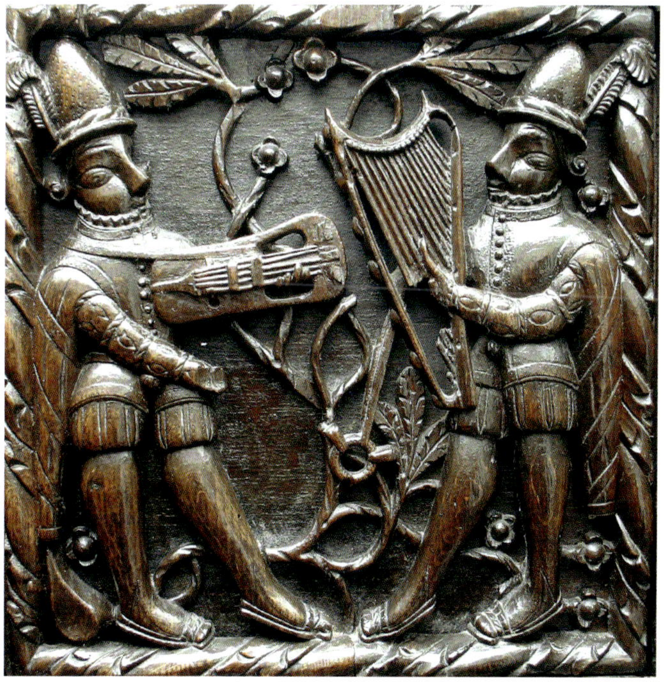

The reign of Henry VIII confirmed the new political order in Wales, both in the Act of Union of 1536, and in the break, two years earlier, with the Church of Rome. Henry's Act of Supremacy initiated the process that brought to the Welsh nation the severe jolt of the religious reformation, transforming cultural practice through much of Europe. Andrew Boorde's illustration of the characteristic Welsh harper was made a decade later, by which time these transformations had dislocated the temporal and spiritual lives of many of those born under the old dispensation of pan-European Roman Catholicism. Boorde's harper is accompanied by a compatriot who kneels before a picture of the Virgin and Child and asserts that 'I loue our Lady, for I am of hyr

11 Inigo Jones, *Welsh Dancers*, c.1618

kynne' – an early acknowledgement of recusant tendencies in Wales. Boorde might be expected to have drawn attention to adherence to Roman Catholic practice amongst the Welsh, given the personal difficulties he himself encountered in negotiating the religious turmoil of his period. He had begun his adult life in a monastery.[12] Recusant tendencies in Wales would become more obvious and problematic to the Church and to the secular authorities during the reign of Elizabeth I. In 1567, Nicholas Robinson, the newly installed Bishop of Bangor, complained to Sir William Cecil, Secretary of State to the Queen, that he found 'images and altars standing in churches undefiled', and the people still practising 'lewd and indecent vigils and watches'.[13] The following year, state control of cultural practice in Wales was manifested in the appointment of a government commission for holding a second Eisteddfod at Caerwys, which sought to regulate professional 'mynstrelles, rithmers, or barthes' who were expert in the 'facultie of the Welshe musick'.[14] The historian Richard Suggett has written of the government's vigorous campaign to prosecute those who operated outside the regulations:

> Fifteenth-century minstrels had been suspected of sedition and their sixteenth-century successors still cultivated the poetry, genealogy and history that helped sustain a sense of a separate Welsh identity. In this sense minstrels maintained 'sinister usages and customs' which the Act of Union (1536) resolved to 'extirpate' because they tended to undermine the unity of the realm. It was probably not coincidental therefore that minstrels were prosecuted so soon after the Act of Union.[15]

Clearly, in mid-century, the distinctness of a persistent integrated musical and poetical tradition was perceived as a threat to the homogenised state that the English government sought to impose. Yet, by the close of the reign of Queen Elizabeth, if representations of Welsh people in the metropolitan arts of the time (and particularly in theatre) can be relied upon as a guide, then the transformation from threatening other to faintly ludicrous bucolic appears to have been well under way. The perceived national obsessions and peculiarities that would characterise the Welsh nation in the English mind for centuries to come, symbolised by mountains, goats, toasted cheese, the natives' miserable attempts to speak the English language, and the music of the harp, were firmly established. In 1618, the playwright Ben Jonson compressed them all in the brief prelude to a masque (the 'antimasque', entitled *For the Honour of Wales*) presented before

12 Boorde had written his text by 1542 and dedicated it to the Princess Mary, subsequently the Roman Catholic Queen Mary. For Welsh content, see Geraint Evans, 'Wales and the Welsh language in Andrew Borde's Fyrst Boke of the Introduction of Knowledge', *Studia Celtica*, 42 (2008), pp. 87–104.

13 *Calendar of State Papers* (London, 1865), p. 301.

14 Given in Richard Suggett, 'Vagabonds and minstrels in sixteenth-century Wales', in Adam Fox and Daniel Woolf (eds.), *The Spoken Word: Oral Culture in Britain, 1500–1850* (Manchester, 2002), p. 157.

15 Ibid., pp. 140–1.

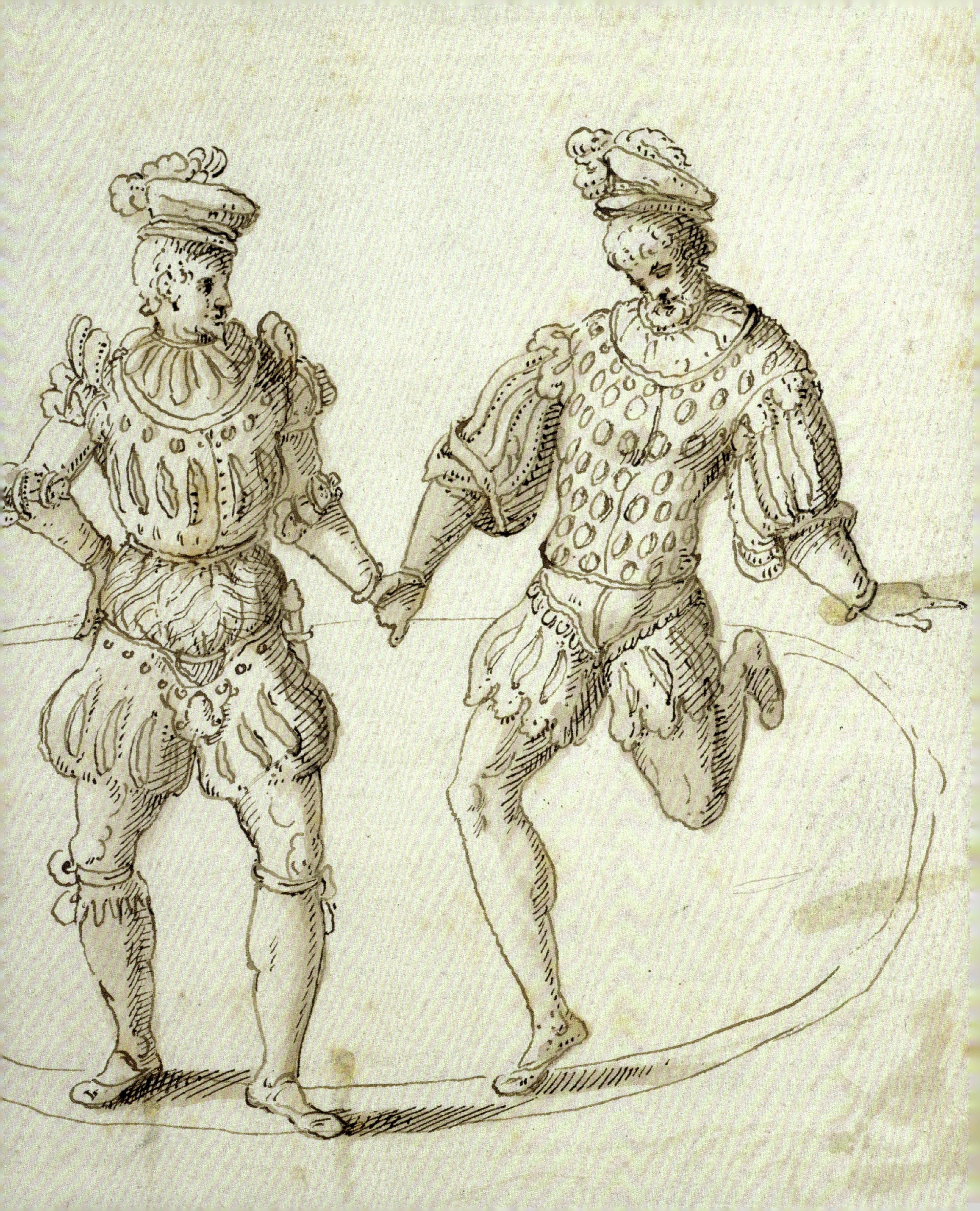

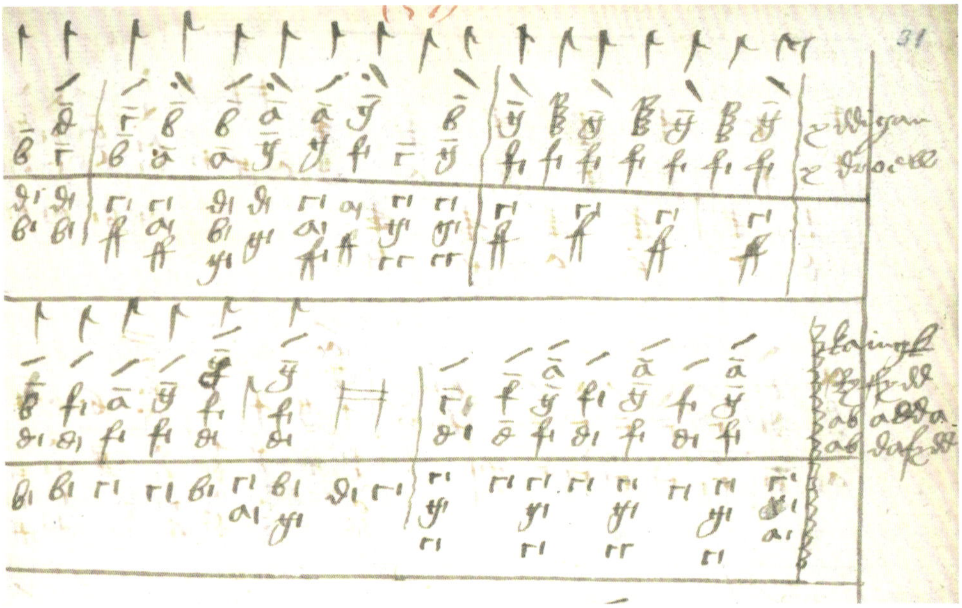

12 Detail of a folio from Robert ap Huw's manuscript, 'Musica neu Beroriaeth', c.1613

13 John Jones of Gellilyfdy, *Bagpiper*, 1583

14 Thomas Price, Carnhuanawc, after John Jones of Gellilyfdy, *The Bardic Order*, c.1830

King James I in London. The masque itself, *Pleasure Reconciled to Virtue*, had strong political undertones, commenting on James's less than successful attempts to reconcile tensions in his native Scotland between adherents to the old religious and cultural order, and the Calvinist inclinations of the new. The King had not been best pleased with the original performance and Jonson attempted in a new antimasque to present Wales as a successful model of assimilation in the construct of the nascent empire. Three Welsh characters in conversation recite the litany of stereotypes, concluding with Howel bragging of Welsh musicality expressed by the music of the harp, the pipes and the crwth (or crowd):

> And yet, is nothing now all this,
> If our musiques we do miss;
> Bothe harps and pipes too, and the crowd
> Must aull come in and tauke alowd …

The musicians play and the men dance in praise of James and Charles, Prince of Wales (the future King Charles I) of whom Jenkin proclaims:

> Calls tru hearts, that is us, he calls us, the Welse nation to be ever at your service, and love you, and honour you, which we pray you understand it his meaning. And that the musicians yonder are so many Brittis bards that sing o'pen the hills to let out the prince of Wales, and his Welse friends to you, and all is done.[16]

16 Ben Jonson, *For the Honour of Wales*, in William Gifford (ed.), *The Works of Ben Jonson, in Nine Volumes* (London, 1816), vol. vii, pp. 333–48. In their loyal testimony, Jonson's characters also cite 'Bangu, Davie's bell' (the bell of St David, that Giraldus Cambrensis reported as held at the Church of St David, Glascwm), and 'our lowder Wrexham organ'. The writer clearly had some knowledge of the Welsh language, using correct Welsh expressions in addition to Wenglish. For the political context of Welsh characterisation in London theatre in the period, see Marisa R. Cull, 'Staging Cambria: Shakespeare, the Welsh, and the Early Modern English Theater, 1590–1615' (unpublished PhD thesis, Ohio State University, 2008). For *Pleasure Reconciled to Virtue* in particular, see Leah S. Marcus, 'The occasion of Ben Jonson's *Pleasure Reconciled to Virtue*', *Studies in English Literature, 1500–1900*, 19, 2 (Spring 1979), pp. 271–93.

At just the same time as Jonson wrote *For the Honour of Wales*, faced both with the earlier attempts at legal regulation of Welsh music and poetry, and the contemporary trend to emasculate it through ridicule, the vulnerability of the tradition was recognised by the earliest Welsh antiquarians of the seventeenth century. Robert ap Huw, who wrote his manuscript in about 1613, was almost certainly aware that the tradition, transmitted aurally in the past, was in danger of loss, and his musical notation provides the only surviving evidence of the Welsh soundworld of the late medieval period. Ap Huw was not merely a copyist, but a sophisticated musician, and although his notation contains elements that relate to the transcription practice of other nations, his method is unique and has proved difficult to interpret.[17] Because of the early date of the music it contains, the manuscript is also of European importance, but additionally, at home, it would become fundamental in the evolution of the thinking of the eighteenth-century revivalists engaged in the construction of a specifically Welsh tradition. A little later, in pursuit of the same agenda, it appears that the copyist John Jones of Gellilyfdy made reference in a manuscript to the Gruffudd ap Cynan tradition. He illustrated the reformed bardic order of precedence by drawing a harp, associated with the Bard (the first rank), and a crwth, associated with the Prydydd (the second rank), one above the other.[18]

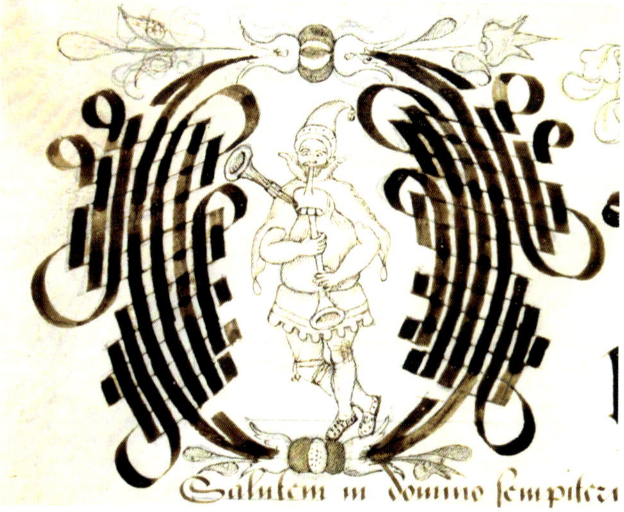

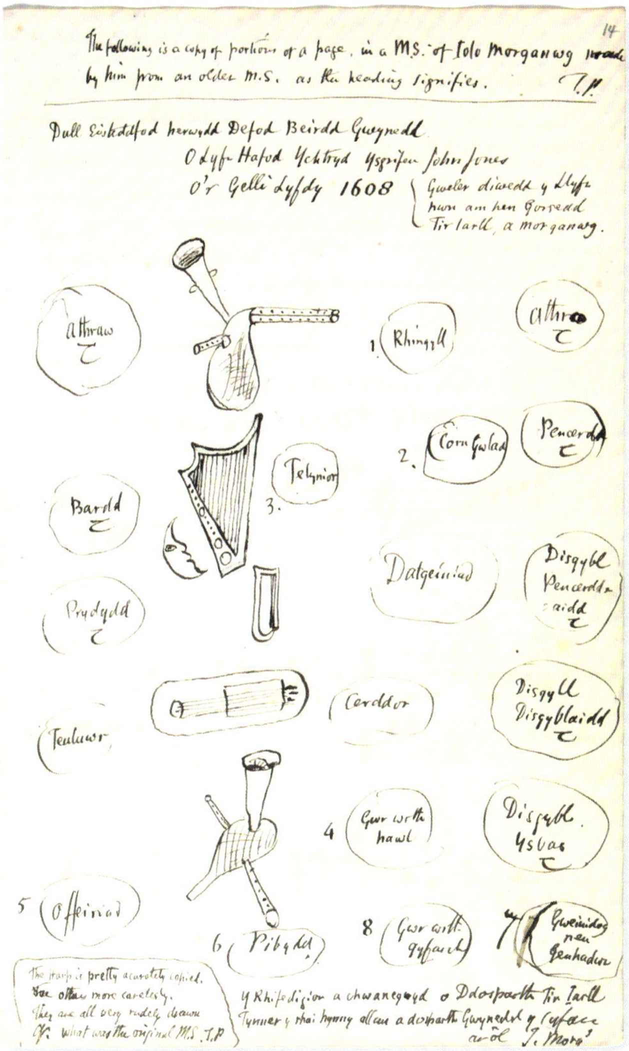

17 See Paul D. Whittaker, 'British Museum Additional MS 14905: An Interpretation and Re-examination of the Music and Text' (unpublished MA dissertation, University College of North Wales, Bangor, 1974).

18 The source for the attribution of the diagram to John Jones of Gellilyfdy is Thomas Price, Carnhuanawc, NLW MS 1464D, f. 14, at the top of which Carnhuanawc says: 'The following is a copy of portions of a page, in a M.S. of Iolo Morganwg, made by him from an older M.S.', dated 1608. We have been unable to trace this earliest source.

THE NATIONAL INSTRUMENT

On occasion, eighteenth- and nineteenth-century commentators would draw two other early pan-European sources into the construction and imaging of Welsh musical tradition. Both concerned the harp, destined to be confirmed by them as the primary visual symbol of Welsh musicality. The Greek myth of the poet and singer Orpheus, accompanying himself on the lyre, was among the most widely familiar classical legends to the modern audience throughout Europe, propagated in particular through visual art. Its familiarity deepened as engravings made art works available to audiences located at great distance from the originals. Artists were able to regenerate the pan-European image in their own national context – a process exemplified in Wales by the painting made for the Myddelton family of *Orpheus Charming the Animals before Chirk Castle*. The painter, Thomas Ffrancis of Montgomery, carried out extensive work for the Myddeltons, and provided his Orpheus not with the classical lyre but with the single-strung harp that would have been familiar to him and his patrons from everyday practice.[19]

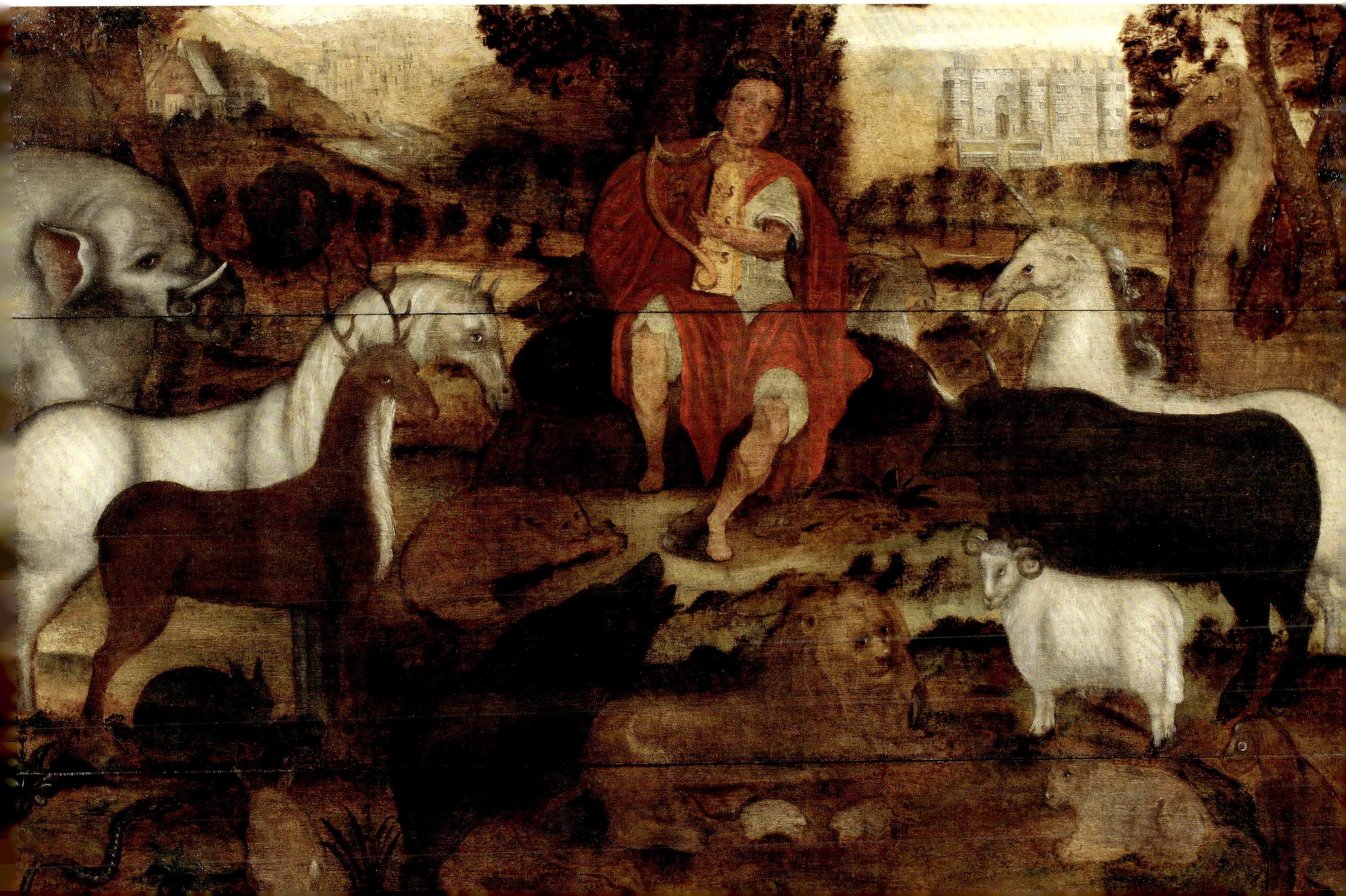

15 Thomas Ffrancis of Montgomery, *Orpheus Charming the Animals before Chirk Castle*, c.1672

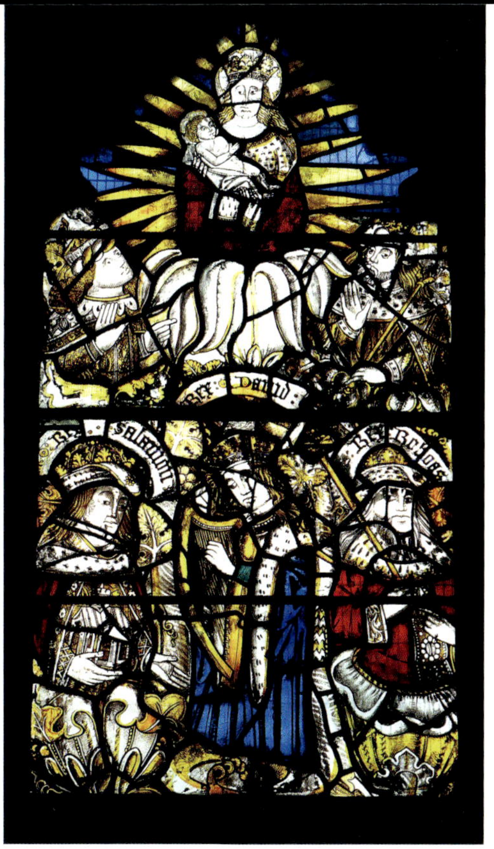

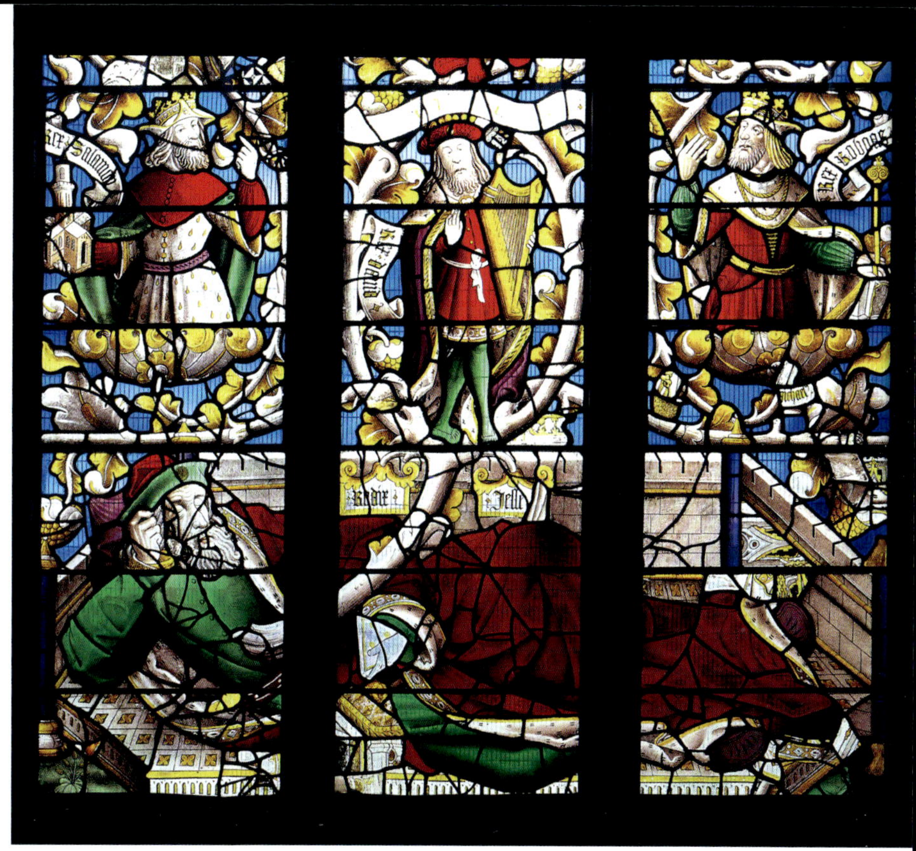

16 Unknown maker, *The Virgin and Child with King David*, *Church of St David, Diserth*, c.1533

17 Unknown maker, *Jesse Window*, *Church of St Dyfnog, Llanrhaeadr-yng-Nghinmeirch*, 1533

In the Judeo-Christian tradition, images of the Jewish King David, regarded as the ancestor of Jesus, were equally familiar.[20] The stained glass windows at Diserth and at Llanrhaeadr-yng-Nghinmeirch, probably both made in 1533, set King David, harp in hand, as the ancestor of Jesus beneath a family tree which leads upward to the image of the Virgin and Child.[21] Again, this iconography was common to the Christian tradition in many continental European countries. Indeed, it is clear that the master who made the Llanrhaeadr window based his image of Jesse, at the root of the tree that leads upward to Christ, on a woodcut from a printed Book of Hours, published in Paris in 1498. Nevertheless, among Welsh intellectuals, imaging of the Jewish King David had a particular and profound national resonance. The self-identification of the Welsh as God's chosen people, re-enacting in the Islands of Britain the exile of the Israelites

19 For Ffrancis, see references in Peter Lord, *The Visual Culture of Wales: Imaging the Nation* (Cardiff, 2000), pp. 59–60, and Peter Lord, *The Tradition: A New History of Welsh Art 1400–1990* (Cardigan, 2016), pp. 72–3, 77.

20 Portraits of David in the specific context of the Psalms were particularly common. Sir William Herbert of Raglan, who shared with his contemporary Sir John Dwnn a taste for Burgundian manuscript art, was probably responsible for the commission of the magnificent 'Pembroke Hours' (Philadelphia Museum of Art MS 1945-65-2). Each of the Psalms in the manuscript was illustrated with a miniature, almost all of which represented King David either holding a harp or identified by the proximity of a harp lying on the ground. See Lord, *Medieval Vision*, pp. 260–2.

21 The window was probably in place in the early seventeenth century, but was taken down and so preserved from destruction by Puritan iconoclasm. The models followed in the medieval imaging of the harp vary. The Llanrhaeadr David has a harp with a straight pillar, whilst the window at Diserth has a curved front, more typical of an Irish harp. D. Roy Saer, *The Harp in Wales in Pictures* (Cardiff, 1991), p. 11, illustrates these together.

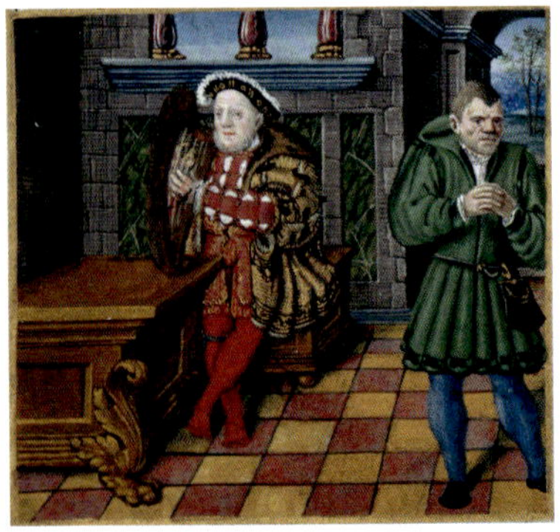

18 Probably Jean Mallard, illumination from *The Psalter of Henry VIII*, c.1540–1

in Egypt, was well established by the sixteenth century. At the same time as Andrew Boorde published his outsider's observations of the Welsh people, in his Chronicle Elis Gruffydd recorded in manuscript a compendium of mythic traditions linking the bard Taliesin and the biblical Moses as leaders of enslaved and dispossessed peoples towards redemption and recovery.[22]

In his early development, Henry VIII, as the son of the Welsh usurper of the English throne, dwelt much on Arthurian legends in his search for a sense of dynastic legitimacy. Later, as his difficulties with the Roman Church intensified, he became more engaged with the notion of King David as an appropriate model. His personal psalter, written and probably also illuminated by the French scribe Jean Mallard, specifically makes the connection in a dedicatory letter. Many of the illuminations – Henry as David slaying Goliath, for instance – illustrate the association, reinforced by the King's own musings in his marginalia. The psalter was presented to the King in the most difficult period of his relationship with Rome, resulting from his complicated marital affairs. Henry sought to justify his separation from Rome on the grounds that his imperial authority, like that of David, derived directly from God, 'with no papal intermediary'.[23] The illumination to Psalm 53 depicts him seated at a table playing a small, single-strung harp. He is accompanied by the court fool, since the Psalm states: 'The fool hath said in his heart, There is no God'.

In 1676, the Benedictine Gwilym Pue depicted in a manuscript a harp similar in general shape to that played by Henry, but encrusted with rich decoration, which suggests gilding. The elaborate nature of the instrument makes it unlikely to have been a simple representation of an everyday harp played by jobbing musicians whom Pue would certainly have known, since his manuscript explained in detail the various tunings used by his contemporaries. Significantly, Pue contextualised his harp with the Christograms 'IHS' and 'MRA' – that is, with initials which are contractions of the names of Jesus and the Virgin. He confirmed the primary biblical context of his drawing with a quotation from Psalm 150: 'Laudate eum in psalterio et cithara' ('Praise him with psaltery and harp'). Surmounting the soundboard is an animal head that seems likely to represent the Lion of Judah. As a Welshman and a Roman Catholic, his image conformed, therefore, not only with the iconography of the Llanrhaeadr window by setting the Virgin and Child above King David, but with the two elements of Andrew Boorde's depiction of a characteristic Welsh person a century earlier. Clearly, Pue's sense of the form of

22 See Amy C. Mulligan, 'Moses, Taliesin, and the Welsh Chosen People: Elis Gruffydd's construction of a biblical, British past for Reformation Wales', *Studies in Philology*, 113, 4 (Fall 2016), pp. 765–96. What is probably a depiction of King David with his harp survives also in the form of a wall painting at the Church of Ystyffan, Llansteffan, for which see Richard Suggett, *Painted Temples: Wallpaintings and Rood-screens in Welsh Churches, 1200–1800* (Aberystwyth, 2021), p. 125.

23 Pamela Tudor-Craig, 'Henry VIII and King David', in Daniel Williams (ed.), *Early Tudor England: Proceedings of the 1987 Harlaxton Symposium* (Woodbridge, 1989), p. 191.

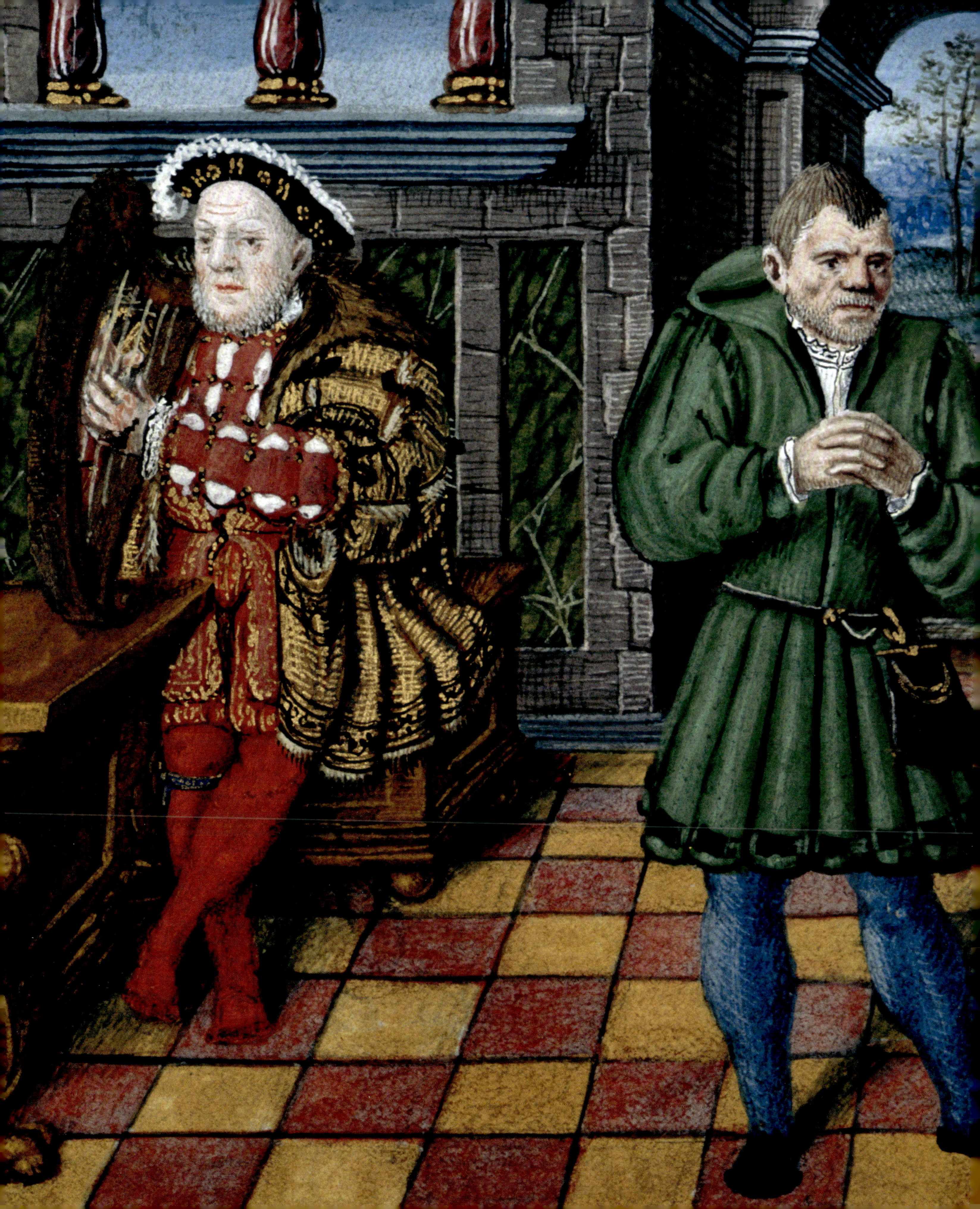

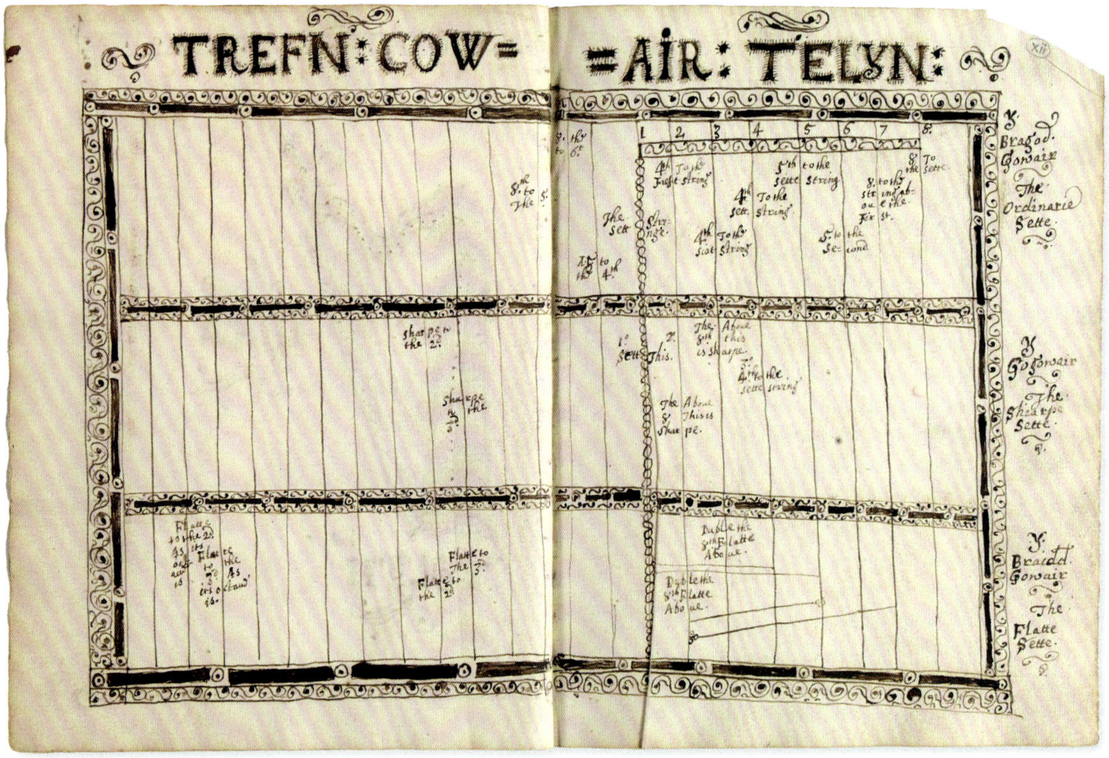

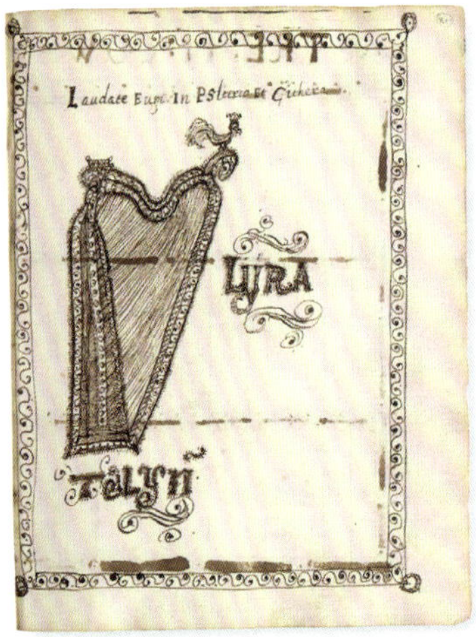

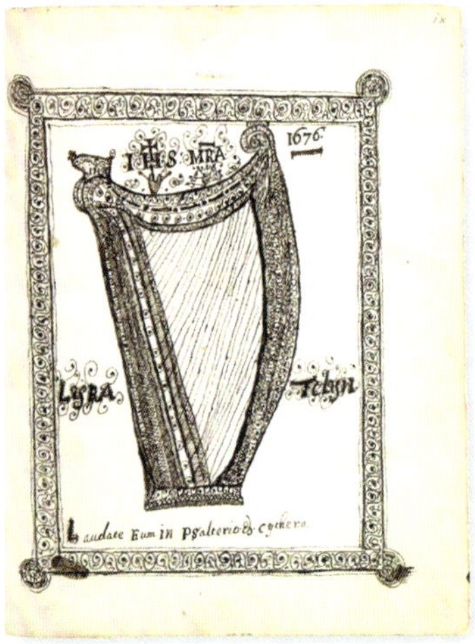

19 Gwilym Pue, *Trefn: Cowair: Telyn* and *Lyra/Telyn*, 1674–6

20 Gwilym Pue, *Lyra/Telyn*, 1676

the harp was as closely related to depictions of King David as the ancestor of Jesus, as to the contemporary Welsh musical practice on which both he and Boorde also drew. The instrument depicted by Gwilym Pue in this folio was surely the Golden Harp of King David.[24] A second depiction of the harp drawn by Pue made a New Testament reference directly to Jesus. Surmounting the instrument, he drew the cock that crowed to fulfil Jesus's prophecy that it would do so when Peter denied knowledge of him, prior to the Crucifixion.[25] But Pue was sensitive not only to these deeply ingrained biblical national identifications, but also to insular tradition, in the form of the prophecies of Merlin and Taliesin, which he recorded in his manuscripts.[26]

24 For the interpretation of Pue's treatise on the tuning of the harp, see Ann Griffiths and André Schaefer, 'Gwilym Puw's "Trefn Cywair Telyn"', *Welsh Music*, 4, 8 (Winter 1974–5), pp. 22–30.

25 The volume containing this depiction, NLW MS 13167B, f. xi, was in the possession of Lady Llanover by 1853.

26 Arising from his particular recusant perspective, Pue copied five 'carols' written by the Welsh Catholic martyr, Richard Gwyn: 'Pump Caroley Mr White'.

THE GENTRY IN THE EUROPEAN MAINSTREAM

A pattern of parallel evolution in traditions of secular art music, of ecclesiastical music, and of folk music, seems to have continued through the eighteenth century, though not without interactions and points of contact. Of these traditions, the engagement of the Welsh gentry with art music is the easiest to track in visual imagery through the century, though the portrait of perhaps the earliest individual musician to be the subject of a picture presents difficulties of interpretation. By the end of the eighteenth century, when the portrait of the liveried young horn player who worked at Erddig, near Wrexham, was painted, he was a figure known only through folk memory. He was visually revived in a portrait commissioned by Philip Yorke, the owner of Erddig, and almost certainly painted by John Walters of Denbigh, probably in the 1790s.[27] In that decade, Walters painted a series of remarkable portraits of servants and tradespeople connected with Erddig, and although the painting of the musician differs in format from the others, it is certainly related to that series since, like the other pictures, it includes descriptive verses written by Yorke:

Of the Condition of this Negre
Our information is but megre;
However here, he was a dweller,
And blew the horn for Master Meller.
Here, too he dy'd, but when or how,
Can scarcely be remember'd now,
But that to Marchwiel he was sent,
And had good Christian interment.
Pray Heav'n may stand his present friend,
Where black, or white; distinctions, end.
For sure on this side of the grave,
They are too strong, tw'ixt Lord & Slave.
Here also liv'd a dingy brother,
Who play'd together with the other,
But, of him, yet longer rotten,
Every particular's forgotten,
Save that like Tweedle-Tum & dee,
These but in notes, could [n]e'er agree,
In all things else, as they do tell ye,
Were just like Handel and Corelli.
O had it been in their life's course
T'have met with Massa Wilberforce,
They wou'd in this alone, have join'd,
And been together of a mind,
Have raisd their Horns to one high tune,
And blown his Merits, to the Moon.[28]

The reference to 'Master Meller' sets the employment of the two musicians in the period before 1733, when John Meller of Erddig died, and the burial record of an African man at Marchwiel in 1721 surely confirms that they worked at the house early in the eighteenth century.[29] The fashion for the acquisition of African servants in gentry households was occasionally reflected in their inclusion in

27 For John Walters, see Peter Lord, 'Deepening the tradition: The paintings of John Walters of Denbigh, *Planet*, 241 (February-May 2021), pp. 68-76.

28 Also published as 'A Black, Aet. 25' in Philip Yorke, *Crude-ditties* (Wrexham, 1802), pp. 30-1.

29 Albinia Lucy Cust, *Chronicles of Erthig on the Dyke* (London, 1914), vol. i, pp. 195-6. Infra-red photography of the portrait revealed that it was painted over an earlier image of a sitter called John Hanby, aged twenty-five, nationaltrustcollections.org.uk/object/115128.

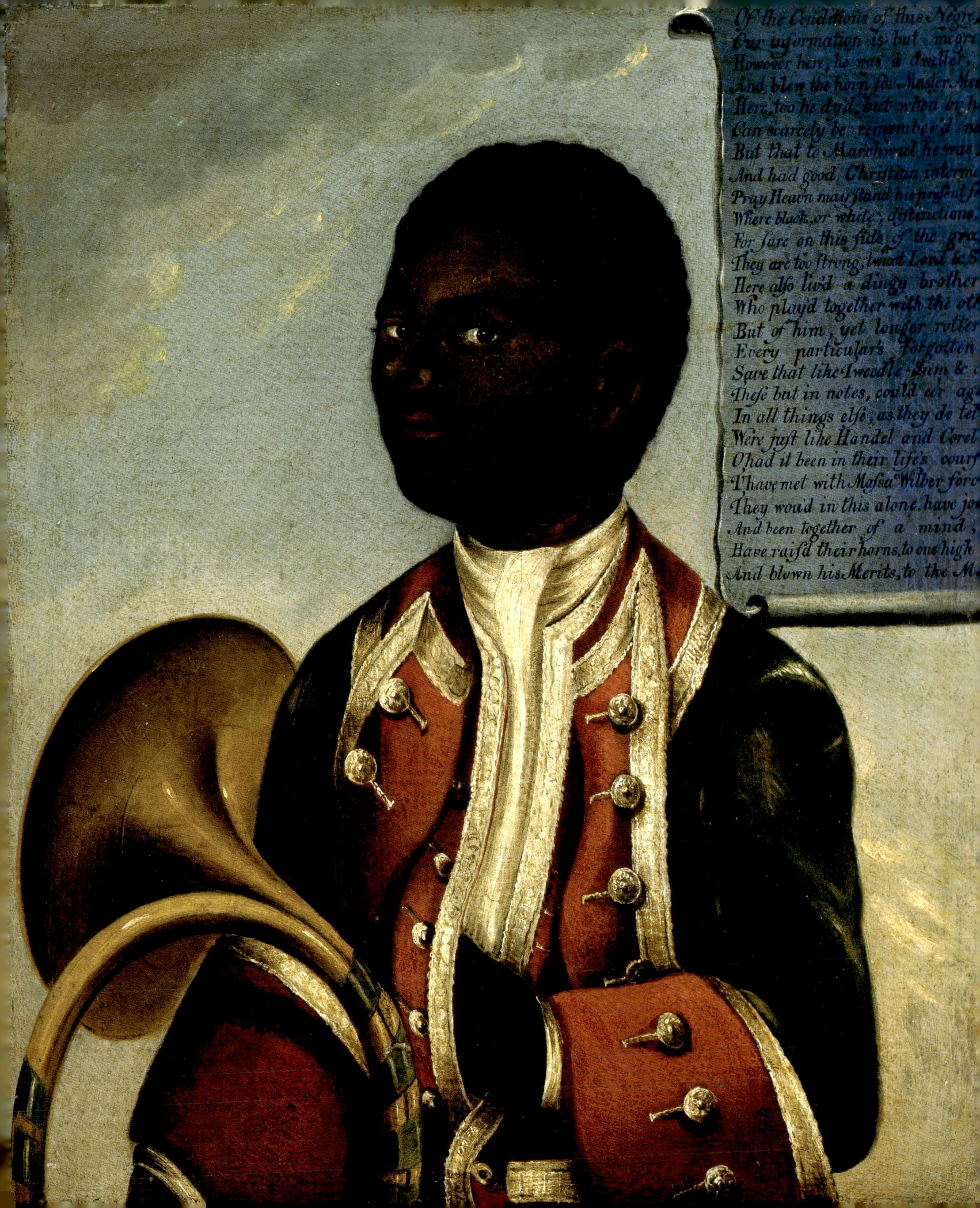
Of the Conditions of this Negro,
Our information is but megre
However here, he was a dweller,
And blew the horn for Master Me
Here, too he dy'd, but when or h
Can scarcely be remember'd no
But that to Marchwiel he was
And had good Christian interm
Pray Heav'n may ſtand his preſent f
Where black, or white, diſtinctions,
For ſure on this ſide of the gra
They are too ſtrong, twixt Lord & S
Here alſo liv'd a dingy brother
Who play'd together with the ot
But of him, yet longer rotte
Every particular's forgotten
Save that like Tweedle-Dum &
Theſe but in notes, could e'er ag
In all things elſe, as they do tel
Were juſt like Handel and Corel
O had it been in their life's cour
T'have met with Maſsa Wilber forc
They wou'd in this alone, have jo
And been together of a mind,
Have raiſ'd their horns, to one high
And blown his Merits, to the M

family or group portraits, though some were painted out as the anti-slavery movement gained momentum after 1787, when the Society for the Abolition of the Slave Trade was founded and William Wilberforce began his engagement with the issue. Philip Yorke's verse, certainly written before 1802, reflects his support for the movement. Since the portrait and the verse are the only surviving evidence of the two men's service, the nature of their musical practice remains obscure, but they were certainly not unique as horn players. A Bristol newspaper reported in 1757: 'Run Away, some time since A NEGRO LAD about 18 years of age near five feet two inches high answers to the name of Starling and blows the French horn very well.'[30] Professor James Walvin has noted that:

> There was a well-established tradition of black musicians in eighteenth-century London, and the French horn was especially popular among them. In part, the rise of black music-making was one aspect of the white belief that Africans and their descendants were especially musical. White accounts of black life, from the earliest encounters frequently referred to black musicality. Not surprisingly, the English encouraged black musicians, in stately and private homes … This was an arena of refinement which would blend African 'musicality' with European sensibility.[31]

With the exception of the retrospective Erddig portrait, with its archaic inclusion of an inscription, the imaging of music among the Welsh gentry in a domestic setting broadly reflected Europe-wide conventions of academic art through the eighteenth century, as did the music played by those depicted. Many of them spent time in London, and were able to acquire the sheet music published there or imported from the continent, as well as to experience public performance. They acquired the notion that music in the home was a central qualification for an individual to be identified as a gentleman or a lady of sensibility. A hundred years after its publication in 1622, Henry Peacham's *The compleat gentleman* continued to set the standard by which a civilised person might be judged. Peacham had asserted that the practice of music placed it among the sciences:

> … which are, the fountaines of our liues good and happinesse: since it is a principall meanes of glorifying our mercifull Creator, it heigthens our deuotion, it giues delight and ease to our trauailes, it expelleth sadnesse and heauinesse of Spirit, preserueth people in concord and amitie, allaieth fiercenesse and anger; and lastly, is the best Phisicke for many melancholly diseases.[32]

21 Probably John Walters of Denbigh, *John Meller's Coachboy*, c.1795

30 *Felix Farley's Bristol Journal*, 19 March 1757, p. 3. The advertisement noted that Starling was 'the Property of Ralph Cook at the sign of the Rising sun in Princes-street, Bristol.'

31 James Walvin, *An African's Life: The Life and Times of Olaudah Equiano, 1745–1797* (London, 2000), p. 92. A painting by John Wootton, *Lamprey, with His Owner Sir William Morgan, at Newmarket* (versions in NMW and the Yale Center for British Art), includes an African servant, Girolamo Bardoletti. It was painted in 1723, two years after the 'Receipts and Expenditure Accounts of James Pratt on behalf of John Morgan 1700–1732' (NLW Tredegar 315-345, 3 April 1721) noted the purchase of French horns for £7/1/0d. John Ystumllyn, brought to Wales by the Wynn family either directly from Africa or by purchase in London, is reputed to have learned to play the crwth, see Alltud Eifion, *John Ystumllyn, neu, 'Jack Black': Hanes ei Fywyd …* (Tremadoc, 1888), no pagination.

32 Henry Peacham, *The compleat gentleman fashioning him absolute in the most necessary & commendable qualities concerning minde or bodie that may be required in a noble gentleman …* (London, 1622), p. 104.

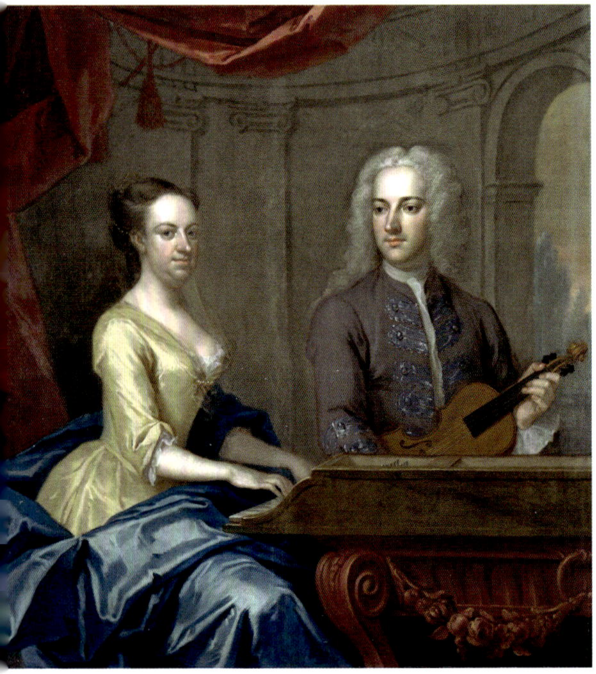

22 Unknown artist, *Thomas and Mary Powell of Nanteos*, c.1730–8

He desired no more of his gentlemen than 'to sing your part sure, and at the first sight, withall, to play the same vpon your Violl, or the exercise of the Lute, priuately to your selfe.' By the time that Thomas and Mary Powell of Nanteos, near Aberystwyth, were painted making music, probably in the early 1730s, the violin had replaced the viol, but their double portrait exemplifies the musical aspect of gentry life that Peacham had espoused. Both sitters had inherited substantial wealth. Mary was the granddaughter of Sir John Frederick, Lord Mayor of London, and Thomas was the son of the Jacobite William Powell of Nanteos and his wife Avarina. It was she who had inherited Nanteos from her father, a mining engineer born in Cologne, who came to Ceredigion to exploit its lead, copper and silver. Mary and Thomas married in 1720 or shortly thereafter, but did not inherit Nanteos until 1738. Although few personal details of their lives have emerged, it seems likely that they spent a considerable amount of their time, before the death of William Powell, in London. Thomas was a Tory Member of Parliament in the mid-1720s. A rare glimpse of his social life in the city is recorded in the diary of the Earl of Egmont in the early 1730s:

> I heard that last Thursday the audience at Drury Lane would not suffer the players to act Lieutenant Bodin's dull comedy, but as soon as the curtain was drawn up, called out for another play. The tumult was great, for several who were curious to see this, cried 'Play, play,' others pulled out of their pockets their catcalls, etc., but Mr. Powell, a Welsh gentleman of estate, offering to speak, silence was made. He told Wilks, the player, that two persons had the night before been hauled out of the gallery by soldiers for showing their disapprobation of the play, which was contrary to the liberty of the subject and right of the playhouse, where those who paid their money were at liberty to approve or disapprove the show. That the highest power on earth should not force the freeborn subjects of England to approve of nonsense, and therefore he required this play should be dismissed and another acted. Wilks, very submissively, told him that they were not prepared on the sudden to change their piece, neither the proper actors nor dresses were ready, but if the audience pleased to take their money again, it should be restored them. The audience were contented, and all trooped home.[33]

33 *Manuscripts of the Earl of Egmont. Diary of Viscount Percival, Afterwards First Earl of Egmont*, vol. i, 1730–33 (London, 1920), p. 216. Thomas Powell trained as a lawyer and was elected and served as a Tory MP in 1725–7. Attempting to win the seat for Cardigan Boroughs in 1729 he was involved in a violent dispute that led to him becoming the prime suspect, on the basis of witness depositions, in the murder of Thomas Howell of Tre-main (see NLW Gogerddan Estate Papers GHA6/2). The election result was disputed by Richard Lloyd, the Whig candidate, and eventually awarded to him on 7 May 1730.

Such 'tumult' was not uncommon in the boisterous atmosphere of the theatre of the period.

In the Nanteos double portrait, Mary Powell plays a harpsichord set on an ornate Baroque table. Mary was somewhat older than her husband, and the ages of the couple suggest that the picture was painted before they inherited Nanteos and commenced its elegant rebuilding in 1739. Mary Powell's attachment to keyboard music was confirmed when she installed an organ in the music room of the new house.[34] However, the architectural setting of the double portrait is almost certainly fanciful, reflecting the fashion of the period set by the court painters. A portrait of Queen Anne, painted in about 1702 by Michael Dahl, has a similar arcaded background.

34 Mary willed the organ to be returned on her death to one of her brothers, probably John Frederick (1678-1755). A single portrait of Mary Powell is at present missing. It was sold by Sotheby's as by 'follower of Michael Dahl' on 19 March 2003. No documentary evidence survives of the repertoire played by the Powells, but it could have included contemporary international composers.

35 NLW Bodewryd Papers 1040.

23 Unknown artist, *Mary Allen of Dale Castle*, c.1745

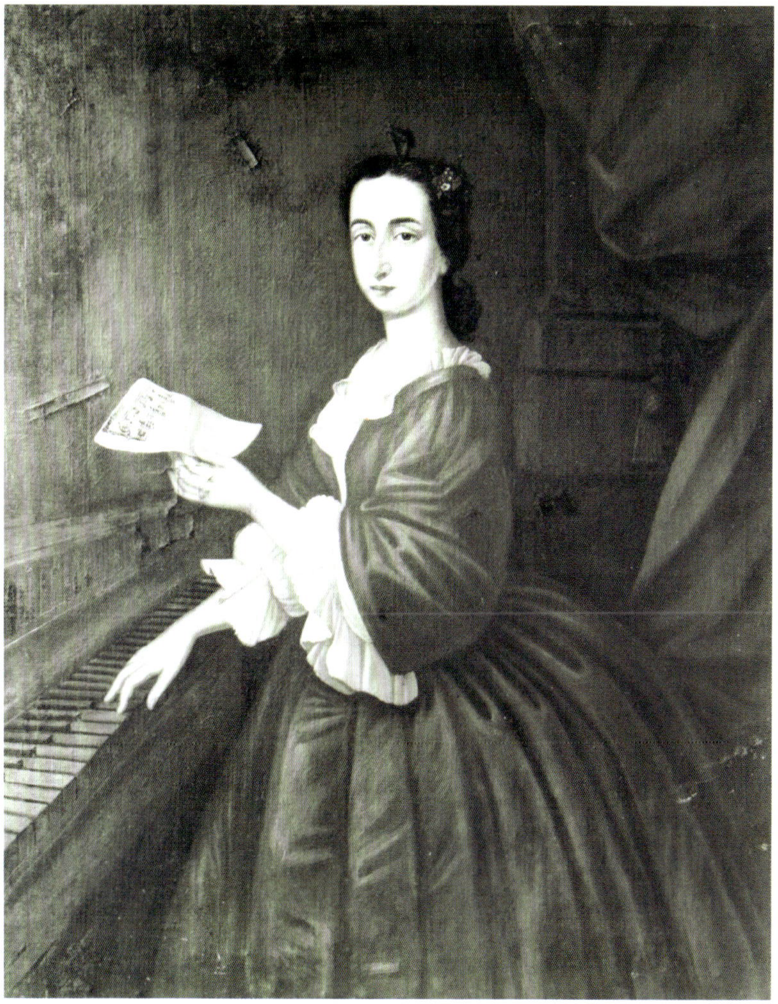

The painter of the Nanteos portrait is unknown. The picture may have been produced in London, and although the young Welsh painter, Edward Owen of Penrhos in Anglesey, was living in the fashionable artistic quarter of Covent Garden during the period, it is unlikely to be his work. Owen is, however, worthy of mention in a musical context since, in 1732, he talked of painting the owners of the Robert ap Huw manuscript, the Meyrick family, when they were visiting the metropolis. Soon afterwards, Edward Owen returned to live at his ancestral home, where he became involved with choral singing at the ancient church of St Cybi in nearby Holyhead. Writing to his brother in 1737, he reported on the state of the choir:

> Our singing goes on pretty well having now upwards of forty schollars we have learn'd two or three psalm's, ye magnificat, & an anthem out of ye Litany since your Departure the Bass improve prodigiously but ye tenor & treble advance but slowly ...[35]

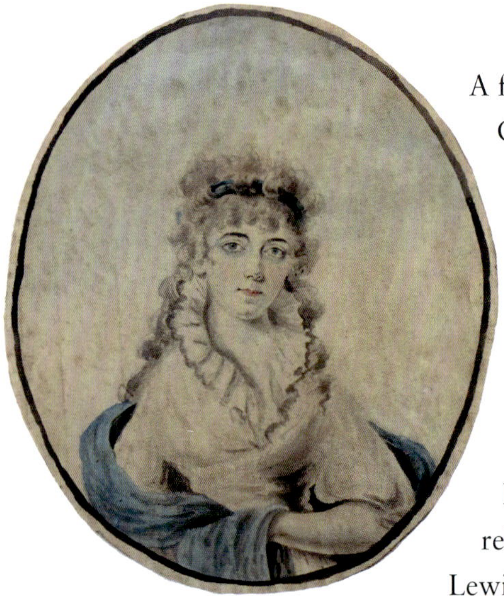

A few years after the Nanteos portrait, in about 1745, Mary Allen of Dale Castle in Pembrokeshire was painted standing at her keyboard with a sheet of manuscript music. Nothing is known of her musical training or ability, though she did have a notable artistic ancestry. She was the great-granddaughter of Anthony van Dyck. But her choice to be painted at the keyboard suggests a deeper interest in music than that of other young women of her class, many of whom would take some musical instruction, just as they would be instructed in drawing, as a normal part of their education. Mary was the daughter of Sir John Stepney of Prendergast. The painter John Lewis carried out a number of commissions related to members of the Stepney family, and the portrait may be his work. Lewis worked in Carmarthenshire and Pembrokeshire over a long period, from the 1730s into the 1760s.[36]

24 Unknown artist, *Catherine Barlow of Colby, later Lady Hamilton I*, c.1755

25 David Allan, *Sir William and the first Lady Hamilton in their Villa at Naples*, 1770

The home of a keyboard player of the next generation, Catherine Barlow, was further east in Pembrokeshire, at Colby.[37] A small watercolour portrait, perhaps painted by an amateur artist, may date from the period before her marriage in 1758 to the Scottish connoisseur, William Hamilton. Through this marriage,

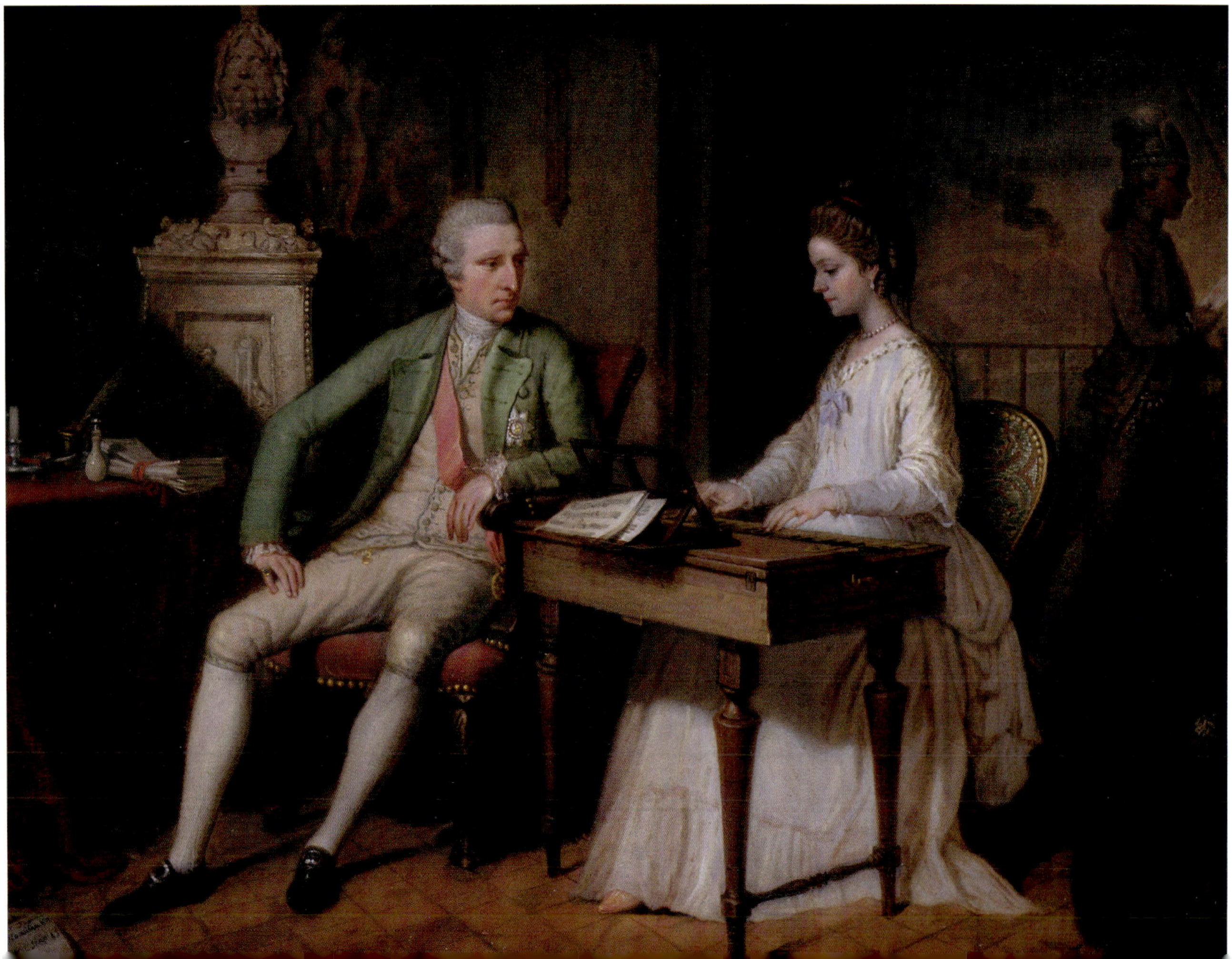

Catherine entered London society at the highest level, since Hamilton had been equerry to the Prince of Wales, a post that was renewed when the Prince became King George III in 1760. Music was important both to Catherine, who was an accomplished keyboardist, and to Hamilton, who had been taught by the celebrated violinist and composer, Felice Giardini. Pursuing their interest, at one of their musical 'at homes', they entertained the young Wolfgang Amadeus Mozart during his visit to London in 1764, when the eight-year-old prodigy also played for the King and accompanied the singing of Queen Charlotte. Six years after their marriage, Sir William took up the post of British Envoy in Naples, where their residences became centres of cultured expatriate life. The Scottish painter David Allan, who travelled to Italy initially under the patronage of Lord Cathcart, Sir William's brother-in-law, was commissioned to paint a double portrait in 1770. The portrait depicts the couple at their villa at Posillipo on the Bay of Naples. Catherine plays a square piano and William's violin lies on the table. Behind him are items from his collection of painting and sculpture – a bust of Zeus and a copy of Correggio's *Venus Disarming Cupid*.[38] William Hamilton would exercise a considerable influence on the classical taste of his period, because of his interest in the vases of Greek manufacture that were being unearthed in great numbers during grave excavations in southern Italy at that time. He formed a large collection and published them as engravings, leading to an increasing awareness of the quality of Greek art, largely obscured until his time by the reputation of Roman work.

In the same year as the David Allan double portrait was painted, the Hamiltons again met Mozart. By then he was fourteen years of age and on tour in Italy. Mozart's father Leopold reported the meeting:

> Yesterday evening we called on the English ambassador Hamilton (our acquaintance from London), whose wife plays the keyboard with exceptional feeling and is a most pleasant person. She trembled at the prospect of having to play for Wolfg. She has a valuable instrument made in England by Burkat Tschudi, with 2 manuals and pedal stops that can be uncoupled by means of the foot.[39]

William Hamilton also played for Mozart on this visit, an event recorded by Pietro Fabris in a painting taken at the residence of Lord Fortrose. Catherine and William Hamilton had recently toured Sicily with Fortrose and the artist. In the

36 Among the Lewis commissions related to the Stepneys is the portrait of Elizabeth Eleanor Lloyd, signed and dated 1744 (Carmarthen Museum), who married Sir Thomas Stepney, 7th Baronet. The portrait of Mary Allen is at present missing, and so attribution to Lewis must remain uncertain. A surviving contemporary portrait of Ann, wife of Rowland Philipps of Laugharne, has stylistic similarities to the portrait of Mary, but seems less likely to be the work of Lewis.

37 Catherine was the daughter of John Barlow (1682–1739), Tory MP for Haverfordwest, and Anne Skrine, his second wife.

38 The original, also owned by Hamilton, is now believed not to be the work of Correggio, but is attributed to Luca Cambiaso. Hamilton was obliged to sell what was at the time generally accepted as a Correggio in 1794.

39 Letter 184, 19 May 1770, given in Cliff Eisen et al (eds.), *In Mozart's Words*, letters.mozartways.com. Lady Hamilton subsequently helped arrange a concert by Mozart at the home of Countess Kaunitz, wife of the Imperial Neapolitan Ambassador.

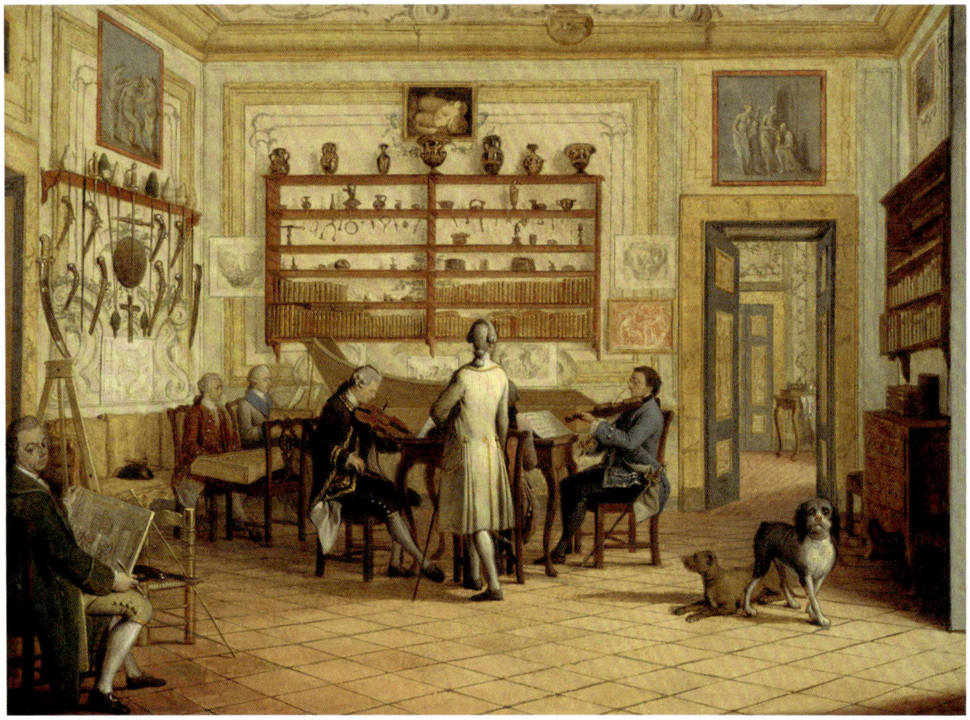

26 Pietro Fabris, *Lord Fortrose (Kenneth Mackenzie, 1st Earl of Seaforth) at home in Naples: a concert party*, 1771

group portrait, Leopold is at the harpsichord with the young prodigy at his side at the spinet. Hamilton is the violinist in the centre of the scene, and the painter included a self-portrait that signified his friendship, as well as his professional relationship, with members of the group. Sadly, the women were absent on this occasion, perhaps because the afternoon levees which were a feature of social life in the period were generally frequented only by men.

Catherine Hamilton's absence was certainly not a reflection on her talent, since the quality of her playing was widely acknowledged. Dr Charles Burney, visiting Italy in 1770 to research what became his *General History of Music*, was impressed, remarking that she was a much better performer on the harpsichord than any Italian he had heard: 'She has great neatness and more expression and meaning in her playing than any lady I ever heard, for ladies, it must be owned, tho' often neat in execution, seldom aim at expression.'[40] Burney's observations on this visit provide an insight into the repertoire that Catherine and her husband enjoyed:

> Mrs H. has a very neat finger and plays the harpsichord with great delicacy, expression and taste. Mr H. is likewise a pretty good performer on the violin; but both are so tired of the music of the Neapolitans as to

> be glad to return to that of Corelli, Geminiani, Handel, Vivaldi etc for the sake of harmony and variety – indeed the general run of Neapolitan music is noisy and monotonous, but while such composers as Jomelli, Piccini, Merula, Mann[a], Paesiello etc are in it one would think no complaint need be made of a scarcity of good music.[41]

On leave from their duties in Naples in 1777, Catherine and her husband re-entered the musical life of London, where she heard of the ability of a young Welsh harper called Edward Jones. They were introduced by a mutual friend, Olivia Wilmot Sims:

> Lady William Hamilton drinks tea with me tomorrow evening. I dined with her last week she then said she would like to hear you play – and if she did she would get you some pupils Mrs Nicols thinks if you would bring your harp in a Coach that Lady Hamilton would be quite delight'd – I am sure I shall feel very happy if my introducing you & Lady Hamilton would Professionally serve you.[42]

Given William Hamilton's close relationship with the royal family, it seems likely that the introduction to Catherine Hamilton did indeed play a significant part in the rise of Edward Jones, who was to become harper to the Prince of Wales, and ultimately to the King.

Just as their shared Scottish origins facilitated David Allan's acquaintance with Sir William Hamilton, it may be that Thomas Jones of Pencerrig was encouraged by the fact that Lady Catherine was Welsh when he decided to leave Rome for Naples to seek the patronage of her husband and his circle. After leaving the London studio of Richard Wilson and painting independently for a decade, Jones had travelled to Italy in 1776. He noted in the account which he wrote later of his life that in the spring of 1780:

> Having no prospect of any more commissions at Rome, & those I was engaged in, being all of them Views in the Environs of Naples I thought it would be more convenient, if not a more Prudent step, to make the latter the place of my future Residence, especially if I should be so fortunate as to obtain the patronage of Sir W'm Hamilton, our Minister – at all Events I should there have fewer Rival Competitors.[43]

40 H. Edmund Poole (ed.), *Music, Men, and Manners in France and Italy, 1770, Being the Journal written by Charles Burney during a Tour through those Countries undertaken to collect material for A General History of Music Transcribed from the Original Manuscript in the British Museum, Additional Manuscript 35122* (London, 1969), p. 180. William Beckford of Fonthill was another admirer of Catherine Hamilton: 'Her power of musical execution was wonderful – so sweetly soft was her touch – she seemed as if she had thrown her own essence into the music,' he recalled. 'I used to listen to her like one entranced.' Lewis Melville, *The Life and Letters of William Beckford of Fonthill* (London, 1910), p. 94.

41 Poole, *Music, Men, and Manners*, p. 177.

42 NLW MS 109B, f. 39.

43 'Memoirs of Thomas Jones, Penkerrig Radnorshire, 1803', in *The Volume of the Walpole Society*, 32 (1946), p. 93.

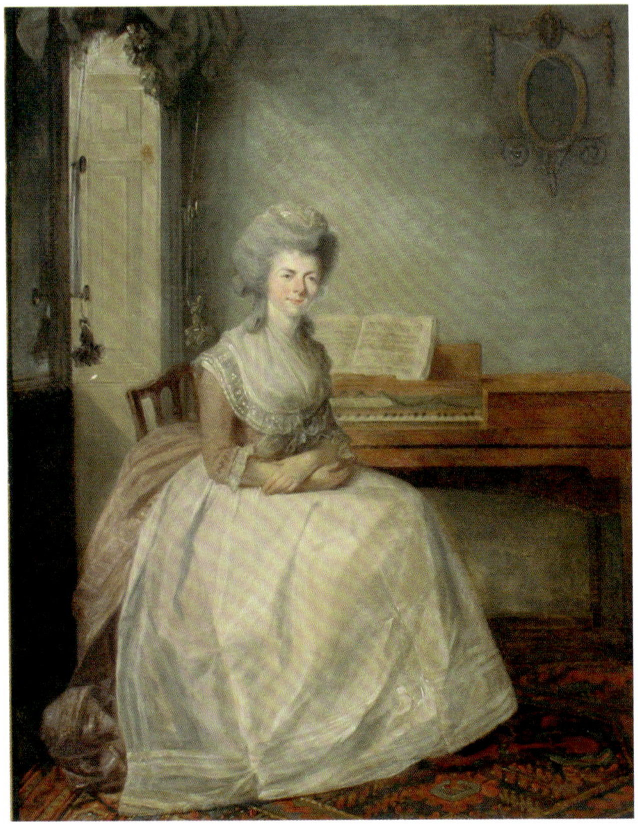

The following day he 'sent off Maria' – his Danish lover, Maria Moncke – to secure lodgings, and followed her to Naples some three weeks later. When eventually he met the Hamiltons, he was received with 'much Civility' and 'attended Sir William's levee as often as delicacy would permit'.[44] Despite Jones's attempts to ingratiate himself with the family, it was not until the beginning of August 1782 that the great man finally saw his pictures and bought one soon after. Sadly, the relationship would have little time to develop because, on 25 August 1782, Catherine Hamilton died. Jones recalled that:

> ... she had long been in a declining State [and] dyed of a bilious fever, rather prematurely, as it is thought, owing to the Sudden Shock she received at hearing the News of that fatal Accident which befell her confidential Physician.'[45]

27 Probably Oldfield Bowles, *Hannah Jones of Pencerrig*, c.1775–82

Catherine's body was returned to Wales and interred at the Commandery Church of St John, Slebech. Her husband soon married the celebrated Emma, the second Lady Hamilton, who had grown up at Hawarden in Flintshire, but Sir William would eventually choose to be interred with his first wife in Pembrokeshire.[46]

Thomas Jones had returned from Italy in 1783 to live not as a professional artist but, eventually, as the squire of Pencerrig, though he continued to paint and to maintain some of the relationships he had made in Italy. Among them was his friendship with the painter Francesco Renaldi, whom he had met in Rome. Subsequently, Renaldi joined Jones in Naples, where they 'lived much together'. They met again in Fleet Street on Jones's return to London, and Renaldi spent the evening with him, Maria, and the children.[47] Given that Renaldi had left Naples before Jones, it is possible that, on his friend's recommendation, he was responsible for a pair of portraits of the painter's parents, Hannah and Thomas. However, the portraits seem more likely to be the work of the painter Oldfield Bowles, a supporter and patron of Jones in the period immediately before he left for Italy.[48]

44 Ibid., pp. 96–7.

45 Ibid., p. 114. Dr Drummond had recently died following a fall from his horse.

46 Hamilton inherited his wife's estates and was responsible for the development of Pembroke Dock and Milford Haven. Like her predecessor, Sir William's second wife, Emma Hamilton, was musical. She sang and was portrayed at the piano, apparently as St Cecilia, by Richard Westall (National Maritime Museum).

47 'Memoirs of Thomas Jones', pp. 106, 138.

48 We are grateful to Jeremy Rye for this attribution.

The Pencerrig estate, where the painter grew up, was Hannah's inheritance. She was unusual among the gentry of the period in having strong Nonconformist religious convictions – her father had founded Caebach Independent Chapel in 1715. The implication of her portrait is that Hannah was musical and played the keyboard at which she is seated. Some fifteen years later, in a group portrait that was certainly painted by Renaldi, a similar instrument is played by Jones's daughter Elizabetha. Both she and her sister, Anna-Maria, who stands behind the instrument, were born in Naples, before their mother's marriage to their father.[49] Maria, who would survive only another two years, sits at her spinning wheel, and the other sitter, relegated to the back of the group, may be Thomas Jones's younger brother, the Revd David Jones. The picture – the last of Renaldi's identified works – was exhibited at the Royal Academy in 1798.

49 They married in London in 1789, two years after Jones became head of the family and heir to Pencerrig following his elder brother's death.

28 Francesco Renaldi, *Thomas Jones of Pencerrig and his family*, 1797

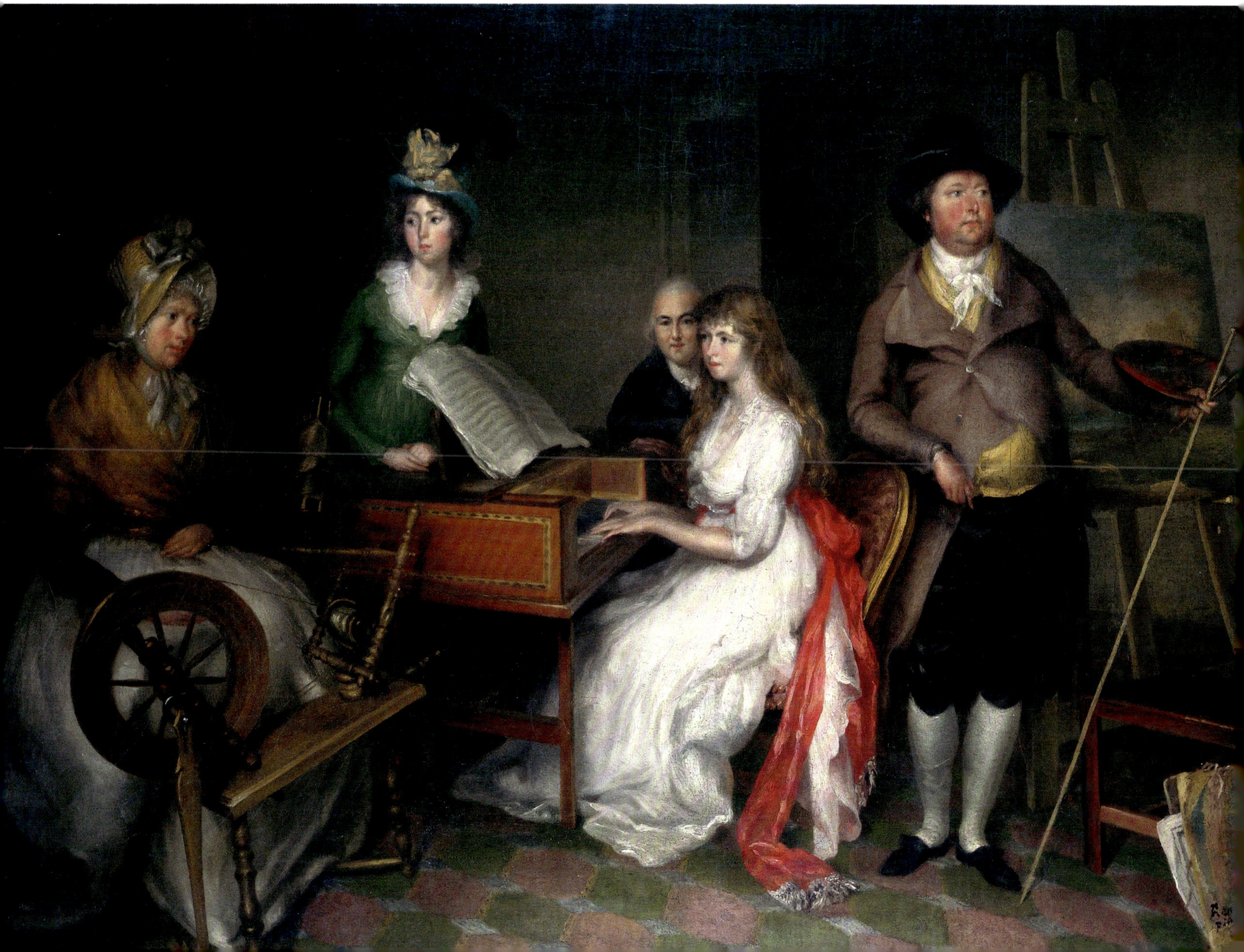

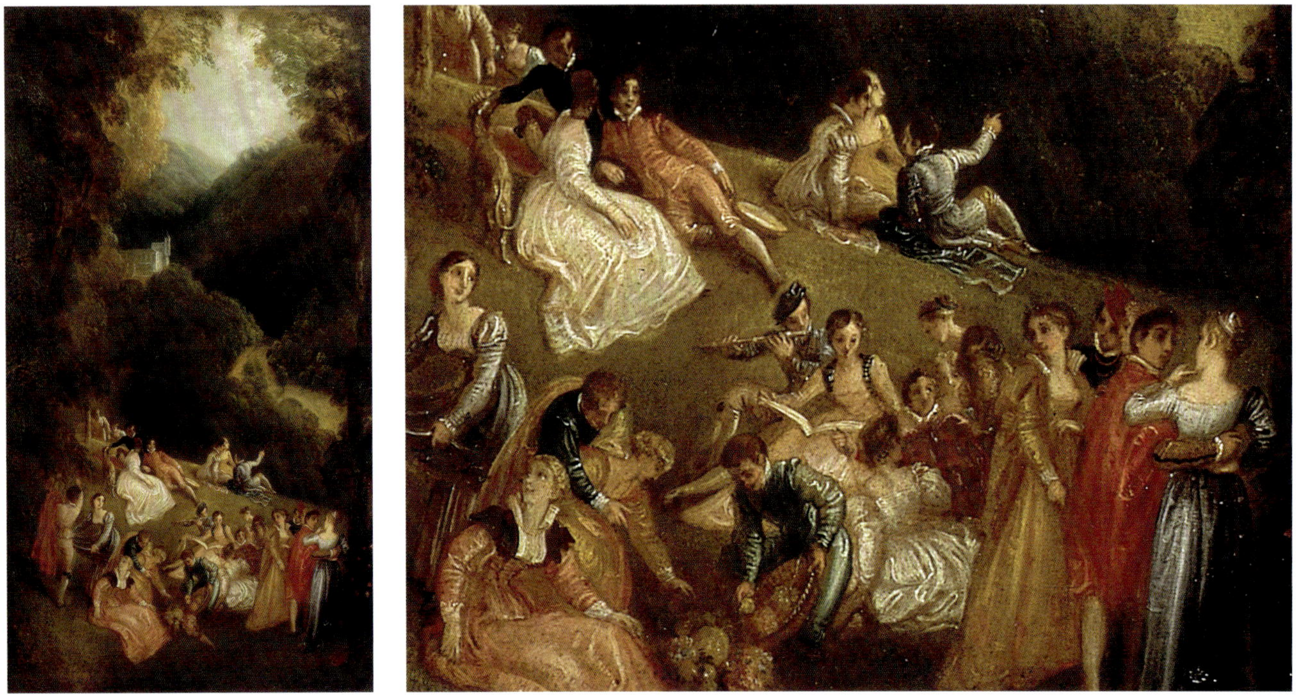

29 Thomas Stothard, *Fête Champêtre at Hafod*, c.1803

Although Thomas Jones himself noted that his professional career as a painter had to all intents and purposes come to an end by 1784, he did continue to take occasional commissions from friends, and to exhibit.[50] Among his supporters in the latter period of his life was Thomas Johnes of Hafod, near Aberystwyth. Although dogged by misfortune, Johnes's attempt to turn Hafod into an exemplar of picturesque taste resulted in visits by many artists and intellectuals. Thomas Jones first journeyed there from Pencerrig in about 1785. He produced drawings and paintings in oil and watercolour, some of which were probably the basis for the Hafod service of porcelain, produced and decorated at Derby in 1787, and exhibited in London the same year.

By 1803, the painter Thomas Stothard had also begun to work at Hafod, primarily as drawing tutor to Johnes's daughter Mariamne, though he also carried out decorative commissions for her father. Indeed, in a letter to his wife, he complained that:

> You have not an idea how my time is filled up … I have no exercise but what the pencil affords me, and sometimes running from one part of the house to the other. Sometimes I get an hour out of doors to get a little air. The small room I paint in affords me none; filled, as it is, with eight canvases, with my colours, oils and turpentines, etc.

50 'Memoirs of Thomas Jones', p. 141.

51 Letter to James Edward Smith, 22 September 1803, Linnean Society of London, Smith, 16, f. 146.

52 Letter to Robert Anderson, 19 April 1804, National Library of Scotland MS Adv. 22.4.12, f. 231.

53 Elisabeth Inglis-Jones, *Peacocks in Paradise* (London, 1950), p. 247.

54 Letter to George Cumberland, 15 October 1806, BL Add MS 36500, f. 405. Francis Gould [Goold] had a substantial financial interest in the King's Theatre in London at this time.

Among the pictures painted by the harassed Stothard for Thomas Johnes was a *fête champêtre*, which was also something of a *capriccio*, since the presentation of the house itself, both its architecture and its elevated location in the Ystwyth valley, inclined towards fantasy. However, the picture may well represent the kind of summer event in which Johnes indulged in his imagined paradise, imitating the practice much favoured at the pre-revolutionary French court and celebrated in the paintings of Watteau and other masters of *L'Ancien Régime*. At the centre of the Hafod group, a flautist entertains the surrounding young ladies, dressed in faux Tudor costumes.

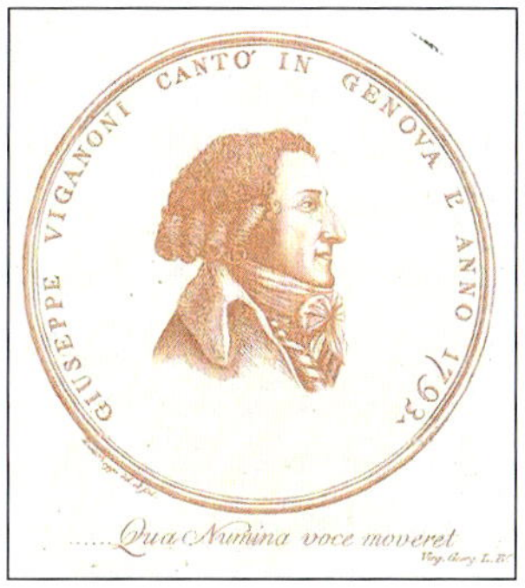

30 Domenico Piaggio, *Giuseppe Viganoni*, c.1793

In the work of teaching Mariamne Johnes, Stothard was joined by a singing master, Giuseppe Viganoni. The Italian tenor had first appeared in London in 1781 without great success, but became more widely appreciated after his return from the continent in 1795. He was at the peak of his London career when his involvement with Hafod began. At the end of the summer of 1803, after Viganoni went back from Wales to London, Johnes reported to a friend that: 'His improvement in Mariamne's playing & singing is wonderful, but I believe her talents for drawing are equally good.'[51] The following spring, anticipating the return of the Italian, Johnes wrote to his close friend, Robert Anderson, in Edinburgh, suggesting that 'if you are fond of Music I shall be able to give you very good as Viganoni & Cramer will both be with us in August.'[52] Well regarded as Viganoni was, the suggestion that Johann Baptist Cramer, friend of Haydn, Mozart and Beethoven, accompanied him to Hafod, takes the patronage of Johnes to an altogether higher level, for Cramer was a prolific composer and widely recognised as among the finest pianists in Europe.

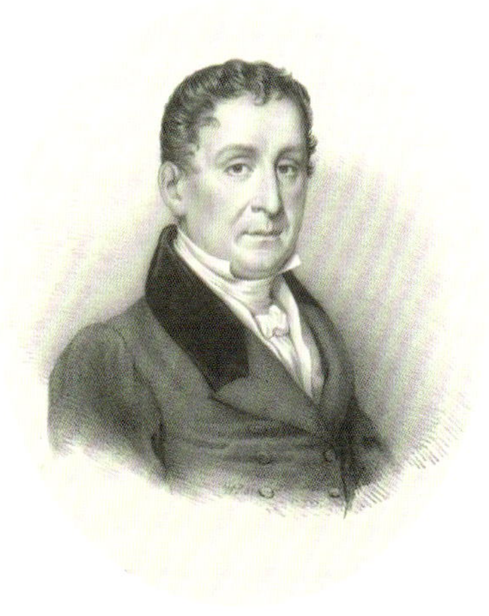

31 William Sharp, *Johann Baptist Cramer*, 1830

The Hafod family's relationship with Viganoni would continue for several years. Johnes had received from the singer himself the gift of a portrait painted by Domenico Pellegrini, in acknowledgement of their association.[53] He was invited to Hafod again in 1806, when Johnes noted:

> Viganoni left us this day sennight on account of Gould [for] the Opera on the 3rd next month. We have now lost our delightful concerts, and the weather weeps his loss, for we have not had one dry day since he went away.[54]

The relationship was maintained in London as well as in Wales after Johnes rented a house each season from 1808. It seems likely that the portrait of

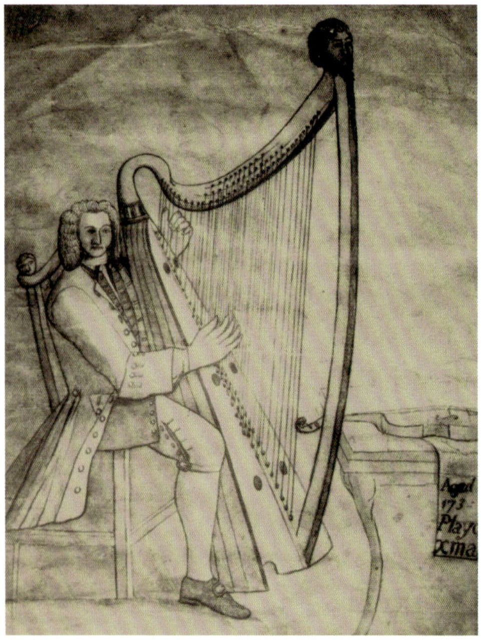

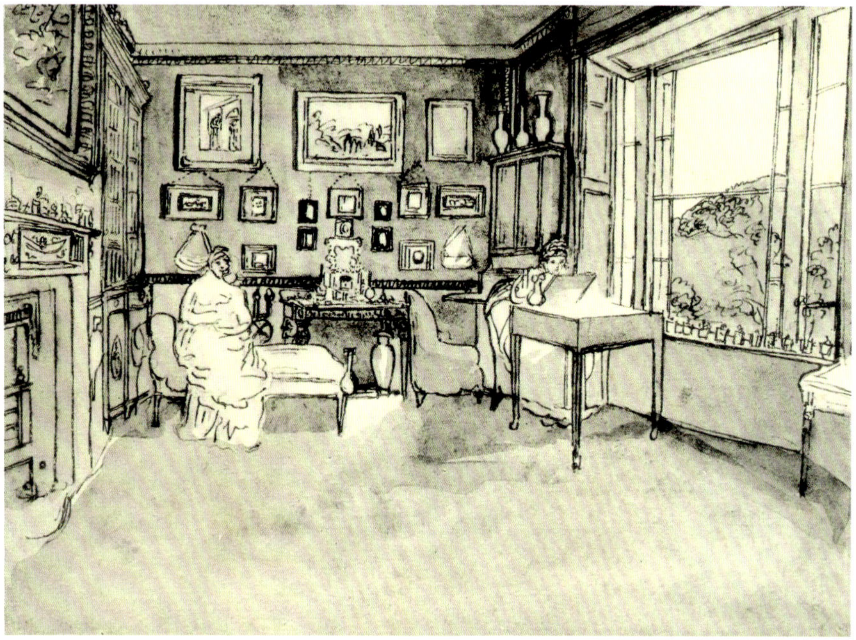

32 Unknown artist, *Griffith Evans of Nanteos*, c.1735

33 Probably Mariamne Johnes, *Music at Hafod*, c.1805

34 George Cumberland, *Mariamne Johnes and Giuseppe Viganoni*, 1804–5

Mariamne, singing to Viganoni's accompaniment, was drawn there. It was the work of George Cumberland, an old friend of her father's, who had published *An Attempt to Describe Hafod* in 1796. In another image which is probably a self-portrait, Mariamne sits at her piano while her mother sews. This drawing certainly depicts an interior at Hafod, and Mariamne's tutoring by Stothard is perhaps evident in the correct perspective of the room, its walls hung with many paintings, though the drawing of the figures is hesitant.

THE GENTRY AND NATIVE TRADITIONS

Such documentary evidence as survives suggests a steady decline through the seventeenth and first half of the eighteenth century in the practice of music that contemporaries regarded as exhibiting particular national characteristics. It was a process for which a weakening of the link between that music and the patronage of an increasingly Anglicised gentry would later be blamed.[55] However, the link had not been entirely broken, and those points of contact that remained, in the form of vestigial elements of the *clera* tradition of hospitality to itinerant musicians, and the maintenance of a family harper, would provide a basis for the work of the patriotic revivalists of the second half of the eighteenth century in their construction of the tradition.

55 For an example of the Anglicisation of music in an ancient Welsh house, Lleweni in Denbighshire, see Sally Harper, 'An Elizabethan tune list from Lleweni Hall, North Wales', *Royal Musical Association Research Chronicle*, 38 (2005), pp. 45–98. The manuscript (Bangor University Archives MS Gwyneddon 4) names seven harpers, three crwth players and three poets present together over Christmas 1595, but the tune list in the same document is almost exclusively English. Harper noted, p. 56, the evidence provided by the manuscript 'that the repertory of old-style harp and crwth players did on occasion encompass popular Elizabethan tunes, despite the limited range of their instruments.'

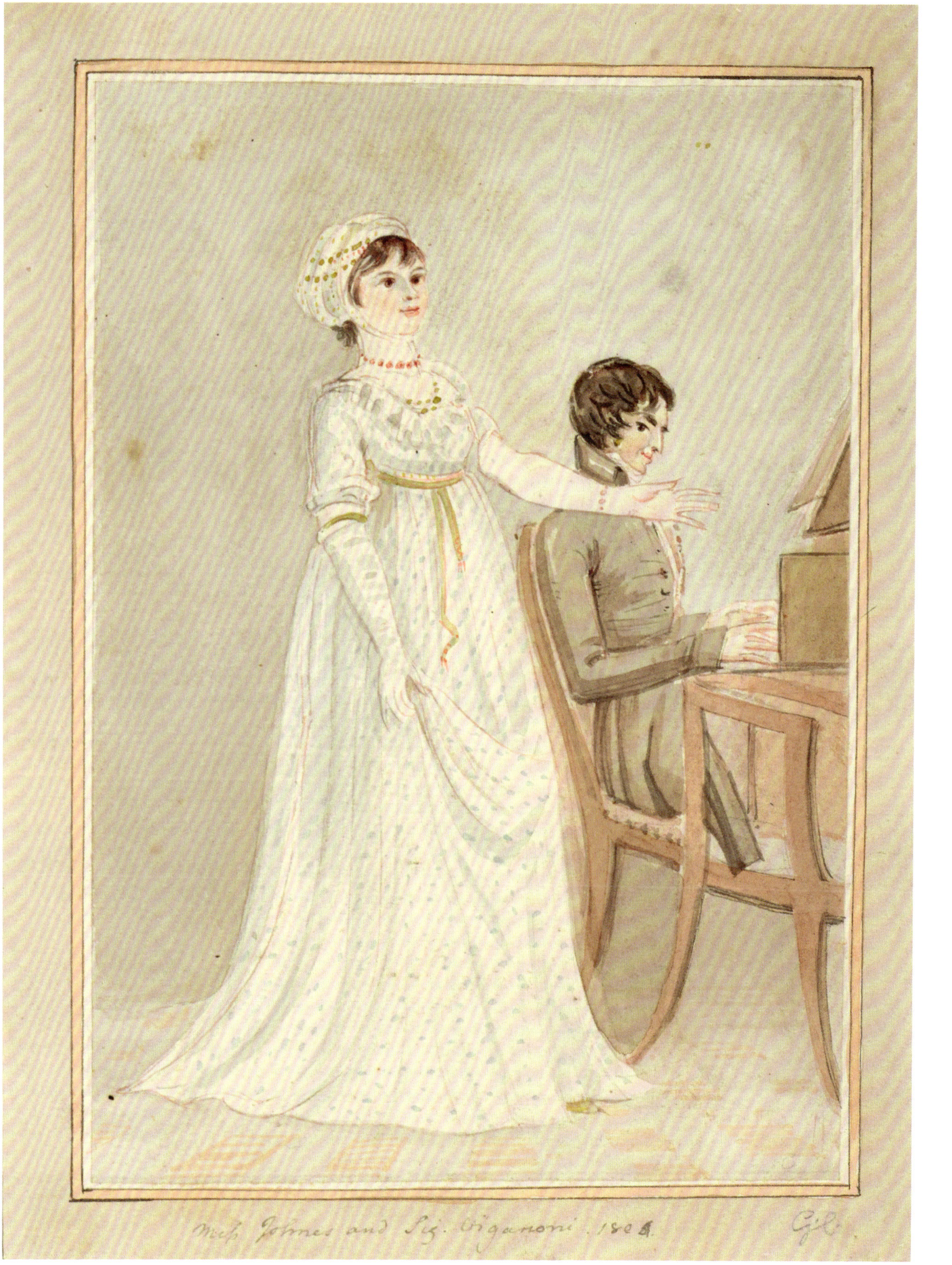
Miss Johnes and Sig. Viganoni

At about the same time as Thomas and Mary Powell of Nanteos were painted in sophisticated trans-national style at their music, perhaps in London, an unidentified artist at their home in mid-Wales made a simple drawing of the harper Griffith Evans. Little is known of this musician, other than that a custom of hosting his visits to Nanteos on an annual basis at New Year appears to have been maintained over many years. Evans's precise dates are uncertain, and it is unclear how far the hospitality offered him extended back into the period of William Powell, but the presence of a violin on a low table at the side of the harper suggests that it was mainly in the period of his son, Thomas, that he frequented the house. Presumably, for the remainder of the year, the harper made a living as an itinerant musician.

For the first time in a visual image, this portrait reveals that the instruments played by working musicians in Wales had changed. The evolution of this fundamental development – the decline of the crwth and the rise of the violin, and the decline of the small single harp and the adoption of the triple harp – are difficult to trace in detail. The process appears to have been driven, as was much else concerning the taste of the Welsh gentry, by London fashion. Nevertheless, in the case of the triple harp, it would have more long-lasting and important implications for Welsh music than for English practice. Though the single harp may still have been in use in the period when Gwilym Pue drew it as the Golden Harp of King David in the mid-seventeenth century, it is doubtful that the instrument was widely played a hundred years later, though the preservation of a few instruments was noted by eighteenth-century antiquarians. The triple harp that superseded it developed in Italy and arrived in London around 1600, with Charles Evans appointed as 'His Majesty's harper for the Italian harp' in 1660. Indeed, this appointment probably marked a transition at court from the use of the single-strung harp of pre-revolutionary days. Charles Evans appears to have been the son, or a close relative, of Lewis Evans, who had been taught by an English court harper to play an instrument of this type, referred to as the Irish harp, in the early seventeenth century. A group portrait of the early 1660s is believed to depict Charles Evans playing the new Italian harp for the acquisition of which he was reimbursed £15 from the royal treasury in 1663. His companions – two violinists, a viola player and a bass violinist – formed King Charles II's 'Private Music', and were attended by a young African servant.[56]

56 Peter Holman, 'The harp in Stuart England: New light on William Lawes's Harp Consorts', *Early Music*, 15, 2 (May 1987), pp. 188–203

Although it seems likely that Lewis and Charles Evans were Welsh or of Welsh descent, there is nothing to suggest that it was their nationality that marked them out as specialist practitioners. Clearly, Charles Evans was playing art music as part of a court ensemble, and there is no evidence that his practice might represent a continuity of particularly Welsh tradition, bridging the transfer from the single to the triple harp. It was not until the first half of the eighteenth century that a particular association between the triple harp and Welsh players – and makers –

35 Unknown artist, *King Charles II's Private Music, with the harpist Charles Evans*, early 1660s

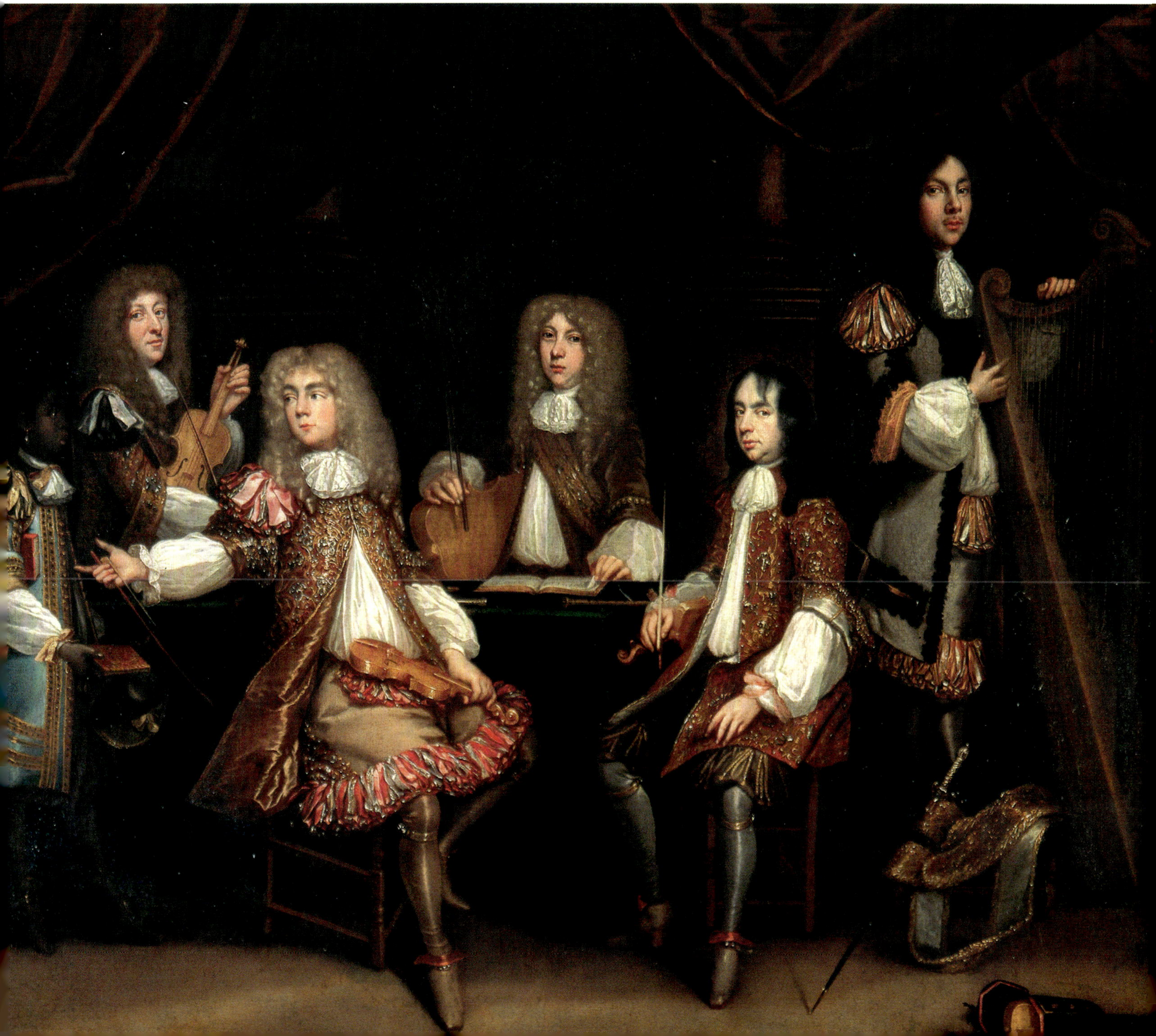

emerged. In London, the instrument maker David Evans, working at Rose Street in Covent Garden, made triple harps in the 1730s – apparently the period of the Nanteos harper. One example survives, dated 1736, and it is probably no coincidence that it was at about this time that the notion of Welsh musicality made a prominent public reappearance in the context of the triple harp, and in the person of the blind harper, John Parry, familiarly known as 'Telynor Dall'.

As we shall see, the celebrity in London of John Parry would be crucial in the construction of the Welsh national musical brand, through the conflation of his virtuoso technique with the idea of the continuity of bardic tradition. But although he would become feted for playing an instrument imported from Italy via the English court, John Parry's career was certainly established as the result of the perpetuation in a few houses of the medieval tradition of gentry patronage. John Parry was born near the Cefnamwlch estate of the Griffith family in about 1710, and the Griffiths were his first patrons. He is reputed to have been taught to play by a relative, Robert Parry of Llanllyfni, and presumably in this early period, he learned the traditional airs which, later, he would perform in England and Ireland side by side with the work of contemporary composers. It is unclear when his services were secured by Sir Watkin Williams Wynn, 3rd Baronet.[57] Unlike Griffith Evans, the Nanteos harper, Parry became a resident member of the Wynn household at Wynnstay, Ruabon, but crucially, his association with the wealthiest family in Wales also propelled him to the highest echelons of London society. Through his association with Sir Watkin, John Parry's playing was heard and admired by Handel, and his growing reputation enabled him also to give concerts independently. In 1742, for example, he appeared at Leeds, where he played 'a Grand Concerto by Mr Handel' and works by Corelli, Vivaldi and Geminiani – in addition to Welsh and Scottish airs. In the same year, he published *Antient British Music*, a seminal event in the evolution of the national brand. Indeed, the career development of Parry from the humblest of origins in Penllŷn to the London salons of the mega-rich, is a barometer of the evolution of a national cultural revival.

In the following year of 1743, Parry's son, William, was born in London to his wife Elizabeth. The family was living at Jermyn Street, near St James's Church, Piccadilly, where John Parry is believed to have played the organ. Sir Watkin died in 1749 but the Parry family continued to receive the patronage of Lady Williams Wynn until the 4th Baronet came of age two decades later. Lady Wynn's support enabled William Parry to train as a painter at the highest level, ultimately in the

57 Parry may have performed in London in 1733, though whether he would have done so independently, or under the patronage of the Griffith family or of Sir Watkin is unclear.

58 A copy of this portrait was made by the Hon. Mary Grace O'Brien in 1879 (NMW) and, significantly, came into the possession of Lady Llanover.

59 'For Mr Parry's Benefit', *Bath Chronicle and Weekly Gazette*, 15 May 1766, p. 4.

60 Anna Maria Bennett, *Ellen, Countess of Castle Howel* (London, 1794), vol. i, p. 4.

61 For instance, at Gogerddan, near Aberystwyth, Jeremiah Wood Jones, 'Jerri Bach Gogerddan', worked for half a century until his death in 1867. He was a member of the celebrated Romany family of musicians. His daughter, Eleanor, married John Roberts, Telynor Cymru, see below pp. 158, 209, 211-15.

studio of Joshua Reynolds, and subsequently to travel to Italy with the support of the young 4th Baronet. William's brother, David, also developed as a musician with the assistance of the Wynns and was often employed by them. A double portrait by William Parry presents his father and brother as family musicians in a domestic setting, probably a room at Wynnstay, and completes the process of fusing the indigenous tradition of gentry patronage with modern music and instrumentation.[58] David Parry holds a score of Handel's *Zadok the Priest,* written as an anthem for the Coronation of King George II in 1727, which he and his father played on two triple harps at Bath in 1766.[59]

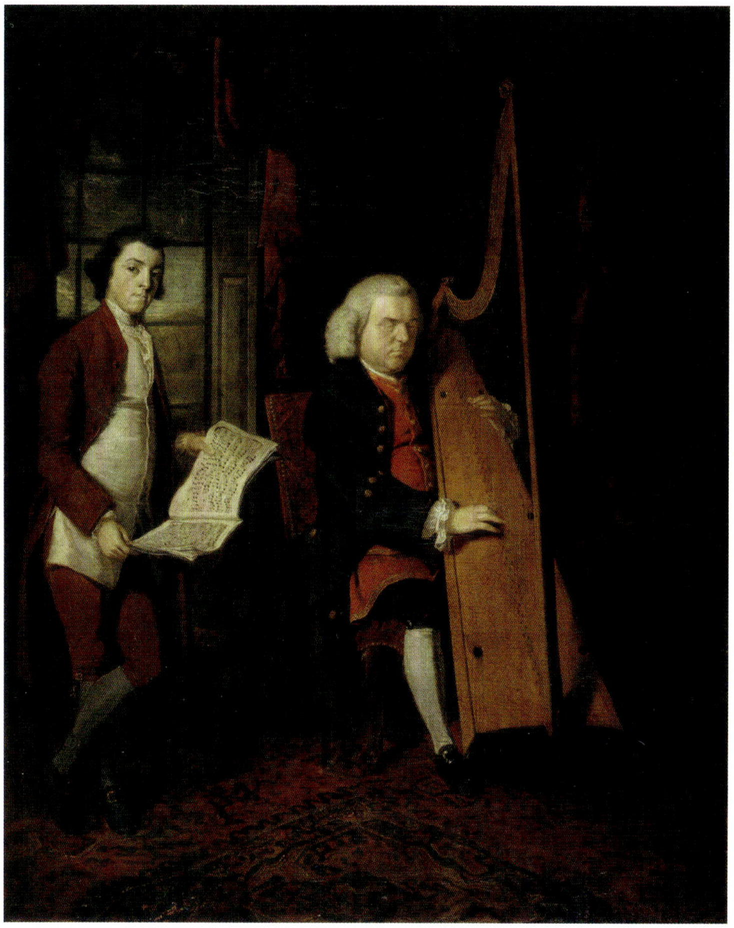

36 William Parry, *David Parry with His Father, the Harper John Parry*, 1770–80

Some twenty-five years after Parry painted the double portrait, in 1794 Anna Maria Bennett published a novel, *Ellen, Countess of Castle Howel*, which was set in a family whose conservative, indeed decayed, Welsh way of life was symbolised by their family harper. In the ancient house:

> The hall appeared to be the bond of union between the heads of the family and the domestics – the harper had his seat, and there the avocations and labours of the day constantly closed with a dance.[60]

The harper was depicted as decrepit an individual as the house itself, but clearly, the idea resonated with a public by that time engaged with myths of Welsh antiquity. The novel achieved considerable popularity. At a few gentry houses, the tradition of keeping a resident harper did indeed persist, even into the early nineteenth century,[61] but the visual record of two of these individuals does not conform to the archaic image presented in the Bennett novel. As in the Parry portrait, Benjamin Marshall depicted the harper Griffith Owen in an unpretentious domestic setting. Owen worked for the Corbett family of Ynysymaengwyn near Tywyn, though his duties as harper were combined with those of a butler. Again echoing the Parry portrait, Owen holds a volume of

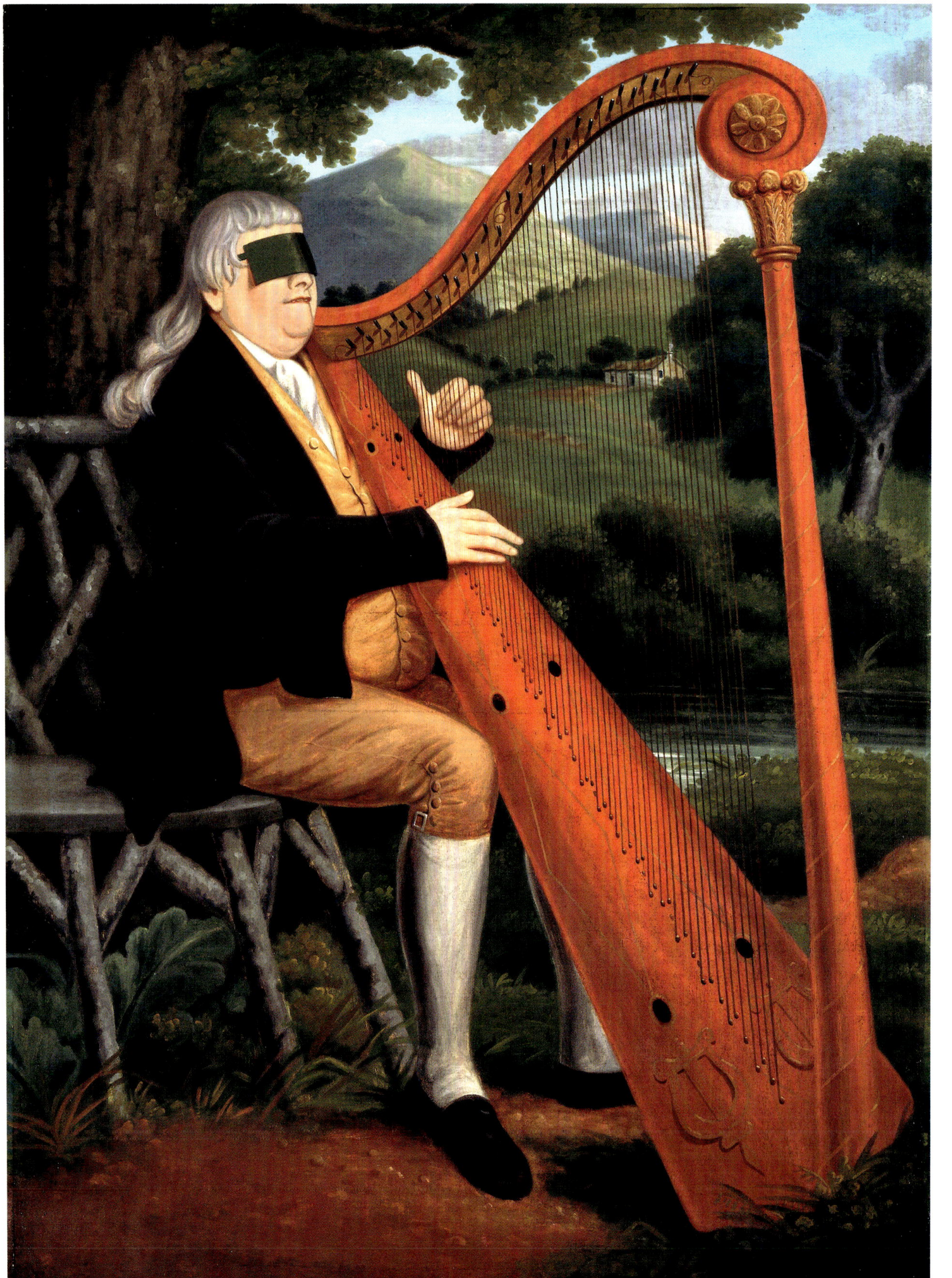

Handel's music, reflecting its continued popularity with either the harper or his employers. The portrait was probably painted in about 1812 and was a somewhat unusual commission for an artist whose popularity in the later part of his career rested mainly on his depictions of sporting subjects.

37 J. Chapman, *William Williams, Wil Penmorfa*, 1826

The restrained tone of Marshall's portrait of the Ynysymaengwyn harper stands in contrast to the brightness and vigour of the remarkable portrait painted in 1826 of William Williams, 'Wil Penmorfa', harper to the Gwynne family of Tre-gib, near Llandeilo in Carmarthenshire. However, the brilliant clarity of the image is not matched by documentary information concerning the sitter and the artist. Williams is believed to have been trained by John Parry, the Wynnstay harper, though how and where is unclear, since Parry spent so much time in London from the 1740s. However, the Wynns did own land in Penmorfa. Equally, how Williams came to work for the Gwynnes in the south is unknown. Clearly, the prominence of the cottage seen through the strings of the triple harp suggests that the picture represents the harper's home – perhaps his home on the Tre-gib estate, or, given the nature of the landscape, an historical reference to his humble origins in the north. The portrait was painted in 1826, two years before the harper died at the age of sixty-nine, by one J. Chapman. No other oil painting by Chapman has been identified, but a number of engravings of the period signed with this name or the name of James Chapman may represent his work.[62] Nevertheless, Chapman's portrait of Wil Penmorfa is a significant as well as a delightful image. It may well be the last portrait to represent the uninterrupted continuity of a tradition of musical patronage which, by the time it had been painted, had already been profoundly changed by the emergence of romantic notions of ancient bards.

38 Benjamin Marshall, *Griffith Owen of Ynysymaengwyn*, c.1812

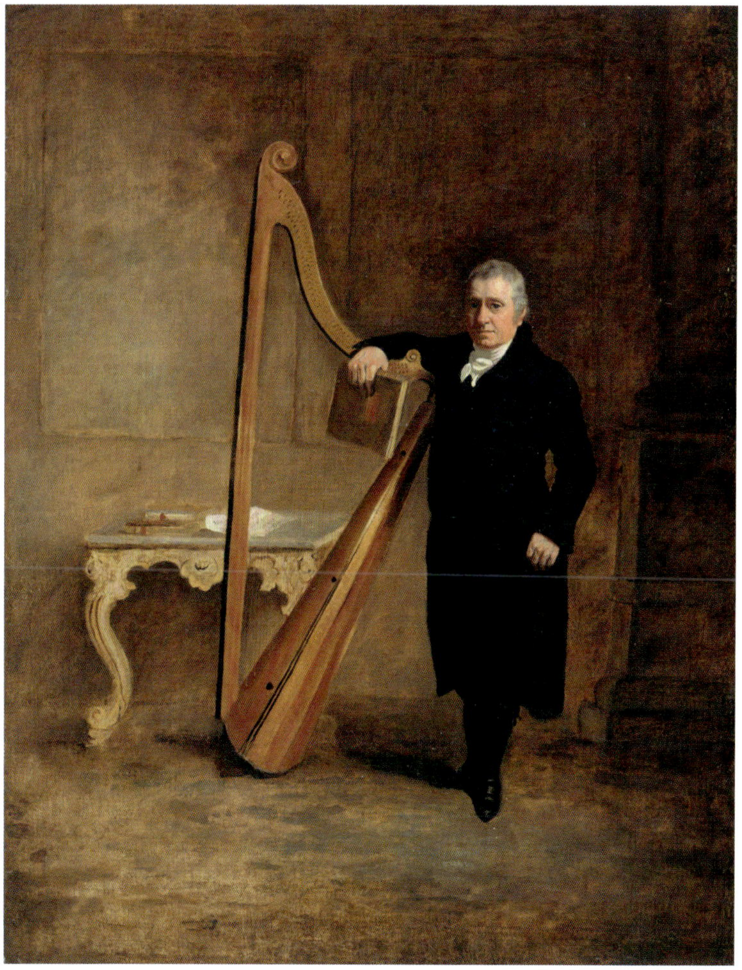

62 See, for instance, *A correct and Beautiful View of the Town and Harbour of Swansea, taken from the Pier Head* in 1825, the simple artisan characteristics of which perhaps suggest the same hand.

CHAPTER TWO

The CONSTRUCTION *of the* BARDIC TRADITION

CAMBRIAN ABORIGINALS – RAISING THE PROFILE IN LONDON

Notwithstanding the grafting by the 1730s of the triple harp on to the much older traditions both of the itinerant harper and the family harper in Wales itself, it was the practice of Welsh musicians in London and the interest that this aroused in intellectual circles that drove the development of the national brand. London would be the source of most printed descriptions and visual images relating to Welsh musical activity – including the earliest extant oil portrait of an individual Welsh harper. No contemporary written documentation survives to indicate the birthplace of David Lewis, who was painted by William Hogarth, but a letter, originally in the possession of the family of the painter, provides some information about him.[1] Hogarth became a nephew of David Lewis by a marriage that took place in 1729, and it was probably shortly afterwards that he painted his portrait. The harper lived at Twickenham, where his wife's brother kept the George Tavern. It is possible that Lewis played there and so met people of influence who congregated in the fashionable village. Perhaps in this way he became known at court and to the Prince of Wales, even before the Prince ascended to the throne as King George II in 1727 and Lewis became his official harper.[2] However, in Hogarth's informal portrait, Lewis is dressed more appropriately for the tavern than for the court. He plays his triple harp on the left shoulder. The painter seems to have had some wider interest in Welsh people. In his sequence of morality paintings, *A Rake's Progress*, created between 1732–4, the bailiffs

39 William Hogarth, detail from *A Rake's Progress III: The Orgy*, 1732-4

40 William Hogarth, *David Lewis*, c.1730

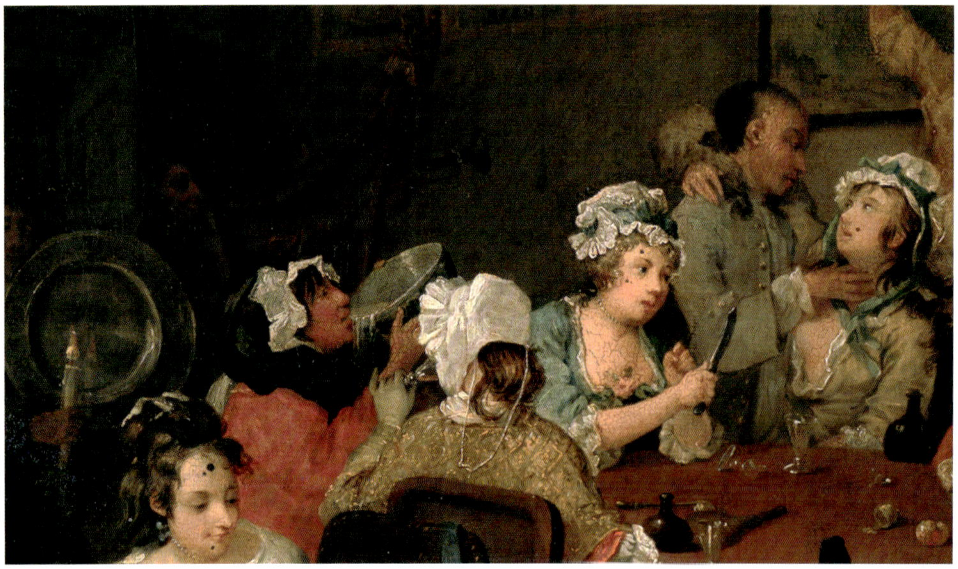

1 The letter, written by one John Phillips, is held at Aberdeen Council (Archives, Gallery & Museums), to which it was donated by a descendant in 1939 along with Hogarth's portrait of David Lewis and that of his daughter Mary, painted in 1755.

2 The length of the service of Lewis at court has not been established, but William Powell was appointed harper to the Prince of Wales in 1736.

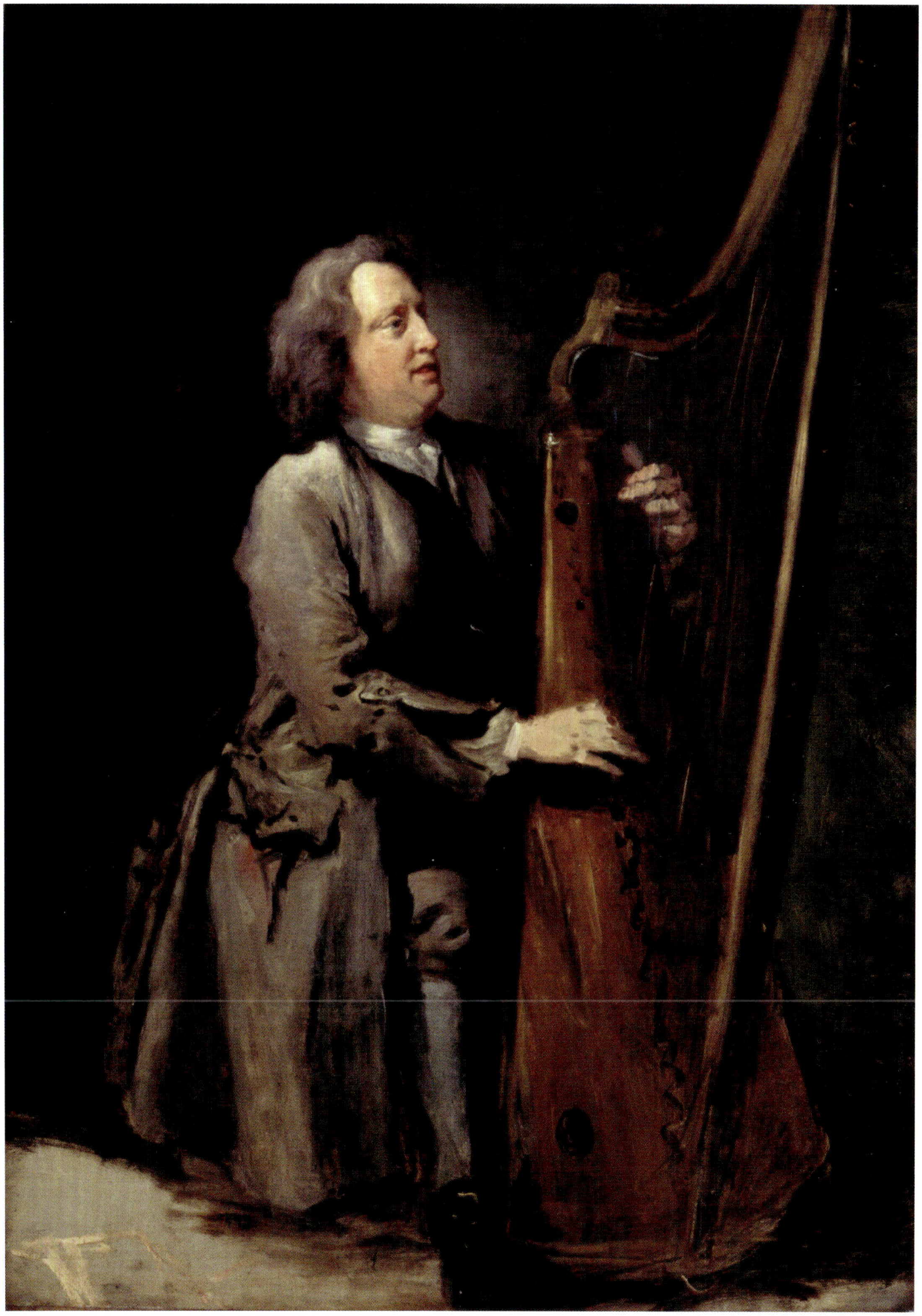

who arrest the Rake in the street do so on St David's Day, indicated by the fact that they wear leeks in their hats. The preceding image of the sequence depicts the Rose Tavern in Drury Lane – not far from the workshop of the instrument maker David Evans – where general debauchery is accompanied by music from a trumpet and what appears to be a triple harp. At least one individual in the scene is known to have been a portrait of a real person who worked at the tavern, so the possibility arises that the harper may also represent a Welsh musician known to the painter, perhaps again Lewis himself. In more general terms, through the engraved versions of the paintings, published in 1735 and widely distributed, the image reinforced the association of Welsh harpers with entertainment in English public houses.[3] It is an association suggested even more directly by the frequent occurrence in England of inns named The Welsh Harp or The Welsh Harper, which displayed appropriate signs.

The Honourable and Loyal Society of Ancient Britons, founded in 1715, had encouraged the celebration of St David's Day in London, providing perhaps the earliest organised focus for the public promotion of expatriate Welsh identity. In 1725 London newspapers reported the Society parading through the streets 'with great Pomp and Magnificence, having Trumpets and Kettle-Drums playing before them.'[4] Through the first half of the eighteenth century, a continued rise in patriotic sentiment amongst Welsh intellectuals in London manifested itself in the establishment in 1751 of the Honourable Society of Cymmrodorion. Investigations into national origins were a particular interest of the antiquarians who joined the Society, reflecting a wider context of the construction of foundation myths in many other European nations. However, English mercantile expansion and the creation of empire in the same period complicated the identity of the Welsh drawn to London, a complexity that resolved into the schizophrenic sense of nationhood that would characterise the Welsh establishment for the next two centuries. Notwithstanding the paradox of the defeat of the 'primary inhabitants' (the *cymmrodorion*) of the islands of Britain by the peoples who became the English, the Welsh gentry and associated intellectual circles sought to identify a place of distinction for themselves in the rise of England as a world power. The enduring influence of the myth of the fulfilment of prophecy represented by the Tudor dynasty provided the link that justified the Welsh claim to supply the new empire with its legitimising foundation myth. Intellectuals revealed that in Wales the ancient British people survived, and they sought to demonstrate that they maintained vestiges of the pre-imperial culture of the whole island.

3 The engraving after the painting was reversed, giving the impression that the harp is played on the right shoulder.

4 Given in Rhys Kaminski-Jones, '"Where Cymry united, delighted appear": The Society of Ancient Britons and the celebration of St David's Day in London, 1715-1815', *Transactions of the Honourable Society of Cymmrodorion*, New series, 23 (2017), p. 56.

The language of that culture was unknown to the English, and the first fragments of the literary tradition that it expressed became accessible only after 1764, with the pioneering translation by Evan Evans, 'Ieuan Fardd', of ten poems published in *Some Specimens of the Poetry of the Antient Welsh Bards*. Music had provided an earlier and more accessible entry point through which to become acquainted with the roots of the new imperial world. By the middle of the eighteenth century, more than any other individual, John Parry came to represent those roots.

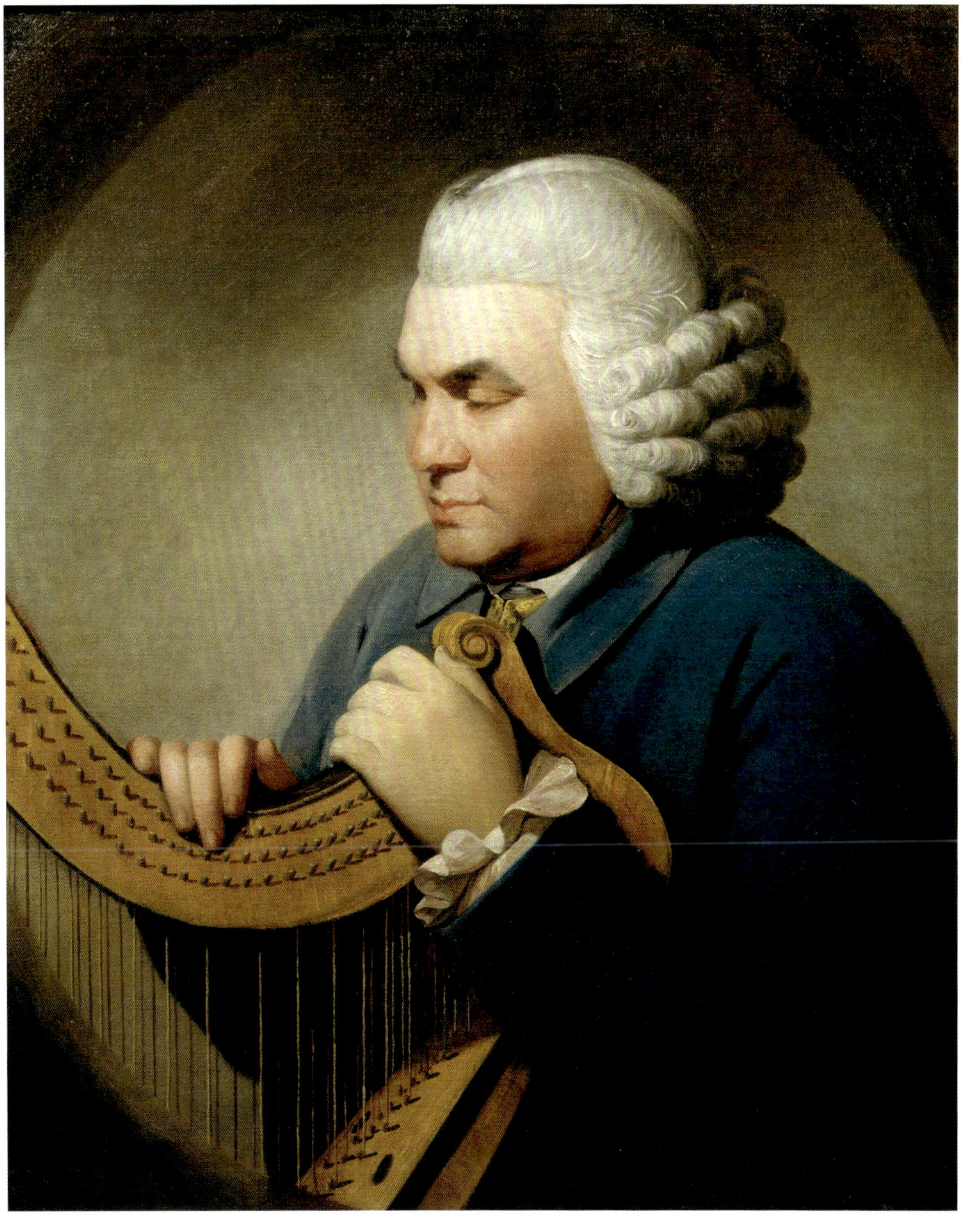

41 William Parry, *John Parry, Blind Harper*, 1780–90

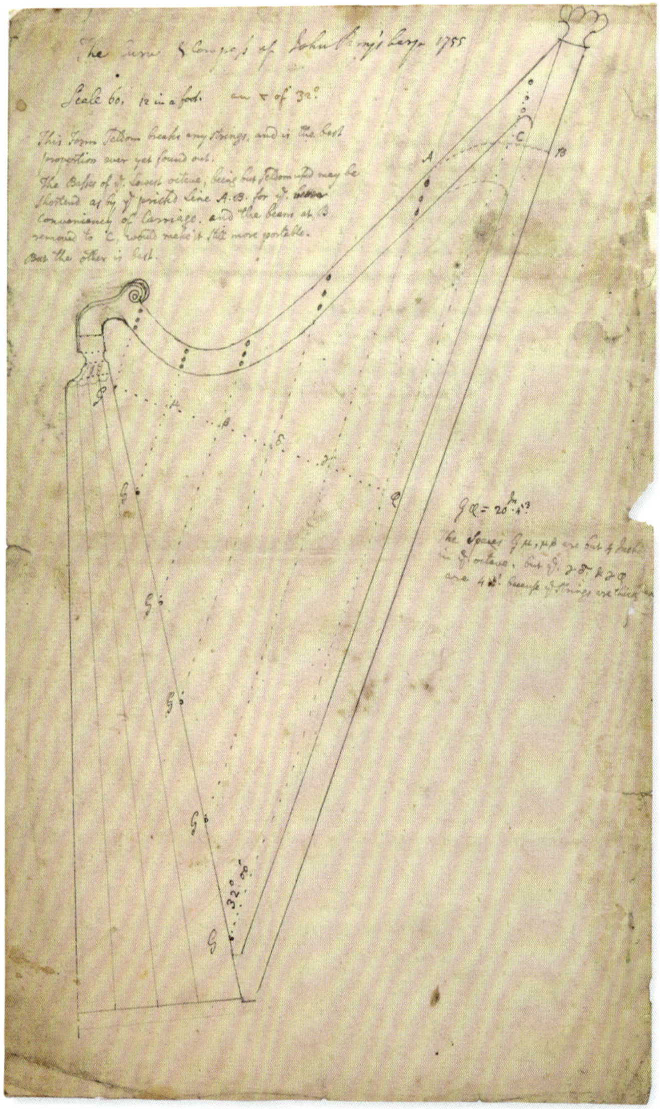

42 Lewis Morris, *The Curve & Compass of John Parry's Harp*, 1755

Parry was a generation younger than David Lewis, depicted by Hogarth. Grafting on to the figure of the popular entertainer and the classical musician the kudos of the myth of Ancient Britain, Parry evolved into what would be described in the language of today as a cultural icon. He was an early member of the Cymmrodorion Society and, alongside his patron and later President of the Society, Sir Watkin Williams Wynn, 3rd Baronet, he was among the most frequently painted Welsh people of his period.

At the time of his early appearances in England, John Parry was a remarkable virtuoso playing fashionable contemporary repertoire. But after the first of his publications of Welsh airs, the proto-Romantic overlay of his association by descent from a mythic tradition as old as the islands of Britain coloured perceptions. *Antient British Music* was published in London in 1742. It made Welsh music (that is, in the terminology of the period, 'British' music) widely accessible for the first time to those who had not inherited it through aural or manuscript transmission.[5] Because of his increasingly iconic status, Parry has tended to become uniquely acknowledged as

5 Some Welsh material had appeared in earlier mixed publications, such as John Playford, *The Dancing Master* (London, 1652). A list is given in Wyn Thomas, *Traditional Music in Wales: A Bibliography* (3rd ed., Llanrwst, 2006), pp. 12–13. The word 'Antient' did not necessarily imply deep history, as in the modern sense. The Concerts of Antient Music, founded in 1776, simply required performance of works more than twenty years old, see below pp. 72–3.

6 J. Lloyd Williams, *Y Tri Thelynor: Arloeswyr Cerddorol Cymru yn y Ddeunawfed Ganrif* (London, 1945), p. 47.

7 BL Add MS 14939, ff. 11–16. Nevertheless, the authorship continues a subject of debate. Given John Parry's blindness, and the intimate familiarity of the writer with earlier texts, it seems likely that if not Lewis Morris, then Evan Williams rather than Parry was responsible for its composition.

8 NLW MS 21300D (Llanover B25).

9 Wynne's work was based on David Powel's *The Historie of Cambria, now called Wales*, published in 1584 and based on earlier texts.

10 William Wynne, *The History of Wales* (London, 1697), p. 159.

the collector of the airs, though in fact the collection was assembled jointly with Evan Williams, a musician whose origins, like those of Parry, were in Penllŷn. The two men may well have known each other for most of their lives.[6] The lengthy introduction to *Antient British Music*, which took the form of a history of the subject, was written in the first person by an individual not identified in the publication. However, a copy of the volume survives with early additions in the hand of the antiquarian Lewis Morris (brother of Richard, the founder of the Cymmrodorion), which suggests that he was the author of the treatise.[7] Morris had drawn John Parry's harp in detail.[8] The text was notable for its patriotic tone, which identified the people represented in the modern world by the Welsh as the founders of music in Britain, and so justified in the most fundamental way the continuing special relationship. The writer took exception to the assertion made in William Wynne's *History of Wales*, published in 1697,[9] that music in the nation had been introduced from Ireland with the formalisation of the bardic tradition, undertaken by Gruffudd ap Cynan in the Middle Ages. Wynne had described Gruffudd ap Cynan's ordering of the bards:

> The next were such as plaid upon Musical Instruments, chiefly the Harp and the Crowd; which Musick *Gruffydh ap Conan* first brought over into *Wales;* who being born in *Ireland,* and descended by his Mothers side of *Irish* Parents, brought with him from thence several skilful Musicians, who invented almost all the Instruments as were afterwards plaid upon in *Wales.*[10]

The writer of the introduction to *Antient British Music* was at pains to correct this piece of antiquarian disinformation, alleging an Irish origin for Welsh music, and deploying a degree of sarcasm in the process that tends to confirm the acerbic Lewis Morris as the author:

> But the Doctor says farther, that the Music, for the MOST PART, in Wales, in his Time, (not the Instruments) either came over from Ireland, with the said Prince and his Irish Musicians, or was composed by them afterwards. Mr. Wynne, the late Editor of Caradoc's History, hath mixed all the Notes with the Text through the whole Book, as well as in this Place, and, mistaking the Sense of this Passage in Dr Powel, by not distinguishing between Instrumental Music and Musical Instruments (i.e. between a Minuet and a Fidle) hath misled all his Readers ever since, in saying, that the Harp and Crowd (as he calls it) came from Ireland …

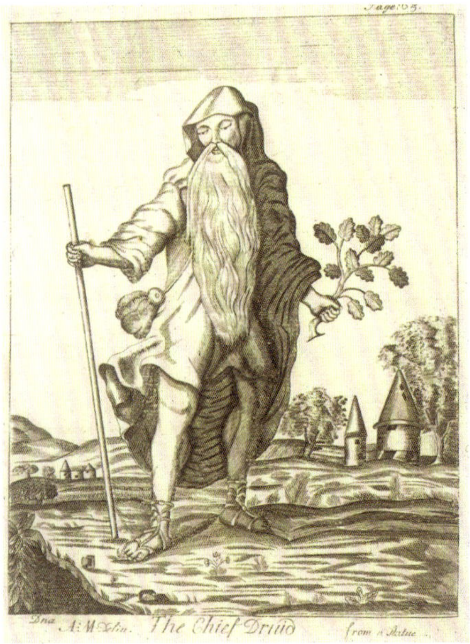

> As to Dr. Powel's Note on Caradoc, before mentioned, where he argues from the Irish Names of the Tunes in our antient Books of Music, that most part of our British Music was had from the Irish: If so, it was but paying what they had borrowed before. But it seems the Doctor had no great Knowledge in that Art, or had not seen many Books of Music; a good Antiquarian may be a bad Musician; it seems to turn out quite otherwise than what he says; for most of the Terms of Art, Names of Tunes, Keys, &c. in our old British Books, (of which I have seen many) are either British, or deriveable from the Greek, as a great part of the Language by its Analogy seems to be, or else are so very obscure, that neither the British nor Irish can account for them; and those, for ought I know, may be the antiquated Terms of the Druids.[11]

43 A.M., *The Chief Druid*, from Henry Rowlands, *Mona Antiqua Restaurata*, 1723

The author's reference to 'British Books' of music, of which many had been consulted in the writing of the piece, alluded not to published English texts (although the author was, no doubt, familiar also with those) but to manuscript sources. The Robert ap Huw manuscript was certainly known to Lewis Morris. Indeed, it was in his possession by 1727, when he made additions to it, again strongly suggesting his authorship of the introduction to the 1742 collection.[12] Morris had acquired the manuscript from the Meyricks of Bodorgan, who were probably also the source of the other early music material, subsequently lost, which he had consulted.[13]

This text, with its identification of the ancient origins of British music with the druids, predating the Roman invasion yet alive in the person of John Parry, stimulated the production of a barrage of mythic representations that conclusively branded the modern nation. Yet despite the fact that Parry and his contemporaries performed on the triple harp, the eighteenth-century branding was crystallised visually in the conjunction of the small single harp and the earlier imaging of druids, such as the engraved depiction of *The Chief Druid* published in Henry Rowlands's *Mona Antiqua Restaurata* of 1723, which was familiar to all interested in Welsh antiquities.[14] The conjunction occurred initially as the result of the work of the poet Thomas Gray. In a letter to the painter Richard Bentley, Horace Walpole noted in 1755 that his friend Gray was working on a 'Pindaric Ode' about the myth of the murder of the bards by Edward I:[15]

11 John Parry, *Antient British Music* (London, 1742), pp. 3-4.

12 Paul D. Whittaker, 'British Museum Additional MS 14905: An Interpretation and Re-examination of the Music and Text' (unpublished MA dissertation, University College of North Wales, Bangor, 1974), p. 10.

13 Lewis Morris's nephew, John Owen, wrote in 1758: 'My uncle Lewis has got a curious manuscript wrote in Charles the 1st time by one Robt ap Huw of Bodwigan in Anglesey ... I am told there are more of the sort in Bodorgan Library.' Hugh Owen (ed.), 'Additional letters of the Morrises of Anglesey 1735-1786', *Y Cymmrodor*, 49 (1947), i, pp. 2-3, and given in Stephen P. Rees and Sally Harper, 'Aspects of the palaeography and history of the Robert ap Huw manuscript', *Welsh Music History*, 3 (1999), pp. 54-5.

14 The image was based, in turn, on that published in Aylett Sammes, *Britannia Antiqua Illustrata* (London, 1676).

> Gray has been here. He has begun an ode, which if he finishes equally, will, I think, inspirit all your drawing again. It is founded on an old tradition of Edward I putting to death the Welsh bards. Nothing but you, or Salvator Rosa, and Nicolo Poussin, can paint up the expressive terror and dignity of it. Don't think I mean to flatter you; all I would say is, that now the two latter are dead, you must of necessity be Gray's painter.[16]

In fact, like Bentley, Gray was suffering from a creative block at the time, and found himself unable to finish the work. But two years later, and fifteen years after the publication of *Antient British Music*, the poet heard John Parry play in Cambridge, and his imagination was fired again. He reported that Parry 'scratch'd out such

15 He had come across the myth in Thomas Carte, *A General History of England* (London, 1747–55).

16 Given in W.S. Lewis (ed.), *The Yale Edition of Horace Walpole's Correspondence* (New Haven and London, 1937–83), vol. xxxv, pp. 251–2. For a discussion of Bentley's illustrations, see Loftus Jestin, *The Answer to the Lyre: Richard Bentley's Illustrations for Thomas Gray's Poems* (Philadelphia, 1990), pp. 218–21.

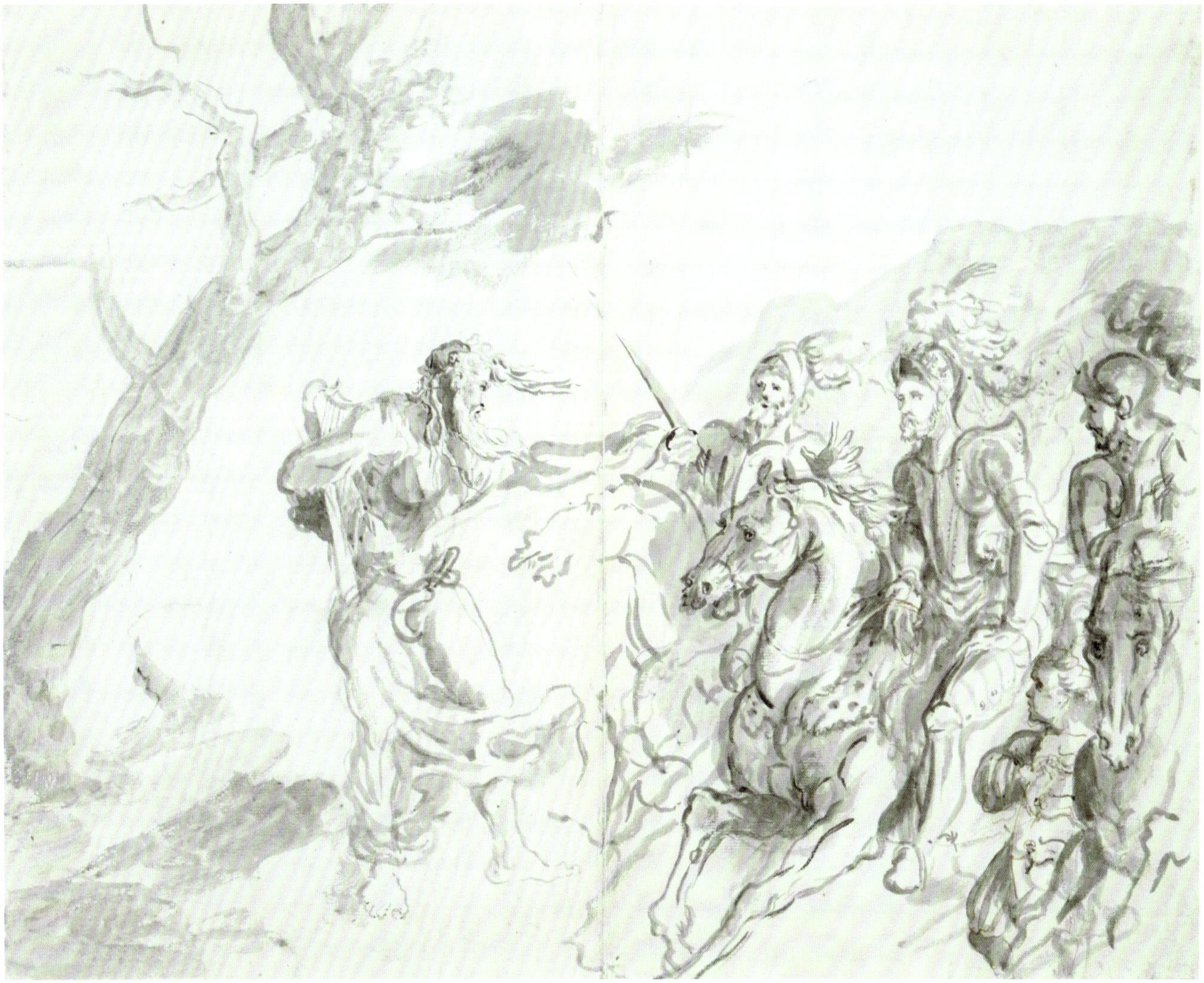

44 Richard Bentley, *The Bard*, 1757

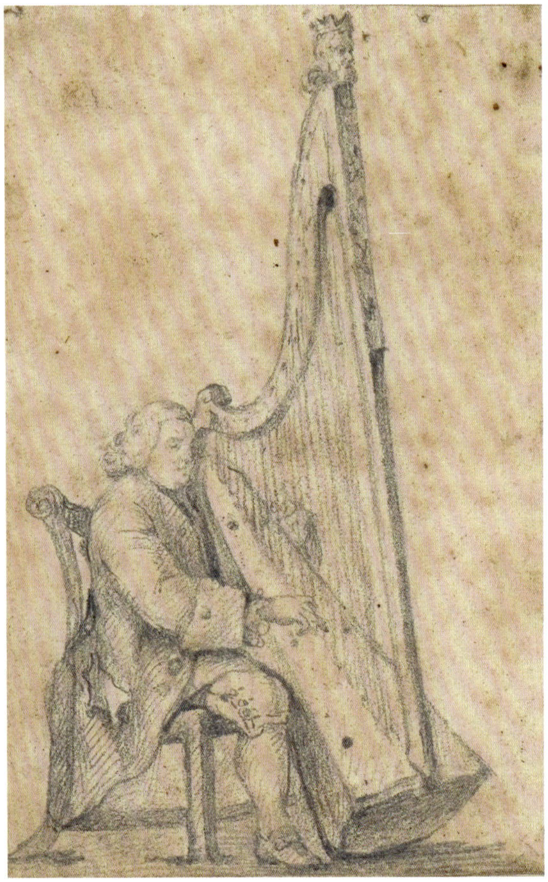

45 William Parry, *John Parry at the Harp*, c.1770–80

ravishing blind Harmony, such tunes of a thousand years old with names enough to choak you, as have set all this learned body a dancing.'[17] Neither did the biblical resonance, reinforced subconsciously no doubt by association of names – King David and St David – fail to impress. In 1744 an English admirer would observe that he played 'as a successor of David's who is come from Wales harp in hand, to exorcise the evil spirit, & raise contributions here; & last Tuesday advertised a benefit for himself without the least ceremony, at halfe a crown a ticket; & this very night is to have another.'[18] From a drawing made by William Parry of his father at the harp, it is clear that the pillar of his instrument was surmounted by the crowned head of King David.

Gray's poem was published in 1757, and although its sentiments failed to please the old order, including the likes of Dr Johnson, it appealed immediately to a younger generation of proto-Romantics. Gray's poetic conception was highly visual, and indeed he had drawn on engravings of celebrated paintings including Raphael's *Ezekiel's Vision* and Parmigianino's *Moses Breaking the Tablets*.[19] These sources would surface again when painters got to work, inspired by the poem, though Walpole's edition appeared without Bentley's drawings.[20] Nevertheless, Bentley's image of the bard, clutching his harp, would prove prescient. Paul Sandby, one of the younger generation, painted the subject and exhibited it at the Society of Artists in that same year. Gray had received advance notice of Sandby's intention to create 'a great picture of M. Snowdon, in Wch the

17 Duncan C. Tovey (ed.), *The Letters of Thomas Gray, Including the Correspondence of Gray and Mason* (London, 1900–12), vol. i, p. 331.

18 Given in Donald Burrows and Rosemary Dunhill (eds.), *Music and Theatre in Handel's World: The Family Papers of James Harris, 1732–1780* (Oxford, 2002), p. 191. The reference is taken from a letter written by Mary Smith to James Harris, 3 April 1744.

19 F.I. McCarthy, '"The Bard" of Thomas Gray: Its composition and its use by painters', *The National Library of Wales Journal*, 14, 1 (Summer 1965), p. 106. Thomas Gray drew also on the Latin treatise of Ieuan Fardd, 'De Bardis Dissertatio', included in *Specimens*, in his other, less celebrated poems on Welsh themes.

20 Bentley had illustrated Gray's poems in 1753 (*Designs by Mr. R. Bentley for six poems by Mr. T. Gray*), and in the 1765 edition, one of *The Bard* illustrations was added as a tailpiece.

21 Given in McCarthy, '"The Bard" of Thomas Gray', p. 110.

22 Ibid.

Bard & Edward the first make their appearance',[21] and it did not disappoint. The image caused a stir. William Mason described it to Lord Newnham:

> My Lord! Sandby has made such a picture! Such a bard! Such a headlong flood! Such a Snowdon! Such giant oaks! Such desert caves! If it is not the best picture that has been painted this century...[22]

Sandby's picture is lost and given its reception it is surprising that it was not engraved. No description survives to indicate if the bard was depicted by the painter with his harp, reinforcing the musical association of the image. However, ten years after his initial venture into Welsh subject matter, in the company of Sir Watkin Williams Wynn, 4th Baronet, Sandby travelled into Snowdonia, providing himself with a body of drawings that he would recycle over a long period and which became highly influential through the medium of prints. The most celebrated group, the *XII Views in North Wales*, published as aquatints in 1776, was soon followed by a massive series issued over three years as *The Virtuosi's Museum*. Among them was *A View of Snowdon*, the mountain looming high over Dolbadarn Castle. A vignette on the decorative frame depicts a harper who seems to combine the bardic image, generated by Gray, of a venerable figure with a long white beard, with observation, since he wears conventional clothes and his instrument, played on the left shoulder, is a large triple harp. The harper is either blind or has closed his eyes in meditation.

46 William Walker after Paul Sandby, *Snowdon in Caernarvonshire*, 1779

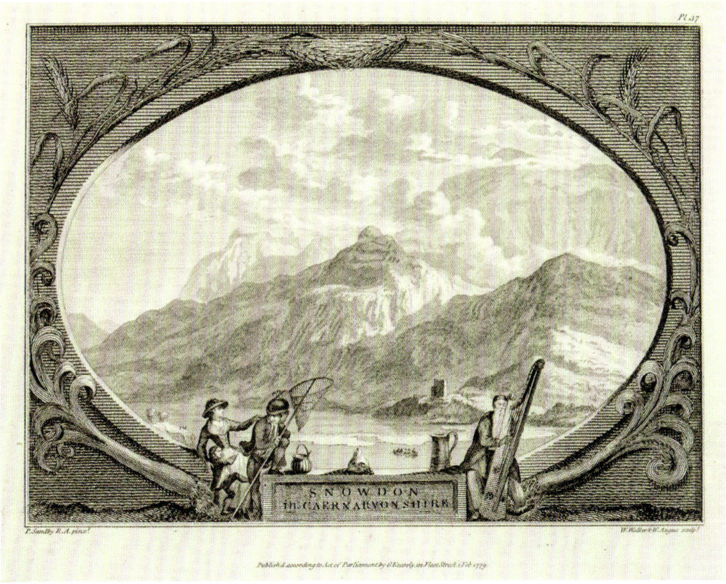

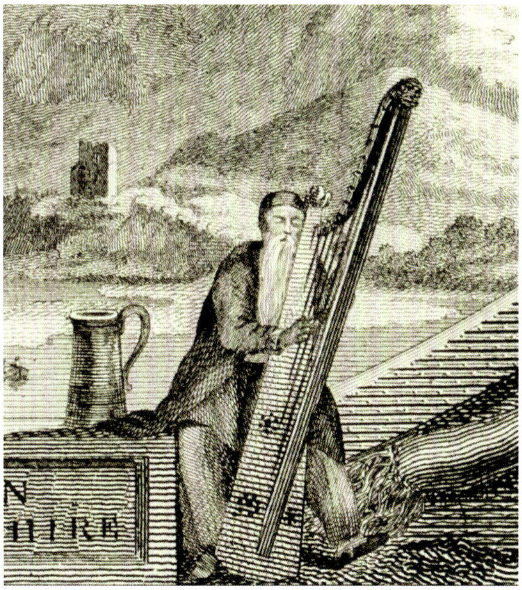

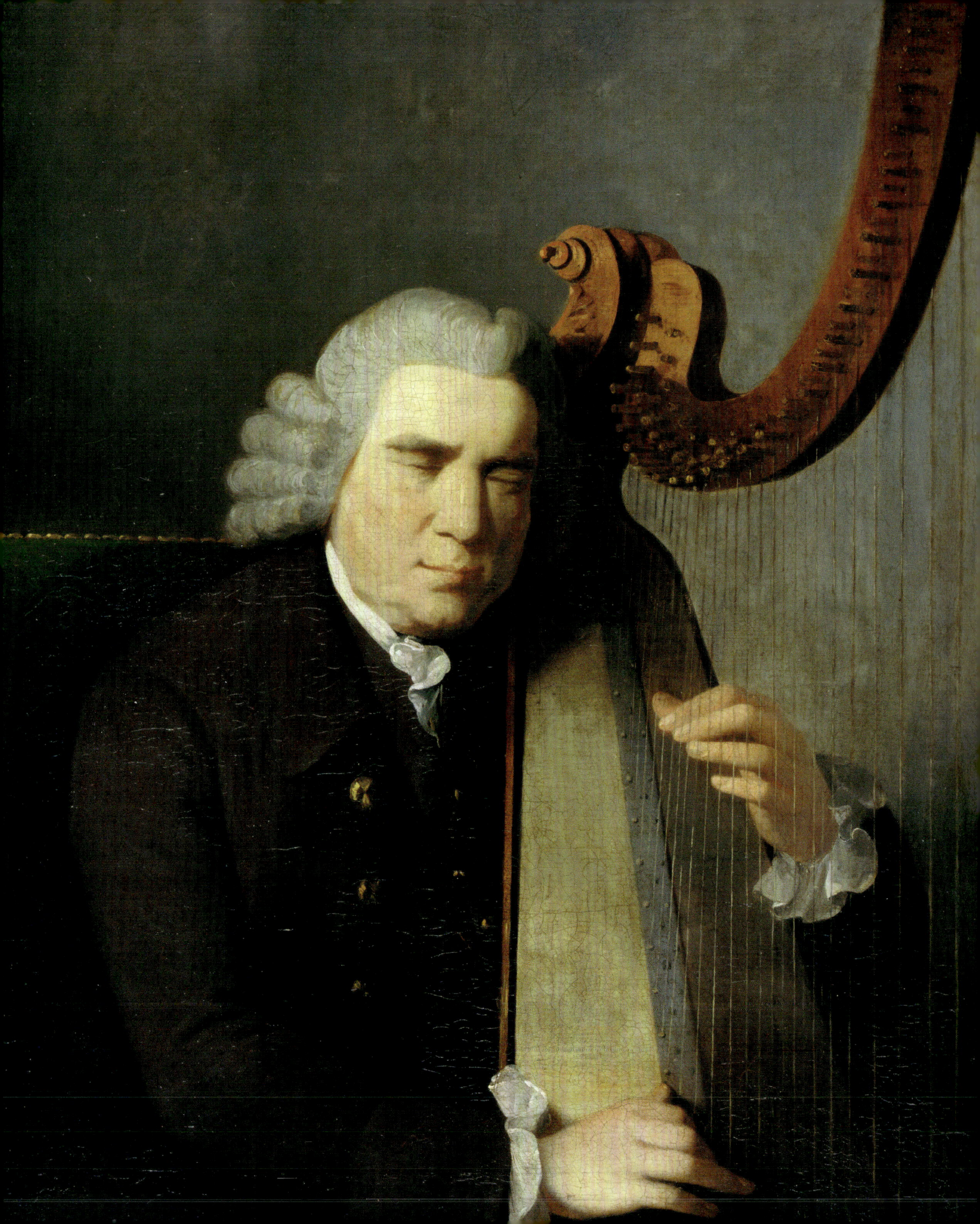

It is likely that the series of individual portraits painted by William Parry of his father date from this same period of the early 1770s, when both he and Sandby were closely associated with the young Sir Watkin. None of the three extant single portraits is dated, though a further two, presently missing, were exhibited at the Royal Academy, following Parry's return from Italy, in 1778 and (after the death of his father) in 1787.[23] Their exhibition surely reinforced the legacy of the harper among the resident intellectual community in London and the gentry who gathered for the season and for parliamentary activities. As late as 1808, over a quarter of a century after John Parry's death, William Parry's first biographer, Edward Edwards, would still identify the painter as 'the son of Parry, the celebrated performer on the Welsh-harp.'[24]

Judging by his appearance in middle age, the depiction of John Parry in the surviving individual portraits is closely related to the double portrait that had so well expressed the domestic role of the harper and his son in the Wynn family. However, in terms of meaning, the individual portraits represent a remarkable transformation. The relaxed informal double portrait had evolved into an image with meditative, almost mystical qualities. The painter's development of the portrait was achieved by a subtle alteration of expression in the shape of the mouth, and a change from the everyday clothes (that in the domestic picture revealed his father's portly figure) to a well-tailored sophistication. The changes suggest a significant development in perceptions of the harpist from his first appearance in England, heavily inflected by the proto-Romantic overlay of association by descent from a mythic tradition as old as the islands of Britain themselves. Given the status of the harper by the 1770s, and the rapid evolution of the myth, it is perhaps surprising that none of the oil portraits was engraved during the sitter's lifetime.[25] They did not become familiar to a wide musical audience until the publication of a lithograph (in slightly modified form) in Nicholas Bennett's *Alawon fy Ngwlad* of 1896. By that time, the mystical associations of the bardic myth had irrevocably transformed perceptions of the original image.

Three years after Paul Sandby's visit to Wales, during which, presumably, he had observed in the shadow of Snowdon the source of his composite bardic image,

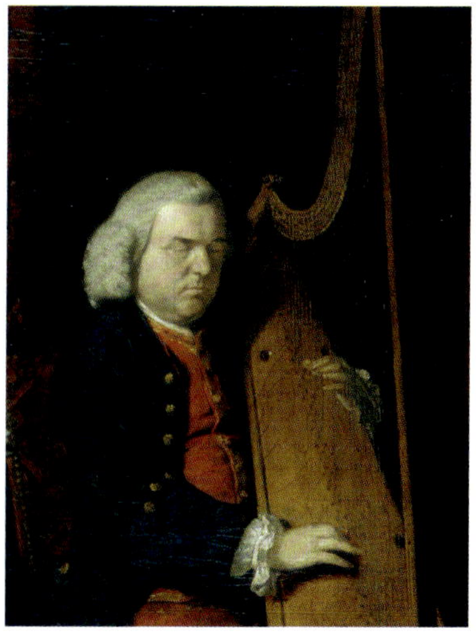

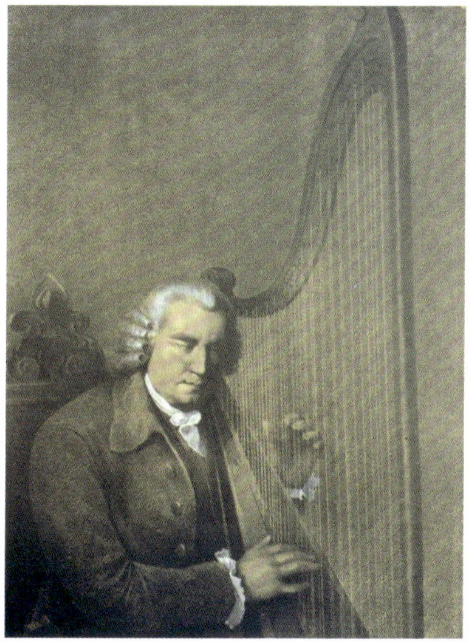

48 William Parry, detail from *David Parry with His Father, the Harpist John Parry*, 1770-80

49 After William Parry, *John Parry, Blind Harper*, from Nicholas Bennett, *Alawon Fy Ngwlad*, 1896

47 William Parry, *John Parry Playing the Harp*, c.1770

23 See Miles Wynn Cato, *Parry: The Life and Works of William Parry A.R.A. (1743-1791)* (private publication, 2008).

24 Edward Edwards, *Anecdotes of Painters* (London, 1808), p. 162.

25 The drawing of Parry made by his son was etched for use as a ticket to a performance.

his friend, Thomas Jones of Pencerrig, painted what has become, by default, the best-known oil painting of the subject. *The Bard*, exhibited at the Society of Artists exhibition in 1774, was an unusual work in the oeuvre of Jones, though he described it in his Memoirs as 'one of the best I ever painted.' He was less constrained by the very specific description of the suicide of the Bard as offered by Gray than would be subsequent interpreters. In particular, he introduced a Stonehenge-like structure apparently as much for aesthetic as for symbolic

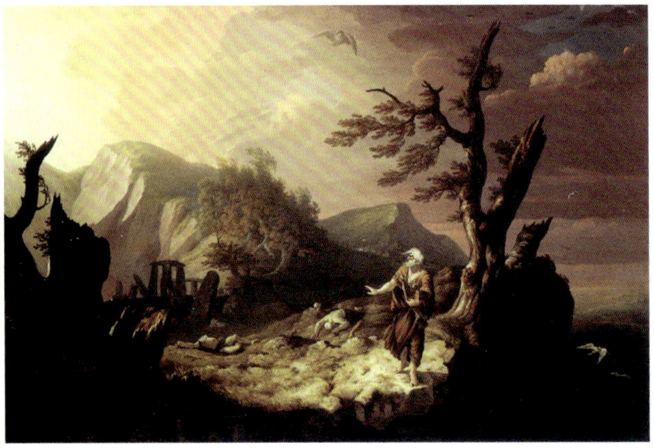

reasons, at which he hinted in the Memoirs. On a visit to the original 'Stupendous Monument of remote Antiquity', Jones had speculated that much of its 'grandeur and Magnificence' derived from its location in the 'void' of the plain:

> ... were this Mass situated amidst high rocks, lofty mountains and hanging Woods – however it might contribute to the richness of the scene in general – [it] would lose much of its own grandeur as a Single Object – The Experiment is easily tried upon Canvass.[26]

50 Thomas Jones, Pencerrig, *The Bard*, 1775

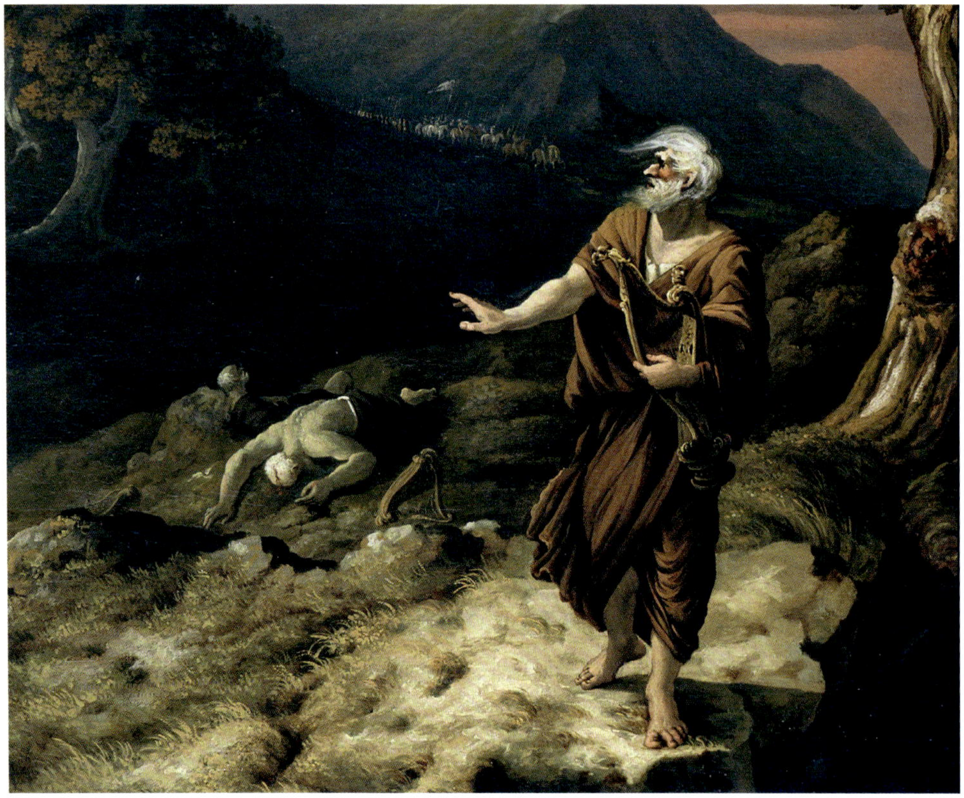

26 'Memoirs of Thomas Jones, Penkerrig Radnorshire, 1803', in *The Volume of the Walpole Society*, 32 (1946), p. 21. The picture was painted during a long stay at the home of Oldfield Bowles, Jones's patron and pupil.

27 Ibid., p. 33.

28 See, for instance, the graphics by Dave Field commissioned for the Welsh Arts Council/Crafts Council exhibition, 'Welsh Harps', 1980 1.

29 See above, p. 35, for the possible role in his rise of Lady Catherine and Sir William Hamilton.

Whatever his motivation, Jones's composition had the effect of emphasising the continuity from druidical to bardic culture, from British pre-history to the Welsh Middle Ages, and carrying the association with music. That said, and notwithstanding its more recent celebrity, the influence of Thomas Jones's painting of *The Bard* in propagating the nascent national brand was limited in its own time because, although it was engraved and a proof copy exhibited in London at the Society of Artists in 1775, no edition was published. Jones himself explained the circumstances:

> This Picture was engraved by Smith, in Mezzotinto – but the Plate being very soon bought up by that great Leviathan, Mr Alderman Boydel, was never that I heard of, published – Another Instance of my illfortune with respect to Engravers.[27]

It is unclear who financed the engraving of the plate, since if it was Jones himself, he is unlikely to have sold it to Boydell without an agreement to publish. Having acquired it, for what reason Boydell chose not to publish an edition remains a mystery, as the subject surely would have been a popular one in the period. Although the painter was not famous, the engraver was rising to become perhaps the most distinguished of his generation. John Raphael Smith was the son of the landscape painter Thomas Smith of Derby. He himself painted and worked in pastel, but would become celebrated as the engraver of works by painters ranging from Joshua Reynolds and George Romney to George Morland, of whom he was a close friend.

51 Hall and Middiman after Philippe de Loutherbourg, *The Bard*, 1784

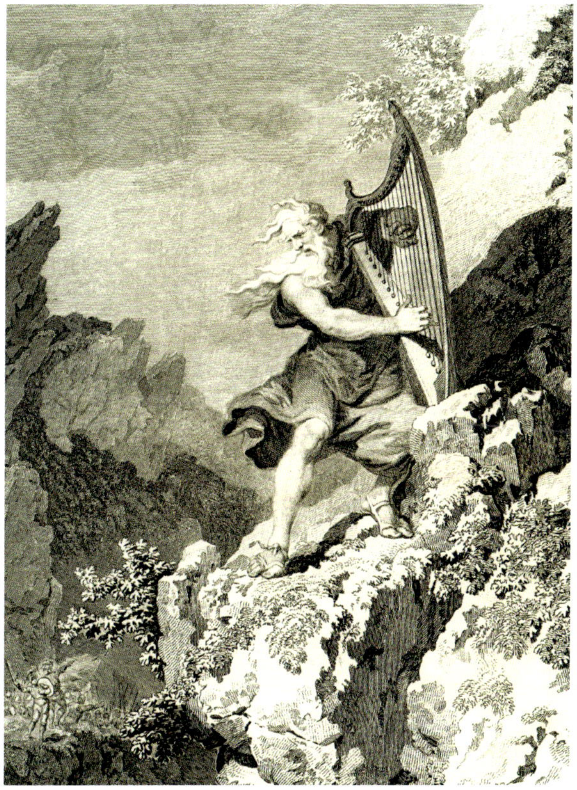

The truly seminal image – the most influential in its own period and subsequently[28] – was without doubt the engraving made in 1784 after a design by Philippe de Loutherbourg, which was first published as the frontispiece to Edward Jones's *Musical and Poetical Relicks of the Welsh Bards* in 1784. Jones had moved from Wales to London in the mid-1770s and, by the time he published the *Relicks*, he was under the patronage of the Prince of Wales, to whom the book was dedicated.[29] Jones's 'attempt to save from oblivion the remaining vestiges of the Bards' was made by developing the melodies to suit modern taste with the addition of 'Variations for the Harp, Piano Forte, Violin or Flute.' De Loutherbourg's heroic frontispiece to the book derived more precisely from Thomas Gray's ode than had the interpretation of Thomas Jones, and the engraving included the famous second section of the poem:

> On a rock, whose haughty brow
> Frowns o'er old Conway's foaming flood,
> Rob'd in the sable garb of woe,
> With haggard eyes the poet stood;
> (Loose his beard, and hoary hair
> Stream'd, like a meteor, to the troubled air)
> And with a master's hand, and prophet's fire,
> Struck the deep sorrows of his lyre ...

52 Unknown artist after Philippe de Loutherbourg, *The Bard*, c.1840–50

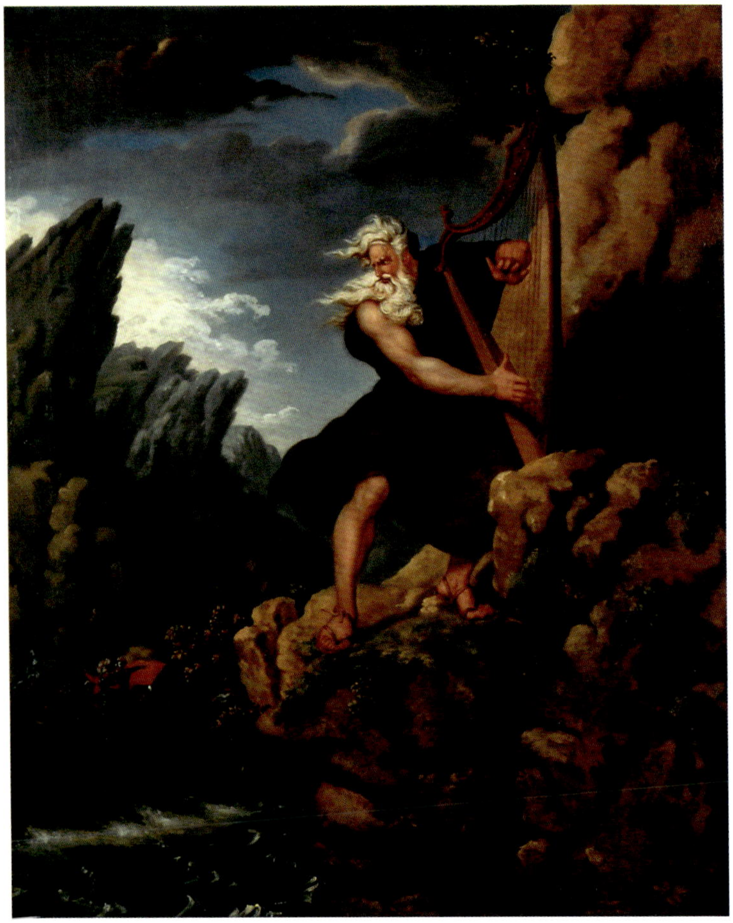

De Loutherbourg was born in Strasbourg but made his substantial reputation in London, where he worked from 1771. When he designed *The Bard* he had yet to visit Wales – a fact that emphasises the grip of the mythic idea of the nation on the imagination of intellectuals in England in the period. The engravers of what became the most widely distributed of bardic images were equally distinguished. The figure was engraved by John Hall, historical engraver to George III, and the landscape by Samuel Middiman.[30] Although understandings of its meaning would evolve, the influence of the print persisted for over two centuries. A well-painted copy was produced probably in the 1840s, for instance, and the image would reappear in graphics associated with the eisteddfod tradition that re-emerged in the second decade of the nineteenth century, and that continues to flourish. Sam Smiles has concisely expressed the appeal of the image and of *Musical and Poetical Relicks*, equally – though differently – to the patriotic Welsh mind and to English Romantics:

> As the frontispiece to a book whose contents celebrated and re-established the bardic tradition which Edward I had attempted to utterly eradicate, the bard is, as it were, vindicated in his prophecy by the text which follows his appearance.[31]

The English were excited by the idea of the British love of freedom; the Welsh continued in thrall to the notion of the fulfilment of the ancient tradition of bardic prophecy that, despite the death of King Arthur at the hands of the Saxons and the subsequent attentions of Edward I, the islands of Britain would eventually come once more under the rule of a native British prince.

The de Loutherbourg engraving has served as a cypher for all that was contained in Gray's poem, but it is precisely this aspect of its appeal that is problematic in considering its role in the evolution of Welsh consciousness. Was the poem an assertion of spiritually undefeated Welsh nationhood, or an act of cultural appropriation by the English author? Did it represent national differentiation or national assimilation, hiding behind the ambiguous use of the terms 'Britain' and 'British'? Edward Jones was in no doubt, since he regarded the poem as in itself sufficient compensation for the loss of political identity to which the conquest of 1282 would lead:

> The lamentable event has given birth to one of the noblest Lyric compositions in the English language: a poem of such fire and beauty as to remove … our regret of the occasion, and to compensate for the loss.[32]

At a personal level, Jones's remarkable assertion, made in his introduction to the *Musical and Poetical Relicks*, becomes comprehensible when we remember that his home was St James's Palace and his employer was the Prince of Wales, later King George IV. It was on the accession of the King, many years later in 1820, that Jones adopted his familiar sobriquet, 'Bardd y Brenin'.

30 It was common practice for painters and engravers specialising in figure or landscape to co-operate on a single picture. Both Middiman and Hall had worked for the publisher John Boydell, whose Welsh connections were strong. He had grown up in Hawarden in Flintshire. Middiman was a friend of William Woollett, who had engraved Richard Wilson's celebrated image of *The Destruction of the Children of Niobe* and his *Solitude* for Boydell.

31 Sam Smiles, *The Image of Antiquity: Ancient Britain and the Romantic Imagination* (New Haven, 1994), p. 56.

32 Edward Jones, *Musical and Poetical Relicks of the Welsh Bards* (London, 1784), pp. 20–1.

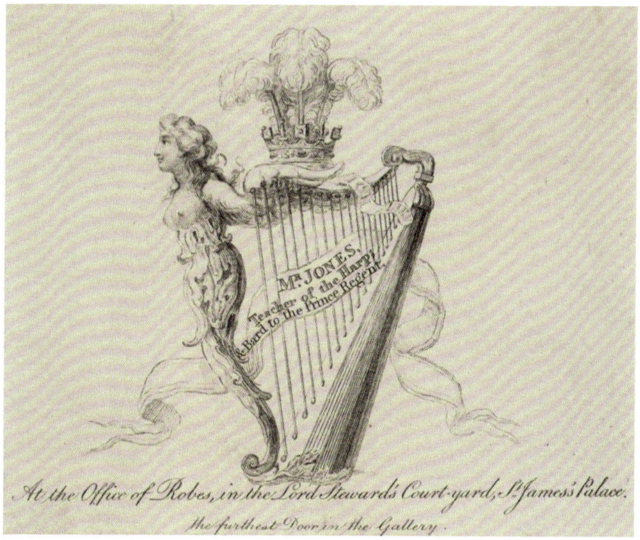

53 Unknown artist, *Trade Card of Edward Jones*, c.1811–20

54 William Blake, *The Bard*, from *The Poems of Thomas Gray*, 1789

Although Gray's poem and its visual cypher by de Loutherbourg were capable of deployment to sustain either conviction about the meaning of the events of 1282, the reality is that intellectuals of the mainstream Welsh establishment adopted a Janus-like attitude, which by facing two ways at once sought to encompass both nationhood and political assimilation – both to vilify Edward I and to celebrate the political reality represented by the Tudor dynasty and its distant German descendants. The work of Evan Evans, Ieuan Fardd, Gray's contemporary, is deeply implicated in the debate about the motivation that lay behind 'The Bard', and the meaning of the visual image.[33] The Welsh poet was still alive when de Loutherbourg's picture appeared. A late poem of his on the same subject that Gray had taken for his magisterial ode spoke to the identity of Wales not only through its primary subject, but also through the association between the Welsh and the Israelites as God's chosen peoples – the association that had been made explicit in the sixteenth-century writing of Elis Gruffydd and was implicit in the seventeenth-century image of the harp of King David made by Gwilym Pue. Ieuan Fardd's poem was inspired by the 137th Psalm:

> By the rivers of Babylon, there we sat down, yea, we wept, when we remembered Zion.
> We hanged our harps upon the willows in the midst thereof.
> For they that carried us away captive required of us a song; and they that wasted us required of us mirth, saying, Sing us one of the songs of Zion.
> How shall we sing the Lord's song in a strange land?

In 'A Paraphrase of the 137th Psalm, Alluding to the Captivity or Treatment of the Welsh Bards by King Edward I', Ieuan Fardd laced a London exile's meditation on the bardic theme (the poem opens with the words 'Sad near the willowy Thames we stood') with musical reference and imagery:

> Silent, neglected, and unstrung,
> Our harps upon the willows hung,
> That, softly sweet in Cambrian measures,
> Used to soothe our souls to pleasures,
> When, lo, the insulting foe appears,
> And bids us dry our useless tears.

33 See Sarah Prescott, *Eighteenth-Century Writing from Wales: Bards and Britons* (Cardiff, 2008), pp. 57–83, for a thorough review of the debate.

34 The poem was first published in 1820, thirty-two years after the poet's death.

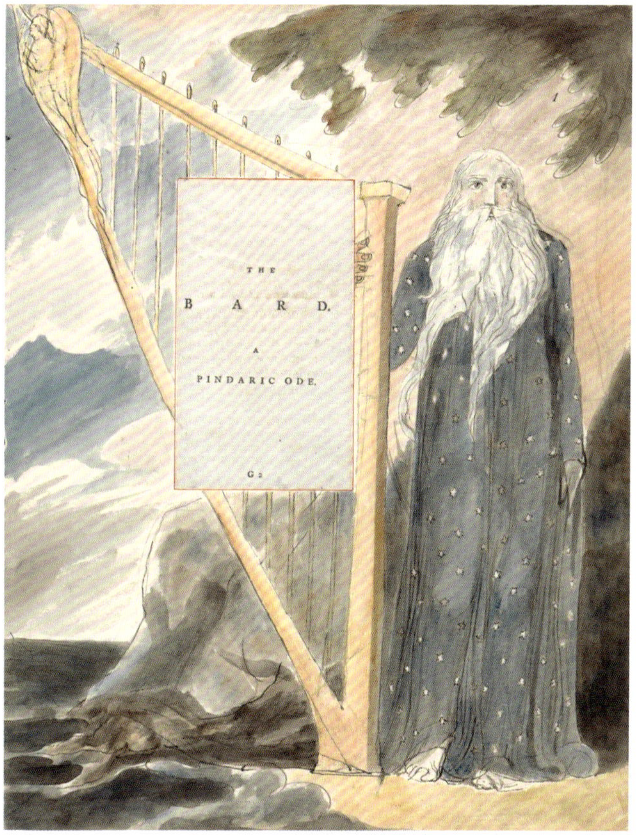

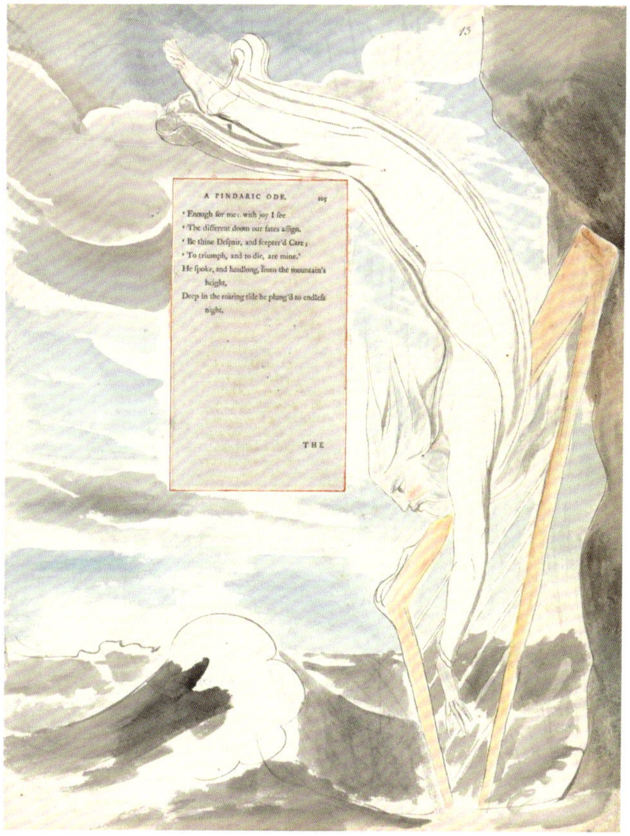

'Resume your harps, the Saxons cry,
'And change your griefs to songs of joy;
'Such strains as old Taliesin sang,
'What time your native mountains rang
'With wild notes, and all around
'Seas, rivers, woods return'd the sound.

What,– shall the Saxons hear us sing,
Or their dull vales with Cambrian music ring?
No–let old Conway cease to flow,
Back to her source Sabrina go:
Let huge Plinlimmon hide his head,
Or let the tyrant strike me dead,
If I attempt to raise a song
Unmindful of my country's wrong.
What, shall a haughty king command
Cambrian's free strain on Saxon land?

May this right arm first wither'd be,
Ere I may touch one string for thee,
Proud monarch; nay, may instant death
Arrest my tongue and stop my breath,
If I attempt to weave a song,
Regardless of my country's wrong! ...

What now avail our tuneful strains,
Midst savage taunts and galling chains?
Say, will the lark imprison'd sing
So sweet, as when on towering wing,
He wakes the songsters of the sky,
And tunes his notes to liberty?
Ah no, the Cambrian lyre no more
Shall sweetly sound on Arvon's shore,
No more the silver harp be won,
Ye Muses, by your favourite son ...[34]

There seems little doubt that de Loutherbourg's visualisation of 'The Bard' was a stimulus to other artists. Immediately after its publication in the *Musical and Poetical Relicks*, in 1785 William Blake exhibited a watercolour of the subject at the Royal Academy. The picture is lost, but Blake would soon return to the idea in a series of extraordinary watercolours made for the sculptor John Flaxman. They formed part of a series of 116 works after Gray, produced in 1789. Although Ieuan Fardd was still alive, Blake's information about the bard and other matters relating to Ancient Britain owed more to the activities of the circle of Welsh intellectuals in London that succeeded him, focused on the Gwyneddigion Society. *The Myvyrian Archaiology*, compiled by Iolo Morganwg and William Owen Pughe, placed information (alongside much disinformation) in the public domain on the publication of the first part in 1801, though just as important was the network of personal relationships that had drawn the gregarious Pughe into English artistic and literary circles considerably earlier. These included Flaxman,[35] the painter Henry Fuseli and William Blake himself. The poet Robert Southey, another of that circle, reported of Blake's picture *The Ancient Britons*, based on one of Iolo's Triads:

> That painter of great but insane genius, William Blake … took this Triad for the subject of a picture, which he called The Ancient Britons, it was one of his worst pictures, – which is saying much; and he has illustrated it with one of his most curious commentaries in his very curious and very rare descriptive Catalogue of his own Pictures.
>
> It begins with a translation from the Welsh, supplied to him no doubt by that good simple-hearted, Welsh-headed man, William Owen [Pughe], whose memory is the great storehouse of all Cymric tradition and lore of every kind.[36]

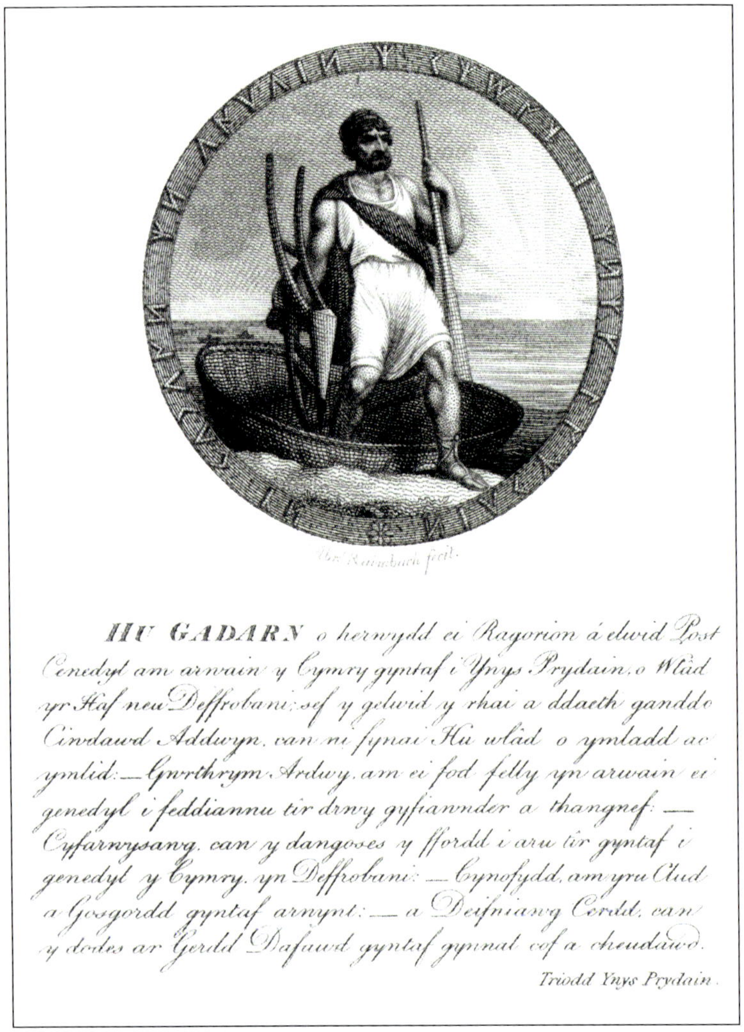

55 Abraham Raimbach, *Hu Gadarn*, 1801

35 In 1820, Pughe was responsible for a commission given to Flaxman by the Cymmrodorion for a medal, modelled by William Wyon. It depicts a bard with a *peithynen* and harp. For the medal, see below, p. 125.

36 Robert Southey, *The Doctor, &c.* (London, 1847), vol. vi, pp. 116–17.

37 The evidence for the relationship between Pughe and Blake is thoroughly reviewed in Glenda Carr, *William Owen Pughe* (Cardiff, 1983), pp. 186–90.

It is unclear precisely when Pughe first met Blake, since Southey, the source of much of the relevant documentary information, was inconsistent in his reporting.[37] However, the contact was almost certainly made through the engraver William Sharp, who sought to draw Blake into the sphere of influence of the millenarian prophetess Joanna Southcote. Like Sharp, Pughe was already among her most dedicated followers.

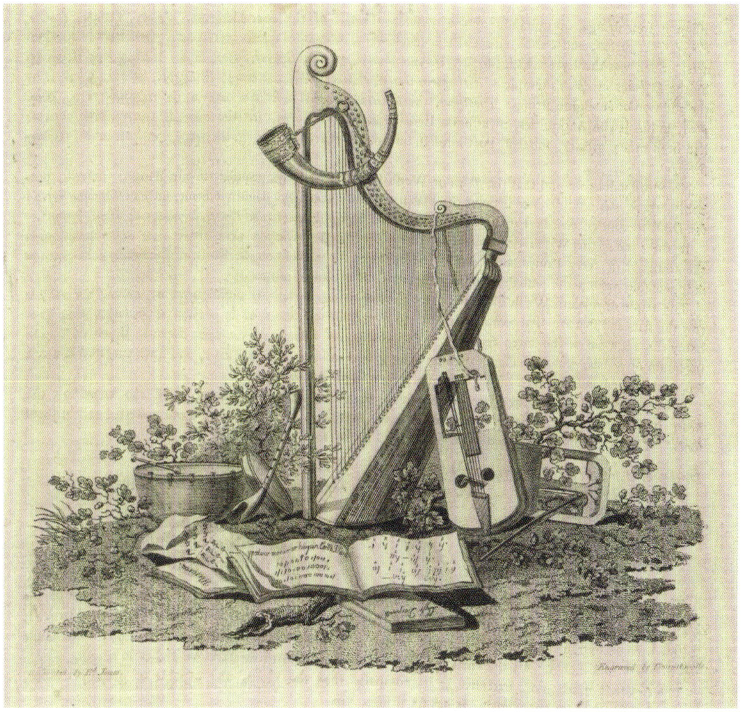

56 Edward Jones, *Musical Instruments of the Welsh* from *Musical and Poetical Relicks of the Welsh Bards*, 1784

William Owen Pughe was the chief proponent of a particular branch of the Welsh foundation myth, based on Iolo's forged Triads, which asserted that a heroic chieftain called Hu Gadarn had brought the race to the islands of Britain, and with it the civilising secret of agriculture. In 1801 Pughe commissioned Abraham Raimbach to engrave the subject based on his design, with an inscription in his new orthography attributing also to Hu Gadarn the invention of song, as the means to secure the native memory.[38] The result was mocked by more grounded contemporaries such as the polemicist Jac Glan-y-gors and the poet Dafydd Ddu Eryri. Pughe's presentation of the proof engraving to his colleagues was described by Glan-y-gors:

> Then W.O. got to his feet and pulled a paper from his pocket and read more of the achievements of Mr H. Gadarn, and that in the most ancient of Ancient British tongues, of which no-one understood a word of what he was saying.[39]

Nevertheless, the image was adopted by the Gwyneddigion for its new medal, funded by Owain Myfyr, modelled by John Minton, and first awarded to Walter Davies, 'Gwallter Mechain'. A subsequent engraving, inscribed in *coelbren y beirdd*, the supposed bardic script, 'Hu Gadarn leading the Welsh to the Island of Britain',[40] confirmed the significance of the chieftain for native British music, surrounding the hero with the harp, crwth, pipe and drum, a version of the image originally engraved for the first edition of Edward Jones's *Musical and Poetical Relicks*, after a drawing made by the author himself.

38 'Deifniawg Cerdd, can y dodes ar Gerdd Dafawd gyntaf gynnal cof a cheudawd'.

39 BL Add MS 14957, given in the original Welsh in Carr, *William Owen Pughe*, p. 180.

40 'Hu Gadarn yn arwain y Cymry i Ynys Prydain'.

57 Unknown artist, *Saint David for Wales*, 1781

For all that it was elaborated in the 'muddy nature of Owen's head',[41] Pughe's fantasy of Hu Gadarn was significant as a patriotic national riposte to an alternative contemporary English construct, which asserted that it was not until the arrival of the Romans that the Ancient Britons were civilised.[42] In the following year, the Revd George Richards offered his lengthy effusion on the subject of 'The Aboriginal Britons', much influenced by Gray, to an audience at Oxford, and again painted an unflattering picture of native savagery. However, his Cambrian aboriginals were blessed with musical knowledge to inspire their love of freedom and bloody resistance to the Roman yoke:

> Hail heav'n-born Seers, whose magic fingers strung
> The Cambrian lyre; who Locrine's triumphs sung
> To the dark haunts of Snowdon's icy caves,
> Plinlimmon's cliffs, and Deva's haunted waves;
> Or where, as Vaga roll'd her winding flood,
> High on the grey rocks wav'd the hanging wood.
> Ye, wandering frequent by romantic streams,
> With harps, that glitter'd to the moon's pale beams,
> Sooth'd by your midnight hymns the warrior's ghost,
> Whose cold bones whiten'd Arvon's dreary coast.

William Owen Pughe's version of the aboriginal myth retained some traction on the minds of Romantics into the 1820s. At the Denbigh Eisteddfod of 1828, a section of the winning *cywydd*, written by 'Merddin Emrys' (the Revd E. Huws, Bodfari) was devoted to 'Mighty old Huw in the forest'.[43]

SIR WATKIN

Notwithstanding the cynicism that in some quarters greeted William Owen Pughe's foundation myth, from the formation of the Society, the Gwyneddigion had certainly identified the harp as the national instrument, and song as the national passion. In 1777 the rules of the Society stated that members must not only speak Welsh but also enjoy singing. W.D. Leathart, the Society's archivist, recorded the song that greeted the reception of a new member:

41 Edward Dowden (ed.), *The Correspondence of Robert Southey with Caroline Bowles* (London and Dublin, 1881), pp. 193-4.

42 For instance, see John Hamilton's didactic illustration to Edward Barnard's *A History of England*, published in 1790, that included a lyre, implying that music was among the arts introduced by the invaders, and not a feature of native British culture.

43 'Hên gadarn HU'n y goedwig ...', see Merddin Emrys, 'Cywydd ar ymdrech Buddug yn erbyn y Rhufeiniaid', *The Gwyneddion* (London, 1828), p. 122. Hu Gadarn was imaged both visually and, as here, in text, felling the trees of the primeval forest of Britain to create agricultural land.

44 W.D. Leathart, *The Origin and Progress of the Gwyneddigion Society* (London, 1831), p. 97. George Thomson, *A Select Collection of Original Welsh Airs* (London and Edinburgh, 1809-17), vol. ii, p. 48, had earlier provided a different text for the occasion, 'translated by Mr Edward Williams [Iolo Morganwg], from the Welsh of Mr Rice Jones.' It was entitled 'The Happy Cambrians' ('Y Cymry Dedwydd') – 'A remnant still, in high renown,/Of Britain's *ancient* race.'

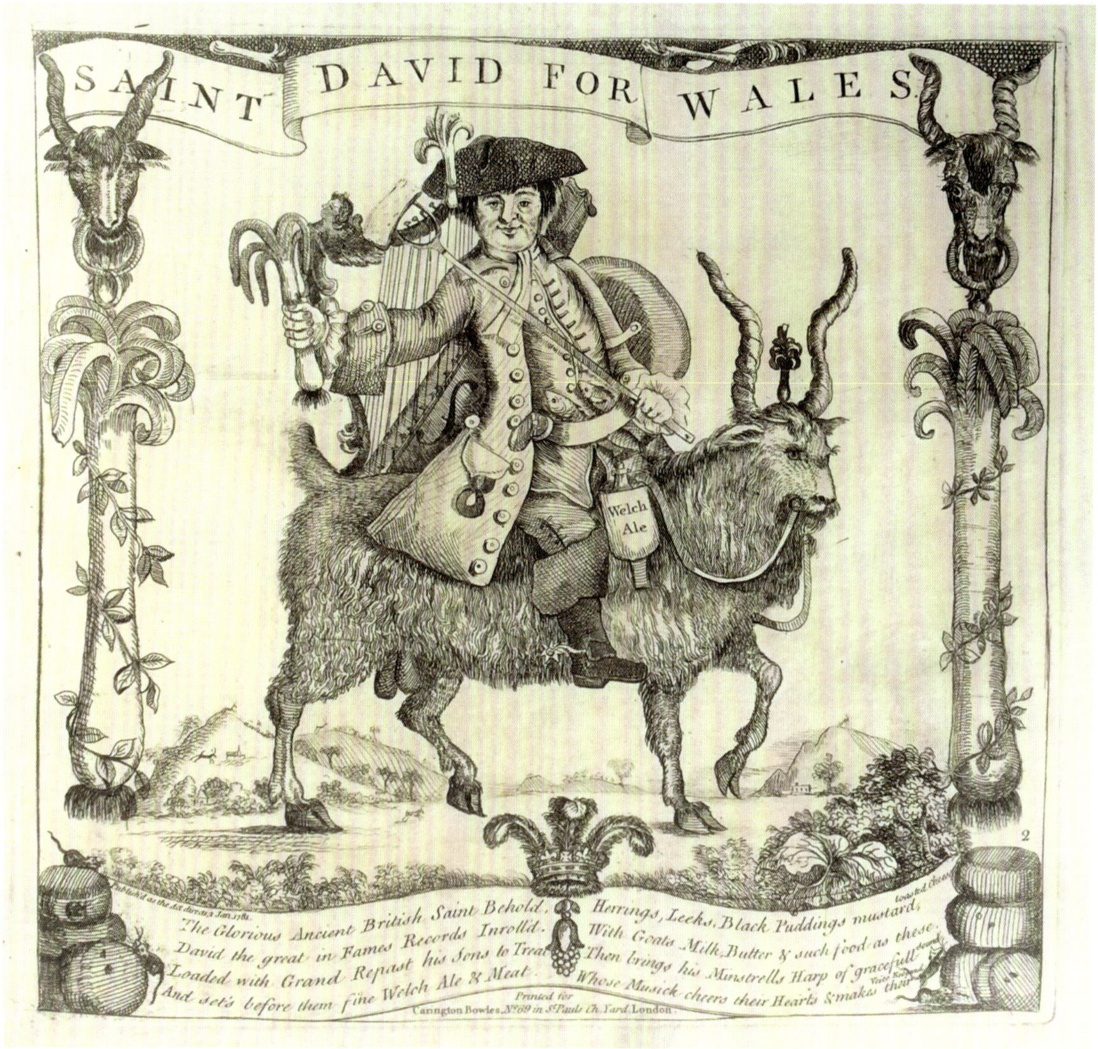

CYDUNWN, GWYNEDDIGION,
brodorion freisgion fryd,
I ganlyn tannau tynion, yn gyson yma i gyd;
Odiaethol wiw gymdeithion yw'r Brython mawr eu bri,
Naturiol lân gantorion, ond mwynion ydym ni?
Nyni, y CYMMRY ydym, ar hoffaf decaf hynt,
Yn dilyn hen arferion ein teidiau gwychion gynt:
Mwynderau tannau tyner y Delyn lwysber lân,
Mae'n fwyniant mawr i'r fynwes, a chynhes yw ei chân.

[WE UNITE, GWYNEDDIGION,
strong-minded brothers,
To follow the taut strings, regularly here together;
The greatly famed Briton is fit fine company,
Naturally pure singers, are we not gentle?
We are the WELSH, on the favourite fairest path,
Following the ancient ways of our splendid forbears:
The gentle tender strings of the pure clear harp,
It is a great pleasure to the breast, and its song is warm.][44]

45 See also below, pp. 108–9, for Thomas Attwood's comic opera *St David's Day*.

46 From the series 'Seven Prints of the Titular Saints'. See Peter Lord, *Words with Pictures: Welsh Images and Images of Wales in the Popular Press, 1640–1860* (Aberystwyth, 1995).

47 Sir Watkin's penchant for dressing up was manifested on another occasion by his entry as a druid, and again, even more remarkably (given his bulk), by his appearance as a milkmaid. See Burrows and Dunhill, Music and Theatre in Handel's World, p. 826.

Along with copious supplies of alcohol, the London societies' annual celebrations of St David's Day always included music. This aspect of living rather than mythological Welshness was once again noted by the English printmakers, two hundred years after its first visual acknowledgement.[45] In 1781, the publisher Carington Bowles turned the Welsh national brand to commercial advantage by issuing an etching entitled *Saint David for Wales*. It brought together the archaic stereotypical tokens that identified a Welsh person – a goat, a leek and toasted cheese – which had featured in hostile representations of the national character since the Civil Wars of the seventeenth century.[46] However, the latest engraving was significant both for a distinct change in tone and for the addition of a symbol absent in the popular press since Andrew Boorde's engraving of 1547. The poverty-stricken Welsh gentleman riding to London on a goat – Shôn ap Morgan, the 'Poor Taff' of earlier representations – was presented with a cheery demeanour and carrying a harp, to which reference was made in the accompanying text. The reinvented Shôn, whose musical talents had previously been passed over, brought to London 'his Minstrells Harp of graceful Sound/ Whose Musick cheers their Hearts & makes their Voice Resound.' The change was a reflection of public awareness of the uninhibited celebration of the national saint's day among the London Welsh, and the general fashion for things Ancient British, represented in the metropolis both by John Parry (still alive at that time) and by his patron, Sir Watkin Williams Wynn, 4th Baronet.

Perhaps the designer of the Carington Bowles engraving had heard of the celebrated entrance of Sir Watkin at a St David's Day celebration in his London home, riding on the back of a goat – a truly stoic animal, since by this time the gentleman had expanded into a figure of considerable bulk.[47] Six years after the St David's Day cartoon, James Gillray presented the enlarged Sir Watkin in the caricature *Ancient Music*. The allusions in Gillray's satire were complex and multi-faceted, but the setting was clear – one of the Concerts of Antient Music. The series had been established in 1776 by the conductor Joah Bates, who is caricatured in the group facing the King and Queen. In the front row, obese under a goat's head, Gillray portrayed Sir Watkin as 'The sleek Welsh Deity who Music Knows/The Alexander of the Tot'n'am Troops' (since the Concerts were held at the New Rooms in Tottenham Street). Sir Watkin had been a leading figure and enthusiast for the Concerts from their inception, and for the performance of music by Handel in particular. Lying on the floor in Gillray's image, a score with the words 'Anointed Solomon, King above all', alludes to

Handel's *Zadok the Priest*, composed in 1727 for the Coronation of the present King's grandfather, George II. In the time of that monarch and of Sir Watkin's father, the 3rd Baronet, John Parry had played Handel's works before the great composer himself and, as we have seen, if his son's double portrait can be relied upon, *Zadok the Priest* was still in his repertoire in the 1770s.

The 4th Baronet's public association with the music had become even stronger of late, since he had been among the prime movers in a festival to commemorate the twenty-fifth anniversary of Handel's death in 1784. Given by large forces before huge audiences in Westminster Abbey and the Pantheon, the concerts had crystallised the curious association between the German composer and English national identity through the medium of the Hanoverian monarchy

58 James Gillray, *Ancient Music*, 1787

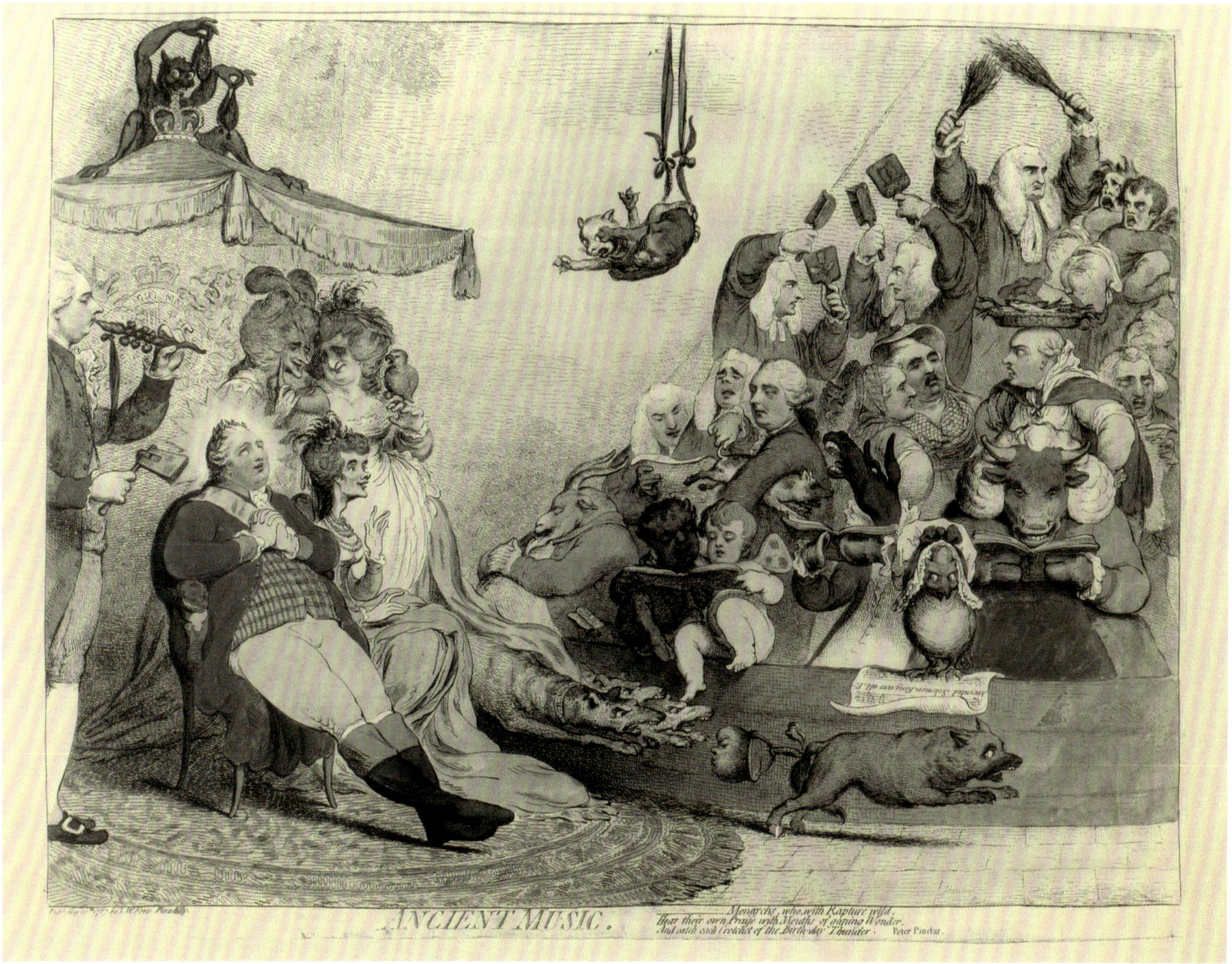

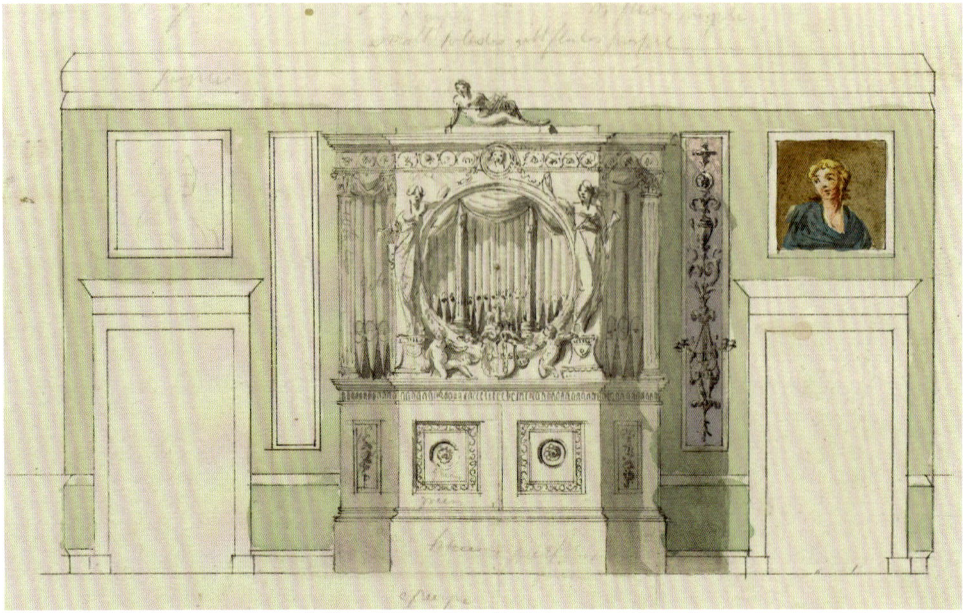

59 Robert Adam, detail from *Plan and Section of the Music Room (The Snetzler Organ Case)*, 1773

that would persist into the twentieth century.[48] In the immediate context of widespread political discontent in the early 1780s, the festival contributed to a reassertion of Tory patrician dominance in a briefly pacified nation. The period of quiet following a contentious election in 1784 was the successful outcome of a political agenda shared by Sir Watkin and that he had pursued not only through his musical interests, but also in his promotion of the patrician imagery of his favoured Welsh painter, Richard Wilson. The most ambitious visual expression of that agenda, commissioned by Sir Watkin in 1770, was a pair of landscapes that, Janus-like, simultaneously presented the patriotic case for Wales as the living archaeology of Ancient Britain. The two extensive views of Castell Dinas Brân would be hung not at Wynnstay, but on view to the fashionable and the empowered who congregated at his new London house, 20 St James's Square, when it was completed a few years later.

The centrepiece of Sir Watkin's house, designed by Robert Adam, was a magnificent music room, the physical focus of which was a chamber organ by the Swiss builder John Snetzler. The case was designed as an integral part of the architectural setting by Adam, whose drawings survive and demonstrate its evolution. The walls of the room were animated by pictures reflecting its purpose. On a design drawing, Adam noted in 1773 that he intended to have a picture of St Cecilia for a panel to the side of the chimney; and 'Over Doors on each sides [*sic*] of Organ was proposed also to have Heads of Great Musicians. Over the Doors at the End, the Muises [*sic*] that honour the Tomb of Orpheus.'[49]

48 William Weber, 'The 1784 Handel Commemoration as political ritual', *Journal of British Studies*, 28, 1 (1989), pp. 43–69.

49 Sir John Soane's Museum, London, SM Adam 40/71.

50 Given in Burrows and Dunhill, *Music and Theatre in Handel's World*, p. 674. Both the St Cecilia and the Orpheus pictures were noted as hanging at Wynnstay in an inventory of 1840, and valued at £500 each. NLW Probate Records, Williams Wynn of Wynnstay, File YB1/4, 1840-3. The Nathaniel Dance *Orpheus* is missing, but it appears to have survived the Wynnstay fire, since it may well be the picture sold in the John D. Wood contents sale in 1947, lot 280, for just £1. We are grateful to Miles Wynn Cato for this information.

These works were commissioned from the most fashionable and expensive painters of the period, and the impression made by the results of the young Welsh gentleman's love of music can be gauged from the report of Mrs Elizabeth Harris, who visited while the house interiors remained incomplete, in May 1775:

> The rooms below are elegant and large; the music room is very judiciously ornamented, a fine picture of St Cecilia by Reynolds, Orpheus by Dance and many smaller paintings in the musical way. The upper floor is not quite finish'd so not open'd. All the fine world were there … The music was all Handelian.[50]

60 James Scott after Joshua Reynolds, *St Cecilia (Mrs Sheridan)*, 1833–37

61 Domenico Zampieri (Domenichino), *King David Playing the Harp*, 1619

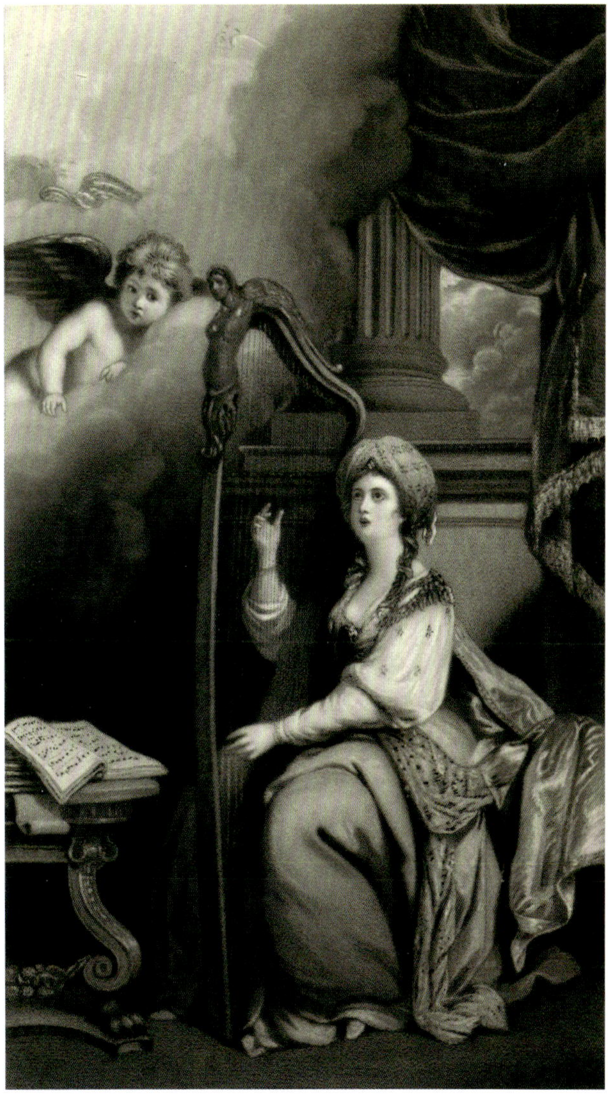

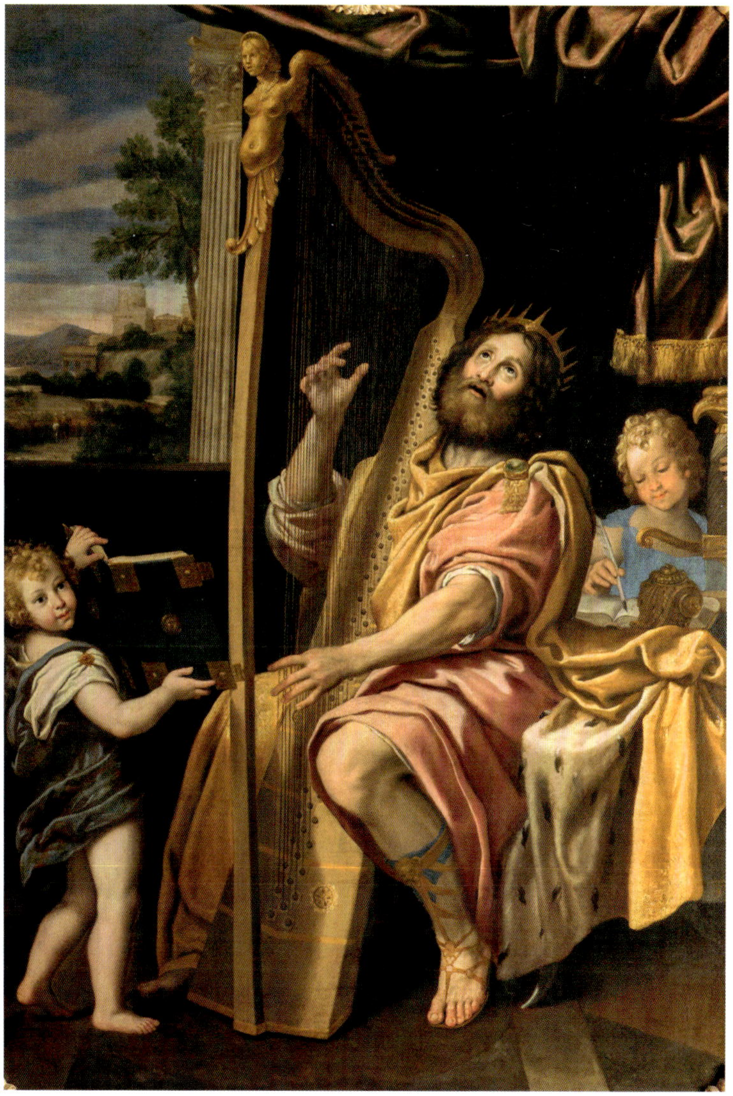

It seems likely that the sitter for the St Cecilia was the singer Elizabeth Ann Linley, recently married to the playwright R.B. Sheridan. But Reynolds's picture involved a long-standing conflation of mythologies, since he modelled his image of the Christian martyr and patron saint of music on King David, as painted in 1619 at his harp by Domenichino. Reynolds greatly admired Domenichino, and if he was not familiar with the picture from a sight of the original in the Royal Collection in France, then he would have known it through engravings.

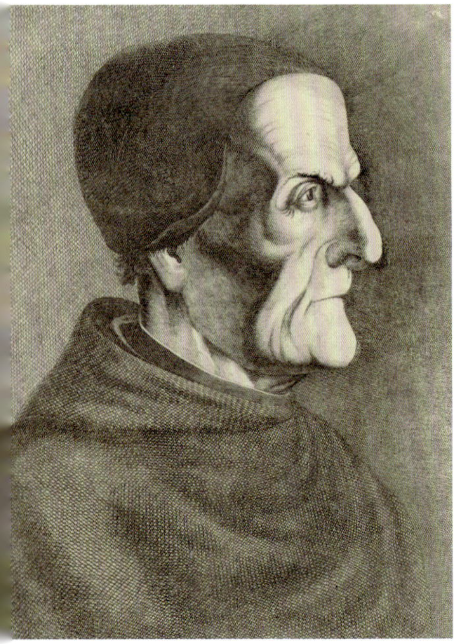

62 Unknown artist, *Gaetano Guadagni*, c.1780

Sir Watkin's musical activities were not confined to London, since the theatre that he constructed at Wynnstay was also graced by London singers and guests, invited to Wales for the season's performances. Similarly, Ruabon Church, which stands in the village opposite the gates to the estate, was enriched with another new Snetzler organ at Sir Watkin's expense. The Italian castrato, Gaetano Guadagni, spent eight weeks at Wynnstay in 1770, during which time he performed in the church at the celebration for the installation of the new organ. The following year, he was employed to give a private performance at Sir Watkin's earlier London house in Grosvenor Square.[51] There can be little doubt that as a leading London patron, and in particular by his association with John Parry, the public image of Sir Watkin – the most celebrated and powerful Welsh gentleman of his period – contributed substantially to the reinforcement of the branding of Wales as a musical nation.

THE FRENCH WARS – NEUTRALISING NATIONALITY

Sir Watkin, the 4th Baronet, died at the age of forty on 24 July 1789, ten days after the storming of the Bastille in Paris. The Revolution would lead from 1793 to long periods of conflict. After Napoleon came to power in 1799, the threat of invasion intensified. Ireland was absorbed by the Act of Union, effective from 1801, and two years later, 'United Kingdom' was added to the earlier title 'Great Britain', emphasising the London government's aspiration to solidify 'national' sentiment in a crisis. The conflict affected in a significant way the representation of Welsh, Irish and Scottish identities in music, literature and in visual imagery produced in England. National crisis, as perceived by unionists, stimulated the creation of a new sub-genre of popular prints, for instance, that presented individually – but collectively, since they were issued in sets – the four

51 See Hilary Peters, blog.library.wales/wynnstay-connections-in-the-papers-of-james-harris. Peters notes that 'James Harris's wife, Elizabeth, wrote to her son, James [future first Earl of Malmesbury] in May 1771: '"Guadagni ... is the finest acter [*sic*], the finest figure, & the finest voice imaginable, & is undoubtedly the most insolent of all fellows; he gives out that he acts only to oblige Sir Watkins Williams [*sic*] & takes no reward whatever".'

52 The English popular press found a market for images encapsulating racial or national identities on a worldwide scale in this period. Native American people became a popular subject, for instance.

53 The print, issued in 1795, was one of a series of at least three pairings under the general title *A Dance in the Temple of Hymen*. Newton produced several Welsh images, see Lord, *Words with Pictures*, pp. 68, 72.

nations of the new United Kingdom.[52] The mocking of national character in grotesque caricature persisted in the work of some artists, such as the London-born Richard Newton, whose particular contempt for the Scots did not preclude mocking also the Welsh and the Irish peoples. Newton's *A Welch Wedding* appeared next to an Irish wedding, both parties identified by their national musical instruments.[53] But a new brand of visual propaganda emerged that promoted the unambiguous loyalty of all the British nations to the English crown in the face of the foreign threat. For instance, *Cambria in a Country Dance*, designed by the Irish painter Adam Buck, formed one of a set of four images of national dance subjects, issued in 1801, that joined a group of feminised – and so, in the mind of the period, implicitly benign – representations of the constituent nations expressive of internal unity. These images represent the earliest manifestation of a regendering process that would proceed through the nineteenth and twentieth centuries which affected Wales in particular, directing representations away from the potentially confrontational image of the masculine bard.

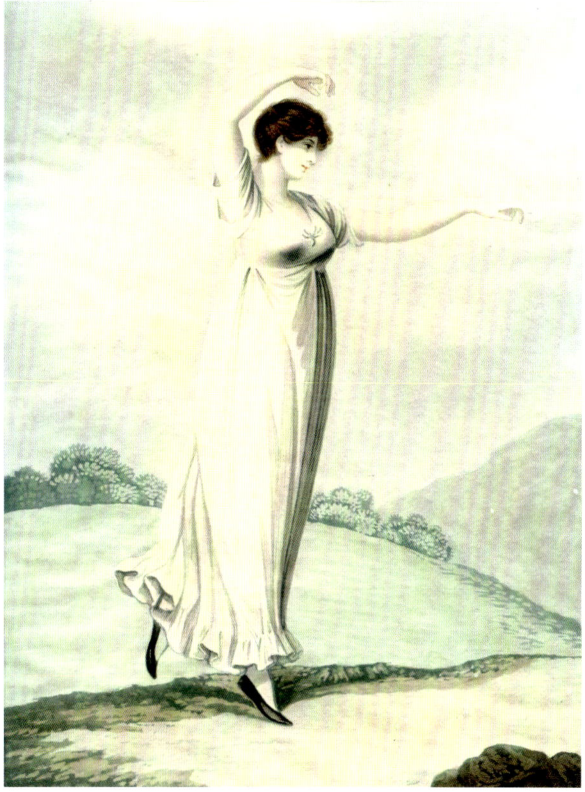

63 Adam Buck, *Cambria in a Country Dance*, 1801

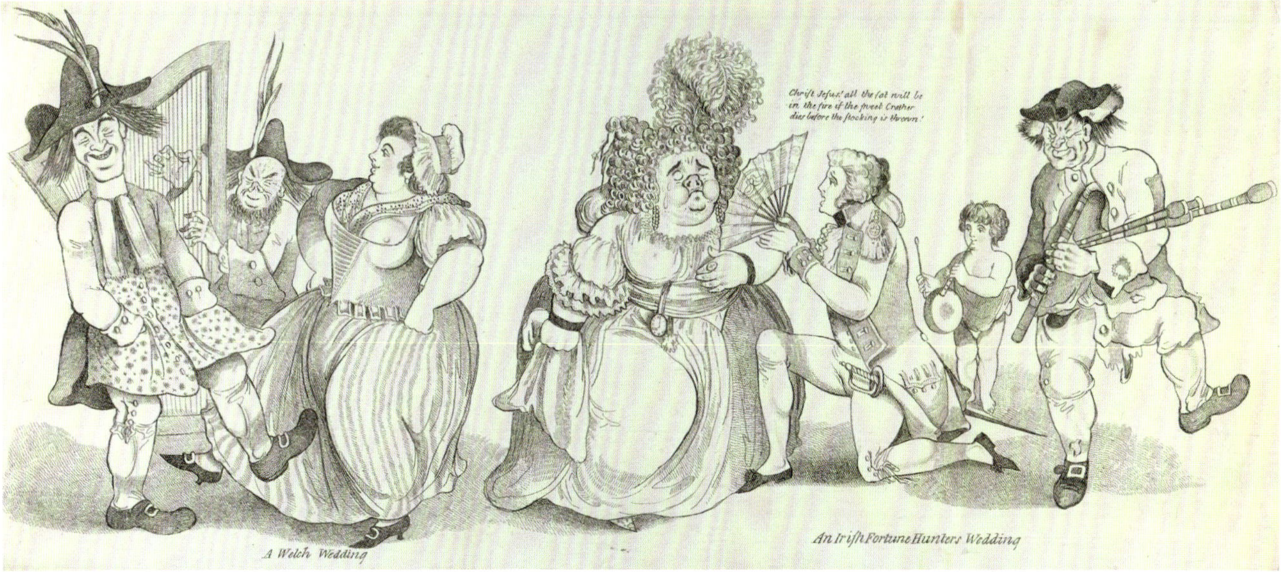

64 Richard Newton, *A Dance in the Temple of Hymen (A Welch Wedding)*, 1794

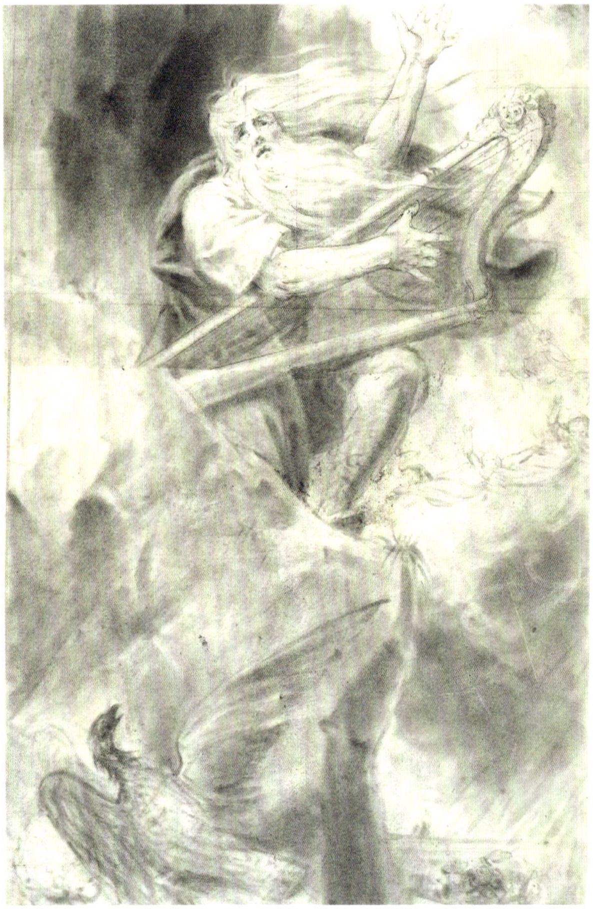

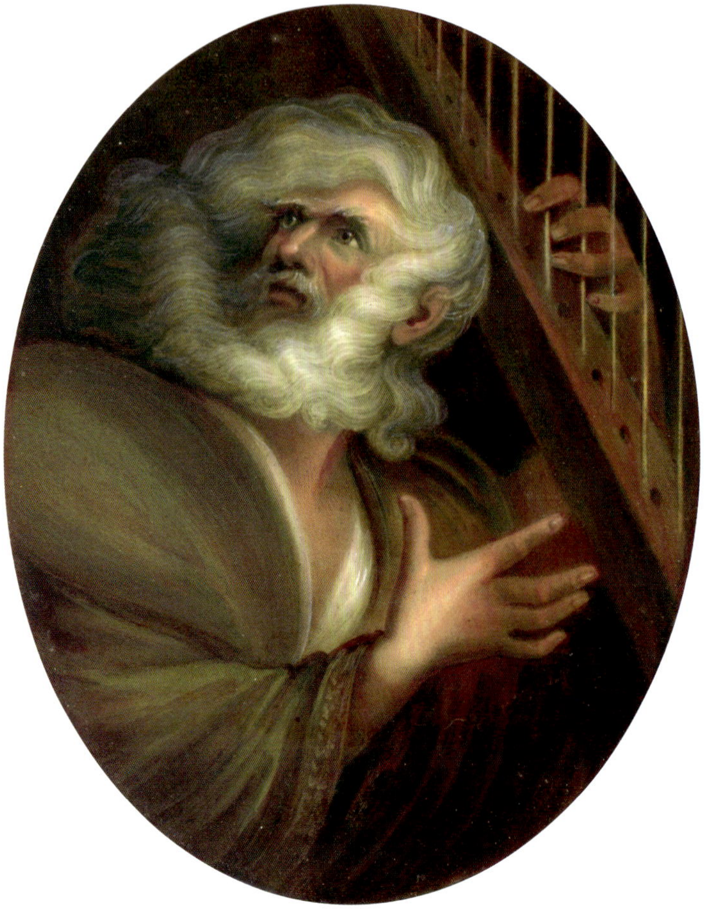

65 John Downman, *The Bard*, c.1800

66 Unknown artist after William Weston Young, *The Bard*, c.1835–45

Imaging of the bard did continue through the French Wars, but by and large in a significantly modified form. The oppositional narrative of the original conception of the illustrators of Gray all but disappeared, as the focus closed in upon the bard himself and his harp, to the exclusion of the invading English army. John Downman produced an interpretation in which the army of Edward I was reduced to a tiny detail. Gray's screaming 'famish'd eagle' assumed the main supporting role. By the time the image descended to the level of kitsch – albeit rather classy kitsch – the association with a Welsh war of resistance against the invading English had entirely disappeared. A bardic image (probably painted by William Weston Young) on mugs produced in about 1805 by the Cambrian Pottery at Swansea was copied on a Davenport patent porcelain plaque some thirty years later, by which time the Last Bard had become, simply, The Bard.

The most radical revision of the brand in the period of the wars was undertaken by Edward Jones in his publication *The Bardic Museum* of 1802. The volume continued the work begun by the author in the *Musical and Poetical Relicks* of eighteen years earlier, but he significantly revised the visual cypher deployed to emphasise the persistence of national tradition from the earliest times. In his lengthy introduction on the subject of Bardism, Jones entirely glossed over the unfortunate events of 1282, constructing instead a story of unbroken continuity:

> Something now remains to be said respecting the national music of the aboriginal Britons, or Welsh, which has been transmitted down to us from time immemorial, and is still, the favourite amusement of the natives.[54]

Jones linked the extensive definition of bardic responsibilities found in the Welsh laws, as codified by Hywel Dda in the tenth century, with post-Edwardian court practice in England, revealing even more clearly than in his previous effusion on musical history his indebtedness to his royal employer. Continuity was also the theme of the visual cypher that Jones now chose, in order to avoid the unfortunate associations of the bard of 1282. Abandoning the original locale and timeframe, Jones pursued the very same agenda with regard to Wales that had been pioneered half a century earlier in the paintings of Richard Wilson, which presented his English and Anglicised Welsh audiences with a contemporary portrait of a timeless topography, a mouldering architecture, and the remnant of a happy aboriginal people, living content with their lot. For the creation of the image, Jones had 'to make his acknowledgement to the Hon. Colonel Greville, a gentleman remarkable for his elegant taste in native picturesque scenery and costume, for the loan of his rural drawing, taken from nature, from a group of Welsh Peasants, singing in alternate theme around the Harp, with a distant view of Snowdon and Dolbadarn Castle in Caernarvonshire.'[55]

54 Edward Jones, *The Bardic Museum, of Primitive British Literature; and Other Admirable Rarities* (London, 1802), p. xi.

55 Ibid., p. xvi.

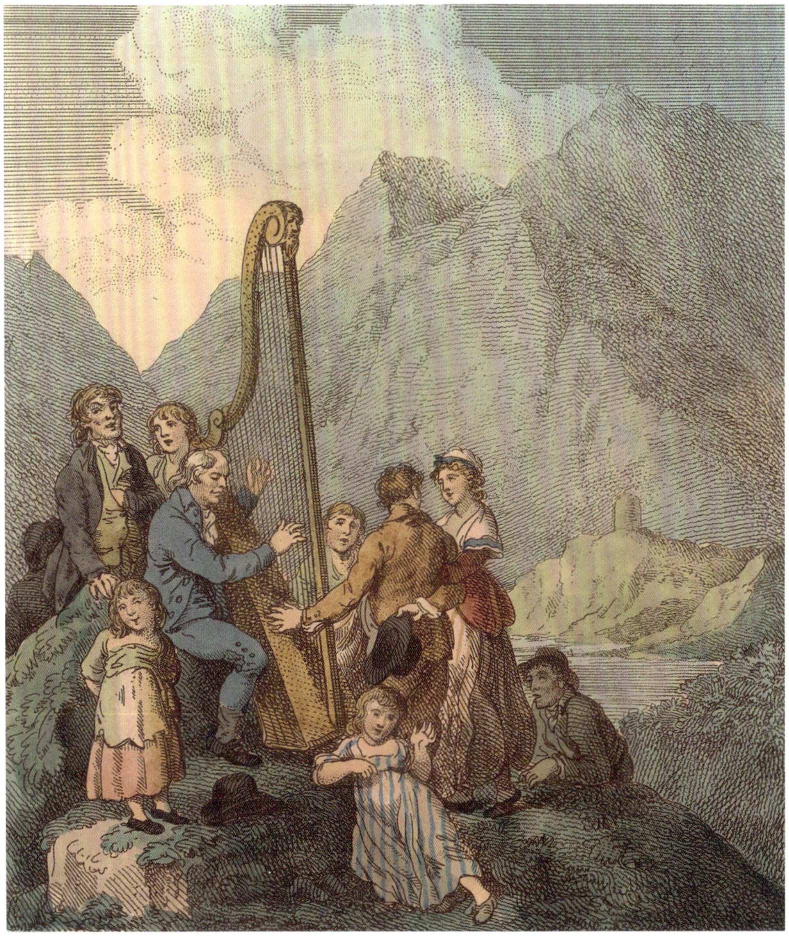

67 Thomas Rowlandson, frontispiece to Edward Jones, *The Bardic Museum*, 1802

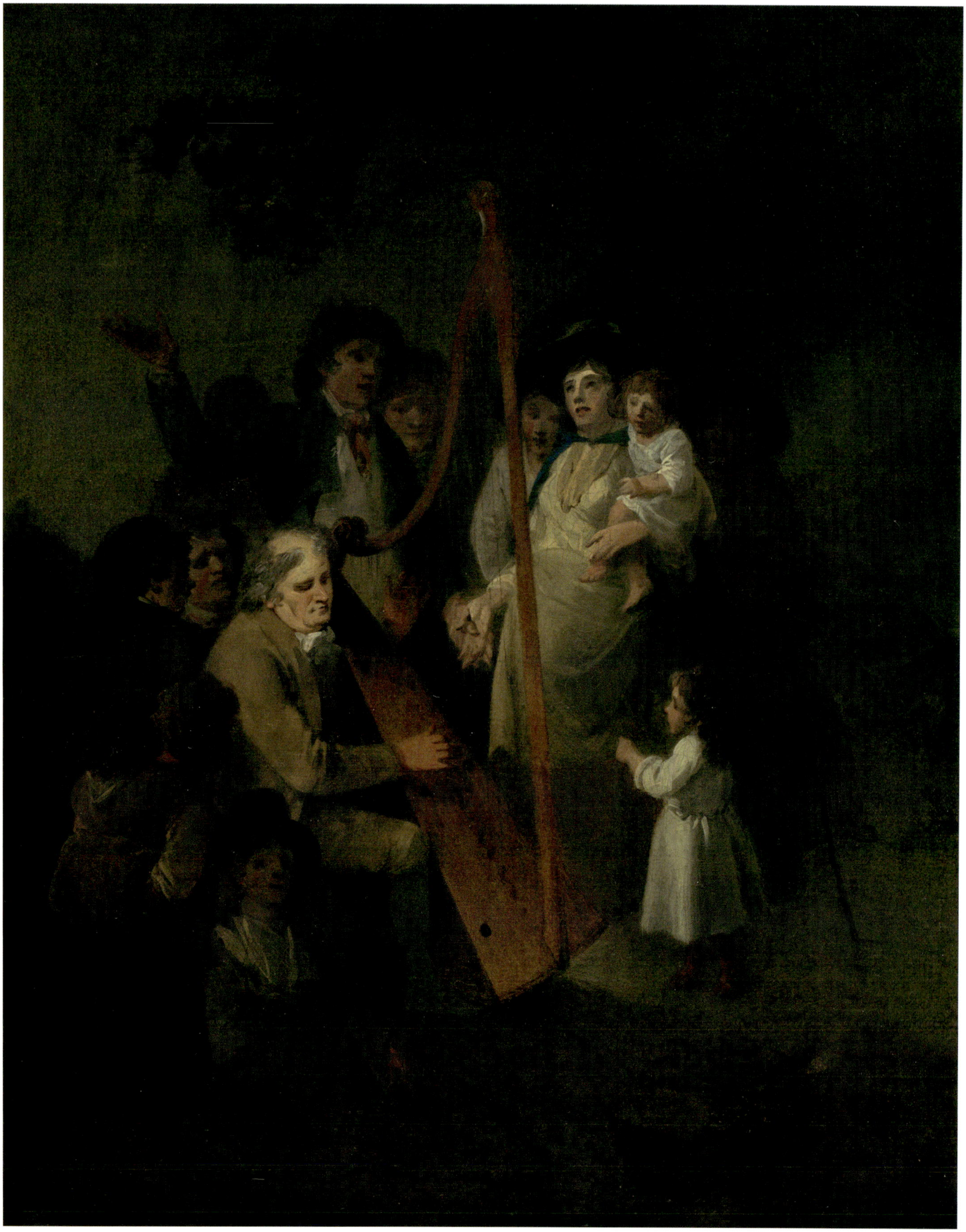

The genesis of the frontispiece reveals the care taken by Jones in pursuit of his political evisceration of the bardic brand. The image was a composite of the work of the two artists, John Warwick Smith and Julius Caesar Ibbetson, who had accompanied Colonel Robert Fulke Greville on his tour of Wales in 1792. Smith was already familiar with the country, having visited on several earlier occasions. His contribution was the landscape of Snowdon with Dolbadarn Castle – rapidly becoming the iconic tourist destination in Wales. Smith's view followed closely an aquatint published by Sandby in 1779, and it had featured recently in J.M.W. Turner's much admired Royal Academy piece of 1800. Ibbetson was the source of the figures, taken from one of several paintings that he made after observing the harper John Smith playing for penillion singers at Conwy. The landscape and the portrait group were blended by Thomas Rowlandson, who himself had toured the area in 1797.[56] Underlining the modern co-option and expansion of the meaning of the terms 'Britain' and 'British', Jones captioned Rowlandson's visual embodiment of the Welsh tradition with lines from a poem by the English Joseph Addison and from the Irish playwright Thomas Sheridan's *Lectures on the Art of Reading*:

> The Muse so oft her silver Harp has strung,
> That not a Mountain rears his head unsung.[57]
>
> And many an amorous, or a humorous Lay,
> Which many a Bard had Chanted many a Day.

In 1803, the year following the appearance of *The Bardic Museum*, the Revd William Bingley published *Sixty of the most admired Welsh Airs*, further adding to the available corpus of national music. In his visual encapsulation of the text, Bingley chose to retain the historic bardic brand but, like Jones, drew attention well away from the contentious issue of the medieval wars of

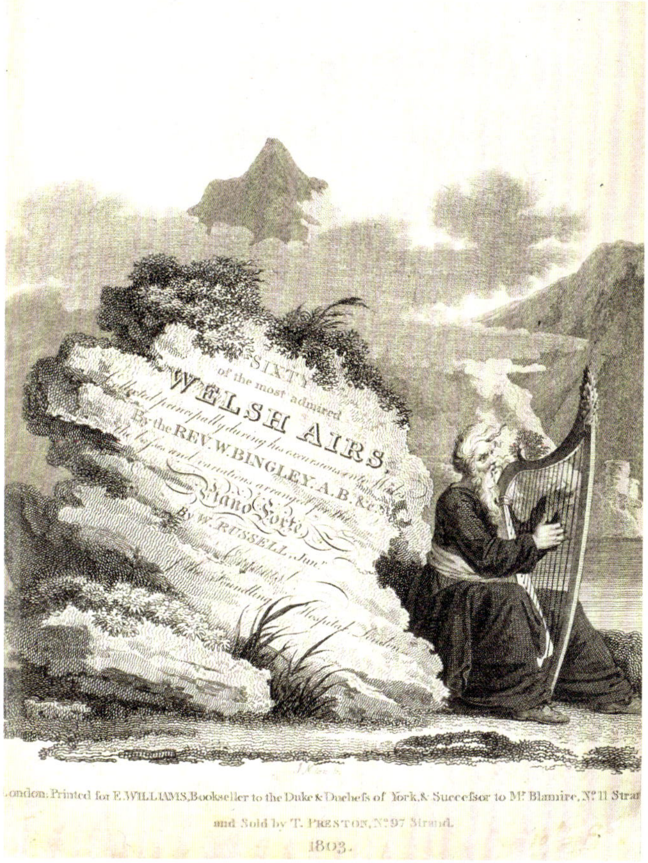

69 James Mitan, title page to the Revd William Bingley, *Sixty of the most admired Welsh Airs*, 1803

68 Julius Caesar Ibbetson, *John Smith, the Blind Harper of Conway, with Penillion Singers*, 1793

56 Edward Jones would call on Rowlandson again in 1804 to engrave the frontispiece for his *Lyric Airs: Consisting of Specimens of Greek, Albanian, Walachian, Turkish, Arabian, Persian, Chinese, and Moorish National Songs and Melodies*.

57 Addison's poem, given as 'A letter from Italy to the Right Honourable Charles Lord Halifax', had been published in Vicesimus Knox (ed.), *Elegant Extracts; or, Useful and Entertaining Pieces of Poetry* (London, 1789).

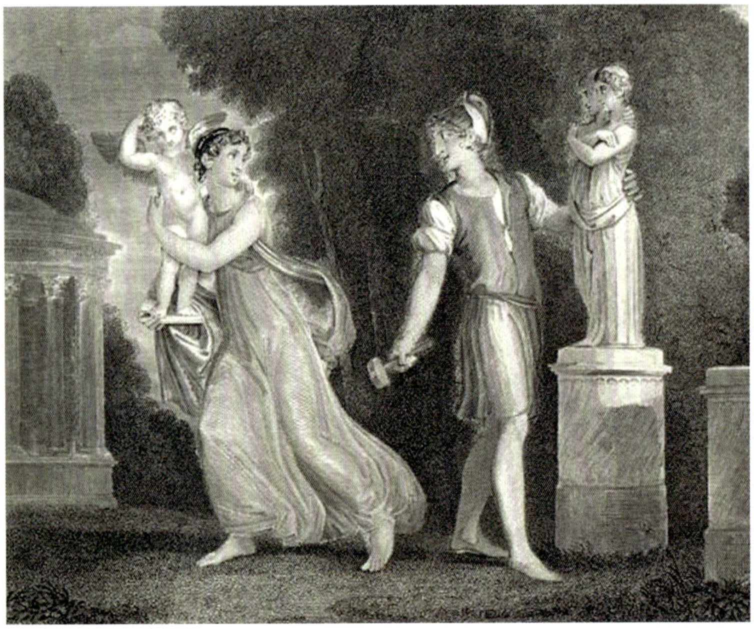

70 James Mitan after Thomas Stothard, title page to Thomas Moore, *Popular National Airs*, 1818

independence. James Mitan's engraving for the frontispiece to the new collection removed the bard from the generally agreed site of his suicide (the River Conwy), and also from the druidical location of Anglesey. Following closely the Rowlandson engraving that adorned *The Bardic Museum*, he relocated the bard above Dolbadarn Castle, though Mitan's sense of its geographical relationship to an Eiger-like Snowdon was somewhat vague. Fifteen years later, Mitan would engrave Thomas Stothard's illustrations to Thomas Moore's *Popular National Airs*, a compilation based on Irish folk melodies. It may be that the Welsh bardic engraving was also designed by Stothard, given that it coincided with the period spent by the painter working for Thomas Johnes at Hafod.

The publication of Edward Jones's *Bardic Museum* in 1802 and William Bingley's *Welsh Airs* the following year was undertaken in the context of the development of folk-song collecting pioneered by George Thomson in Scotland. As in Wales, Thomson made use of the earliest published collections of airs, but had them encased in 'symphonies and accompaniments' for pianoforte, violin and violoncello by contemporary composers with words by living writers. The objective was to popularise the airs by adapting them to the polite taste and rational morality of his period, with the effect of turning what had been a folk tradition into art music for performance in private drawing rooms and public assembly rooms. Thomson's ambitions were high, and he had been able to draw on the talents of Robert Burns and other distinguished individuals such as R.B. Sheridan for his lyrics, and no less a figure than Joseph Haydn, along with his pupil Ignaz Pleyel and others, for the musical development. Each volume was introduced by an engraving, illustrating the subject matter. Thomson's first volume of *A Select Collection of Original Scottish Airs* was published in 1793, and its success and that of the subsequent volumes encouraged him to begin work in 1802 on what became the three volumes of *A Select Collection of Original Welsh Airs*. His relationship with Haydn continued and resulted in the composer setting a substantial number of the Welsh tunes. After Haydn's death, Ludwig van Beethoven and Leopold Kozeluch provided settings. The verses were commissioned from a curious assortment of writers, ranging from William Roscoe to Walter Scott and other Scottish authors who had worked on the *Collection of Original Scottish Airs*, with some Welsh contributions, including two from Edward Llwyd, 'Bard of Snowdon'.

From Edinburgh, Thomson established contact with Llwyd and a network of others who had an interest in Welsh material, including Iolo Morganwg and Owain Myfyr. In 1806 he visited Wales accompanied by his brother, David Thomson, as his visual artist. They stayed with Sir Foster Cunliffe of Acton, near Wrexham, a relationship facilitated no doubt by the fact that the gentleman had married a Scottish lady, Harriet, daughter of Sir David Kinloch. It was probably at Acton that Thomson heard the Wrexham harper Edward Randles play in a manner that struck him as 'graceful, animated, and expressive.'[58] No doubt, David Thomson would also have been interested by Sir Foster Cunliffe's substantial art

58 Thomson, *A Select Collection of Original Welsh Airs*, vol. i, p. 2. The Thomsons also stayed with Owen Williams (son of the celebrated Thomas Williams, the 'Copper King') and his wife Margaret, at Llanidan.

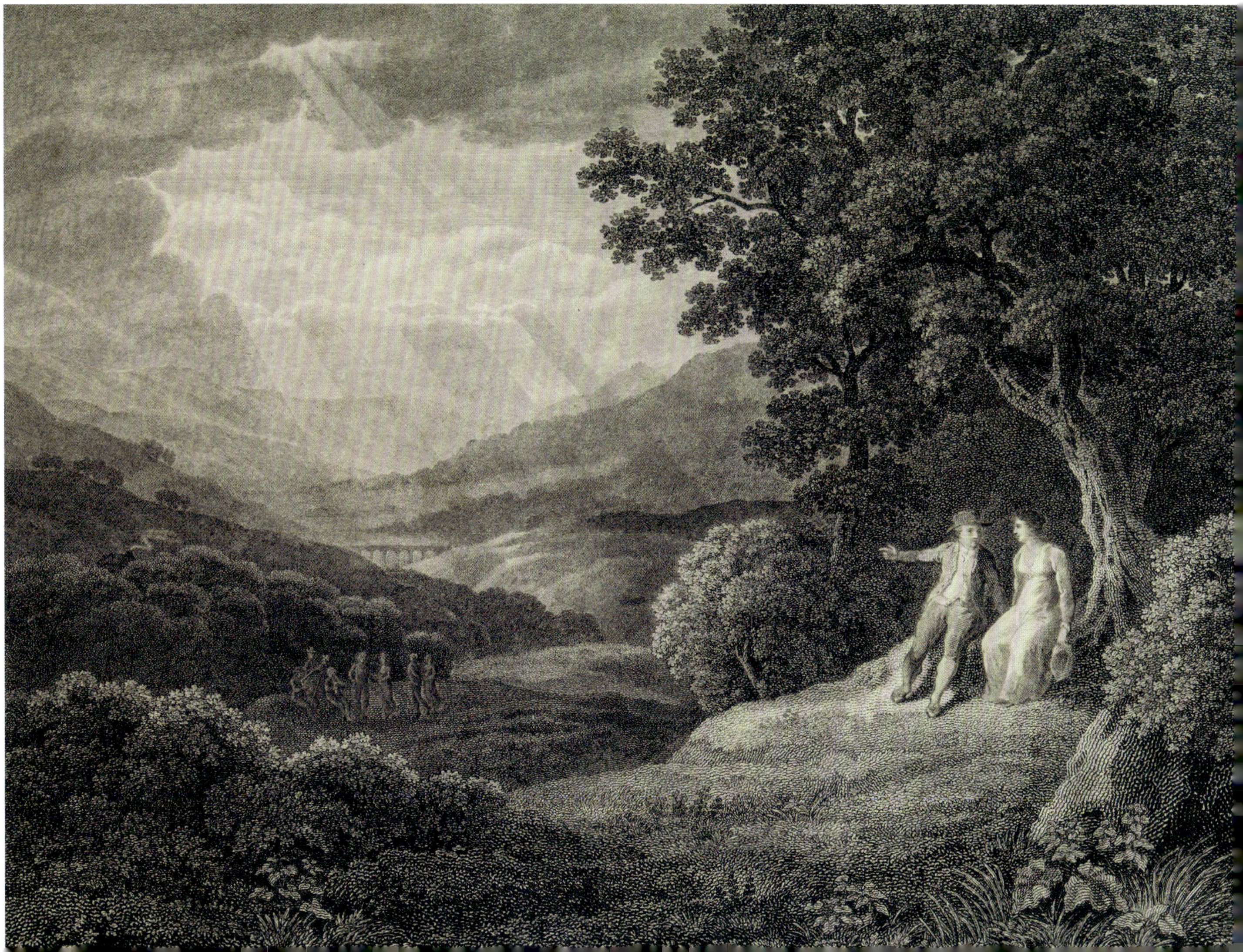

71 David Thomson, *Llangollen Vale*, 1809

collection. The first volume of *Welsh Airs* appeared with a pastoral landscape engraving entitled *Llangollen Vale*, a view taken by Thomson looking towards Pontcysyllte. A shepherd indicates to his lover a group of dancers accompanied by musicians. Rays of light shine down through breaking clouds in the manner pioneered in an aquatint of Llangollen Vale made by Paul Sandby in 1776, which, it would appear, Thomson had seen. The musicians included a harper, but the benign contemporary pastorale contrasted with the historicist imagery favoured by most of the Welsh antiquarians, keen to stress their particular agenda of Welsh bardic continuity, notwithstanding its awkward ambiguities in a time of war.

George Thomson was a unionist of conviction, who sought to sanitise the internal national traditions not only in a political sense, avoiding any suspicion of Jacobite tendencies, but also in pursuit of his conception of polite good taste. Clearly, subsequent Welsh writers and musicians would have been well aware of Thomson's publications, but despite his distinguished musical collaborators, they seem to have remained marginal to the Welsh mainstream. In contrast to the success and influence exerted by his Scottish publications, *Welsh Airs* never went to a second edition. Whatever Thomson's unionist intentions, like Thomas Moore's *Irish Melodies*, published between 1807 and 1834, the *Scottish Airs* – with many of the words created by Burns – would contribute substantially to sustaining patriotic sentiment, and would in due course be frequently deployed in national politics.[59] Although the politics of Burns continue a subject of academic debate, poems such as 'A Parcel of Rogues in a Nation' (1791), that lambasted those who signed the 1707 Treaty of Union, have been potently deployed ever since in the nationalist cause. The reinvented Welsh material, pioneered by John Parry, 'Bardd Alaw',[63] in *A Selection of Welsh Melodies*, published in 1809, after the *Scottish Airs* and the *Irish Melodies*, would remain politically dormant.

BARDD ALAW SETS THE AGENDA

Bardd Alaw was the rising star of Welsh music. The bardic frontispiece to *A Selection of Welsh Melodies* maintained the eviscerating trend of the earlier historicist images of the period of the French Wars. It depicted Cadwaladr, a seventh-century King of Gwynedd, 'Presiding at an Eisteddvod … and presenting the successful Candidate with a Medal for his superior skill in Music and Poetry.'

59 *The Anti-Jacobin Review and Magazine: or, Monthly Political and Literary Censor* discerned a threat to the prevailing order in Moore's lyrics, since 'several of them were composed in a very disordered state of society, if not in open rebellion. They are the melancholy ravings of the disappointed rebel, or his ill-educated offspring.' Moore described the airs as 'our national music', and that his lyrics 'reflect an unmistakable intimation of dispossession and loss in the music itself.' Given in Harry White, 'Thomas Moore', https://www.dib.ie/biography/moore-thomas-a5948.

60 John Parry, *A Selection of Welsh Melodies* (London, 1809), pp. 1-2.

61 Jones, *Musical and Poetical Relicks*, p. 10. Jones cited as his source John David Rhys, *Cambrobrytannicae Cymraecaeue Linguae Institutiones* (London, 1592), p. 103.

62 The triad is among those recorded in the *Red Book of Hergest*. See Rachel Bromwich (ed.), *Trioedd Ynys Prydein* (3rd ed., Cardiff, 2006), p. 150.

63 The engraver is usually noted as being active only from some twenty years later. However, Turnbull engraved two portraits of *Signor Sampieri* (one after Charles Hayter), an Italian opera singer in London and Dublin, which tend to confirm that he was active *c.*1809.

64 Parry 'dedicated to his highly respected friend Dr. W.O. Pughe' his *Original Melodies: composed in the style after the manner of the ancient British airs for pennillion singing with Welsh harps* (London, n.d.).

The tradition that Cadwaladr (known in the early sources as 'the Blessed') had called an eisteddfod was familiar, but Parry's image suggested a more particular narrative. Three apparently unsuccessful bards appear to resent the award – as we shall see, a situation increasingly familiar in the reviving eisteddfod tradition of Parry's own times – but although he wrote humorous songs and parodies, a light-hearted contemporary comment seems unlikely to have been in his mind on this occasion. In his *Musical and Poetical Relicks*, Edward Jones had cited a legend of dissent at Cadwaladr's eisteddfod arising from a performance on the harp given in a minor key. The bard 'was censured for the inharmonious effect he produced.' Furthermore, on the king's order, the use of the key was 'interdicted under a heavy penalty … ever after', an outcome clearly inconsistent with the award of a medal.[60] Equally, the legend given in the Triads that Cadwaladr's Chief Bard, Golyddan, had on some occasion struck the king a blow, seems inappropriate, and the narrative remains obscure.[61] Below the engraving, James Macpherson's Ossian was invoked, also for no apparent reason other than the presence of harpers at the Scottish scene described in 'Croma. A Poem': 'They poured forth their burning souls and the string answered to their voice.' But whatever the precise narrative of the visual context within which Bardd Alaw set his *Welsh Melodies*, the image effectively served to distract observers from the medieval perception of King Cadwaladr the Blessed as a messianic militant, associated with the prophecy of the ultimate return of rule over the islands of Britain to the Welsh people.

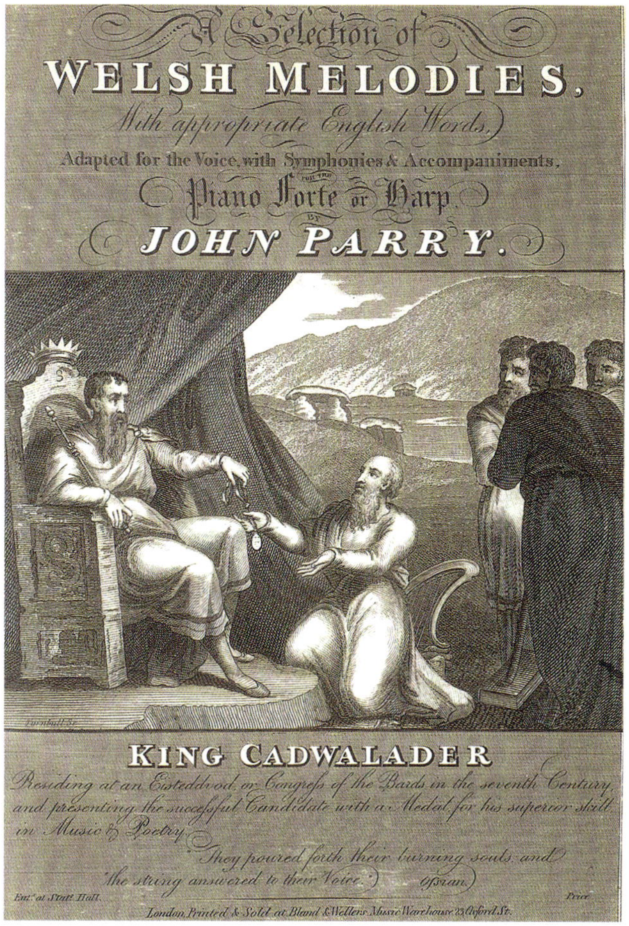

72 Thomas Turnbull, title page to John Parry, Bardd Alaw, *A Selection of Welsh Melodies*, 1809

The engraver of the picture was Thomas Turnbull, but it seems likely that the fertile imagination of William Owen Pughe lay behind the design.[62] Pughe had been an informant for Edward Jones, who acknowledged his contribution in *The Bardic Museum*, as now did Bardd Alaw. The two men would become close associates in the succeeding decade, as the musician assumed a place of authority on the tradition among the London Welsh.[64] Bardd Alaw became an increasingly important influence on the performance of national music, but he would also

73 John Downman, *Edward Randles and His Daughter Elizabeth*, 1807

achieve celebrity in the field of popular music in England. From 1809, coinciding with the publication of *A Selection of Welsh Melodies*, he became closely involved with the direction of music at Vauxhall Gardens.

John Parry, Bardd Alaw, was born in Denbigh in 1776. He was largely self-taught as a musician, but became a competent performer on numerous instruments including the flageolet, clarinet and harp. His initial engagement with music developed through the band of the local militia.[65] A highly sociable and energetic man, he became involved with an extensive network of musicians living in the north-east quadrant of the country. Among them was the harper and organist at Wrexham Church, Edward Randles, who, as we have seen, would play for George Thomson in 1806. As Bardd Alaw pointed out in the introduction to his *Selection of Welsh Melodies*, Randles had been taught by none other than John Parry of Wynnstay. Randles also composed several pieces, one of which, 'Four Waltzes: for the piano forte or harp: the Cambrian, Albian, Caledonian and Hibernian', tidily reflected in music the fashion of his period for unionist four-nation visual imagery. Randles's daughter, Elizabeth, born in 1800, developed exceptional musical talent at a very early age. She emerged first as a pianist, was exhibited in public, and came to the attention of Sir Watkin Williams Wynn and others of the gentry. From 1803 Bardd Alaw undertook her musical education. Through the influence of her admirers among the gentry, at the age of three and a half, she was presented as a prodigy at court, where she performed for King George III:

> Shortly after this a public breakfast was given at Cumberland Gardens, for the benefit of Miss Randles: tickets (one guinea each) were to be had at Sir W. W. Wynn's house, in St James's-square. The morning was very fine, and no less than five hundred persons of the first rank in the kingdom attended, and the child's performance was the admiration of every one. The profits of the breakfast, together with various sums of money presented to Miss Randles, were vested in the funds, in the names of trustees, for her sole benefit; and in order to accumulate enough to defray the expenses of her education, it was recommended that she should perform at the principal provincial towns in the kingdom.[66]

The Randles undertook some engagements jointly with Bardd Alaw, and it would seem that the latter's association with the 'Cambrian Musical Prodigy' greatly facilitated his introduction to both Welsh and English musical circles in London

65 He published *The Ancient Britons' Martial Music*, two sets of Welsh airs arranged for wind band.

66 John S. Sainsbury and Alexandre Choron (eds.), *A Dictionary of Musicians from the Earliest Ages to the Present Time* (London, 1825), vol. ii, p. 335.

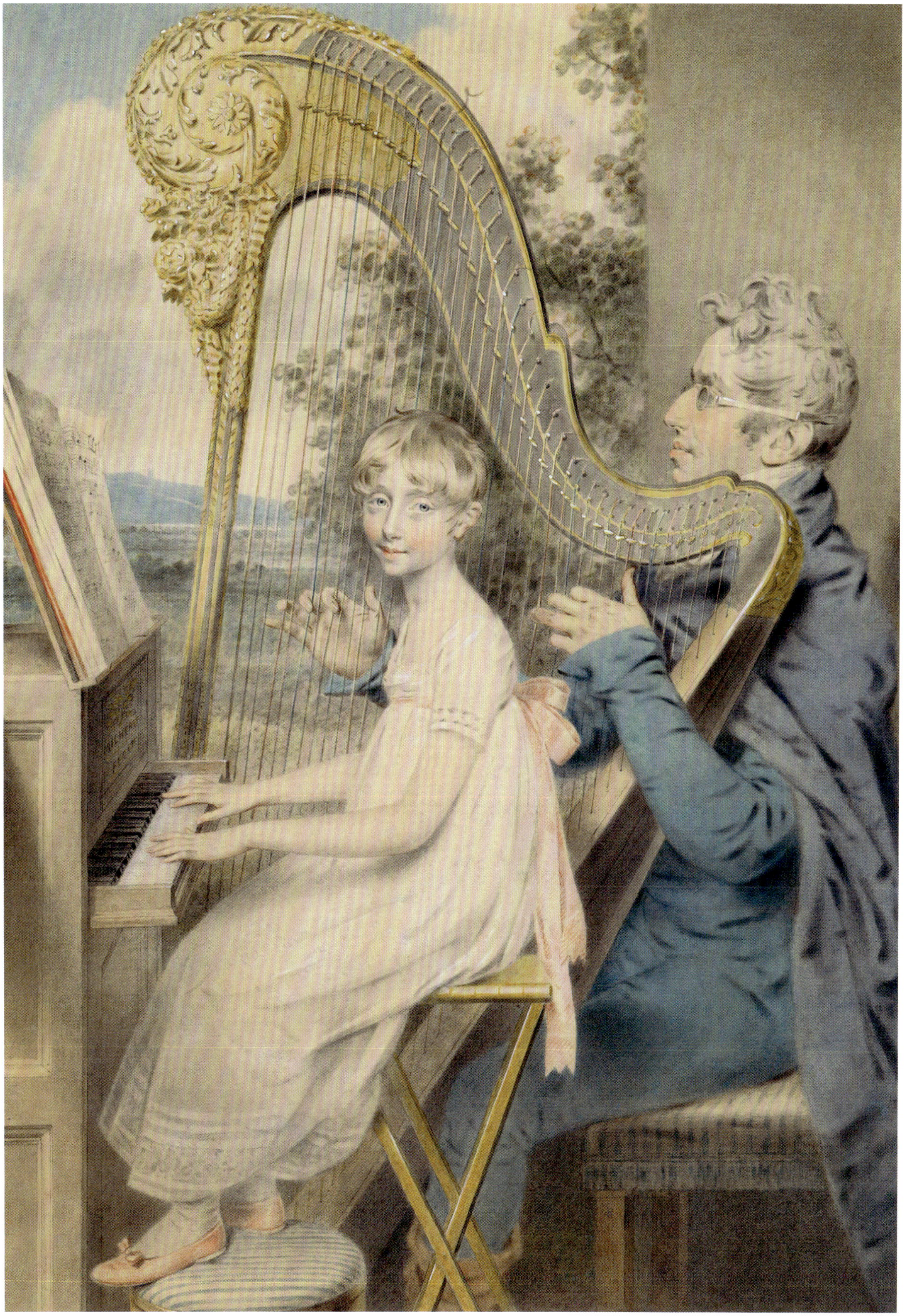

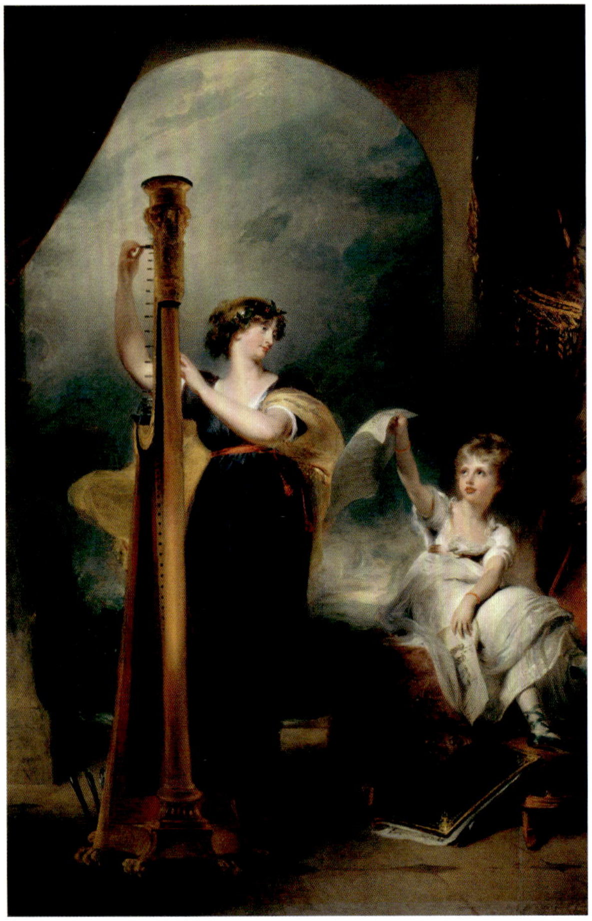

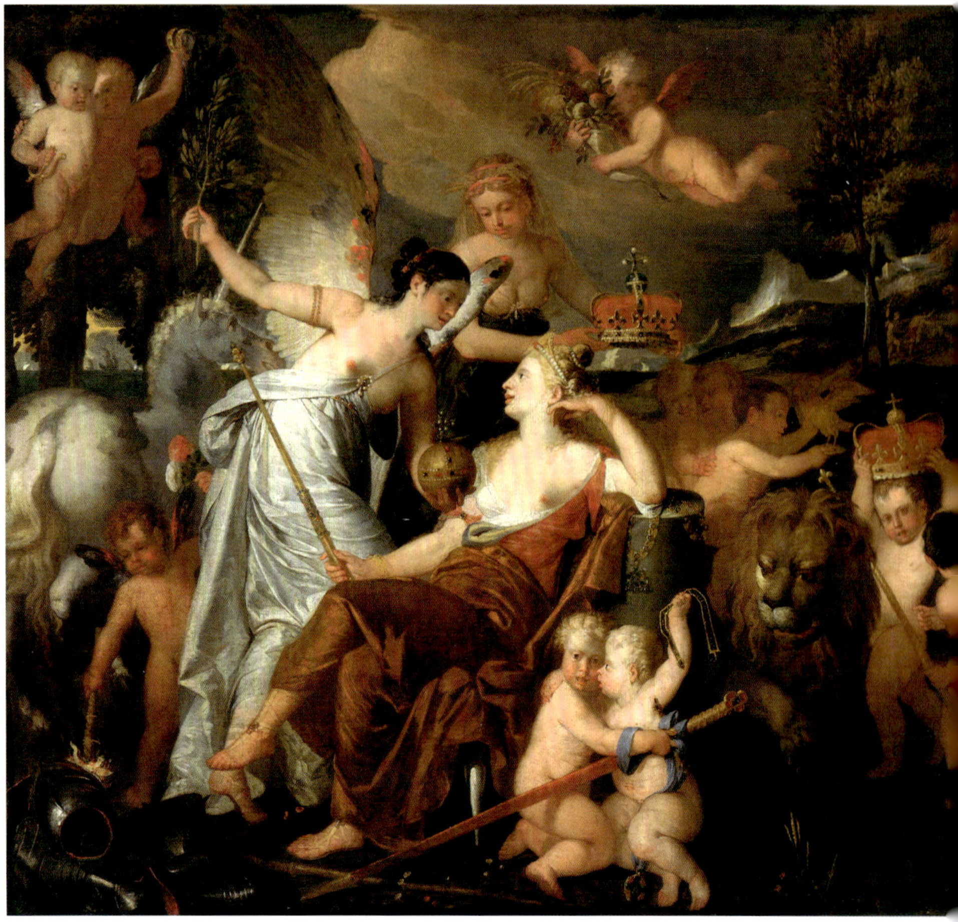

74 Thomas Lawrence, *Caroline, Princess of Wales, and Princess Charlotte*, 1801

75 John Downman, *A Late Princess Personifying Peace Crowning the Glory of England Reflected on Europe*, 1819

from 1807. It was also in that year that Elizabeth Randles and her father were painted by John Downman. The identity of the patron is unknown, but he or she is unlikely to have been one of the family, or indeed Bardd Alaw, since Downman was an expensive and fashionable painter. The double portrait would go eventually into the Royal Collection, identified as 'Queen Charlotte as a child' – a confusion presumably caused by the interest taken in the actual sitter by the Queen's daughter-in-law, Caroline of Brunswick, Princess of Wales. Caroline was the unfortunate but publicly popular wife of the Prince Regent, subsequently George IV.[67] She had been memorably portrayed by Thomas Lawrence at the harp with her daughter (and heir to the throne), Charlotte, who extends a sheet of music towards her.

Caroline of Brunswick encouraged a friendship to develop between Charlotte and Elizabeth Randles. Caroline 'took great interest in her', and Princess Charlotte 'soon became very much attached to her.'[68] The young Princess

Charlotte of Wales became a popular figure among the Welsh in London, and perhaps at home also. She died in November 1817, following the stillbirth of her first child. Bardd Alaw wrote the words and music of an elegy, *Mourn, England, Mourn*, published in London in a black-bordered edition, in which he asked, rhetorically, 'But ah! what must thy Parents, Husband feel?' As far as her father, George IV, was concerned, probably considerable guilt, since his hatred for his wife, mother of the Princess, had resulted in a troubled childhood and adolescence for his only legitimate daughter.

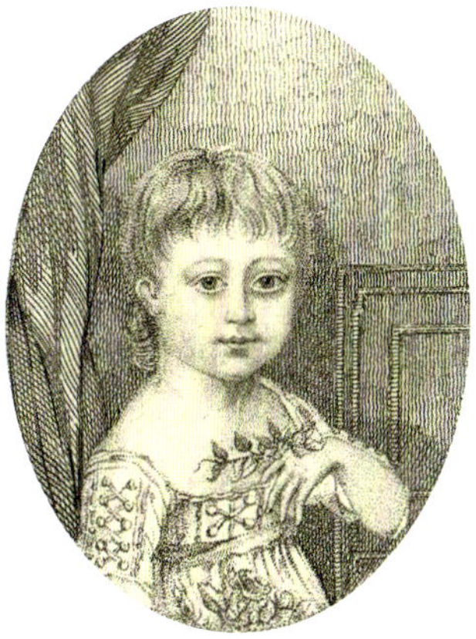

76 Unknown artist, *Miss Randles*, c.1804

John Downman grew up at Ruabon,[69] trained at the Royal Academy, and worked in the studio of Benjamin West at the same time as William Parry was at work in the studio of Joshua Reynolds. Towards the end of Parry's stay in Italy, Downman was also in that country. But despite these close parallels in the career of the contemporary painters, there is no evidence that Downman had any connection with Wynnstay. Indeed, in general, Welsh sitters were rare in the painter's output. It was not until 1819 that Wynnstay acquired a painting by Downman, bought at the Royal Academy. Nevertheless, *A Late Princess Personifying Peace Crowning the Glory of England Reflected on Europe* was a significant purchase, reinforcing the impression of a sense of national loss experienced among the Welsh establishment on the untimely death of Princess Charlotte. Although the origins of the commission to paint the Randles remain obscure, remarkably – and perhaps a testimony to the fame of the sitters –

77 John Downman, *Elizabeth Randles*, 1807

78 John Downman, *Edward Randles*, 1807

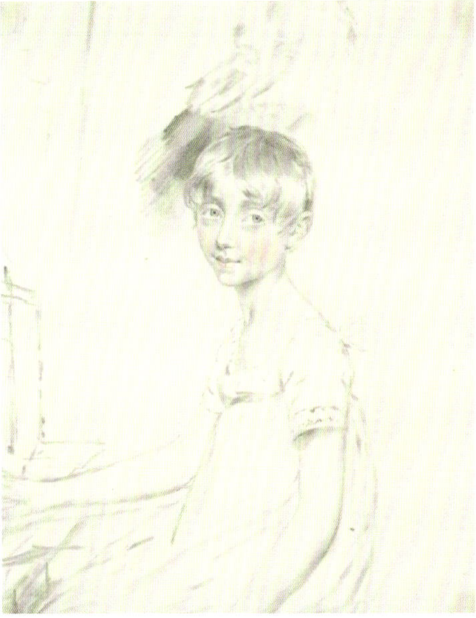

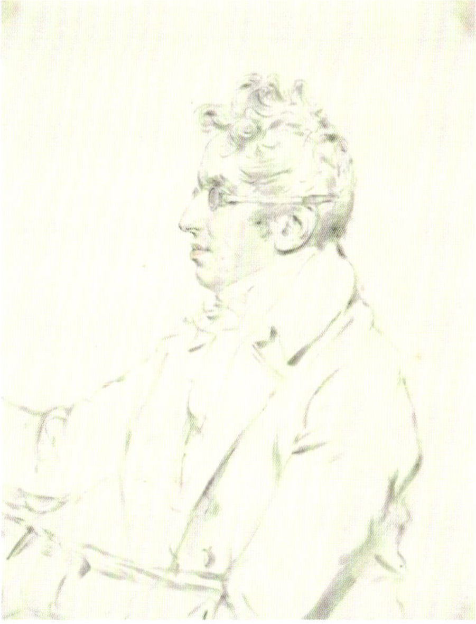

67 When it entered the Royal Collection, the portrait was attributed to Micheau. Previously it had been in the collection of the sculptor Joseph Edgar Boehm, best known for his Jubilee head of Queen Victoria, which appeared on the coinage.

68 Sainsbury and Choron, *A Dictionary of Musicians*, vol. ii, p. 335.

69 Downman's birthplace, previously presumed to be Ruabon, is uncertain, since a baptismal record at Eynesbury in Huntingdonshire suggests he may have been born there, see britishmuseum.org/collection/term/BIOG25601.

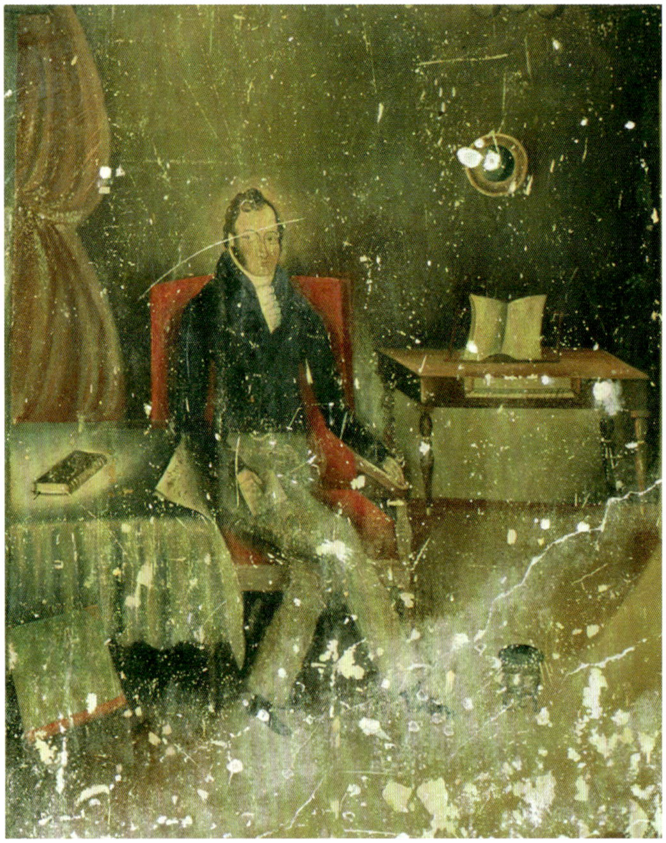

79 Probably Albin Roberts Burt, *Henry Hayden of St Asaph*, c.1823–6

both of Downman's drawings for his finished watercolour have survived. But, notwithstanding the celebrity of Elizabeth Randles, the double portrait was not engraved, probably because it was painted shortly before she retired to Wrexham to pursue her studies, and rapidly faded from public view. An earlier woodcut is the only surviving engraved image. In later life Downman too would return to Wales to live in Wrexham.

Bardd Alaw's *A Selection of Welsh Melodies* of 1809 had been popular enough to encourage the publication of a new version, which would prove to have more significance musically, visually and in literary terms. It seems certain that its publication in 1822 was financed by the publisher James Power in London. Indeed, the project itself may well have been undertaken on his initiative, since the Dublin company of William Power, brother and original partner of James, had been responsible for funding Thomas Moore's *Irish Melodies*. The ongoing publication of the ten Irish volumes had begun in 1806, and was proving highly successful. Parry's new venture followed the pattern of the Scottish and Irish precursors, transforming folk tunes into art music with new accompaniments and verses. Parry himself provided new harmonisations for a stock of Welsh melodies inherited from the eighteenth-century publications while the work of writing the 'characteristic' new verses was undertaken largely by Felicia Hemans, already by this time widely recognised as a considerable poet. Hemans had grown up at Gwrych, near Abergele, and lived subsequently, from 1809 until 1828, at Bronwylfa, near St Asaph. There she was in touch with the hymn writer Reginald Heber, a canon of the cathedral and son-in-law of the celebrated Dean Shipley. Presumably she associated also with others of the small intellectual community in the city. Among them was Henry Hayden, the cathedral organist, pictured along with Heber and Shipley in the remarkable series of mural paintings of the mid-1820s that decorate a room at Elwy Bank, a house near the cathedral. Behind Hayden stands his square piano. The series was probably the work of Albin Roberts Burt.[70]

The high status of Felicia Hemans had been acknowledged by the Honourable Society of Cymmrodorion when it was relaunched at a meeting in London in May 1820, along with the contribution of five other women, who included the harper Fanny Luxmore of St Asaph and the folk music collector Mary Richards of Darowen.[71] The new Welsh periodical, *The Cambro-Briton*, noted that the meeting received 'a beautiful copy of verses, entitled "The Wakening of Cambria", by Mrs. Hemans, of Bronwhylva, a lady before well-known and deservedly admired in the land of the Muses.'[72] At a safe distance from the war, the poem picked up again the music of the bards as the accompaniment to the expression of the Ancient Britons' love of liberty in their last Welsh stronghold, before 1282:

80 Edward Scriven after William Edward West, *Felicia Hemans*, c.1825–30

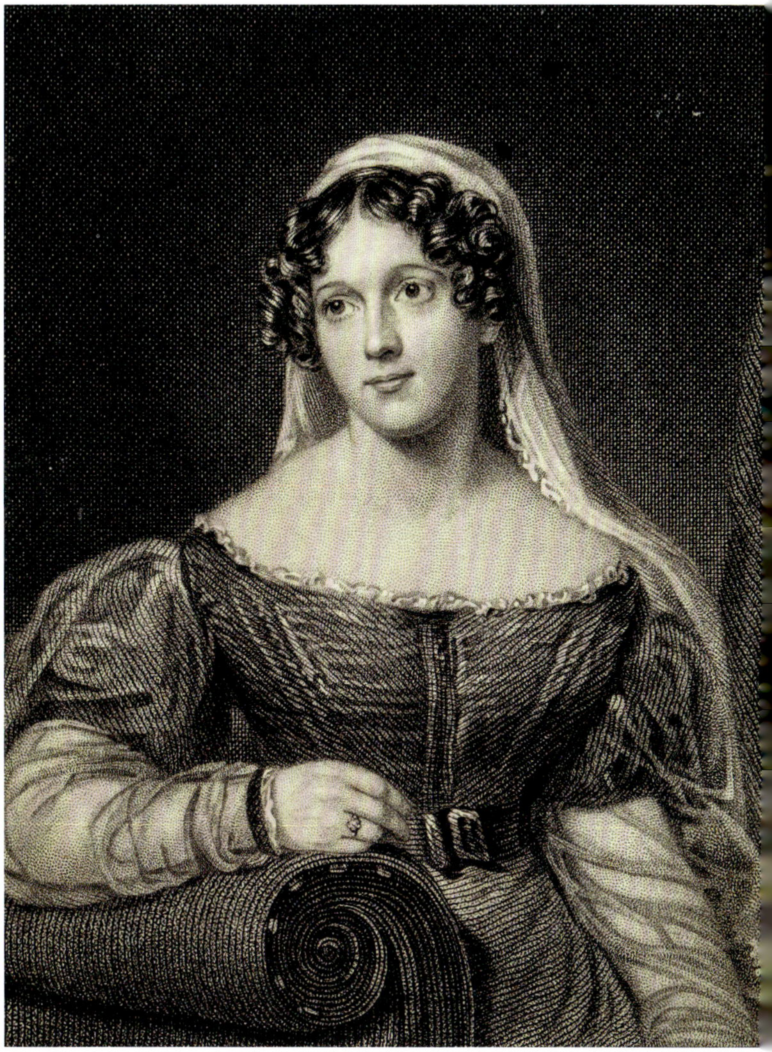

And thou, O Harp! To whose deep tone
  Was given a power, in elder time,
A might, a magic all thine own,
  The burning soul of Cambria's clime;

Thou, hallow'd thus by freedom's breath,
  To guard her fastness on high,
With sounds, inspiring scorn of death,
  Instinct with Immortality:

Then to the winds, at that proud call,
  Didst pour thine old, majestic strains,
As when they fir'd, in bower and hall,
  The hearts that were not born for chains.[73]

70 Peter Lord, *Looking Out. Welsh Painting, Social Class and International Context* (Cardigan, 2020), pp. 61-2.

71 Fanny Luxmo[o]re was the daughter of John Luxmoore, Bishop of St Asaph, and lived at the Bishop's Palace. She was an amateur harpist. Her brother was Dean from 1826, but a notorious pluralist. Among the other posts he held was that of Rector of Darowen, home of Mary Richards. For Richards, see Leila Salisbury, '"Melusder mwyn ar danau per odlau": Mair Richards 'Darowen' (1787–1877) and Thraddodiad Gwerin Maldwyn' (unpublished PhD thesis, Bangor University, 2012).

72 'Cymmrodorion Report', *The Cambro-Briton and General Celtic Repository*, 3 (November 1821), pp. 59-62.

73 Published in T.J.Ll. Prichard, *The Cambrian Wreath* (Aberystwyth, 1828), p. 63.

Bardd Alaw was almost certainly present at the Cymmrodorion meeting, at which he was appointed to the Council of the institution, and this may be how he became aware of Hemans's willingness to apply her literary talent to Welsh sentiment. The meeting was followed in September 1820 by the Wrexham Eisteddfod, which would have presented an opportunity for the development of their relationship. By the summer of 1822, Hemans was at work providing new words to the melodies. She found it 'a very interesting employment, as it made me acquainted with many traditions and legends of the country, some of which are extremely striking.' In particular, 'The idea entertained of the bardic character appears to me particularly elevated and beautiful … One of the general titles of the order was, "Those who are free throughout the world," and their

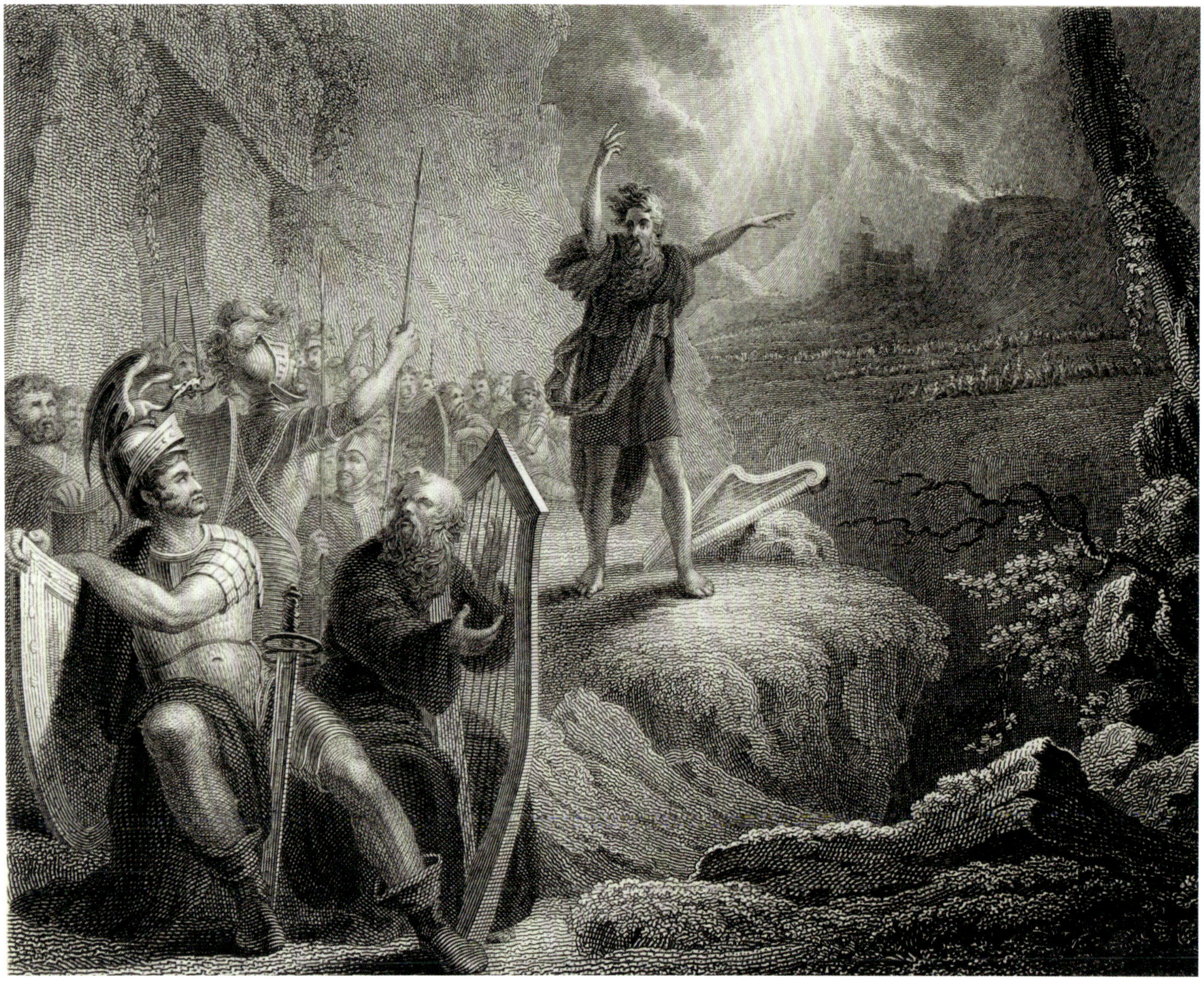

81 H.F. Rose, title page to John Parry, *A Selection of Welsh Melodies*, 1821

motto, "The Truth against the World".'[74] In her poems, Hemans suggested that she wanted to convey 'the true Welsh spirit', an aspiration entirely consistent with the general perceptions of her generation.[75] Unfortunately, Parry was obliged to marry her Romantic sentiments to the stock of available airs, some of which were jauntily inappropriate. It was a conjunction that would upset the antiquarian purists, as we shall see.

Hemans emphasised the Ancient Britons' love of liberty by the example of their resistance both to the Romans and to Edward I, and the importance of prophecy, expressed to the accompaniment of the harp. However, she widened the post-war agenda by reintroducing the subject of the Glyndŵr Revolt into the range of subjects considered appropriate as exemplars of the Welsh pursuit of national freedom. Without doubt, when composing 'Owain Glyndŵr's War Song', Hemans was well aware not only of the Irish 'War Song' written by Thomas Moore,[76] but of the earlier radical Welsh precedent set in the opening part of Anna Seward's celebrated poem 'Llangollen Vale', published in 1796 – a very different view of the scene to that presented in David Thomson's pastorale that had introduced his brother's *Select Collection of Original Welsh Airs*. In Seward's poem, Glyndŵr's forces, fired by 'Fredom's flame', had brought him victory over 'the English host' – 'the Myriads he abhorr'd.'

Hemans's opening lines imaged the scene as Glyndŵr's forces faced the English at Denbigh Castle in 1402, inspired by the appearance of a brilliant comet in the sky:

> Saw ye the blazing star?
> The heavens look down on freedom's war,
>   And light her torch on high!
> Bright on the dragon-crest
> It tells that glory's wing shall rest,
>   When warriors meet to die!
> Let earth's pale tyrants read despair,
>   And vengeance in its flame.
> Hail ye, my bards! the omen fair
>   Of conquest and of fame,
> And swell the rushing mountain-air,
>   With songs to Glyndŵr's name.

74 Letter to a female friend, written from Bronwylfa and dated 31 January 1823. Henry F. Chorley, *Memorials of Mrs Hemans, with Illustrations of Her Literary Character from Her Private Correspondence* (London, 1836), pp. 79-80.

75 Given in Winston Gwynne John, 'John Parry, Bardd Alaw, 1776-1851' (unpublished MA dissertation, University of Liverpool, 1951), p. 30.

76 Published in Thomas Moore and John Stevenson, *A Selection of Irish Melodies* (Dublin, [1808]), vol. i, pp.10-11.

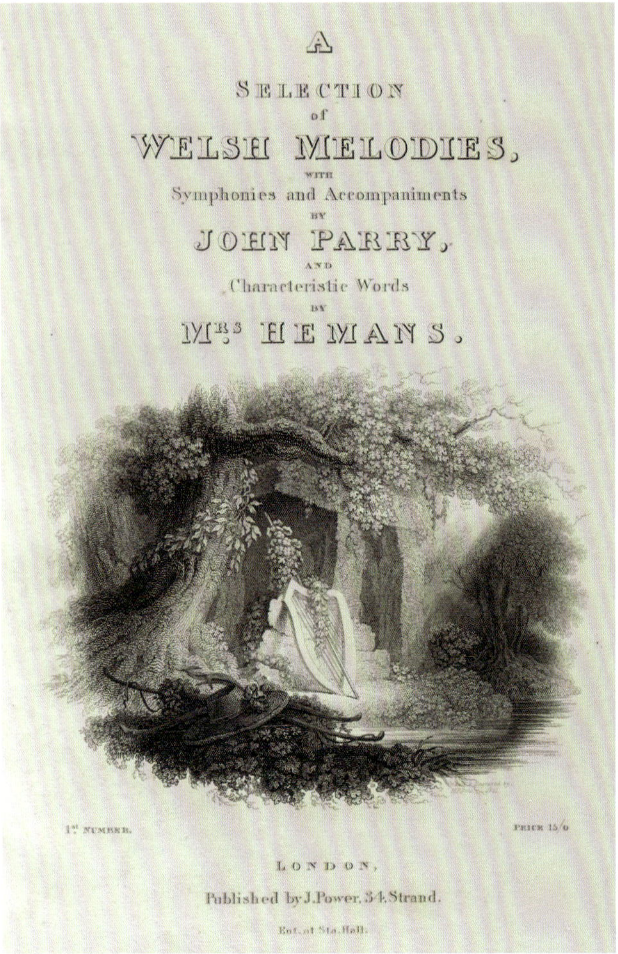

82 H.F. Rose, *Owain Glyndŵr's War Song*, frontispiece to John Parry, *A Selection of Welsh Melodies*, 1822

It was this moment that was chosen for a keynote visual preface to the volume, again following the pattern of Moore's *Irish Melodies*. Indeed, the visual image was both designed and engraved by H.F. Rose. The artist was not a prominent figure during the dozen years of his known activity, but he had designed one of the illustrations which adorned the fifth volume of *Irish Melodies* in 1813. He also created a frontispiece for Parry's volume, which depicted the massive entrance to a cromlech, with a harp lying before it. He deployed the same cromlech as the background to his ambitious Glyndŵr composition.[77] The comet silhouettes the castle, from which the English army emerges. The leader of the revolt, the 'dragon crest' clearly delineated on his helmet, prepares for battle. But the focus of the image is upon the two bardic visionaries, one in voice and the other accompanying him on the harp.

Hemans's poems conjoined with Parry's settings of traditional airs would never fulfil the potential for political exploitation that the Scottish and Irish publications of Thomson and Moore achieved. The fact is that the London Welsh, largely responsible for shaping what passed for national sentiment in the period, were much more interested in continuing to promote the unionist agenda in which the Welsh love of freedom had lately manifested itself on the side of the English and against the French, than in the revolt of Owain Glyndŵr. The reconstituted Cymmrodorion published the words to the Society's song, 'Caniad y Cymmrodorion', a text carefully preserved by Bardd y Brenin:

A gwnawn i'r FLRANGCOD [*sic*] DUON,
Fyn'd ar eu Gliniau noethion:
Gwae nhwy erioed y Dydd a fu
Ffyrnigo CYMRY a SAESON.

[And we cause the BLACKGUARD FRENCH,
To go on their bare Knees:
Woe to them for ever the day
They angered the WELSH and ENGLISH.]

The might of the Prince of Wales, defender of the faith, and his pious family, was again extolled:

Hir Jechyd a fo ein TWYSOG,	[Long life to our PRINCE,
A Theulu'r Ffydd GATHOLIG;	And the family of the CATHOLIC faith;
I daflu yr CONSUL ar i din	To throw the CONSUL on his arse,
A ffrwyno'r DIAWLED FFREINIG.	And bridle the FRENCH DEVILS.][78]

The melody to which the stirring words were sung is unknown.

Even in this period of high Romanticism and of Welsh excitement about the generic idea of national liberation,[79] the myth of the Tudor fulfilment of the ancient prophecies of Merlin and Taliesin was all-powerful in conditioning the attitudes of the intellectual community. The Tudor succession of 1485 had irrevocably cemented Welsh loyalty to the English crown. A glee for three voices of the period expressed concisely the historical construct that resolved for Anglophiles the paradox of Welsh birth or descent within the modern United Kingdom. It opens with a description of the state of affairs following the events of 1282:

> O'er Cambria's russet hills and verdant dales,
> No more the bard's celestial strain prevails;
> Their harps by discord's jarring hand unstrung,
> On blasted oaks despondingly were hung.

An instrumental march provides an interlude, followed by the happy resolution of the woes of Wales, sung as a chorus:

But now a prince ascends the throne,	Hail Tudor, heaven-descended king,
Who makes the bardic cause his own:	Who wak'st the harp's long silent string,
A thousand harps in concert join,	The bards thy glory shall prolong,
And Tudor's name salutes the skies.	And praise thee in immortal song.[80]

It is remarkable that Welsh loyalty to the English crown reached its Romantic peak at the time of the disreputable Regency and the subsequent reign of George IV. Less remarkable was what appears to have been the particular attraction of the Tudor construct of history to the expatriate community. Edward Parry of Chester, among the competitors at the Denbigh Eisteddfod of 1828 (graciously

77 Some confusion surrounds the publication date of the new *Selection of Welsh Melodies*, resulting from the ambiguous wording of Parry's 'Advertisements' to the first two numbers, which might suggest that the second number was issued prior to the first. The suspicion that this may have been the case is strengthened by the dating of the engraving of the frontispiece to 1821 and of 'Owain Glyndŵr's War Song' to 1822, to which is added the reference 'Vide Welsh Melodies Vol. I P.P. 38', where Hemans's related poem was printed.

78 NLW MS 171E, f. 73. Napoleon's official title between 1799 and 1804 was First Consul.

79 See, for instance, 'Gwarediant Groeg' ('The Liberation of Greece'), a poem written by Eryron Gwyllt Walia in 1827. Given in Peter Lord, *Hugh Hughes Arlunydd Gwlad 1790–1863* (Llandysul, 1995), p. 175.

80 Apparently first published in Prichard, *The Cambrian Wreath*, pp. 163–4, but of uncertain date.

83 Unknown maker, chair back, *c.* 1840

attended by the Duke of Sussex, brother of George IV), adopted a particularly obsequious tone in concluding his 'Historical account of the Flintshire Castles':

> We, however, acknowledge with gratitude 'that we were conquered to our gain, and undone to our advantage.' When English generosity appeared, Welsh loyalty increased; our countrymen soon found out that the change was beneficial. Instead of precarious liberty, they now began to enjoy a permanent and solid freedom, secured by equal and fixed laws, and established under one august monarch. We shall find the remnant of the ancient British nation, after being the victims of ambition for so many centuries, now rivalling their conquerors in their duties as loyal subjects, and uniting in interest and mingling in friendship with their old enemies – at last both nations cemented together and became one. Now the highest point of our ambition is, who shall be the most useful to the arts and best affected to the British crown! …
>
> Henceforward, therefore, the sons of Albion, Erin, Caledonia, and Walia, may harmoniously join in the noble sentiment of the Bard –
>
> The Shamrock of Erin so brilliant and green,
> Entwined with the Leek and the Thistle has been;
> Oh! may they for ever a safeguard compose,
> To shelter from danger Old England's fair Rose:
> And grant that *Great Britain*, for ever may be,
> The terror of tyrants, the friend of the free:
> Mewn awen fwyn lawen byw byth y bo hi!![81]

The verses chosen by Edward Parry that encapsulated his sense of Welsh identity under the 'British crown' were the work of Bardd Alaw. They had been written for the centenary meeting of the Society of Ancient Britons on St David's Day 1814 a few weeks before the abdication of Napoleon. They encapsulated the unionist spirit that would permeate the attitudes of most Welsh intellectuals and the gentry class until mid-century. In about 1840, an unknown embroiderer worked an ambitious needlepoint to upholster a slipper or nursing chair – perhaps for their own use. On the seat the embroiderer set a harp against a mountain landscape, and on the back, The Bard in his musical manifestation, rather than in the ambiguous context of the conquest, surmounted by the three feathers of the Prince of Wales, and his motto, Ich Dien.

81 *The Gwyneddion*, p. 49. The occasion was identified in Prichard, *The Cambrian Wreath*, p. 191, which published the poem in full: 'It has since become very popular, and has been loudly applauded at several Eisteddvods, or Cambrian Literary and Musical Meetings.' The meeting was reported in *The Cambrian*, 12 March 1814.

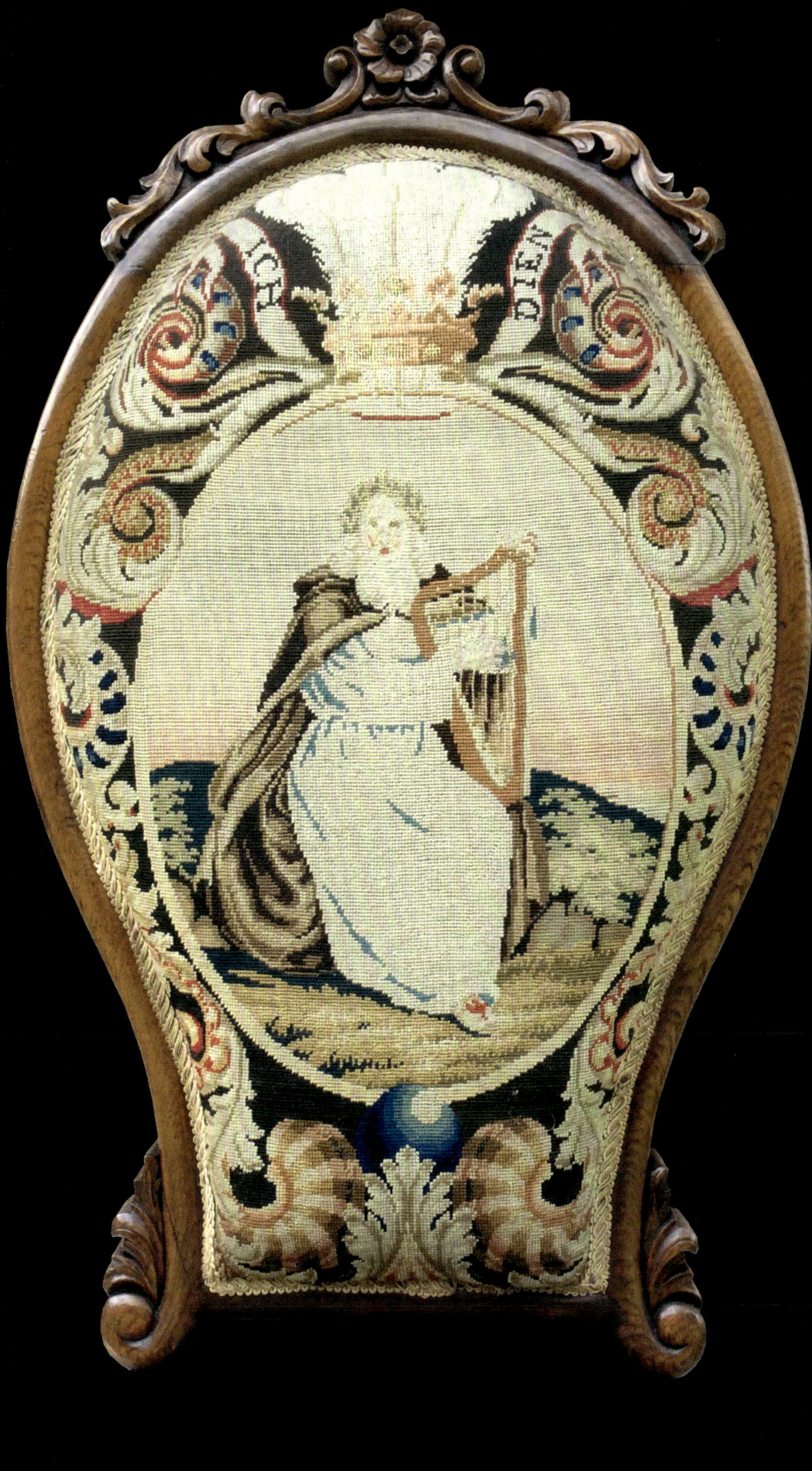
ICH
DIEN

CONTINUITY OR CONSTRUCT?

Notwithstanding the multitude of assertions in the late eighteenth century of the continuity of the musical tradition from druidic times, in the preface to *The Bardic Museum*, in 1802 Edward Jones, Bardd y Brenin, had presented native Welsh music as being under threat. He had transcribed the melodies that he published from 'hearing them sung by the old people, and from their being played by the most venerable Harpers, in North Wales; and it is very fortunate that I did so', he added, 'because most of them are since dead.'[82] This impression of a serious decline of traditional music and in particular in the use of the national instrument was shared by other observers in the earliest years of the nineteenth century, though not without a degree of ambiguity. As we have seen, in the same pessimistic introduction to *The Bardic Museum*, Bardd y Brenin himself had also declared that the ancient music remained 'the favourite amusement of the natives.' Similarly, in his introduction to *A Selection of Welsh Melodies*, Bardd Alaw acknowledged a decline in the popularity of traditional music among the common people, whilst at the same time noting that 'There is scarce a parish in the principality but it contains a harper of some kind or other.' The painter Edward Pugh, touring his native country between 1804 and 1813, was similarly ambivalent in his observations, published after his death in his illustrated tour, *Cambria Depicta*. Like Parry, he described the popular singing of penillion and, on one occasion, having crossed the Menai Straits, he again heard the harp while he rested at Bangor Ferry. However, whilst there he also reflected on its general decline:

84 Pye after Craig, *The blind harper of Llaneltid*, c.1820

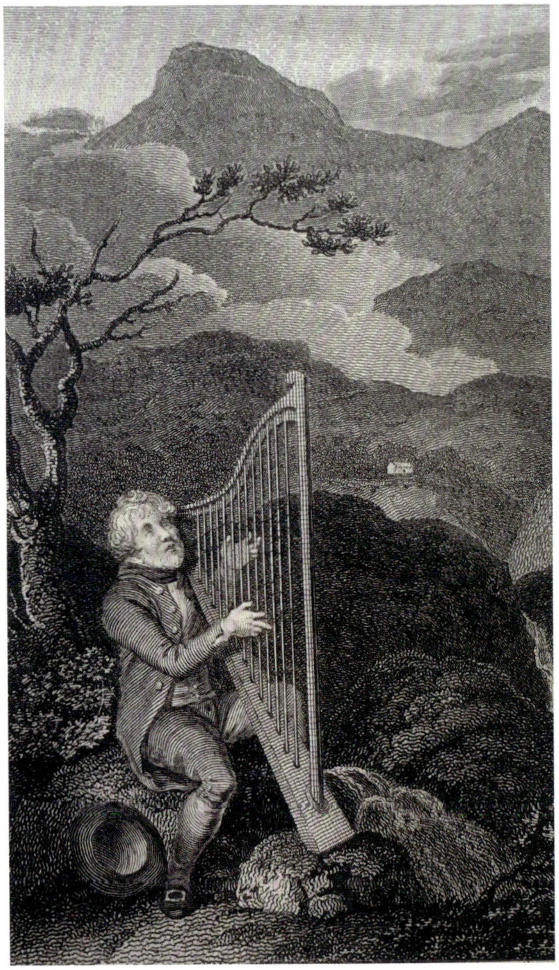

> The sound of the harp, in this house, the ingenious musical instrument of the country, fully accordant with the situation, vibrating amidst water, rock, and wood, has a very agreeable effect upon the ear of a stranger unaccustomed to these pleasurable sounds. Mr Skrine, speaking of the Welsh-harp, says, 'And through the whole of North Wales it is cultivated with a degree of veneration, and scarce a family exists, in the meanest cottage, without at least one performer.[83]

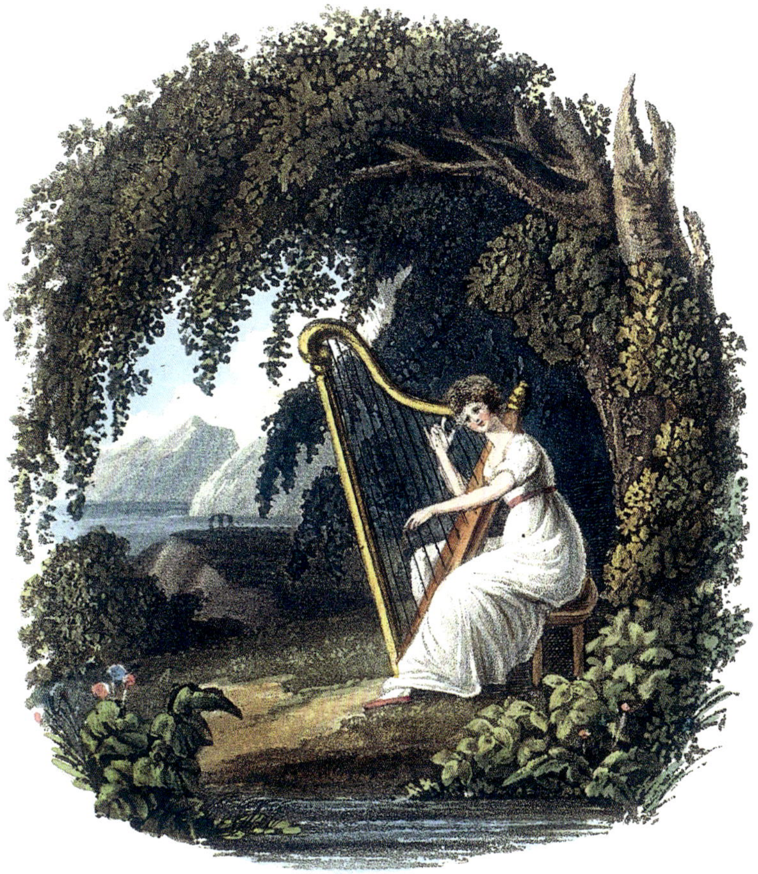

85 Edward Pugh, frontispiece to *Cambria Depicta*, 1816

But Pugh himself was clear that 'The truth is the harp is by no means now so much in vogue, as it was in former days.'

Influenced by his broader democratic and patriotic agendas, Edward Pugh had no hesitation in pointing the finger of blame at the gentry for his perception of decline in contemporary musical practice:

> When the most distinguished families of landed property, to whom descended the manners and habits of their ancestors, resided constantly upon their estates, with them, indeed, the harp was held in high esteem … This is not the case at present; the gentry, in general, seem to have lost their taste for the instrument; its sounds are no longer heard, except in a few of their houses. The intercourse with England, indeed, has long been so general and so close, and the English taste and manners so incorporated with those of the aboriginal districts, as in great measure to efface them; and the ancient provincial customs and peculiarities, whether estimable or not, are, in great measure, discarded.[84]

82 Jones, *The Bardic Museum*, p. xi.

83 Edward Pugh, *Cambria Depicta* (London, 1816), p. 94. Pugh quoted from Henry Skrine, *Two successive tours throughout the whole of Wales: with several of the adjacent English counties* … (London, 1798).

84 Ibid.

86 Paul Sandby, title page to *Twelve Views in North and South Wales*, 1786

87 Paul Sandby, detail from *Overton Bridge over the Dee*, 1776

85 The drawing was made on his tour with Sir Watkin Williams Wynn, but apparently not engraved as the title page to a collection of his work until 1786.

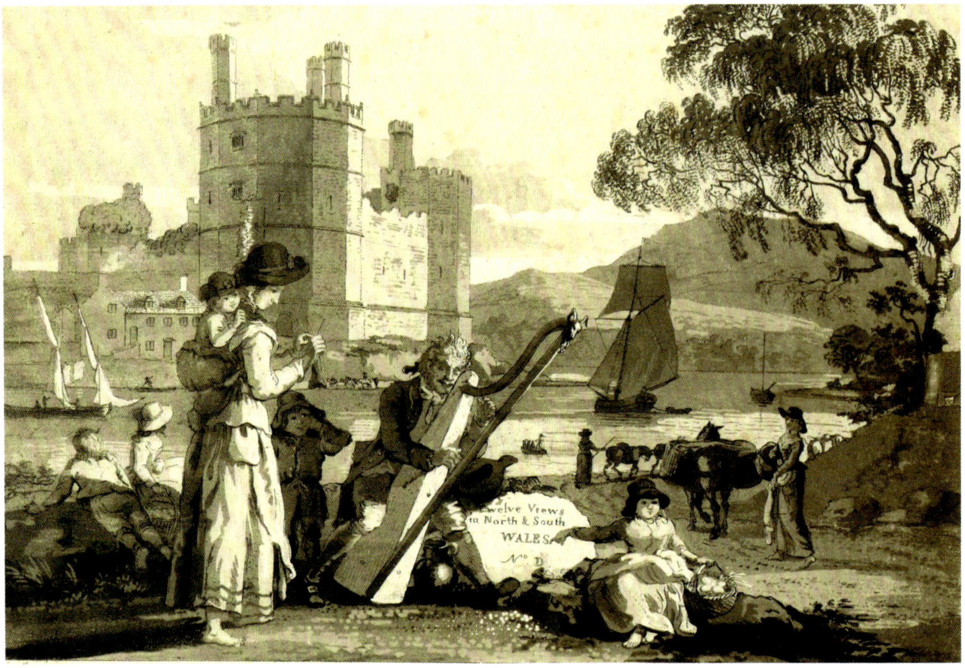

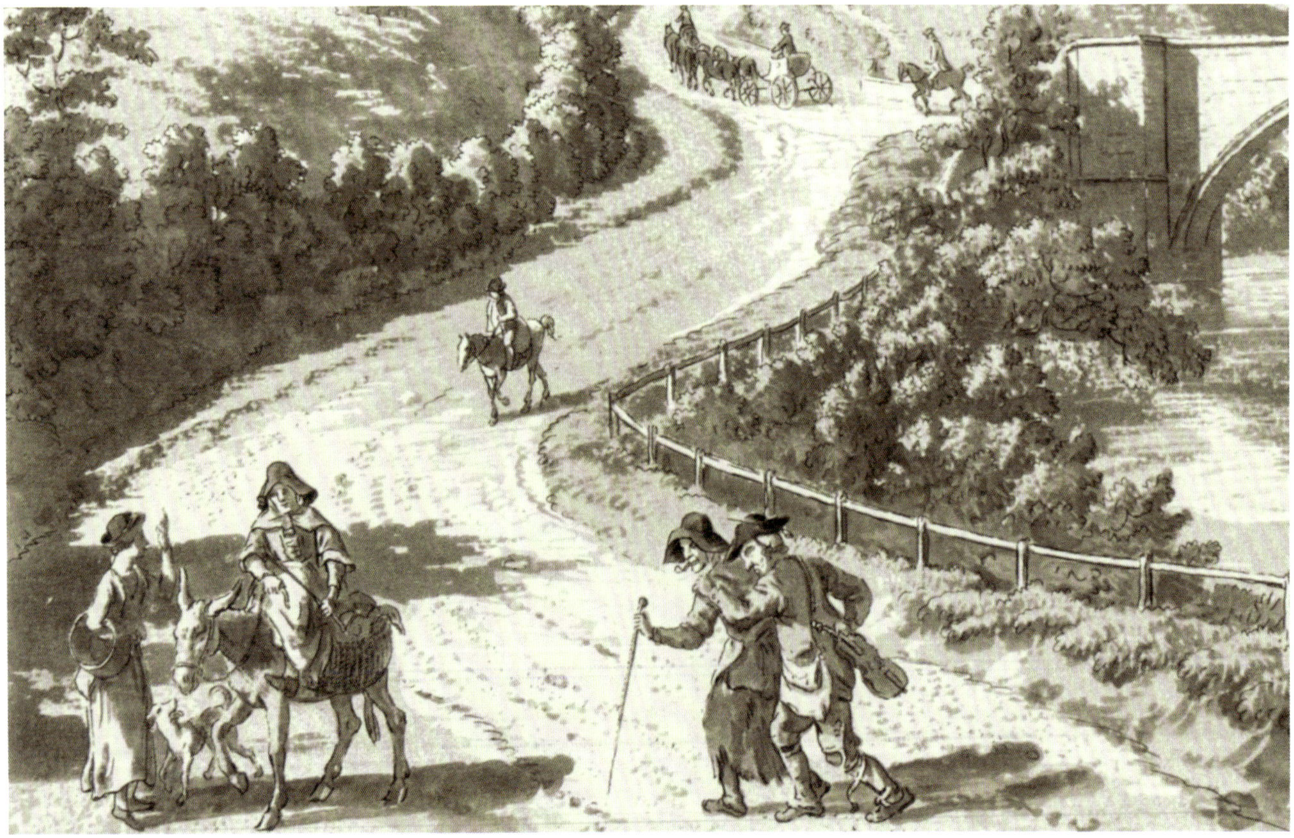

It is perhaps significant that unlike many late eighteenth- and early nineteenth-century travellers, Pugh included not a single musical image among the nearly seventy pictures that illustrate his text. Contrarily, his frontispiece to *Cambria Depicta* broke new and prescient ground by illustrating a female harper. However, her classical attire and her self-conscious bardic location under an oak tree made clear that she was not one of the several women known to have worked as harpers among the common people in the eighteenth century. Pugh's harper reflected the painter's awareness of a developing fashion among gentry ladies for playing the instrument.

But musical practice among the common people was not dependent on gentry patronage. A drawing made by Paul Sandby in 1771 suggests that he had witnessed the genuine continuity of tradition in the streets. His engraving of a harper in Caernarfon, observed by a mother and her child, has the convincing character of observation.[85] The visual record confirms an evolving folk tradition of music, particularly in association with dance, though it does also illustrate

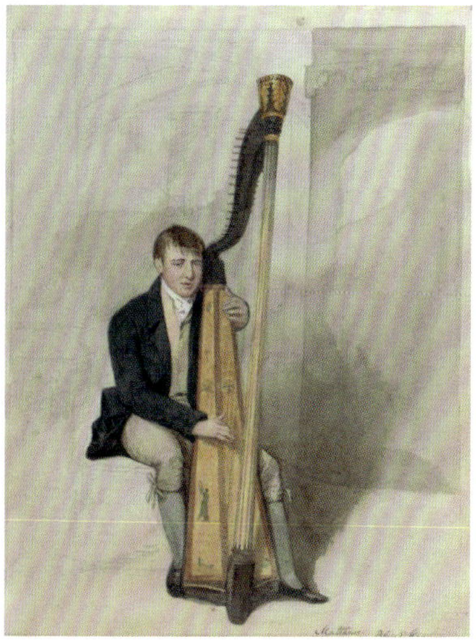

88 George Delamotte, *William Matthews, Blind Harper*, c.1820

89 Paul Sandby, *View of the Copper Works at Neath*, 1779

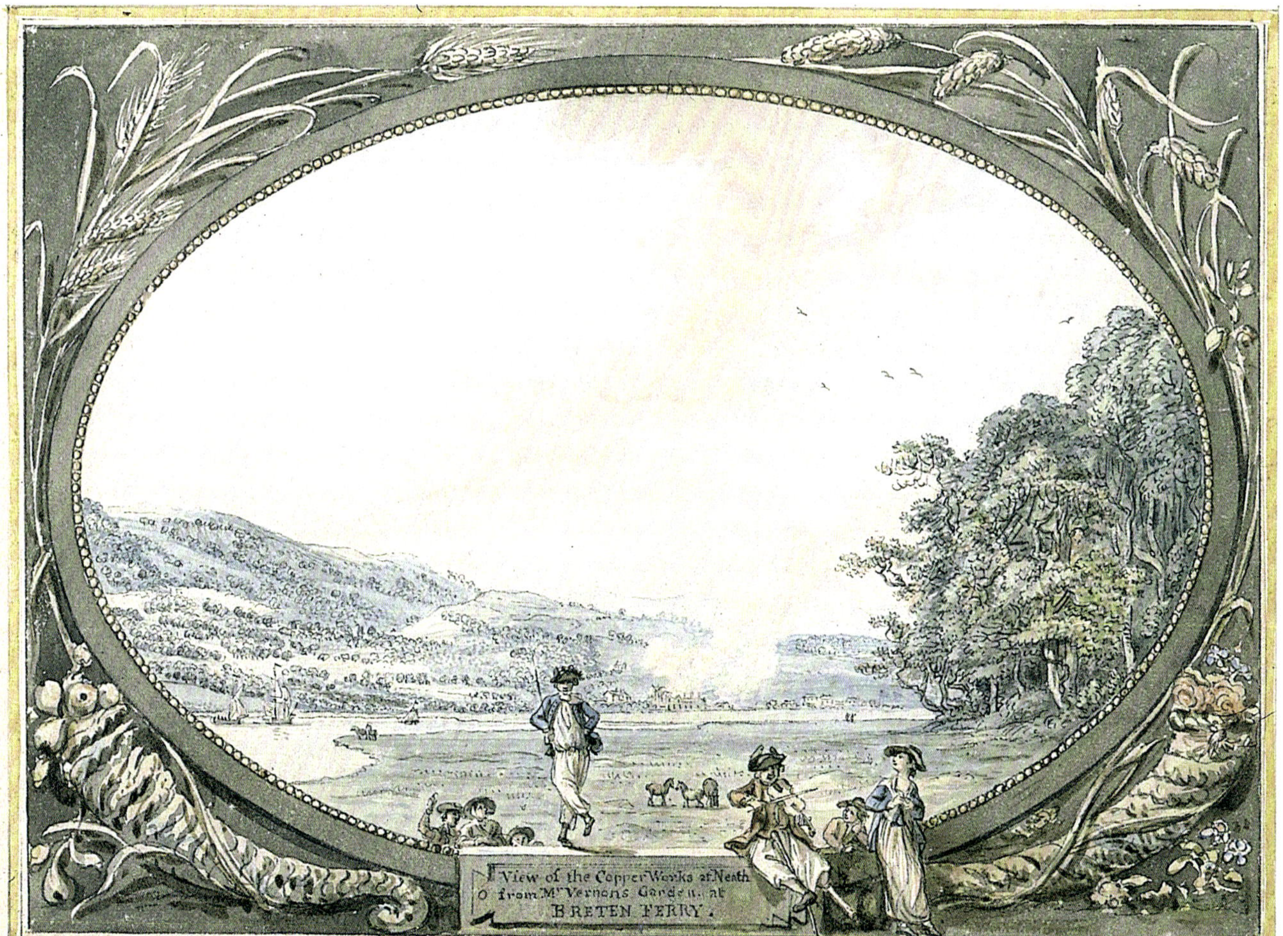

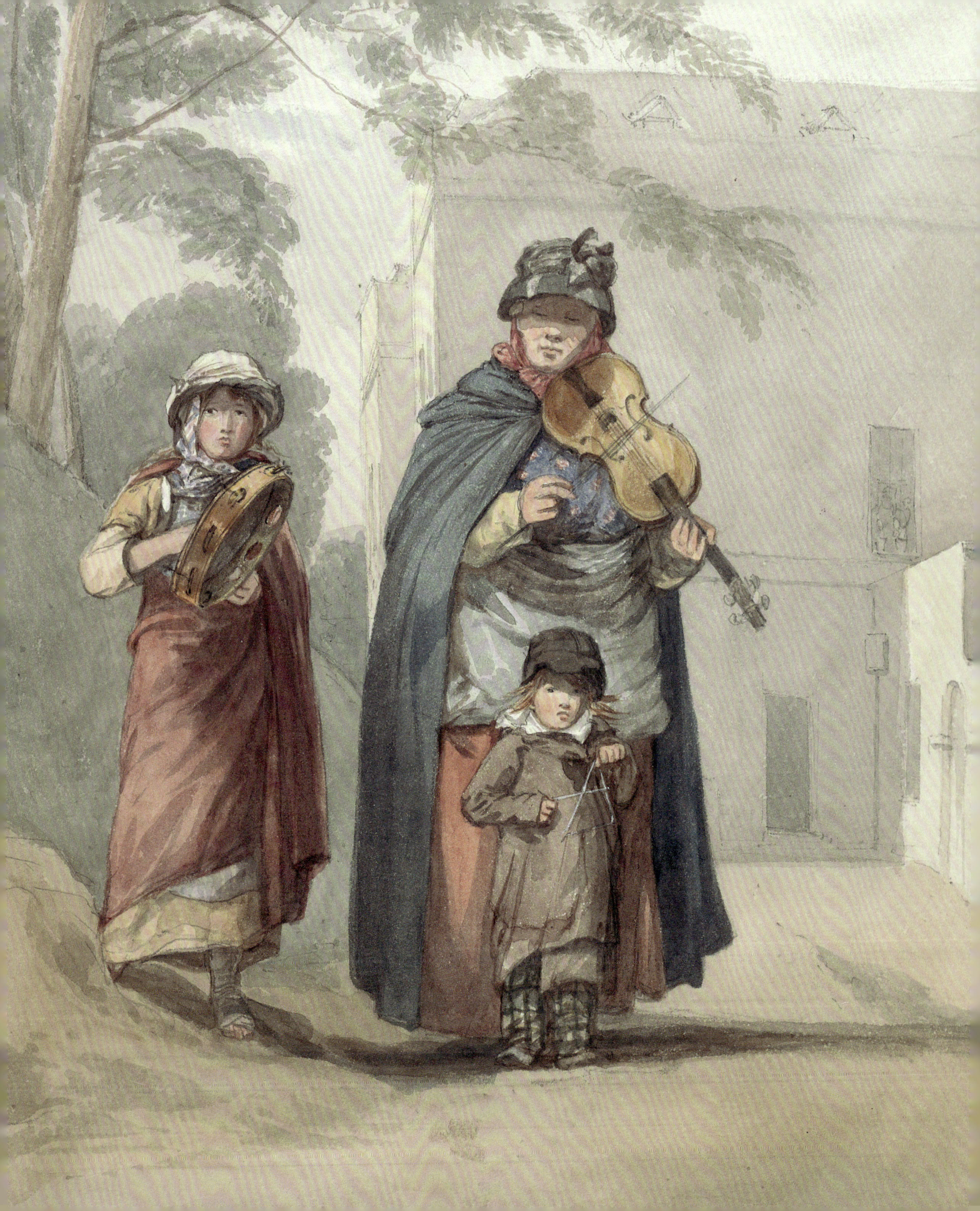

the increasing infiltration of the fiddle as the primary instrument of itinerant practitioners. In 1776 Paul Sandby observed a blind fiddler being led towards Overton Bridge over the River Dee. A watercolour painted by Sandby in the south in 1779 depicted the copper works at Neath. Enlivening the decorative frame, which the artist often employed for his finished views and engravings, are a fiddler and a dancer, attended by a small audience.[86] The drawing was made from the garden of Mr Vernon, whose house stood on the main route west, near the point at which travellers to and from Ireland could cross the Neath River by ferry. Nearly forty years later, George Delamotte would paint at much the same place *An Irishman Going to Cork* – an itinerant fiddler passing Vernon House, presumably *en route* for Swansea and the boat home.[87] The painter was the son of a French refugee and brother of the better documented William Alfred Delamotte. George Delamotte seems to have had a particular interest in itinerants, and from the same group of drawings survives a sensitive portrait of the blind harper William Matthews[88] and a remarkable image of a female fiddler and her two children, one with a tambourine and the other a triangle, entitled *Scotch Beggars*. The conjunction of these three images among the Delamotte drawings, made at the height of the efforts of antiquarians in Scotland, Ireland, and Wales to construct pure and distinct traditions of national music, suggests a reality of rather more complicated interactions and cross-cultural transmission at the level of the street, the fair and the marketplace.

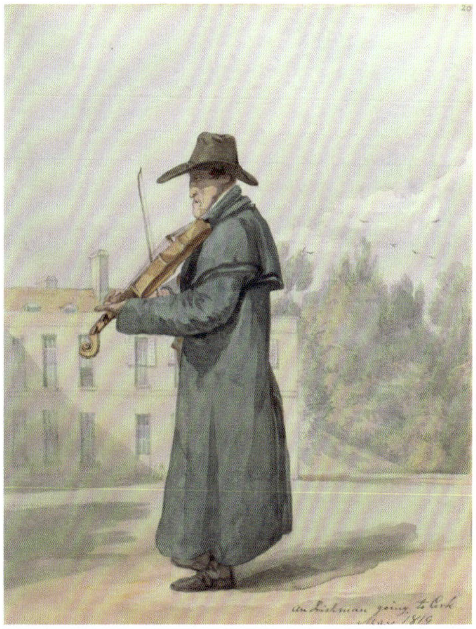

91 George Delamotte, *An Irishman Going to Cork*, 1819

90 George Delamotte, *Scotch Beggars*, c.1820

The difficulty of distinguishing continuity from construct, of folk practice from patriotic intellectual aspirations – indeed, of reality from fantasy – in the period of national musical revivalism is well illustrated by an incident recorded by Hester Thrale. On a tour with Dr Samuel Johnson in 1774, Thrale returned to the country in which she had spent her childhood. While she and Johnson were at Caernarfon, they made the acquaintance of Colonel Glyn Wynn, younger brother of Sir Thomas Wynn of Glynllifon. The Colonel's wife, Bridget Pugh of Penrhyn Creuddyn, took the visitors on a trip on horseback to Llanberis, which Thrale recorded in her diary:

> It is the wildest, stoniest, rockiest road I ever yet went, and in fifteen miles' riding we came to a cottage by the side of the lake, where we found a Harper, and Mrs. Wynn sang Welch songs to his accompaniment.[89]

86 The frame also includes cornucopia, suggestive of the increasing prosperity of the area as a result of industrialisation. See Peter Lord, *The Visual Culture of Wales: Industrial Society* (Cardiff, 1998), pp. 31–3.

87 The caption does not specify the location, but the group of works from which it comes was painted in the Swansea and Neath area. The drawing closely resembles the back of the right-hand side elevation of Vernon House. See Bernard Morris, *George Orleans Delamotte: A South Wales Sketch Book, c.1816–35* (Swansea, 2007), and Julian Mitchell, 'The Rolls family and George Delamotte', *Monmouthshire Antiquary*, 23 (2007), pp. 75-86.

88 William Matthews was taught by Thomas Evans of Nottage.

89 Alexander Meyrick Broadley, *Doctor Johnson and Mrs. Thrale: Including Mrs Thrale's Unpublished Journal of the Welsh Tour Made in 1774 …* (London, 1910), pp. 204-5.

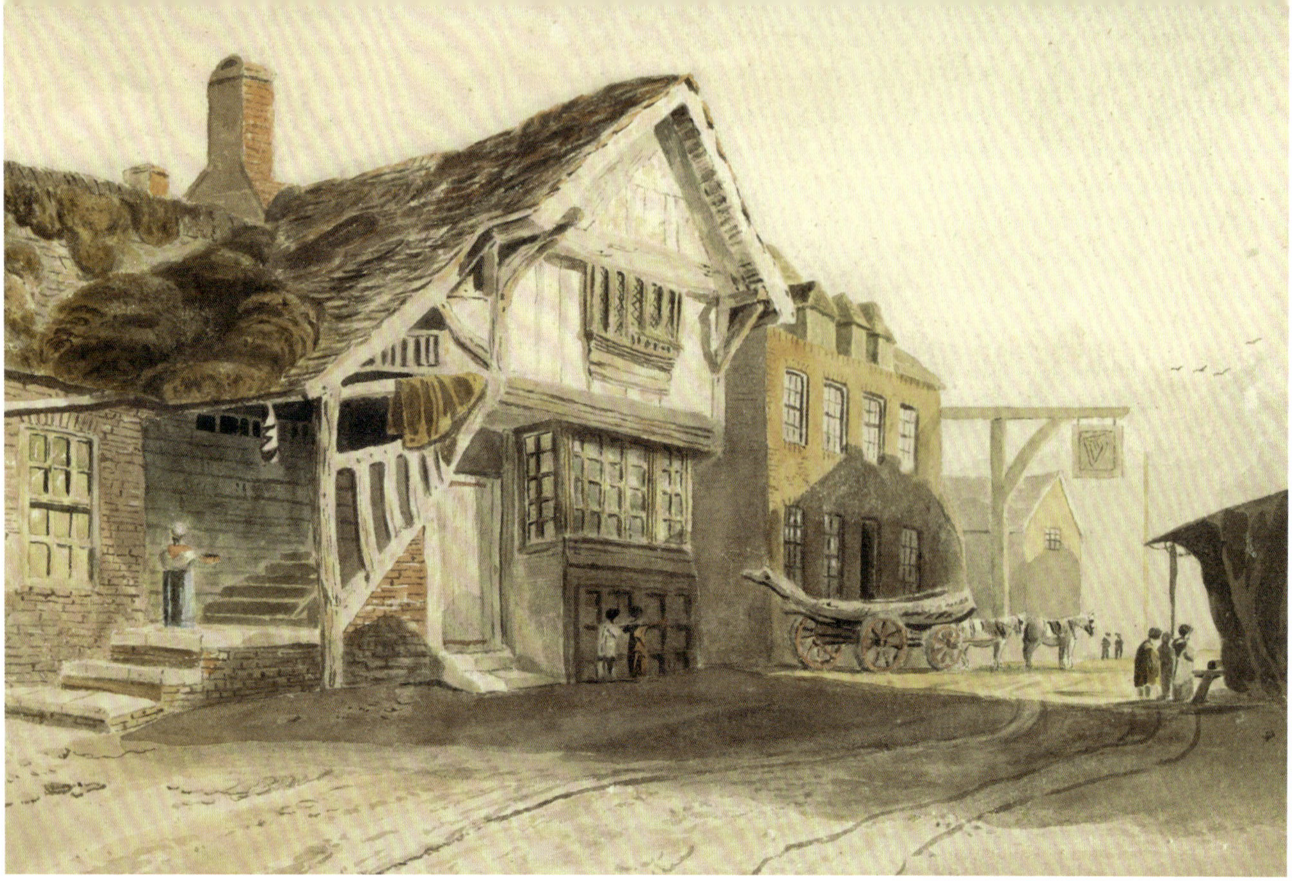

92 John Varley, *The Welsh Harp Inn, Conwy*, 1809

It is difficult to judge the significance of this incident – if it represented a continuity of gentry knowledge of the musical tradition, inherited by Bridget Wynn, or Hester Thrale's exposure to an early manifestation of fashionable reinvention, planned for her benefit and based on her companion's familiarity with the publications of John Parry, Telynor Dall. However, in the same year as the unnamed harper was accompanying Bridget Wynn near Snowdon, in the more prosaic setting of a Conwy inn, Henry Penruddocke Wyndham heard John Smith at work, a chance encounter that seems to reflect genuine common practice:

> As Chester fair was now approaching, the inns of Conway were filled with linen merchants from Ireland; and as there were not beds for the whole company, a party of them, not unwillingly, sacrificed the night to Bacchus, in the adjoining room to my chamber, the melody of a blind harper, accompanied with Welsh songs of the maid of the inn, encouraged by libation; which, to my agreeable surprise, was unattended with either riot or noise. This was the only harp I heard in the principality, both the instrument and voice were perfectly pleasing, and the music being truly Welsh, was plaintive and melancholy. I thought my situation so happy, that I did not lament the interruption of my slumbers, or with the harmonic society at a greater distance.[90]

90 Henry Penruddocke Wyndham, *A Gentleman's Tour through Monmouthshire and Wales in the Months of June and July, 1774* (London, 1775), pp. 160-1. An unidentified tourist at Conwy, annotating in 1779 his or her copy of the *Gentleman's Tour* (NLW 6747B, p. 161), noted: 'I not only was entertained with the harp here, but at many other places in the Tour; & frequently met Harpers in the Road, travelling from one village to the other, with their Instruments upon their Backs.'

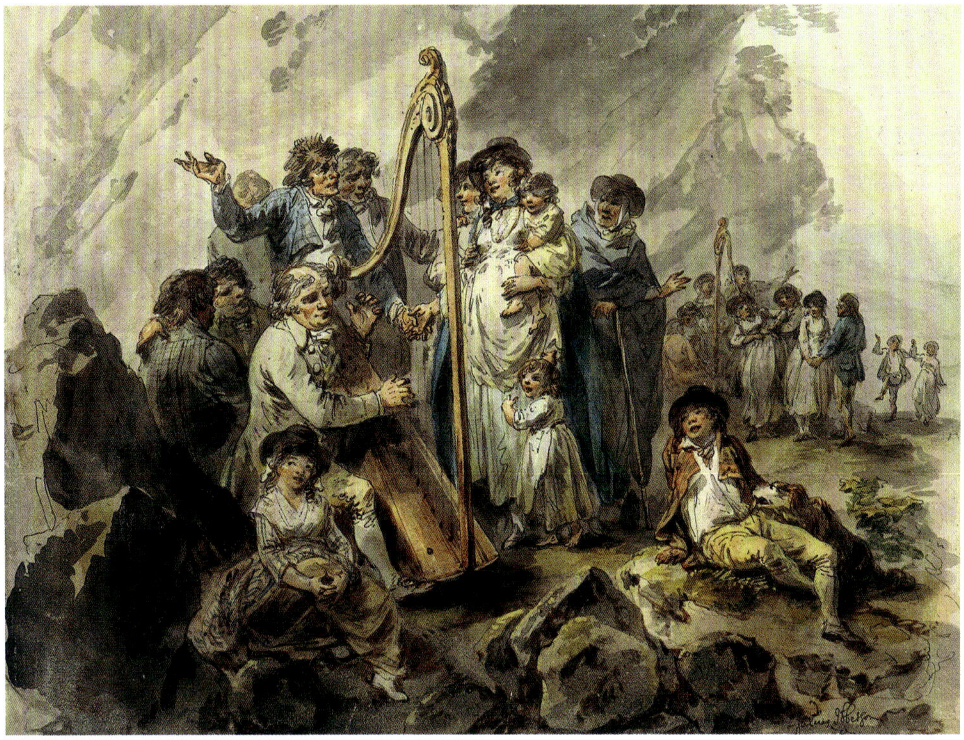

93 Julius Caesar Ibbetson, *Peasants Singing with the Blind Harpist John Smith*, c.1792–3

94 Julius Caesar Ibbetson, *Conway Castle with John Smith*, 1796

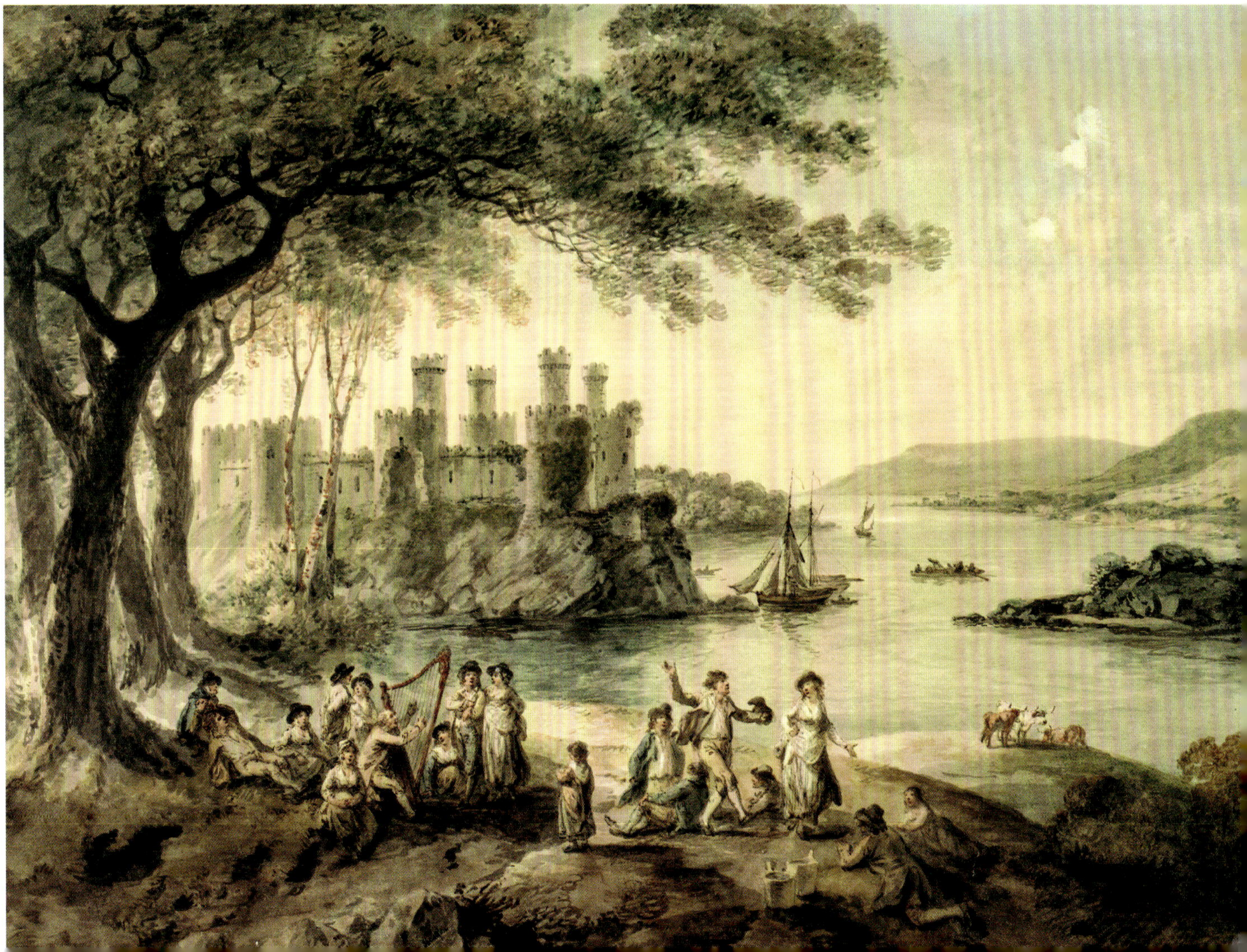

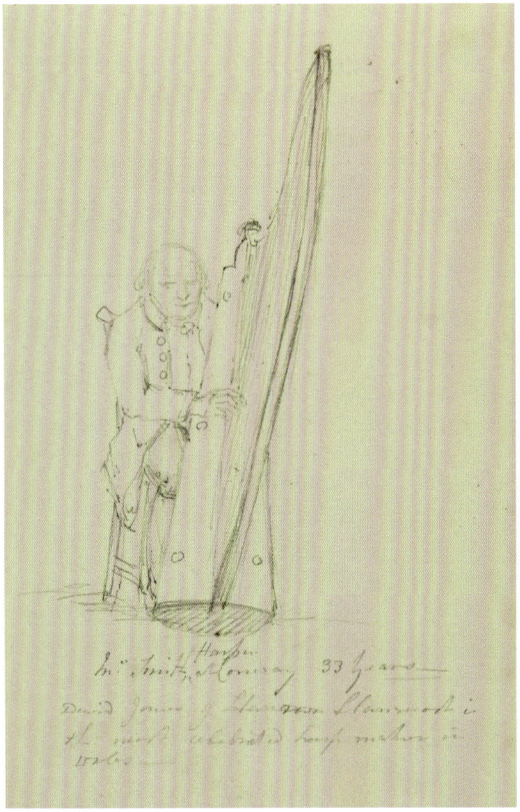

John Smith of Conwy was the focus of the most sustained visual documentation of musical practice in the period. Julius Caesar Ibbetson produced at least five pictures in which Smith figured, the first of which was exhibited at the Royal Academy in 1793 and so was seen by many among the fashionable London audience. It may have been this image that evolved into the frontispiece to Edward Jones's *The Bardic Museum*, which became even more widely disseminated.[91] The watercolour identified by its traditional title as specifically representing penillion singing shows the harper surrounded by a large group. Later, Bardd Alaw would suggest that he too had 'often seen from thirty to forty persons sitting around the harper, and each, in his (or her) turn, sing a *penill* or stanza – and the person who could sing the greatest number of stanzas to the different airs, was considered the best singer.'[92] Nevertheless, in this version of Ibbetson's image, a second but unidentified harper is certainly playing for dancing. One of the figures surrounding Smith gestures towards this second musician, suggesting some sort of comparison or competition.

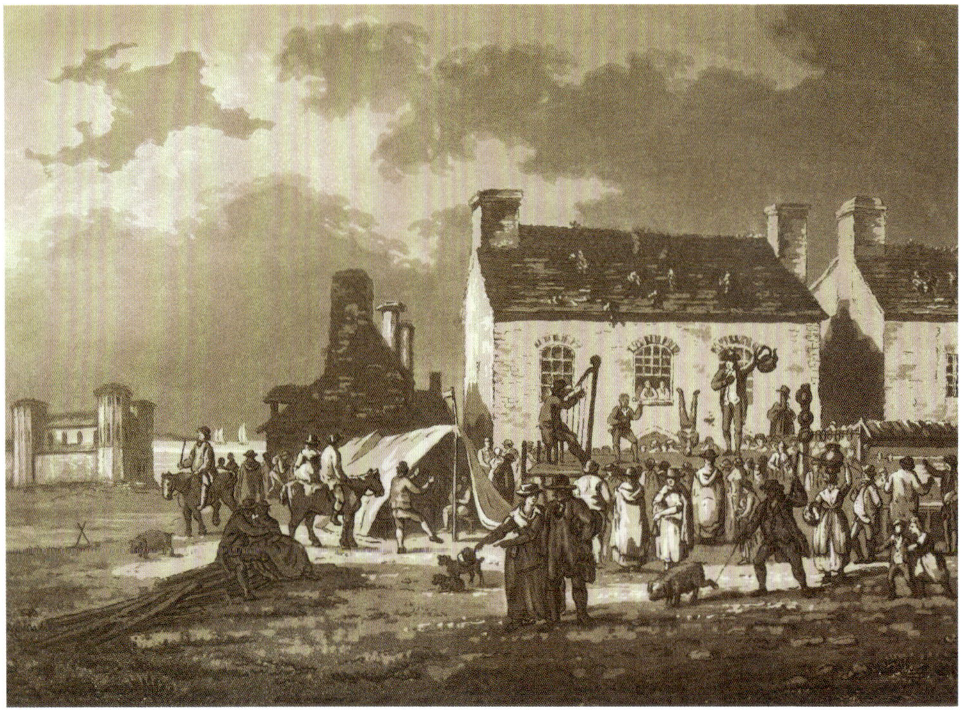

95 Unknown artist, *Mr Smith, Harper at Conwy 33 Years*, *c.*1800

96 Samuel Ireland, *Market at Aberystwyth*, 1797

91 It is not entirely clear which version is primary. Rotha Mary Clay, *Julius Caesar Ibbetson, 1759–1817* (London, 1948), p. 110, identifies a lost version exhibited in Germany and, apparently, copied by Princess Elizabeth, daughter of George III.

92 Parry, *Selection of Welsh Melodies*, p. 2.

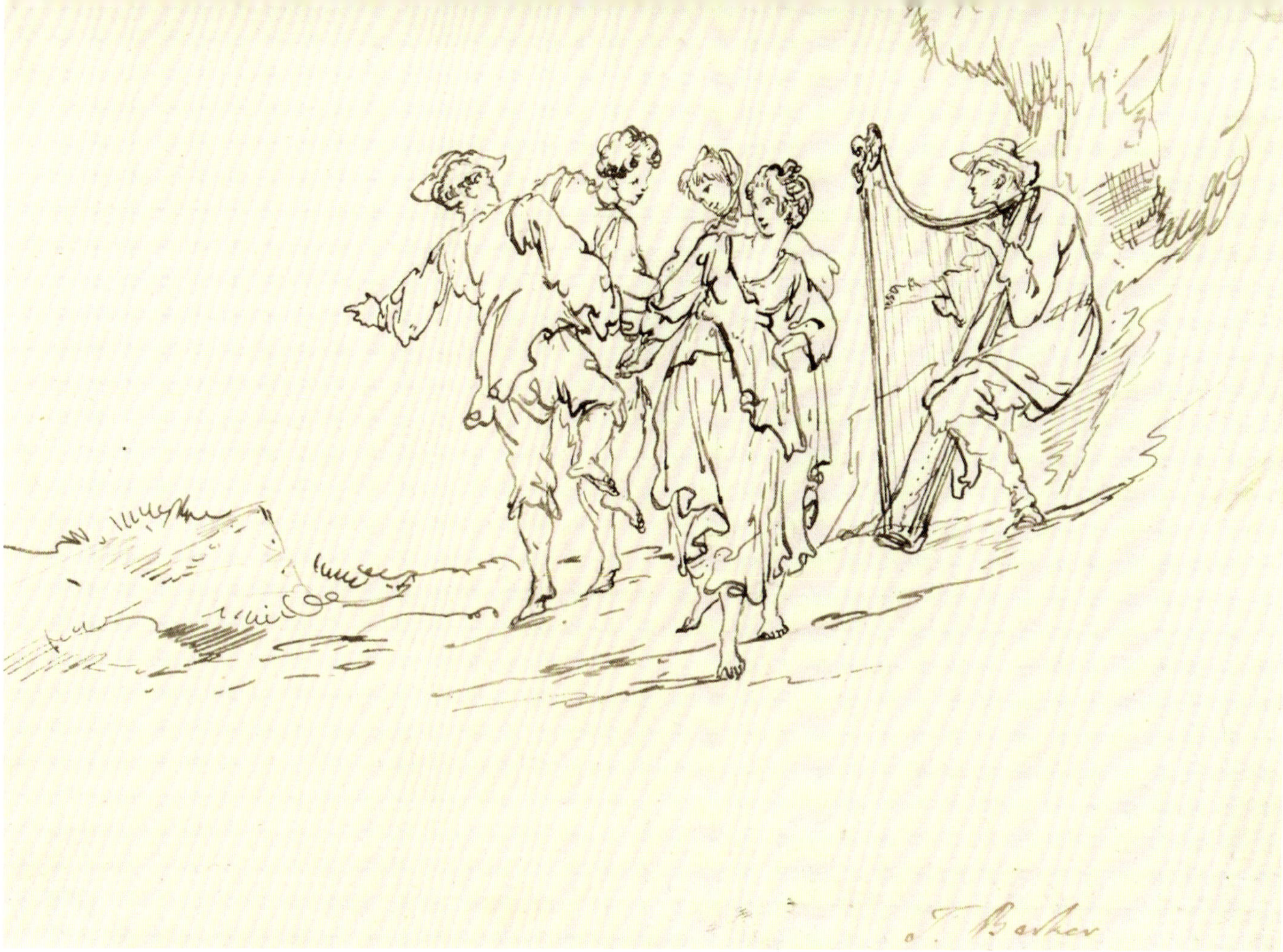

A further view in watercolour, taken from a high level so as to include the castle, shows Smith clearly playing for dancing rather than for singing. The celebrity of John Smith suggested by the multiplicity of these Ibbetson portraits is reinforced by the survival of a pencil drawing of the harper, produced by an unidentified tourist, who noted that he had played at Conwy for thirty-three years.

97 Probably Thomas Barker, *Dancing to the Harp*, c.1798

Perhaps because of the later emphasis on the unique indigenous form of penillion singing, the role of the harp as an accompaniment for dance has become somewhat sidelined. It seems clear that, in late eighteenth- and early nineteenth-century practice, dance figured prominently in the living tradition of the common people, and that was certainly the perception of outsiders. It was a perception that extended to representations of the Welsh on the London stage. According to its own publicity, a two-act comic opera entitled *St David's Day* played to 'unbounded applause' at the Theatre Royal, Covent Garden, in 1800. It was written by Thomas Attwood with a libretto by Thomas Dibdin, and featured Charles Incledon, who was among the most popular stage performers of the period. He was celebrated in costume in his role of William in an engraving. The musical foundations of the

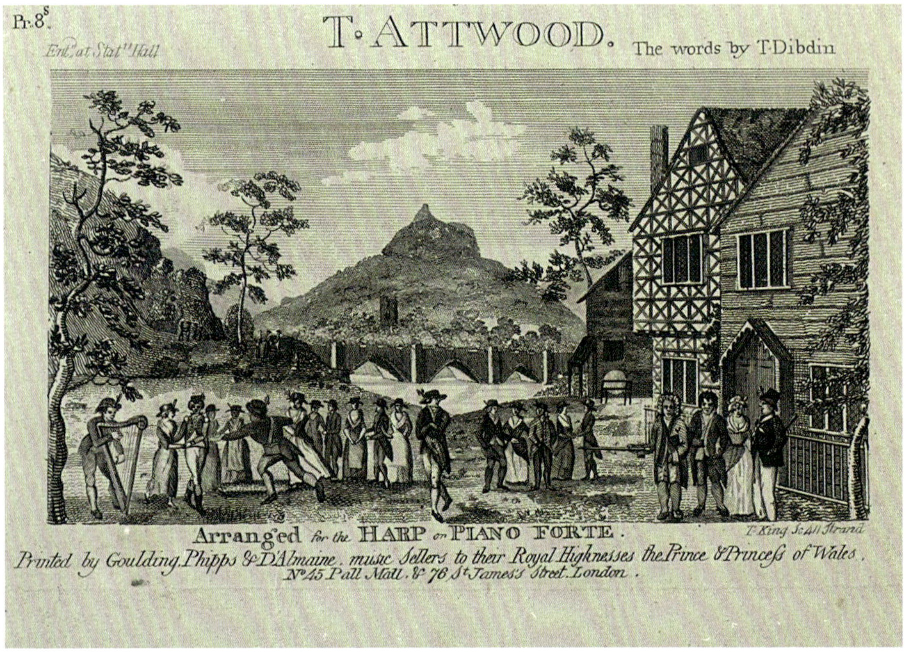
Pr. 8s.
Entd. at Statrs. Hall
T. ATTWOOD.
The words by T. Dibdin
Arranged for the HARP or PIANO FORTE.
T. King Sc. 411 Strand
Printed by Goulding, Phipps & D'Almaine, music Sellers to their Royal Highnesses the Prince & Princess of Wales,
No. 45 Pall Mall & 76 St. James's Street, London.

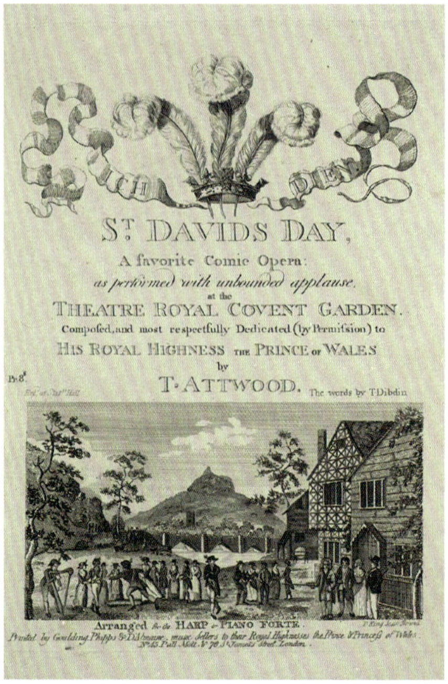
St. DAVIDS DAY,
A favorite Comic Opera;
as performed with unbounded applause,
at the
THEATRE ROYAL COVENT GARDEN.
Composed, and most respectfully Dedicated (by Permission) to
HIS ROYAL HIGHNESS THE PRINCE OF WALES
by
T. ATTWOOD.
The words by T. Dibdin
Arranged for the HARP or PIANO FORTE.

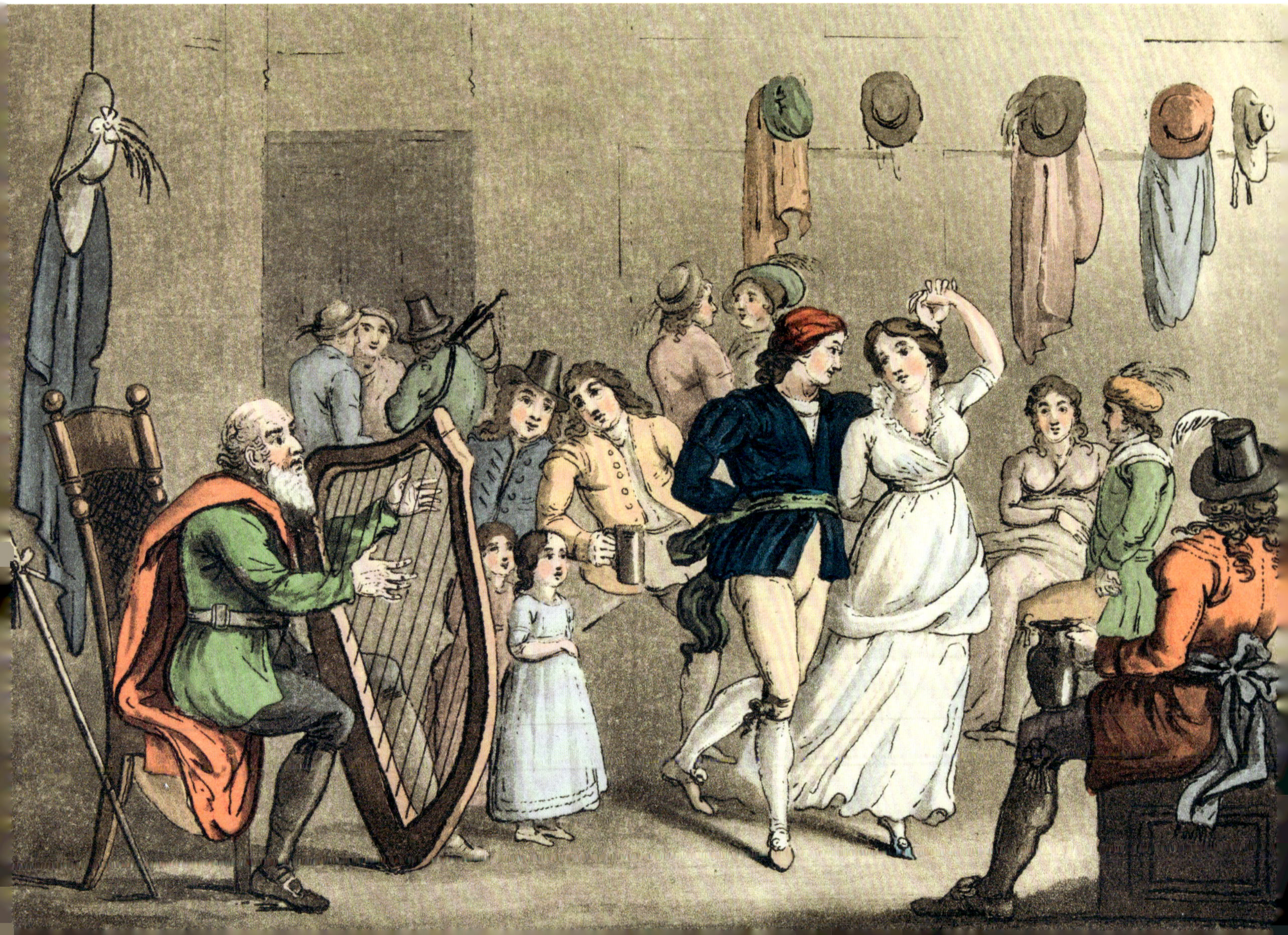

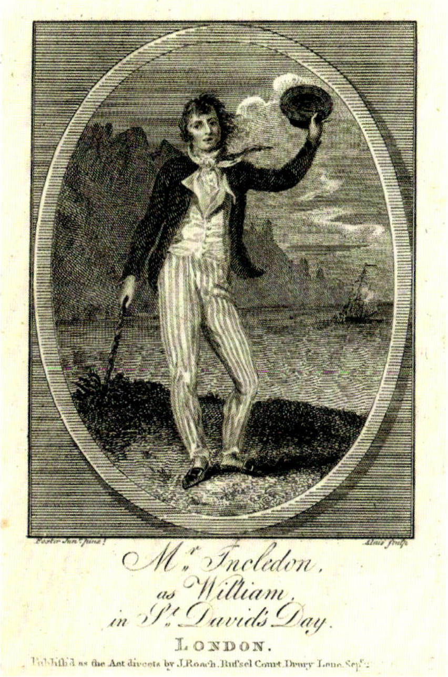

98 John Alais after Thomas Foster, *Mr Incledon, as William, in St. David's Day*, 1820

99 Thomas King, cover for Thomas Attwood, *St. David's Day*, 1800

100 Robert Havell, *Singing to the Harp and Dancing*, 1815

piece were laid in the overture based on three well-known Welsh melodies, 'Y Gadlys', 'Rhyfelgyrch Gwŷr Harlech' and 'Codiad yr Haul'. Reflecting both the fashion for Welsh tourism and the wartime agenda of a united four-nation British kingdom, the portrayal of the common people of Wales was positive. It stood in remarkable contrast to the long tradition of racist abuse of Welsh people in London popular culture.[93] In the opera, the upshot of the honesty and generosity of a Welsh yokel towards an English sailor, stranded in the remote country, was a wedding to which the locals were 'seen descending from the hills with wands, flowers and leeks.'[94] This concluding scene was depicted on the cover of the published score in an engraving featuring dancing to the accompaniment of the harp.

In one of the most successful of the many descriptions of Wales published in the brief period of positive imaging, dancing to the music of the harp again featured as a trope of national identity. Like Edward Pugh's *Cambria Depicta*, the Revd Peter Roberts's *The Cambrian Popular Antiquities*, although published in London and in English, was the work of an insider. The widely travelled antiquarian was serving a parish in Shropshire when he published the book in 1815, though he would return to Wales as Vicar of Halkin in Flintshire a few years later. The London engraver Robert Havell (who also worked for Pugh on *Cambria Depicta*) produced a dance scene of indeterminate period, apparently set in a tavern. Its temporal ambiguity was enhanced by a nod in the direction of the ancient bardic tradition in the form of the aged and bearded harper himself, whose loose robe flows over his shoulders.

93 See references in Lord, *Words with Pictures*.

94 Given in Meirion Hughes, 'Attwood's St David's Day: Music, Wales, and War in 1800', in Rachel Cowgill and Julian Rushton (eds.), *Europe, Empire, and Spectacle in Nineteenth-Century British Music* (Aldershot, 2006), p. 137.

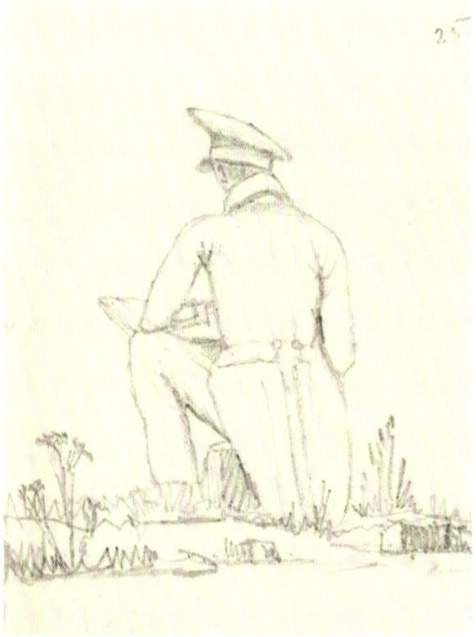

101 Unknown artist, *Young Man Sketching (Felix Mendelssohn-Bartholdy)*, 1829

The apparent contradictions in the reports of the state of the national tradition among the common people at the beginning of the nineteenth century are certainly explicable in the context of the development of the tourist market, guided by the long succession of writers that extended over the half century from the accounts of Thomas Pennant in the 1770s to Edward Pugh and Peter Roberts, four decades later. Innkeepers in the most favoured parts of the north increasingly took advantage of the expectation of visitors to find a harper at every hostelry.[95] While the collective enjoyment of traditional music by various degrees of the Welsh people themselves may well have been in decline, the presence of a harper at inns appealed strongly to tourists – though there was at least one notable exception. In 1829, after a visit to Scotland that became celebrated as a result of his composition of the *Hebrides Overture*, Felix Mendelssohn-Bartholdy visited popular tourist destinations across north Wales. He stayed with the mining engineer John Taylor at Coed Du, Rhydymwyn, near Mold, where he composed piano pieces for the daughters of his host, the *Three Fantaisies*, Op. 16. He found time also for the sketching that he enjoyed. But his written observations on the veracity as well as the quality of the musical offerings provided at a tavern in Llangollen were particularly revealing:

> Anything but national music! May ten thousand devils take all folklore. Here I am in Wales, and oh how lovely, a harpist sits in the lobby of every inn of repute playing so-called folk melodies at you – i.e., dreadful, vulgar, fake stuff, and simultaneously a hurdy-gurdy is tootling out melodies, it's enough to drive one crazy, it's even given me a toothache. Scottish bagpipes, Swiss cow's horns, Welsh harps – all playing the Huntsmen's Chorus with ghastly variations or improvisations, not to mention the lovely songs in the lobby – it's the only real music they have! It's beyond comprehension. Anyone like myself, who can't abide Beethoven's Nationallieder, should come here and hear them howled by shrill nasal voices, accompanied by doltish bumbling fingers, and then hold his tongue.[96]

Clearly, the indiscriminate commercial exploitation of Romantic fashion among the intellectual community of the early nineteenth century had infected small-nation nationalism not only in Wales but all over Europe. Furthermore, monetisation was no longer directed solely at the gentry and fashion-conscious intellectuals who had been able to afford travel to exotic regions in the eighteenth century, since increasing numbers of middle-class persons were now also touring, as Edward Pugh

95 See, for instance, the encounter between the Revd Richard Warner and the resident blind triple harper named Jones at The Bull in Conwy. Jones played 'David of the White Rock' and 'the solemn dirge-like music of Morfa Rhuddlan'. Revd Richard Warner of Bath, *A Walk through Wales, in August 1797* (Bath, 1798), pp. 148–9.

96 Given in Rudolf Elvers (ed.), transl. Craig Tomlinson, *Felix Mendelssohn: A Life in Letters* (London, 1986), p. 89. Weber's 'Huntsmen's Chorus' from *Der Freischütz*, first performed as recently as 1821, had rapidly entered popular consciousness, reinvented in a variety of contexts all over Europe.

97 Pugh, *Cambria Depicta*, p. 93.

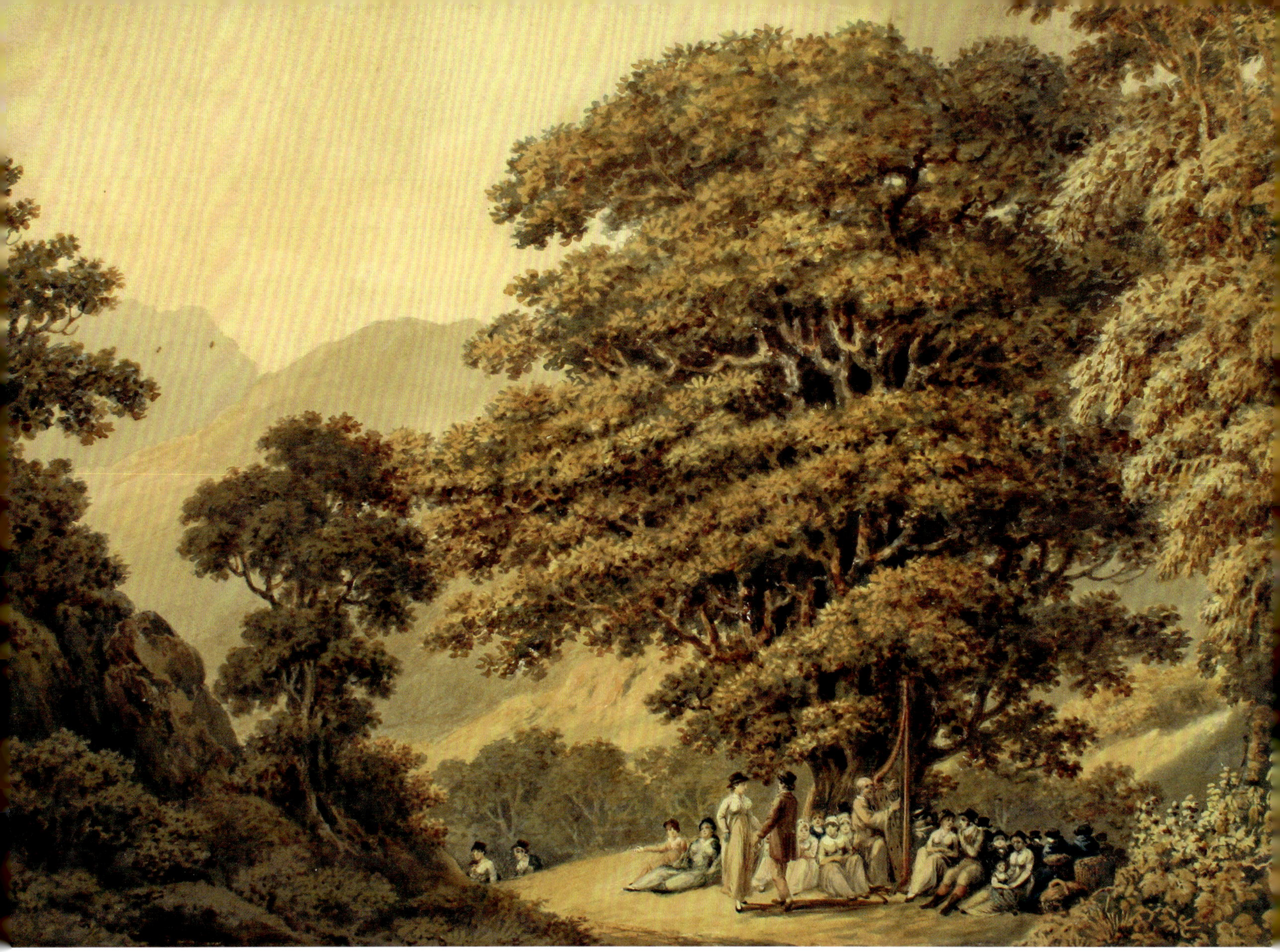

pointed out in *Cambria Depicta*.[97] By the second decade of the nineteenth century, harp music was a manifestation of the national character of the natives which all expected to witness. Providing this necessary accompaniment to the experience of the mountain landscape was profitable for publicans and practitioners alike. By contrast, the positive economic implications of national music coincided with an intense debate about the true tradition, and some tension within the world of Welsh musicians and intellectuals, that developed inside the framework of the Eisteddfod movement. But whatever the concerns of patriotic Welsh intellectuals about the true state of affairs, the burgeoning number of published accounts of tourists who had experienced the playing of a harp did nothing but confirm the association of Wales with music. The fusion of bardic myth and observed if vestigial reality had firmly established the national brand in the mind of outsiders.

102 Unknown artist, *Dancing to the Harp*, *c.*1820

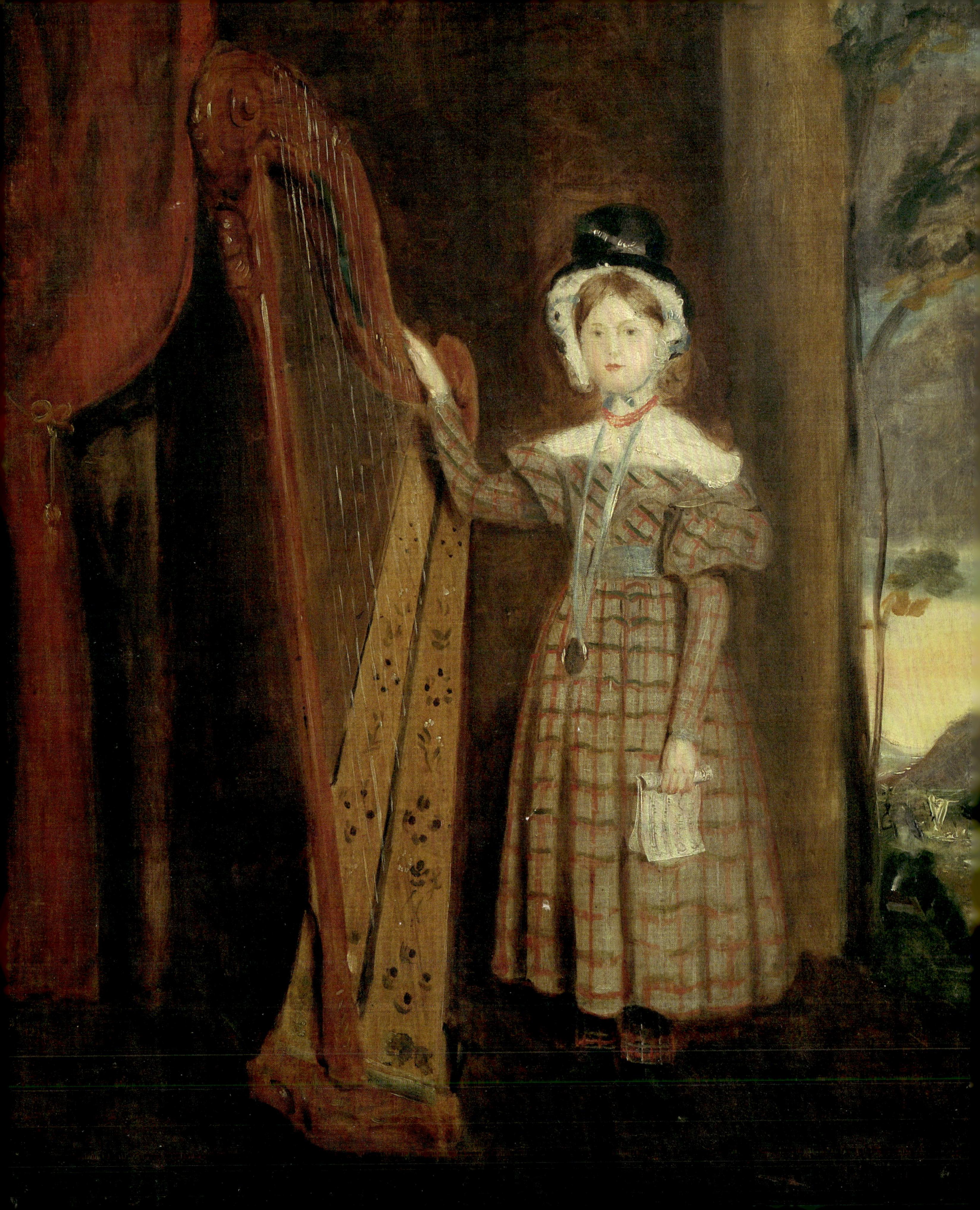

CHAPTER THREE

The EISTEDDFOD MOVEMENT: REVIVAL – *and* RIVAL UNDERSTANDINGS

In the late 1770s or early 1780s, Thomas Pennant had his painter, Moses Griffith, illustrate the idea of musical continuity in Wales with a portrait of his friend and colleague, John Lloyd, Rector of Caerwys, holding the Mostyn Harp – the silver miniature that had been awarded to the winning instrumentalist at the Caerwys Eisteddfod of 1567–8. Lloyd sat in a spindle chair of a kind that was known in the sixteenth century and, in that period, probably signified particular authority,

103 *The Mostyn Harp*, c.1567

104 Moses Griffith, *The Revd John Lloyd, Caerwys*, c.1778–81

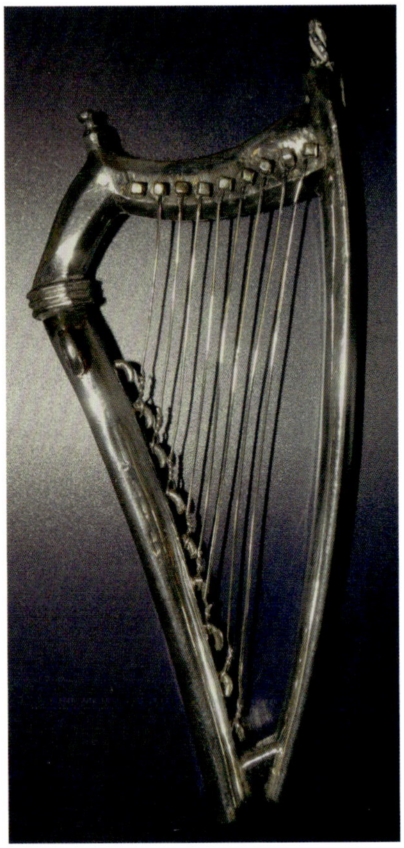

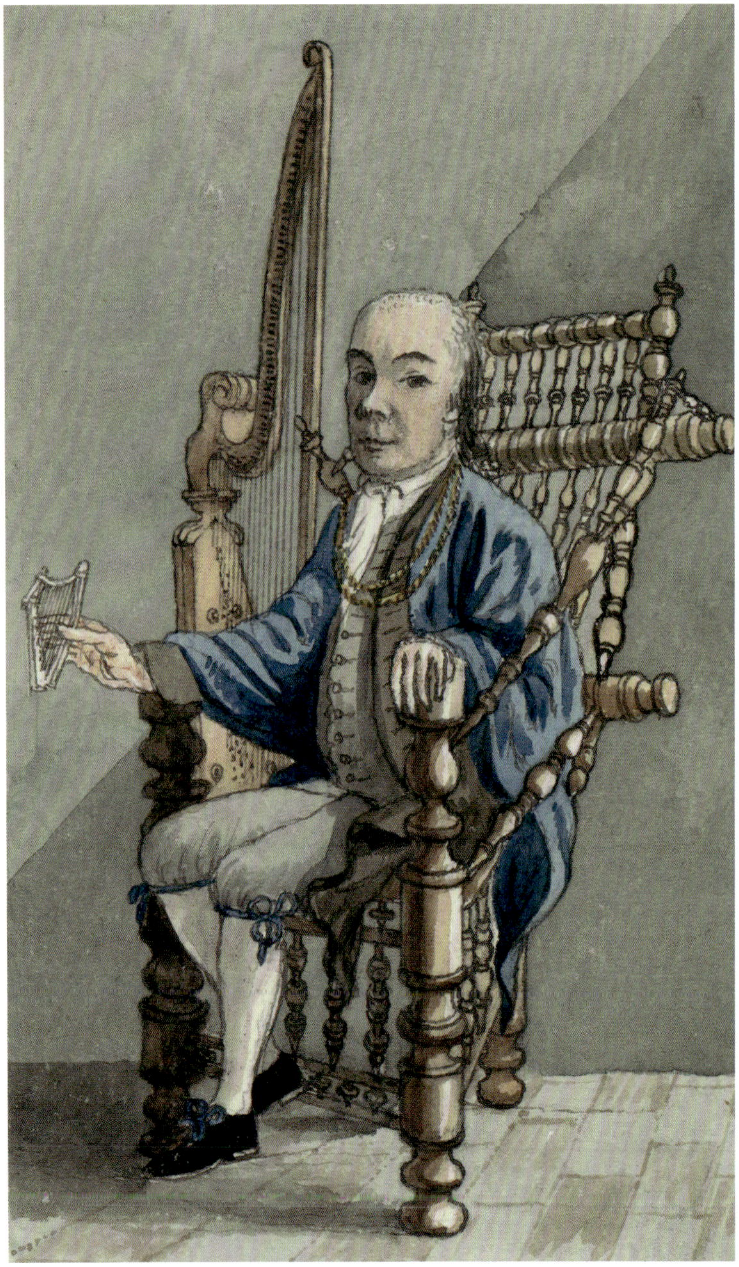

and so it may be that Pennant intended to illustrate also the custom of chairing the bard.[1] In his *Tour in Wales*, Pennant's writing about the eisteddfod exemplified the growing interaction of antiquarian interest in the idea of tradition among the largely English-speaking gentry and their intellectual circle, and the continuing practice among the lower orders of competitive extemporised poetry in the Welsh language. A competition held at Corwen in 1789 proved particularly significant in this context because the winning poet, the Revd Walter Davies, Gwallter Mechain, would become a leading figure in formalising eisteddfod practice during the remaining four decades of his upwardly mobile life, directed for the most part by prominent members of the Gwyneddigion Society in London. Indeed, it seems to have been his success at the Corwen Eisteddfod that brought Gwallter Mechain to the attention of William Owen Pughe and of Owain Myfyr, the Society's founder, who was able to facilitate his rise from local craftsman to Rector of Manafon. He had left school at twelve years of age to become a cooper and, during his ascent, gained degrees at the Universities of both Oxford and Cambridge.

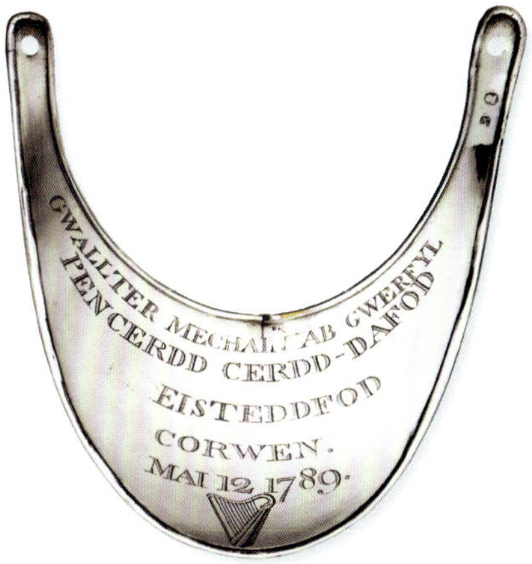

105 *Medal of the Corwen Eisteddfod*, 1789

The revived eisteddfod tradition would provide the most important public platform for the promotion of the idea of Welsh musicality throughout the nineteenth century. Sadly, the beginnings of the revival in the previous century were not documented visually, though engraved medals survive. The poet Jonathan Hughes wrote on behalf of the bardic community to the Gwyneddigion in 1789 urging them to provide such medals as an incentive,[2] and a medal awarded to Gwallter Mechain at Corwen in that year survives. In the shape of a military gorget, engraved with a harp, it is unique among the early eisteddfod medals in its allusion to music. The piece was made by a Chester silversmith, and paid for by subscription. However, the Bala Eisteddfod medal of 1789, again won by Gwallter Mechain, is also worthy of note both because of its maker and its donor. The medal, depicting a female head representing Liberty and a Phrygian cap, was designed by the French medallist and student of Jacques-Louis David, Augustin Dupré. The donor was that great British royalist, Bardd y Brenin, who was presumably in ignorance of the original inscriptions that the medal had carried, as also the meaning of the allegorical image on the reverse. It depicts France, defending the child America from the English lion. The medal had been commissioned in 1783 by Benjamin Franklin, when American

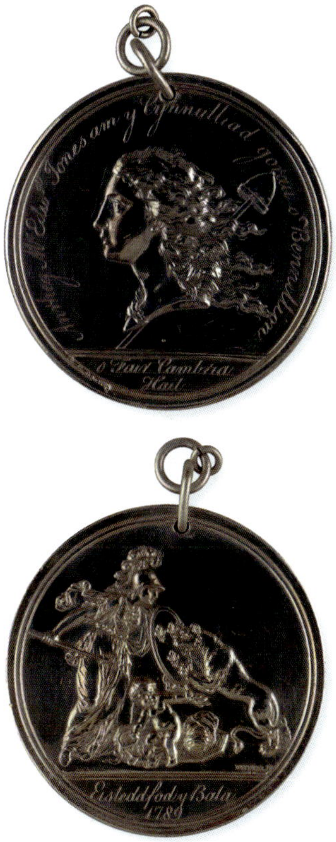

106 After Augustin Dupré, *Medal of the Bala Eisteddfod*, 1789

1 John Rhys (ed.), *Tours in Wales of Thomas Pennant* (Caernarfon, 1883), vol. ii, pp. 79–102.

2 BL Add MS 9848, 25 February 1789. For Hughes's embroilment in an eisteddfodic dispute with Gwallter Mechain that resulted in the painting of a satirical image of himself, see Peter Lord, *The Visual Culture of Wales: Imaging the Nation* (Cardiff, 2000), p. 203.

ambassador in Paris, to celebrate the Revolution. It carried then the inscription 'Libertas Americana' and the date '4 Juil. 1776', not an anniversary that Bardd y Brenin's employer would have wished to celebrate. Perhaps the musician had drawn the wrong conclusion from the *fleur-de-lis* motifs on France's shield.[3]

No eisteddfod has bequeathed a contemporary visual record of its musical component between 1789 and a seminal meeting that took place at Carmarthen in 1819. The meeting was the outcome of the deliberations of an informal group who met on an annual basis over New Year at the home of the Revd John Jenkins, 'Ifor Ceri'.[4] Jenkins and his Anglican clerical neighbours, Gwallter Mechain and W.J. Rees of Casgob in Radnorshire, formed the core of the group who came together to enjoy poetry, the music of the harp and discussion of their shared antiquarian interests, in what became known to them as a 'clerical eisteddfod'. Among those present in January 1818 was David Rowland, 'Dewi Brefi', who had recently returned from a period of six years spent evangelising in Newfoundland, and it was from him that the suggestion came to establish a more formal society with the purpose of awakening the Anglican clergy of Wales to the literary and musical traditions of their country. In their turn, they might then lead a revival. His suggestion was passed on to Thomas Burgess, Bishop of St Davids who, unusually for an English clergyman, was a scholarly man with a genuine interest in Welsh antiquarian matters – though he was equally engaged with his contemporary world. In particular, he sought to address the perceived estrangement of the Anglican clergy from the people of Wales in order to win back the ground being lost all over the country to Nonconformist denominations. Burgess saw that the proposed society, led by the clergy, reinforced that agenda. By the autumn, a public meeting had been organised at Carmarthen (the Bishop's Palace stood just outside the town) and the foundations of the Dyfed Cambrian Society were laid. As a part of the Society's programme, an Eisteddfod was planned for July 1819, and notwithstanding its clerical leadership, it was made clear that it was open to all with an interest in reviving the tradition.

The Carmarthen Eisteddfod would have far-reaching consequences, the most long-lasting of which was the result of an event that had not been planned by the Society. Iolo Morganwg attended the meeting and attached to it the faux druidic ceremonies that he had been devising over the past decades. Iolo presided in person, presenting himself as the venerable and distinguished heir to an ancient tradition. The theatricality of his appearance at the novel ceremony

3 The reverse inscription reads: 'Non sine diis animosus infans' ('The infant is not bold without the aide of the gods'), from Horace's ode 'Descende coelo'. At the St Asaph Eisteddfod of 1790, Gwallter Mechain was victorious again with an essay on the subject of Liberty, fashionable for the moment as a generic idea in the wake of early events in France, but soon to acquire its specifically British inflexion, directed against that country. Augustin Dupré was designer of French currency between 1791 and 1803.

4 Jenkins's bardic name was a reference to Ifor Hael (*fl.* 1340-60), renowned for his generosity to the medieval poets and in particular for his patronage of the most celebrated of them, Dafydd ap Gwilym.

5 See the observations of Joseph Harris, *Seren Gomer*, 2 (1819), p. 233.

6 Ifor Ceri seems also to have drawn on the knowledge of friends and family members, though his manuscripts do not record all his sources.

7 Bowen (c.1747–1835) lived at 13 Portland Place and was a graduate of Oriel College, Oxford. He was active as Minister of Margaret Chapel, Bath, but also Priest Vicar of Wells Cathedral, and Vicar of Mudford (1796-1828). He and his wife, Elizabeth, had two children who died in infancy, but they adopted two nieces as daughters.

8 Letter from Bowen to Iolo, 1801, expressing appreciation of the latter's poems, and regretting that they had failed to meet in Cowbridge (NLW MS 21280E, f. 32).

made a considerable impression on many of those present in the garden of the Ivy Bush Hotel.[5] However, a second precedent set at the meeting met with less universal approval. Ifor Ceri had a particular interest in music, playing the 'cello and other instruments, and he had for some four or five years been transcribing melodies and words familiar to him from a lifetime of listening to musicians working both in an ecclesiastical context and in the folk tradition.[6] It was this heritage which he wished to celebrate and sustain as a part of the work of the new institution, but others took a broader view of the opportunity presented by the regional, if not national, reach of the reformed eisteddfod. Alongside the various traditional competitions involving poets and musicians, choral concerts and dances were organised as fringe events, and they proved highly popular. The renowned Bath Harmonic Society was invited to perform as part of the proceedings under the Revd John Bowen, their conductor. Bowen was a native of Swansea, though he had made his ecclesiastical career, which included several no doubt lucrative and probably absentee posts, based in Bath.[7] Nevertheless, he had not entirely turned his back on Welsh affairs, and was indeed in contact with Iolo Morganwg in 1801, nearly twenty years before his engagement in the regional eisteddfod movement.[8]

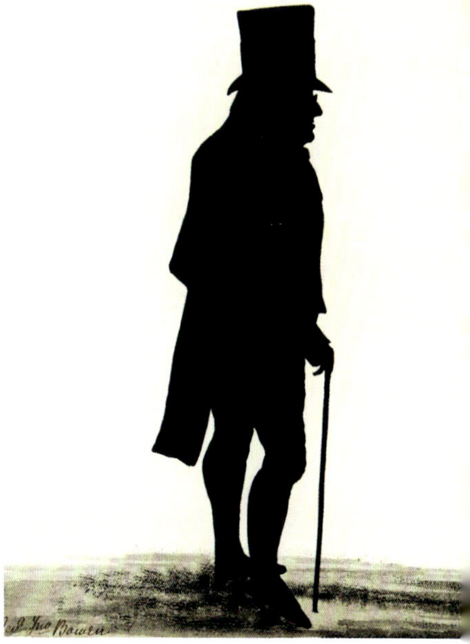

107 Unknown artist, *Revd. Jno. Bowen*, *c.*1800–20

In 1795 Bowen had founded the Bath Harmonic Society, at a time when the city was at the height of its celebrity. It attracted innumerable artists, in particular portrait painters, miniaturists, and cutters of silhouettes, who met the demand from residents and also from visitors, who were keen to acquire a memento of their season at the fashionable resort. Printed caricatures of celebrated men and women seen about town provided visitors with one such memento. It is a mark of the status of John Bowen that he was the subject of just such a portrait, part

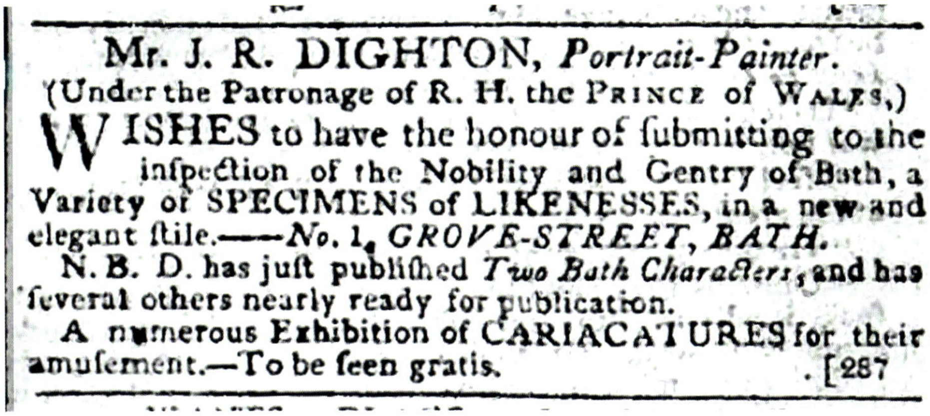

Mr. J. R. DIGHTON, *Portrait-Painter.*
(Under the Patronage of R. H. the PRINCE of WALES,)
WISHES to have the honour of ſubmitting to the inſpection of the Nobility and Gentry of Bath, a Variety of SPECIMENS of LIKENESSES, in a new and elegant ſtile.——*No. 1, GROVE-STREET, BATH.*
N. B. D. has juſt publiſhed *Two Bath Characters*, and has ſeveral others nearly ready for publication.
A numerous Exhibition of CARIACATURES for their amuſement.—To be ſeen gratis. [287

108 *Mr J.R. Dighton*, advertisement from the *Bath Chronicle and Weekly Gazette*, 1809

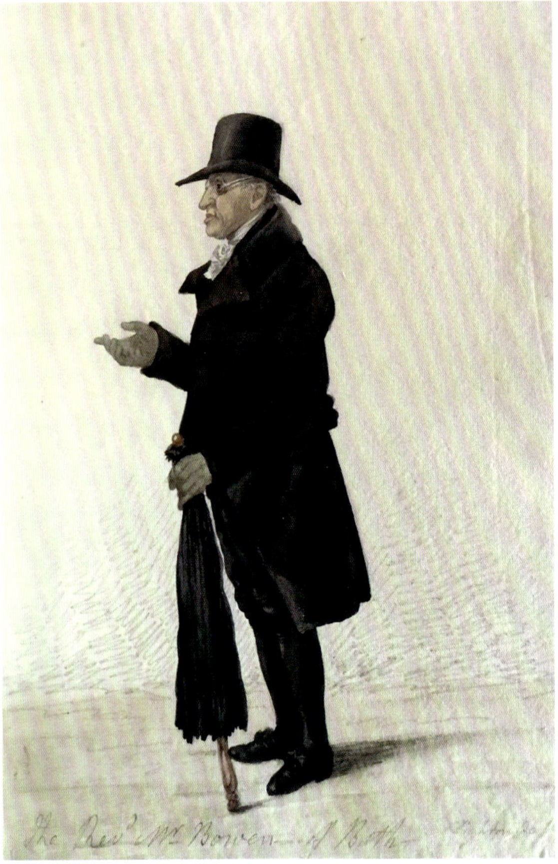

of a series of etchings made by Robert Dighton. The artist's original drawing (in which he holds an inverted umbrella rather than a walking stick) also survives. In another life, Dighton had been a singer and actor on the London stage, but when he drew Bowen in 1809, he was steering clear of his native metropolis. Some three years earlier, a scandal had followed the discovery that he had been stealing prints from the collection of the British Museum and selling them in his London shop.

Dighton's image of Bowen linked him with his home in Bath at Portland Place, in the most fashionable part of the city. The artist caught the determined set of the clergyman's jaw, which conveyed something of what appears to have been a pugnacious temperament. In May 1805, William Siddons wrote to Hester Thrale of an unfortunate confrontation at Sydney Gardens, during the course of a gala concert by the Harmonic Society:

109 Robert Dighton, *The Revd Mr Bowen of Bath*, *c.*1809

110 Robert Dighton, *A View Taken from Portland Place, Bath*, 1809

I suppose there was about a thousand people – seven hundred of which I shoud think were Ladies beautifully dressd. The weather was lovely – and all went on charmingly till the Ices and Jellies were to be distributed. And then such a confusion and scramble, I never saw – waiters running to particular Boxes – Gentlemen, nay Ladies too – snatching as they passed. Tis not to be described but the worst of all a serious discord happened – which is likely to make some work for the long Robe – The Revd Mr Bowen – (who I believe every body knows) one of the principal of the Society – was accosted by Sir George Colebrooke, and chargd with being inattentive in his office. Mr Bowen, being from Wales – look you went into a passion, and spoke hot words, when Sir George thinking to cool him threw a Glass of Ice in his face. But this had a contrary effect when fists were held up and sticks brandished – but the combatants were separated – without the appearance of blood outwardly. However Sir George is looked upon as the aggressor, and the Rev'd is to proceed against him accordingly.[9]

9 William Siddons at Bath to Hester Piozzi at Brynbella, Denbigh, 22 May 1805, given in Kalman A. Burnim, 'The letters of Sarah and William Siddons to Hester Lynch Piozzi in the John Rylands Library', *Bulletin of the John Rylands Library*, 52, 1 (1969), p. 79.

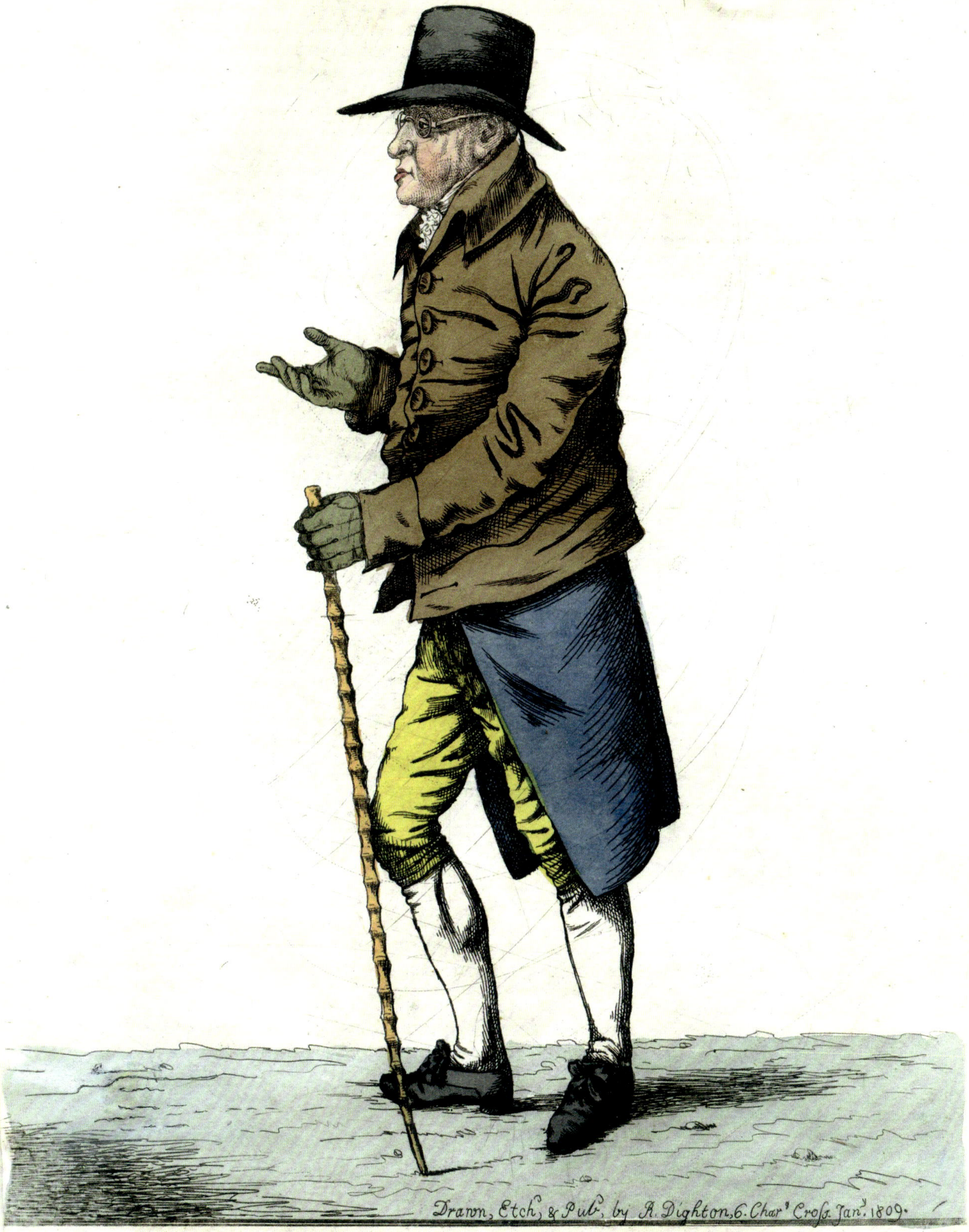

A VIEW taken from PORTLAND PLACE, BATH.

Bowen would live at Portland Place until his death in 1835, and it is clear from the contents of his home, sold the following year, that he lived a sophisticated life, surrounded by his musical instruments (two violins, a 'cello, a chamber organ and a glass harmonica), his musical and antiquarian library (that included the works of Thomas Pennant and Edward Pugh), and his pictures. It would seem that a silhouette of the musician was cut at about the same time as the Dighton portrait.[10] Bowen had a penchant for the medium. An earlier image had him raising his hat in salutation, and a head and shoulders appears to depict him in old age.

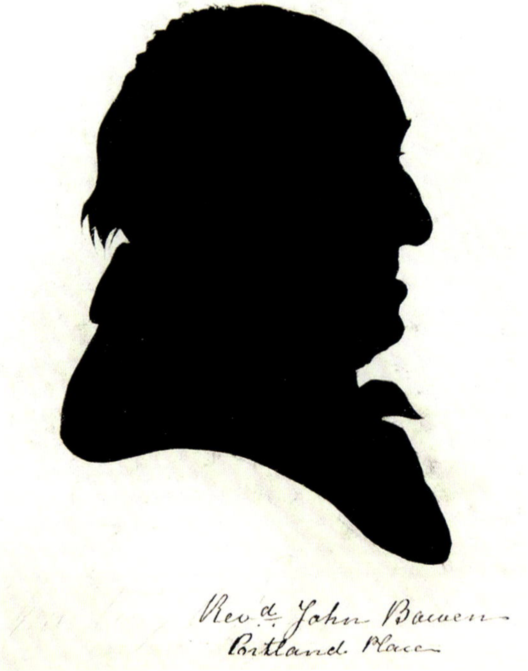

111 Unknown artist, *Revd. John Bowen, Portland Place*, c.1820–35

By the time of its appearance at Carmarthen in 1819, the Bath Harmonic Society was a distinguished group that included professional musicians and enjoyed the patronage (and membership) of the Prince Regent:

> The Rev. John Bowen … having engaged Miss Bartlett, and Messrs. Loder, Garbett and Rolle, Professional Members of that Society, to render their gratuitous services at a Concert for the benefit of Decayed Harpers, on Friday evening, the Cambrian Society, acknowledging the liberality of their offer, most handsomely patronized a Vocal Concert, which they gave the preceding evening at the Town-Hall, which was generally allowed to be as rich a treat as was ever enjoyed in the Principality: such an assemblage of rank, fashion, and respectability, taking it for all in all, had not been witnessed in Carmarthen for some time. There were upwards of three hundred persons present at this Concert.[11]

Following the precedent set by George Thomson, Bowen had taken traditional airs and attached to them 'classically appropriate words', which 'were sung as songs and glees, in the first style.'[12] The repertoire does not appear to survive, but it seems likely that it was responsible for the serious reservations expressed by Ifor Ceri after the event. He was critical of the association of modern music with a festival expected by him to be a celebration of what he understood as pure, traditional material. In a memorable phrase, he suggested that the Eisteddfod had been turned into an 'Anglo-Italian farce'. Even worse, the concert at the Town Hall had been followed by a ball, which led to Dewi Brefi complaining about what the world might think 'if the grave deliberations of the clergy should end in a hop and a jig.'[13] Neither was Bardd y Brenin, who had adjudicated the competition for the silver harp, best pleased. In a letter to Ifor Ceri about arrangements for the next regional eisteddfod at Wrexham, the harper expressed his concern both about the possible dilution of Welsh content in the main competition, and in particular about the employment of Bowen's singers from Bath:

> Permit me to suggest, if it should concur with the approbation of the committee, that is, to have it mentioned, (in the advertisement of the intended Eisteddvod or Congress of the Welsh Bards & Musicians,) to inform the performers on the Triple Harp, who intend to be Competitors for the prize of the Silver Harp, that no Composition would be allowed to be played on that occasion, but the native Music of the Principality of Wales; & by that means some of the oldest & best of the Welsh Airs would be resorted to, brought forth & remembered; I conceive that these would be more characteristic for the purpose than any other Music, and certainly more congenial with the ancient custom of the Eisteddvod; But if English tunes & others are permited to be performed on that occasion, we shall soon loose almost the only original National Music that this Island can boast of.
>
> If it is intended to have any other Music, besides the Competition between the Harpers – such as a Concert, I would most willingly assist in my professional line, by performing on the Harp, some of the unpublished Welsh Airs with Variations; also a Duet or two with the Piano Forte; & surely we might select 3 or 4 good Welsh Singers that could sing songs & glees without having recourse to England for performers; & if we can find native singers I think they would give more satisfaction; & at the same time would be more in character with a Welsh Congress of Bards, & Musicians.[14]

Nevertheless, the popularity among the less discriminating public resulted in a return visit of Bowen and his professional singers to Carmarthen in 1820. The ecclesiastical association was maintained when the group performed 'appropriate anthems' in St Peter's Church, before presenting two secular concerts at the Town Hall in aid of church charities. Proceedings opened with an 'Ode on the Patron

10 The Dighton portrait has been identified previously as one 'Mr Banks', on the basis of a note added in pencil under a copy of the etching in the National Portrait Gallery (NPG D8721). The source for this inscription is unknown, and it replaces an earlier attribution, crossed out, identifying the sitter as the Duke of Portland. The original drawing, inscribed with Bowen's name, apparently in the artist's hand, is in the Royal Collection. The silhouette of Bowen, identified by the maker (possibly Edouardt, who was working in Bath in the period), in the same ink as used for the ground on which the cut-out was set, clearly represents the same individual as that depicted by Dighton, and further confirms the identity of the subject.

11 William Cathrall, *History of North Wales* (Manchester, 1828), vol. i, p. 292. The volume included woodcut illustrations. *Esus* was certainly the work of Hugh Hughes, and probably also *Bardism*.

12 *Bath Chronicle and Weekly Gazette*, 15 July 1819. The success of the concert led to invitations from other venues, and resulted in performances at Swansea, Cardiff, Newport and Chepstow on the way back to Bath (*The Cambrian*, 10 July 1819).

13 NLW MS 1894, f. 109.

14 Bardd y Brenin, draft of a letter to Ifor Ceri, 24 November 1819 (NLW MS 171E, f. 99).

112 John Woodhouse, *The Revd John Bowen of Bath*, c.1800–20

of the Royal Bath Harmonic Society's accession to the Throne'[15] as the lengthy reign of George III had at last come to a close. There was little Welsh sentiment expressed in the choice of songs for these Carmarthen concerts. The second event did open with an 'Ode to Harmony', sung to 'Gorhoffedd Gwŷr Harlech', taken from a recently published collection of traditional airs married to modern words that had been assembled by John Dovaston.[16] But, on the whole, the repertoire was similar to that performed in the growing number of public assembly rooms opening in towns throughout the country.

When the Wrexham Eisteddfod, organised by the Powys Cambrian Society, took place in 1820, the precedent of parallel choral events, set at Carmarthen, was followed, except that they were organised, to the annoyance of John Bowen, by John Parry, Bardd Alaw. Perhaps mindful of the criticism voiced by Bardd y Brenin and others in the previous year, emphasis was placed on the reinvented Welsh material that Bardd Alaw had published in 1809 in *A Selection of Welsh Melodies*, and on some traditional airs more recently arranged for his next publication project:

> On Friday morning the Committee met for the purpose of awarding gratuities to the Bards and Minstrels who had not obtained prizes, and for granting each other rewards as might be deemed necessary; when a Piece of Plate, of the value of fifteen guineas, was voted to Mr Parry, Editor of the 'Welsh Melodies', for his great zeal and unwearied exertions in the cause of the Eisteddvod. A concert took place every evening at the Wynnstay Arms, under the direction of this Gentleman; which from the national airs and music introduced, formed an appropriate appendage to the festivities of each day. The sum collected at the three Concerts amounted to nearly £180; a sufficient proof of the general patronage they experienced. The entertainments consisted, for the most part, of Welsh Melodies, with English words, adapted to the occasion; there were also a few Pennillion with English translations. And it deserves to be recorded, to the praise of the ladies of Cymru, who attended this musical festival, that they appeared to take the warmest interest in the national traits by which it was distinguished.[17]

In 1821, at Caernarfon, Bowen's ensemble was again favoured, and received a substantial fee of 100 guineas. Their success resulted initially in an invitation to perform at Brecon in 1822. However, the Brecon organisers were presented with a less expensive option by Bardd Alaw, and the result was a row that was made

15 'The First Miscellaneous Concert, For the Relief of Superannuated Curates, and the Widows and Orphans of Poor Clergymen', 13 July 1820 (NLW MS 11116E, f. 10). The Society toured as far as Aberystwyth on this occasion.

16 Ferneat of the Breidden [J.F.M. Dovaston], *The Cambrian and Salopian Minstrel: or, Legendary ballads, incidental poems, hymns, sonnets, British melodies and other poems, &c. of the Welsh border* (Shrewsbury, c.1818). The Bath Harmonic Society would again visit Carmarthen under Bowen in 1823 (*Bath Chronicle and Weekly Gazette*, 9 October 1823).

17 Cathrall, *North Wales*, vol. i, p. 295. At the Caernarfon Eisteddfod of 1821, the Bath Harmonic Society was again in attendance. By this time, they had expanded their Welsh repertoire: 'The Rev. Mr. Bowen then proposed that they should ascend the platform, and sing a Pennillion; the chaste style in which this was executed, and the correctness of the pronunciation, drew forth the greatest plaudits' (*The Cambrian*, 6 October 1821). In addition to their eisteddfod performance, the Bath Harmonic Society sang a programme dominated by Handel at Bangor Cathedral to coincide with the second day of the meeting.

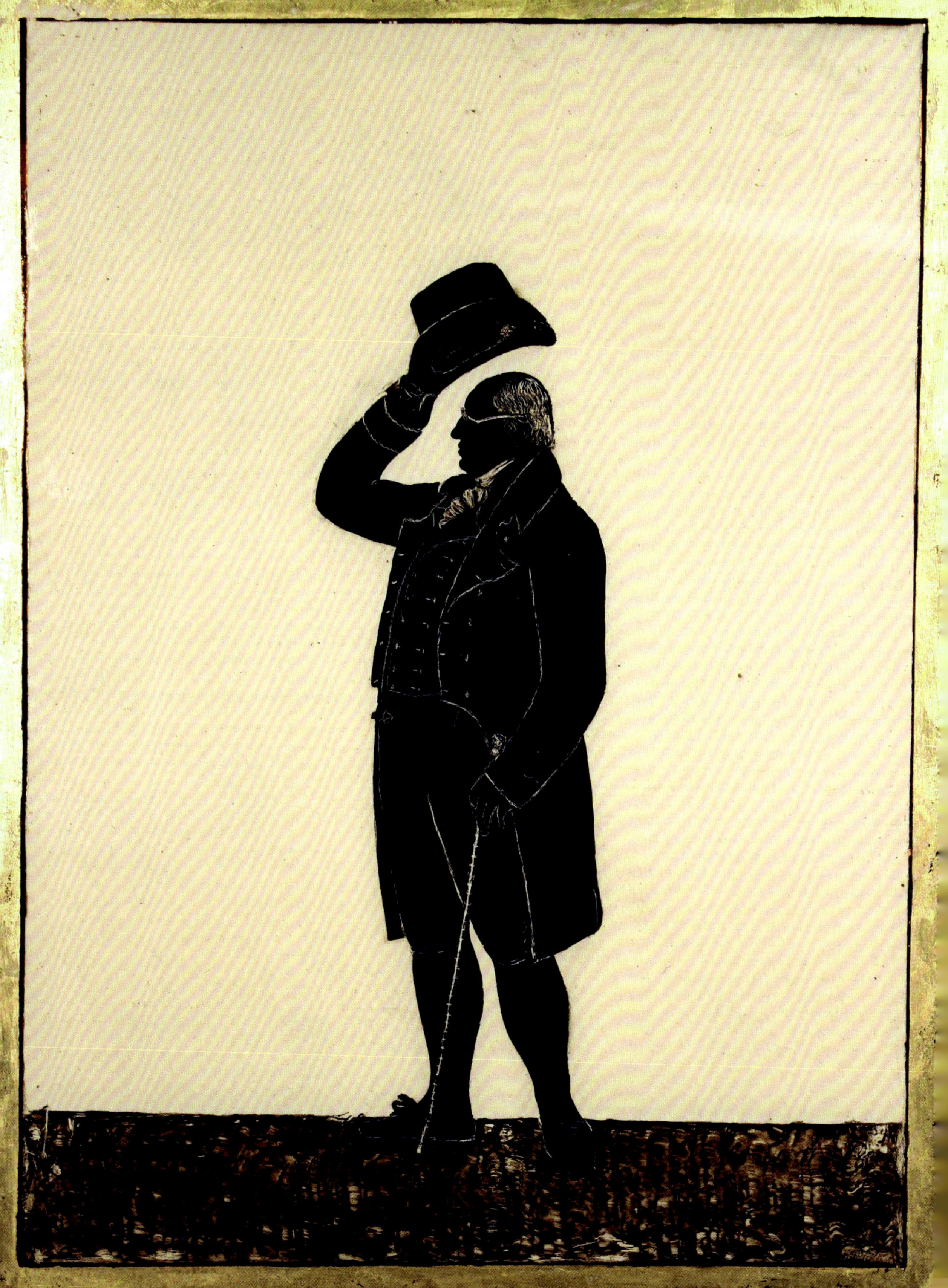

public by Bowen, who had his letter of complaint about being undercut printed and published.[18] The competition between the two rival groups rather obscured the central issue, though not for the antiquarian Angharad Llwyd, who was equally irritated by the 'Saxon singing' of both parties: 'My opinion of the Bath Harmonica [*sic*] ... is not singular', she observed, referring to criticism published in the *Morning Post* newspaper, 'and those horrid Denbigh trumpeters, etc., making such noises in a Hall where none but harps should have been admitted was excess of bad taste.'[19] Her reference to the 'Denbigh trumpeters' implicated Bardd Alaw, whose career had begun with the Denbigh Militia and developed in the world of popular entertainment on the London stage and at Vauxhall Gardens, a context that was clearly anathema to her. Again, she expressed her displeasure to W.J. Rees:

> I have been gratified much by you and Mr. Jenkins's awakening feel *at last* to our own unadulterated Welsh music. – *Datgeiniaid*, etc., without I hope any further interference from that coxcomb Parry who has been making cat's paws of our eisteddfodau to get himself and his fiddling friends, some money when London is empty. I cannot forgive him anglicising our tunes & gobbling up the profits of last 22nd May – getting 15£ at Wrexham & 40 or 50£ at Welshpool – more than was divided among our men of genius.[20]

The tension between the two views of the scope of the modern eisteddfod would persist for some time.[21] Nevertheless, the popular success of the choral concerts from their initiation was indicative of the fact that the modernisers would not only win the day, but that the widening of the musical content of the meetings begun at Carmarthen would have long-term implications. Among those present in 1819 had been the young John Thomas, 'Ieuan Ddu', who was to become a pioneer of the popularisation of choral music in the second half of the nineteenth century. In his lengthy poem, 'Cambria upon Two Sticks', that satirised the eisteddfod movement, he reflected on the early meetings, where 'all was dreariness'. For him, it was the appearance of Bowen's singers from Bath that had saved the day, since no Welshmen had previously sung 'song, duet, or glee/With any skill; though ear and voice might be/Evinced like those of any company':

> To make amends for this – there was each night
> A concert given, in which, for ear's delight –
> English professionals came to perform,
> And not a Welsh voice came to spoil the charm.[22]

18 Letter to Charles Morgan, 14 September 1822 (NLW MS 1888E, f. 47).

19 Mary Ellis, 'Angharad Llwyd, 1780-1866', *Publications of the Flintshire Historical Society Journal*, 26 (1973-4), p. 91.

20 Ibid.

21 See Rachel Ley, 'Lady Llanover and the Triple Harp', for a very late manifestation of the difference of opinion, library.wales/fileadmin/fileadmin/docs_gwefan/amdanom_ni/cyfeillion/darlithoedd/cyfn_dar_RLey_000916S.pdf: 'The Eisteddfod had her ladyship's most cordial support when it was the true Welsh eisteddfod, but not when it was of the mongrel sort that had recently taken place at Cardiff (laughter and applause).' *The Cambrian*, 26 October 1883.

Immediately prior to the Wrexham Eisteddfod, Bardd Alaw had issued an advertisement for the new edition of his *Welsh Melodies*, in which he thanked 'Literary Gentlemen, Natives of the Principality' for the verses already submitted and set by him, which would be performed at Wrexham for the first time. They would be printed in what became the second of two parts of the new publication, although it was the first to be issued. The reference to the 'ladies of Cymru' who attended the Wrexham concerts suggests that Felicia Hemans may have been among them, since the Eisteddfod came only four months after she presented 'The Wakening of Cambria' on her admittance to the reconstituted Cymmrodorion Society. Although no documentary evidence survives to confirm the supposition, it seems likely that Hemans's subsequent intensive co-operation with Bardd Alaw, that resulted in the first part of the new *Welsh Melodies*, adorned by its engraving after her 'Owain Glyndŵr's War Song', dates from this time.[23]

Despite his earlier suspicions, the generosity of spirit of Ifor Ceri sustained his relationship with Bardd Alaw. Back in London, in February 1821, the professional musician attended a meeting of the Cymmrodorion Society, where he was excited to see the designs for the medal which was belatedly to be awarded to W.J. Rees for his prize essay at Wrexham. The medal marked the return of the visual imaging of music, and became the standard award given by the Society for some years:

> I long to hear what Mr Rees thinks of his medal – we have determined our designs for our medal – the Cambrian Institution – on one side – a figure of a primitive Bard in full vigour – with a Coelbren in his hand – on the obverse an aged Bard, just rising from a sleeping posture, a ray of light darting (from) him – the first is by Flaxman and the other by Capt. Jones – two of our first artists – It will be a very handsome thing.[24]

Bardd Alaw appears not to have realised that the two designs must have been alternative proposals for a single image, so that the reverse of the medal was available to carry an engraved inscription for each winner. Perhaps unsurprisingly, given his high status as Professor of Sculpture at the Royal Academy, the design by John Flaxman was chosen. It seems likely that William Owen Pughe, whose relationship with the sculptor extended back into the previous century, was responsible for facilitating the commission. Consistent

22 J.L.Thomas, 'Ieuan Ddu', *Cambria upon Two Sticks* (Pontypridd, 1867), p. 21. The 'two sticks' support the aged nation staggering forward. Ieuan Ddu was fulsome in his praise of the role of Bishop Burgess at Carmarthen, and his support for the innovation of Iolo's Gorsedd: 'He, in his carriage took – placed by his side,/And afterwards – o'en with a pupil's pride –/From aged Iolo took a bard's degree/As Christ would by a John baptized be!' Ibid, p. 20.

23 See above, p. 92.

24 Bardd Alaw to Ifor Ceri, 6 February 1821, given in Winston Gwynne John, 'John Parry, Bardd Alaw, 1776–1851' (unpublished MA dissertation, University of Liverpool, 1951), p. 167. 'Capt. Jones' is untraced.

113 John Flaxman, *Medal of the Honourable Society of Cymmrodorion*, 1821

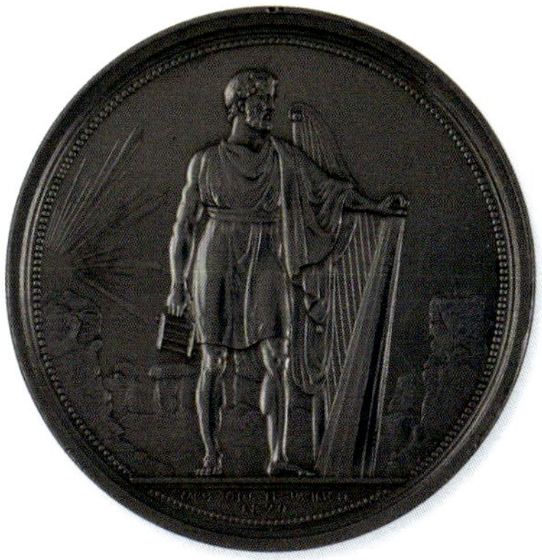

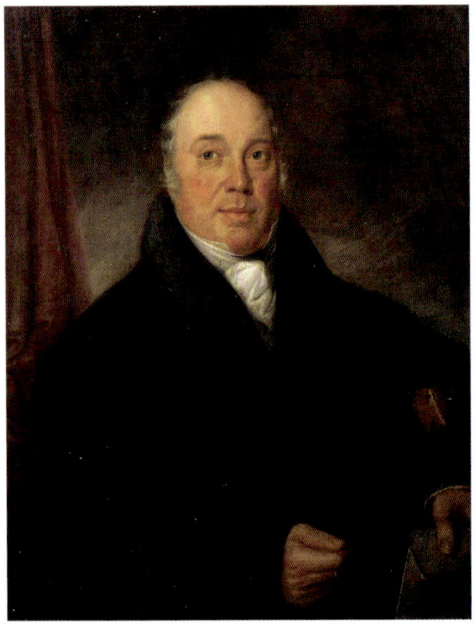

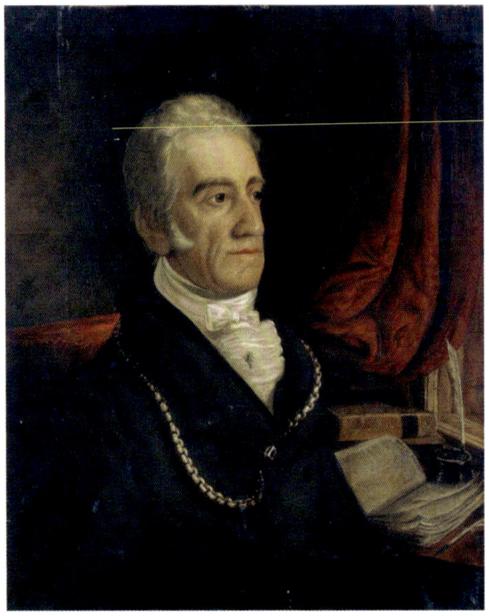

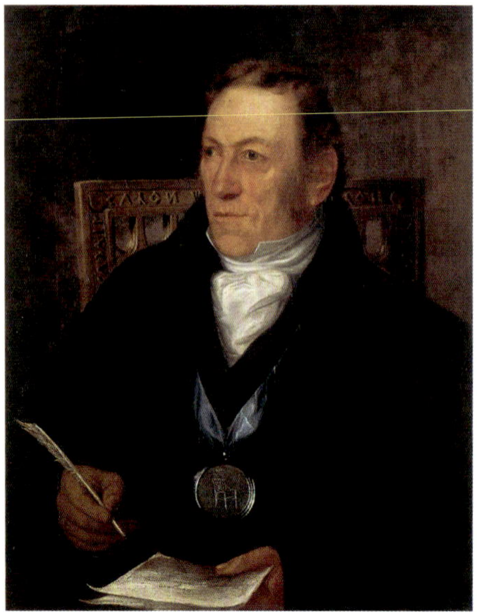

114 Hugh Hughes, *John Jenkins, Ifor Ceri*, 1826

115 Hugh Hughes, *W.J. Rees, Casgob*, 1826

116 Hugh Hughes, *Walter Davies, Gwallter Mechain*, 1825–6

with his usual style, Flaxman classicised the bard most inappropriately by dressing him in a Roman toga and trimming his beard in a tidy imperial manner. The design was a remarkable concoction, since the bard was portrayed leaning on a modern triple harp, against the background of Stonehenge, struck by the light of the sun.

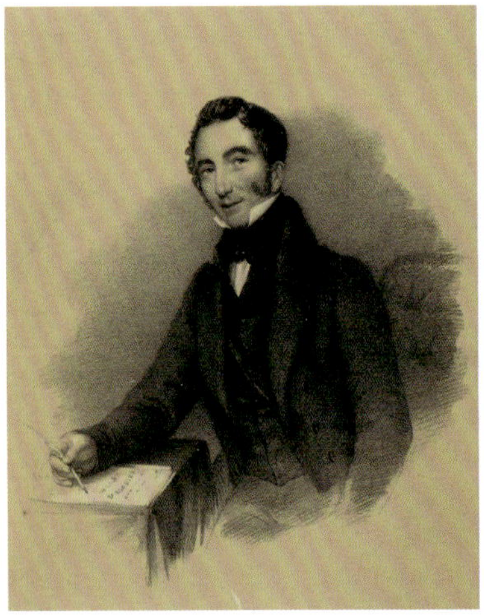

117 Edward Morton after Cornelius, *John Parry, Bardd Alaw*, c.1835

118 Unknown artist, *John Parry, Bardd Alaw*, c.1820–5

Although those who purchased Bardd Alaw's latest *Selection of Welsh Melodies* might have been disappointed that, contrary to the suggestion in the author's advertisement, only one of the airs was accompanied by an engraving, the 1820s saw an increase in the visual imaging of musicians themselves, and the intellectual community in general. Among those present at Wrexham in 1820 had been the painter Hugh Hughes, and it was there that he met Ifor Ceri, W.J. Rees, Gwallter Mechain, and the other prime movers in the regional eisteddfod movement, all of whom he would be commissioned to paint in the next few years. The increase in portraiture reflected a wider fashion among the middle classes that was met by the emergence of artisan painters such as Hughes, and the increasing demand for engraved images, both to be included in texts and published as individual prints. Bardd Alaw was painted at about this time by an unknown and relatively unsophisticated artisan, sitting at a window with a distant view of a winding river in hilly country, presumably intended to suggest the Afon Chwiler and the Clwydian Hills near his birthplace, Aberwheeler (Aberchwiler). In his hand he holds a score and behind him stands his harp. The identity of the score is unclear, but in an engraving of the same period he is directly associated with the *Welsh Melodies* of 1821–2, which lie on the table

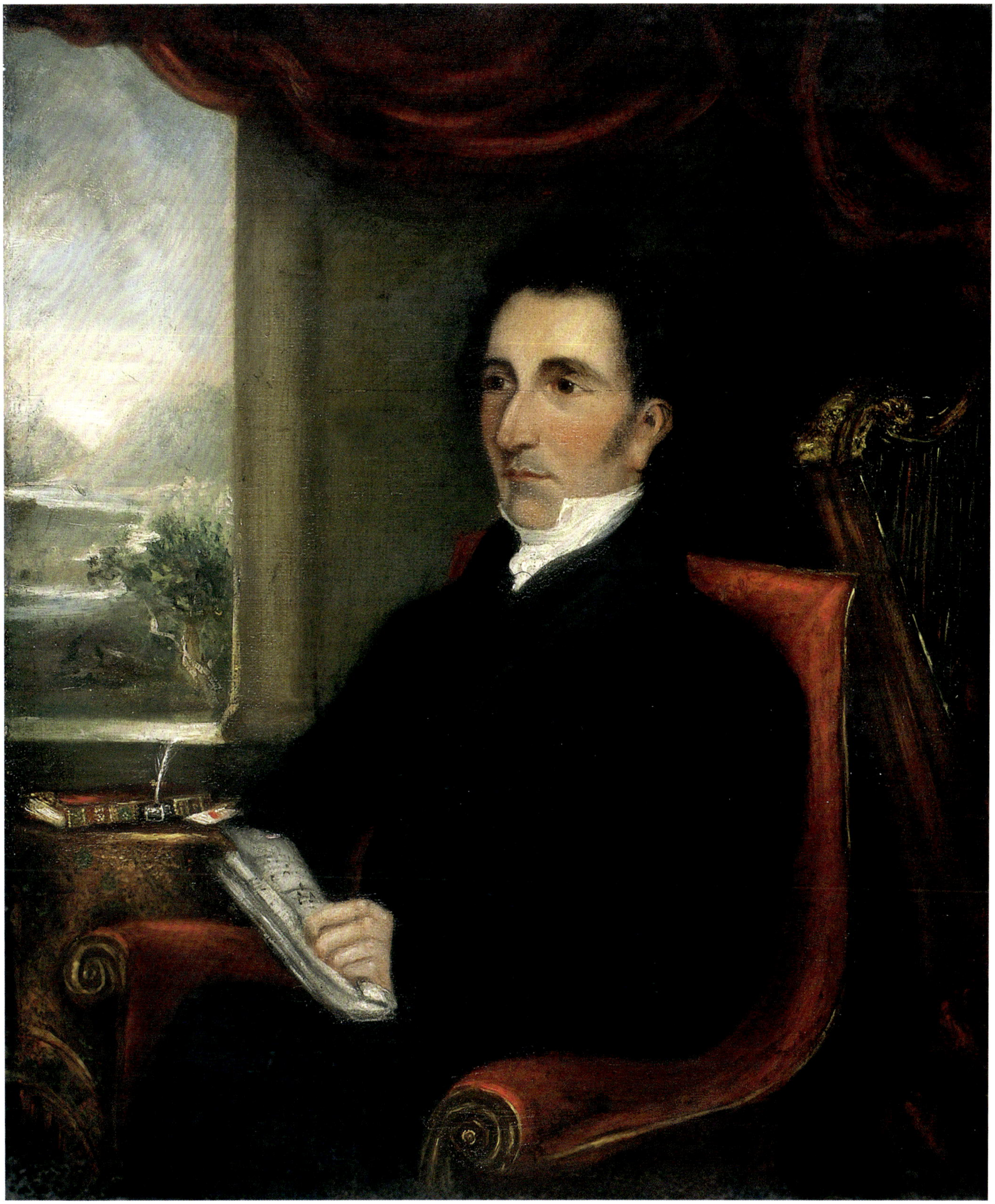

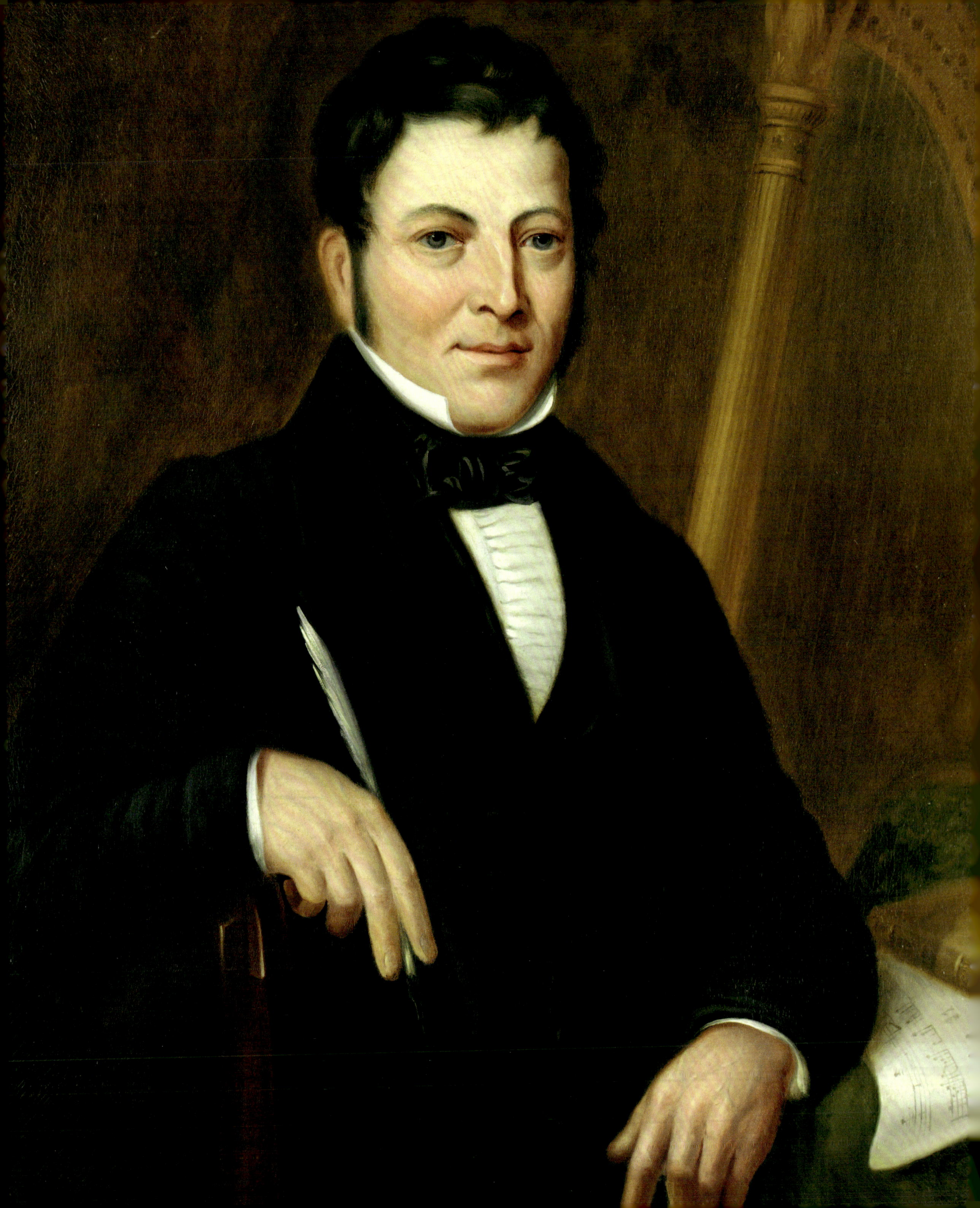

toward which he leans. The portrait was based on a miniature by Cornelius[25] and lithographed by Edward Morton, an artist who produced theatrical and musical subjects, in addition to portraits.[26]

Two more of the most prominent harpers of the period, Benjamin Cunnah and Richard Roberts, were also celebrated in portraits. Cunnah came from a middle-class Flintshire family in trade. He was praised by Bardd Alaw in *Welsh Melodies* in 1809, and was successful in attracting the patronage of many gentry families in the borders. He settled at Ruabon, where he secured the post of organist at St Mary's Church. His portrait celebrates him as a harper and also as a composer. His *New Welch Music ... for Harp or Piano Forte*, had been published with the support of nearly 300 subscribers sometime between 1805–6. The painter of the portrait is unknown, but it is a competent work which, on the basis of the sitter's elegant apparel, was apparently produced in about 1820, though he appears younger than his late forties. At this time, Cunnah was much in the public eye as the result of an unfortunate series of disputes with Richard Roberts, who was a generation younger. In a close contest at the Wrexham Eisteddfod, Cunnah had been placed second to Roberts, contrary to the opinion of some among the audience.[27] Cunnah felt that he had been unfairly treated, and when he was beaten again the following year at Caernarfon, where the adjudicator was none other than Roberts himself, personal animosity was suspected. The reporter for the *Chester Courant* made the point that Cunnah's 'sweet and enchanting' performance 'drew forth the loudest cheering and bravo from every quarter.'[28]

25 Unidentified, but possibly Cornelius Beavis Durham.

26 His signature appears on the illustration to *Jenny Jones*, one of the most popular of the many Parry song settings published as sheet music. See below, pp. 188–9.

27 Following the victory of Roberts in 1820, the rules surrounding the harp competitions were questioned by Bardd Alaw in *The Cambro-Briton*, 12 (November 1820), pp. 139–42, although he had not himself been present at the event.

28 *Chester Courant*, 2 October 1821.

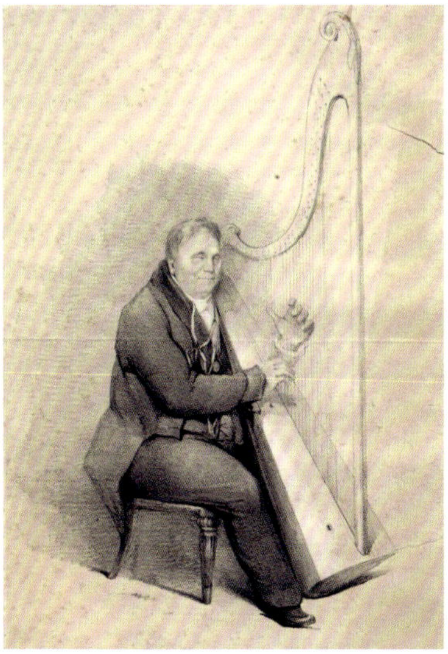

120 Unknown artist, *Richard Roberts*, 1829

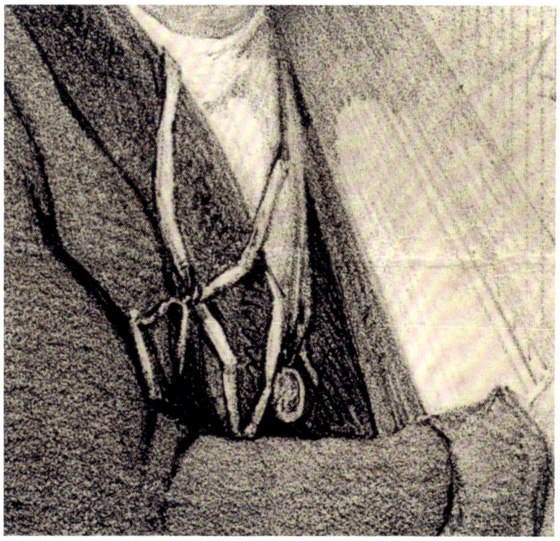

119 Unknown artist, *Benjamin Cunnah*, c.1820

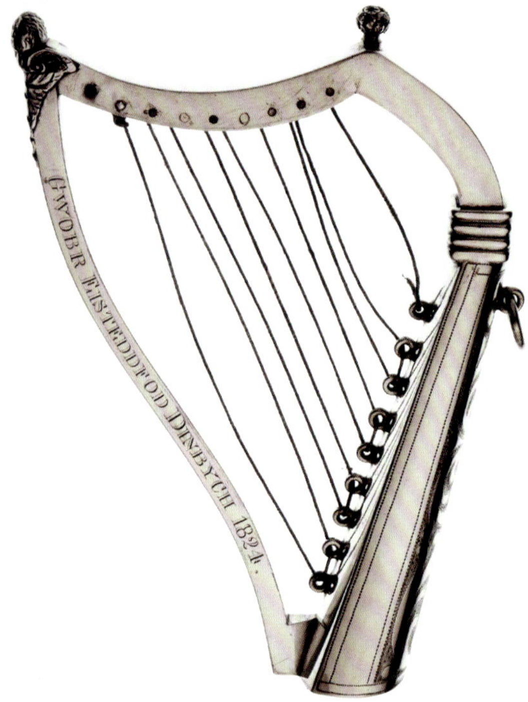

In 1822, the ongoing spat was revived in the public mind, when the *Salopian Journal* reported that Cunnah had been heard to say 'that he had been wronged at Wrexham as well as at Caernarvon, and it has also been hinted by some of his friends, that Mr Roberts had manifested towards him what they called "Gwenwyn" [poison].'[29] In an act of solidarity, Cunnah's supporters resolved to award him a retrospective silver medal, which was presented to him at a meeting of the Chester Cymmrodorion on 1 March 1823, where the harper performed. A portrait of Roberts, known only in its engraved version, was taken some years later, since the harper was depicted adorned with both the silver harp that he had won over Cunnah at Wrexham, and the gold harp which he would win at Denbigh in 1828. In the following year, the portrait was presented as the frontispiece to Roberts's *Cambrian Harmony: Being a Collection of Welch Airs Never Before Published, Arranged as they were originally performed By The Ancient Britons, Adapted for the Harp & Piano Forte.*[30]

121 *Silver Harp awarded to Henry Humphreys, Denbigh Eisteddfod*, 1824

Between his most notable victories, Roberts had been involved at the Denbigh Eisteddfod of 1824 in another spat. Henry Humphreys won the silver harp – a trophy that survives – but the *North Wales Gazette* reported a remark made by Roberts to the effect that he had not deserved to do so. To resolve the matter, Humphreys challenged Roberts to compete for a prize of twenty guineas, but Roberts raised the stakes to forty.[31]

The year of 1824 was notable also for the earliest visual record of an eisteddfod competition in progress. The scene was drawn at the event organised in Welshpool by the Powys Cymmrodorion where Bardd Alaw was in charge of the music and Viscount Clive presided:

> Mr Parry called the Vocalists to accompany the Welsh Harp, after the manner of the Antient Britons. There were eight candidates, namely:
>
> Pierce Jones, Evan Jones, Richard Williams, Richard Jones,
> John Hughes, Thomas Edwards, John Evans, Owen Griffith.

29 *Salopian Journal*, 18 September 1822.

30 'Dublin: Published for the author, and to be had at his residence, Carnarvon: 1829.'

31 *North Wales Gazette*, 25 November 1824.

This excited considerable interest. Such was the enthusiasm of two of the candidates, that they even applauded those competitors against whom they were contending. Mr Parry, on behalf of the judges said, that there was peculiar difficulty in deciding on the merits: for the question was not merely who sang best with the Harp? but the merit and difficulty lay in the art with which the singer changed the metre.

The candidates were at length reduced to two, namely, John Evans, and Thomas Edwards, both residents of the vicinity of Corwen. These two men with great simplicity and kindly feeling towards each other, then declared that as they were neighbours, they declined contending against one another. On this being announced, the Noble President applauded such honest and warm-hear[t]ed friendship, and said, that he would personally confer a Medal upon the unsuccessful candidate.– (Immense cheering.)

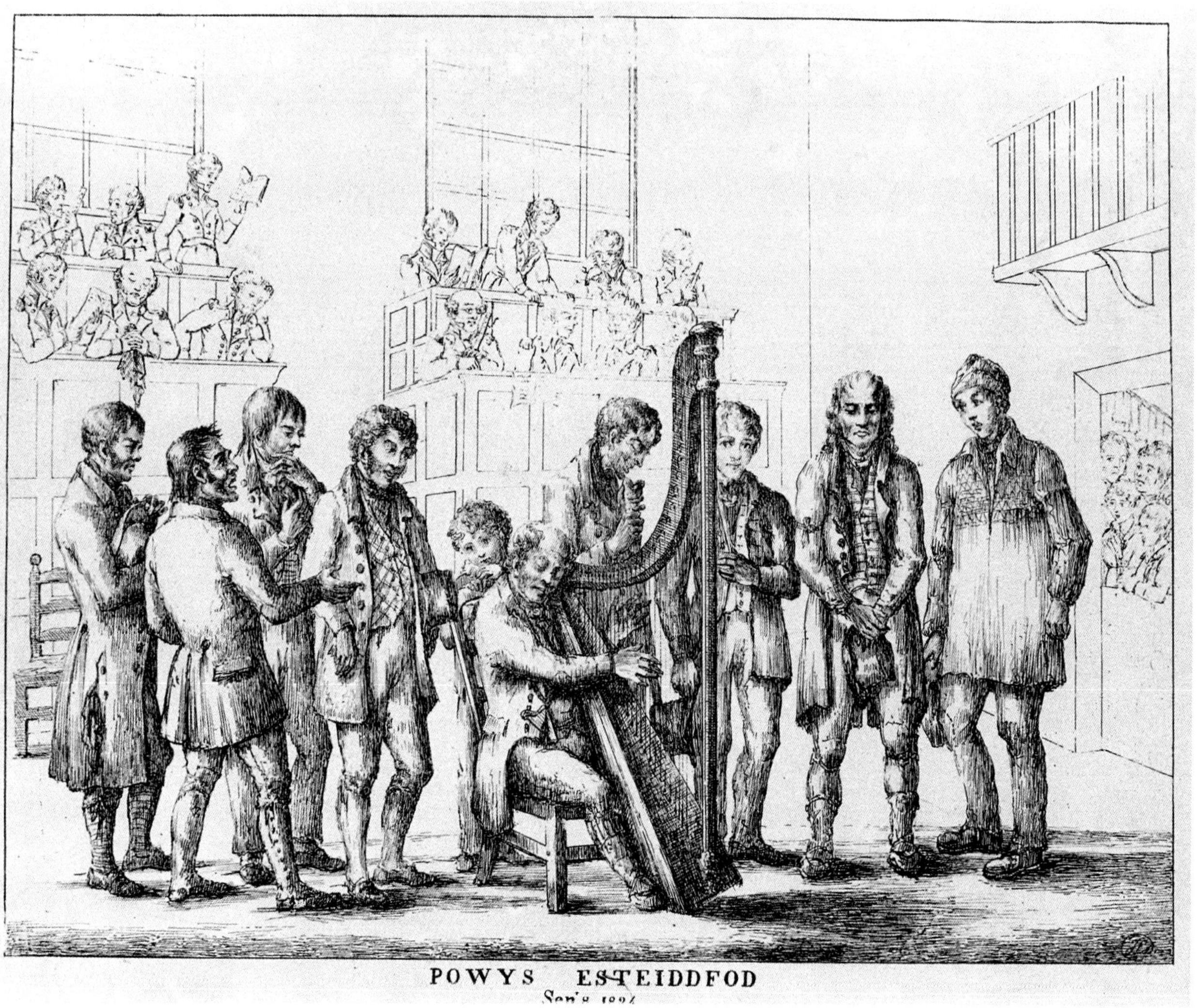

122 Unknown artist, *Powys Esteiddfod*, 1824

> His Lordship added, that a noble Lady near him, was so much interested by the manner and appearance of the blind Vocalist, Richard Williams, that, she requested to present him with a Medal also.– The blind man sung several humorous stanzas which convulsed the meeting with laughter. He was then led along the platform to his noble and amiable Patroness on this occasion, whose benevolent feelings were agitated even to tears while she hung upon the neck of the lowly-clad and blind, but merry Cambrian, the Silver Medal. The peasant, as he receded, grasped the token of kindness which the fair hand conferred upon him, and with genuine native gallantry kissed it with ardour, and, held it up in triumph to the company.[32]

It seems likely that this particular incident stimulated the production of the image, since Richard Williams is clearly distinguished, directly behind the harper – who is, perhaps, Henry Humphreys, once again the winner of the silver harp. The portrait is notable because it shows Williams with a *pastwn*, indicating the continuing tradition of recitation or chanting while marking the beat with a heavy staff – a tradition first imaged by Moses Griffith for Thomas Pennant, nearly fifty years earlier.

123 Moses Griffith, *Datceiniad*, c.1778–81

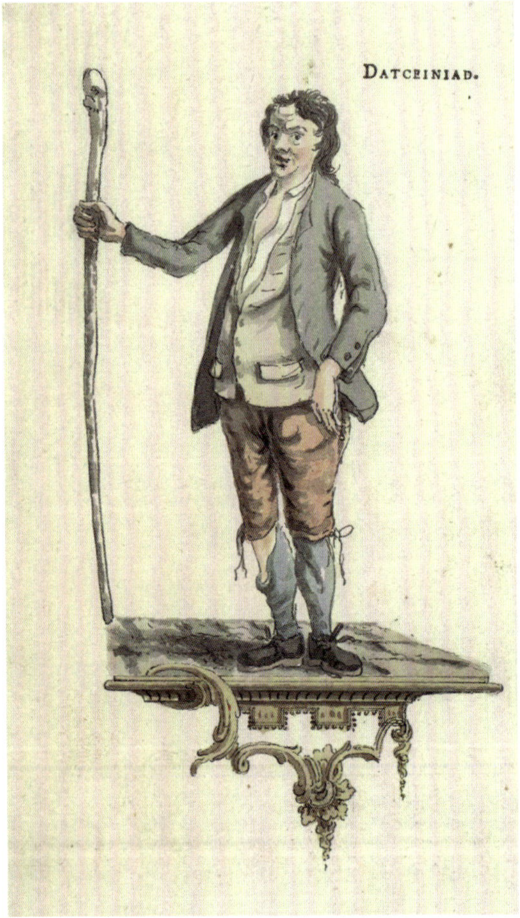

The 1824 Powys Eisteddfod engraving emphasises the distinction, equally clear in the written commentary, between the class status of the audience, dressed in their finery and seated in the lofty boxes, and the competitors, who wear the everyday clothes of the common people – and whose supporters, excluded by convention and the price of tickets, crowd at the door for a glimpse of the proceedings. The patrons belonged to a world at a huge remove from that of the patronised – as also were the intellectuals engaged in the construction of tradition at a social remove from the practitioners. The fact that the *Chester Courant*, three years earlier, at Caernarfon, had chosen to single out the appearance of the only harper from a middle-class background and with close gentry associations, Benjamin Cunnah, tends to reinforce the rule: 'His harp was beautifully clean and elegant, and in appearance alone worthy to bring before an audience, chiefly composed of the first rank and consequence in the country.'[33]

THE RELIGIOUS DIVIDE

In 1802, in *The Bardic Museum*, Edward Jones, Bardd y Brenin, had pointed to a new force in the land that threatened to undermine the efforts of the bardic revivalists to strengthen the national brand. Jones raised the spectre of Methodism:

> The sudden decline of national Minstrelsy, and Customs of Wales, is in a great degree to be attributed to the fanatic impostors, or illiterate plebeian preachers, who have too often been suffered to over-run the country, misleading the greater part of the common people from their lawful Church ... In the course of my excursions through the Principality, I have met with several Harpers and Songsters, who actually had been prevailed upon by those erratic strollers to relinquish their profession, from the idea that it was sinful. The consequence is, Wales, which was formerly one of the merriest, and happiest countries in the World, is now become one of the dullest.[34]

Bardd y Brenin's perception of the current situation was a highly prejudicial interpretation of an evolution of Welsh identification with song and melody that would lead not to the destruction of music but to its reorientation towards praise in a Christian context, outside the Established Church. Like many of his contemporaries in the employ of that Church, of the gentry and, in his case, also of the court, Jones regarded the rise of Nonconformist denominations (but in particular the Methodists within his own English Church) as a threat as dangerous as Napoleon to the social order on which he depended. Beneath his words, the distant echo of the Tudor legislation regulating minstrelsy resonates. During the French wars, Methodists suffered accusations of disloyalty and Jacobinism on the grounds of their increasing alienation from the Established Church and, by implication, from the crown. The accusations were of sufficient seriousness to cause their leader, Thomas Charles, to write a response, *The Welsh Methodists Vindicated*, in 1802 – the same year in which Bardd y Brenin's complaint was published. His allegation of Methodist suppression of the tradition voiced a widespread perception among the old guard that would prove influential over a long period.[35]

It is certainly the case that some Methodists regarded popular secular music with disapproval. One of the earliest female harpers known by name, Elen Owen of Dolgellau, was reported to have 'put her harp under her bed forever'[36]

32 Ibid., 23 September 1824.

33 *Chester Courant*, 2 October 1821.

34 Edward Jones, *The Bardic Museum, of Primitive British Literature* ... (London, 1802), p. xvi.

35 Bardd y Brenin developed an international perspective on musical affairs that was unique among his Welsh colleagues, and that surely affected his perception of events at home. In touch with musicians and antiquarians in many parts of the world, his knowledge of musical practice extended from Portugal to China and even Australia. In London, his international associates were distinguished. Johann Christian Bach wrote a Sonata 'purposely' for him to play, which he published in his *Musical Remains: or the compositions of Handel, Bach, Abel, Giuliani, &c: selected from original manuscripts never before published* ... (London, 1796), p. 28.

36 Robert Griffith, *Llyfr Cerdd Dannau* (Caernarfon, 1913), p. 258.

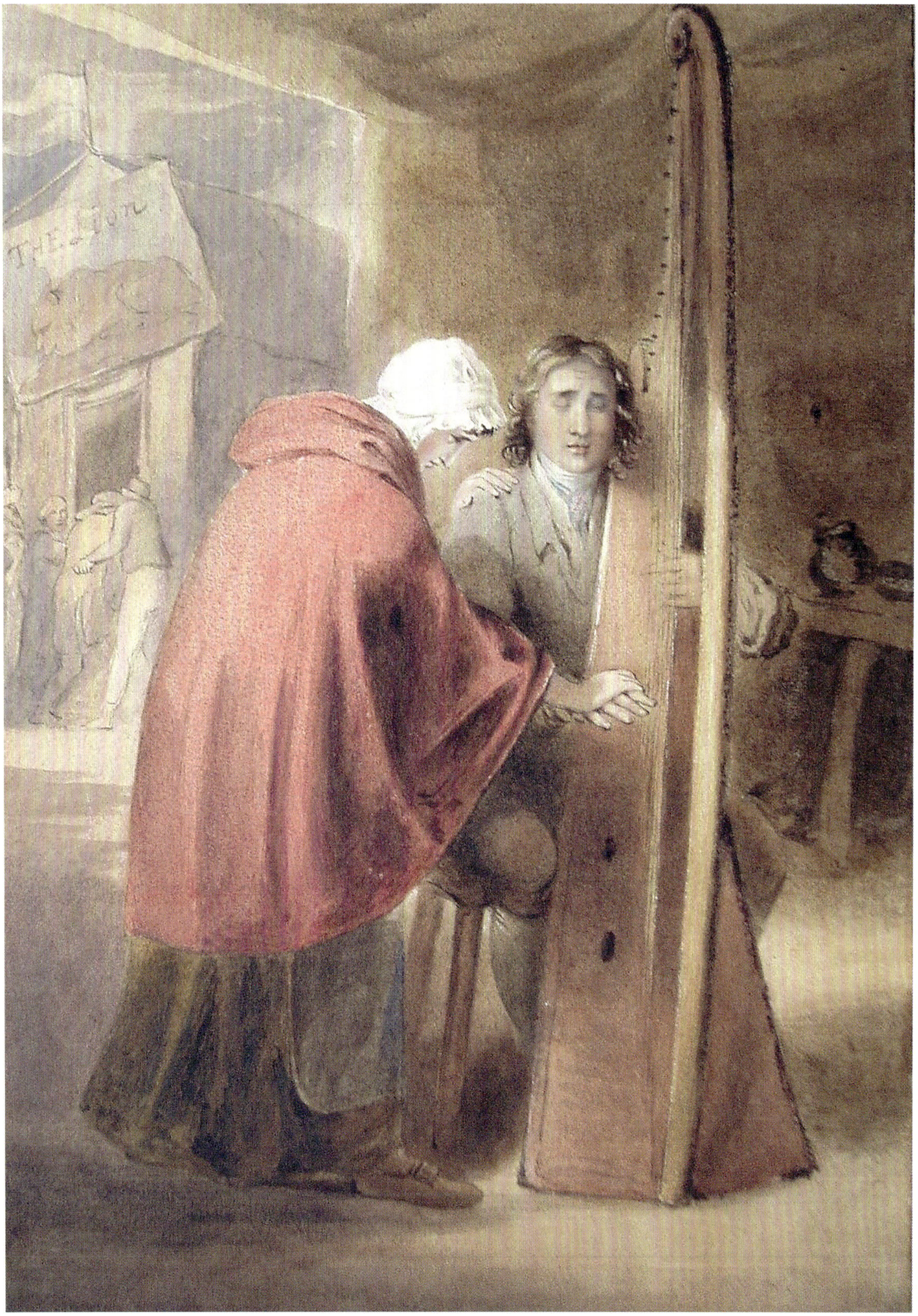
THE Lion

after joining the Methodists. Much of the disapproval of Nonconformists arose because the harp was so often to be heard in the taverns of the country and was associated in their minds, therefore, with drunkenness – with 'carousing in alehouses',[37] licentiousness, and the generally unruly behaviour which it was their mission to eradicate. Thomas Charles himself campaigned to rid Wales of the music of the harp – excepting only 'the golden harps of heaven'. He described the custom of the people in Bala from the middle of the eighteenth century into his own time:

> On Saturday nights, especially in the summer, the young people, men and women, held what they called 'singing evenings', in which they amused themselves, singing to the harp and the dance, till the break of dawn on the Sabbath. In this town (Bala) on the Sabbath afternoons they would sing and dance in the Taverns and play tennis at the Hall … In the summer, Interludes would be played in the Hall on Sabbath afternoons; the gentry and the common people coming together in this way, to pollute the Lord's day.[38]

The editor of Charles's letters noted the leader of the Methodists' particular distaste for 'the national instrument of Wales': 'It is said that Mr Charles was so much under the influence of the recollection of the interludes, that it was quite painful to him, in after years, to remain anywhere near where a harp was being played.'[39] On the other hand, Charles was certainly not opposed to singing, if it took place in the appropriate context. Writing of the hymns of William Williams, Pantycelyn, he noted that 'Some of the verses in his Hymns are like burning embers, heating and enflaming all the emotions when sung, causing them to be repeated often until the people leap with rejoicing.'[40]

At the Liverpool Academy art exhibition in 1811 – the very year in which the Methodists broke with the Church of England and established themselves as an independent denomination – the London painter Henry James Richter exhibited a picture entitled *A Blind Welsh Harper*. Uniquely, it alluded to the place of the harp in this national moral debate. Significantly, it was owned by Hester Frances Williams Wynn, who was married to Sir Henry Watkin Williams Wynn, the third son of the 4th Baronet of Wynnstay, patron of the iconic John Parry and owner of at least two portraits of that earlier blind harper. The original painting by Richter is lost but it is known through a copy made by Lady Mary Leighton.[41] It depicted a blind young man instructed by a woman, who guided his hand on

124 Lady Mary Leighton after Henry James Richter, *A Blind Welsh Harper*, c.1830

37 Thomas Charles, *The Welsh Methodists Vindicated* (Chester, 1802), p. 69.

38 'Ymddyddan rhwng Scrutator a Senex …', *Trysorfa Ysbrydol*, 1, 1 (1799), p. 31.

39 William Hughes, *Life and Letters of the Rev. Thomas Charles B.A. of Bala* (Rhyl, 1881), p. 19.

40 *Trysorfa Ysbrydol*, 2, 11 (1813), p. 454.

41 Lady Mary Leighton (1810–64) is best known as an artist for her double portrait of Sarah Ponsonby and Eleanor Butler, the Ladies of Llangollen, which was engraved by Richard James Lane in 1836 and distributed widely. While staying at their home, Plas Newydd, Leighton also painted views in the grounds. Mary Leighton's brother, the Revd John Parker, painted extensively in Wales. An inscription on *The Blind Welsh Harper* records that the original painting was burnt in the Wynnstay fire of 1858.

to the strings of a triple harp, played on the left shoulder. Clearly the painter was well informed about Welsh practice, and he did have at least an indirect association with Wales. Before studying at the Royal Academy, he was taught by Thomas Stothard, and the two remained friends. Stothard was painting at Hafod for Thomas Johnes in the period when Richter exhibited his harper, and although no Welsh tour by him is documented, the possibility arises that he visited Wales in pursuance of this friendship.

But whether the picture was based on an observed incident or was an imaginative construct, its narrative differed profoundly from the work of tourists such as Ibbetson, who was either unaware of, or felt unconstrained by, moral debate about music in Wales. In the background of Richter's picture, a group of drunken men enter a tavern, The Lion, with a mountain scene beyond. One of the men glances over his shoulder towards the young harper and his instructress, who work inside a house or barn. They have turned their backs on the tavern. In contrast with the mainstream eighteenth-century tradition, whether that of the historical bard or of his modern descendant, Richter's harper was conspicuously decoupled from the mountain wilderness with which the Romantics associated him, and relocated in the company of a chaste and musical country maiden, a type soon to become representative of Welsh identity through the work of mid-nineteenth-century artists. Richter located the music of the harp in the context of Christian virtue, though exemplified here not by angels in heaven but by a woman's kindness and empathy in the real world. Clearly, it was not difficult for Christians to perceive a metaphor in the contrast between the blindness that afflicted many Welsh harpers and the beauty of the music they played. The blindness of the harper represented both the inability to see God and the beauty of the vision revealed when their eyes were opened to Him through music. It was certainly a metaphor that appealed to Richter. In 1812, he painted what would become his most celebrated work, *Christ Giving Sight to the Blind*. The close relationship between the subject matter of this picture and *A Blind Welsh Harper*, painted in successive years, seems unlikely to be coincidental.[42]

Eight years after the exhibition of Richter's painting in Liverpool, the 1819 Eisteddfod at Carmarthen brought the question to the fore. Prior to the Eisteddfod, it appears that pious middle-class Nonconformists living in Wales had paid little attention to the cultural revival and its musical aspect, which was largely in the hands of the London intelligentsia and the gentry. The high

42 *Christ Giving Sight to the Blind* was bought by the trustees of the British Institution for the considerable sum of 500 guineas, and later presented to the New Church, Greenwich, as an altarpiece. The metaphysical significance of light for Richter, and the use of painting as a medium for moral enquiry, was apparent again in 1817, when he published the pamphlet *Day-light; a recent discovery in the art of painting, with hints on the philosophy of the fine arts, and on that of the human mind, as first dissected by Emanuel Kant.*

43 *Seren Gomer*, 2 (1819), p. 233. The Bishop was Burgess.

44 Ibid., 'Pob un a'i delyn aur,/Mab Mair a gaiff y clod.'

profile of the Carmarthen Eisteddfod and the subsequent meetings at Wrexham and Caernarfon, which they were invited to attend and did so in considerable numbers, forced them to face the issue. Writing in *Seren Gomer*, the editor, Joseph Harris, approached the matter from a personal standpoint in his review of the proceedings which, perhaps to his surprise, he had much enjoyed:

> There was nothing indecorous associated with this music that the ignorant could despise; aside from a Bishop and large numbers of priests of the Established Church, many ministers were present, and many believers of different denominations among the Nonconformists. As it happens, I had never heard a harp before, other than in passing a tavern, and since dissipation and immorality are commonly attached to such places, it was not appropriate for me to stay and listen.[43]

Although Joseph Harris, 'Gomer', was a Baptist, it may be that the death of Thomas Charles in 1814 facilitated a general liberalisation in attitudes. Indeed, Gomer himself offered a biblical justification of the harp, adding that 'misuse of anything on one occasion is not a reason why good use should not be made of it on another.' The sight of the silver harp, worth five guineas, to be awarded as a prize to the best harper only brought to mind the wonderful vision of angels:

> Each with his golden harp,
> The son of Mary to praise.[44]

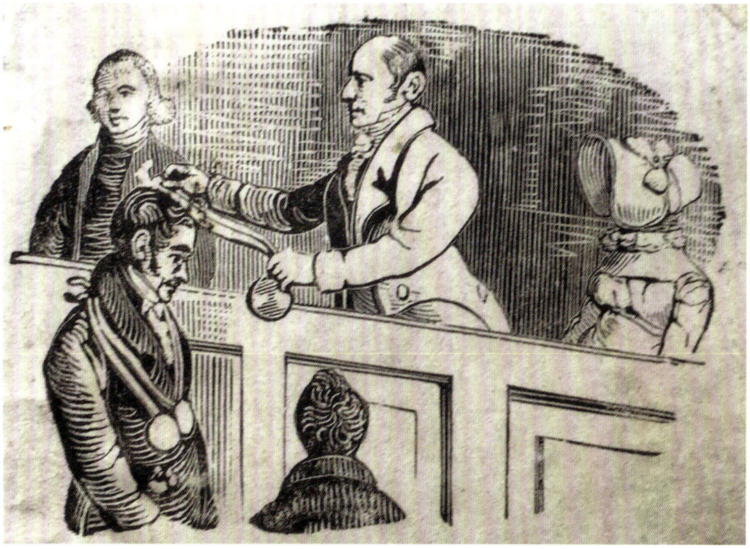

125 Hugh Hughes, *Awarding an Eisteddfod Medal*, *c.*1820

The Wrexham Eisteddfod in 1820 attracted young Nonconformists such as William Williams, 'Caledfryn', who were soon to become prominent public figures. As we have seen, the painter Hugh Hughes, on tour in Wales from his London home, would profit by commissions given by the distinguished company that he met there for the first time. Notwithstanding his religious views – he was a Methodist of deep conviction – he enjoyed what he saw and heard:

> There is but little in the concert that is not consistent with reason and with simple morality, and much that is wonderful and beautiful and expressive of marvellous human talents that seem perfectly sensible.[45]

Hughes came to this opinion from an awareness of the importance of music as praise. He recorded in his diary on several occasions his enjoyment of the company of singers. At Llanidloes in 1820, he noted spending a Sunday morning with the Cleaton family, fellow Methodists who were celebrated for their singing. On another occasion, working in Radnorshire in September 1820, he met unexpectedly with John Cleaton at a fair:

> Figs, and beer, and nuts, and agreeable company, and wonderful singing, were the last things I enjoyed in the mountains of Radnorshire. T.J. is a wonderful singer, and in this respect every one of his numerous family are like him, he is also a poet and a good linguist, and a wise and entertaining story-teller … Mr J. Cleaton, perhaps the best singer in Wales, was one of the three I met at the fair, and he is at present among the melodious family of T.J., and their music is so lovely that I forget the speed of passing time, and it is turned nine o'clock in the evening before we begin our journey of thirteen miles.[46]

On the other hand, a year later in Haverfordwest, Hughes was dismayed by the congregations that he joined for Sunday worship:

> In the three places of worship that I attended I noticed only a very few singing at all, just four or five men and one or two women in a corner, and those in the last chapel remained seated. The sight of them was disgraceful, and the sound rather embarrassing.[47]

45 NLW MS Cwrt Mawr 130A, The Diary of Hugh Hughes, 14 September 1820.

46 Ibid., 26 September 1820.

47 Ibid., 30 September 1821.

The earliest attempt to improve standards and the understanding of music with the object of improving its use in chapel among Welsh speakers had been made by John Williams, known as 'Sion Singer'. In his youth he had become a travelling teacher of music, and in 1797 he committed his knowledge to paper in his *Cyfaill mewn Llogell*, which explained the gamut and gave examples of hymns appropriate to various occasions. Nothing further on the subject was published in the Welsh language until 1816, when Hugh Hughes, working with Ishmael Davies, the Trefriw printer, produced a frontispiece to a pioneering book of settings in Welsh, entitled *Mawl yr Arglwydd*. It was the work of John Ellis, a saddler from Llanrwst. Facing the title page, placed in a rondel formed by Ellis's setting of words from Psalm 41, was Hughes's portrait of the author. Ellis would develop his career as a composer and a peripatetic teacher of music, later moving

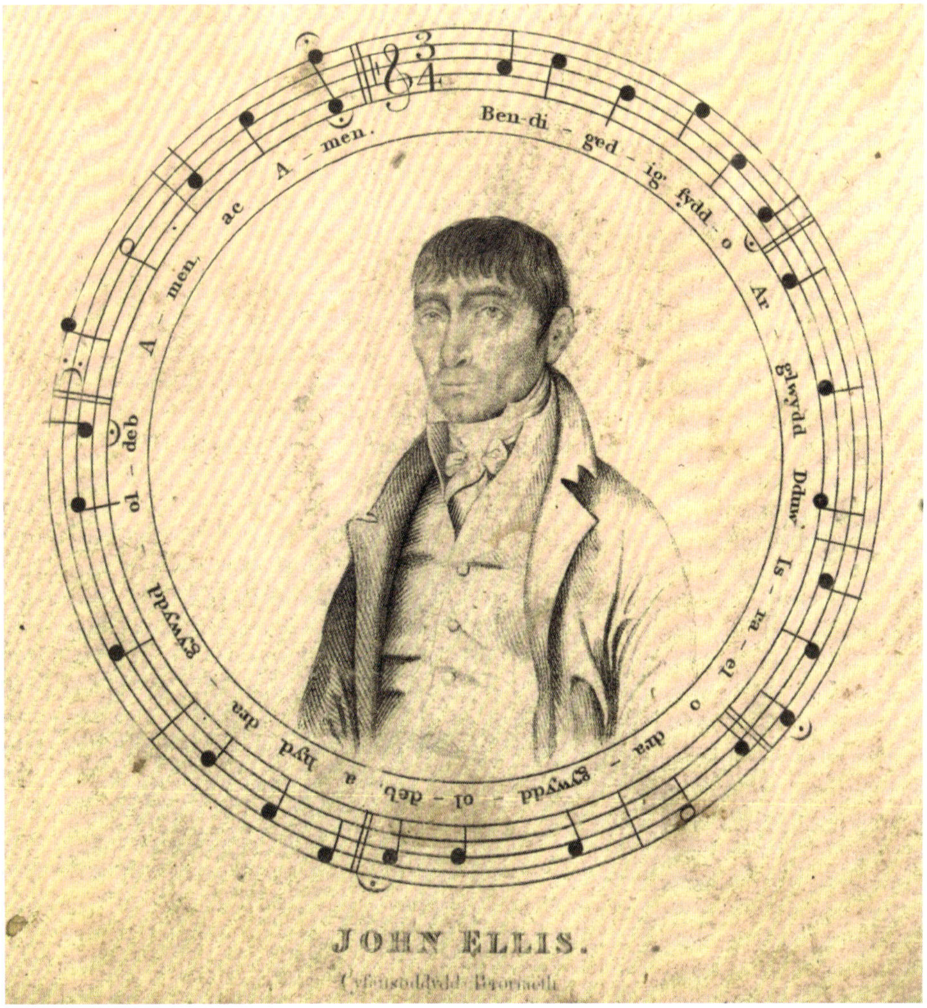

126 Hugh Hughes, *John Ellis, Cyfansoddydd Peroriaeth*, 1816

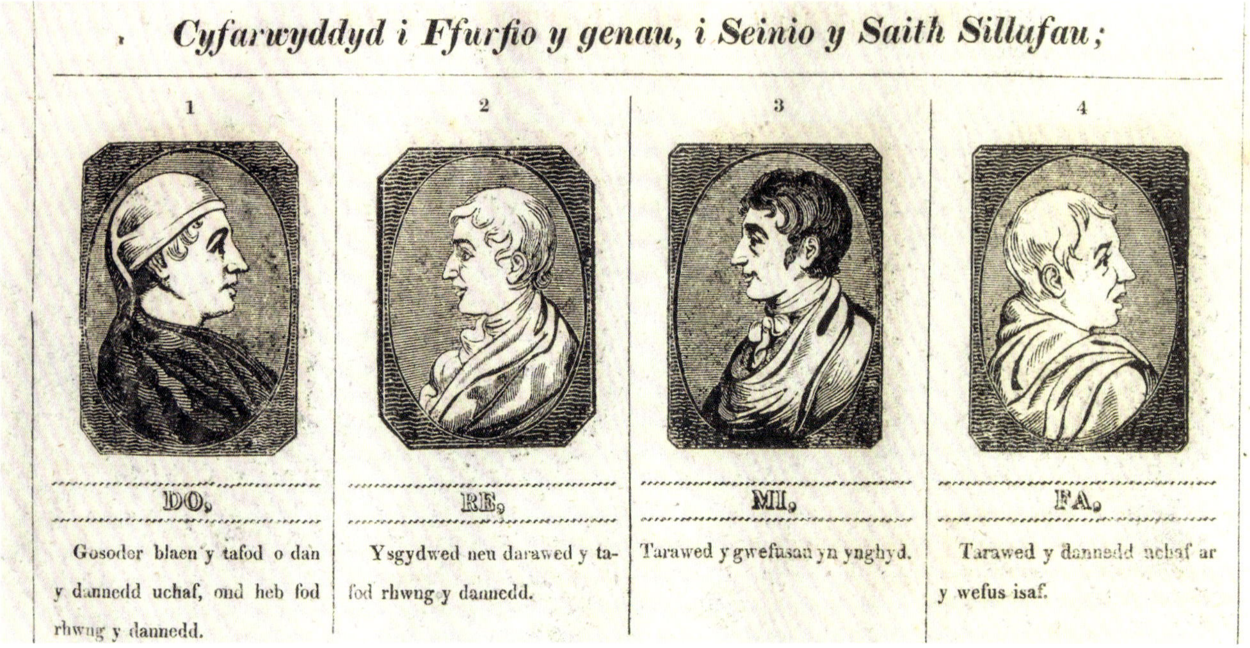

127 Hugh Hughes, illustrations to Owen Jones Williams, *Egwyddorion Canu*, 1817

to Liverpool to lead the singing at Pall Mall, the city's original Welsh Calvinistic Methodist chapel, where Hugh Hughes himself had been a member.[48] Whether the idea of the circular settings, which framed the author's portrait and was repeated on two further pages, was that of the engraver or of the author is unclear.

Underlining the growing desire among the Welsh-speaking Nonconformist community to strengthen the role of song in their practice, in the following year of 1817, another musician, Owen Jones Williams, published a more theoretical work on the subject, *Egwyddor-ddysg Ragegorawl, neu Gatecism ar Reolau Cerddoriaeth*. An addition to Williams's original text appeared in 1818, known more simply as *Egwyddorion Canu*. Once again Hugh Hughes was involved, producing a series of wood engravings to teach the voicing of the sol-fa system on its first appearance in Wales. The syllables used to sound the notes had been formalised some five years earlier by Sarah Ann Glover in Norwich, completing a process of evolution in many parts of Europe over centuries. However, Glover's system was not published until 1835, and Williams's source is unknown. His system varied only in detail from that of his English contemporary for Williams adopted the syllable 'Si', rather than 'Te' for the seventh note.

The history of the publication had been troubled, to say the least, as the exasperated author himself explained. He had been at work on his book since 1793. The original engraver commissioned to illustrate the text in London was

48 NLW CMA 5971, proof sheets of an essay by William Williams, Plas Llecheiddior, 'John Ellis y Cerddor, 1760-1839', 1927.

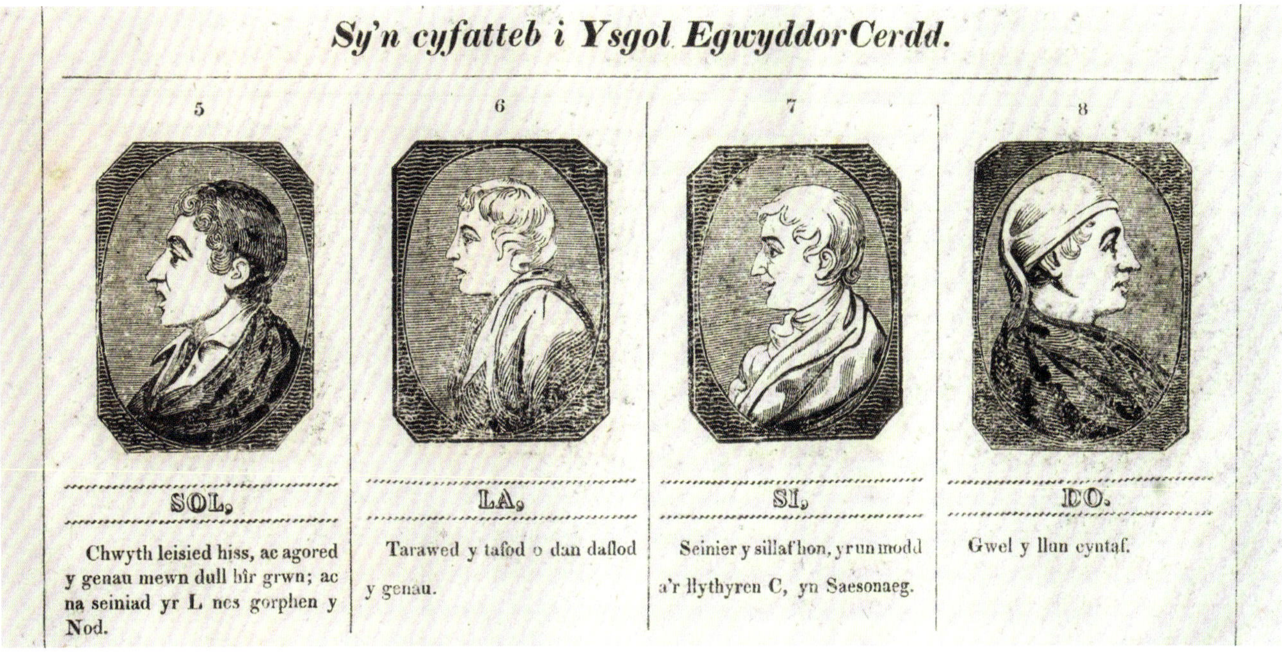
Sy'n cyfatteb i Ysgol Egwyddor Cerdd.
5
6
7
8
SOL.
LA.
SI.
DO.
Chwyth leisied hiss, ac agored y genau mewn dull hîr grwn; ac na seiniad yr L nes gorphen y Nod.
Tarawed y tafod o dan daflod y genau.
Seinier y sillaf hon, yr un modd a'r llythyren C, yn Saesonaeg.
Gwel y llun cyntaf.

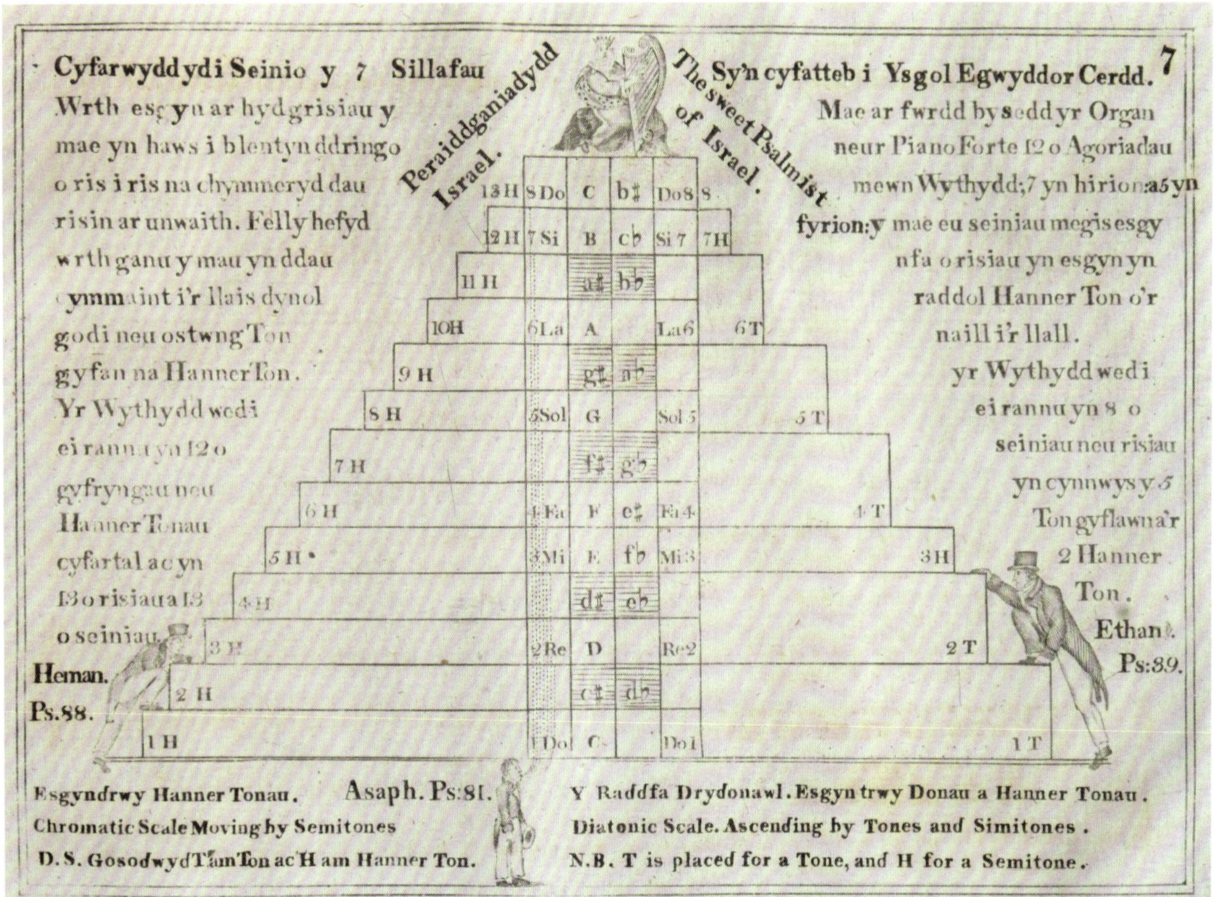
Cyfarwyddyd i Seinio y 7 Sillafau
Peraiddganiadydd Israel.
The sweet Psalmist of Israel.
Sy'n cyfatteb i Ysgol Egwyddor Cerdd. 7
Wrth esgyn ar hyd grisiau y mae yn haws i blentyn ddringo o ris i ris na chymmeryd dau risin ar unwaith. Felly hefyd wrth ganu y mae yn ddau cymmaint i'r llais dynol godi neu ostwng Ton gyfan na Hanner Ton. Yr Wythydd wedi ei rannu yn 12 o gyfryngau neu Hanner Tonau cyfartal ac yn 13 o risiau a 13 o seiniau.
Mae ar fwrdd bysedd yr Organ neu'r Piano Forte 12 o Agoriadau mewn Wythydd; 7 yn hirion a 5 yn fyrion; y mae eu seiniau megis esgynfa o risiau yn esgyn yn raddol Hanner Ton o'r naill i'r llall. yr Wythydd wedi ei rannu yn 8 o seiniau neu risiau yn cynnwys y 5 Ton gyflawn a'r 2 Hanner Ton.
Heman. Ps.88.
Ethan. Ps:89.
13 H
8 Do
C
Do 8
8
12 H
7 Si
B
Si 7
7 H
11 H
10 H
6 La
A
La 6
6 T
9 H
8 H
5 Sol
G
Sol 5
5 T
7 H
6 H
4 Fa
F
Fa 4
4 T
5 H
3 Mi
E
Mi 3
3 H
4 H
3 H
2 Re
D
Re 2
2 T
2 H
1 H
1 Do
C
Do 1
1 T
Esgyn drwy Hanner Tonau.
Asaph. Ps:81.
Y Raddfa Drydonawl. Esgyn trwy Donau a Hanner Tonau.
Chromatic Scale Moving by Semitones
Diatonic Scale. Ascending by Tones and Simitones.
D.S. Gosodwyd T am Ton ac H am Hanner Ton.
N.B. T is placed for a Tone, and H for a Semitone.

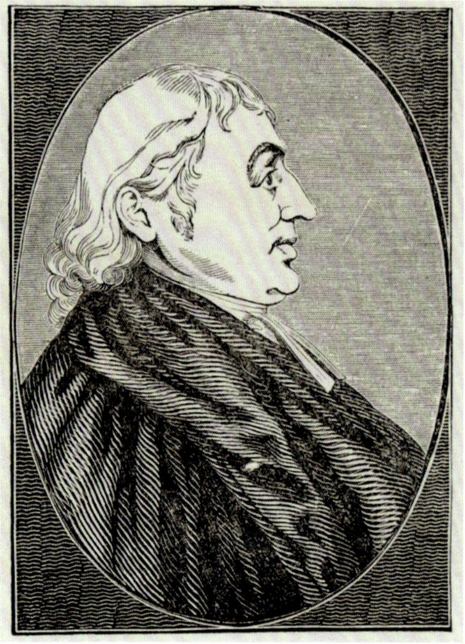

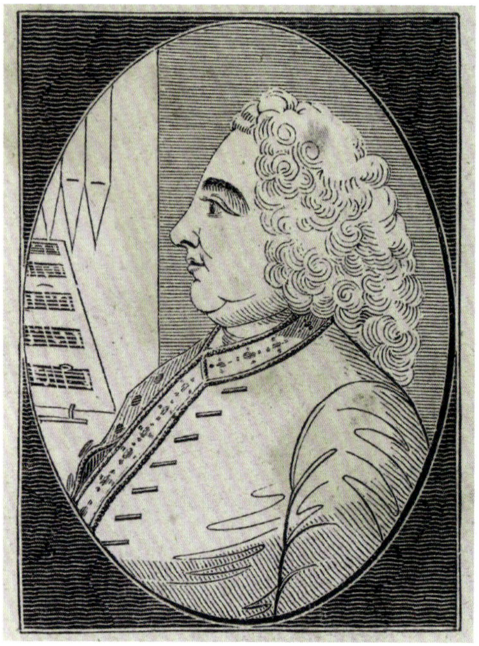

128 Hugh Hughes, *The Revd Edmwnd Prys*, 1817

129 Hugh Hughes, *George Frideric Handel*, 1817

130 J. Smith after Owen Jones Williams, *The Harp of David King of Israel*, 1839

one Skarrat, who received £18 in advance but failed to complete the plates and refused to release them to the author, as a result of what Owen Williams regarded as fraud on the part of the volume's original sponsor, an unnamed but musical gentleman in Caernarfon. The author reworked his text and proceeded to publish it himself, followed by the second volume with Hughes's illustrations. They included a schematic representation of the scale in the form of a pyramid, surmounted by King David with his harp.

Owen Williams came from a poor background, stating that:

> … his first employment was the same as that of the Patriarch Jacob's sons, namely Joseph's brethren, when Pharaoh King of Egypt asked them, what is your occupation, and they said 'thy servants are shepherds, both we and also our fathers.' Thus the author was in like predicament, at seven years old, when he was sent in his shepherd's dress to the field to keep his father's flock … At the age of nine he began to drive the plough, two horses abreast; at this age his father gave him a small reaping hook (about a span in circumference) to try his hand at reaping barley; at twelve he began to hold the plough.[49]

He was indebted to Charles Watkin Williams Wynn for getting him a job as a hall porter in the Stamp and Tax Office in 1827, which was then to him 'as a life from the dead.' The position enabled Williams to develop his work, the

49 Owen Williams, *The Harp of King David of Israel or Royal Psalms of Zion* (London, 1839). The convoluted history of Owen Williams's musical publications was explained by him firstly in *Egwyddorion Canu* and later, in more detail, in *The Harp of King David*.

"Yea, upon the harp will I praise thee, O God my God. Psalm 43. 4.
Unto thee will I sing with the harp, O thou Holy One of Israel. Psalm 71. 22.
Sing unto the Lord with the harp; with the harp, & the voice of a Psalm. Ps. 98. 5.
Praise him with the psaltery & harp: praise him with stringed instruments & Organs. Ps. 150. 3. 4.

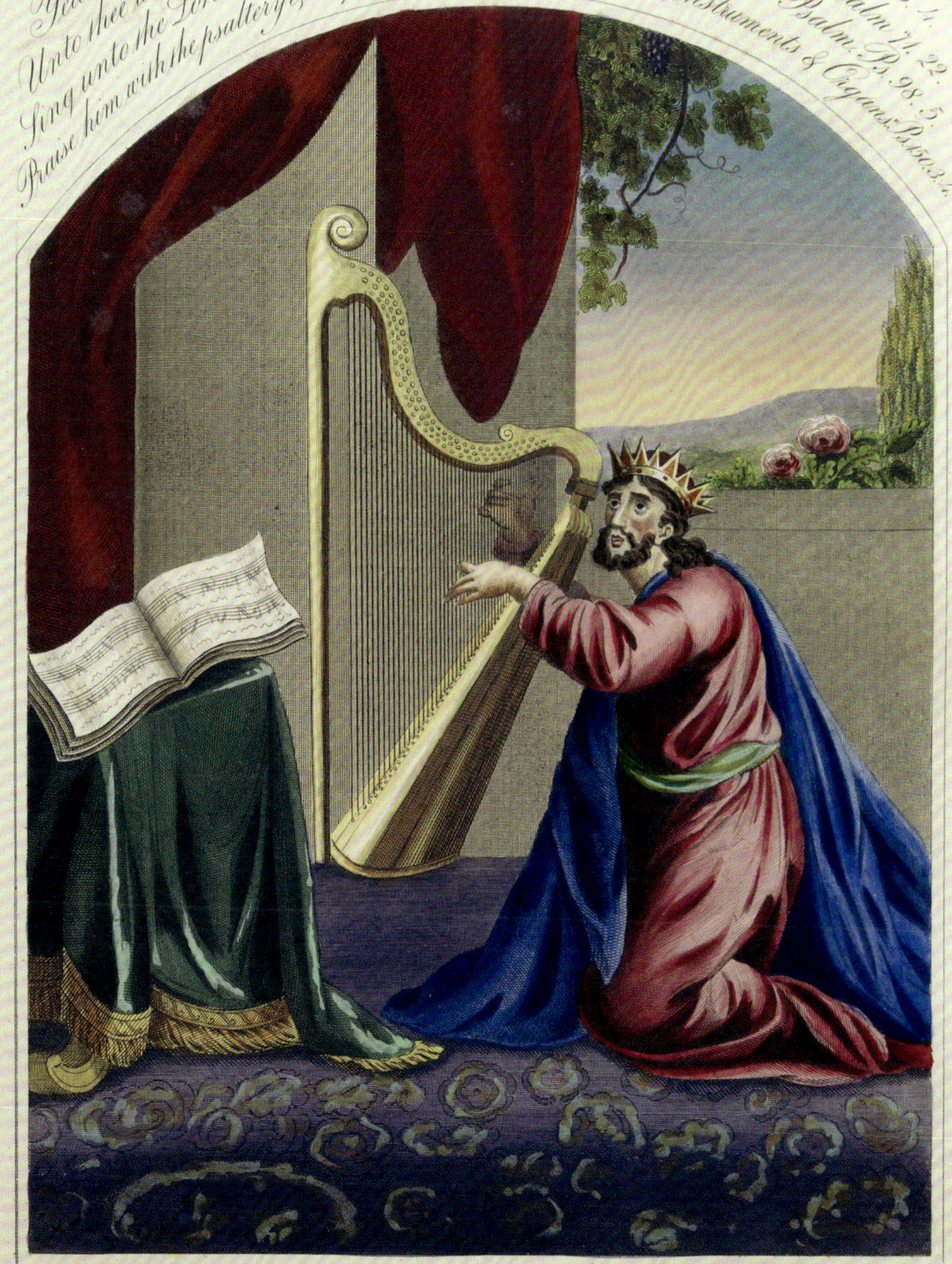

ENGRAVED BY J. SMITH, 10 KING STREET WEST SMITHFIELD, LONDON

"THE HARP OF DAVID KING OF ISRAEL"

Delineated by P. J. Williams.

April 23rd 1839

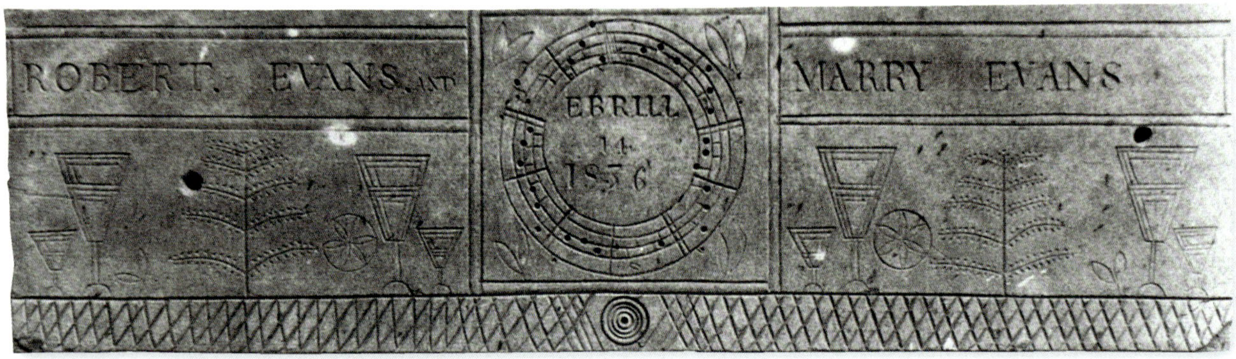

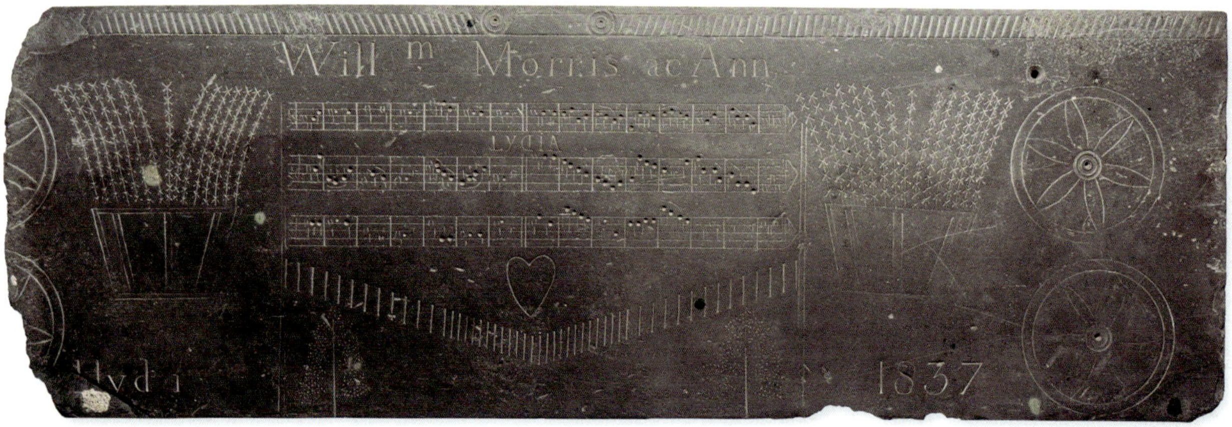

131 Probably John Parry, *Slate Lintel with Rondel*, 1836

132 Unknown maker, *Slate Lintel with the Hymn Tune 'Lydia'*, 1837

final version of which emerged in 1839. It included portrait wood engravings by Hughes of George Frideric Handel and Edmwnd Prys, originally intended for the earlier publications. The frontispiece was drawn by Williams himself. *The Harp of King David of Israel or Royal Psalms of Zion* was published on an ambitious scale, and apparently at the author's expense. But a copy belonging to Lady Llanover noted the pathetic end to his lifetime's labour: 'There was only 32 copies printed – The author drop [*sic*] down in Chancery Lane dead before any more were worked off.'[50]

133 James Cope, *Dirwest*, c.1835

The representation on a slate carving of 1836 of the psalm setting engraved in rondel format by Hugh Hughes to contain the portrait of John Ellis in *Mawl yr Arglwydd* suggests that the publication soon had an effect on musical practice among the common people in chapel. The slate is one of a group of remarkable mantelpieces made in Dyffryn Ogwen from the 1820s to the 1840s by quarry workers for their own community.[51] The slates are decorated with a range of figurative designs and patterns, and at least four include music. Three of the

50 Inscribed in NLW XM 2062 W72 (4to).

51 For the slate work, see Gwenno Caffell, *Llechi Cerfiedig Dyffryn Ogwen/The Carved Slates of Dyffryn Ogwen* (Cardiff, 1993).

CAN NEWYDD

AM LESHAD

DIRWEST.

Cenir ar "Belisle March."

Prydferthwch y Meddwyn.

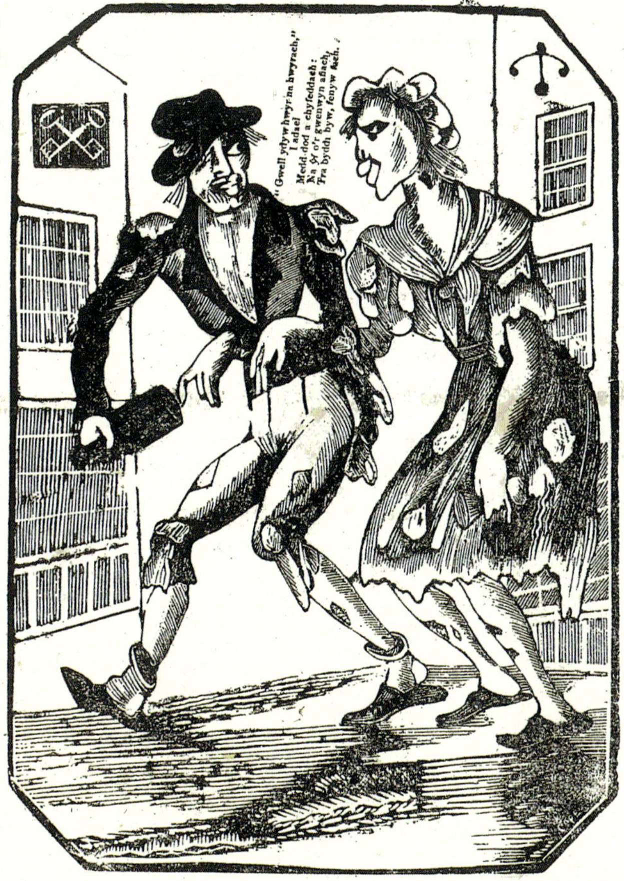

I'R Cymdeithion, dethol, doethion
Rai mwynion, fawr a mân.
Y Cymru diddig, mwyn, caredig,
'Rwy'n awr yn cynyg cân:
Yn erbyn medd'dod hynod henwaf.
Ymdrechai hyn o dro;
Gwnaeth yr hen gena anferth gynwr
Mae'n fradwr yn y fro.
Dwys holed pawb ei hun,
Pa dd'ioni ddaw i ddyn,
Wrth ddilyn meddwdod ar gwrw a
gwirod.
Mae'n bechod ar bob un;
Fe grogodd rai *transportiodd* lawer
I ddyoddef digter dwys,
A gyrodd filoedd yn annharod,
I'w gosod dan y gwys.
Fe dwyllodd lawer dyn
Yn afiach legach lun,
'Rol gwerthu eu tiroedd wedi tori,
I bob drygioni a gwŷn:
I ladd eu gwragedd, rhai i foddi,
Annedwydd ydyw'r nod,
A rhai i saethu a chrogi eu hunain,
Yn rhyw fan is y rhod.

2

Fe yrodd lawer gwr bonheddig,
Nid perygl dwedyd pwy,
I fyw i fwthyn gwael yn fethiant,
A'u plant ar hyd y plwy';
Bu llawer gwr yn siopwr siapus,
A pharchus ddawnus ddyn:
Wrth fod yn feddw nid oes gan
hwnw
Run swllt i'w elw ei hun:
Cadd llawer llongwr llon
Eu diwedd ar y don,
Trwy fod y Captain yn ei feddw-
dod,
Bu'r hynod ddamwain hon.
A llawer tref yn ulw losgwyd,
Mae'n arswyd dweyd yn wir;
Tylodi beunydd ddaeth o'i herwydd
Trwy'r gwledydd oll yn glir;
A'r hen dafarnwr tew
Yn llyncu megys llew,
Ac yntau'r meddwyn wedi cysgu,
Bron rhynu yn y rhew;
A'i wraig a'i blant fydd bron a
ll'wgu,
A'u lliw a'u lletty'n llwm,
Fel hyn trwy feddwdod daw baich
o bechod,
A llawer trallod trwm.

3

Gwell yw cymdeithas y Tee-total,
I'w chynnal tra bo chwyth;
Nid all rhai pobol, mae'n wirion-
eddol,
Mor byw'n gymedrol byth:
Ar ol i ddyn gael hanner peintyn,
Yn ddygyn fe fyn ddau,
Heb lwyr ymwrthod fel hyn mae
meddwdod,
Pur hynod yn parhau:
Chwi feddwon ffolion ffowch,
Yn dirion yma dowch,
I'r Gymdeithas a'ch ymgeledda,
Yn rhwydd â'ch enwau rhowch:
Llawer un o'r domen gododd,
A rhoddodd aur i'w rhan;
Mae effaith hon yn sobri'n union,
Y meddwon yn mhob man:
Mae sir y Fflint hoff lân,
A Dinbych fel ar dân,
A Môn ac Arfon, a muriau Meirion,
Yn hoywlon heb wahan,
[illegible] faldwyn hyfwyn hefyd,
Yn unfryd oll un iaith,
Ceir clywed miloedd yn ei moli,
A gwaeddi, Da yw'r gwaith.

4

Mae'r dynion meddwa ag oedd
ffordd yma,
Yn garpiau bylla o hyd,
Yn prynu tanwydd, cynfasa, a
rhrysa,
A bwyd rhag eisia i gyd;
Mae Doli, mawsmawr, a'i gywnau
drudfawr,
A Sianl fawr, Sir Fon,
Gadd siwt i Elis, a chôt a throwsus
Gysurus iawn i Sion;
Cadd Lowri fantell lâs,
A gywn merino i Gras
Mae Gwen a'i bonnet yn llawn
rhubana'
A Lydia a chap a *lace*;
Mae Harri, o'r Reinallt, a Huw o'r
Ynys,
Mor barchus yn y byd,
Eu gwragedd fydda yn cardota,
A'u plant yn garpia i gyd,
Am Lewis, Pen y lôn,
Trwy siroedd byddai son,
A fyddai'n curo, rhwygo a rhegi,
Gan dyngu'n hyll ei dôn;
Mae hwn a'i frodyr yn Ymwrthod-
wyr,
Mor gywir bob ag un;
Prin gallech goelio, heb eu gweled,
Mor lloned yw eu llun.

5

Fe syn i dynion y dillad n'wyddion
A brynodd Sion y Sais,
A gywn i Mari, a siôl i Sali,
Cadd Begi ddefnydd pais
Roed yntau Robin Llwyd o'r
Yn talu i'r Hawker Tea, [Aber,
A phrynu bwyd a dillad taclus,
Yn drefnus iawn o'r dre;
A Simon, mab i Sam,
A fyddai'n curo ei fam,
Sy'n awr i'w deulu yn garedig,
Heb gynyg iddynt gam.
Mae Jack y Saer, a Will y Colier,
A Deio'r Miner mawr,
A'u plant a'u gwragedd yn gysurus
A threfnus weddus wawr;
Ceir gweled Twm y crydd,
Ac yntau, Gutto'r gwŷdd,
Yn byw yn sobor a chariadus,
A Siencyn Morris sydd
A'u dillad n'wyddion, a'u tai yn
llawnion,
A'u cigau breision braf;
Ac enwi chwaneg, heb achwynion,
Yn union i chwi a wnaf.

6

Mae son trwy'r gwledydd, gwn ar
gynnydd
Am Griffith, Tan y graig,
Sy'n mynd a'i gyflog adre'n gyfan,
Yrwan at ei wraig,
A Dic y Ffatri, a'r hen Sion Hari
A Luke, gwr Neli o'r Nant,
A Ffoulk y llifiwr, a Roli'r garddwr
A'r panwr o'r Cae pant;
A Grasi o'r Berthen gron,
A gwraig i Ned, Llwynon,
Sydd yn cael lluniaeth 'nawr i'w
lloni,
'Rwy'n henwi y ddwy hon,
A gwraig Will Aaron, o Gapel
Garmon,
A digon ganddi o Dea,
Oedd er ys dyddiau yn cardota,
Yn llyma o fewn i'r lle;
Caiff merched y Pant mawr
Ddilladau gorau 'n gwawr,
A Morgan Dafydd, esgidiau new-
ydd,
Ac Elis fydd yn gawr,
A Morris Rolant, y chwarelwr,
A James y cariwr coed,
'Rol gado'r dafarn sy'n perchen
arian,
Yr wan twy na 'rioed.

7

Ffarwel bellach yn ddiballu
I'r cwrw a'r brandi brwd,
Caiff llawer gwraig fywoliaeth
gryno
Fu gynt yn cario'r cwd;
A bwyd a dillad i'w diwallu,
Yn lle eu dyrnu'n dost,
Bydd llai o bwysau ar y plwyfydd,
Nid cymaint fydd y gost;
Tylodion fydd trwy lwydd
Yn talu eu rhenti'n rhwydd:
Bydd llai o alwad am failiaid,
Ceir gweled yn ein gŵydd.
A'r Twrna tew a'r Auctioneer,
Ar fyrder aiff ar feth,
Bydd fawr trwy Gymru
Cyn hir yn methu,
Drwy dristwch dalu'r dreth;
Ffarwel i'r tafarndai,
Na fwriwch arnom fai,
Ond chwi gewch wel'd cyn hir o
amser,
Eich llawnder aiff yn llai;
Ffarwel i lywcio cwrw a *licer*,
Ces lawer chwerwder chwith,
Ffarwel i feddwdod a chyfeddach,
Tee-total bach am byth.

YWAIN MEIRION.

Llanrwst, argraffwyd gan J. Jones.

four are identifiable as hymn tunes. 'Lydia' was attributed to Thomas Phillips, a brushmaker of Bristol, whose circumstances were as firmly rooted among the common people as the craftsmen of Dyffryn Ogwen.[52] The American hymn tune 'Sabbath', written by Lowell Mason, was carved for a mantelpiece that names William and Marry Morris, though whether the work was made by William himself is unclear. Few of the slates were signed. However, the tune 'Friendship' is believed to have been carved by its composer, John Parry. It carries his name and that of Marry, presumably his wife, with designs of a tree and wine glasses – perhaps communion cups – and the precise date of January 1838. The motifs and overall structure of the decoration, in addition to the eccentric anglicised spelling of the name 'Mari' are closely similar to the designs inscribed two years earlier on the slate carrying the circular musical motif, suggesting that they were probably both the work of Parry. The suspicion is reinforced by the fact that John Parry was a celebrated musician in the locality. He was born at Llanllechid in 1816, and despite the fact that he had little musical education as a child, he became a member of the Carneddi Chapel choir at the early age of ten. He would develop into a composer of many choral pieces and in later years led his choir at Capel Jerusalem to victory in Eisteddfod competitions.[53]

It was from the congregational singing in those chapels, and in the meetings of the temperance movement which emerged in the mid-1830s, contemporary with the Dyffryn Ogwen carvings, that the choral tradition which flourished and came to be regarded as characteristic of the nation would develop in the second half of the nineteenth century. The visual record of the music of the temperance movement, so important in attracting supporters to its meetings and its marches,[54] emerged first in the hands of the last of the ballad singers, who would surely have been familiar to John Parry and his neighbours through visits to fairs, such as those at Llanllechid and Menai Bridge, where they would have performed. Their tradition among the common people would soon be rendered largely an anachronism as the sanitised ballad form transferred to the middle-class parlour in the high Victorian period. But in the last years before that transformation was complete, the printer John Jones of Llanrwst, in association with the Caernarfon wood engraver James Cope, presented ballads on large format sheets with especially cut illustrations that marked the end of the old tradition of popular song in the service of the new temperance movement. James Cope illustrated his publication of Ywain Meirion's lengthy ballad on the evils of drink, which was to be sung to the eighteenth-century Scottish tune, the 'Belisle March'.[55]

52 'Lydia' was written by Charles Wesley.

53 William Parry, Llechidon, *Hanes llenyddiaeth ac enwogion Llanllechid a Llandegai: sef, Traethawd buddugol yn Eisteddfod Gadeiriol Bethesda, 1867* (Bangor, 1868).

54 For song as an attraction to the temperance movement, see W.R. Lambert, *Drink and Sobriety in Victorian Wales c.1820–c.1895* (Cardiff, 1983), pp. 105–9. Temperance eisteddfodau were held in Merthyr chapels from 1848–79.

55 For the work of James Cope and John Jones of Llanrwst, see Peter Lord, *Words with Pictures: Welsh Images and Images of Wales in the Popular Press* (Aberystwyth, 1995), pp. 93–134.

56 She would edit her ancestor's work for publication as *The autobiography and correspondence of Mary Granville, Mrs. Delany: with interesting reminiscences of King George the third & Queen Charlotte* (London, 1861).

LLANOVER – REGENDERING THE BRAND

At the other end of the social scale, the fact that Augusta Hall, Lady Llanover, owned a scarce copy of Owen Williams's *The Harp of King David of Israel or Royal Psalms of Zion* signifies her understanding of music as a central part of a broader Welsh cultural tradition that she assiduously promoted throughout her long life. She had grown up in Monmouthshire as Augusta Waddington until, in 1823, she married Benjamin Hall, the owner of the neighbouring estate to that of her father. Hall was a progressive thinker who was to become the Member of Parliament for the county. As a young woman, Augusta developed strong opinions about Welsh cultural identity that first came to widespread public attention in 1834 when her essay on the advantages of the preservation of the Welsh language and of Welsh costume won a prize at the Cardiff Eisteddfod – the last of the regional meetings. Among her ancestors had been the painter and craftsperson Mary Delany, in whom she took a great interest, following her example in practising a range of visual arts and crafts.[56] In 1837, at the age of about thirty-five, she painted a miniature self-portrait, identifying herself with her bardic name of Gwenynen Gwent. By this time, in addition to illustrating

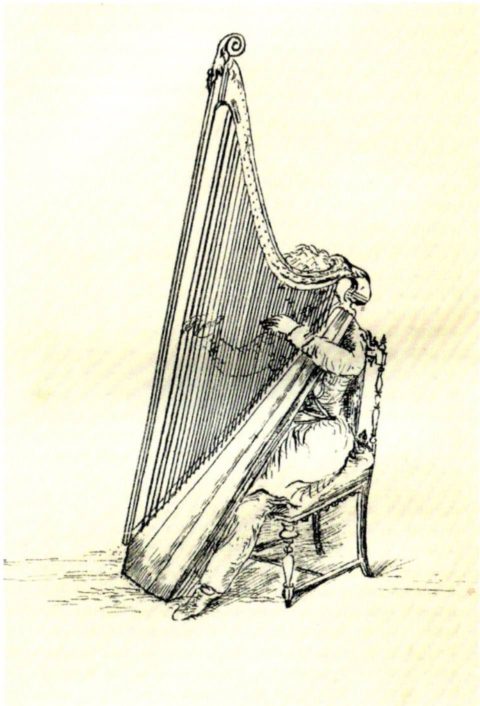

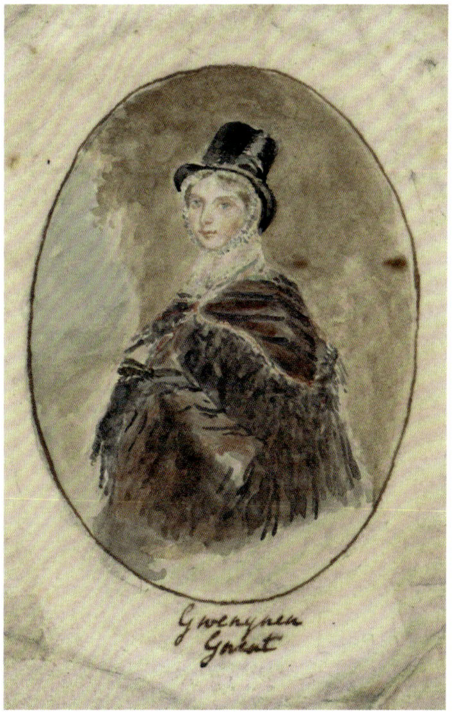

134 Augusta Hall, Lady Llanover, *John Jones, Harper*, c.1840

135 Augusta Hall, Lady Llanover, *Gwenynen Gwent*, 1837

books written by her friend Jane Williams, 'Ysgafell', she had produced the series of delicate watercolours in which she formalised regional Welsh costumes. From them she standardised a version of what she would, for the rest of her life, energetically promote as the national costume of Wales.

Augusta Hall's support for Welsh music was initiated by her revival of the fading practice of employing a family harper. She heard John Wood Jones play for the first time at the Brecon Eisteddfod of 1826, and subsequently took him into her household, where he remained until his death. Jones was the son of Adam Wood, harper to the Gwynne family of Glanbrân, and was taught the triple harp both by his father and by Richard Roberts of Caernarfon. He inherited, therefore, the Romany tradition and also a line of tutelage that extended from John Parry, Telynor Dall, through William Williams, Wil Penmorfa.

The 1826 Eisteddfod had been a seminal event in the life of Augusta Hall. The meeting was attended both by the ageing generation of late eighteenth-century antiquarians, including William Owen Pughe and Ifor Ceri, but crucially also

136 Unknown artist, *Maria Jane Williams*, c.1815–20

137 Unknown photographer, *Maria Jane Williams*, c.1865

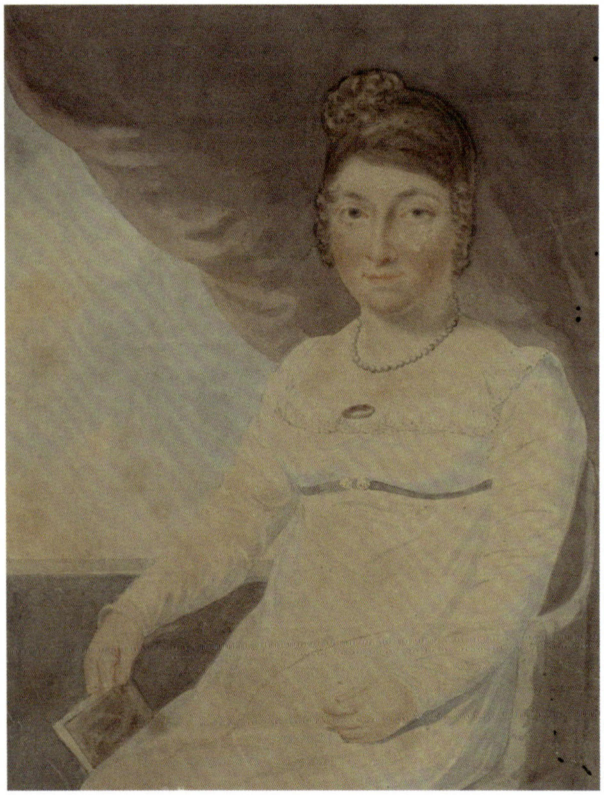

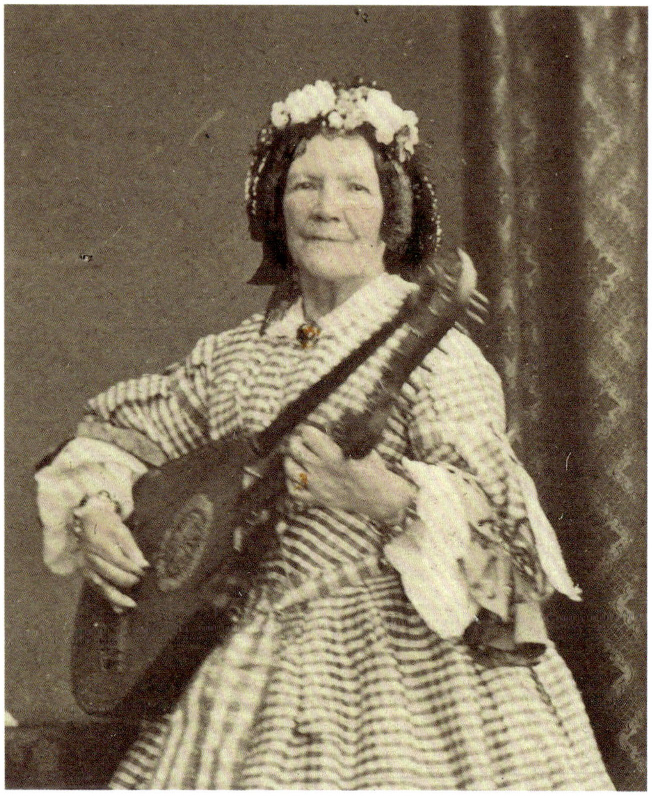

by the leader of the next generation, Thomas Price, 'Carnhuanawc'. Price would reinforce her own ideas, and exercise an important influence on other crucial figures who would coalesce into a new group of cultural revivalists. Among them was Maria Jane Williams of Aberpergwm in the Neath Valley. Williams was acknowledged by her contemporaries as a fine singer, and as an instrumentalist she played both harp and guitar. Before the 1826 Eisteddfod, she and Carnhuanawc had been together on a visit to Ireland, where they met the folklorist Thomas Crofton Croker. From Croker, Williams absorbed the methodology of collecting folk tales, and by 1837 she had extended her work to folk music. At the Abergavenny Eisteddfod of that year, she was awarded the prize for the 'Best Collection of Unpublished Welsh Music'. Her work represented a significant change in methodology from the adulterations of her predecessors, Bardd Alaw and Bardd y Brenin, in that it presented without adornment the airs and Welsh-language words of the material she had collected. The forty-three songs would be published in 1844 as *Ancient National Airs of Gwent and Morganwg*, with a dedication to Queen Victoria arranged through the good offices of the Llanover household.

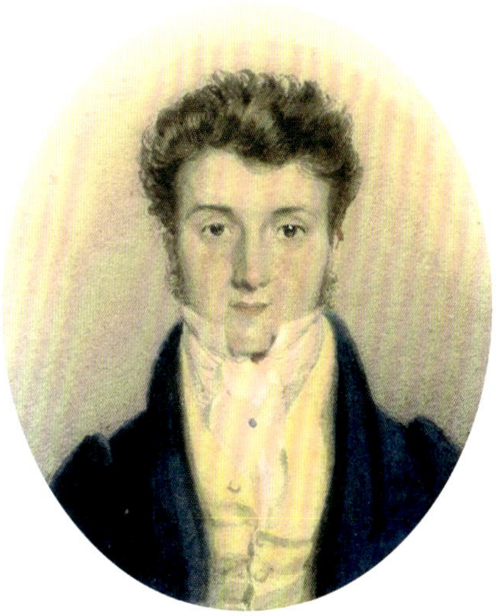

138 Penry Williams, *William Williams, Aberpergwm*, 1825

Two painted portraits believed to represent Maria Jane Williams survive, though neither is well documented, and the faces of the sitters do not seem consistent. They date from the 1820s, but are different in style. The facial features recorded in a miniature portrait seem consistent with photographs taken of Maria Jane in middle age. It may be an early work by the painter Penry Williams. A miniature of Maria Jane's brother, William (who was also involved with antiquarian affairs) was inscribed by Penry Williams in 1825. The painter was born into an artisan family in Merthyr in 1802, and had emerged as an aspiring artist by 1816, when he painted a pair of pictures depicting the civil disturbances of that year in his home town. He may well have been encouraged in his vocation by his schoolmaster, Taliesin Williams, son of Iolo Morganwg. He first worked at Aberpergwm in 1819 when, according to Maria Jane's account, she came upon him drawing a bridge near the house: 'I saw Penry Williams thereabouts, 17 years old sketching it: after which I sent him to the house where he remained a month filling albums and drawing everybody and everything.'[57] It seems likely that 'everybody' included Maria Jane herself, then only some twenty-four years old. The portrait of her brother William is considerably more sophisticated than her own, since it was painted by Williams after he had trained at the Royal Academy.

57 Note inscribed on a drawing, *Bridge near Aberpergwm*, given in Derrick Pritchard Webley, *Cast to the Four Winds: The Life and Work of Penry Williams* (Aberystwyth, 1997), pp. 13, 22-3.

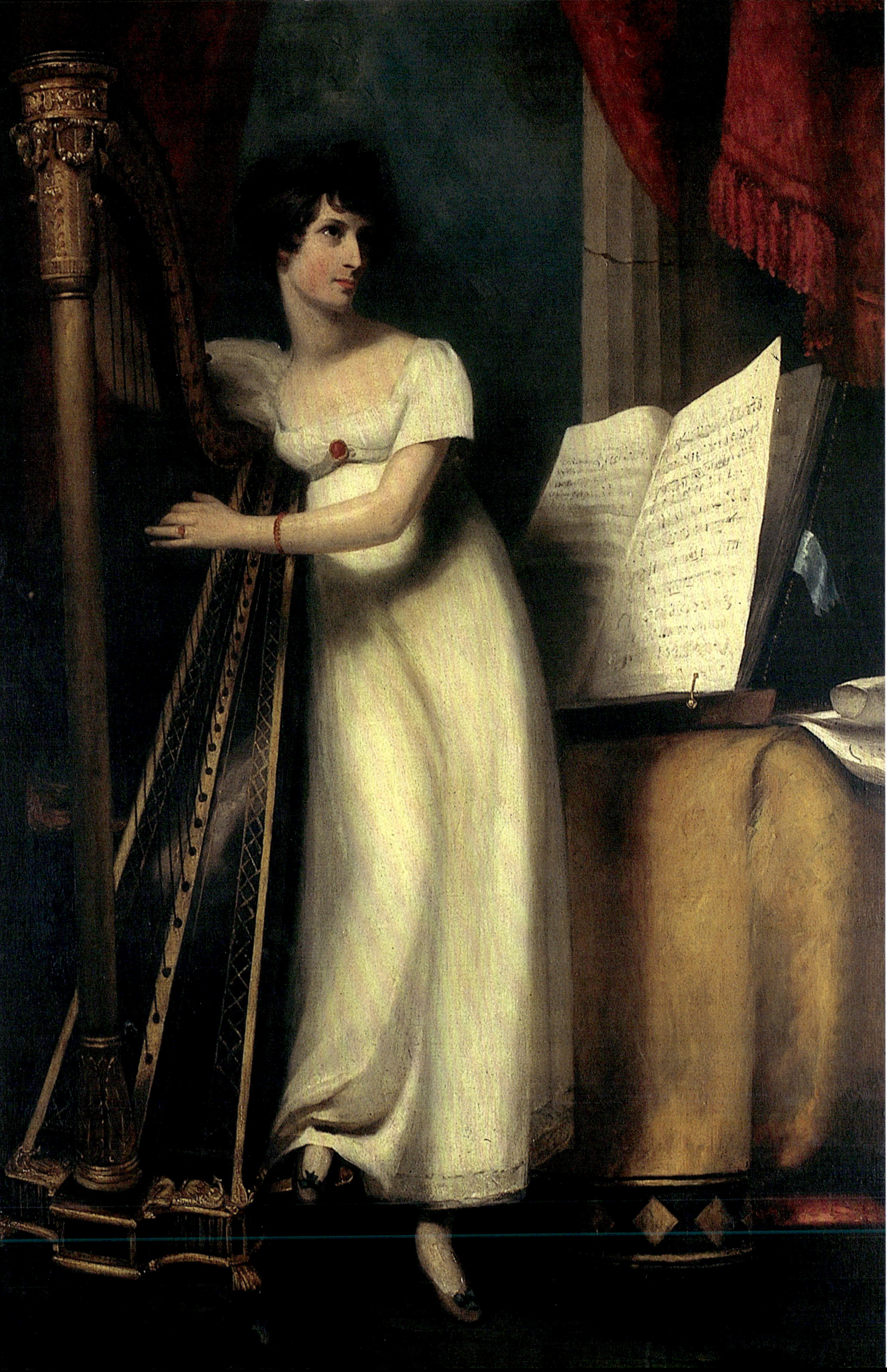

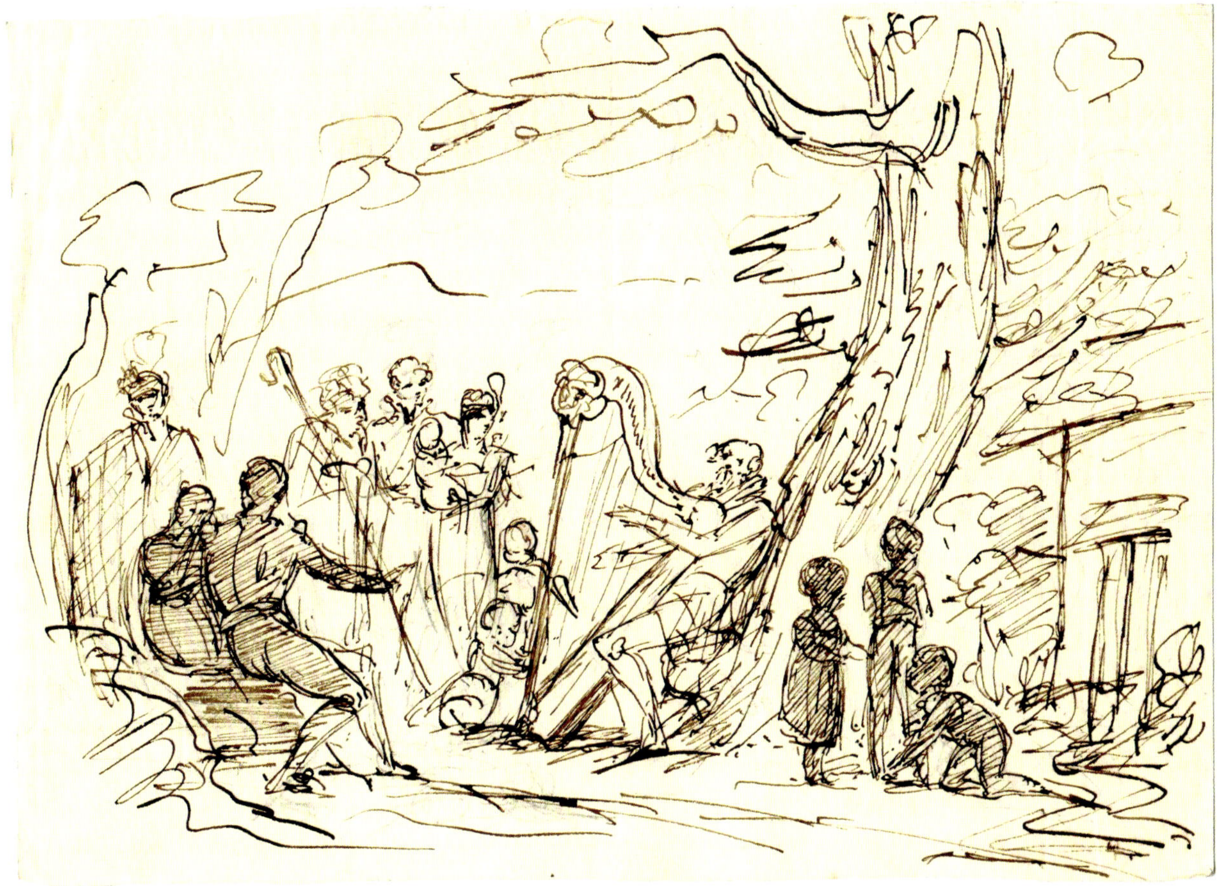

The writer Thomas Matthews would later report in an essay about the artist that 'it was chiefly through the faith of Miss [Maria] Jane Williams in him that Penry Williams went to London and then to Italy', and although this seems likely to overemphasise Maria Jane's role compared with that of other early patrons, it implies an ongoing relationship.[58] A full-length oil portrait, in which the sitter is apparently tuning her pedal harp in preparation for performance, is firmly reputed by family tradition to represent Maria Jane, and may well be the work that Williams exhibited at the Royal Academy in 1822. By this time, he was resident in London. Maria Jane's harp teacher, Elias Parish Alvars, appears to have begun teaching there at about that time, and so it is possible that she sat to Williams in London.[59] In composition the picture reflects what had become, by the 1820s, a Europe-wide genre of portraits of female harpers.

140 Lady Henrietta Antonia Williams Wynn, *A Harper under an Oak Tree*, c.1820

139 Probably Penry Williams, *Maria Jane Williams, Aberpergwm*, c.1822

58 Thomas Matthews, 'Penry Williams', *Cymru*, 42 (1912), p. 118. Penry Williams probably trained at the Academy under the patronage of William Crawshay of Cyfarthfa, though others may also have been involved.

59 However, a tiny detail of the portrait may present a problem with the identification of the sitter. The harper wears a Regency gown with a matching brooch, bracelet and ring, which is on the fourth finger of her left hand. Maria Jane Williams did not marry. Nevertheless, photographs reveal that it was her practice in later life to wear a ring on that finger.

In Wales in the eighteenth century, professional public performance on the harp was undertaken predominantly, though not uniquely, by men. Several women performers have been identified, of whom the earliest appears to have been Angharad James of Dolwyddelan but, sadly, none was imaged.[60] However, in the second half of the century, it became fashionable for upper-class women to play the instrument in a domestic setting. Indeed, Evan Williams, John Parry's collaborator in publishing *Antient British Music* in 1742, is known to have supplemented his income when living in London by teaching the harp to society ladies.[61] Among the upper-class Welsh women who adopted the fashion was Lady Henrietta Antonia Williams Wynn, the daughter of Edward Clive, Earl of Powis. She married Sir Watkin, the 5th Baronet, in 1817, three years before the Wrexham Eisteddfod in which he featured prominently. No doubt, as a competent harper, she was involved, though with a lower public profile.

141 Thomas Price, Carnhuanawc, *Membership Certificate of Taliesin Williams, Cymdeithas Cymreigyddion y Fenni*, 1834

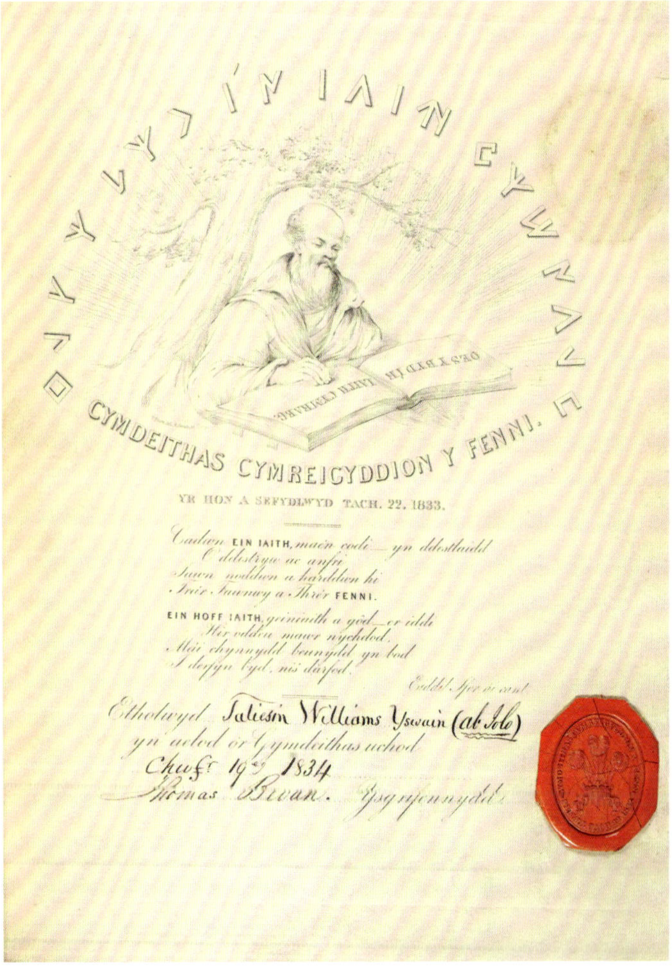

Lady Henrietta also drew and painted. It is impossible to say if her fluid sketch of a male harper at work represents an observed event or is a fantasy. It certainly reproduces many of the features that had become visual tropes by the beginning of the new century. The harper plays before his cottage in the shade of an oak tree attended by a group of the common people (including a shepherd) and children at play.

The regendering of the harp in polite society was first suggested in Wales in Anna Maria Bennett's *Ellen, Countess of Castle Howel*. As we have seen, the novel of 1794 was set in a family whose traditional but decayed Welsh way of life was symbolised by their aged male harper.[62] On the other hand, Bennett's young heroine, Ellen – like Maria Jane Williams – was possessed of 'a naturally sweet as well as a strong voice.' She learnt to play the harp by listening to the old harper's renditions of tunes such as 'Of Noble Race was Shenkin'.[63] However, closely reflecting in the novel the agenda of those prominent Welsh musicians who had migrated to London in the second half of the eighteenth century, Ellen's native talent could be refined and brought into the modern world only under the paternal influence of the English, since 'the *science* of music was a matter she was totally unacquainted with' in her native condition.[64] The musical image served, of course, as a political metaphor for the dependent relationship of Wales to England, as perceived by political unionists. Bennett predicted precisely the complaint about native practitioners made by Bardd Alaw in *A Selection of Welsh Melodies*. There were many Welsh harpers, he observed, but 'few of them play well, most of them being totally unacquainted with music, they generally play by ear.'[65]

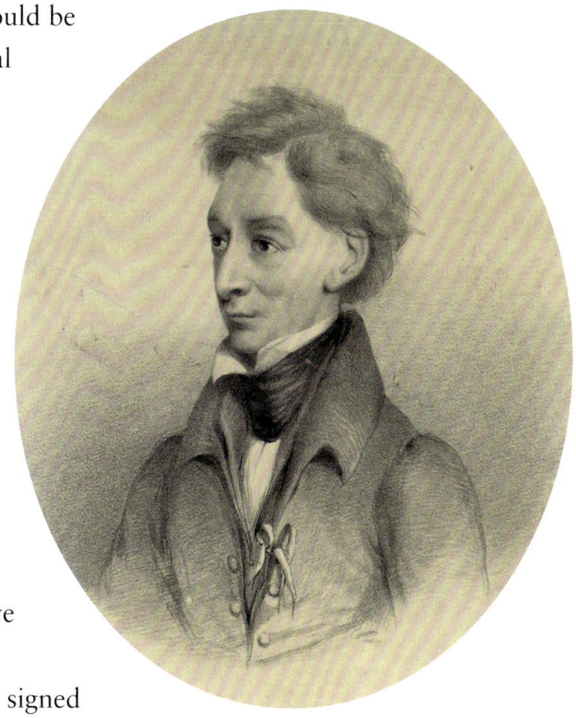

142 Charles Lucy, *Thomas Price, Carnhuanawc*, *c*.1836

In 1833, Augusta Hall facilitated the founding of the Abergavenny Cymreigyddion Society, and their first Eisteddfod took place the following year. The Society developed with the active engagement of Carnhuanawc, whose name headed the list of the original members. The membership certificate of Taliesin Williams, signed by Thomas Bevan, 'Caradawc', the first secretary and another driving force behind the Society, carries a bardic image designed by Carnhuanawc himself. His own engraved portrait dates from about 1836. It was published after a drawing made early in his career by the painter Charles Lucy, who was born and grew up in Herefordshire.[66] Lucy maintained his association with the county throughout his life, which may account for this link with Carnhuanawc. An associate of his, Lady Elizabeth Coffin Greenly, was another enthusiastic supporter of the Cymreigyddion. She lived at Titley Court in Herefordshire, but kept a house in Abergavenny, and was an important figure in the development of the ideas of both Lady Llanover and Maria Jane Williams. Greenly vividly described the meeting in 1837 that took place between the accession of Queen Victoria to the

60 For Angharad James (1677–1749), see Owen Thomas, *Cofiant Y Parchedig John Jones, Talsarn* (Wrexham, 1874), pp. 24–6. The first record of women harpers present at eisteddfodau appears to be at Caernarfon in 1821, when Margaret Edwards of Corwen and Elizabeth Hughes were among the competitors.

61 J. Lloyd Williams, *Y Tri Thelynor, Arloeswyr Cerddorol Cymru yn y Ddeunawfed Ganrif* (London, 1945), p. 49.

62 Anna Maria Bennett, *Ellen, Countess of Castle Howel* (London, 1794), vol. i, p. 4.

63 Ibid., p. 213. The popularity of this tune was satirised with verses by Dryden, see T.J.Ll. Prichard, *The Cambrian Wreath* (Aberystwyth, 1828), p. 192.

64 Bennett, *Ellen*, p. 122.

65 John Parry, *A Selection of Welsh Melodies* (London, 1809), p. 292.

throne and her Coronation. At the ball, 'the refreshments [were] served in the library by the Ladies maids dressed in complete Welsh costume':

> Lady Charlotte Guest appeared first in Welsh costume, as did her husband. She then changed this garb for a superb Crimson Velvet with Diamonds ... Many of the young people were very correctly dressed from Mrs Hall's Book of Welsh costumes, and looked extremely well ... My God-daughter Miss [Augusta Charlotte] Hall, looked very nicely in a checked Jacket and Petticoat of silk in imitation of Welsh colours, and an apron to match. Her mother was, in the same attire, with a superb diamond leek in her black silk hat.[67]

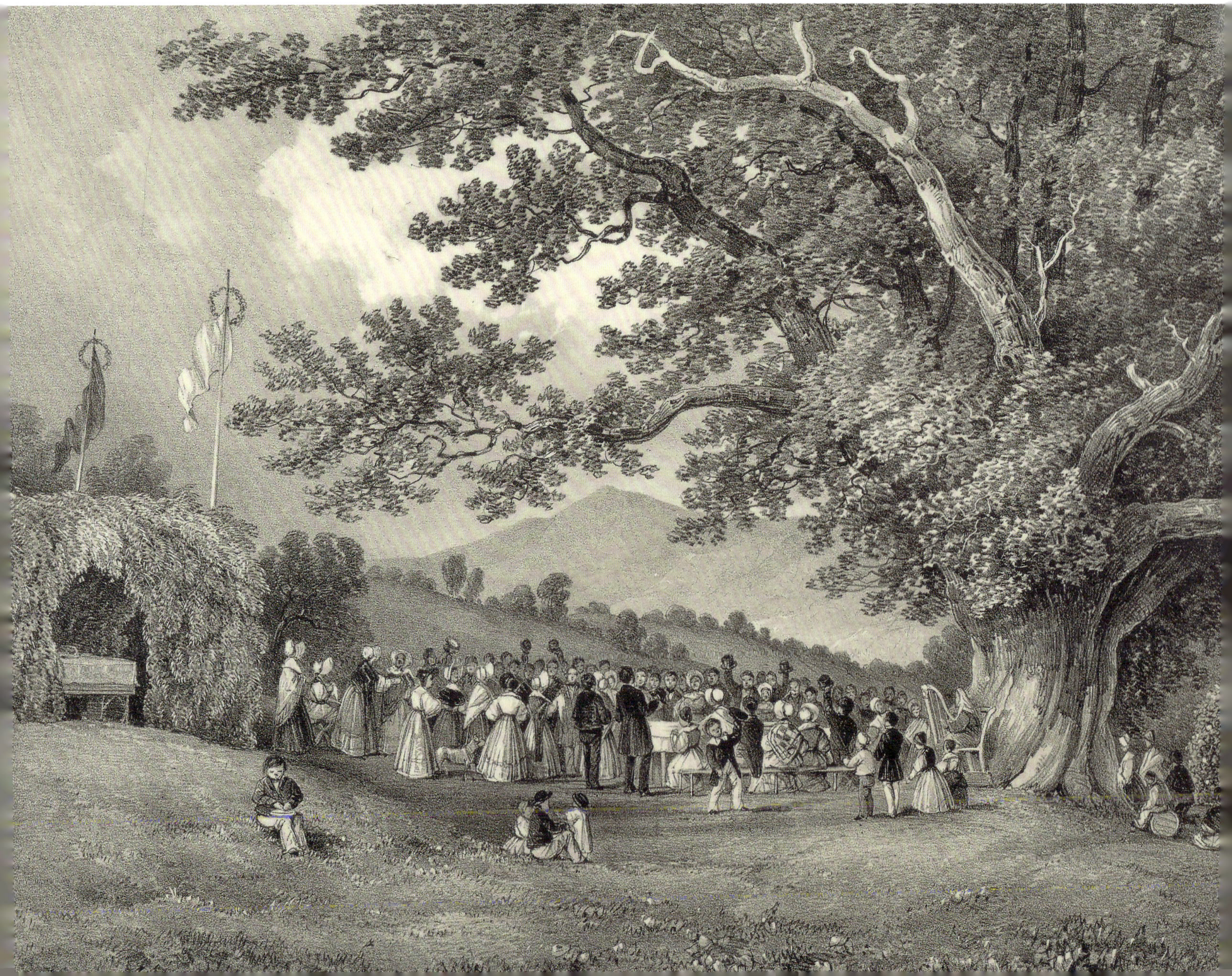

143 Henry Francis Worsley, *Coronation Fête of Queen Victoria under the Caeryder Oak, Usk*, 1838

In June the following year, at Llanhenock, not far from Abergavenny, the celebration of the Queen's Coronation provides an instructive comparison with the proceedings of the Cymreigyddion. The celebration was funded by the local landowner, Sir Digby Mackworth, who presumably also paid for a depiction of the event by Henry Francis Worsley to be engraved. Worsley was resident in Bath, though he appears also to have lived at Caerleon for a time. The event took place in the shadow of the celebrated Cae-ryder Oak, against which a harper sat to accompany the dancing, enacting in reality the image presented in Lady Williams Wynn's earlier drawing. The harper was not named in contemporary reports, but the absence of the Llanover family among the gentry guests suggests that John Wood Jones was not involved and that, therefore, at least one other triple harper was at work in the area. National costume is also conspicuous by its absence. The weather was fine, and 'Aeolus himself, became a powerful auxiliary in refreshing the company by wafting his still soft breezes through the beams of the burning sun;– thus counteracting their strong effects, and at the same time causing the strings of the harp to vibrate in such a manner as to give the appearance of a sweet Aeolian':

> One table consisted of about forty children (rich and poor) under 12 years of age, who were waited upon by six young persons appointed for the occasion. The rest of the tables were indiscriminately occupied by all persons who were present. This was another pleasing sight – all grades of society dining together, on so joyous an occasion! – the Baronet carving for the labourer, and the child of the Baronet seated by and dining with the child of the peasant, each one manifesting the greatest satisfaction … at the close of which the harp struck up 'God save the Queen,' when the whole of the company united their vocal powers in accompanying the harp with song.[68]

Down the road at Abergavenny, during the two decades that bridged the late Georgian and high Victorian periods, the Eisteddfodau would develop the role of the lapsed regional meetings as a focal point of national cultural celebration, featuring the harp and the costume. As early as 1835, a newspaper report of the proceedings resounded with the words that by the end of the century would come to encapsulate the national brand of Wales at home and around the world – the 'Land of Song'.[69] The elevated connections in London of the Hall family were important in achieving for these Eisteddfodau a higher profile outside

66 An oil portrait, apparently painted at about the same time (University of Wales Trinity St David, Lampeter) was signed by one Emmanuel Giaconi, probably a pseudonym.

67 NLW Maxwell Fraser Bequest, CB5, pp. 73-6.

68 *Monmouthshire Merlin*, 7 July 1838, p. 4.

69 *The Cambrian*, 5 December 1835. For the use of the phrase, see A.D.J. Cusworth, 'Towards a Digital Land of Song: A Digital Approach to the Archival Record of Welsh Traditional Music, its Performance and Reception' (unpublished PhD thesis, The Open University, 2016).

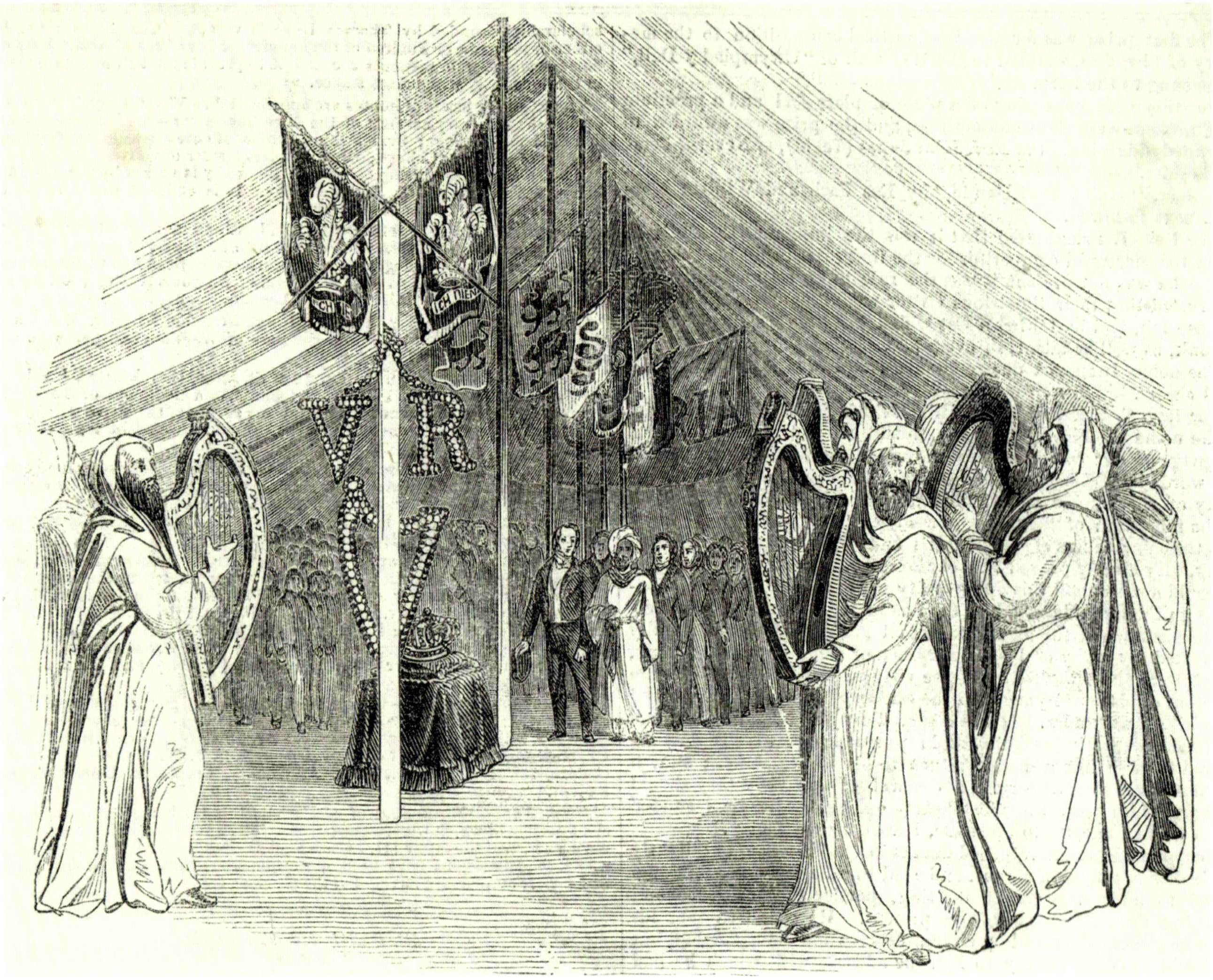

144 Unknown artist, *The Welsh Bardic Festival*, 1842

Wales than had been attained by the earlier series. A fortunate coincidence in the development of the popular press in England facilitated the publicity. In May 1842, the first issue of *The Illustrated London News* was published, establishing a new standard of pictorial journalism in England. Just five months later, the paper illustrated *The Welsh Bardic Festival* with a woodcut in the style that became characteristic of its pioneering work.[70]

The paper sometimes sent its own artists to draw events that the editor wished to feature, and on other occasions relied on locally based artists. Drawings were dispatched to London where teams of engravers worked, sometimes overnight, to transfer the originals to wood blocks for immediate printing. However, on this occasion, the woodcut appears likely to have been an imaginative reconstruction made in London after the event, and based on a written description of the opening ceremony. The account, which was clearly the work of an insider, noted that 'On the president entering the room and taking his seat, he was received with a grand chorus of harps.'[71] In reality, the instruments in question must have been modern triple harps, rather than the single harps of bardic mythology imagined by the artist, who was clearly working under the influence of the de Loutherbourg tradition of 'Last Bard' images. The floral harp that adorned the central pillar of the pavilion was formed of dahlias, set beside 'A splendid crown, mounted on a velvet cushion', the function of which was not explained for the presumably mystified English readership. The President, Rhys Powell of Wonastow, was depicted entering the pavilion with the nephew of the Bengali financier and industrialist Dwarkanath Tagore, to whom praise poems were addressed.[72] In his speech, Rhys Powell was fulsome in his celebration of the work of the Cymreigyddion in promoting the triple harp as the national instrument. Five harps were offered as prizes, 'calculated, from their different value, to suit the practised harper, who deserves reward for excellence attained, or the timid, crippled, or perhaps blind, or orphan child, who, with fine musical talent, is destitute of the means of obtaining a harp of his own on which to practise and improve, and by means of which he may eventually gain his daily bread':

> I can with confidence declare that the Abergavenny Cymreigyddion has done more for the restoration of our various and beautiful national instrument, the triple stringed harp, than has been effected in the last one hundred years, by any society in North or South Wales; and were – which heaven forbid! – this patriotic society to be annihilated to-morrow, the effects of their past labours would be apparent for another century, although the sound of the numerous harps which they have been the means of dispersing in this district, where once the soft tones of its strings were common to every village, and where the ancestors of many still-existing families would have parted with every luxury, rather than resign their own family harper, to soothe or enliven them as they were inclined.[73]

Though the President's rhetoric was florid, the essence of his prediction would be borne out by events. Indeed, although it was yet to become apparent, one of the many prize harps made by Bassett Jones of Cardiff for the Cymreigyddion would prove particularly significant. It had been awarded in 1838 to an eleven-year-old

70 *The Illustrated London News*, 22 October 1842, p. 377.

71 Ibid.

72 Dwarkanath Tagore was the grandfather of the celebrated poet and writer Rabindranath Tagore. For a discussion of the international context of the Llanover circle, see Geoffrey Powell, 'The Llanover Project: The European Dimension', library.wales/fileadmin/fileadmin/docs_gwefan/amdanom_ni/cyfeillion/darlithoedd/cyfn_dar_GPowell_000916S.pdf.

73 *Monmouthshire Merlin*, Supplement, 15 October 1842. Notwithstanding the hype, the report noted that on both the first and second days of the meeting 'the attendance was rather thin, neither the platform nor the body of the Pavilion being at any time fully occupied.'

from Bridgend called John Thomas, who in due course would become one of the most influential Welsh musicians of the nineteenth century. He acquired the bardic name 'Pencerdd Gwalia' in 1861 and ten years later was appointed harper to Queen Victoria and a teacher at the Royal Academy of Music.[74] Similarly, in 1842, a harp was won by John Roberts who, as we shall see, became an important figure in the development of the national brand as 'Telynor Cymru'.

Visual coverage in *The Illustrated London News* of the 1845 Abergavenny Eisteddfod, held in the new hall especially designed to accommodate it, was even more extensive. Music was again prominent. As in 1842, the opening parade through the streets of the town had been led by 'A band, composed principally

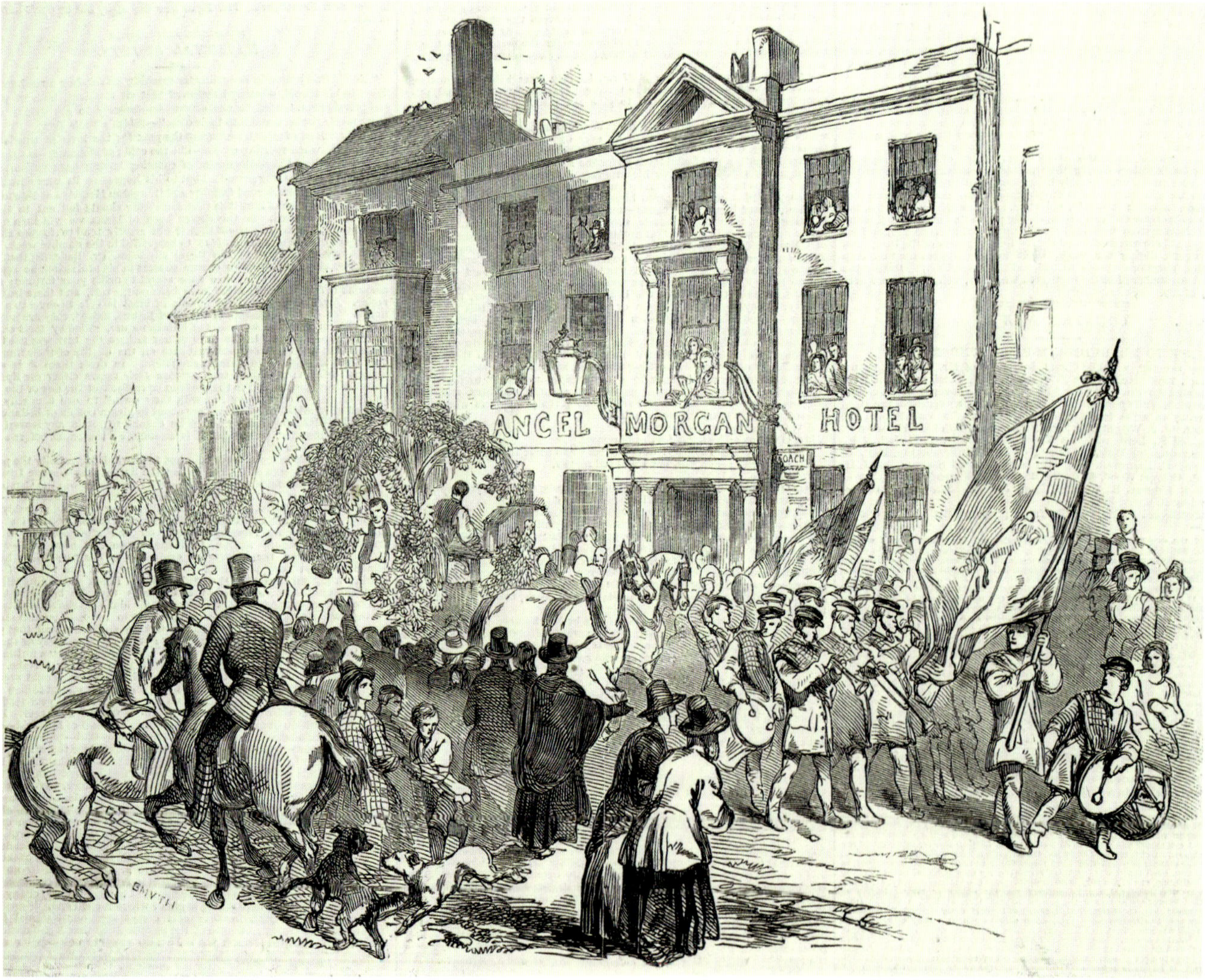

145 Unknown artist, *The Abergavenny Eisteddfod Procession*, 1845

of workmen from the neighbouring works.' An interior view concentrated on the assembling dignitaries, though the harpers were just visible in the left margin of the image. The local newspaper, the *Monmouthshire Merlin*, carried an enthusiastic eye-witness account:

> When the waves of the rushing crowd had somewhat stilled, and people had an opportunity of calmly looking around them, the coup d'oeil was singularly striking … On the left side of the gallery, from the front entrance, a row of harpers – male and female – attired in Welsh costume, had seated themselves, and were pouring forth a flood of matchless harmony from their triple harps.[75]

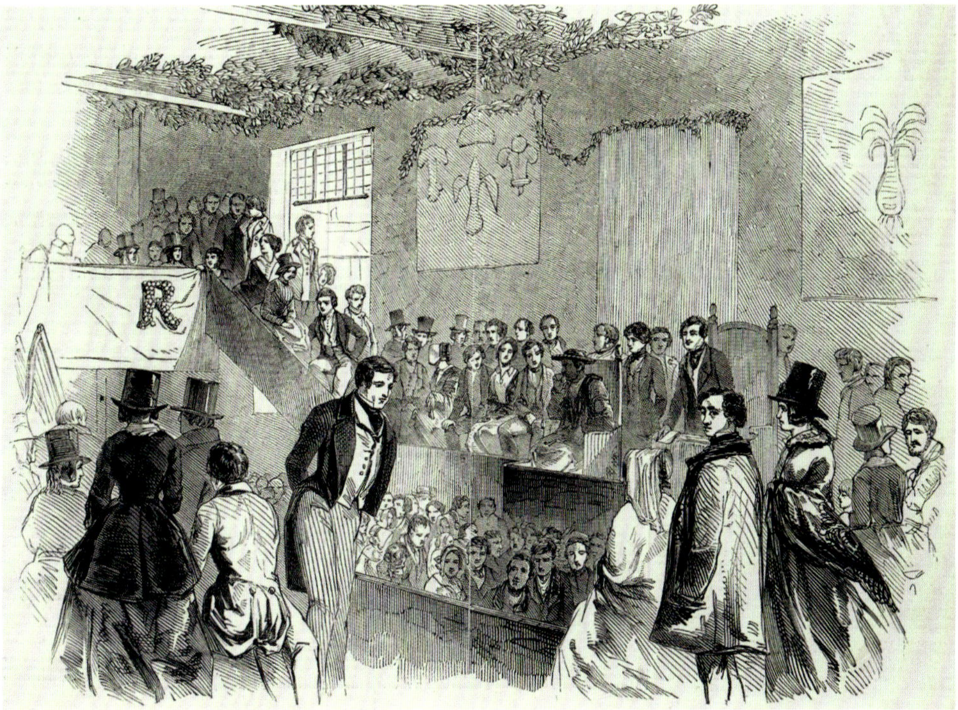

146 Unknown artist, *The Abergavenny Eisteddfod*, 1845

74 As his reputation grew, Lady Llanover became excessively protective of him. At an Abergavenny Eisteddfod ball, Mary Elizabeth Lucy recalled an embarrassing incident: 'Miss Bickersteth who … had really lost her heart to Mr Thomas, asked him to dance which he modestly declined, saying that perhaps it might annoy Lady Hall … Lady Shelley said, 'Nonsense, Mr Thomas, you cannot refuse a lady when she asks you to be her partner,' so he stood up and they danced together. Lady Hall, seeing them, flew at him like a tigress and insisted on his retiring. Then we all attacked her and defended Mr Thomas, Mrs Herbert too came to the rescue and remonstrated with her mother and there was quite a scene. But Mr Thomas was triumphant and danced and enjoyed himself for the rest of the evening, the young ladies vying with each other who should secure him for her partner.' Mary Elizabeth Lucy, *Mistress of Charlecote* (London, 1983), p. 99.

75 *Monmouthshire Merlin*, 18 October 1845.

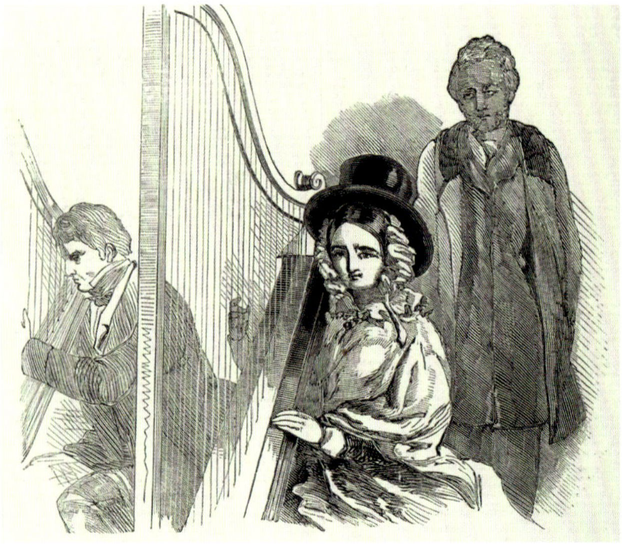

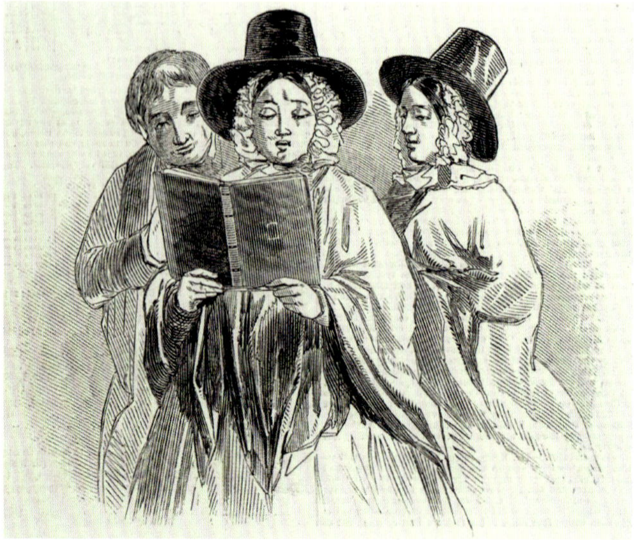

147 Unknown artist, *Harpers at the Abergavenny Eisteddfod*, 1845

148 Unknown artist, *Singers at the Abergavenny Eisteddfod*, 1845

However, two smaller and simpler images would prove to be more significant – indeed, perhaps seminal – in the evolution of the national brand. For the first time, images of Welsh costume and Welsh music, and especially of the national instrument, were conjoined in the form that would carry the brand for the next century and a half. The name of the artist who created these informal but prescient images is unknown but, clearly, he or she was present at the event. Behind the young female instrumentalist and singer, a shadowy and slightly unkempt figure studies the harp and the score. It is a detail that exudes documentary veracity and records the continuing participation of the common people under the patronage of the gentry in the evolving eisteddfod tradition.

The association of heroic if tragic nationhood conveyed by the image of the male Bard had yet to lose entirely its grip on the imagination of patriotic individuals. Indeed, a copy made in pastel after Benjamin West's 1778 painting of the subject, if not the work of Augusta Hall herself, certainly has Llanover provenance. But a simple portrait, probably that of her daughter, Augusta, standing at the harp, score in hand and wearing a medal over her dress of Welsh fabric, represented the contrasting future of the national brand. It was a future in which Victorian conventions of submissive and dependent femininity supplanted masculine defiance and independence, with all that that implied for perceptions of the political relationship between the nations.

149 Unknown artist after Benjamin West, *The Bard*, c.1835

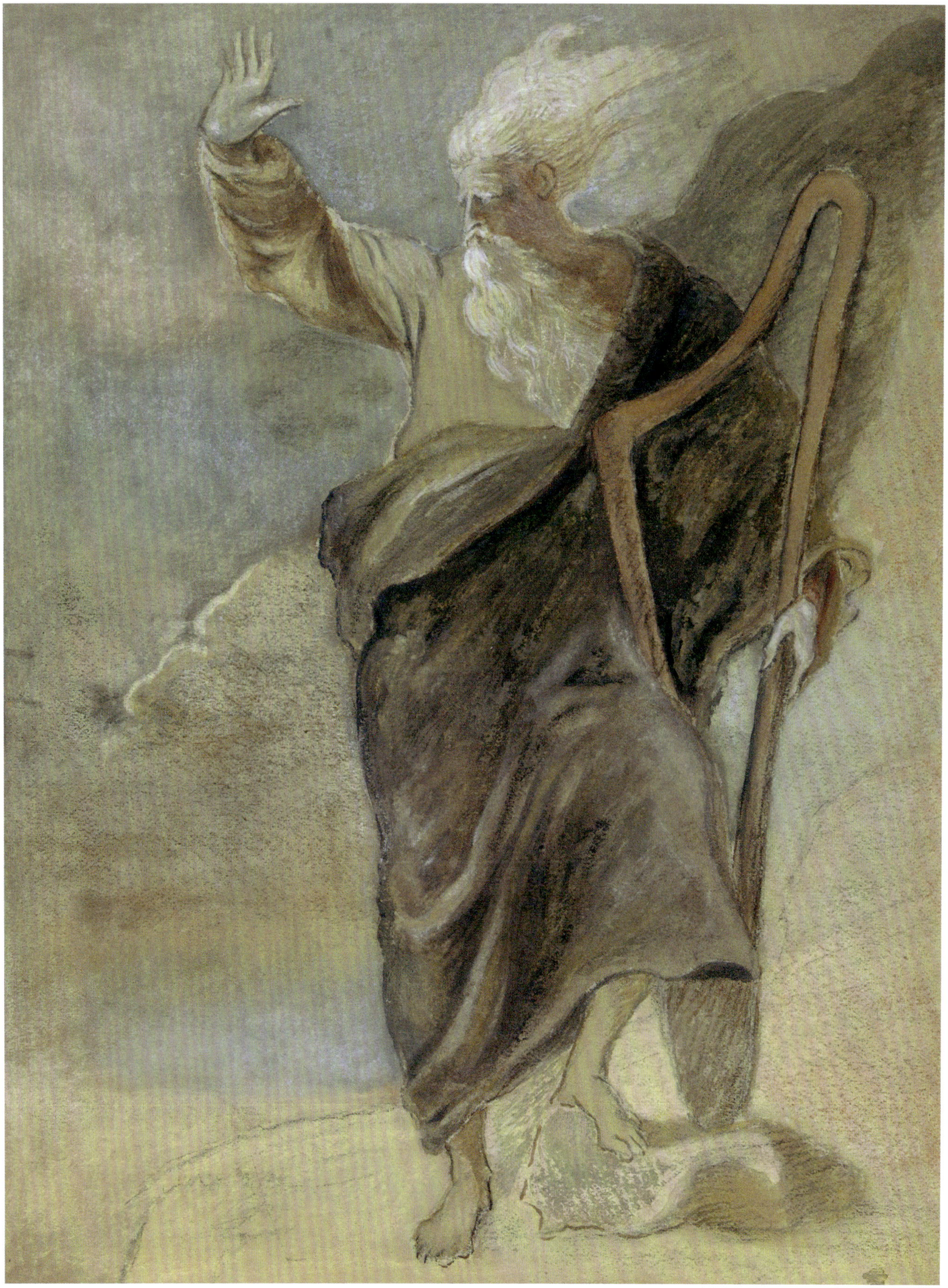

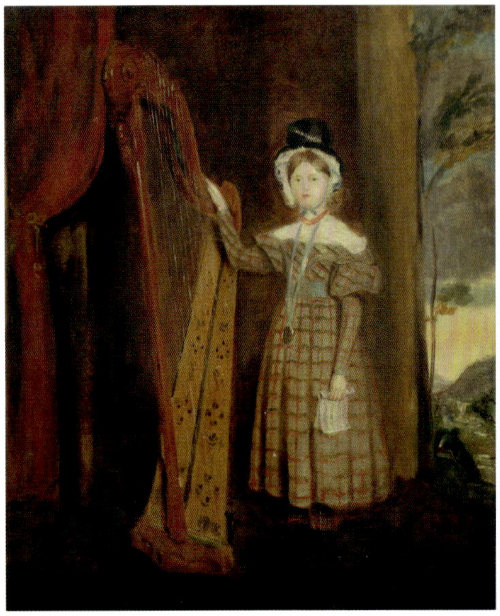

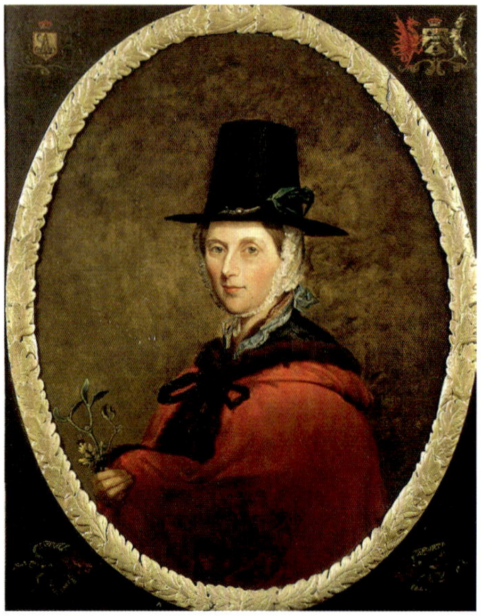

150 Augusta Hall, Lady Llanover, *The Painter's Daughter, Augusta*, c.1835

151 Charles Augustus Mornewicke, *Augusta Hall, Lady Llanover*, 1862

152 Daniel Maclise, *John Orlando Parry*, c.1850

Probably during the early 1830s, the Llanover circle expanded to include Charles Augustus Mornewicke, an English painter whose history remains obscure. How his relationship with Llanover was established is unknown, but he was favoured with several commissions. His portrait of Lady Llanover herself has become the most familiar image of the sitter.[76] That of Carnhuanawc, probably painted in the mid-1840s, confirms the description given by others who knew him or heard him speak as a handsome individual of a romantic cast of mind. But of most immediate interest from the perspective of music is Mornewicke's less formal portrait of the young John Orlando Parry, apparently completed a decade earlier, since the sitter was born in 1810 and can hardly have been older than his early twenties when the picture was painted.

John Orlando was the son of John Parry, Bardd Alaw, and as such was brought up with access both to Welsh music and to the popular English tradition exemplified by his father's engagement with the London stage and Vauxhall Gardens. John Orlando became a professional singer and a performer on the pedal harp and piano in both of these contexts, and in London, by the time he was eighteen, he was performing regularly for the Gwyneddigion Society.[77] He was also a talented draughtsman and, like his father, an individual of boundless energy and curiosity, to which his illustrated diaries bear witness.[78] Of his more finished works, the earliest survivor (dated 1837) is a portrait of a blind harper, perhaps in a tavern, accompanied by his dog and a jug of ale. Under the bench

76 The portrait is dated 1862, though the apparent age of the sitter suggests a much earlier period. Among Mornewicke's other sitters at Llanover was Miss F. D. Port (Fanny Port). Augusta Hall's mother was Georgina Mary Ann Port.

77 For Parry's London career, see Janet Snowman, *John Orlando Parry and the Theatre of London* (London, 2010).

78 Groups of diaries are held both by NLW and NMW.

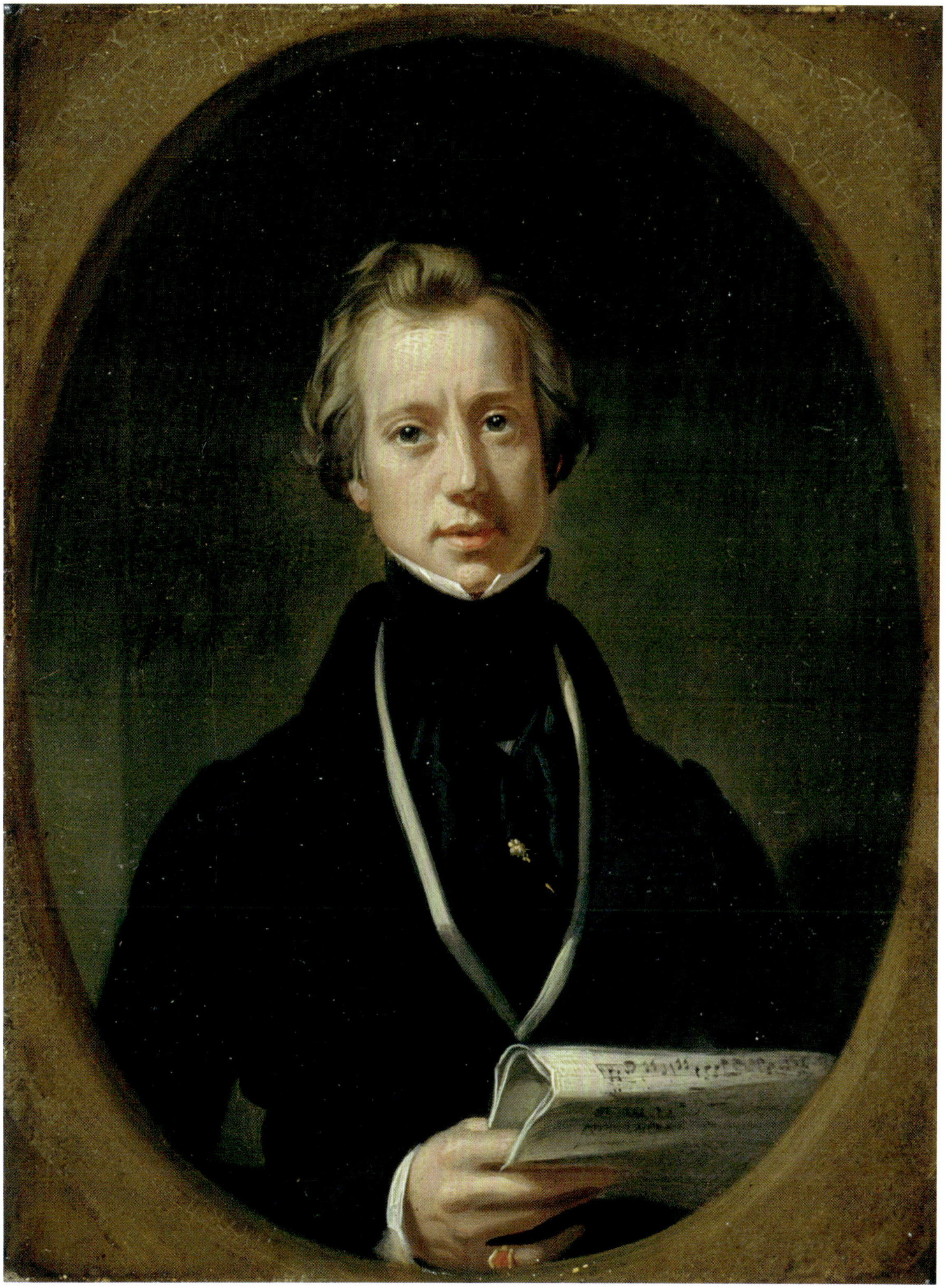

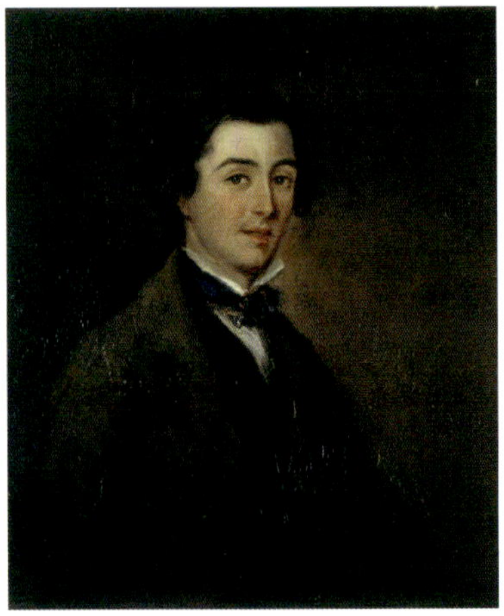

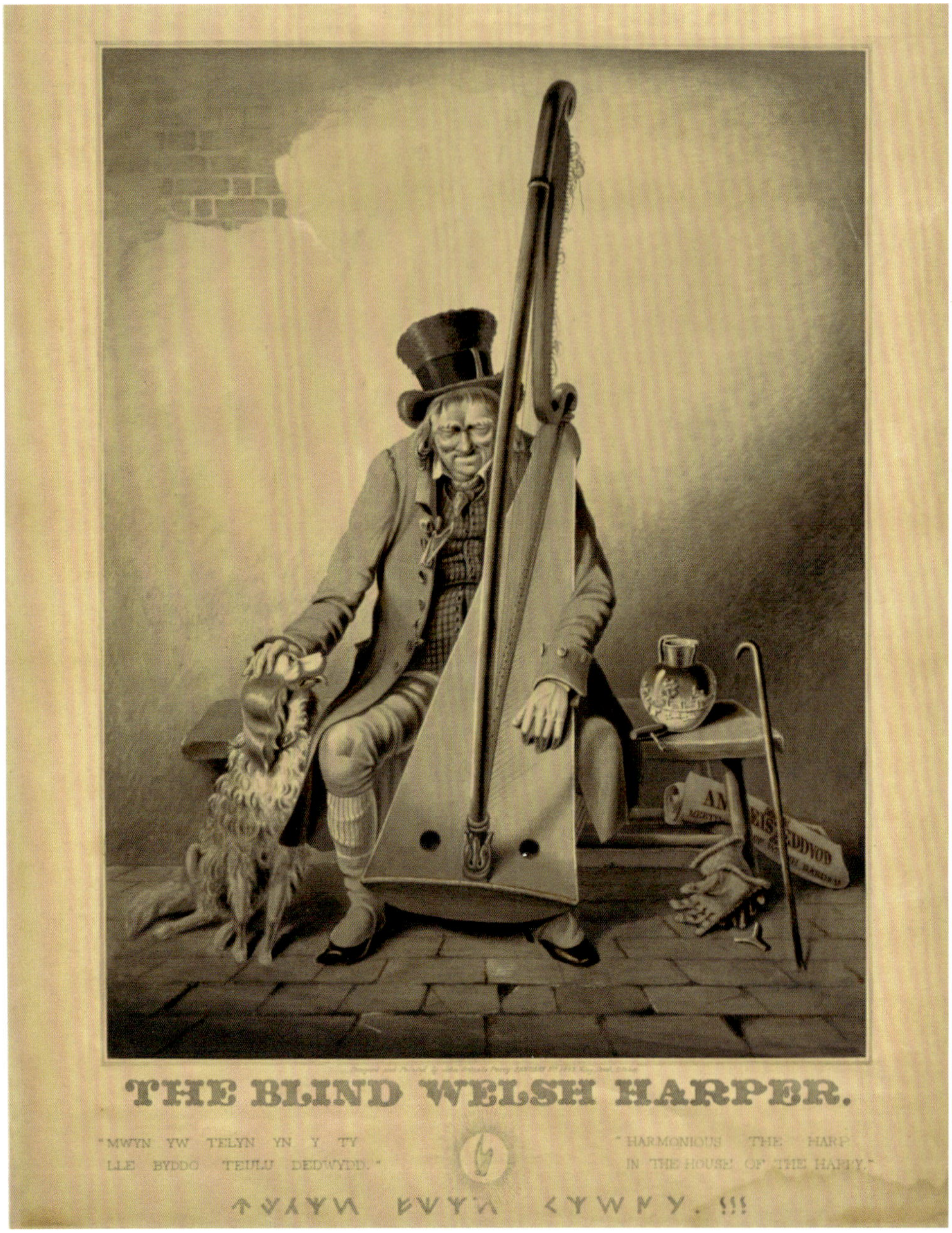

153 Charles Augustus Mornewicke, *John Orlando Parry*, c.1835

154 John Orlando Parry, *The Blind Harper*, 1837

on which he sits is a poster advertising an eisteddfod, and he wears on his lapel a silver harp that testifies to his victory in a competition. The lithograph, for which the original sepia drawing survives, may be generic rather than a representation of a particular individual, though Richard Roberts seems a likely candidate for the sitter if it is, indeed, a portrait. It is inscribed: ‘Mwyn yw telyn yn y ty lle bydd teulu dedwydd. Harmonious the harp in the house of the happy’, followed by a second inscription written in *coelbren y beirdd* that reads ‘telyn vwyn cymry’ (‘the sweet harp of Wales’).

John Orlando Parry was a welcome visitor to Llanover. In 1848, when Parry was in residence, he drew and described domestic preparations for the forthcoming Eisteddfod. The first Llanover harper had recently died, to be replaced by Thomas Griffith, who accompanies the house choir rehearsing 'Serch Hudol'. The rehearsal turned into an extended musical evening, during which Parry rendered 'Jeannette and Jeannot', one of the songs that he popularised in his now frequent public performances.

Also preparing for the 1848 Eisteddfod were the Brecon sculptors John Evan and William Meredyth Thomas. They were responding to one of two art competitions announced at the previous event to produce works on national subjects. There were no entries in the painting competition, for which William Williams, Aberpergwm, had sponsored the prize, but the Thomas brothers were awarded the substantial sum of 70 guineas for their sculpture on the subject of *The Death of Tewdrig*. The adjudicators were Williams and Benjamin Hall. The engagement of Hall with the competition was significant. It had been announced in the immediate aftermath of the highly publicised exhibition at Westminster Hall in London of competition pieces for sculpture to decorate the new Houses of Parliament, then

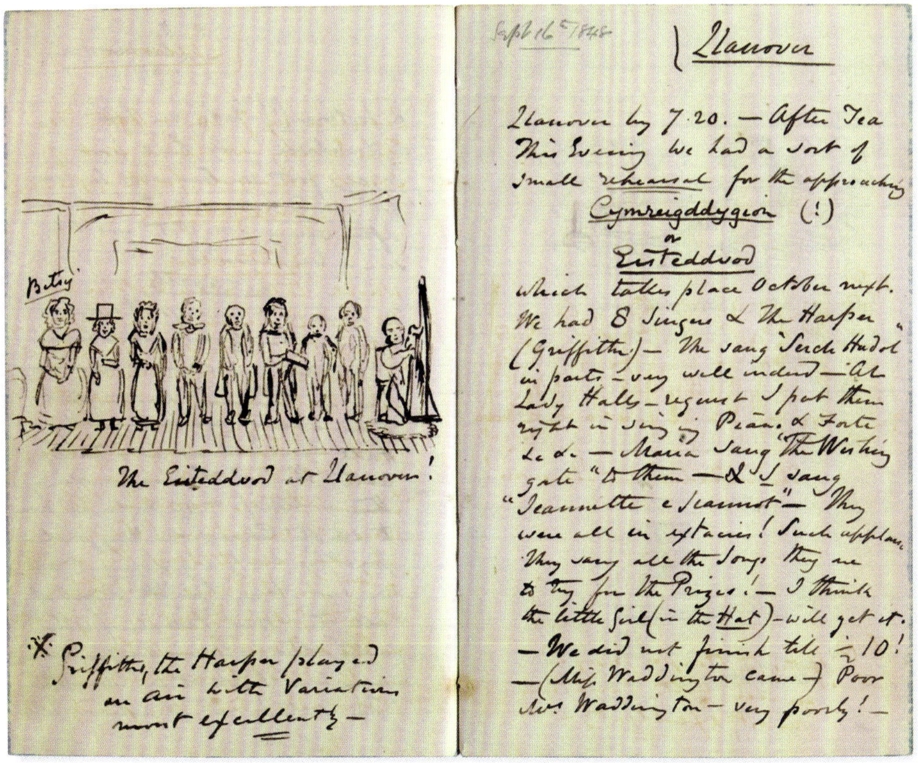

155 John Orlando Parry, *The Eisteddvod at Llanover*, 1848

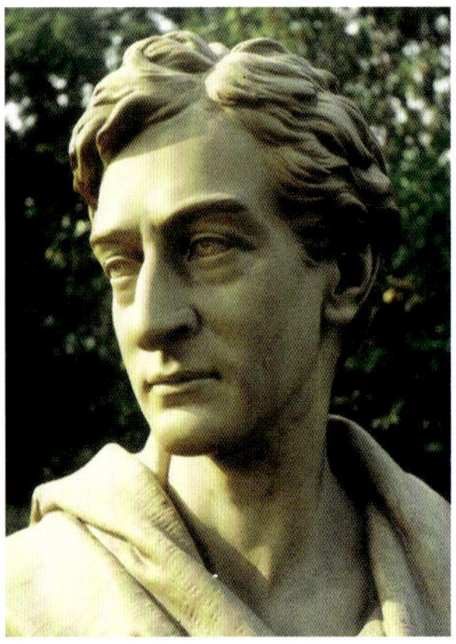

156 William Meredyth Thomas, *Thomas Price, Carnhuanawc*, 1848

rebuilding after the fire of 1836. Hall had been an active Member of Parliament since 1831 and indeed, in 1855, would become Commissioner of Works during the lengthy building process at Westminster. William Meredyth Thomas had been amongst the competitors who exhibited at Westminster Hall in 1844, where he showed *Prince Harry*. Although it was his elder brother, John Evan, who was awarded the prize at Abergavenny four years later, presumably on the basis of the work being his conception, the piece was in fact modelled by William Meredyth:

> The subject was the Death of Tewdrig, the King of Gwent, in the moment of victory over the Saxons at Mathern. The King is here represented, after having been wounded in the battle, supported by his faithful daughter Marchell, mother of Brychan Brycheiniog, attended by his faithful bard.[79]

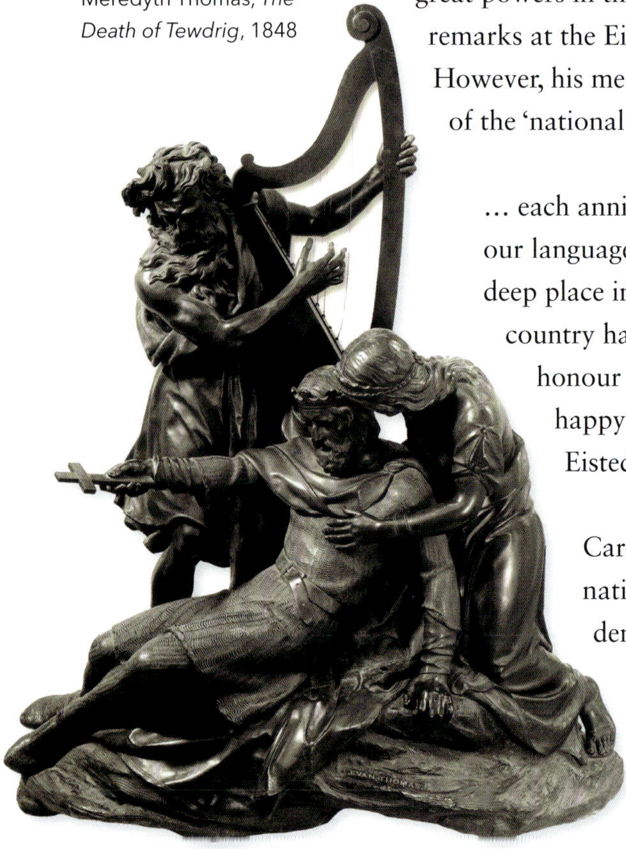

157 John Evan and William Meredyth Thomas, *The Death of Tewdrig*, 1848

The Death of Tewdrig was a major work of nineteenth-century historicist Welsh art.[80] Created in the year of revolution all over the European continent, it is tempting to place it in the context of the many expressions in art of the struggles of the small nations that fought for their freedom from the domination of the great powers in that extraordinary period. Indeed, Carnhuanawc's opening remarks at the Eisteddfod made reference to the events of the past year. However, his message ran counter to the turbulent spirit of the time. He spoke of the 'national object' of the festival, and felt gratified that:

> ... each anniversary brought with it an increase of strength; our music; our language, &c. were progressive, national feeling had always found a deep place in the hearts of the masses, but now this feeling in behalf of our country had found its way to royal hearts; and well might royalty thus honour us, for while other nations are engaged in revolutions, the happy people of the principality are employed in composing odes for Eisteddfodau and singing pennillion with the harp.[81]

Carnhuanawc's fantastical vision of the mindset of the Welsh nation in the year of revolution (within a decade of Chartist demonstrations and disturbances at Newtown and Llanidloes, and the Newport Rising) exemplified the continuing and pervasive Janus-like patriotism of the Welsh establishment. Carnhuanawc's ingratiating celebration of the patronage of the infant Prince of Wales came in response to the future king having been prevailed upon to donate a prize at the Eisteddfod.[82] The irony of the fact that the sculpture in close proximity to which he gave his loyal speech memorialised the resistance of a Welsh military leader to an invading English army had, apparently, passed him by: 'The war song of the aged bard is heard amidst the din of arms. The harp is struck, and the victory is celebrated.'[83]

Clearly derived from de Loutherbourg's familiar frontispiece to *Musical and Poetical Relicks*, the sculpture redeployed its eighteenth-century bardic iconography emasculated and sanitised by a pietà-like composition that emphasised the dominant myth of nineteenth-century national identity, the piety of the people, embodied in the notion of the primacy of Welsh Christianity. King Tewdrig, dying after the Battle of Mathern, points a crucifix at the invading English pagans. A further and deeper irony lies in the fact that, in the very year of the creation of the sculpture, the roots of a far more potent deployment of Welsh bardic mythology were laid down in one of the European nations most profoundly aroused by the revolutionary spirit of 1848. Through Russian intervention, the nascent Hungarian republic was suppressed and returned to Austrian rule in 1849. Eight years later, the restored Austrian Archduke ventured his first visit to the subjected nation. The most celebrated Hungarian poet of the period, János Arany, was asked to compose a celebration of the event. His response was a lengthy subversive metaphor – an ode describing the suppression of the Welsh bards by Edward I. The ode, 'A walesi bárdok' ('The Bards of Wales') rapidly became celebrated in Hungary, though it differed from the version of the myth familiar from Gray's English poem by setting the events in Montgomery. An edition published in 1896 visualised the Welsh bardic myth with engravings based on the work of Mihály Zichy – a painter renowned for his evocations of Hungarian national sentiment.[84]

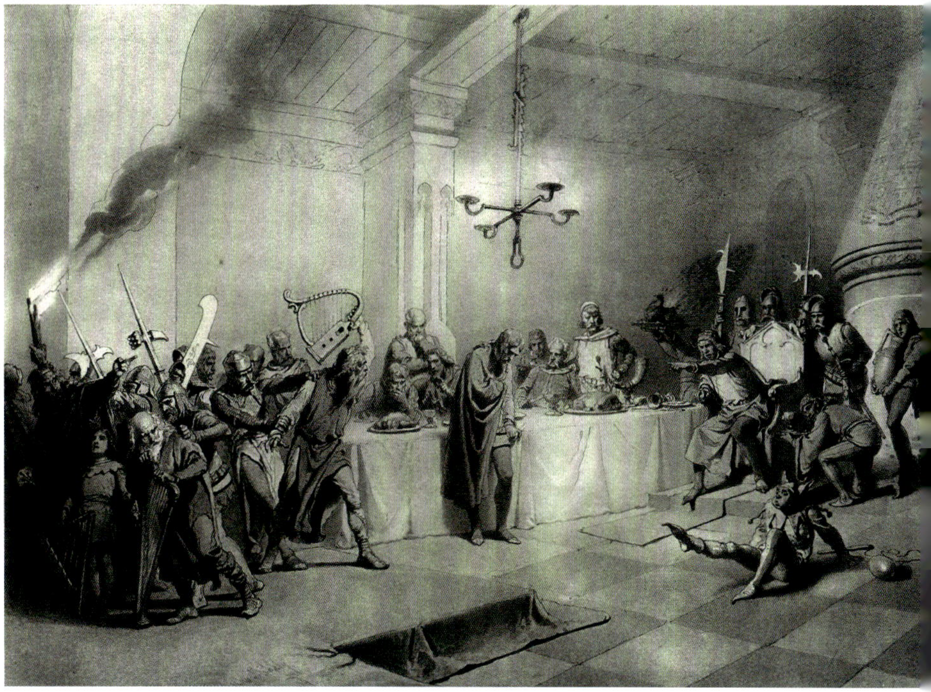

158 Mihály Zichy, *A walesi bárdok*, 1898

79 *The Welshman*, 20 October 1848, p. 4.

80 When exhibited at the Eisteddfod the sculpture was in plaster. Two copies in bronze were produced later by the electrotype process.

81 *The Welshman*, 20 October 1848, p. 4.

82 The prize for 'The best critical essay on the history of the language and literature of Wales' was won by Thomas Stephens and was published as *The Literature of the Kymry* (Llandovery, 1849).

83 *The Welshman*, 20 October 1848, p. 4.

84 Among his most celebrated works was his painting of the declamation of the national song, 'Nemzeti dal' by its author, Sándor Petőfi, at the high point of the revolution in 1848. The lasting importance of 'A walesi bárdok' in Hungarian tradition was reinforced in 2011 when the first performance of Karl Jenkins's setting of the poem was given at the Béla Bartók National Concert Hall in Budapest.

WALES

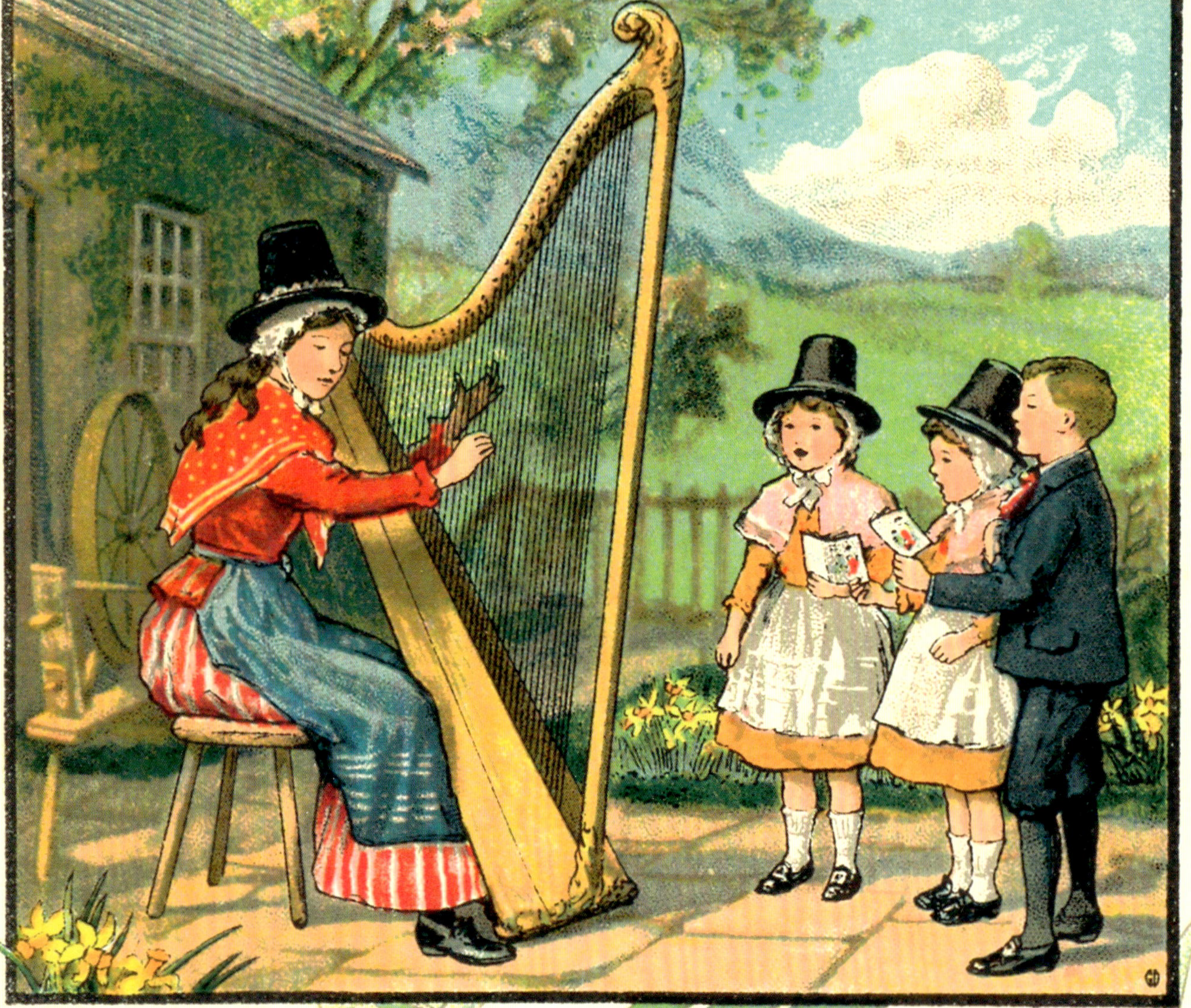

Hen Wlad fy Nhadau,

The Land of my Fathers.

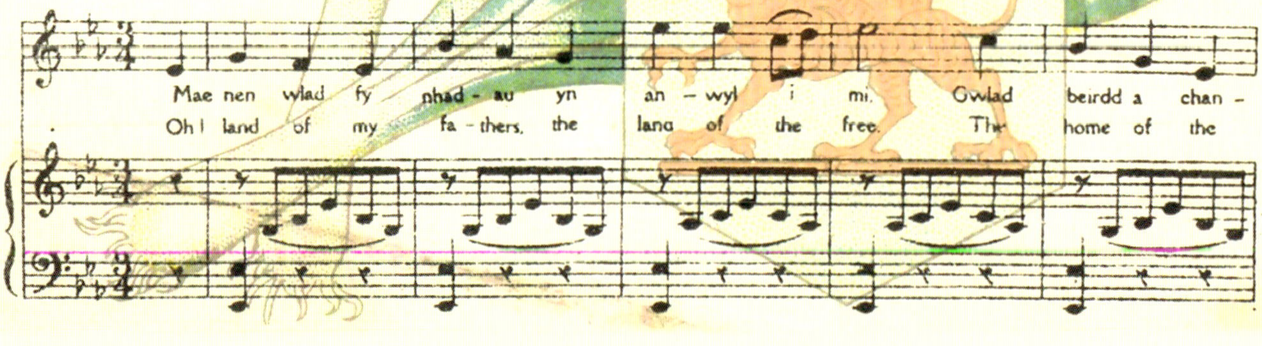

CHAPTER FOUR

WALES: *The* LAND *of* SONG

Carnhuanawc died shortly after the 1848 Abergavenny Eisteddfod, and although the Cymreigyddion Society continued to function, with the loss of its most charismatic supporter, its influence declined. A new generation of intellectuals emerged as the leaders of artistic activity, though some had developed their public profiles at Abergavenny. The composer Brinley Richards had adjudicated the choral and harp competitions in 1848, for instance. The victorious harper that year was John Roberts, and at an Eisteddfod held in the Town Hall at Cardiff in the spring, two years later, he was again successful. Under these new leaders, the first two decades of the second half of the nineteenth century would see fundamental changes in the way in which national sentiment was expressed through music, poetry and the visual arts, as the national brand evolved.

In many ways, the Rhuddlan Eisteddfod, held in 1850, marked the turning point, characterised both by an extension of the material presented and the means by which it was disseminated. The Eisteddfod was directed by John Jones, 'Talhaiarn', whose career as a poet at home and as an engineer and architect in London was approaching its peak.[1] Talhaiarn designed an Eisteddfod pavilion which accommodated thousands of people – many more than the elite audiences that had attended previous events in extant small venues such as at Wrexham in 1820, or even the specially built Abergavenny Cymreigyddion Hall and the relatively commodious Cardiff Town Hall. The extensive report of the event published in *The Illustrated London News* stated that early on the first day at Rhuddlan, 'pedestrians from various towns within a circle of twenty miles, *of all classes*' were making their way to the castle, in addition to those arriving by special trains from London, and from Chester, Liverpool and Manchester.[2] Rhuddlan reset the scale of public participation in the Eisteddfod, providing an enlarged national stage for the traditional competitions, alongside the performance of international repertoire and of new Welsh scores in order to benefit the emerging generation of composers. John Owen, for instance, acquired his bardic name, 'Owain Alaw', at the meeting, when the first performance of his anthem 'Deborah a Barac' brought him to public attention. Nevertheless, the decade inaugurated at Rhuddlan would continue to be marked by the periodic rumblings of disagreement amongst patriotic intellectuals that had surfaced at Carmarthen in 1819 about the true nature of the musical tradition. On this

1 Talhaiarn's 'Awdl y Greadigaeth' was published in 1849. He worked on the Crystal Palace in London, 1850–1.

2 *The Illustrated London News*, 28 September 1850, p. 262, authors' italics.

matter, it would seem that *The Illustrated London News* had been well briefed by the London modernisers. Reviewing the history of music in the Eisteddfod, the correspondent observed that: 'In 1828, under the direction of Mr Parry, there was an attempt to introduce at Denbigh music of other masters besides the Welsh composers, but it does not appear that Wales was sufficiently ripe for

159 Unknown artist,
The Cardiff Eisteddfod, 1850

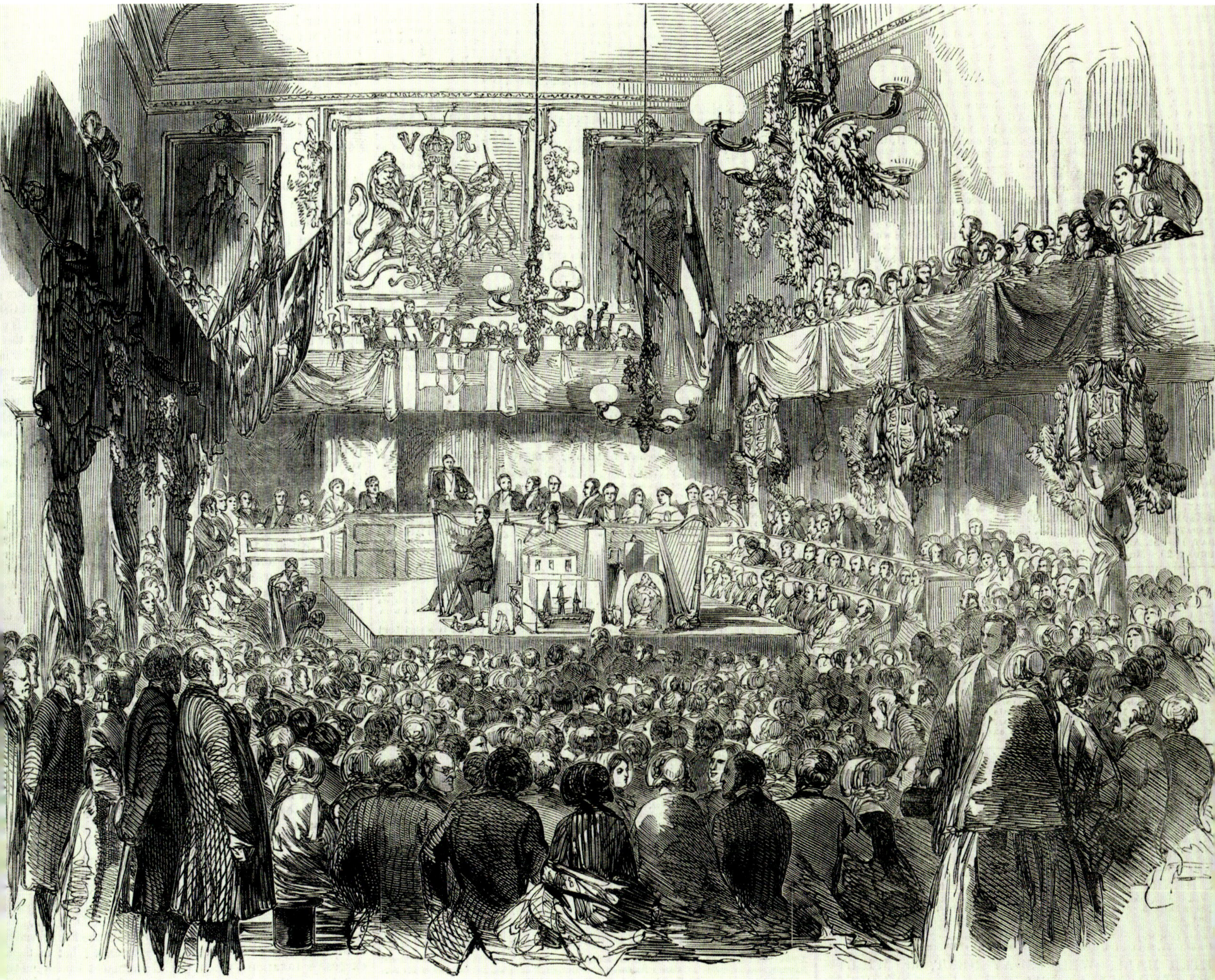

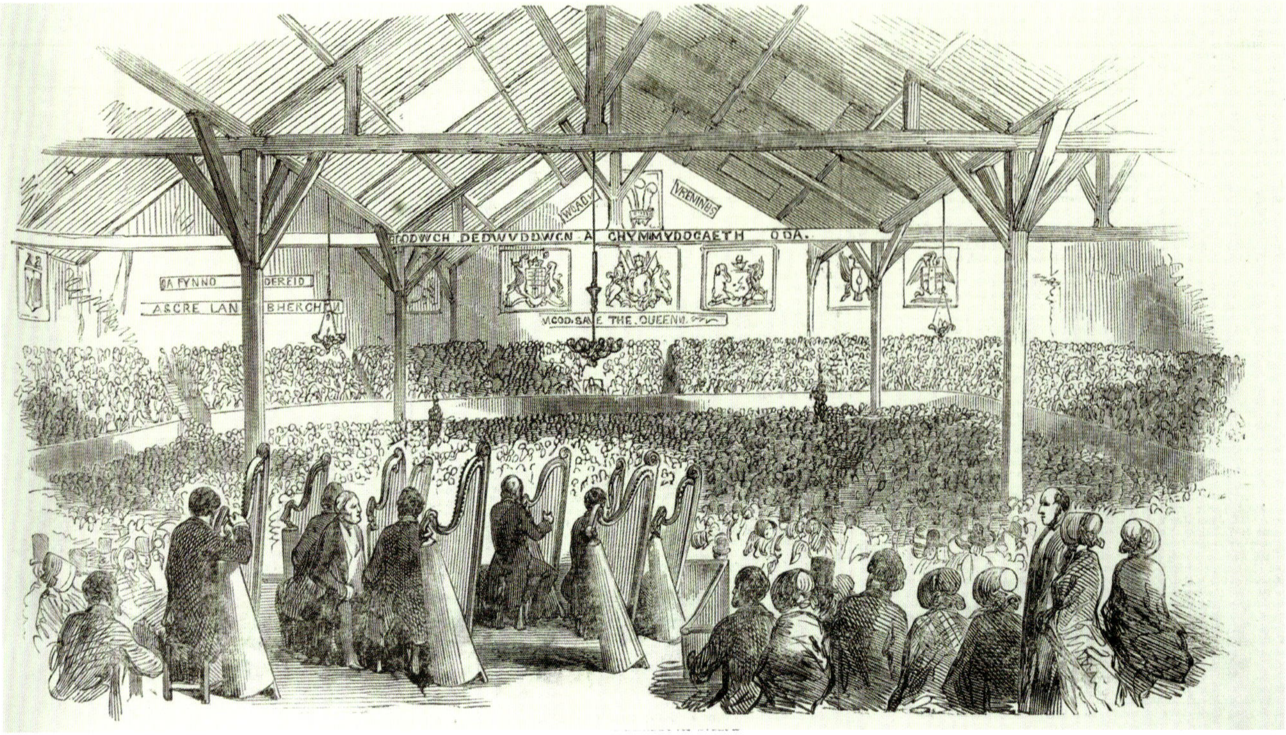

160 Unknown artist, *The Rhuddlan Eisteddfod*, 1850

161 William Roos, *John Jones, Talhaiarn*, 1864 or earlier

this innovation.' In the first concert at Rhuddlan, works by Beethoven, Weber, Mendelssohn and Donizetti were performed before a large audience. In his speech at the opening ceremony, 'without excluding nationality' the Dean of Bangor 'argued in behalf of the progress exhibited in this age in the fine arts and education generally.' But there were dissenters:

> The learned Dean was listened to with some impatience by the Welsh 'purists' and was replied to with immense energy by the Rev. Hicks Owen, who was for everything Welsh and against everything English. This exhibition of nationality, or of antipathy, found responsive echoes in some portions of the auditory.[3]

The concert concluded in an inauspicious manner for the modernisers: 'A heavy shower of rain coming down whilst Miss Luscombe was singing "Within a mile of Edinboro' town" a precipitate retreat of the company took place, and Sir H.R. Bishop's glee, "Blow gentle gales" was omitted.'[4]

The considerable coverage granted the Rhuddlan meeting by *The Illustrated London News*, whose reach extended beyond England throughout the Empire, confirmed the pattern initiated at Abergavenny, with views of both the Eisteddfod

3 Ibid. The Revd William Hicks Owen, Senior Vicar of St Asaph and Vicar of Tremeirchion, was the second husband of Harriet Mary Browne, sister of Felicia Hemans. Among the competitions at Rhuddlan was one for a poem to 'The Memory of Mrs Hemans'. The hostile response to the speech of James Henry Cotton, Dean of Bangor, is perhaps surprising since the Dean was an educationalist sympathetic to the Welsh language (which he had learnt to speak). He had been offended by the methods employed by the Commissioners for Education, published in the Blue Books of 1847.

4 Ibid.

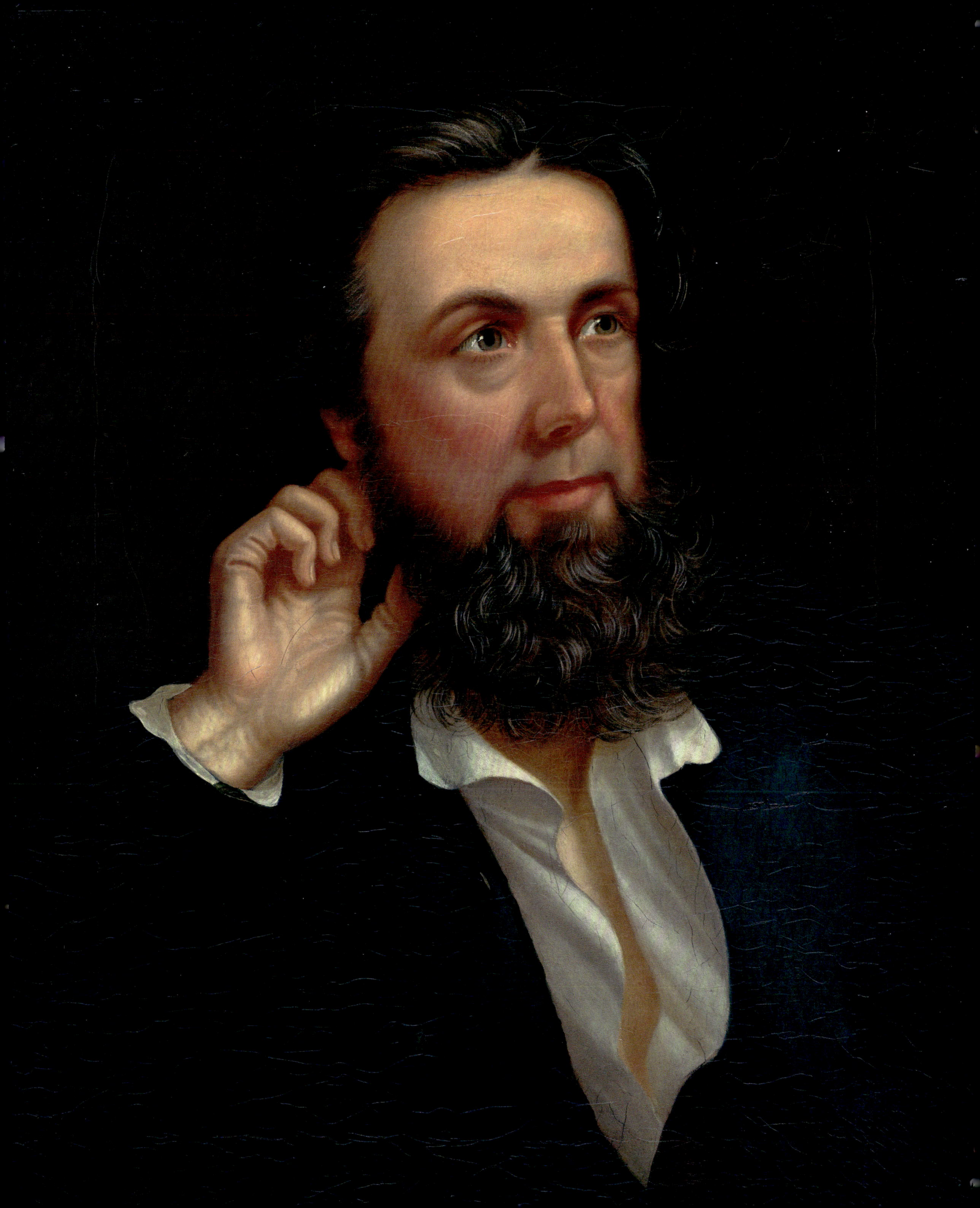

environs and the pavilion interior. In the age of photography, but before it was technically possible to print photographs in newspapers and journals, the ambition to document the world with the realism of the new medium dominated aesthetics, and the sophistication of the work of artists and wood engravers – sometimes the same individual – reached a high level. Sadly, few of the many engravings based on the Rhuddlan pattern were signed, but most were probably cut after drawings made on the spot, rather than being imaginary interpretations based on written reports. The interior view of the Rhuddlan pavilion depicts the harp competition won by Ellis Roberts. The documentary character of the engraving rings true – one competitor, waiting his turn to perform at the rear of the stage, tunes his instrument. Clearly visible at the rear of the pavilion were an impressive array of armorial pictures 'painted by Mr Atkins, the conductor, who, to his accomplishments as a musician, super-adds those of a painter.' With 'truly artistic enthusiasm', he 'had supplied these well-decorated specimens of heraldic art, ten feet by twelve each coat of arms, at his own expense.'[5] An equally remarkable series of portraits of notable literary figures, on loan from John Williams MP, was displayed above the President's chair, and so behind the artist. Some of the portraits were copies of originals painted by William Roos and he may have been responsible for the reproductions. Roos developed a close relationship with Talhaiarn, and would paint a formal portrait of him in the following year. His more remarkable portrait of the same sitter, inscribed 'The Bard in Meditation', carries an amended date of 1864, and it seems possible, given the apparent age of the sitter and his engagement at Rhuddlan, that Roos may have painted it in 1850. The informality of the portrait, which shows Talhaiarn looking beyond the painter, with flowing beard and open-necked shirt, indicates that Roos was well acquainted with the long tradition of bardic imagery. It was a sophisticated reinvention of tradition that did not resort to pastiche and pantomime bardic costume.[6]

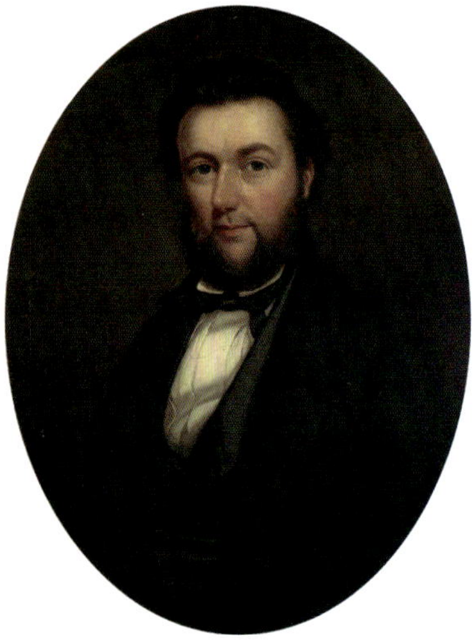

162 William Roos, *John Jones, Talhaiarn*, 1851

It was as well that the artist working for *The Illustrated London News* attended the harp competition on the Wednesday of the Rhuddlan Eisteddfod, since the competition for women harpers on the following day was interrupted:

> ... when the entire audience, consisting of some thousands, were suddenly terrified by a loud crash. There were instantaneous cries of 'the building is falling in', and the rush to the different doors was positively frightful. In a few moments after the crash the platform fell in at its centre.[7]

5 Ibid. In another report, Atkins was noted as 'professor of music, St Asaph'.

6 For the Roos portraits and his relationship with Talhaiarn, see Peter Lord, *William Roos and the Itinerant Life* (Llangefni, 2020).

7 *The Welshman*, 4 October 1850, p. 4.

8 *The Illustrated London News*, 28 September 1850, p. 262.

9 NLW MS Evan James 1.

There were some broken bones and, mysteriously, 'Miss L'Estrange was hurt by a combe going into her head', but fortunately nothing worse. *The Illustrated London News* reported that 'The heroism of the sufferers is beyond all eulogium.'[8] Recriminations directed at both the architect and the contractor would continue for some time.

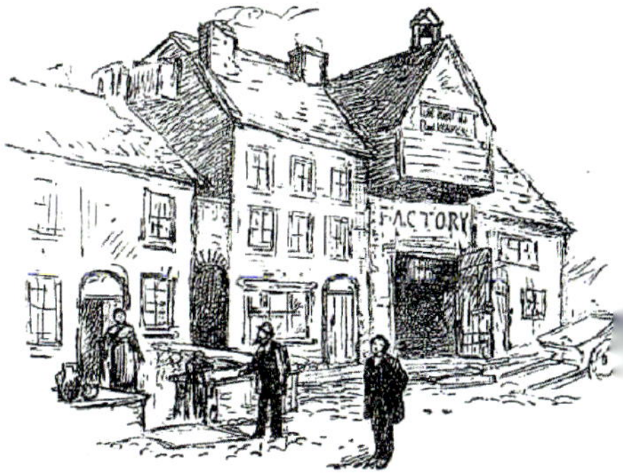

163 Unknown artist, *The Woollen Factory of the James Family, Pontypridd*, 1893

The first years of the second half of the nineteenth century saw the composition of a potent group of definitive national melodies and poems. The first to emerge, in 1856, was a melody originally called 'Glan Rhondda', but it soon became known as 'Hen Wlad Fy Nhadau'. It was the work of James James, a harper from Pontypridd. The words were written by his father, Evan James, a weaver and woollen merchant – though the retrospective accounts of those who knew both the poet and the composer differ as to whether the words preceded the melody or the melody preceded the words. With commendable foresight on the part of his parents, James James had been born at the Ancient Druid Inn at Hollybush. The evidence of his tune book[9] suggests that he was self-taught, but he was a professional musician, who played for dancing in public houses. An artist working for *The Illustrated London News* recorded a scene that would have been familiar

164 Unknown artist, *Stepping, Merthyr*, 1873

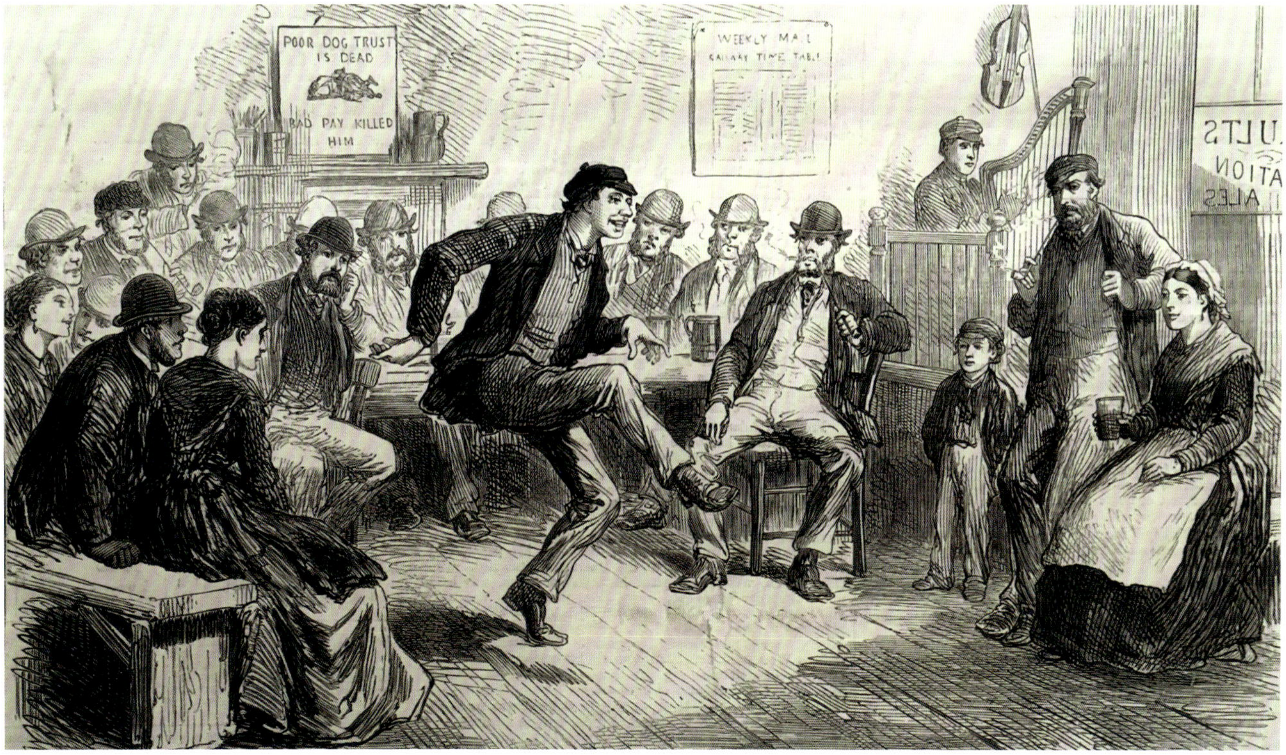

to him. A serious industrial dispute in 1873 drew the paper's artist to Merthyr where, despite the dire poverty that he or she depicted in other parts of the town, music and dance continued to provide relief. The harper, playing for 'stepping', appears also to have been a fiddler, though there is no evidence to suggest that James James played both instruments. The company in the pub is mixed – women and children are present along with the men – and on the back wall hangs what appears to be a loose copy of a lithograph, politically appropriate for the times, entitled *Poor Trust is Dead. Bad Pay Killed Him*. The print which was probably the source of the image was published in about 1868 by the American company of Currier and Ives. Interaction between mining communities at home and Welsh émigré workers in the United States characterised the period.[10]

It seems that 'Glan Rhondda' soon became popular locally, and was in print as early as 1858.[11] In the same year it reached a national audience at the Llangollen Eisteddfod, where it was included by two competitors in their entries for a new collection of Welsh airs. Owain Alaw was the adjudicator and, two years later, he included it in the first volume of his collection *Gems of Welsh Melody* as 'Hen Wlad Fy Nhadau'. By then, he had already been busy facilitating its dissemination at a personal level. Along with Talhaiarn, in 1859 he performed the piece regularly on a concert tour, which was advertised as 'A Night with Tal and Alaw'.

The debate about the nature and purpose of the Eisteddfod flared up once more at Llangollen in 1858. The meeting was boycotted by Lady Llanover, who disapproved of the Celticist fantasies of the organiser, the Revd John Williams, 'Ab Ithel'. It has been remarked of this Eisteddfod that 'every odd-bod in Wales

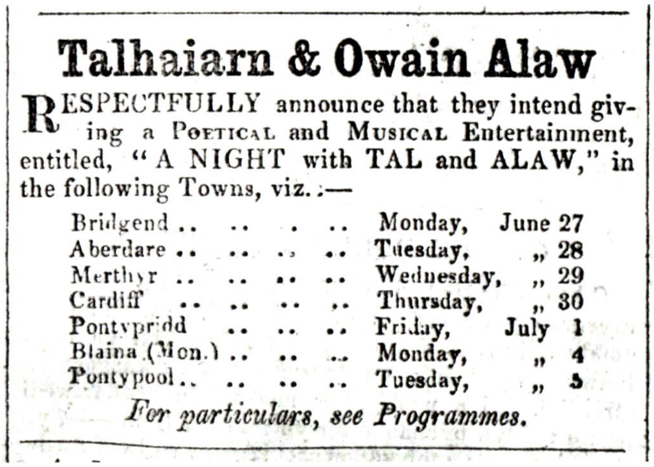

Talhaiarn & Owain Alaw

RESPECTFULLY announce that they intend giving a POETICAL and MUSICAL Entertainment, entitled, "A NIGHT with TAL and ALAW," in the following Towns, viz.:—

Bridgend	Monday,	June 27
Aberdare	Tuesday,	„ 28
Merthyr	Wednesday,	„ 29
Cardiff	Thursday,	„ 30
Pontypridd	Friday,	July 1
Blaina (Mon.)	Monday,	„ 4
Pontypool	Tuesday,	„ 5

For particulars, see Programmes.

165 *Talhaiarn and Owain Alaw*, advertisement from *Y Gwladgarwr*, 1859

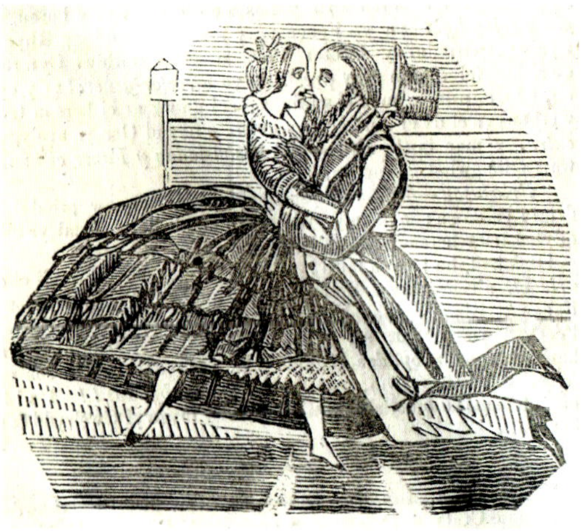

166 Ellis Owen Ellis, *John Jones, Talhaiarn*, 1860

took himself off there, and no doubt felt quite at home in the company',[12] which included the remarkable Thomas Price of Pontypridd. Ab Ithel himself was satirised in the magazine *Y Punch Cymraeg* by its cartoonist Ellis Owen Ellis. It was at this event that the Last Bard appeared for the final time in his eighteenth-century incarnation – the invading English army minutely suggested rounding a perilous outcrop of rock in the background. Significantly, the picture was the work of an artist based in the new industrial Wales. William Edward Jones had established himself at Merthyr in 1853, following a period in London working for the illustrated press. His original picture is missing, but other works of his which survive, including national subjects such as Hywel Dda, confirm that he was a competent painter. The adjudicator, John Francis of Manchester, thought the work 'full of national character':

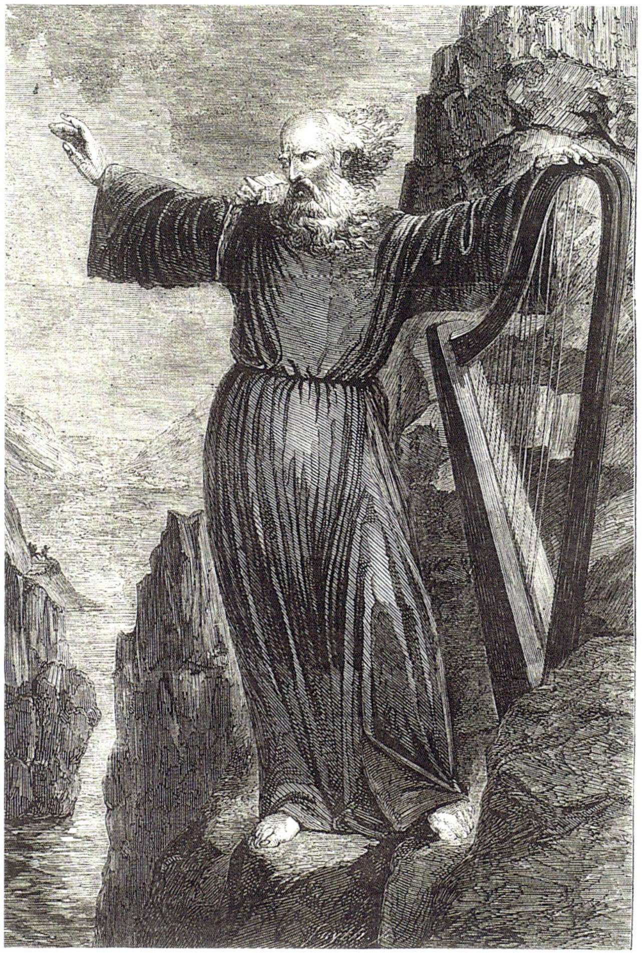

167 William Edward Jones, *The Bard*, 1858

> The attitude of the venerable bard, standing undismayed on his dizzy height, is boldly conceived. His face wears a severe expression, his sparse grey hairs being agitated by the wind. The ribbon bound round his uplifted arm denotes that he is a man of high rank.
>
> Far below, and far into the distance, winds the struggling and broken flood of the Conway. The sunset in the background is probably intended as a practical figure emblematic of the 'Decline and Fall of Wales'.[13]

Like Ab Ithel, Talhaiarn fell victim to the satirists of *Y Punch Cymraeg*. Ellis Owen Ellis lampooned him on several occasions on the basis of his alleged fondness for drink and for ladies. But the poet's public popularity was undeniable, and the concert tour he undertook with Owain Alaw in 1859 was characteristic of an appetite throughout the country for performers who provided, in halls and assembly rooms, a national twist to their offerings. As we have seen, John Parry, Bardd Alaw, had accompanied the child prodigy Elizabeth Randles on an extensive tour with her father, Edward, in 1807. Thirty years later, public fascination with child prodigies focused on another Welsh harpist, who became known simply as Master Hughes.

10 For the group of Merthyr engravings documenting the industrial dispute, see Peter Lord, *The Visual Culture of Wales: Industrial Society* (Cardiff, 1998), pp. 146–52.

11 Percy A. Scholes, 'Hen Wlad Fy Nhadau', *NLW Journal*, 3, 1 & 2 (Summer 1943), p. 5.

12 Isaac Foulkes, Llyfrbryf, given in G.J. Williams, Ab Ithel, *Y Llenor*, 12, 4 (Winter 1933), pp. 216–30, and 13, 2 (Summer 1934), pp. 88–100.

13 *The Illustrated London News*, 16 October 1858, p. 348.

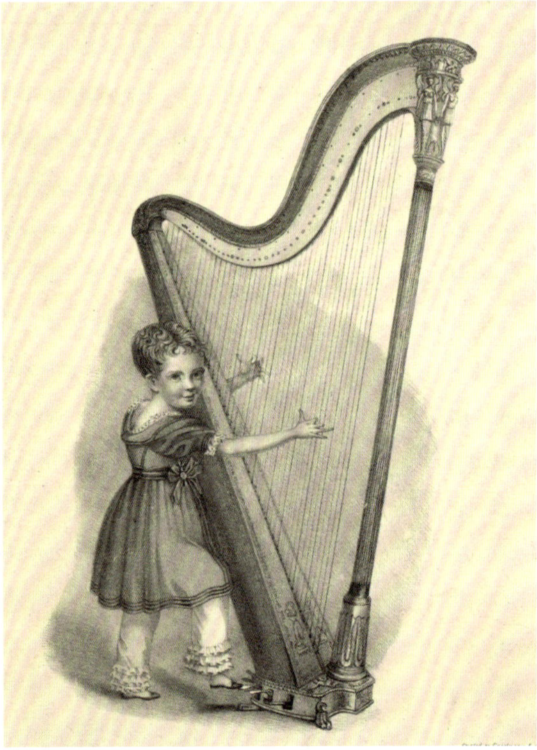

Joseph Tudor Hughes was born at Bala in 1827, and showed prodigious musical talent from a very early age. He is reputed to have performed in public on a harp when only three years old. An advertisement for a concert in Bath in 1832 acknowledged one T. ap James as his tutor.[14] A lithograph of the harper made at about this time, when Hughes was five years of age, was drawn from life by Benjamin Waterhouse Hawkins, though Master Hughes did not play the pedal harp on his left shoulder. The artist had not troubled to reverse his drawing when transferring it to the stone.[15] The occasion on which the portrait was taken is unknown, but by the mid-1830s, Hughes was being exhibited all over Wales and in England and Ireland by his entrepreneurial father, Dafydd. In June 1835 at an eisteddfod at Llannerch-y-medd, his son was made a member of the Gorsedd in the name 'Blegwryd ap Sitsyllt' and awarded a gold medal. His elevation was accompanied by concerts and by a competition to celebrate the young harpist in verse, which stimulated twenty-two entries.[16] The news was reported throughout the country. The *Glamorgan, Monmouth and Brecon Gazette* reprinted an account of the events:

168 Benjamin Waterhouse Hawkins, *Master Hughes. Five Years of Age*, c.1832

169 Albin Roberts Burt, *Master Hughes*, 1834

> This precocious genius has delighted the denizens of our good borough during the week, at two evening concerts; and has been attended by numerous and fashionable audiences. On Thursday evening, at his first concert, the programme contained a selection of the most favourite airs, calculated to display to advantage the brilliancy of his execution, and his exquisite taste. The variations to 'Poor Mary Ann' and 'My lodging is on the cold ground', were most tastefully given, and elicited loud applause. He also excited general admiration in the 'Welsh battle piece', 'Napoleon's March,' and the 'Melange.' ... We understand Master Hughes intends giving concerts at Pwllheli, Conway, Denbigh, &c. and after receiving his gold medal at Llwydiarth, will exhibit in Chester, Liverpool and Manchester, previous to his departure for Dublin.[17]

The iconography of Master Hughes expanded rapidly. The itinerant painter Albin Roberts Burt had caught up with the prodigy at Southampton in 1834,

14 *Bath Chronicle*, 6 February 1834.

15 Benjamin Waterhouse Hawkins (1807–94) was not noted for this type of work. Indeed, he would become celebrated twenty years later at the Great Exhibition for his life-sized sculptures of dinosaurs.

16 *North Wales Chronicle and Advertiser*, 28 July 1835.

17 *Glamorgan, Monmouth and Brecon Gazette*, 4 July 1835.

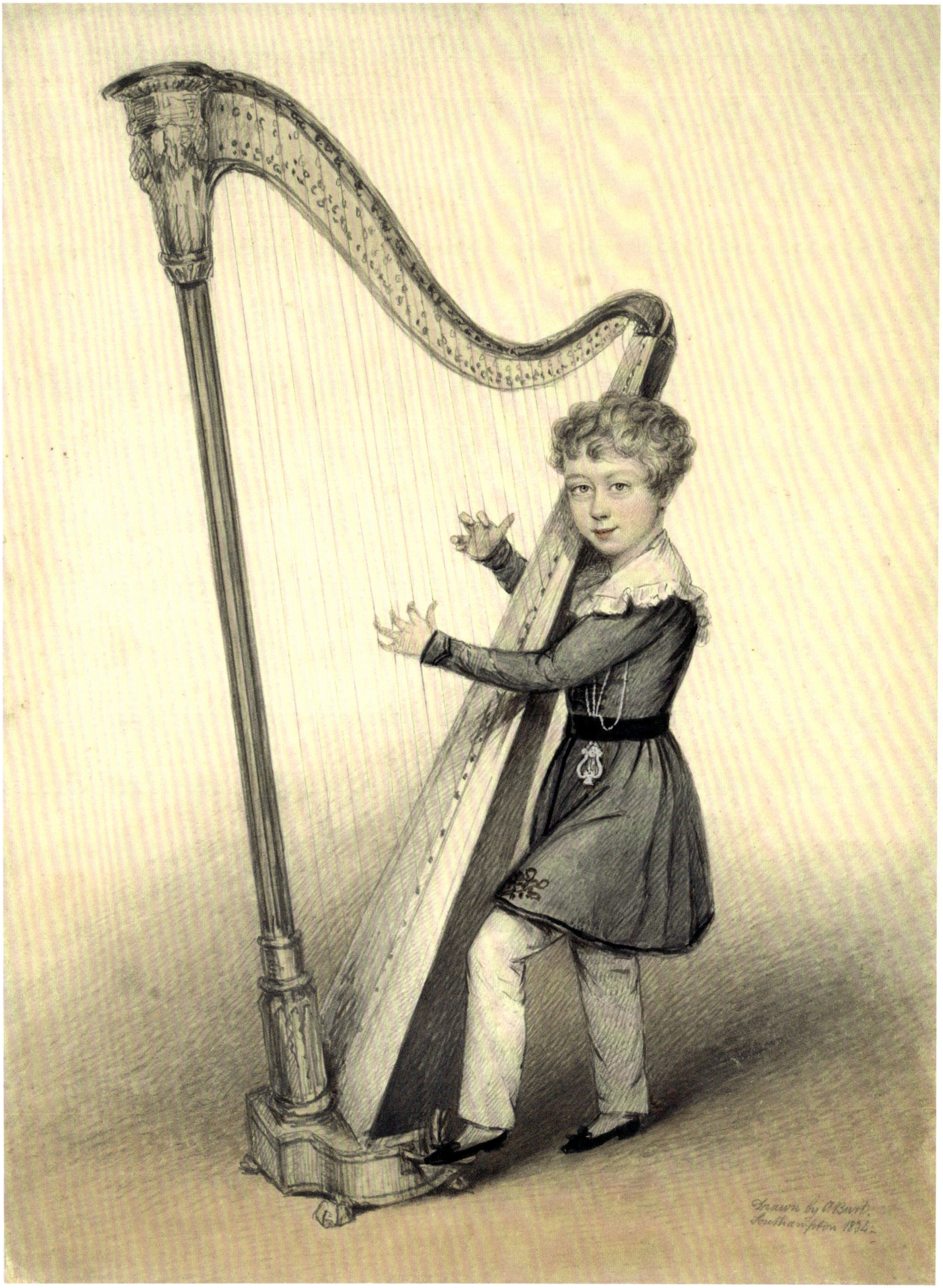
Drawn by A Burt.
Southampton 1834.

and painted a portrait of him in watercolour. Burt had a long track record of drawing celebrated individuals specifically as a basis for engravings, which would provide a steady income stream, rather than as commissions from the sitters. A closely similar lithograph, noting the fact that the harper had enjoyed royal patronage (he had played for the Dowager Queen), seems likely to have been based on the Burt original.[18] A further variant, differing only slightly, was published with a dedication to Frederick Chatterton, acknowledging him as the child's tutor. Chatterton was himself a young but already distinguished harper, and presumably had taken the place of ap James.[19]

By the late 1830s, the two younger brothers of Master Hughes were performing with him, and his iconography continued to expand:

> Last Wednesday and Thursday evenings the inhabitants of Merthyr were favoured with Concerts, by the justly celebrated juvenile Harpists, Master Hughes, and his younger brothers ... The concert on Wednesday opened with a Solo, Glan Meddwdod Mwyn, on the Harp by Master Hughes. We cannot ever recollect hearing this old favourite national Welsh Melody played with better effect; the new variations composed expressly by Master Hughes, and his excellent performance of the same, riveted the attention of the audience, causing a glow of national feeling, which brought to our minds 'the happy days of yore.' The duet performed by the two brothers on *one* Harp was admirably executed; the appearance of two boys, (the eldest only 11, and the other, 7 years of age), playing on the same Harp had a singular and pleasing effect, particularly as their performance was so correct, and evinced such good taste and judgement. The popular tune of *Jenny Jones*, was sweetly played on the Violin by Master John A. Hughes, only four years old, with much precision and spirit, and called forth violent applause.[20]

The brothers were depicted together in a composite print of three lithographs. The central image, also issued as a separate print, depicted the youngest, John A. Hughes, playing the violin, David Edward Hughes playing the harp, and Joseph Tudor Hughes with a concertina. The flanking images depict the party pieces of each of the brothers. On the right, Joseph plays two harps simultaneously, while on the left Joseph and David Hughes play a duet on a single harp.

18 To coincide with the Denbigh Eisteddfod in 1820 Burt had drawn and engraved Sir Watkin Williams Wynn on this speculative basis. The Master Hughes engraving carries the inscription 'drawn by J. Mitchell', which – although it has been taken to imply that the original was Mitchell's – probably identifies the lithographer, though the detail differences between the lithograph and Burt's watercolour make the provenance of the work uncertain. For Burt, see Peter Lord, *Looking Out: Welsh Painting, Social Class and International Context* (Cardigan, 2020), pp. 50–67.

19 In August 1832, Master Hughes and Chatterton shared the stage at a concert in the Royal Assembly Rooms, Leamington Spa (*Leamington Spa Courier*, 25 August 1832, p. 2).

20 *Glamorgan, Monmouth and Brecon Gazette*, 30 November 1839.

21 *The Illustrated London News*, 15 June 1844, p. 389. 'No man was ever more deservedly respected for ability and character than Mr P. senior, and the junior has walked the same path with honour and success, under the fondest of parental care.'

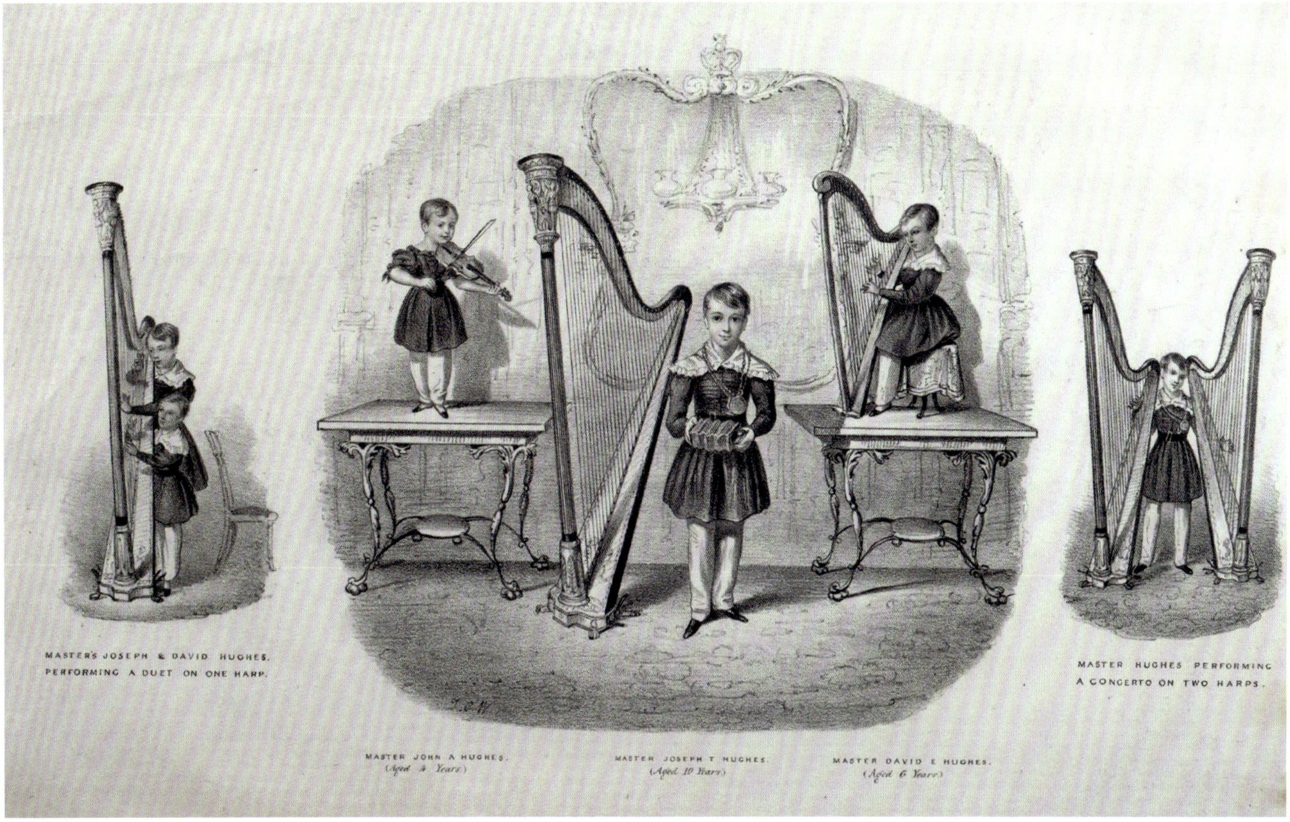

170 Unknown artist, *Master Hughes and His Brothers as They Appear at Their Concerts*, *c.*1838

To exploit their celebrity further, the children's father arranged a concert tour of the United States. In 1841 it ended abruptly, when Joseph Tudor Hughes was drowned in the Hudson River, a tragedy reported in both the Welsh- and English-language press on both sides of the Atlantic.

By this time, John Orlando Parry was beginning to acquire a public profile as a performer that extended beyond the confines of the London Welsh societies and the Llanover circle. After studying with Luigi Lablache in Naples and appearing in burlettas on the London stage, in 1840 he toured England and Ireland with Franz Liszt. Four years later he gave a concert performance at the Hanover Square Rooms that excited the correspondents of *The Illustrated London News*. They 'enjoyed one of the most delightful concerts we had ever been at', of which the contribution of 'glorious John' was the centrepiece, and noted that Parry 'is of Cambrian descent, being we believe, the only son of an ancient Briton, of similar name, who has "done some service" to music and poetry both in the Saxon and his native measures.' John Orlando 'at first used to sing sentimental ballads to his own harp accompaniment, but now he gives comic musical narratives and recitations at the pianoforte in a style that is quite *sui generis*.'[21]

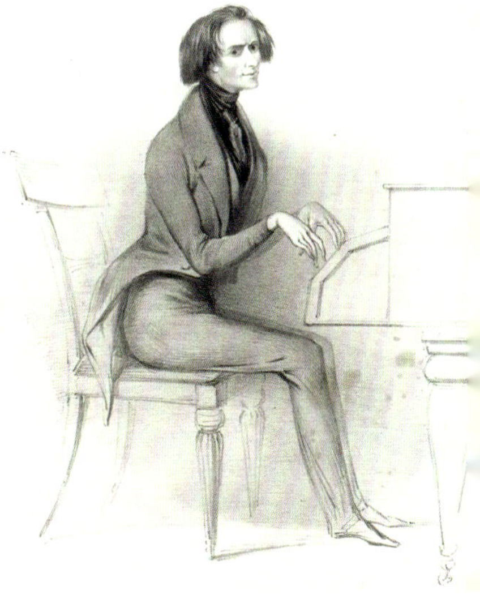

171 Unknown artist, *Monsieur Liszt. The Celebrated Pianist*, 1840

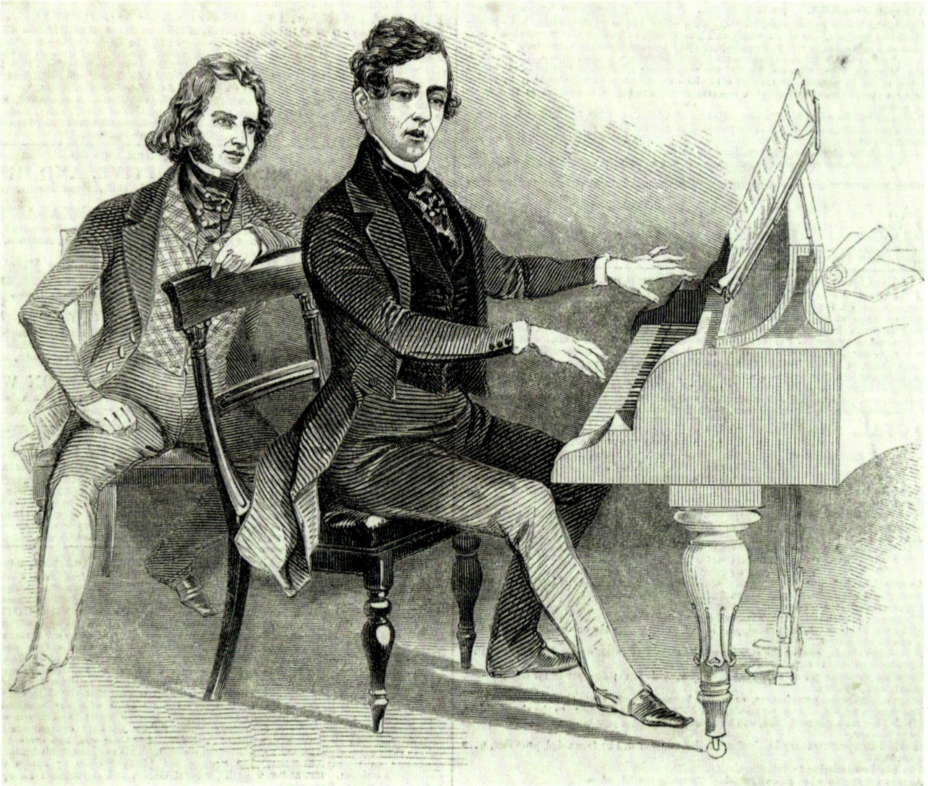

172 Unknown artist, *Mr Albert Smith and Mr John Parry*, 1844

173 Henry Tilbury, *Mr John Parry as the Artist*, 1850

Over the next thirty years, Parry's popularity was celebrated in the most extensive iconography of any Welsh performer of the nineteenth century.

In his entertainment *Notes, Vocal and Instrumental*, first given at the Store Street Music Hall in 1850, Parry included a pastiche of himself as 'An Artist', which was recorded by Henry Tilbury.[22] Parry's own visual talent continued to contribute to the imaging of musical practice. His diary for 1848, in which year he made a tour of small venues in Wales, records the primitive conditions in which sometimes he performed, in addition to notes about his repertoire and the audience reaction to it. At Bangor, the Broadwood square piano on which he was to perform arrived in the nick of time from Caernarfon, its legs still in their protective wrapping. The instrument was supplied by the organist and piano dealer Henry Hayden, son of the St Asaph cathedral organist who had been painted, years earlier, by Albin Roberts Burt with a similar instrument standing behind him. At Dolgellau, the celebrated London performer was forced to perch on boards placed across the box seats of the courthouse: 'very poor attendance. It poured with rain again! & the wind howled.' Nevertheless, he was encored

22 Reviewed in *The Times*, 25 June 1850.

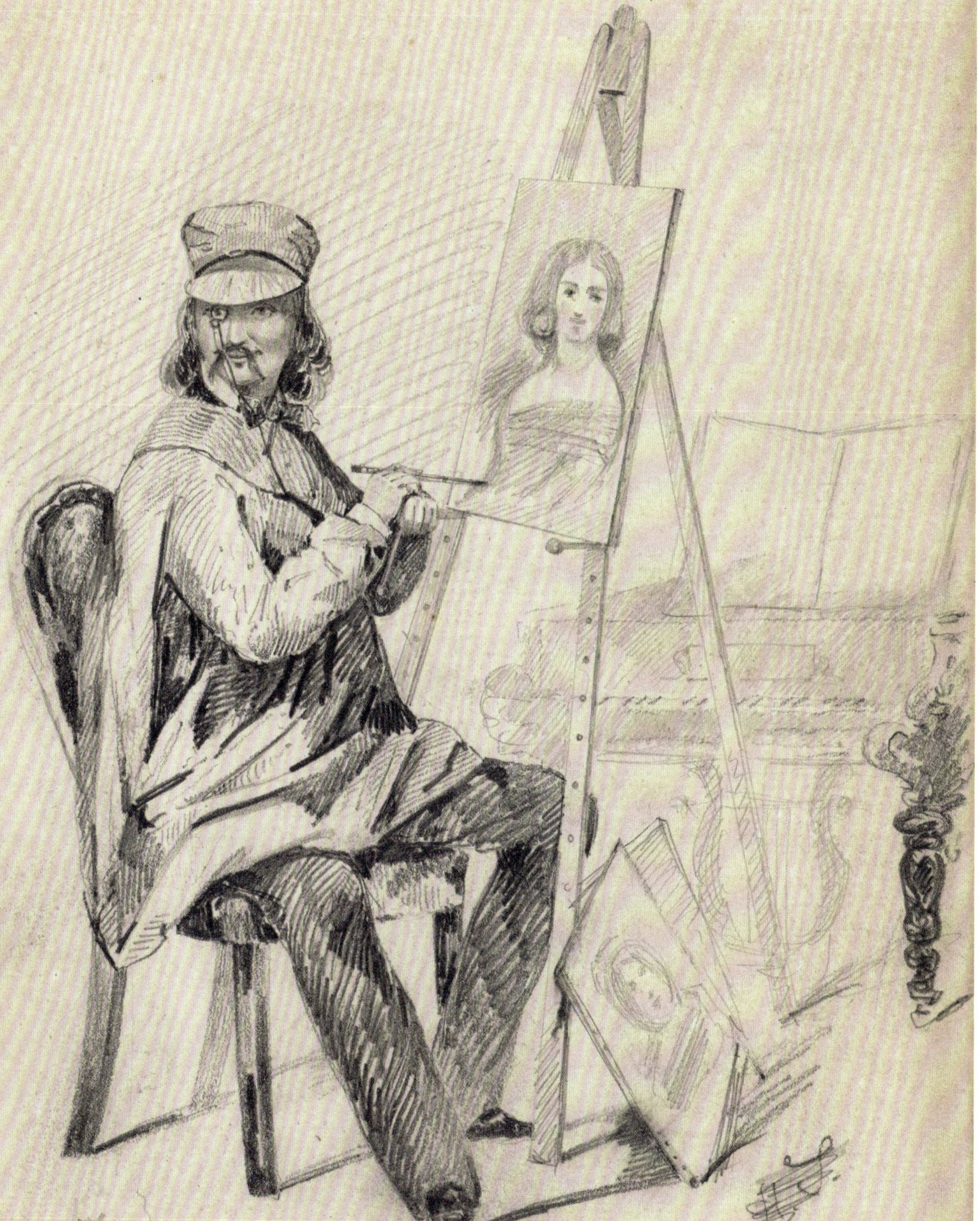

Drawn by Henry Tilbury London

Mr. JOHN PARRY
as the Artist
IN HIS "NOTES, VOCAL AND INSTRUMENTAL"

92

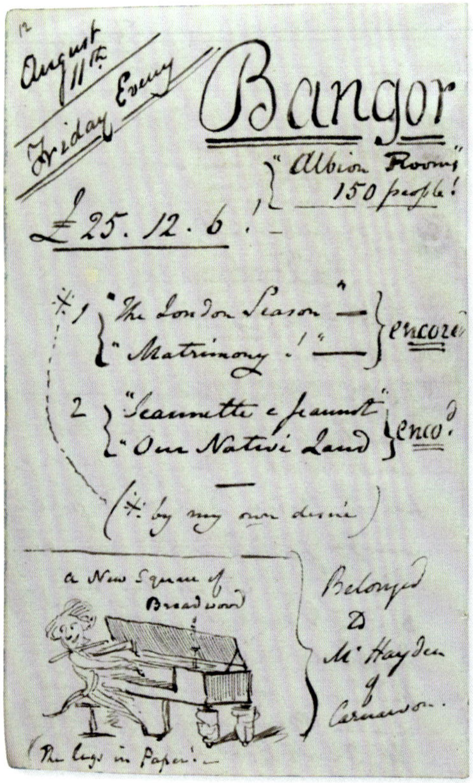

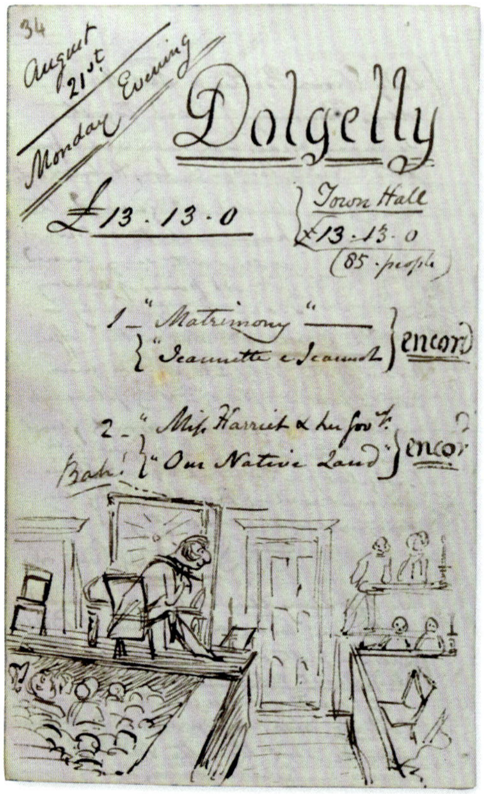

174 John Orlando Parry, *Diary Entries*, 1848

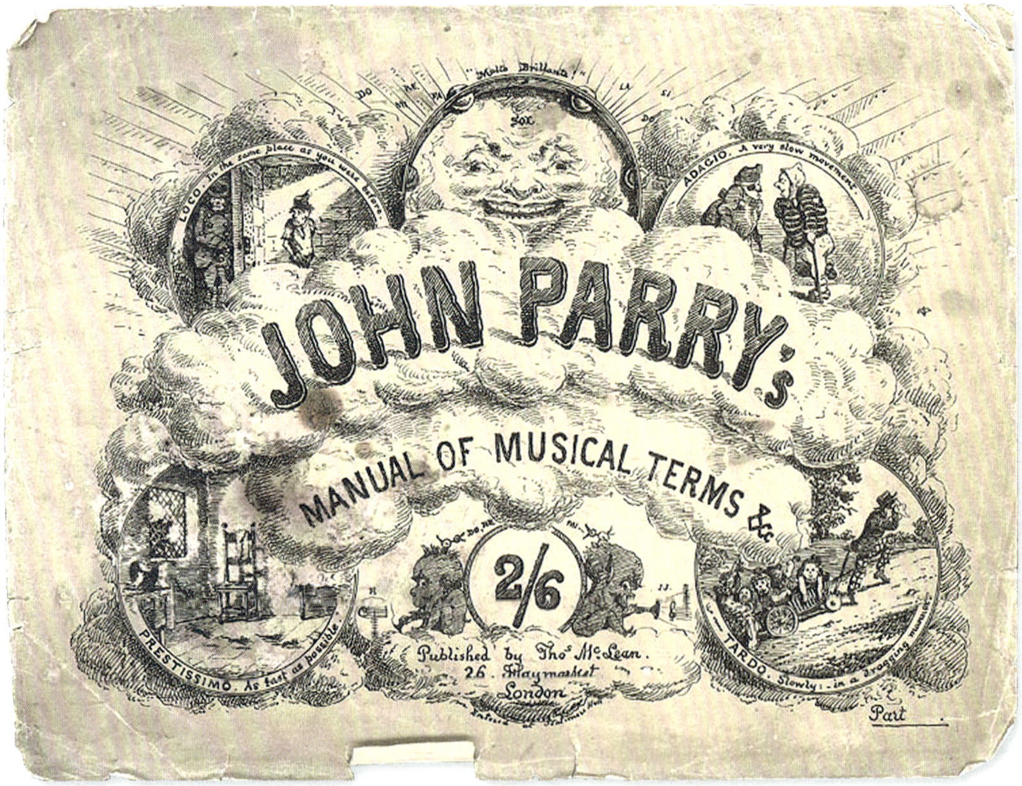

for his performance of 'Our Native Land'.[23] In due course, Parry would publish a collection of his musical caricatures, entitled *John Parry's Manual of Musical Terms*. It would have a long shelf life. First published in 1863, a new edition appeared as late as 1920.

With the notion of Welsh musicality now well established in the public mind, John Orlando Parry was by no means the only Welsh performer of the mid-nineteenth century for whom 'Cambrian descent' was regarded as an advantage in the promotion of a career. Appearing in London and the United States but, like Parry, touring also to small venues in Wales during the period, was the soprano Miss Elizabeth Lucy Williams. Trading on the huge celebrity of Jenny Lind, who by the mid-1840s had become widely known as 'the Swedish Nightingale', Williams promoted herself as 'the Welsh Nightingale'. Her portrait in character appeared on sheet music published in London for at least two popular songs, 'Tapping at the Window' and 'Wait, Till I Put On My Bonnet', by Charles Swain and Carlo Minasi, and she was identified as the composer and arranger of the 'national Welsh song', 'The Bells of Aberdovey', on a third.[24]

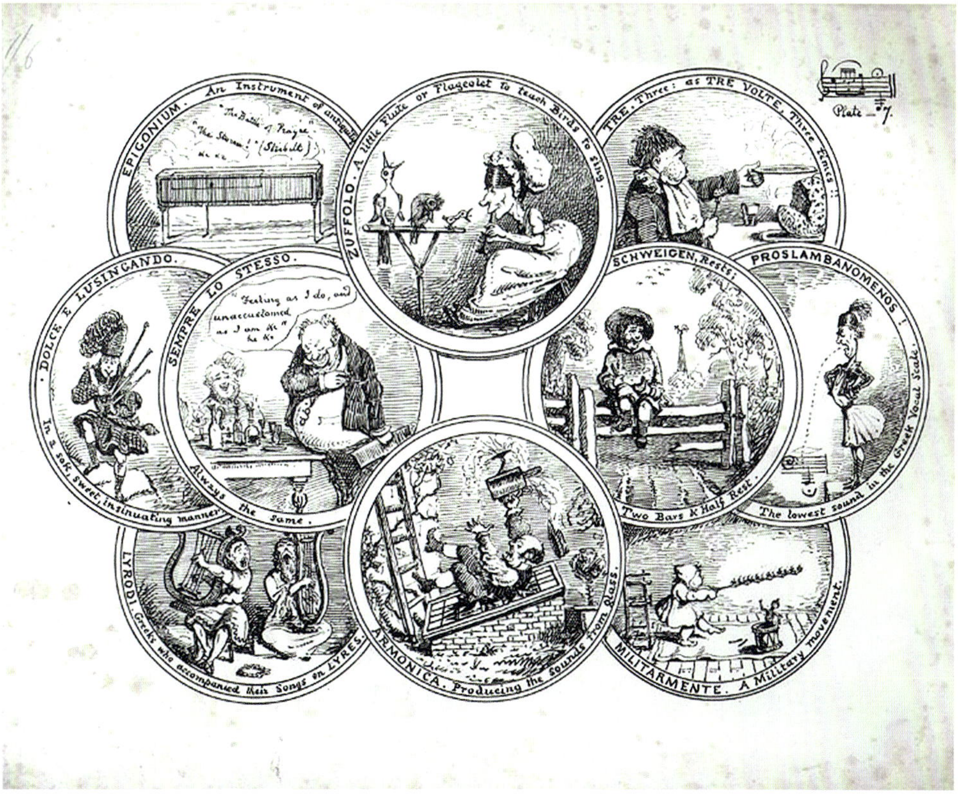

175 John Orlando Parry, *John Parry's Manual of Musical Terms*, 1863

23 NLW MS 17728A, f. 35. A flyer for the Conwy concert, 14 August 1848, advertised the song as 'New Work, "Our Native Land," In Three Short Volumes (from Julius Caesar to Queen Ann.) Written by J.W. Roe, and arranged by John Parry', and therefore not to be confused with the hymn of the same name.

24 For the career of Williams (1828–1902), see kurtofgerolstein.blogspot.com/2019/10/the-welsh-nightingale-miss-lucy-williams.

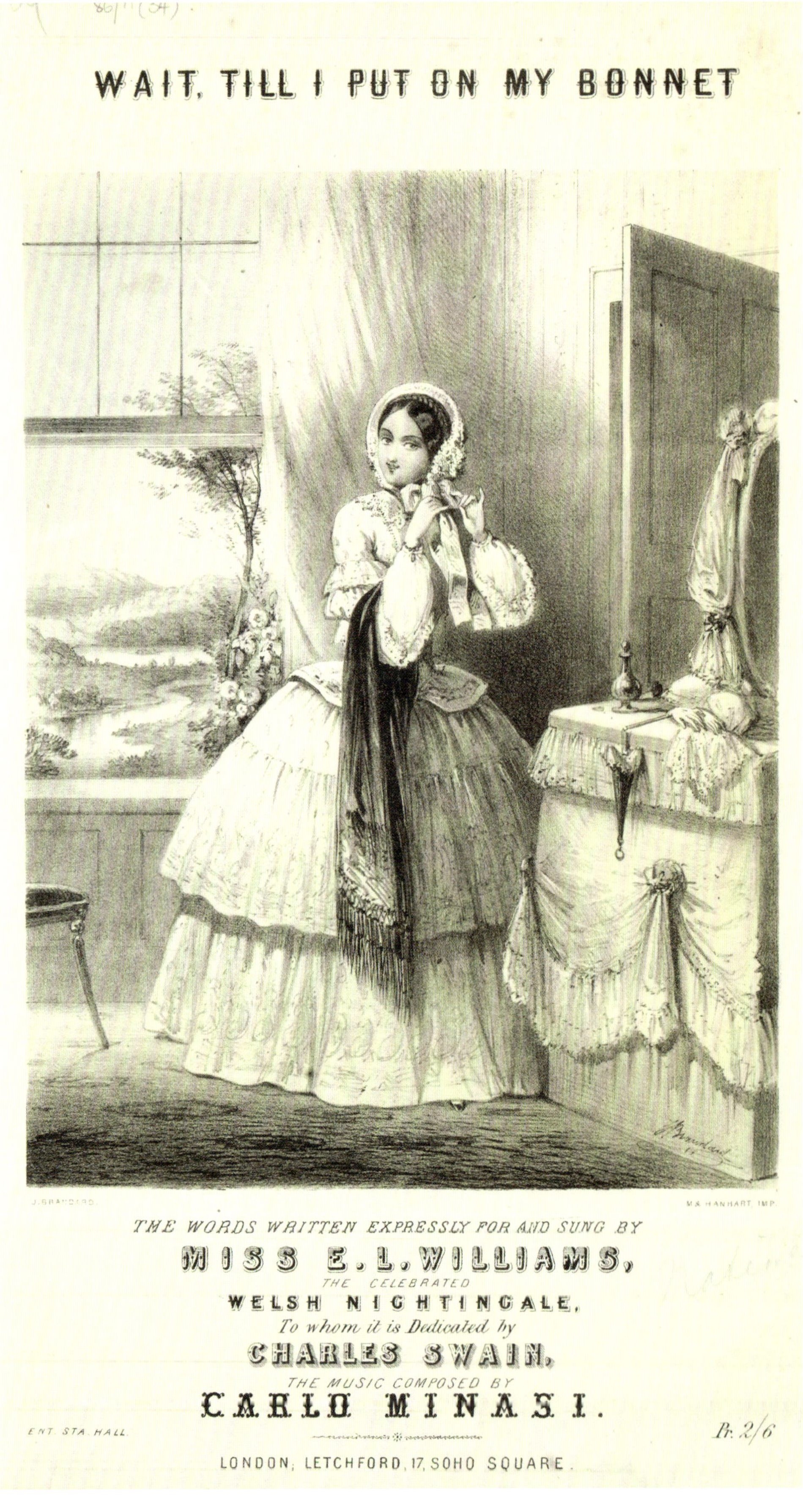

176 John Brandard, cover for *Wait, Till I Put on My Bonnet*, c.1855

In 1848, it had been necessary for the organisers of the Abergavenny Eisteddfod to advertise the fact that they required ladies wishing to attend events to dress in the newly-defined national costume.[25] Contrary to the impression gained from the press publicity, Lady Llanover's zeal in this respect had not proved universally popular, and indeed, there had been a revolt, led by a woman of impeccable Welsh pedigree, Mary Elizabeth Lucy of Charlecote Park in Warwickshire. She was born and grew up at Bodelwyddan, the daughter of John Williams, and she played the harp well. In 1851, preparing to attend the first meeting of that year at Abergavenny, there was a knock at her door:

> Lady Hall's maid entered carrying two frightful linstey petticoats and bodies, two Welsh chimney-pot black hats with coarse mob caps and said, 'If you please, her Ladyship wishes you and Miss Lucy to wear these Welsh costumes today at the Eisteddford,' laid the things down and, before I could give an answer for laughing, she went off.

Not wishing to offend, Mary's daughter, Carry, pressed her mother to conform with the Llanover dress code:

> So Carry and I took off our pretty dresses and put on the frights. The hat was much too large for me and was so heavy it did nothing but come down half over my nose, and the linstey so hot, I never was more uncomfortable, and vowed I would never wear such horrible things again to please any Lady Hall, nor did I, and all the other ladies agreed with me and we returned our linsteys and hats etc. to her Ladyship that same evening and made her very angry.[26]

The revolt at Abergavenny suggests what the visual records of mid-century Eisteddfodau confirm. National costume is conspicuous only by its absence in documentary illustrations of public gatherings, including depictions of those ceremonial events, such as the Cardiff and Rhuddlan Eisteddfodau, where it might have been expected to be in evidence. Nevertheless, thanks to an ever-increasing flow of costume prints, the idea that the uncomfortable national garb represented a reality of ancient tradition gained ground with surprising

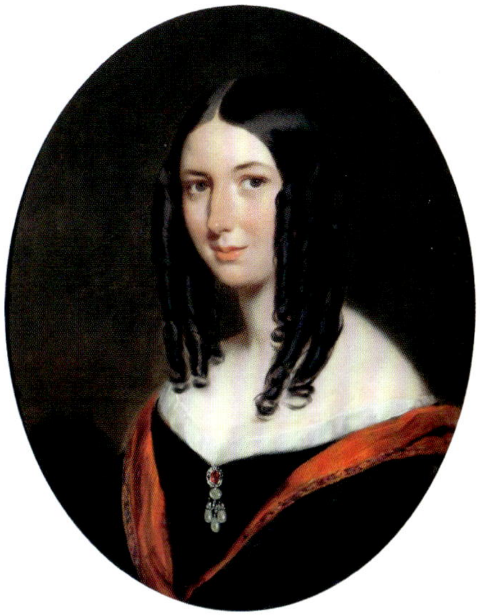

177 Richard Buckner, *Mary Elizabeth Lucy*, 1847

25 *Monmouthshire Merlin*, 7 August 1848, p. 4.

26 Mary Elizabeth Lucy, *Mistress of Charlecote* (London, 1983), pp. 95–6.

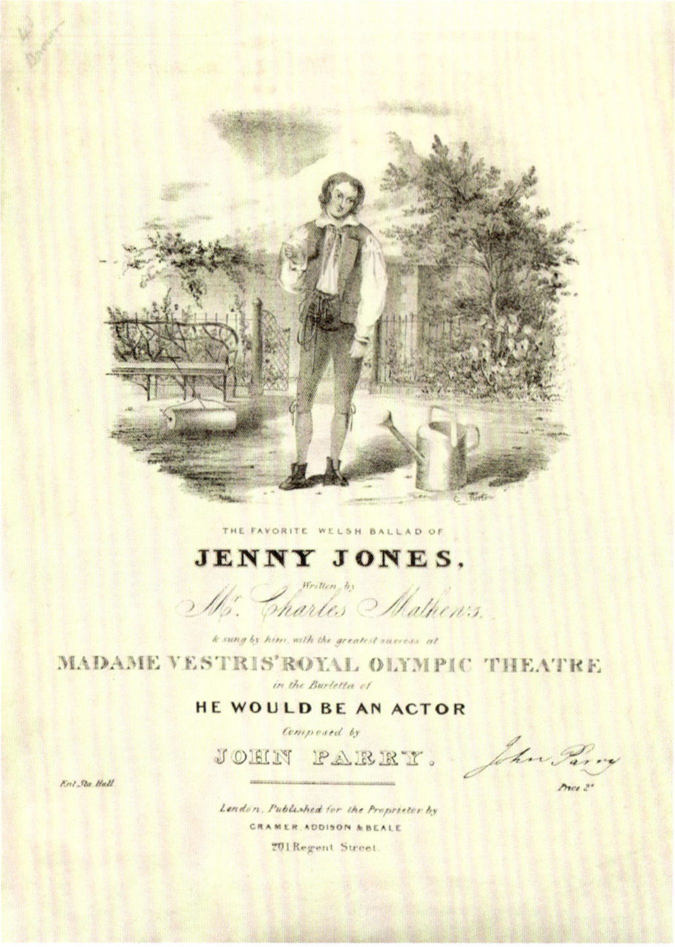

178 Edward Morton, cover for *The Favorite Welsh Ballad of Jenny Jones*, c.1835-8

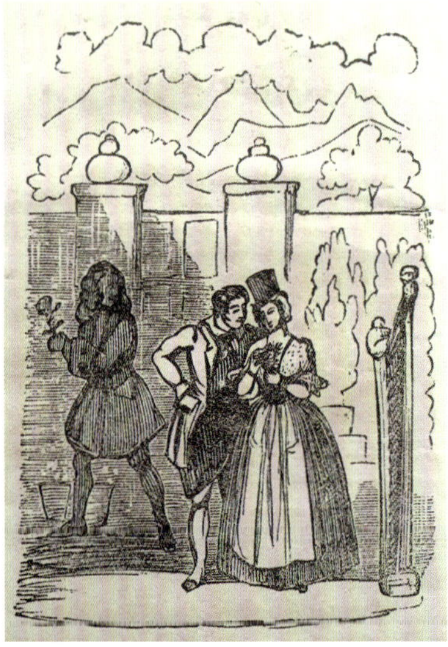

179 Unknown artist, illustration from Fox Cooper, *Jenny Jones: An Operetta*, 1838

speed, joining Welsh airs and bardic effusions as a stage phenomenon. In 1838, the printed text of an operetta based on the story of Jenny Jones and Edward Morgan of Llangollen reached the Royal Theatre at St James's in London. The published text of the performance was given a woodcut frontispiece that illustrated the opening scene. It included both a harp, on which Edward would accompany his songs, and a costume supplied for Jenny Jones, described in the stage directions as simply 'Welch girl's dress – hat, &c.'[27] Clearly, by 1838, and independent of goings-on at Abergavenny, the concept of national costume was common knowledge in London, where it now cohabited with the harp as an easy shorthand for Welshness. The author of the operetta was Fox Cooper, though he had taken great liberties with the ballad which had initially stimulated his imagination. The original verses had been the work of the actor Charles James Mathews, who described in his autobiography collecting the story on a visit to Llangollen when his father was working in the north-east of the country. Jenny Jones had been parted from Edward, her lover, who travelled the world in the Navy for twenty years. She remained faithful to him and when he came home, they were married:

> I parted a lad from the vale of my fathers
> And left Jenny Jones then a cockit young lass,
> But now I'm returned a storm-beaten old mariner,
> Jenny – from Jones into Morgan shall pass!

Mathews fitted his verses to what he took to be a traditional air that he had heard performed in a hotel by a 'venerable white-bearded druid'. It was not until some years later that he was informed by an irritated Bardd Alaw that the air had nothing to do with druids, but was a composition of his own called 'Cader Idris'. It had won for him a prize at an eisteddfod in 1804.[28]

Fox Cooper's operetta was reviewed by one 'Philo Dramaticus', who was of the opinion, not complimentary to Mathews, that:

> Mr Cooper has very skilfully worked up a story out of very rare materials. The Welsh verses of Jenny Jones are contemptible trash; but the playwright has grafted a story of his own upon them, which tells very well with the audience.[29]

180 Unknown artist, *Jenny Jones*, c.1850

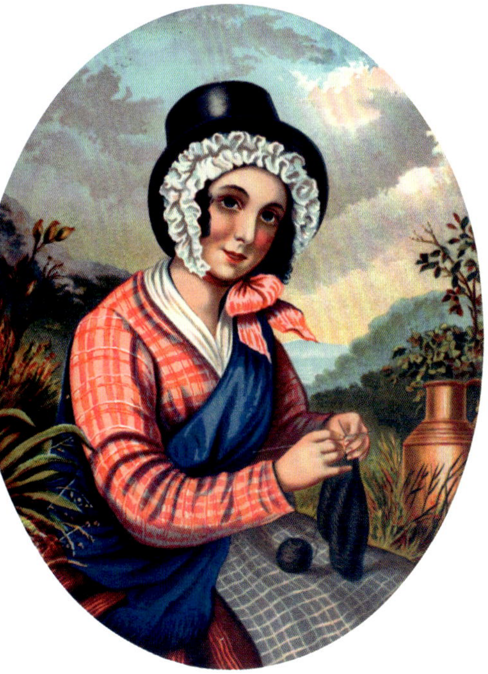

The original ballad had been in print well before the London operetta, but it seems that it was through a performance of an entertainment written by Mathews called *He Would Be an Actor*, performed at his wife's Royal Olympic Theatre at about the same time as Cooper's piece, that words and music together became popular on the streets.[30] A degree of confusion continues to surround the evolution of the piece, since what appears to be a flyer for the

27 Fox Cooper, *Jenny Jones: an Operetta ... as performed at the Theatre Royal, St James's* (London, 1838), and reissued in the United States under the imprint *The British Theatre and America Acting Drama, embellished with engravings* (New York; Philadelphia; Boston, c.1838).

28 Charles Dickens (ed.), *The Life of Charles James Mathews, chiefly Autobiographical with Selections from His Correspondence and Speeches* (London, 1879), pp. 170-86. For a list of variants and sources for Jenny Jones, see welshhat.wordpress.com/images/prints/jenny-jones/. Parry did not publish the air until the first volume of *The Welsh Harper* (London and Chester, 1838).

29 *Pattie's Modern Stage* (1839), vol. i, p. 6.

30 Mathews joined the company managed by Lucia Elizabeth Vestris in 1835, and they married in 1838.

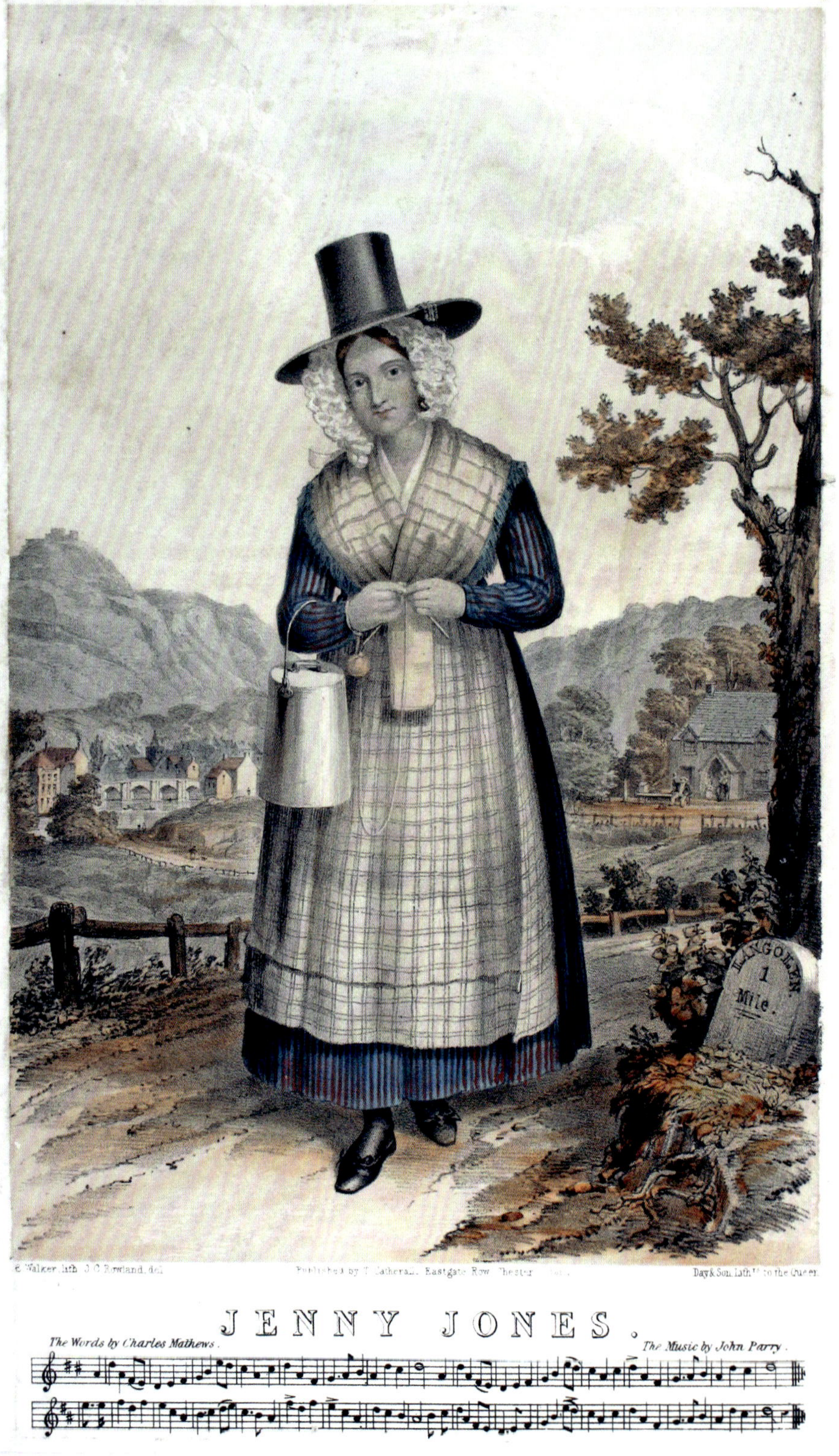
LLANGOLLEN
1
Mile.
Day & Son. Lithrs to the Queen
JENNY JONES.
The Words by Charles Mathews.
The Music by John Parry.

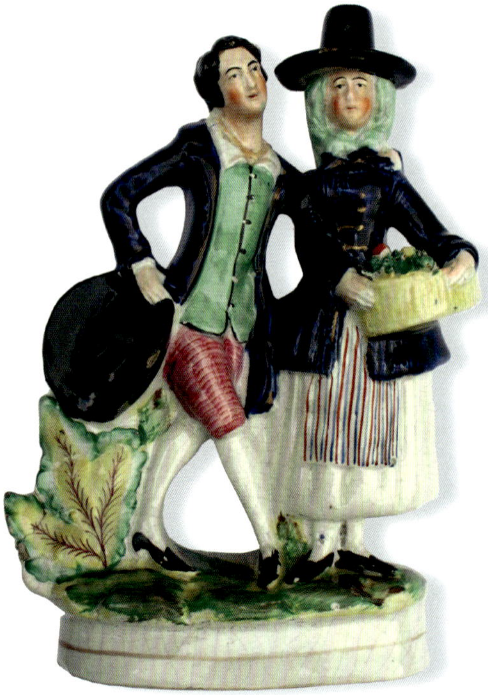

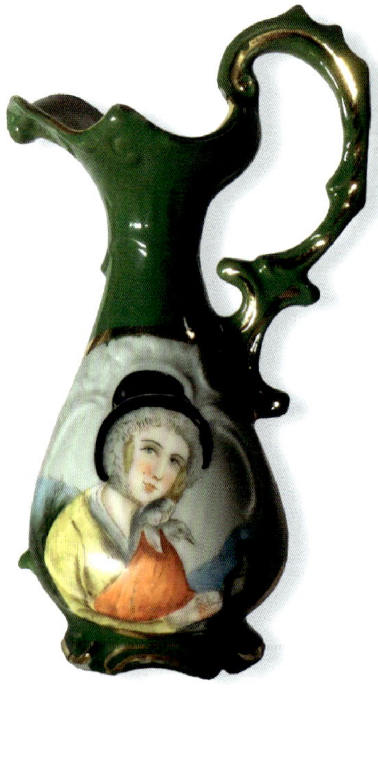

Mathews performance clearly illustrates the first scene of Cooper's operetta, in which Edward Morgan enters with a 'watering pot'.

181 John Cambrian Rowland, *Jenny Jones*, c.1849-53

182 Staffordshire ceramic, *Jenny Jones and Edward Morgan*, c.1850–1914

183 Unknown maker, *Jenny Jones Jug*, late 19th century

The images, words and music of the Jenny Jones story were now firmly entwined. Jenny Jones assumed her place as a mythic embodiment of the demure Welsh maiden who would promote the national brand for the remainder of the nineteenth and twentieth centuries. At least two further engravings of Jenny that included Parry's melody appeared in mid-century. Among the most widely distributed and influential of the costume prints of the period were those drawn by John Cambrian Rowland, an artist born in Ceredigion, who later established himself in Caernarfon. His prints, allegedly based on observation of living characters in his native county, were published in several variants from 1849.[31] They included a pair that illustrated Jenny Jones and Edward Morgan. Bardd Alaw's melody appeared under Rowland's engraving of Jenny – presumably the same melody as that performed by Master John Hughes on the violin a decade earlier in Merthyr. The engravings were joined by a deluge of ceramic representations of Jenny herself, and sometimes the couple. At the bottom of the market, German factories exported many variants on the theme. The Staffordshire factories produced rather larger and more expensive variants.

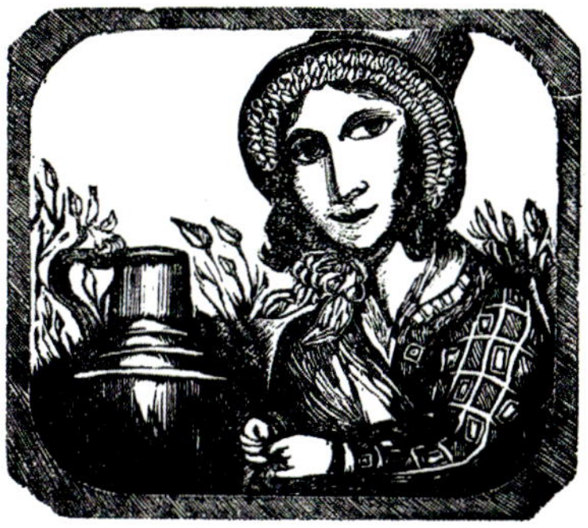

184 John Richard, *Jenny Jones*, 1865

In 1856, binding together the visual and the musical manifestations of the national brand and carrying it back into physical reality in Wales itself, the *North Wales Chronicle and Advertiser* printed an advertisement for 'Welsh Concerts. Welsh songs in the Welsh Costume'. The concerts were given by a fourteen-year-old performer known at the time as Miss Sarah Wynne, 'the talented Welsh songstress'.[32] In due course, she would become one of the cornerstones of the London Welsh artistic establishment, as the stately diva Edith Wynne, 'Eos Cymru'.

In the light of the deluge of musical maidens that was to follow at the beginning of the twentieth century with the development of postcard imagery, the direct linkage between national costume and national music is less common than might be expected in the proliferation of prints published in the 1850s. Somewhat downmarket from Rowland's prints were those produced by Newman & Co. in London, which became particularly important in disseminating costume imagery when transferred to the cheap ceramics that were sold as souvenirs at tourist destinations, and for home consumption at fairs and markets. A second

31 See 'John Cambrian Rowland (1818-90)', in Lord, *Looking Out*, pp. 86–101.

32 *North Wales Chronicle and Advertiser*, 20 September 1856, p. 1.

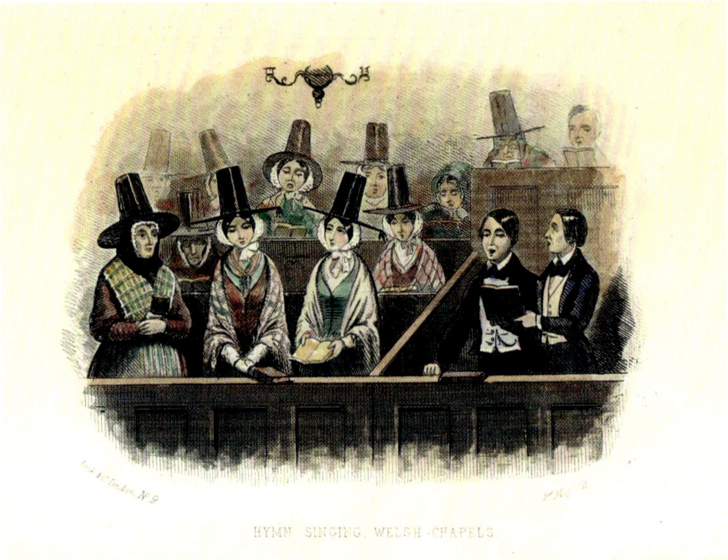

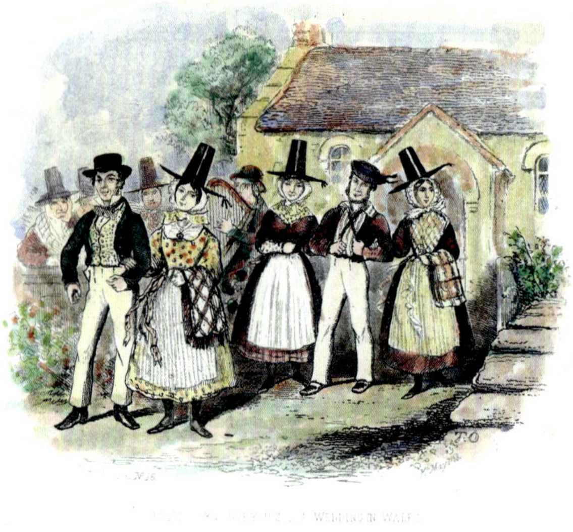

185 Thomas Onwhyn, *Hymn Singing. Welsh Chapels*, 1853

186 Thomas Onwhyn, *Priodas yn Nghymru – A Wedding in Wales*, 1853

London publisher, Rock & Co., made frequent use of the work of the artist Thomas Onwhyn, who produced images for popular publications dealing with a wide variety of subjects. His Welsh works, published between 1852 and 1860, seem to have been particularly popular. They were issued as sets in book form, though surviving complete copies are scarce since it appears that the prints were generally extracted for display singly or for pasting into albums. Although the impression given that uncomfortable and expensive national costume was widely in use among working women in Wales must be considered as highly misleading, it is clear that Onwhyn worked from experience gained on a walking tour or tours through Wales. It seems likely, therefore, that the essence of his engraving, *Hymn Singing. Welsh Chapels*, is accurate, even if the tall black hats are a picturesque embellishment, included to conform to the expectations of potential consumers of his employer's products. Depictions of the intimate context of chapel interiors during meetings are rare, and Onwhyn's image is, perhaps, unique in its acknowledgement of the foundation on which the wider choral tradition was building in the period, in parallel with developments in popular image-making. Appropriately, Onwhyn's picture was published in 1853, the very year in which Griffith Rhys Jones, soon to become famous above all other conductors as 'Caradog', took his first choir to compete at Aberafan. Caradog was just nineteen years of age but it proved to be the initial step on a career path that would lead to his South Wales Choral Union, or Côr Mawr, winning the most prestigious choral trophy on offer in England at the Crystal Palace in 1872, and again in 1873. That high point in the development of the tradition was grounded in congregational singing, in the temperance movement and in chapel, as illustrated by Onwhyn.

Other references to music in Welsh popular prints of the 1850s were incidental, though intriguing and perhaps more reflective of reality for not being the core subject matter. Onwhyn's *Priodas yn Nghymru – A Wedding in Wales* is remarkable for the appearance in the procession leading away from the church of a harper, playing a small instrument on his left shoulder, precisely in the manner first imaged on Sir Rhys ap Thomas's bedstead, nearly three hundred and fifty years earlier. The engraving is notable also for its bilingual title, a feature common to several images in the Rock & Co. Welsh series. Whether this bilingual marketing strategy is to be interpreted as an attempt to interest Welsh-speaking clients or simply as an addition to the appealing curiosity value to tourists of the pictures is unclear, though an engraving made in about 1860 in Ceredigion, *Wesleyan English Chapel, Lisburne Mines*, was certainly of interest mainly to local people.

187 Thomas Kilner, *Wesleyan English Chapel*, c.1860

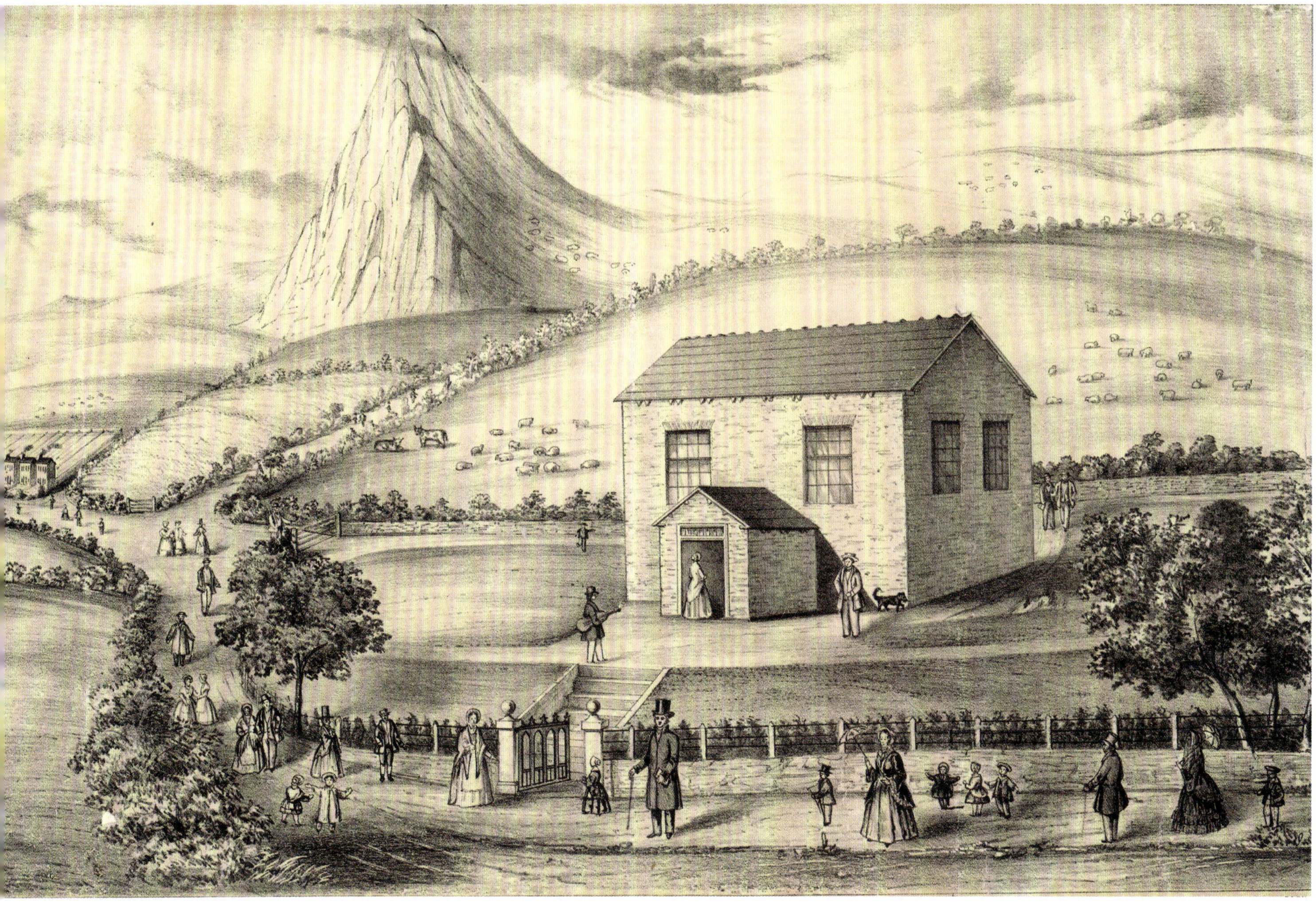

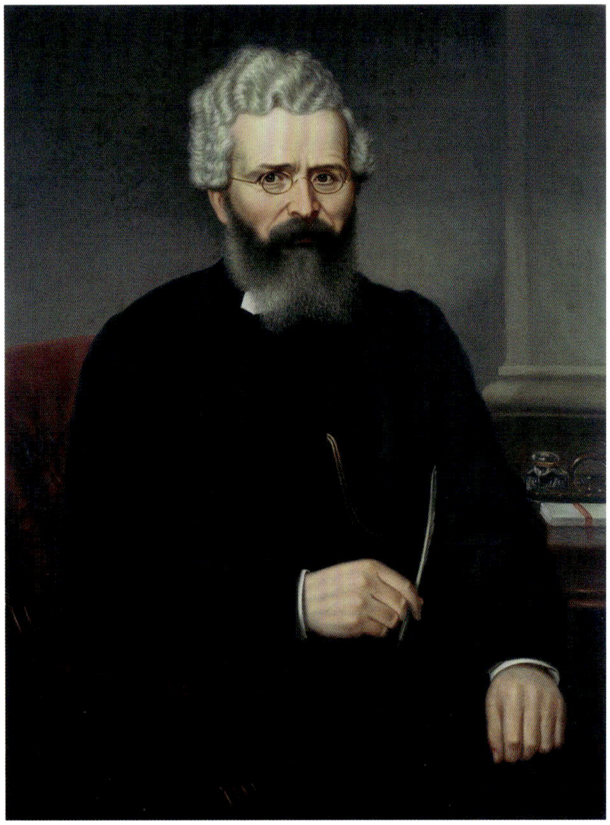

It reveals an intriguing facet of sacred musical tradition. The chapel at New Row, Pont-rhyd-y-groes, was built to serve a population rapidly expanding as a result of metal mining in the area. A gentleman in a top hat, placed in the centre foreground and holding a book, may represent the minister himself, who was also the artist, the Revd Thomas Kilner.[33] None of the many women depicted wears Welsh costume. However, the portrait of a gentleman approaching the door of the chapel, is of considerable interest. Beyond the use of the organ or harmonium, little documentation survives of musical accompaniment to the singing of hymns and psalms in chapel, in the manner of the West Gallery Anglican tradition but, under his arm, the gentleman carries a 'cello or bass viol into the meeting.

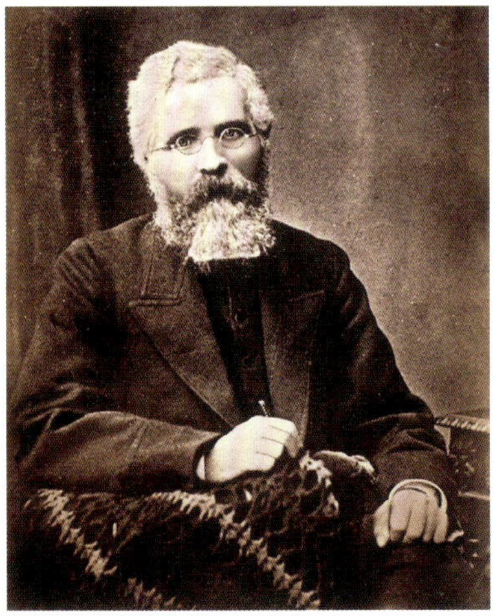

The source of a substantial body of the sacred choral music sung in chapel during this period was John Ambrose Lloyd of Mold. When only sixteen years of age, he had composed the hymn tune 'Wyddgrug', named after his birthplace. Later in life he became celebrated for his anthem, 'Teyrnasoedd y Ddaear'. His first collection of hymns had been published in 1843, shortly after he took charge of music at Salem, in Brownlow, Cheshire. On leaving the chapel and the Liverpool Welsh Choral Society, of which he was the first conductor, he was presented with portraits of himself and his wife, painted by the Liverpool artist Richard Norbury. The practice of presenting a portrait, though usually that of a minister on his retirement or departure, was a well-established tradition among Welsh Nonconformist congregations, from which artisan painters such as Hugh Hughes, William Roos and Evan Williams all benefitted. The quality of the Lloyd portrait reflects the high esteem in which he was held by 1850, when it was presented to him at the age of just thirty-five.[34] At the end of the decade, a

188 Evan Williams,
John Roberts, Ieuan Gwyllt, 1877

189 Hugh Humphreys,
John Roberts, Ieuan Gwyllt, c.1877

190 Richard Norbury,
John Ambrose Lloyd, 1850

33 Thomas Kilner (c.1806 78) had worked as a missionary in Sri Lanka. He published *Sketch of the Wesleyan Mission on the Negombo Station in the Island of Ceylon* (J. Mason, 1850). Several engraved drawings of the mission and surrounding areas survive in a simple style, not dissimilar to his own. His service in Ceredigion may have been of short duration, but the 1861 census recorded Esther Kilner, head of household, married, 55, missionary's wife, living at 148 North Parade, Aberystwyth, documentation that provides an approximate date for the engraving. Among the miners in Ceredigion were many immigrants from Cornwall and west Devon who were Wesleyan rather than Calvinistic Methodists.

34 The partner portrait of Catherine Lloyd is missing.

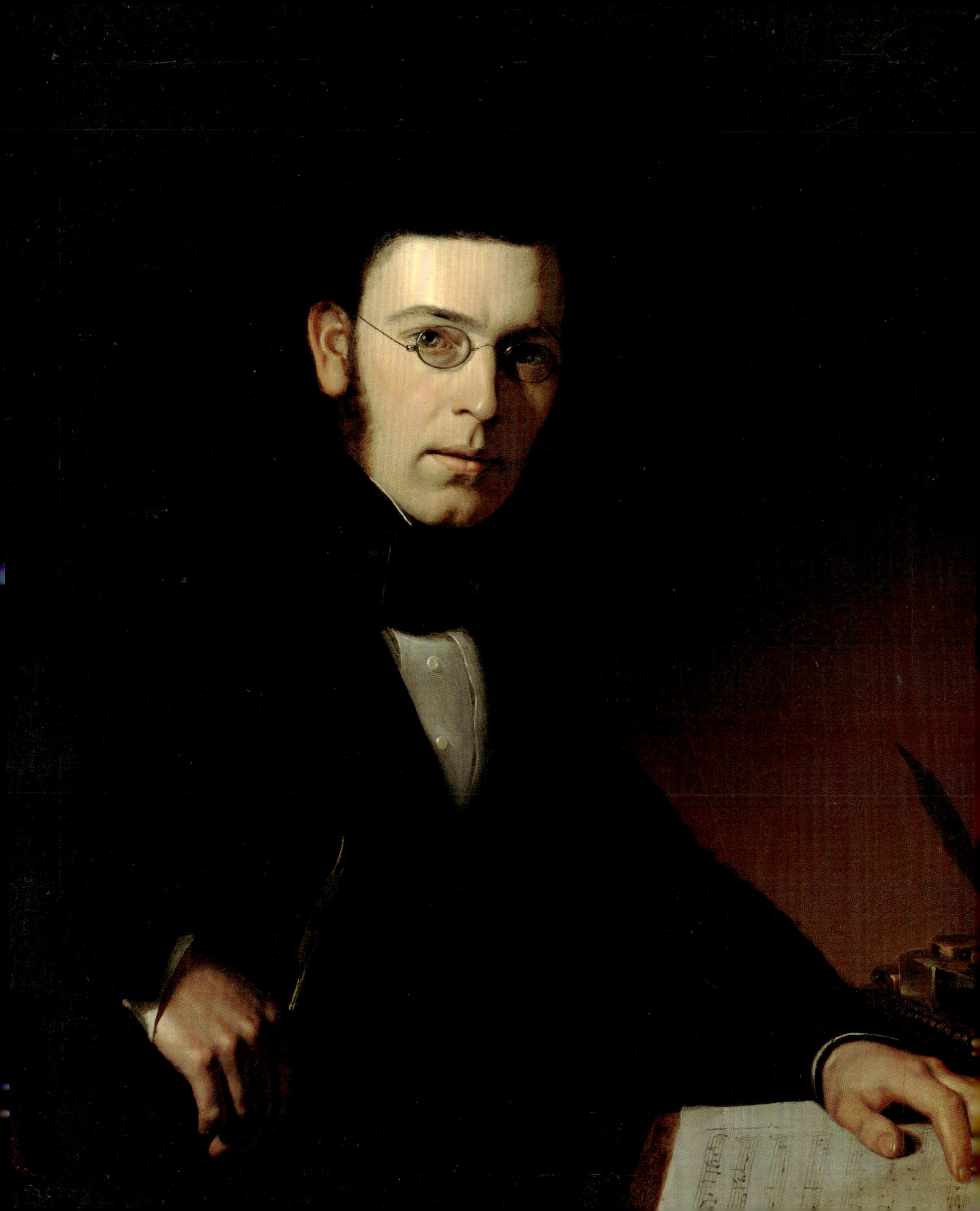

second major contributor to sacred choral music, John Roberts, 'Ieuan Gwyllt', published his *Llyfr Tonau Cynulleidfaol*. In a late manifestation of the same visual tradition that had celebrated John Ambrose Lloyd, the contribution of Ieuan Gwyllt as a musician and minister was commemorated in a portrait by Evan Williams. The picture was unusual in that it was painted on the basis of a photograph in the year of the sitter's death. It seems likely that the commission was related to the National Eisteddfod, held in 1877 in Caernarfon, close to the area in which Ieuan Gwyllt had spent the last decade of his life.[35]

REFORMING THE NATIONAL EISTEDDFOD

The image of the Welsh as a musical people continued to be reinforced by the visualisation of the Eisteddfod in the London illustrated press. From the 1860s, the imagery became largely generic, though by the turn of the century, photography, both as a source for engraving and, eventually, reproduced directly by the half-tone process, caused some evolution in the style of presentation. The large scale of a series of 'reformed' National Eisteddfodau, that began at Aberdare in 1861, attracted most attention. It may be that the consistent reporting of the annual events was facilitated by the fact that this new Eisteddfod movement was promoted largely by the expatriate Welsh establishment. Indeed, the picturesque location of the second meeting of the series, held within the castle walls at Caernarfon, attracted attention even further afield. The event coincided with the visit to Wales of a French writer, Alfred Erny, whose observations were published in 1867 with illustrations based on his own sketches. The harps at the centre of attention in his sketch of the interior of the Caernarfon pavilion were convincingly delineated, and it appears that a competition was in progress, with the adjudicators seated at their table close by. Erny was well disposed to Wales and to the idea of a Celtic culture shared with the Bretons, and had spoken with Lady Llanover in the course of his travels.[36] In the process of translating Erny's original sketches into the published images, via worked-up drawings prepared back in France by Pierre-Eugène Grandsire and various engravers, some distortion occurred. That the size of the interior of the Caernarfon pavilion was exaggerated is evident by comparison with the more convincing exterior view published by *The Illustrated London News*. On the other hand, in 1865, both *The Illustrated London News* and *The Illustrated Times* had presented images

35 Evan Williams also painted notable portraits of John Jones, minister of Brynrodyn Chapel, Y Groeslon, and his wife Ellen. Brynrodyn provides a good case study for the intense musical activity based in chapels in the north-west of Wales that extended into the secular competitive tradition. See Lord, *Looking Out*, pp. 12–19.

36 M. Alfred Erny, *Voyage dans le Pays de Galles* (Paris, 1867). For an analysis of the attitude of Erny to Wales, see Kathryn N. Jones, Carol Tully and Heather Williams, *Hidden Texts, Hidden Nation: (Re) Discoveries of Wales in Travel Writing in French and German (1780–1891)* (Liverpool, 2020), pp. 77–82.

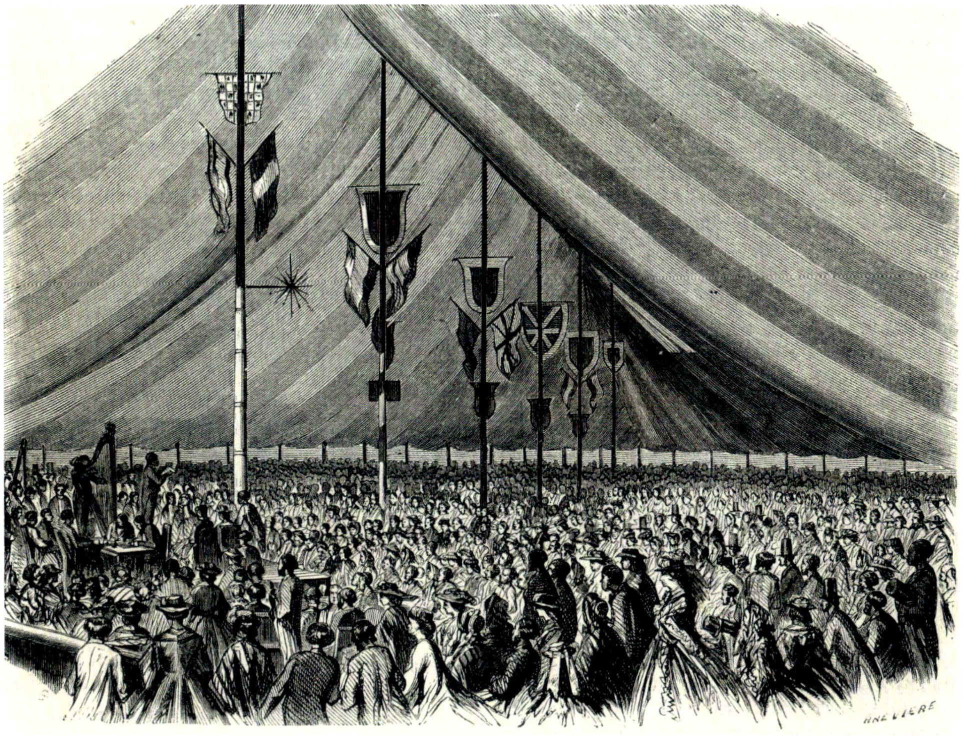

191 Pierre Eugène Grandsire after Alfred Erny, *L'Eisteddfod, à Carnarvon*, 1867

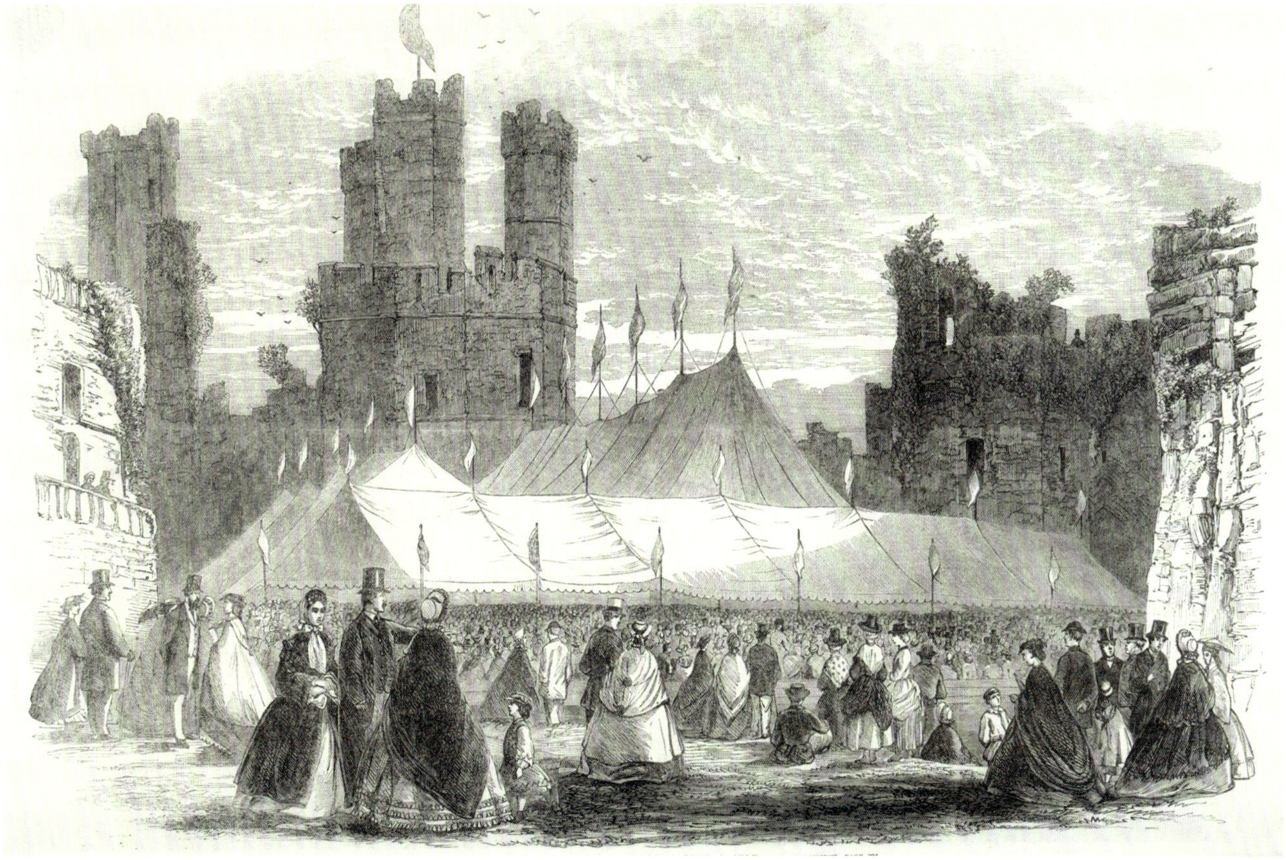

192 Unknown artist, *The Pavilion of the Caernarfon National Eisteddfod*, 1862

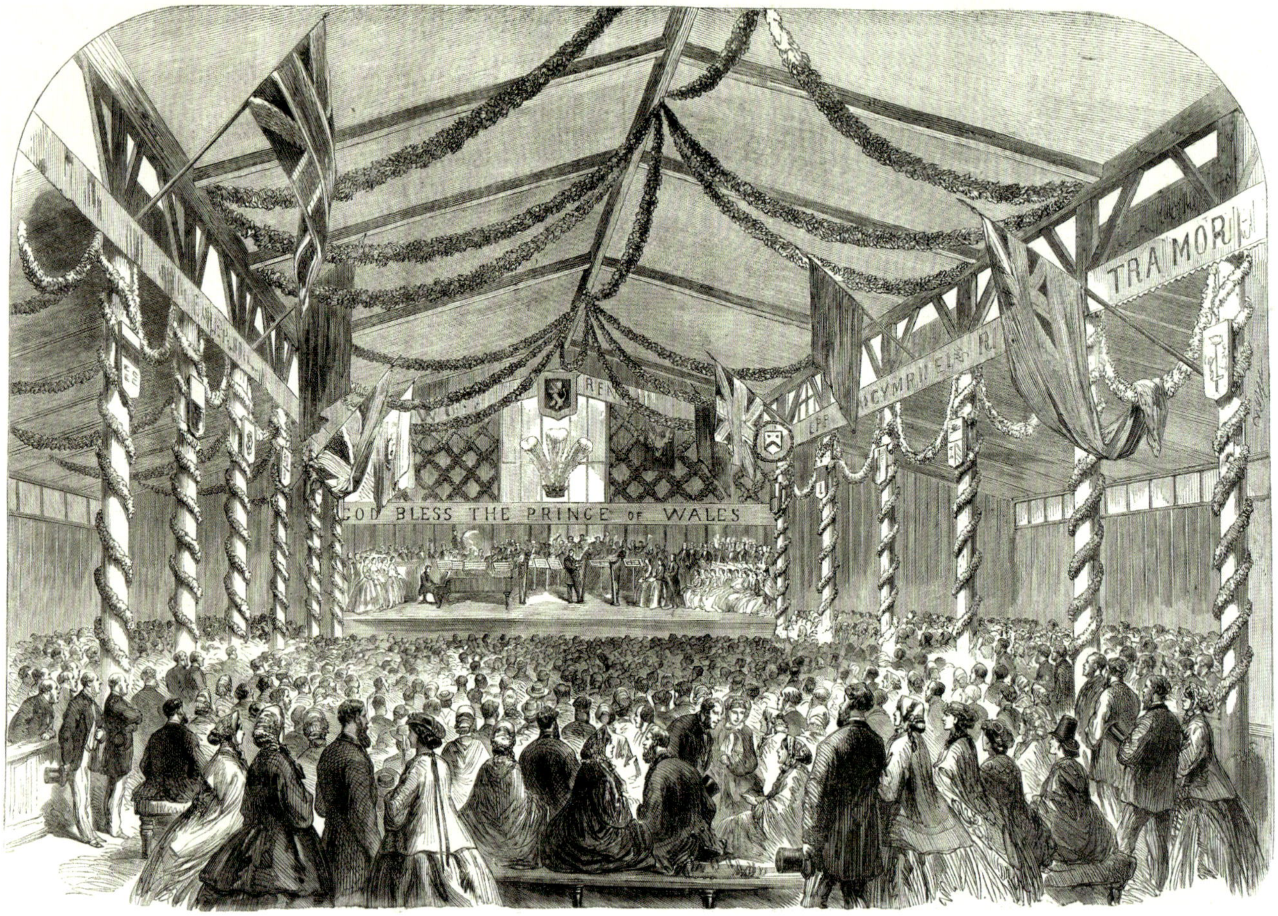

193 Unknown artist, *Interior of the Pavilion of the Aberystwyth National Eisteddfod*, 1865

of the interior of the Aberystwyth pavilion. It is unclear if the two papers were reliant on a single artist as their source or if they both sent representatives, but a comparison of the images of the concert presented by a mixed choir, with vocal and instrumental soloists, tends to confirm the documentary accuracy of the representations. The original drawings taken on the spot and translated into print by the London engravers show remarkably few variations, and those only of detail.

Even larger musical forces were recorded on the platform at Chester in the following year, before an audience of six to seven thousand. Major works by both Brinley Richards and by John Thomas, Pencerdd Gwalia, were staged, though neither was composed specially. Richards's Overture in F minor had first been published in 1840 in Paris, where he had studied with Frédéric Chopin, and the dramatic cantata, *Llewelyn*, by Pencerdd Gwalia with words by Talhaiarn, was performed first at the Swansea Eisteddfod of 1863. By the time of the performance at Chester in 1866, an edition of the English-language version of *Llewelyn*, written by Thomas Oliphant, had been published by subscription with a series of seven photographs of illustrations drawn by Deborah Elizabeth Wageman. Among the subscribers were many of the Welsh diaspora, including the redoubtable Mary Elizabeth Lucy. Notwithstanding her refusal to don the national costume at Abergavenny, she had retained in England her sense of Welsh identity, and had become close to Pencerdd Gwalia, who gave her lessons to improve her harp technique, so that she was able to play 'many a difficult duet with him.'[37]

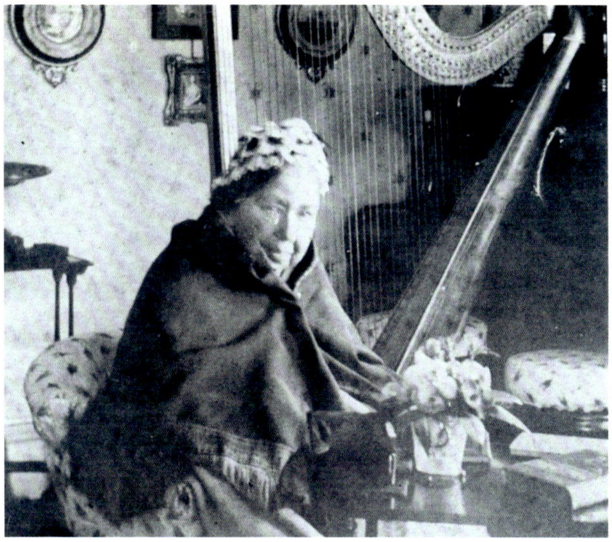

194 Unknown photographer, *Mary Elizabeth Lucy*, c.1880–90

Deborah Elizabeth Wageman was the daughter of Thomas Charles Wageman, a prolific portrait artist, in particular of theatrical characters. Unlike her brother, Michael Angelo Wageman, who also became a professional painter, Deborah Elizabeth trained at the Royal Academy of Music under William Sterndale Bennett and became a school proprietor and teacher, first in London and subsequently in Brighton. She was a friend of Pencerdd Gwalia, Eos Cymru, and others associated with the Academy.[38] As she seems to have had no other

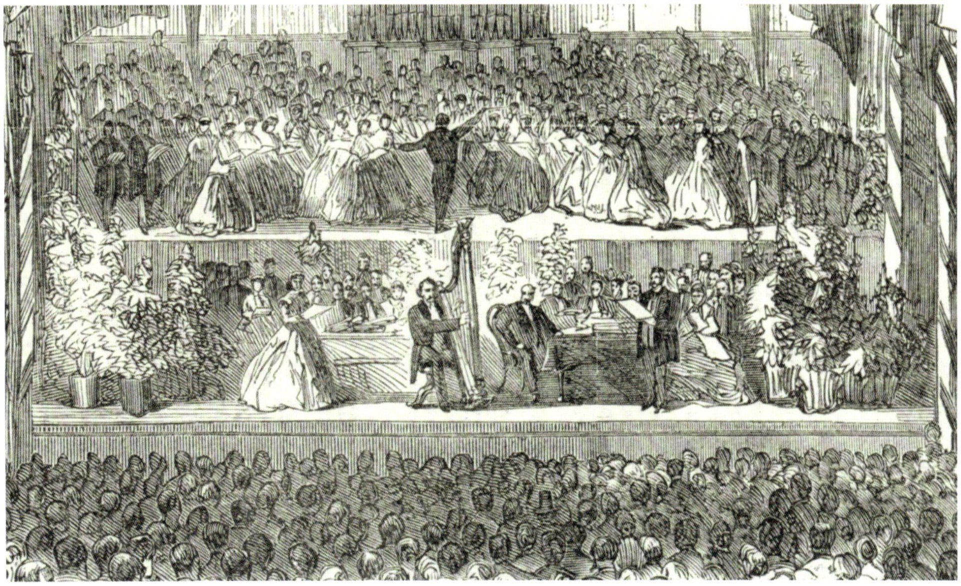

195 Unknown artist, *The Stage at the Chester National Eisteddfod*, 1866

37 Lucy, *Mistress of Charlecote*, p. 100.

38 *Brighton Gazette*, 10 July 1884, p. 8, noted that at one of her fortnightly musical evenings at her school in Brunswick Square, Pencerdd Gwalia and Eos Cymru were among the two hundred guests. Her Llewelyn drawings are not traced.

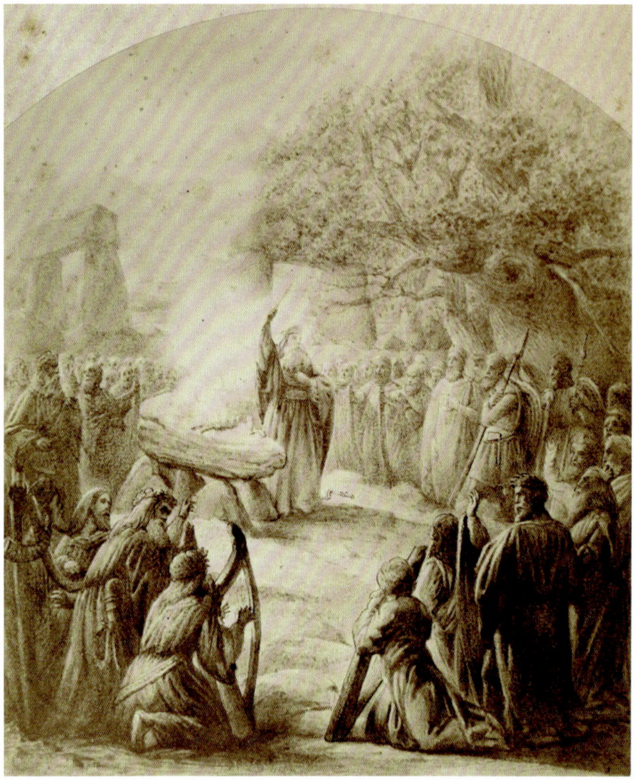

196 Deborah Elizabeth Wageman, *Morning Hymn,* 1865

connection with Wales, presumably it was these friendships that led to the production of the drawings and to her attendance at the Aberystwyth Eisteddfod, where they were awarded a silver medal. They follow the libretto, which refers to each picture at the appropriate point in the narrative. Among the sections illustrated from the cantata is the story of the dog Gelert, by this time attracting substantial numbers of visitors to view what was promoted as the unfortunate animal's grave at Beddgelert.[39]

The presence of the Eisteddfod on English territory at Chester in 1866 affected the spoken and written commentary on the event and the nation it represented. From the platform, John Griffiths adopted a defensive unionist tone from the outset:

> When nothing but Welsh is to be spoken at the gathering of the nation, no longer distinct and isolated, but happily and profitably blended with people that speak another tongue, united with them under one government, and deriving from them what tends to develop our resources, and raise our positions; when this becomes a rule, my sympathy with the Eisteddfod becomes greatly diminished. If we wish to provoke the ridicule of others, that is the right way to do it.[40]

The Times was delighted to confirm that Wales was, indeed, ridiculous:

> Wales, it should be remembered, is a small country, unfavourably situated for commercial purposes, with an indifferent soil, and inhabited by an unenterprising people. It is true that it possesses valuable minerals, but these have been chiefly developed by English energy, and for the supply of English wants. A bare existence on the most primitive food of a mountainous race is all that the Welsh could enjoy if left to themselves. Under such circumstances, what can be more out of place than an exhibition designed to foster satisfaction with Welsh productions and Welsh virtues? All the progress and civilisation in Wales has come from England, and a sensible Welshman would direct all his endeavours towards inducing his countrymen to appreciate their neighbours instead of themselves ... There is more good music produced in England in a single year than has been played at all the Eisteddfods that were ever held ... The sooner all Welsh specialities disappear from the face of the earth the better.[41]

'GOD BLESS THE PRINCE OF WALES'

Notwithstanding the aspersions cast by the editor of *The Times*, the year of the Caernarfon Eisteddfod of 1862 had seen the publication of further songs that became closely entwined with national identity and reinforced the influence of 'Hen Wlad Fy Nhadau'. 'Men of Harlech' had a long pedigree, being among the airs first published in the 1794 edition of Bardd y Brenin's *Musical and Poetical Relicks*, but it did not acquire words until 1862, when it appeared in Owain Alaw's *Gems of Welsh Melody*. The English-language lyric was written by Thomas Oliphant and the Welsh by Talhaiarn, who also provided two alternative English versions. His opening line, 'Glyndŵr, see thy comet flaming', closely echoed Felicia Hemans's 'Saw ye the blazing star'. But it was two phrases from lines in Talhaiarn's Welsh text for the song that would have the greatest impact: 'Cymru lân' and 'Cymru, gwlad y gân'. Indeed, reformulated simply as 'Cymru lân, gwlad y gân' for a new song, published in the next volume of *Gems*, it is no exaggeration to say that it would come to define the nation for the next century: 'Pure Wales, the land of song'.[42]

39 Walter R. Cassels had recently published a lengthy narrative poem, 'Llewellyn', recounting the legend in his *Poems* (London, 1856).

40 *Report of the National Eisteddfod of Wales, held at Chester* (Carnarvon, 1866).

41 *The Times*, 14 September 1866.

42 Talhaiarn wrote the less resonant English words and title, 'Beauteous Wales, dearest Wales'. The year 1862 also saw Pencerdd Gwalia publish the latest manifestation of *Welsh Melodies*, with English words by Thomas Oliphant, publicised by concerts given with Eos Cymru at St James's Hall and the Crystal Palace in London.

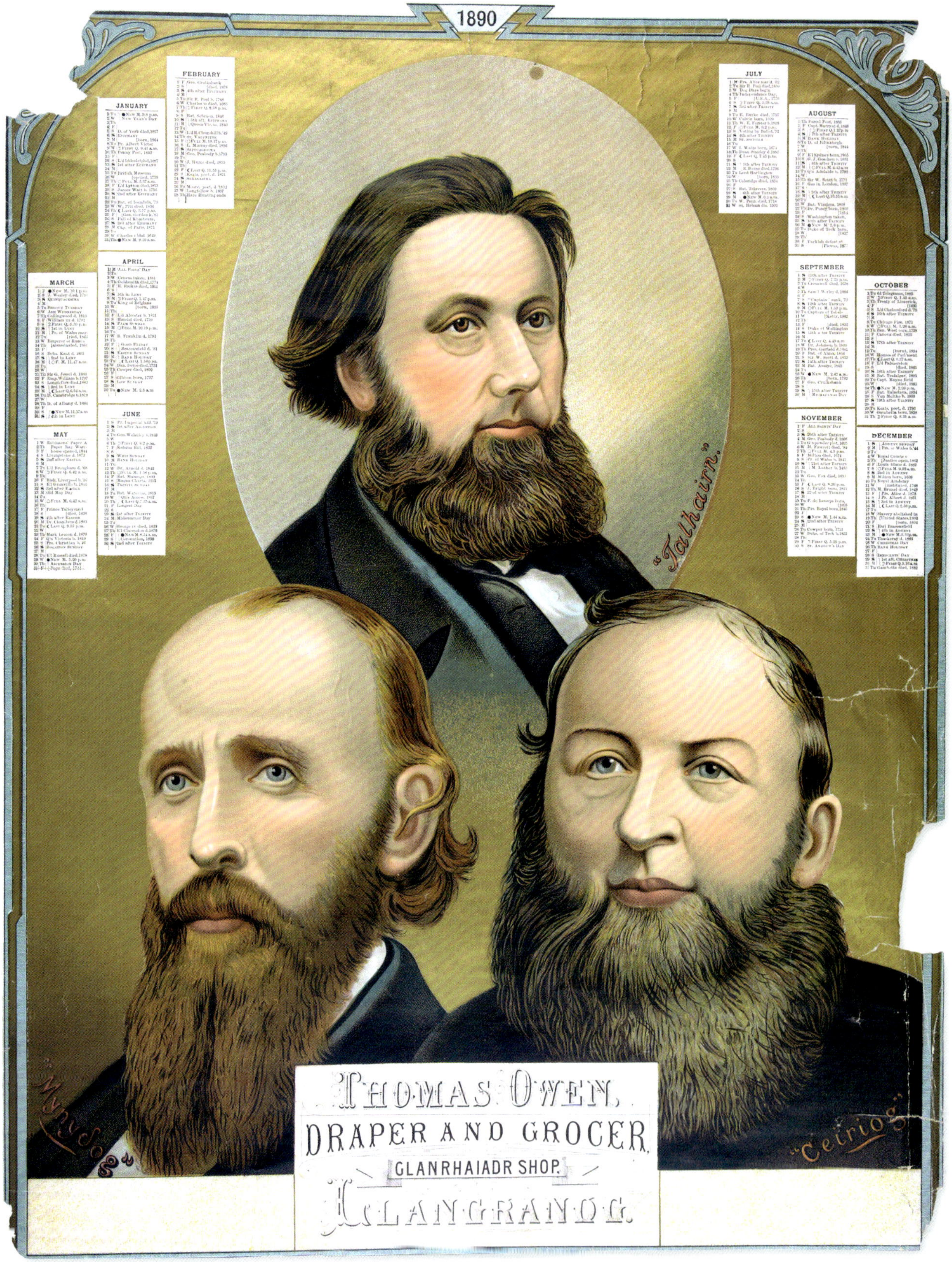
1890
JANUARY
FEBRUARY
MARCH
APRIL
MAY
JUNE
JULY
AUGUST
SEPTEMBER
OCTOBER
NOVEMBER
DECEMBER
"Talhaiarn."
"Mynyddog"
"Ceiriog"
THOMAS OWEN,
DRAPER AND GROCER,
GLANRHAIADR SHOP,
LLANGRANOG.

The popularity of the new songs was facilitated by the evolution of visual imagery both within the advertising industry in general, and in the music publishing industry in particular. The development of chromolithography and, in the last quarter of the nineteenth century, the offset process, presented opportunities for the first time for all but the poorest in society to acquire coloured pictures. Few Welsh national images emerged for the mass market sincc the printers and publishers who dominated the use of the technology were based outside Wales, and it is all the more significant, therefore, that among those few was a portrait group, headed by the image of Talhaiarn, supported by John Ceiriog Hughes and Richard Davies, 'Mynyddog', who wrote not only 'Myfanwy', but also 'Bedd Llywelyn', the party piece of the most celebrated Welsh tenor of the period, Robert Rees, 'Eos Morlais'. The portraits of these poets, whose words inspired so many of the most popular Welsh-language patriotic song settings of the period, adorned an almanac for 1890, designed to be customised for distribution by local traders to their loyal customers.[43]

197 Unknown artist, *Talhaiarn, Mynyddog, Ceiriog*, 1890

In 1903, one of the most prolific exploiters of modern marketing methods, the Colman company of Norwich, promoted their starch in a free booklet illustrated by a comprehensive assemblage of Welsh symbols – mountain, daffodils, and spinning wheel but, above all, a young female harper in national costume, performing 'Hen Wlad fy Nhadau', with the words and music printed below. The specialist publishers of sheet music had been early in the field, and in this format Welsh material featured more strongly. Their publications, aimed at middle-class people of sufficient means to own a harp or a piano, were often enhanced in the period by covers designed with elaborate typography or colour pictures. The London company of Stannard and Dixon published and printed several compositions by Brinley Richards, of which the most visually notable was 'The Vale', his setting of 'Ar Hyd y Nos'.[44] The words, expressing the longing of an expatriate for the homeland, were written by George Linley, who also supplied libretti for several other compositions or arrangements by Richards.[45]

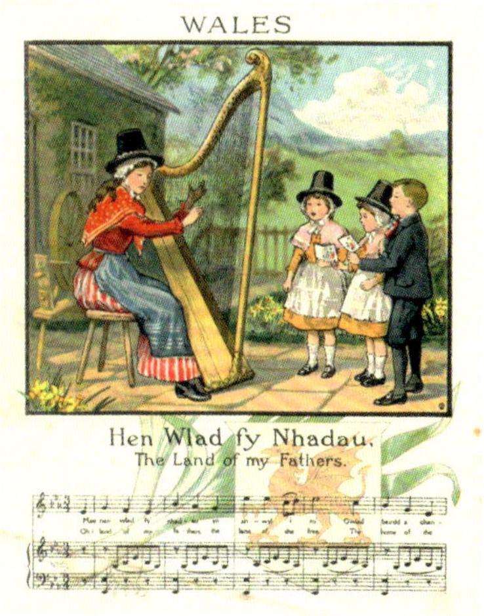

198 Unknown artist, *Wales. Hen Wlad fy Nhadau*, 1903

43 T.H. Thomas, *John Elias preaching in the Association at Bala*, 1892, was also distributed through shopkeepers as a customised almanac, see Lord, *Industrial Society*, p. 107. The music for 'Myfanwy' was written by Joseph Parry, and for 'Bedd Llywelyn' by D. Emlyn Evans. For Eos Morlais, see Hywel Teifi Edwards, 'Y gân y ganai Morlais', in *Codi'r Hen Wlad yn ei hôl: 1850–1914* (Llandysul, 1989), pp. 83–139.

44 The company was owned jointly by William Thomas Stannard and Francis Dixon, until Dixon's retirement in 1868, giving a terminal date for music carrying both their names. The most prolific artist employed by them was Alfred Concanen.

45 'Hunting the Hare' ('Hela'r 'Sgyfarnog'); 'Forth to the Battle' ('Rhyvelgyrch Cadpen Morgan'); 'The Ballad Singer', etc. Linley also composed the air 'The Lone Hills of Arvon', with words by Mrs Crawford. Among other Richards compositions published with illustrated covers by Stannard and Dixon were 'The Albert Edward March'; 'Annie Laurie'; 'Alexandra', and 'The Christian Soldier'.

GOD BLESS THE PRINCE OF WALES.

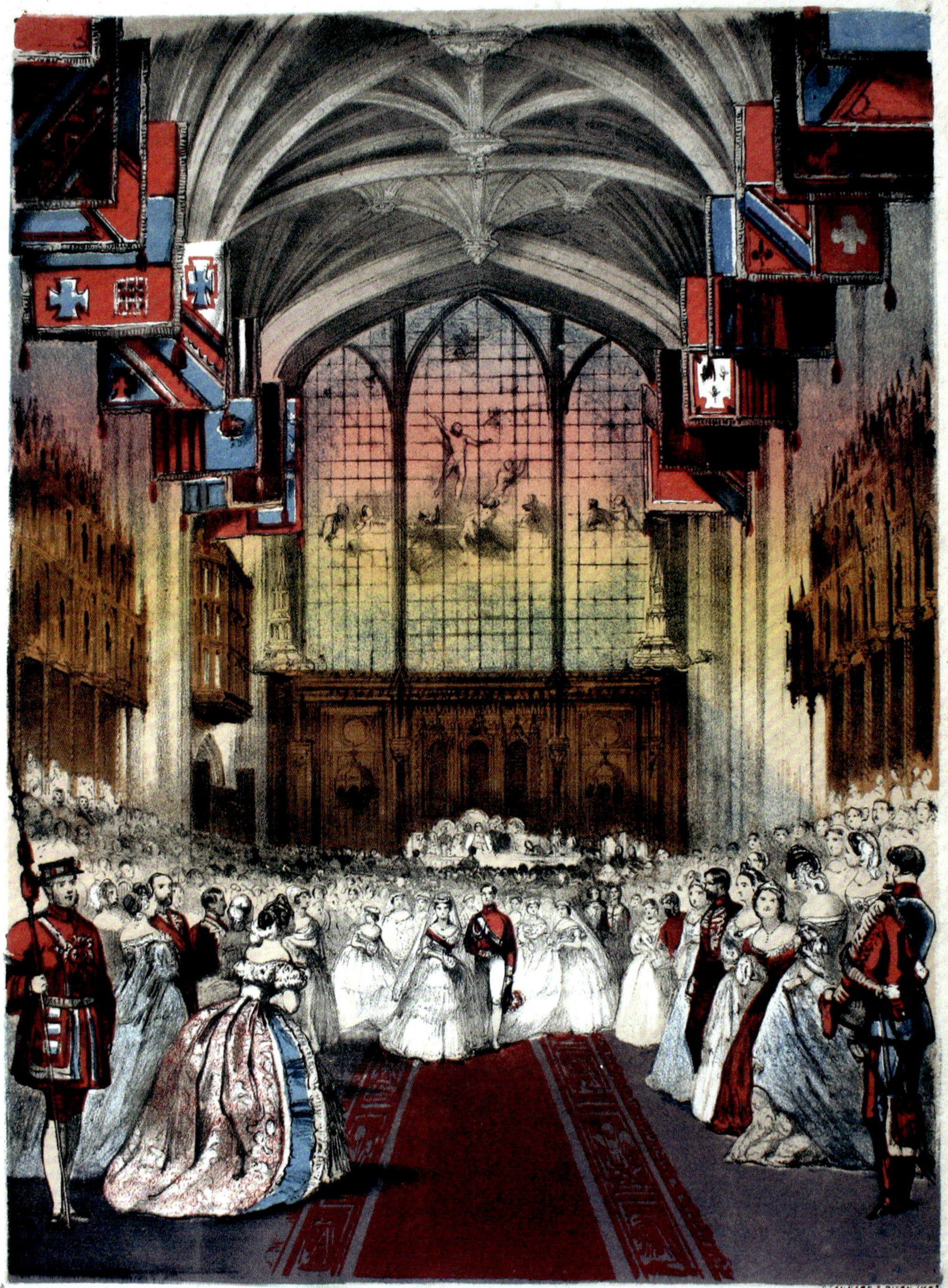

STANNARD & DIXON, IMP.

(THE NEW NATIONAL SONG.)

COMPOSED & ARRANGED FOR THE

PIANO-FORTE,

BY

BRINLEY RICHARDS.

Piano Solo 4/-
Piano Duet. 4/-
Song. 3/-

LONDON, ROBERT COCKS & Co NEW BURLINGTON STREET, W.
BY SPECIAL APPOINTMENT

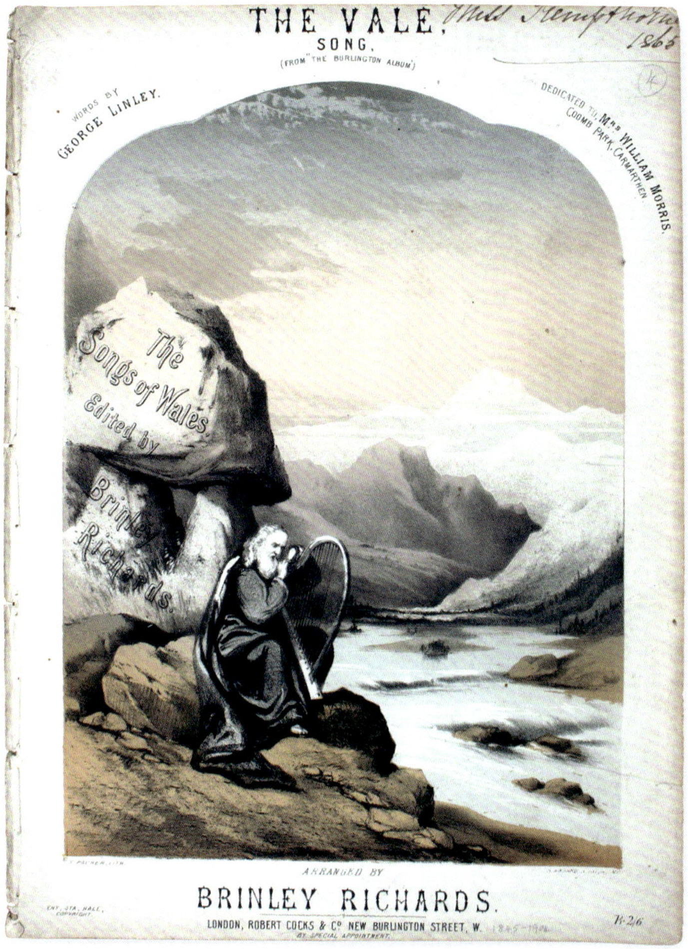

For 'The Vale', the lithographer Thomas Packer was clearly inspired by the Revd William Bingley's *Sixty of the most admired Welsh Airs* of 1803. He presented the bard in his most benign and meditative incarnation in the mountains of the north, apparently unaware that the vale in question was 'The "Vale of Towy" in South Wales' as the arranger took care to point out on the first page of the music itself.[46] Furthermore, Richards dedicated his arrangement to Mrs Mary Morris of Coombe in his native Carmarthenshire. She was the great-grand-daughter of the triple harper Sackville Gwynne of Glanbrân.[47]

199 Unknown artist, cover for Brinley Richards, *God Bless the Prince of Wales*, 1863

200 Thomas Packer, cover for Brinley Richards, *The Vale*, 1873

46 Surviving copies of the sheet music were published by Robert Cocks & Co., who took the opportunity presented by the rocky outcrop in the shadow of which the bard eased his weary soul, to advertise Richards's collection, *The Songs of Wales*, first published in 1873. However, the image itself carries the inscription of Stannard and Dixon and so must predate 1868, when the partnership came to an end. It seems, therefore, that the image was recycled from an earlier publication and that the prominent advertisement for *The Songs of Wales* was superimposed on the original.

47 Bardd y Brenin regarded Sackville Gwynne as among the finest triple harpers of his day. Gwynne acquired one of William Parry's portraits of John Parry, Telynor Dall. The later Gwynnes were patrons of John Wood Jones. Although set for piano, Linley's words to 'The Vale' include the line that begins 'When my harp to song shall waken.'

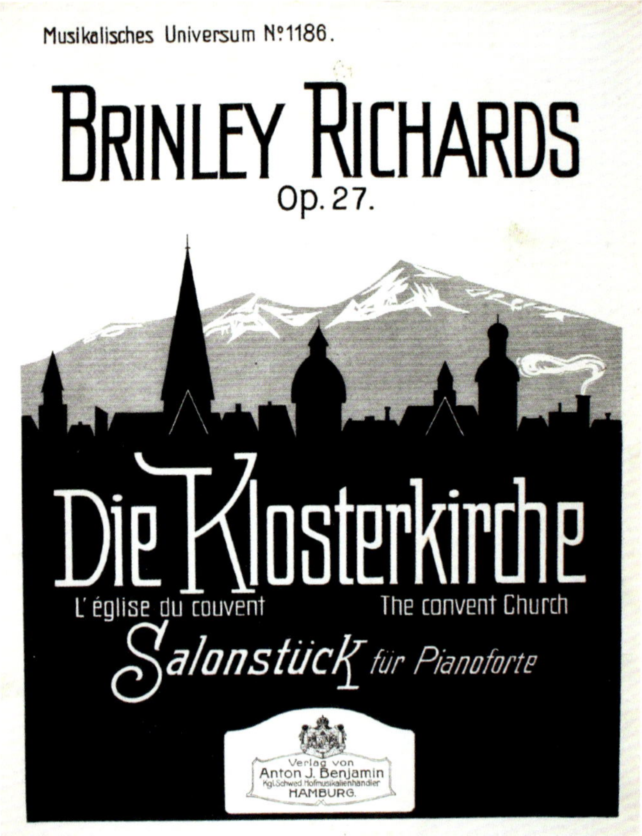

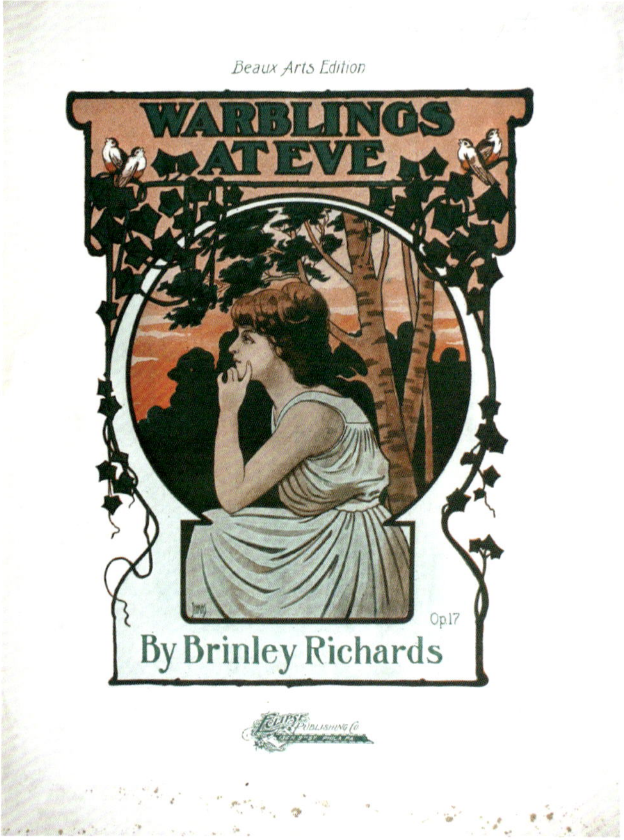

201 Unknown artist, cover for Brinley Richards, *Die Klosterkirche*, c.1910

202 Jenkins, cover for Brinley Richards, *Warblings at Eve*, c.1905

Ten years after 'Men of Harlech', and eloquently voicing the Janus-faced national spirit of the times, in 1873 Brinley Richards's 'God Bless the Prince of Wales' was published in the composer's collection *The Songs of Wales*. On this occasion, Ceiriog provided the Welsh words. A sheet music version had appeared earlier with a colour lithograph of the marriage of the future King Edward VII to Princess Alexandra of Denmark, which took place in 1863 at St George's Chapel, Windsor.[48] George Linley was again the librettist for the English-language version of the song, the success of which elevated it to the status of a second national anthem in the minds of many. Indeed, through the medium of sheet music, Brinley Richards's audience was now international, and far exceeded that of any Welsh contemporary. His prolific output of compositions and arrangements was distributed in illustrated editions by publishers in France, Germany, Italy and the United States.

Immediately after the publication of 'God Bless the Prince of Wales' and firmly in the tradition of Bardd y Brenin, Richards was again able to exploit his loyalty to the crown in order to promote a patriotic Welsh song. His composition,

'Let the Hills Resound', with words written by a London lyricist, L.H.F. Du Terreaux, was in the repertoire of Caradog's South Wales Choral Union by the time they took the prize at the Crystal Palace on the second occasion in 1873. Following their victory, the Prince of Wales invited the five hundred members of the choir to perform in the garden of Marlborough House for his extended family, including his wife and her sister, the future Empress of Russia, and the Grand Duchess of Mecklenburg-Strelitz. They were accompanied by a gallery of London Welsh hangers-on, eager to be associated with the national triumph. These ranged from the Prime Minister, William Gladstone, through the Marquess of Bute, Henry Richard MP, Thomas Charles Edwards and Hugh Owen, to Owain Alaw. The Royal Command performance was extensively reported, revealing much about the needy state of mind of the Welsh establishment of the period. The *Llandudno Register* recorded that 'Mr Brinley Richards has, with great truth, observed that the South Wales Choral Union has done more than anything to lift the veil that had divided Wales from England. The Principality now shines before England in a bright light.' Of Caradog, the paper noted with pride that 'the hand of the honest Welshman from Treorkey was pressed in that of Cambria's titular prince.'

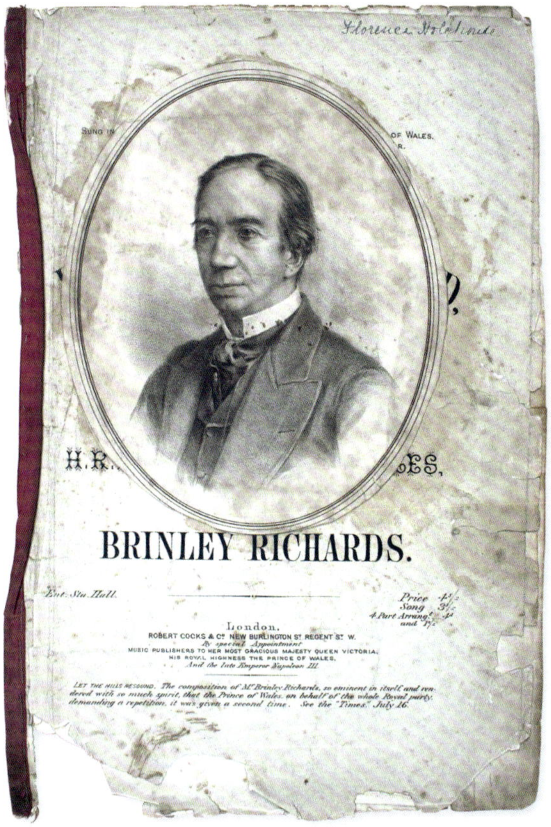

203 Unknown artist, *Brinley Richards*, c.1875, and cover for his song *Let the Hills Resound*, 1863

The Prince of Wales had been particularly enamoured of 'Let the Hills Resound':

> A spirited and effective delivery of this work so gratified the Prince and Princess that its repetition was commanded, and her Royal Highness signified to the composer that she would accept its dedication to herself.

Richards responded with a particularly sycophantic expression of his loyalty, distancing himself from the political sentiments of others of his compatriots:

> In a conversation with the Prince of Wales at Marlborough House, Mr Brinley Richards made a most appropriate remark. 'You belong to a national people,' observed the Prince. 'We have nothing to do with another kind of nationality, your Royal Highness,' replied Mr Richards, 'Our nationality is founded on self-respect, love of home, and loyalty to the throne of England.'[49]

48 The illustrated edition provided only the music. The words were published separately, without the illustration.

49 *Llandudno Register*, 19 July 1873, p. 3.

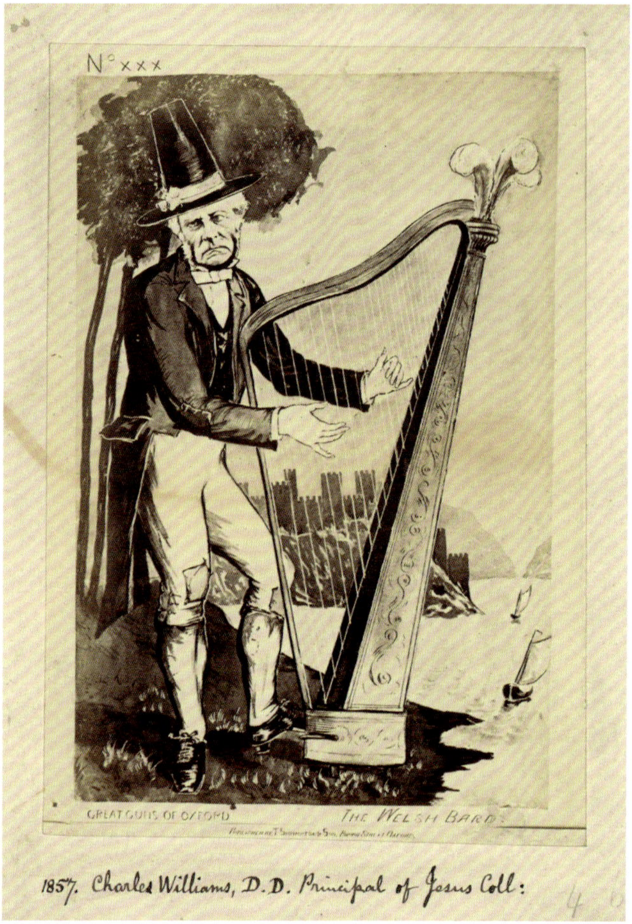

204 Unknown artist, *The Welsh Bard: Charles Williams of Jesus College, Oxford*, c.1870

At this summit of national approbation, a devotee of Richards pasted a copy of an engraving of the composer on the cover of her copy of 'Let the Hills Resound', above the publisher's marketing pitch. Quoting *The Times*, the publisher reminded the public that the new hymn was 'So eminent in itself', and had been 'rendered with so much spirit, that the Prince of Wales, on behalf of the whole Royal party, demanding a repetition, it was given a second time.'

Perhaps it was not coincidental that in the immediate aftermath of this well-publicised moment of royal favour, an unknown but talented cynic at Oxford produced a significant caricature of a prominent Welsh leader of academic life in the city. Charles Williams, formerly perpetual curate of Holyhead, had returned to academic life at his *alma mater*, Jesus College, in 1857, when he was elected Principal. A decade or so later, the printsellers and photographers, Shrimpton and Son of Broad Street, set up a unique business venture, reproducing photographically portraits and caricatures of the prominent academics of the city, made mainly by students. The rather dour Williams was caricatured playing a harp and wearing a tall black hat – suggesting both that the national brand, whether exemplified by bearded bards or behatted harpists, was now thoroughly well established in the public mind – and that its artificiality made it seriously vulnerable to parody.

The damp proclamation of the London Eisteddfod of 1887, held in the garden of the Inner Temple, resulted in a group of images in which the harper John Roberts featured. He had acquired recently the title of Telynor Cymru and, with a clear sense of its marketing potential, as he aged he moulded himself increasingly into the shape of the ancient bard. The son of a ballad singer who had served at the Battle of Waterloo, Roberts had spent nearly ten years in the Royal Welch Fusiliers, before settling to live at Newtown. His nephew and pupil, William Roberts, subsequently became harper to the Fusiliers, adopting also his uncle's visual sense of druidic heritage. In 1876, Herbert Johnson of *The Graphic* depicted William performing to greet the Prince of Wales on a visit to Gibraltar:

> When the Prince of Wales entered Gibraltar the officers of the regiment rigged up a rocky cave, placed over the entrance to their mess, with the harper inside, and a plentiful supply of leeks around him, playing 'God Bless the Prince of Wales'.[50]

50 *The Graphic*, 6 May 1876, p. 435. The Prince presented the Fusiliers with a new regimental goat. The artist and author of the account of the event, Herbert Johnson, is notable for his work documenting the dire social conditions endured by the people of Merthyr during the industrial dispute of 1875. See Lord, *Industrial Society*, pp. 144–51.

205 Unknown artist, *Welsh Bards Proclaiming the Eisteddfod*, 1886

206 Herbert Johnson, *William Roberts at Gibraltar*, 1876

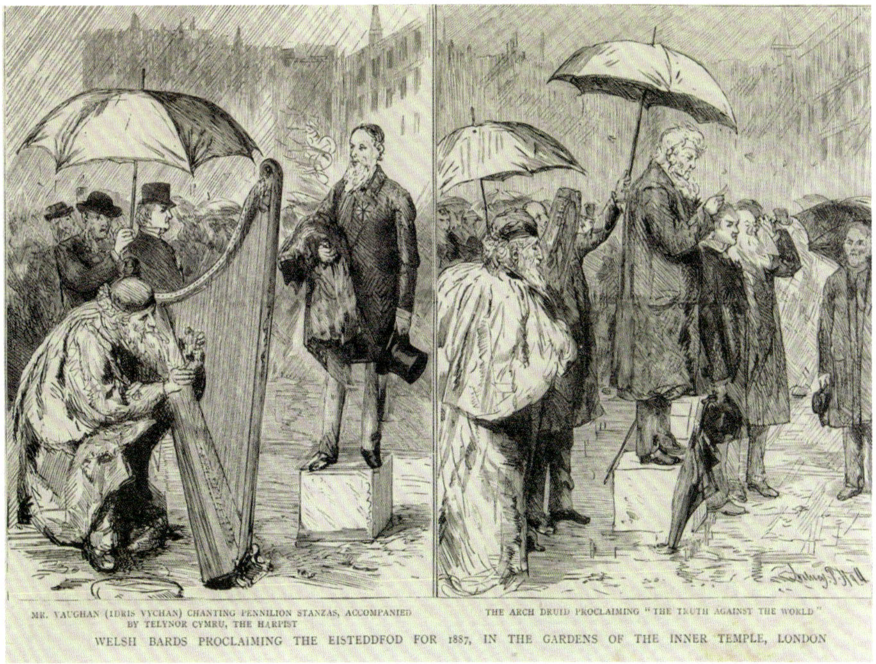

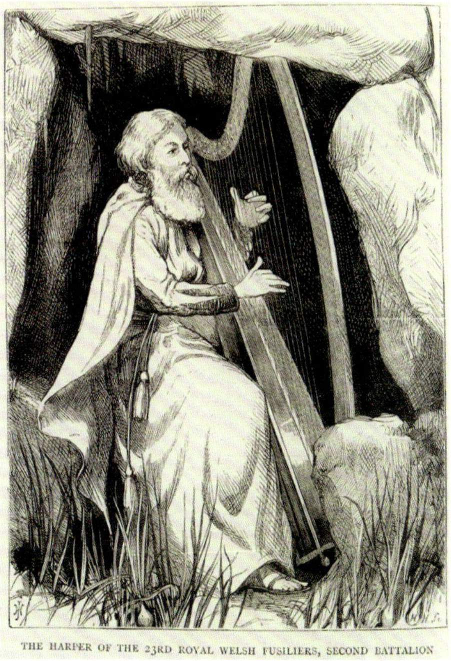

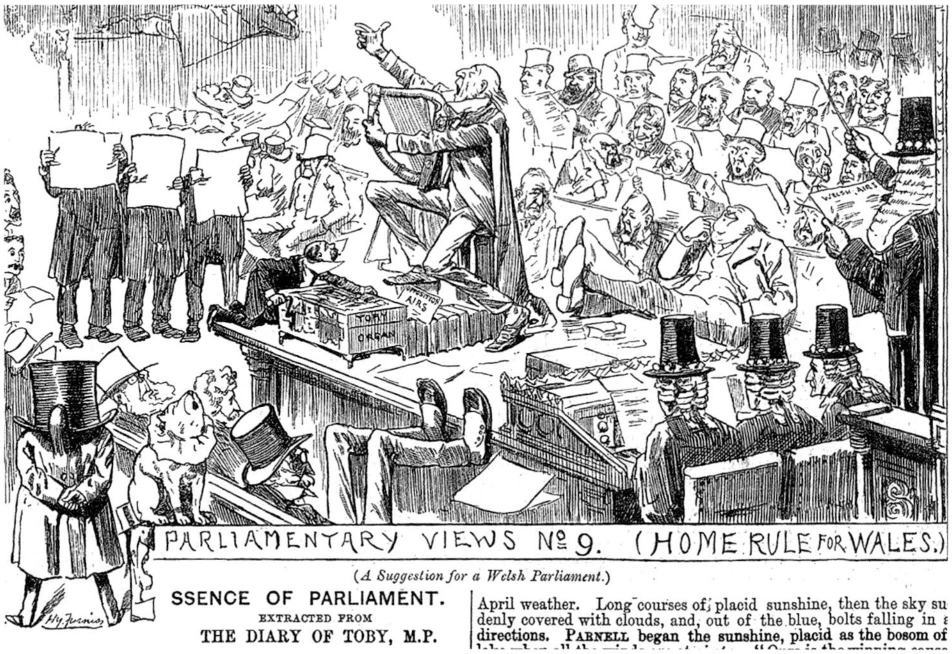

207 Harry Furniss, *Parliamentary Views, No. 9. (Home Rule for Wales)*, 1886

The 1887 proclamation ceremony, at which William's uncle John performed, took place just a few months after the establishment in London of the nationalist movement, Cymru Fydd, and coincided with a parliamentary debate on Home Rule for Wales, addressed by Mr Gladstone. The coincidence did not go unnoticed by the *Punch* cartoonist, Harry Furniss. Although as a young man Furniss had moved in nationalist circles in Ireland (where he was born and grew up), by this time he was an ardent unionist. With the image of Telynor Cymru at the proclamation clearly fixed in his mind, he lampooned Gladstone as the bard, addressing the House of Commons. Fellow Home Rulers among the members sing 'Welsh Airs', apparently conducted by the Speaker who, along with officers of the House, wears a tall black hat for the occasion.[51] English members on Gladstone's own side of the aisle are not amused, reflecting the split in the party that the Home Rule issue caused.

A year later, the Eisteddfod itself was held in the Royal Albert Hall. The title set for the *cywydd* was 'Cymru Fydd'.[52] Waxing lyrical in opening its account of the proceedings, the *Llangollen Advertiser* announced unequivocally that:

> The Welsh are essentially a musical people. The spirit of music is in every breast, and wherever the race of Cymry may be, in their own sweet valleys, or on their own rugged mountains, or in distant America, or still more distant Australia, it burns with unceasing ardour.[53]

The composite presentation of the event in *The Illustrated London News* was not among its more visually distinguished achievements, but it did include one of the earliest portraits of a successful female competitor. Although unnamed, she was almost certainly Lucy Clarke, a Cardiff contralto trained by Clara Novello Davies, who would develop her career into the twentieth century, performing in opera, concerts, and on the music hall stage.

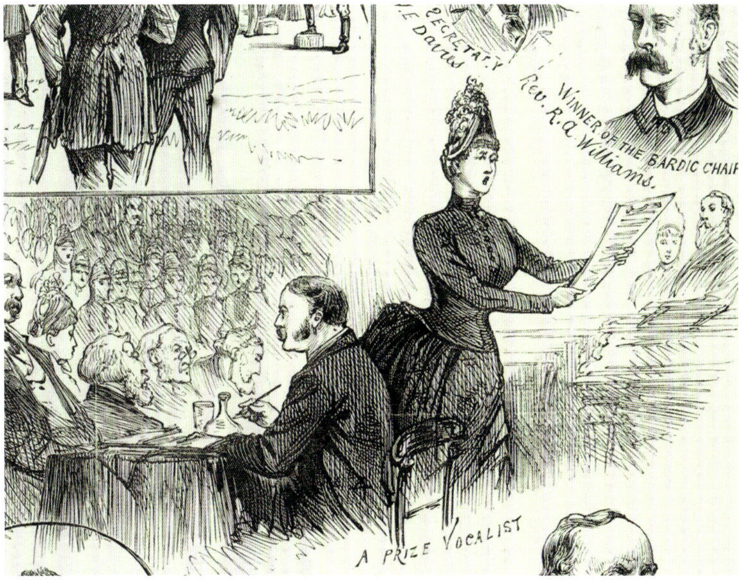

208 Unknown artist, *The London National Eisteddfod*, 1887

The Royal Albert Hall proved an appropriate location for an enthusiastic demonstration of Eisteddfodic loyalty to the English crown. George Linley's words to Brinley Richards's song of 1863 that had presented unionists with the slogan 'God Bless the Prince of Wales', were to be seen on banners and inscriptions decorating many Eisteddfod venues of the period. It had been emblazoned before all others at Aberystwyth, across the full width of the platform. In London, the Eisteddfod was briefly graced by the presence of the current incarnation, Prince Albert Edward, who found himself ensconced, amidst a forest of harps, at the front of the platform:

> Splendid weather again, and a large and noble audience, and all boiling with enthusiasm to see the Prince and Princess of Wales, and their children. When the time came, the bards had formed a procession in the corridors of the Albert Hall … At 12 o'clock, the Prince and his family appeared, and under the hands of Haydn Parry, from the great organ flowed forth 'God Bless the Prince of Wales' – the wonderful crowd waving their handkerchiefs, and shouting terrifically. Indeed, the Prince and his beautiful Princess become constantly more popular. The three princesses, their children, looked simple and unassuming. Under the direction of Pencerdd Gwalia, the eisteddfod choir thundered out 'God Bless the Prince of Wales,' Eos Morlais singing the solo.[54]

Two years later, suitably dressed down for the occasion, John Roberts, Telynor Cymru, would perform for the Prince's mother. In 1836, Roberts (who was a Romany speaker) had married Eleanor Wood Jones, daughter of Jeremiah

51 *Punch*, 4 September 1886, p. 119. Furniss published a collection of his cartoons two years later, *Parliamentary Views; Extracted from the Diary of Toby, MP*. The accompanying texts in *Punch* were written by Sir Henry Lucy.

52 Dewi Rowland Hughes, *Cymru Fydd* (Cardiff, 2006), p. 30.

53 *Llangollen Advertiser*, 12 August 1887, p. 3.

54 *Y Drych*, 25 August 1887. Brinley Richards's melody was adopted with new words by unionists in Ireland as 'Derry's Walls', a song that celebrated the siege of Derry in 1689. Haydn Parry was the son of the composer Joseph Parry.

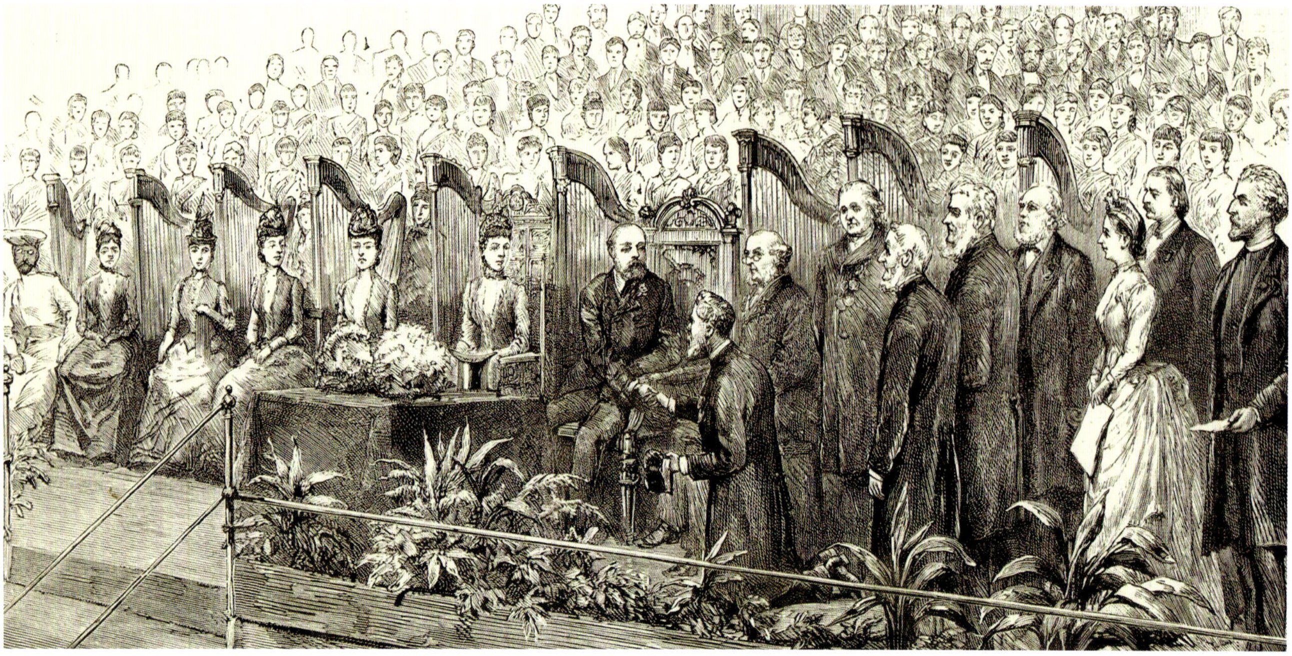

209 Unknown artist, *Notes at the National Eisteddfod of Wales*, 1887

Wood Jones, the Pryse family harper at Gogerddan. They produced a veritable orchestra of musical children, and by the 1870s they were performing together as The Original Cambrian Minstrels. They took the stage at the St David's Day concert in the Royal Albert Hall in 1889 and, later that year, eight of Roberts's sons joined him in a command performance at Palé Hall, near Bala, where Queen Victoria was staying on a progress through north Wales. *The Illustrated London News* depicted the Queen and her courtiers observing the proceedings with bemused condescension. The paper's correspondent noted that:

> … many places in Wales are equally romantic with those of the wilder parts of Scotland … Welsh history, romance, and poetry, however, remain comparatively obscure to the majority of English people, not for their lack of intrinsic interest, but for want of a great English-writing author to make them widely known.[55]

Reporting on the same visit and attempting to rectify the inadequate representation of Welsh specialities, *The Graphic* featured on its cover a portrait of the Queen's fifth daughter and companion, Princess Beatrice, tentatively wielding a pickaxe, down one of Sir Watkin Williams Wynn's coalmines.[56]

In the later part of his life, John Roberts was photographed by John Owen of Newtown, who had been awarded a medal for his work at the 1865

Aberystwyth Eisteddfod. Before the age of half-tone photographic reproduction in newspapers and magazines, Owen's images became familiar mainly in the *carte de visite* format. Conscious like his sitter of the long tradition of bardic painting and engraving, Owen reconstructed the myth in his studio with the 'realism' of the modern medium. Cardboard rocks and a painted backcloth cause the observer to wonder how seriously the image was taken during the harper's lifetime, even allowing for the acceptance of such familiar conventions in the period. A more straightforward photograph, apparently from the same session, was more widely distributed than the meditating (or sleeping) bard. It was reproduced for instance by *The Graphic* in its Eisteddfod report of 1895,[57] a year after the harper's death, and it stimulated the production of an oil painting. After suffering a stroke in 1893 that prevented him from playing, John Roberts had given his harp to his friend Nicholas Bennett, the folk-song collector. Bennett displayed it in his home, Glanyrafon, at Trefeglwys in

55 *The Illustrated London News*, 24 August 1889, p. 242.

56 *The Graphic*, 14 September 1889, p. 317.

57 Ibid., 3 August 1895, p. 146. In its commentary, the number of Telynor Cymru's sons who had played for Queen Victoria at Palé had swollen to eleven.

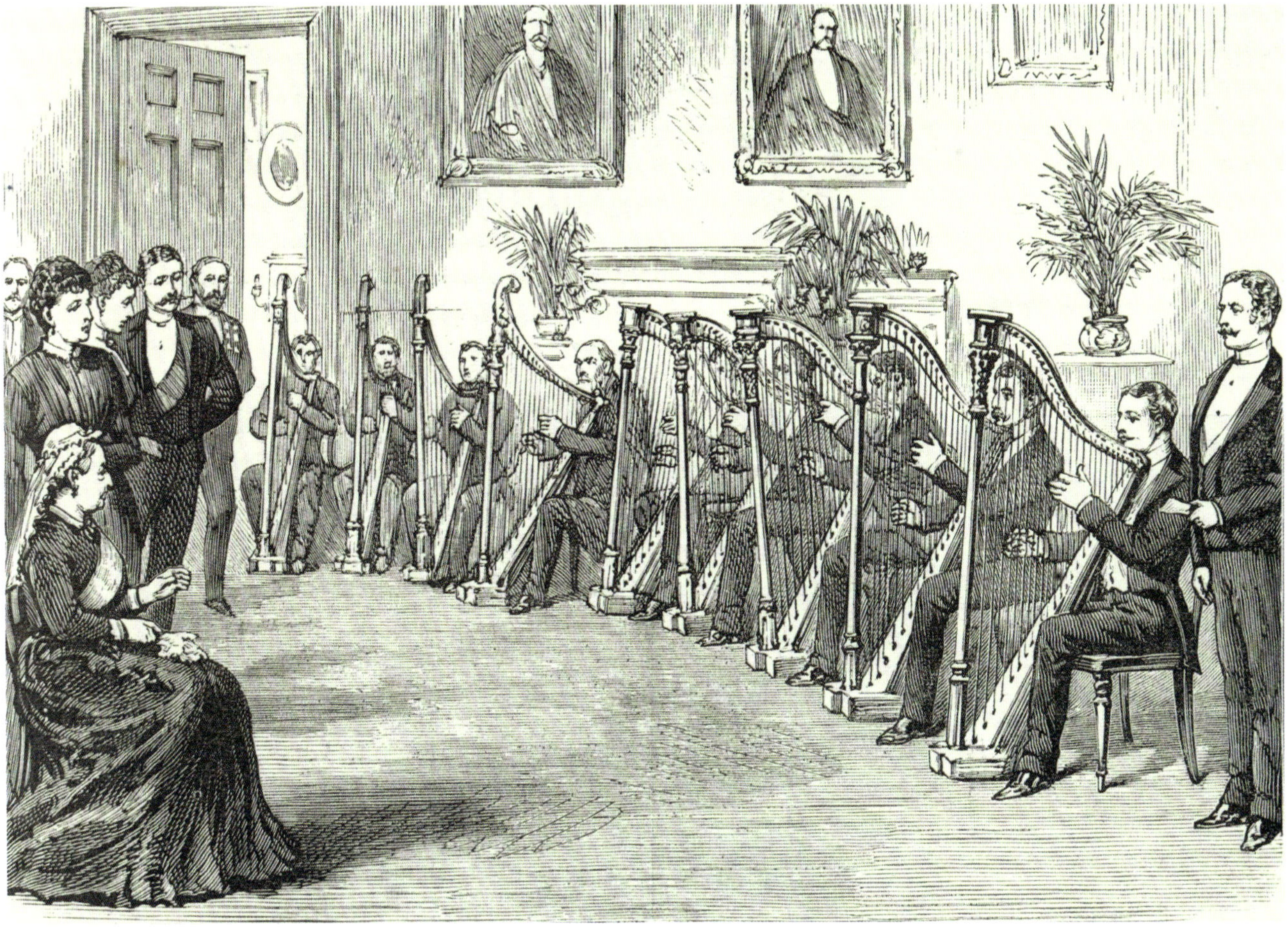

210 Unknown artist, *John Roberts and Family at Palé*, 1889

211 John Owen of Newtown, *John Roberts, Telynor Cymru*, c.1890

212 Probably Richard Henry Jerman, *John Roberts, Telynor Cymru*, c.1890–95

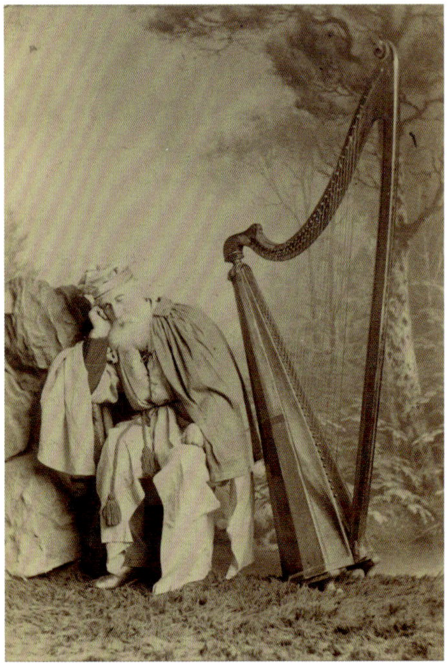

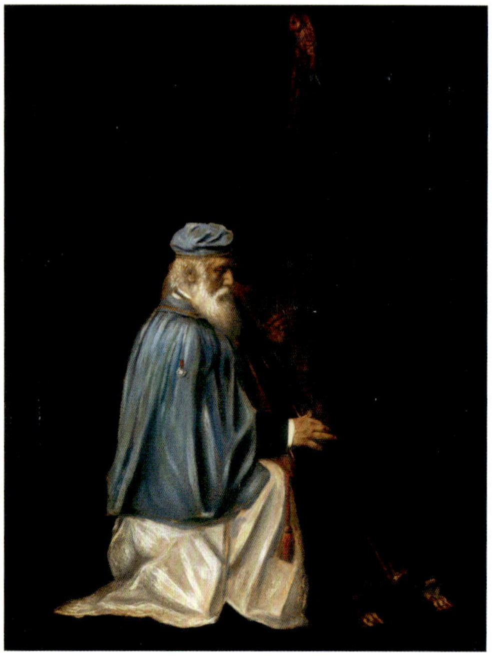

Montgomeryshire, and hung the oil painting above it.[58] Combined with an image of Idris Fychan to recall the London proclamation ceremony of 1886, the final manifestation of the image as an engraving came on the title page to Bennett's collection of folk tunes, *Alawon fy Ngwlad*, in 1896, opposite a frontispiece based on William Parry's portraits of John Parry, Telynor Dall.

DEMURE YOUNG HARPERS AND PIN-UP DIVAS

By the end of the nineteenth century and with the emergence of Cymru Fydd, the imaging of Welshness in the person of John Roberts, Telynor Cymru, was an anachronism that had been largely overtaken by a feminised visual vocabulary. It was manifested in pictures that appealed to all sections of society – the devotees of academic art, the middlebrow audience who enjoyed the reportage of the illustrated press, and before long a broad swathe of the public who sent postcards and purchased kitsch memorabilia on their holidays. The first of six volumes entitled *Cambrian Minstrelsie*, that in 1893 marked the entry of Joseph Parry into the long tradition of arrangers of traditional airs, was illustrated with a transitional coloured lithograph. An ancient bard entertains two young women who manifest outsider perceptions both of the national costume and of the national preoccupation with knitting socks.

58 *Montgomery and Radnor Echo*, 10 March 1900. Presumably the portrait was commissioned by Bennett himself although the evidence of style suggests that it was probably not the work of the Llanidloes painter Hugh Jerman, who knew Bennett well. It may be the work of Hugh Jerman's son, Richard Henry Jerman, also a painter.

In 1891, at about the same time that Nicholas Bennett had commissioned his painted portrait of Telynor Cymru, the Scottish artist John Robertson Reid attended the National Eisteddfod at Swansea. He was moved to paint a portrait that would encapsulate those essential elements of demure femininity, first presented at Abergavenny, and express Welshness through a combination of musicality and costume. It was a formula to which image makers of popular art in particular would persistently return in their characterisations of the nation

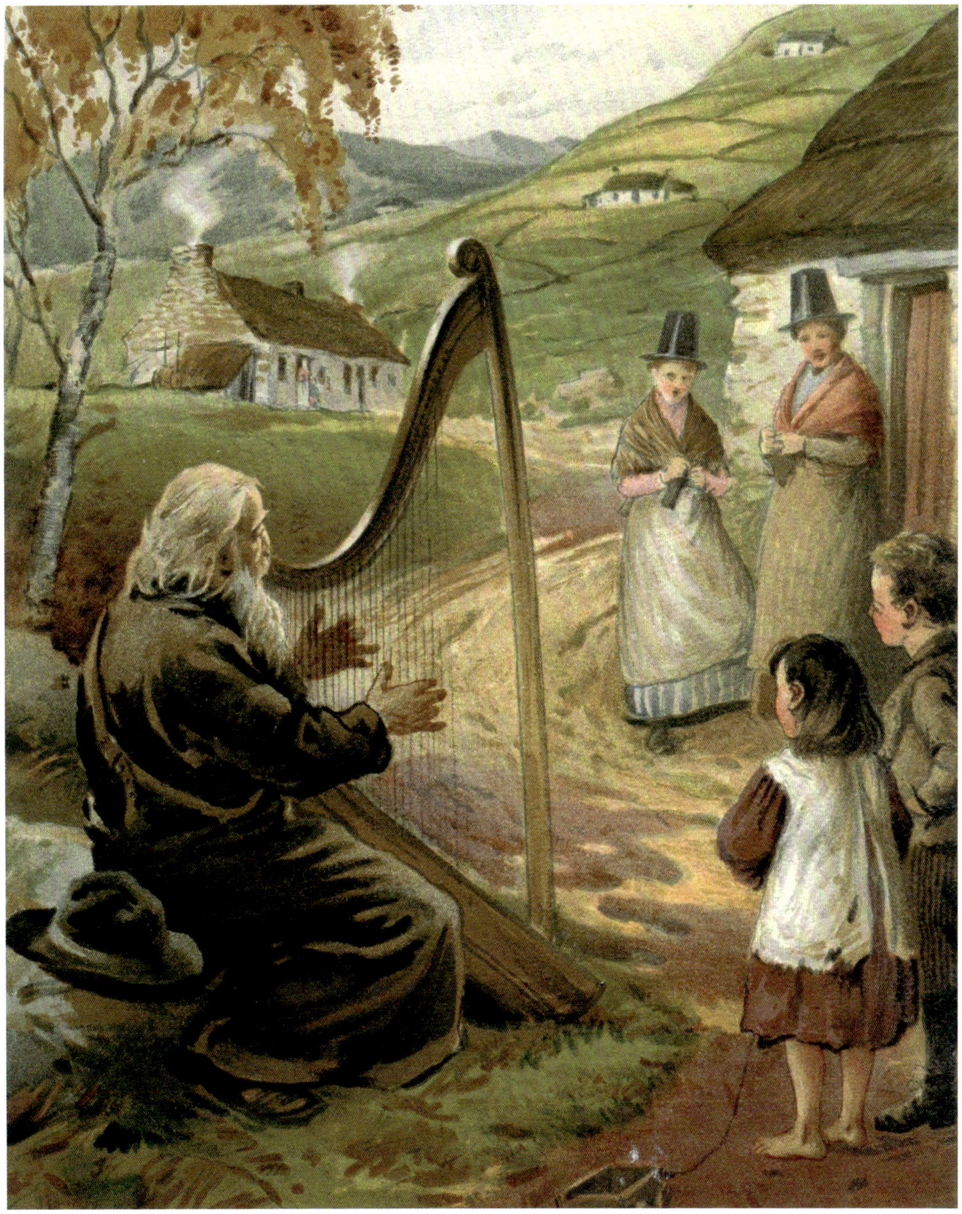

213 J. Michael Brown, *The Old Blind Harper*, 1893

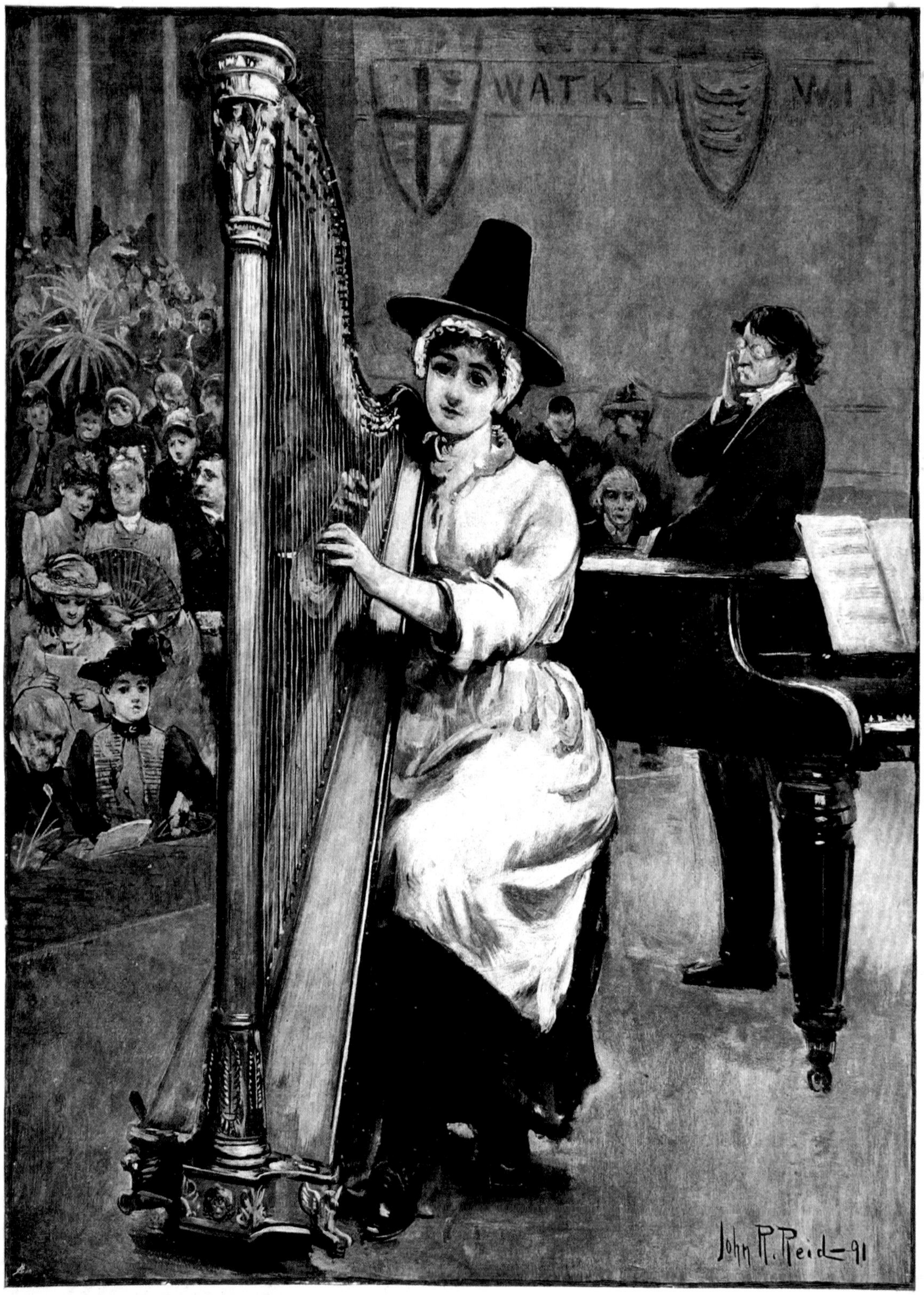

A POPULAR SOLOIST

THE RECENT EISTEDDFOD AT SWANSEA

throughout the twentieth century. J.R. Reid had trained in Scotland but by the 1880s he was working primarily in the south-west of England, painting scenes of Cornish fishing communities and the like. It is unclear if his visit to Swansea at Eisteddfod time was coincidental, perhaps the result of coming to the area to paint cocklewomen at Penclawdd, a popular subject for artists of his kind, or if he was specifically commissioned by *The Graphic*. Whatever its origins, Reid's painting was regarded as sufficiently characteristic for the editor to reproduce it as a full-page feature. The paper's cursory written account of the Eisteddfod named neither the harpist nor the gentleman leaning on the grand piano behind her, presenting to the sober audience a contrasting and well-cultivated romantic self-image. The written report concentrated on reinforcing the message of the painting:

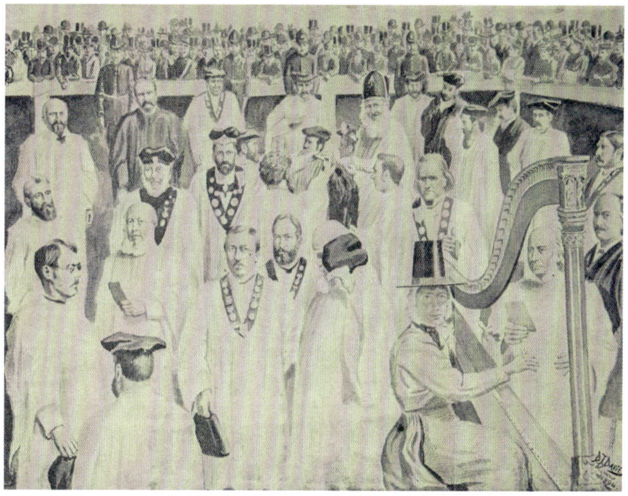

215 David John Davies, *The Bards of the Isle of Britain*, 1894

214 John Robertson Reid, *A Popular Soloist*, 1891

> There are all sorts of competitors … But the [competition] that moves the people most is the national harp, especially when accompanied by the national costume, as in Mr Reid's picture. A pretty young girl, he says, came on to the platform, and, in her Welsh dress, played a Welsh air on a Welsh harp. All Cymri [*sic*] folk who were present; young and old, man, boy, and girl, wore an expression of proud happy contentment in their nationality.[59]

Four years later, a Welsh illustrator presented closely similar iconography, though it was directed at a different audience. It was the second year of publication of O.M. Edwards's magazine *Wales*, which was aimed specifically at the English-speaking people of the nation. The young illustrator was David John Davies, a native of Carmarthenshire, who became better known, subsequently, as Dyer Davies. In 1894 and 1895, he worked throughout Wales in a flurry of activity stimulated by commissions from Edwards.[60] His visual memoir of the 1894 National Eisteddfod at Caernarfon presented the assembled intelligentsia, among whom were Edwards's contemporary from his Oxford days, John Puleston Jones, the Archdruid Clwydfardd and Hwfa Môn, all in their Gorsedd attire, but the core message is carried by the unidentified female harper and Pencerdd Gwalia, to whom the eye is immediately drawn by his contrasting everyday attire. The musician stands in precisely the same position relative to the female harpist, encased in her national costume, as the unidentified companion of the harpist painted three years earlier at Swansea by Reid.

59 *The Graphic*, 29 August 1891, p. 254. Clearly, the soloist does not play 'the national harp' but a Grecian-style pedal harp.

60 See D.J. Davies's letters to O.M. Edwards (NLW O.M. Edwards Papers, Class A, General). Supported by several prominent local figures, Davies trained at Kidderminster School of Art and at Antwerp. In particular he noted the support of 'Mrs Gwynn Hughes, Tregib, Llandeilo, whose Protégé I practically always have been', and Maria V.G. Havergal, sister and biographer of the hymn writer and poet Frances Riley Havergal, who resided for a time at Caswell Bay, Swansea. He went to the Boer War as a correspondent and illustrator, and appears to have remained there subsequently.

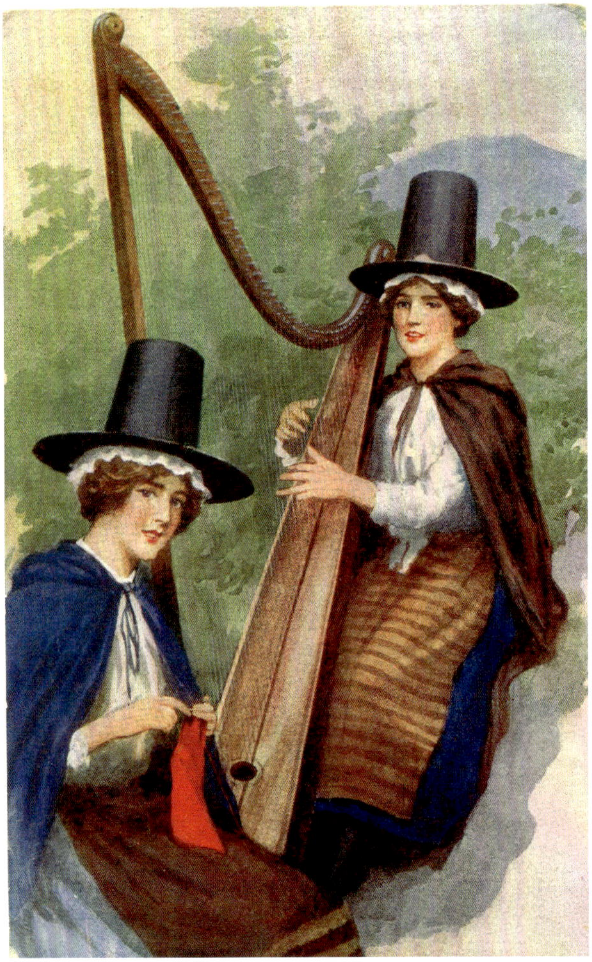

The social reach of imagery that presented the identity of the Welsh people in terms of femininity and musicality was about to expand on an unprecedented scale with the advent of the picture postcard. The fashion for sending postcards arrived relatively late in Britain, as the format was not regularised by the Post Office until 1899, when *The Standard* reported that 'The illustrated postcard craze, like the influenza, has spread to these islands from the continent, where it has been raging with considerable severity.'[61] The cards produced in the period before the Great War, when the craze was at its height, ranged widely in style to suit all tastes and all requirements, since their use was not confined to greetings sent by seaside tourists to friends at home. The reliability and frequency of the postal service in the period encouraged the public to use cards for everyday communication, when only a brief message, such as an arrival time at a railway station, needed to be conveyed. Although this element of functionality declined after the Great War, initially with the advent of the telephone, postcard designers would continue to produce variants on Reid's image of feminine Welshness and musicality until the end of the twentieth century.[62]

216 Unknown artist, *Costume Postcard*, c.1900–14

Prolific designers based in England, including F.G. Lewin and G.F. Christie, produced many of the early Welsh designs, although not all cards were of English origin. Welsh artists, notably Lloyd Hughes and Howard Lloyd Roberts, produced many designs,[63] and work by both was published by the Everton company of the Liverpool Welsh Thomas brothers, and by the Scottish company Valentine. Cards often featured the Welsh and English languages together. The titles and, occasionally, the words and the music of particularly celebrated national songs were a popular feature. The legend of Jenny Jones was reincarnated in the new format. 'Sospan Fach' joined the internationally recognised Welsh repertoire and many cards quoted 'Hen Wlad Fy Nhadau'.

The universally popular genre of mildly vulgar holiday cards was manifested in Welsh costume, and the difficulties experienced by English visitors in

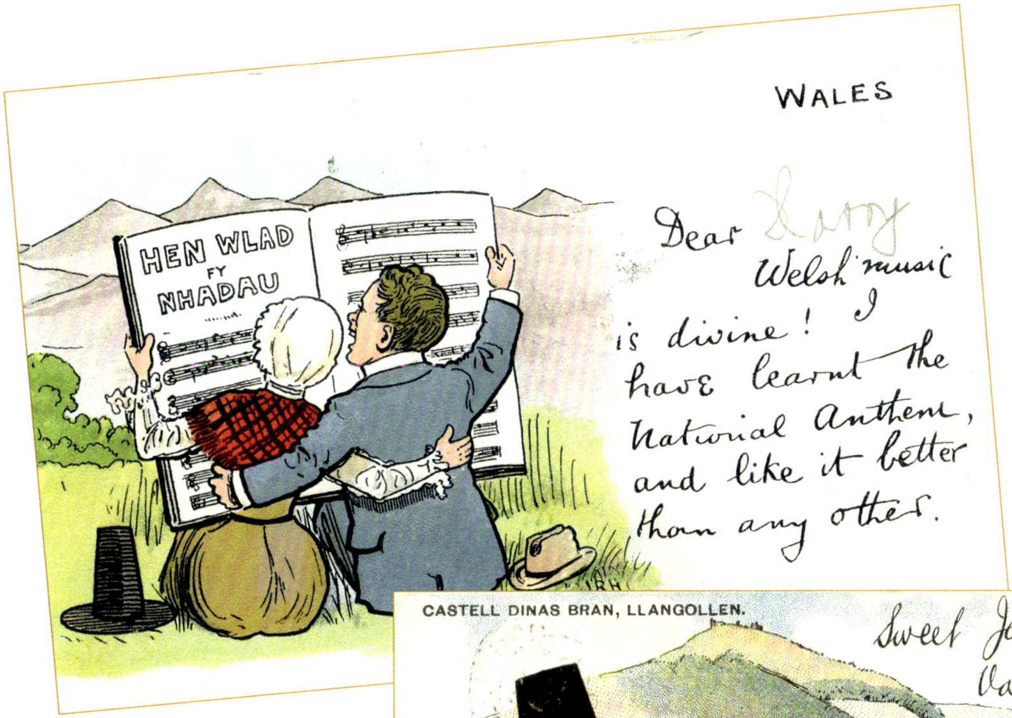

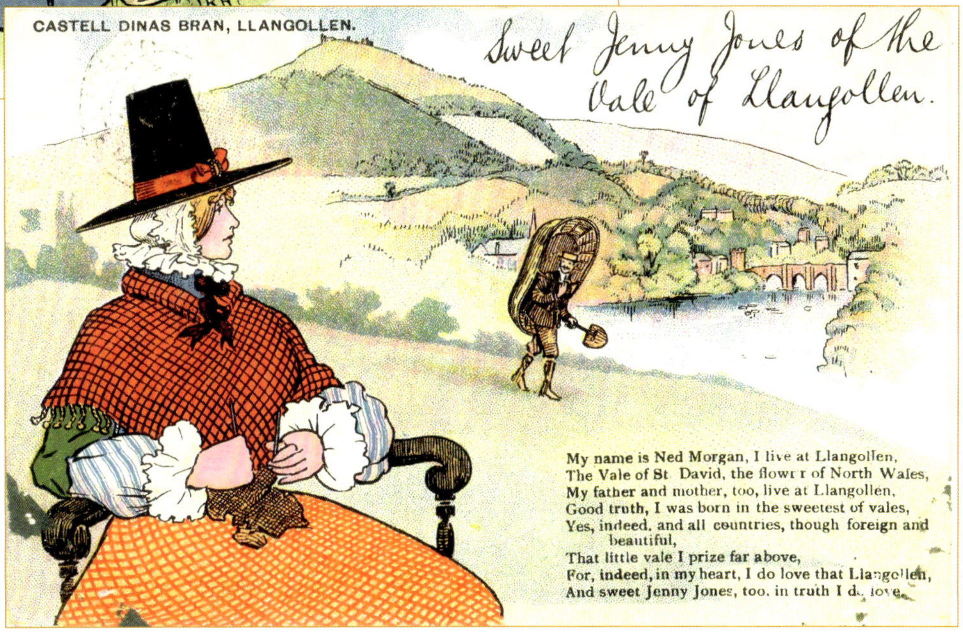

217 J.R.H., *Hen Wlad Fy Nhadau: Welsh Music is Divine*, c.1900–14

218 Unknown artist, *Sweet Jenny Jones*, c.1906

219 Unknown artist, *Cymru*, c.1900–14

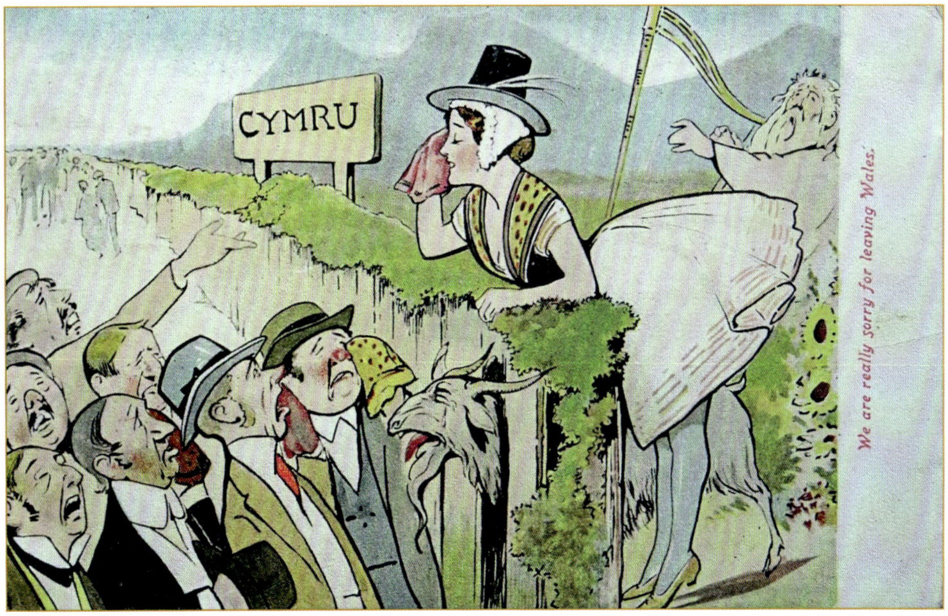

61 *The Standard*, 21 August 1899.

62 The cartoonist Rupert Besley continued the tradition of seaside postcards, including Welsh imagery and using a style closely related to that of the pre-Great War pioneers, into the twenty-first century.

63 Lloyd Hughes was from Anglesey, and trained at the Slade School in London. Howard Lloyd Roberts was from Borth, Ceredigion, and also used the professional names of Llwyd Roberts and Ap Rhobert. After the Great War he worked as a school teacher. See E.G. Millward, *Cymru'r Cardiau Post* (Llandysul, 1996), pp. 26, 30.

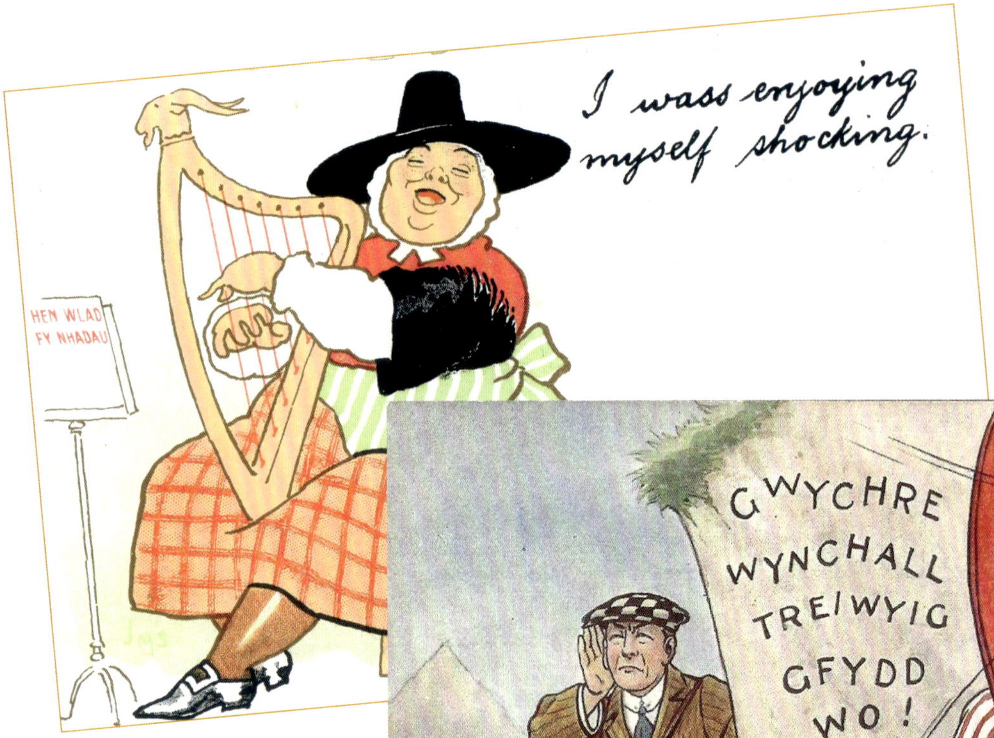

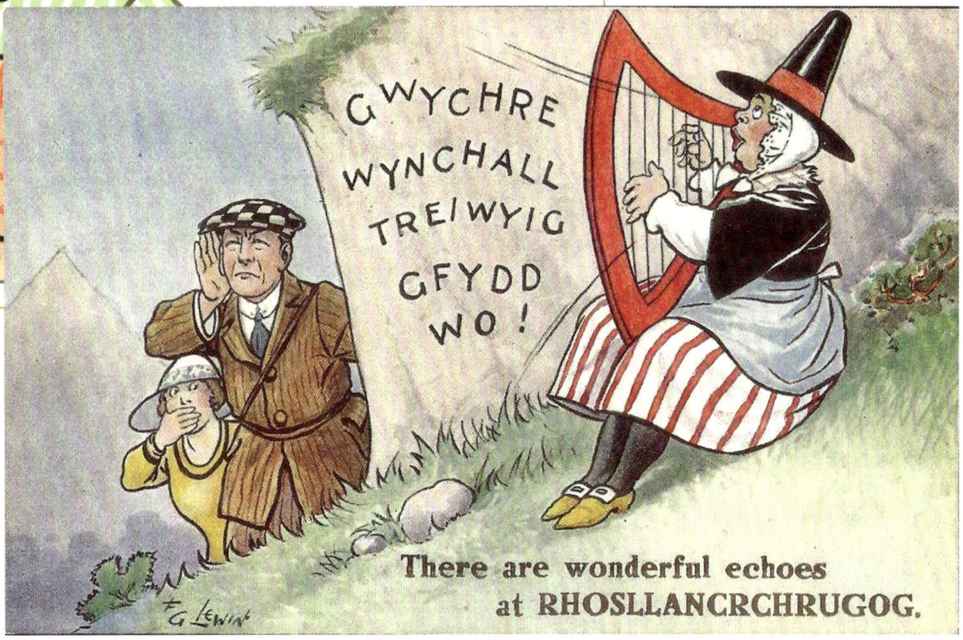

220 J.M. Staniforth, *I wass enjoying myself shocking*, c.1900–14

221 F.G. Lewin, *There are wonderful echoes at Rhosllancrchrugog*, c.1900–14

pronouncing Welsh words also proved a fertile area for humour. F.G. Lewin's evocation of the celebrated choral tradition of Rhosllanerchrugog was accompanied by gobbledegook, but his card is of particular interest because it seems to reflect the influence of the home-grown reinvention of national costume imagery created by J.M. Staniforth. His character Dame Wales, popularised from her first appearance in 1893 in the artist's many cartoons for the *Western Mail*, transferred well to the postcard format.[64]

Dame Wales coexisted with the rather more sober insider perception of Welshness promoted by the nationalist generation of university-educated intellectuals led by O.M. Edwards and T.E. Ellis. In their writings and speeches, the myth of the *gwerin Gymraeg*, the common people of Welsh-speaking Wales, reached its fullest expression. In their construction of history, it was they who had kept alive the core values, the language and the cultural traditions of the nation, within the framework of their everyday lives working on the land and

64 Staniforth was a native of Cardiff who had been apprenticed at the age of fifteen in the lithographic department of the *Western Mail*, whilst at the same time he studied at art classes in the town.

as craftspeople. Although Edwards had begun to address and depict industrial workers in his English-language magazine, *Wales*, it was through the image of the musicality of a Welsh-speaking family of craftspeople that Dyer Davies presented the editor's concept of essential Welshness in his drawing *In the Land of Song*. A cobbler's daughter sings to the accompaniment of her father's harp. A copy of Edwards's Welsh-language magazine, *Cymru*, lies on the floor. More subtly, the *gwerin* mythology was reinforced on an annual basis at the National Eisteddfodau, where the large audiences who flocked to the musical events depicted in the London illustrated press implied a uniquely cultured common people, appreciative both of their indigenous tradition and of pan-European art music. The choral tradition, in particular, sustained by the common people, constantly reinforced the message of the tag lines 'Everyone in Wales sings', 'Wales: a sea of song', and 'Cymru lân, gwlad y gân'.

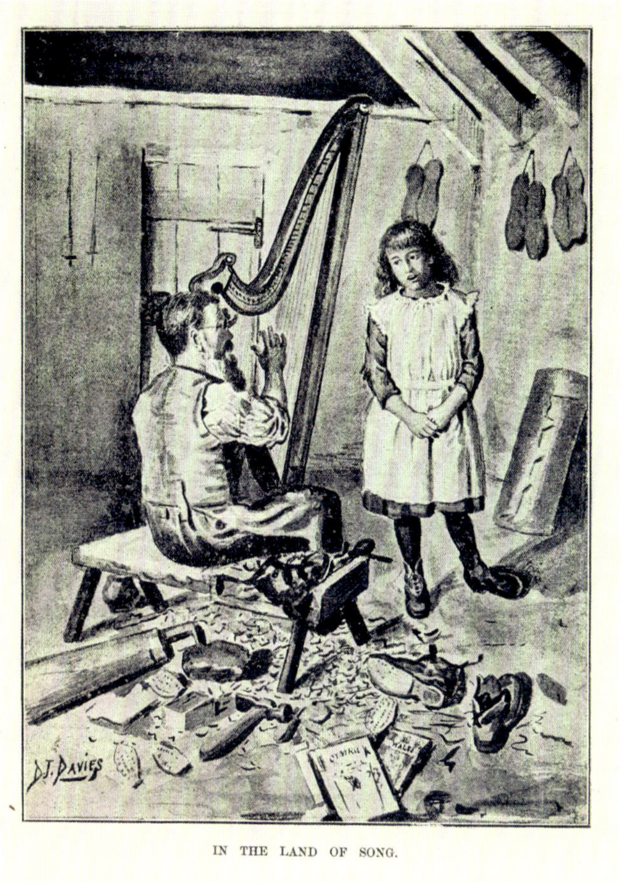

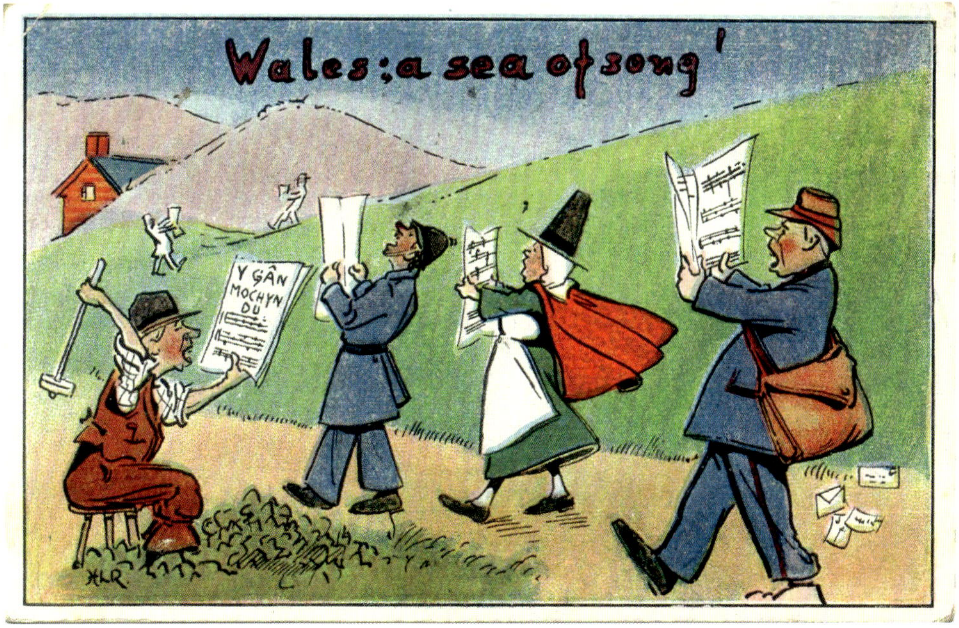

222 David John Davies, *In the Land of Song*, 1894

223 Howard Lloyd Roberts, *Wales: a sea of song*, postcard, c.1900–14

Because of his large output of images, J.M. Staniforth became a well-known name in the 1890s. Behind the scenes of his day job as a cartoonist, he associated with a group of intellectuals and artists of the Cymru Fydd generation in Cardiff who supported the visual arts and campaigned for the development of art institutions. The Cardiff Naturalists Society and the South Wales Arts Society provided a focus for many of their activities, which included organising a series of large-scale art exhibitions in the town, notably at the National Eisteddfod in 1883. The group included the architect Edwin Seward and the graphic artist Thomas Henry Thomas, 'Arlunydd Penygarn'. Thomas was born in Pontypool and had trained as a painter in Bristol and London. By the time he settled in Cardiff he had travelled widely on the continent and to north America, from where he had provided illustrations for *The Graphic*. His association with the paper continued on his return to Wales.[65] Because of his close association with the Gorsedd (which included designing its banner – a prominent feature of all the outdoor ceremonies), at the Pontypridd Eisteddfod of 1893 he was able to draw for *The Graphic* from an advantageous position at the side of the stage. His subject was the lyric soprano Madame S.A. Williams-Penn, singing at the chairing of the bard. Sarah Williams was a native of Pontypridd who, after singing with Caradog's choir and studying at the Royal Academy of Music, returned to live in the town following her marriage to Charles Penn, manager of the Chainworks, and continued to sustain a professional career. But when she took to the Eisteddfod stage in 1893,

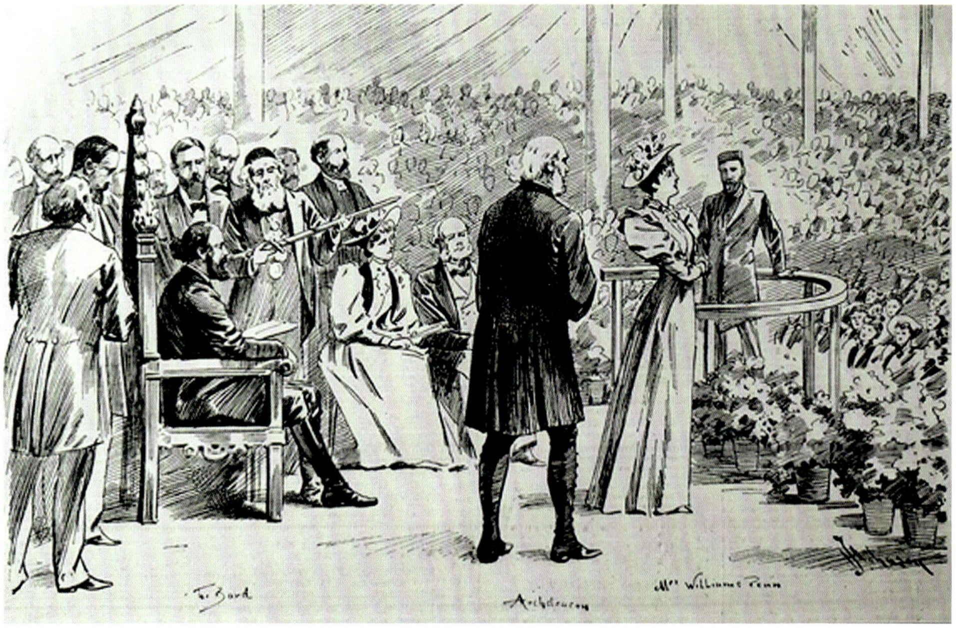

224 T.H. Thomas, *Mrs Williams-Penn at the Pontypridd National Eisteddfod*, 1893

she was following in the footsteps of an even more distinguished diva. Four years earlier, at Brecon, the most famous soprano in the world, Adelina Patti, had led the singing of 'Hen Wlad Fy Nhadau'. Patti was born in Spain and grew up in the United States, but in 1878, when she was still at the height of her career, she bought Craig-y-Nos, at the head of the Swansea Valley, which became her home until her death in 1919. For her performances, Patti was able to command huge fees (presumably waived when she took the stage at Brecon), and she invested a good deal of her wealth in developing Craig-y-Nos, to which she added a fully equipped private theatre adorned with the names of her favourite operatic composers and a fire curtain on which she drove a chariot in the title role of Rossini's *Semiramide*. Patti lived at Craig-y-Nos with her second husband, Ernesto Nicolini, and both of them were portrayed by John Ernest Breun in an unusually informal portrait on the banks of the River Usk, near Trecastle, where they enjoyed the salmon fishing.[66]

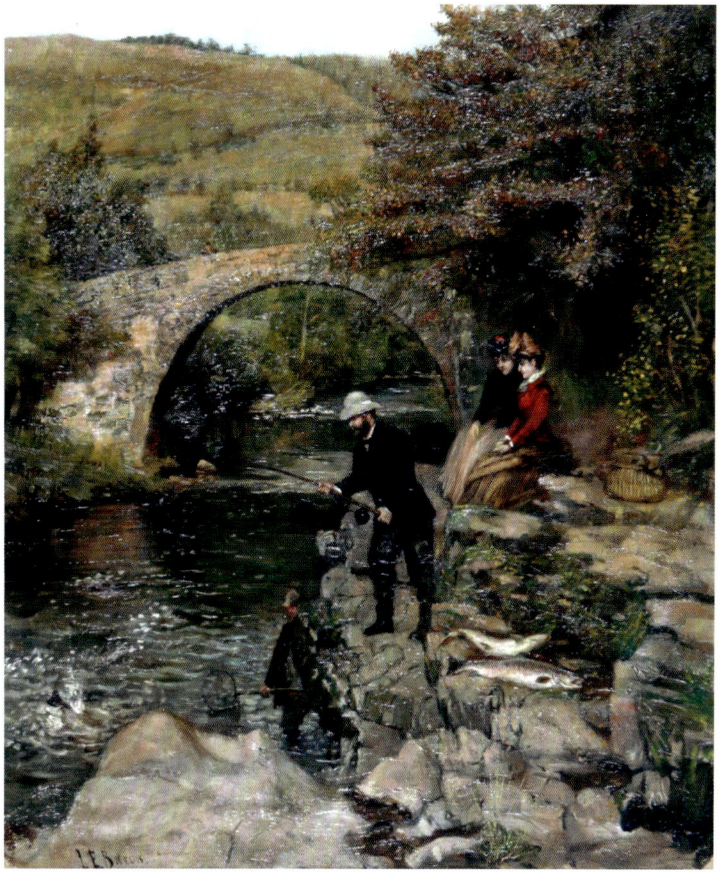

225 John Ernest Breun, *Madame Patti Watching Nicolini Landing a Salmon, Pont Pantysgallog*, c.1880

The close association with Wales of a singer of worldwide renown surely reinforced the national brand in the public mind. Although it was perhaps the postcard more than any other genre that fixed for the twentieth century the notion of Wales as the 'Land of Song', academic art imagery nevertheless played its part. In the late Victorian and Edwardian periods, major portraits of celebrated figures like Patti attracted considerable press attention when exhibited at the Royal Academy and other London galleries. Patti was among the most frequently portrayed women of the period, and distinguished artists ranging in their approach from the intensity of Gustave Doré to the superficial gloss of Queen Victoria's favourite, Franz Xavier Winterhalter, had painted her. A portrait by a less celebrated German, Karl Friedrich Steinhardt, while certainly not the most flattering representation of the diva, is of particular interest since it shows Patti as Desdemona in Rossini's lesser-known opera *Otello*, in which she performed widely on the continent and in London. Her role début at Covent Garden in 1871 attracted the attention of the illustrated press, as well

65 Thomas's work for *The Graphic*, including his eyewitness reporting of the 1887 Cwtch colliery disaster, is illustrated in Lord, *Industrial Society*, pp. 154–7.

66 The painter, John Ernest Breun, carried out several more formal portrait commissions in the Swansea area.

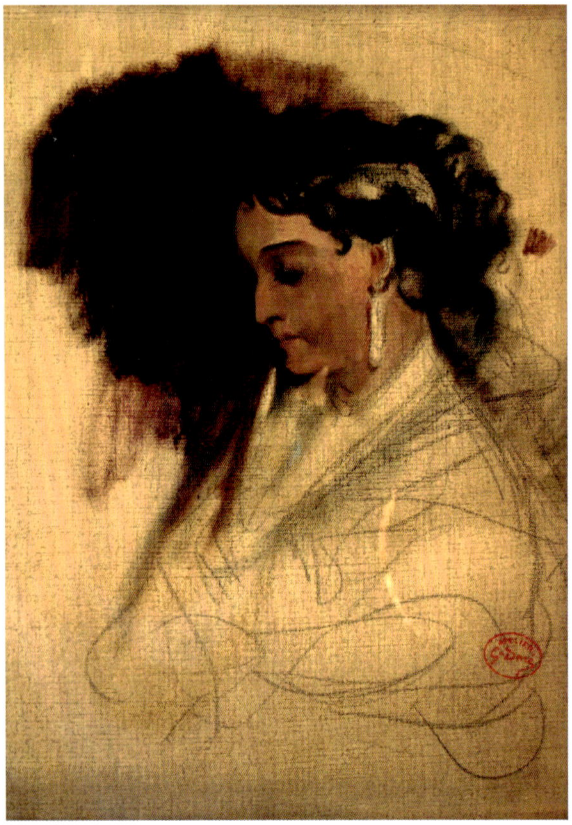

as the academic art world, and *The Graphic* published a portrait of her in character made by one of its regular lithographers, James Dromgole Linton.[67]

The development of a sub-genre of full-length portraits of late nineteenth- and early twentieth-century divas reflected the earlier fashion for portraits of female harpers. In 1897, John Singer Sargent painted an opulent portrait of the singer Elizabeth (Elsie) Ebsworth, who was still an amateur at that time but who would later sing professionally under her married name of Mrs George Swinton. Elizabeth Ebsworth's father was the tenant of Llandough Castle in the Vale of Glamorgan, where his daughter and her Scottish husband also spent much time when not at their London home. Among their elevated artistic circle was the composer Gabriel Fauré, who was invited to stay with them at Llandough, where the portrait was hanging, in August 1898. It appears

226 Gustave Doré, *Madame Adelina Patti*, *c.*1865–75

227 James Dromgole Linton, *Adelina Patti as Desdemona*, 1871

228 Karl Friedrich Steinhardt, *Adelina Patti as Desdemona*, *c.*1871

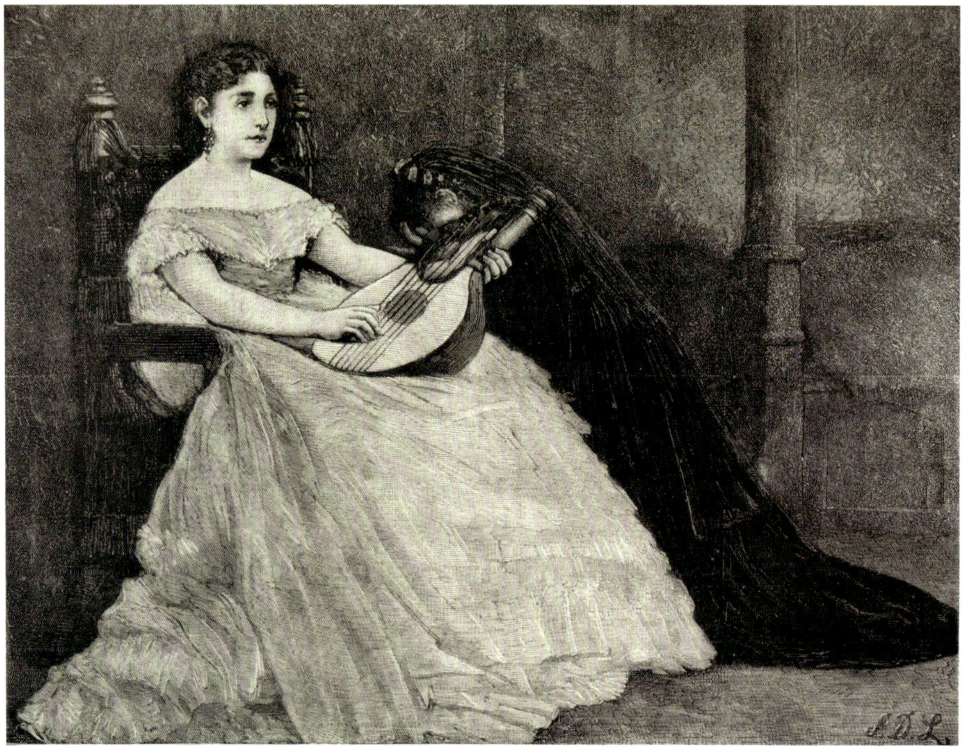

67 The *Morning Post*, 12 May 1871, p. 4, suggested that the 'Canzone del Salice', from the final act of the opera, had been arranged for Patti some years earlier by Rossini himself (he had died in 1868). Her London performance was given with the Royal Italian Opera.

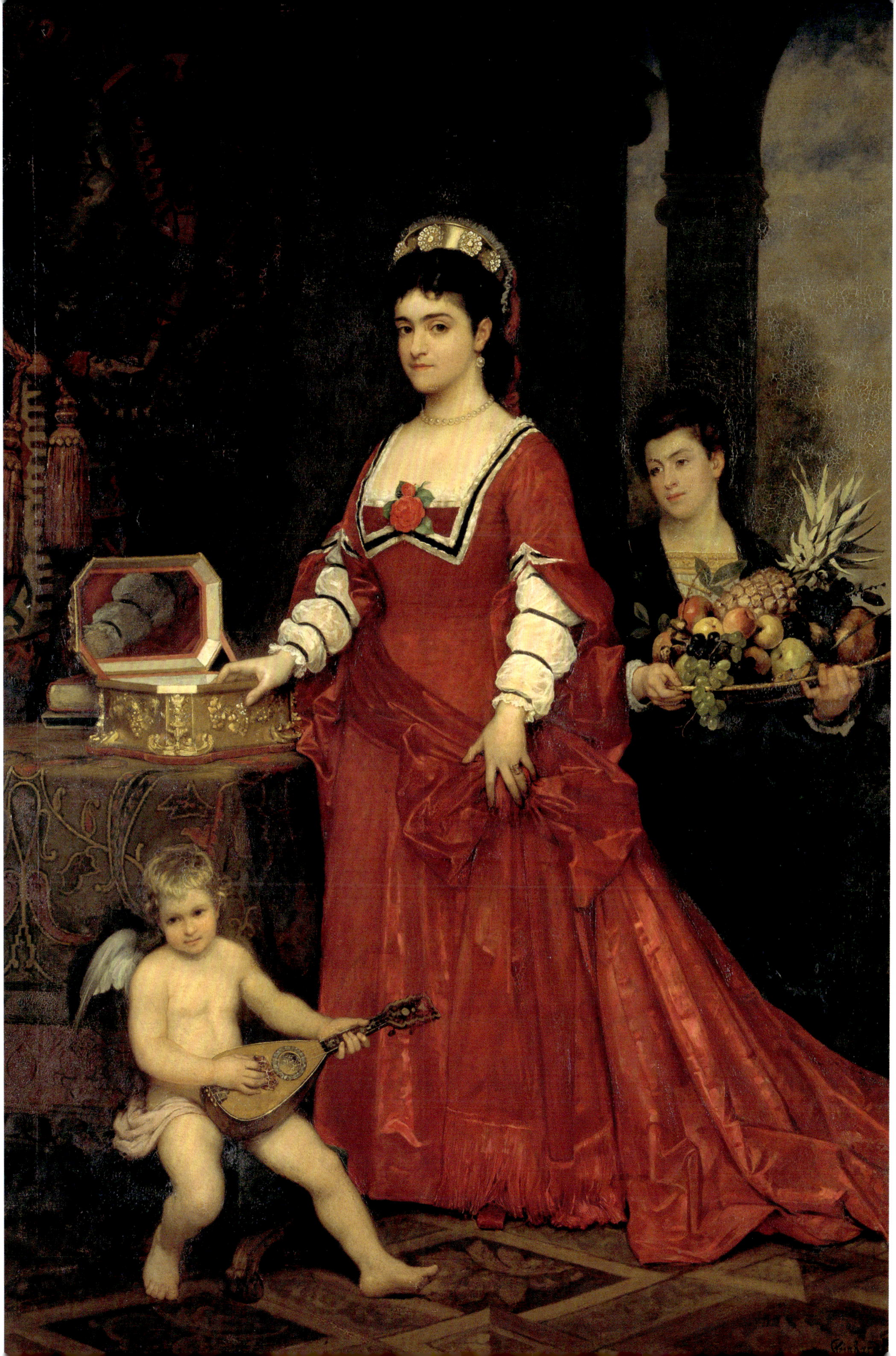

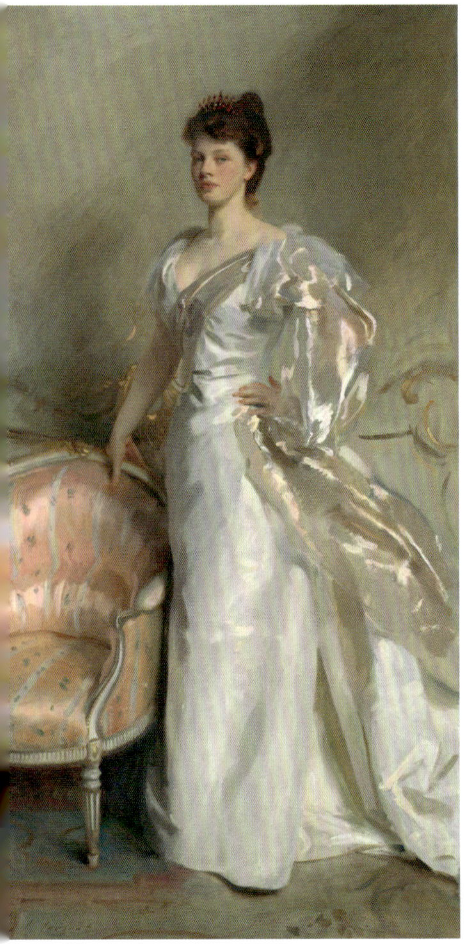

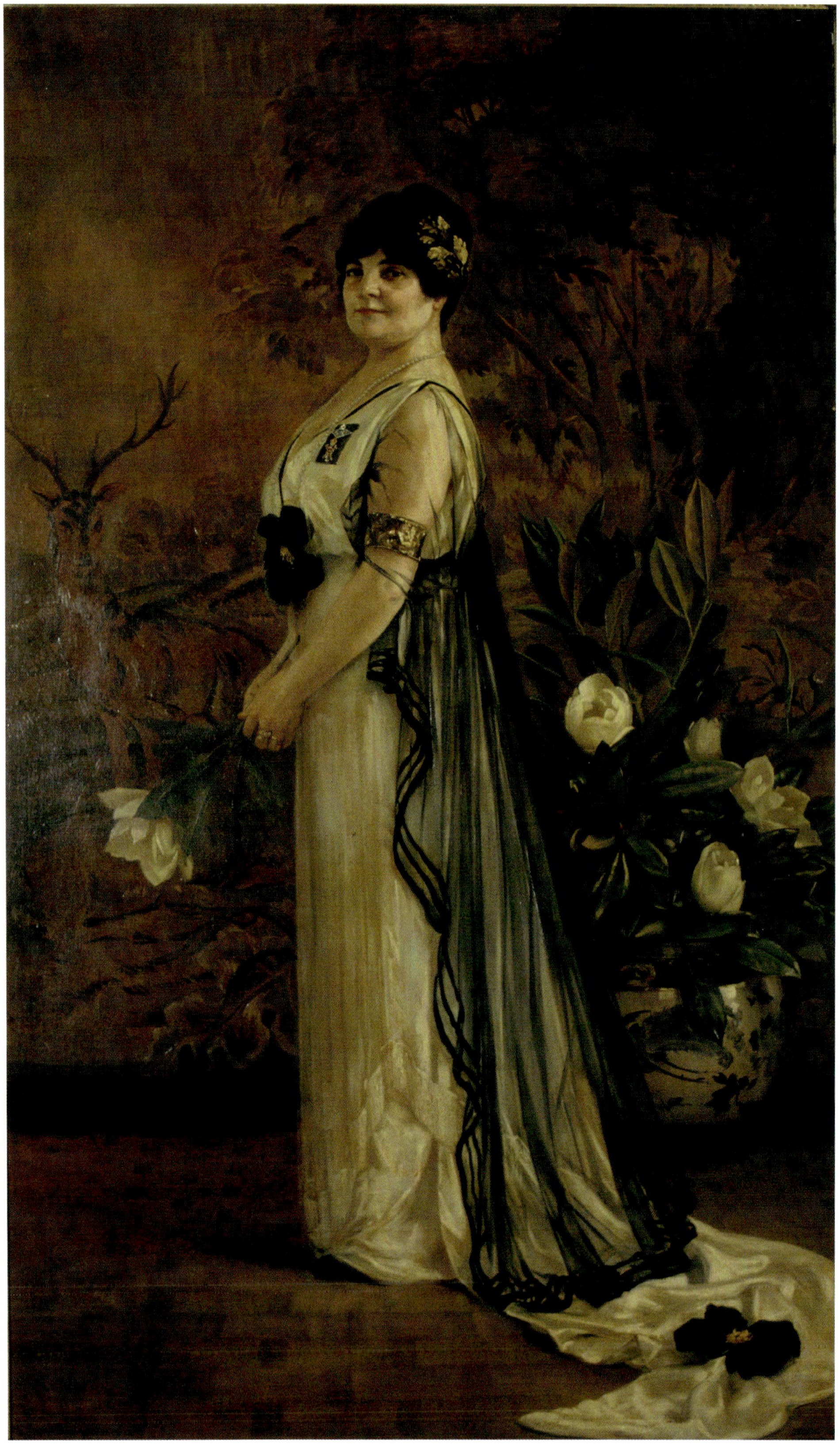

229 John Singer Sargent, *Mrs George Swinton (Elizabeth Ebsworth)*, 1897

230 Margaret Lindsay Williams, *Clara Novello Davies*, 1914 that Elsie demanded of her celebrated guest a masterclass in his setting of Victor Hugo's 'Tristesse d'Olympio'. Fauré, much enamoured of his hostess, requested in payment a photograph of Sargent's portrait.[68]

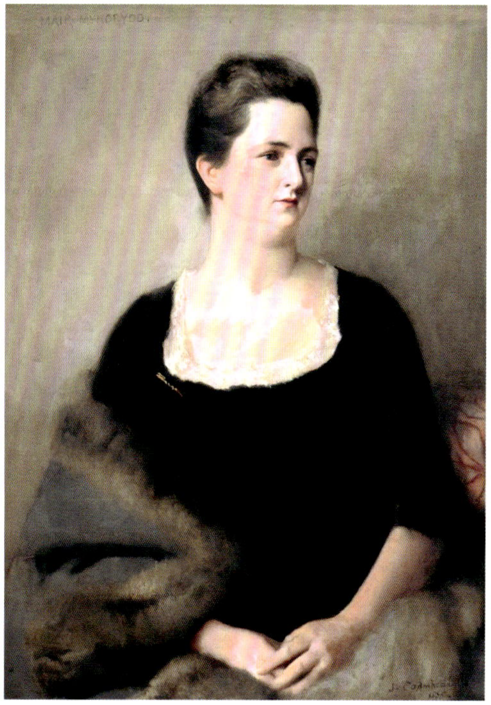

231 James Cadenhead, *Mair Mynorydd (Mary Davies),* 1885

Not far away in Cardiff, although Clara Novello Davies was not celebrated as a soloist, her portrait may also be counted among the diva genre since, as a vocal coach and choral trainer, she was highly influential. In the public mind, Davies became famous for the ladies' choir that she formed in 1883 and which, ten years later, won the prize at the World's Fair in Chicago, confirming in the United States the reputation of Wales as the 'Land of Song'. The painter, Margaret Lindsay Williams, trained at the Royal Academy and was much influenced by Sargent. She became a friend of Clara, and also painted her celebrated son, Ivor Novello.[69]

Amongst the London Welsh who provided so much of the creative energy in national music during the *fin de siècle* period, two sopranos stand out. Both Edith Wynne, Eos Cymru, and Mary Davies, 'Mair Mynorydd', were the subjects of academic portraits, though that of Eos Cymru took the form of a sculpture by Joseph Edwards. It was made in 1873 – the year of the second victory at the Crystal Palace of Côr Mawr Caradog, and a high watermark in the status of Welsh music – and was presented to the singer at an event given by the London Welsh Choral Union in the following year.[70] Contemporaries regarded it as among the sculptor's most distinguished pieces, and he was invited to exhibit it at the Centennial International Exhibition in Philadelphia in 1876. Edwards was born in Merthyr, the eldest of a remarkable clutch of sculptors from the town who migrated to London in the middle of the nineteenth century. William Davies, 'Mynorydd', followed Edwards, and became a pillar of London Welsh society, prominent among

68 Graham Johnson, *Gabriel Fauré, The Songs and their Poets* (London, 2017), p. 48. For an account of the relationship between the composer and the singer, see Hilary Thomas, 'Llandough Castle and Gabriel Fauré', *Morgannwg*, 47 (2003), pp. 47-60. Fauré completed his seventh Nocturne in C sharp minor at Llandough. His work was promoted in London by Sargent (himself a competent musician), who had painted the composer in 1889.

69 Angela Gaffney, *Wedded to her Art: Margaret Lindsay Williams, 1888-1960* (Aberystwyth, 1999), pp. 16-17.

70 The event was chaired by William Cornwallis West of Ruthin Castle, who created two remarkable eisteddfod art exhibitions, at Ruthin in 1868 and at Wrexham in 1876. See Peter Lord, *Y Chwaer-Dduwies: Celf, Crefft, a'r Eisteddfod* (Llandysul, 1992), pp. 41-8.

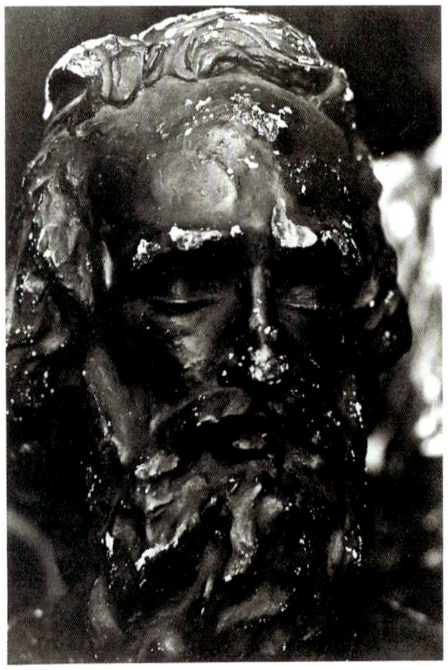

232 William Davies, Mynorydd, *The Bard*, c.1860

those responsible for the establishment of the reformed Eisteddfod series of the 1860s. Mynorydd was himself a musician as well as a sculptor and led the singing at Nassau Street Chapel. At a 'Grand Concert of Welsh National Music' given by Eos Cymru and Pencerdd Gwalia at St James's Hall (and again at the Crystal Palace) to publicise the composer's new edition of the *Welsh Melodies* in 1862, Mynorydd's 'large ideal bust of a bard' was prominently placed,[71] although English reviewers were, at best, condescending, both about the music and the sculpture:

> The orchestra presented a peculiarly striking and David-like appearance, with its 20 harpists and a large bardic bust which occupied the centre. Not remembering the name of any Welsh Carolan,[72] we were somewhat puzzled to make out who this statuesque embellishment was intended to represent. Upon enquiry, however, of competent authorities, we discovered he was nobody – that is, that he was everybody as regards lyric Wales; in other words, an ideal illustration of the bardic power and beauty of the leek-appreciating Principality.[73]

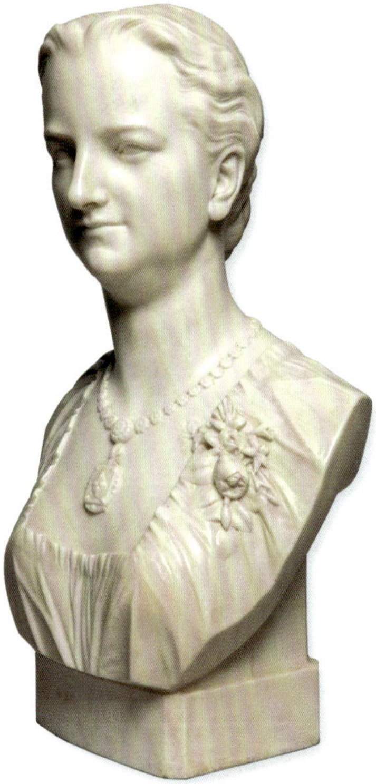

233 William Davies, Mynorydd, *Mrs Mary Davies (Mair Mynorydd)*, 1883

234 Joseph Edwards, *Edith Wynne, Eos Cymru*, 1873

Mary Davies, Mair Mynorydd, was the daughter of the sculptor. Moving from childhood in her father's world of musical and artistic London-Welsh energy, she benefitted early in her career from the encouragement of Pencerdd Gwalia and Brinley Richards – though as a young performer, she interested herself mainly in contemporary repertoire. Indeed, she gave some of the earliest British performances of *La Damnation de Faust* by Hector Berlioz.[74] Both the bust made by her father and her painted portrait by the Scottish artist James Cadenhead were created while she continued to pursue her career in London. However, following her marriage to W. Cadwaladr Davies, Registrar of the University College of North Wales, Bangor, she reoriented her career towards the idea of national music that had so much engaged her father's circle. As a distinguished President of the Welsh Folk-Song Society, she became deeply involved in the study and dissemination of traditional music and recorded it on the wax cylinders of an early Edison phonograph.

71 *Carnarvon and Denbigh Herald*, 23 August 1862.

72 An allusion to the blind Irish harper Toirdhealbhach Ó Cearbhalláin or Turlough Carolan (1670–1738)

73 *North Wales Chronicle and Advertiser*, 12 July 1862, p. 11, reprinted from the *Morning Post*.

74 With Charles Hallé's choir and orchestra, Mair Mynorydd performed the work in Manchester and London in April and May 1880 (*The Illustrated Sporting and Dramatic News*, 29 May 1880, p. 254).

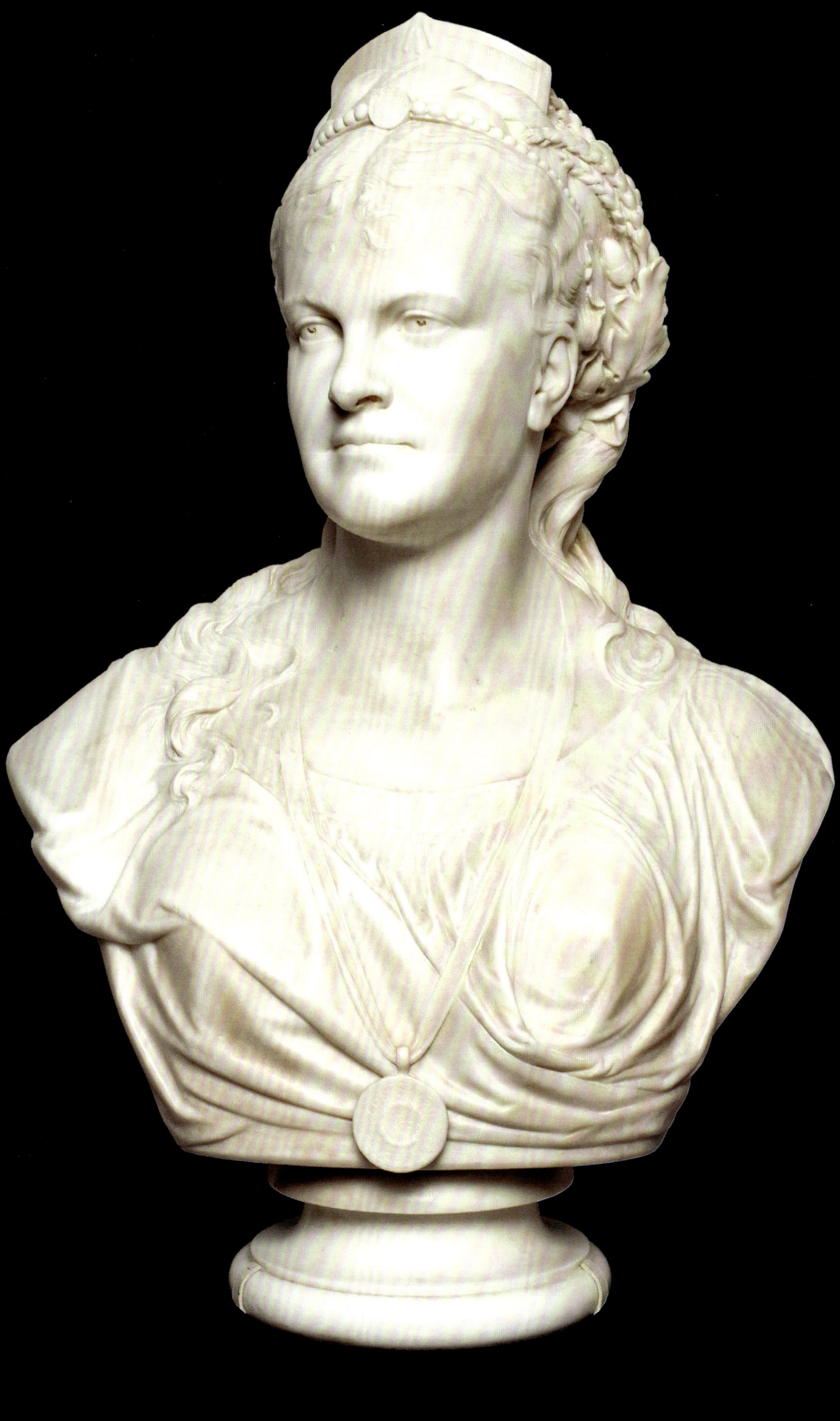

PERPETUATING THE NATIONAL MEMORY

The centrality to the evolution of the national brand of two events in the 1850s – the emergence of Caradog as a choral conductor and the composition of 'Hen Wlad Fy Nhadau' – would be confirmed at the turn of the century by moves to create public memorials. The project to celebrate Caradog began immediately after his death in 1897, with high ambitions on the part of those involved. The committee established to move the memorial project forward received a letter from Judge Gwilym Williams, a native of Aberdare:

> I wish it to be known that I heartily sympathise with the movement, and will do all I can to make it worthy of him. My view is that, whatever form it takes, it should be a thoroughly national one not confined to Glamorganshire or, indeed, to South Wales, but open to all Wales.[75]

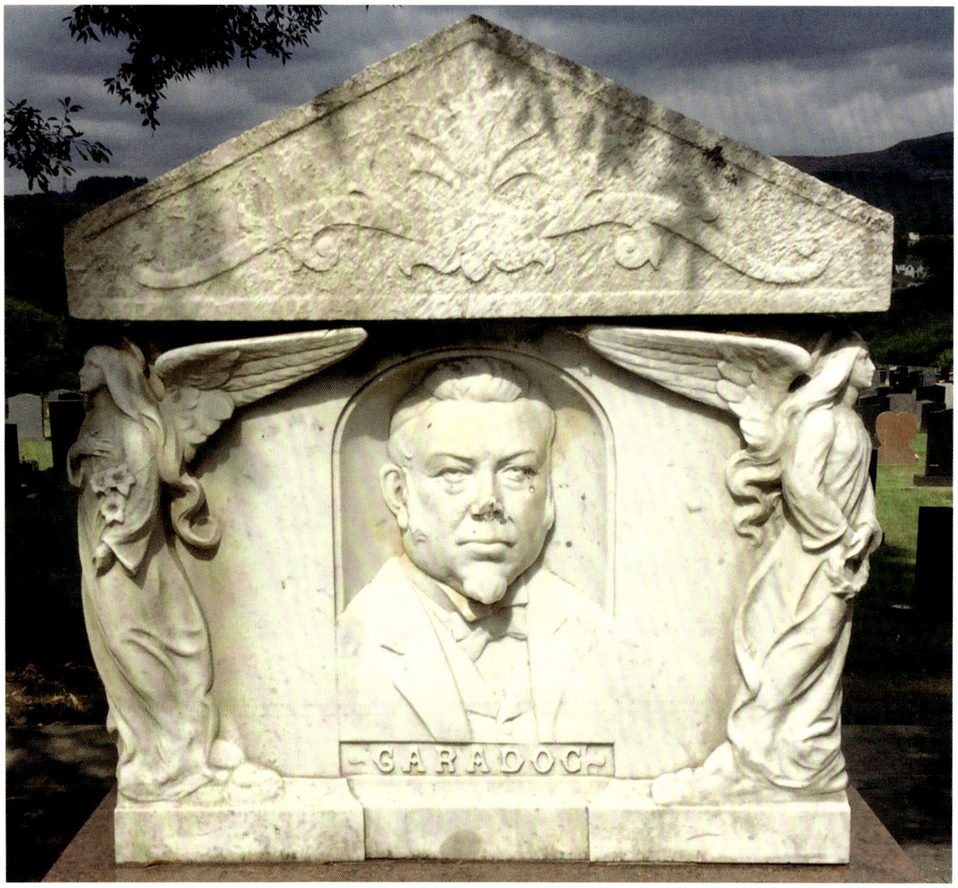

235 Unknown maker, *Tomb of Griffith Rhys Jones, Caradog*, c.1898

75 *Evening Express*, 21 January 1898, p. 4.

76 *The Welsh Coast Pioneer and Review for North Cambria*, 26 October 1906.

77 John Rowlands, Waunarlwydd, *Cardiff Times*, 3 July 1909, p. 5.

The Judge's enthusiasm (and, no doubt, his wealth) resulted in his being appointed chairman, and it was resolved to raise funds for a statue in Aberdare. Unfortunately, the committee also noted 'the want of enthusiasm on the part of those connected with choral singing' for the project, an indifference that meant it did not bear fruit until 1920 – ten years after the Judge himself had been memorialised by the sculptor William Goscombe John in a statue located outside the law courts in Cardiff. No doubt focus was lost also because of fundraising for the extraordinary tomb created for the conductor in the graveyard at Trecynon.

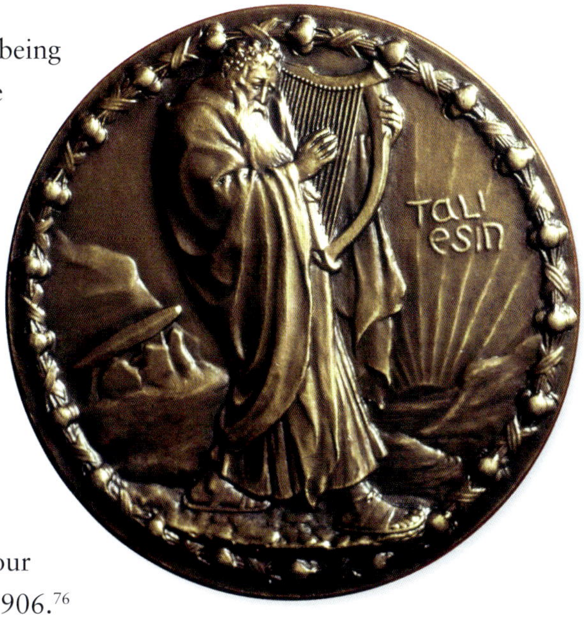

236 William Goscombe John, *The Taliesin Medal of the National Eisteddfod Association*, 1899

The project to memorialise the creators of the national anthem became even more attenuated. A proposal to erect a statue to honour Evan and James James was suggested first in the United States in 1906.[76] A committee was established in 1909, apparently with the involvement of the Cymmrodorion in London, but failed. There appears to have been disagreement as to the form the memorial should take, one correspondent to a newspaper proposing the establishment of a school of music.[77] The idea of raising a statue was revived in 1914, but fell foul of the Great War, and it would not be completed until 1930.

Ultimately, the beneficiary of the movements to memorialise both Caradog and the Jameses was Goscombe John – the last in that line of distinguished nineteenth-century Welsh sculptors that led back through Mynorydd, the Thomas brothers of Brecon and Joseph Edwards, to John Gibson. Goscombe John's training as a sculptor began in the Bute estate workshops in Cardiff, where his father was one of many skilled craftspeople employed to rebuild Cardiff Castle and Castell Coch. He proceeded, via the London studio of Thomas Nicholls (who also worked extensively for the Marquess of Bute), to the Royal Academy. Ten years later, in 1884, his career had developed sufficiently to be celebrated in an article published in O.M. Edwards's *Wales* and, from that point, his engagement with the establishment led to his receiving most of the major public sculpture commissions given in Wales into the 1930s. These included works carried out for the National Eisteddfod and the Gorsedd. He designed the Hirlas Horn in 1898, and in the following year, the medal of the National Eisteddfod Association. Reverting from the radical style that he had deployed in the same year for a memorial to literary figures associated with

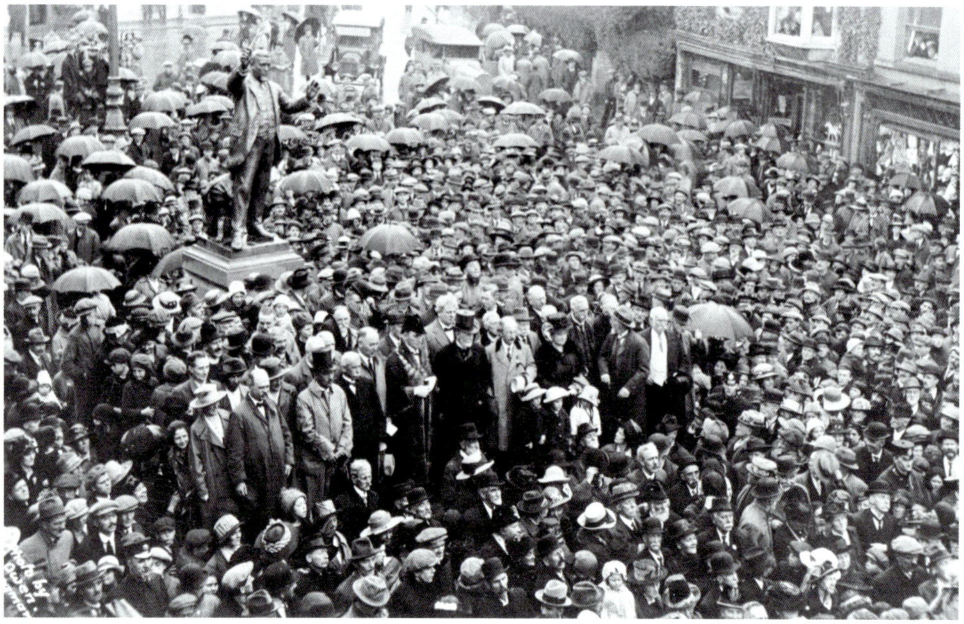

237 Unknown photographer, *Unveiling of the Caradog Statue*, 1920

238 Garth Jones, *The National Eisteddfod of Wales*, 1909

Llansannan, Goscombe John revived generic druid imagery for the medal, except that he identified the figure specifically as the poet Taliesin. The rays of the sun illuminate the name of the poet, who plays his harp with a cromlech in the background. The generic bard seems to have retained his currency among the London Welsh intelligentsia, since he was deployed again, a decade later, in one of the most memorable of his innumerable incarnations as the logo for the National Eisteddfod, held in the metropolis in 1909. The designer was Garth Jones, who went on to make a successful career in the United States.

Goscombe John's statue of Caradog followed the convention that he had adopted in his earlier portrayal of T.E. Ellis at Bala, depicting the subject in vigorous action rather than in meditative mood. Caradog stands with his arms raised, holding a baton aloft. Behind him is placed a violin, a reminder that the conductor was also an instrumentalist. However, the iconography deployed by the sculptor in his memorial to the Jameses, ten years later, was less straightforward. In 1914, when the sculpture commissions had been awarded for the Pantheon of National Heroes at the City Hall in Cardiff, Goscombe John was given the central figure of St David, rather than one of the two figures with musical associations, William Williams, Pantycelyn, and Dafydd ap Gwilym. Following the generic pattern though applying it to an historic individual (as John had done with the Taliesin medal), the sculptor William Wheatley Wagstaff placed a harp in the hands of his Dafydd ap Gwilym.[78] But when the opportunity arose for John himself to celebrate the musical tradition in the James memorial

78 In one of many series of cards published by Wills & Co. to encourage the sale of its cigarettes, a photograph of Leonard Merrifield's energetic statue of William Williams, Pantycelyn, was curiously identified as 'Welsh Singer'. Presumably the identification arose from a misunderstanding of the Welsh verb *canu*, to sing, but also used to describe the production of verses by poets.

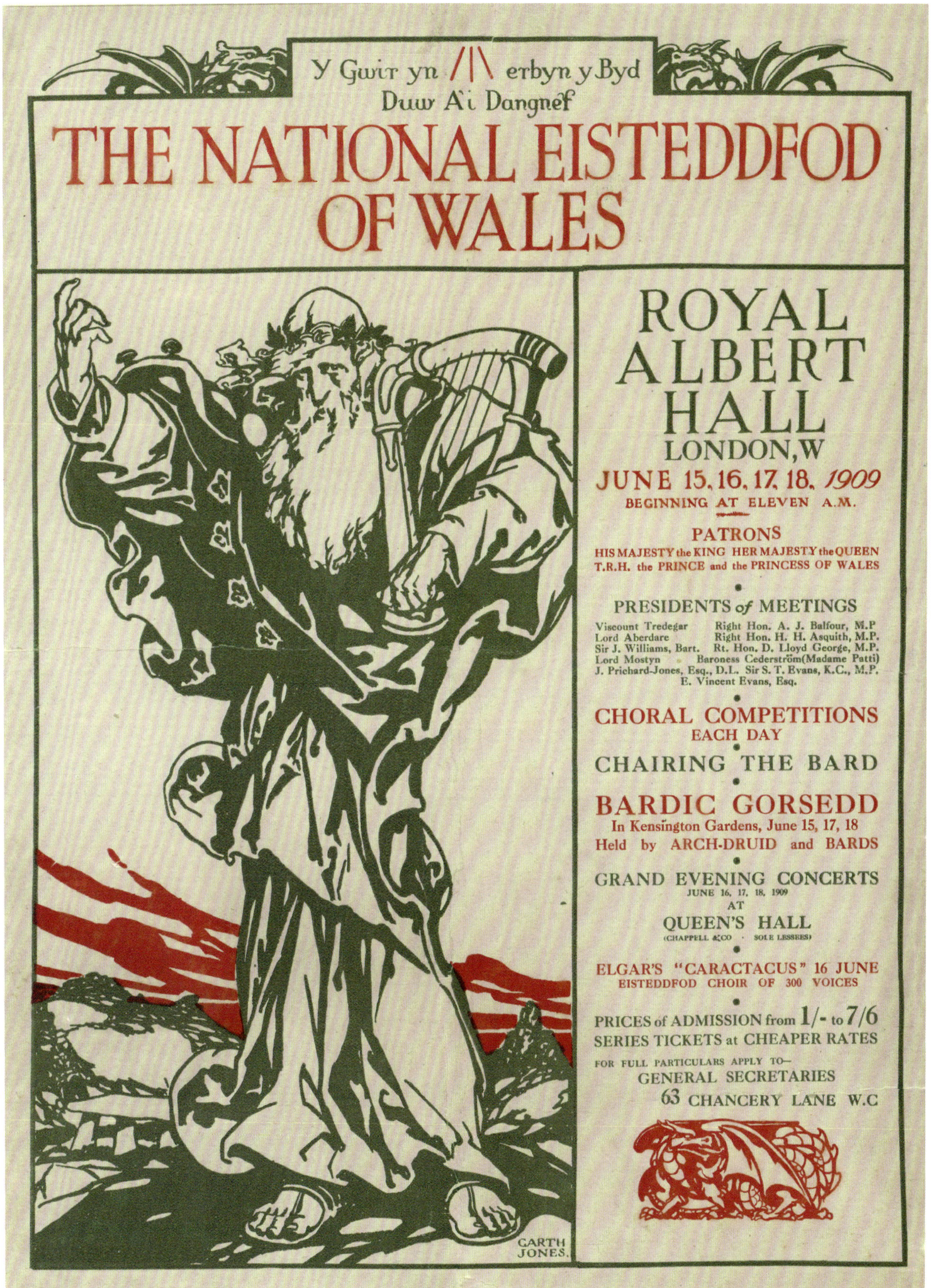
Y Gwir yn /|\ erbyn y Byd
Duw A'i Dangnef
THE NATIONAL EISTEDDFOD OF WALES
ROYAL ALBERT HALL
LONDON, W
JUNE 15, 16, 17, 18, 1909
BEGINNING AT ELEVEN A.M.
PATRONS
HIS MAJESTY the KING HER MAJESTY the QUEEN
T.R.H. the PRINCE and the PRINCESS OF WALES
PRESIDENTS of MEETINGS
Viscount Tredegar
Right Hon. A. J. Balfour, M.P
Lord Aberdare
Right Hon. H. H. Asquith, M.P.
Sir J. Williams, Bart.
Rt. Hon. D. Lloyd George, M.P.
Lord Mostyn
Baroness Cederström (Madame Patti)
J. Prichard-Jones, Esq., D.L.
Sir S. T. Evans, K.C., M.P.
E. Vincent Evans, Esq.
CHORAL COMPETITIONS EACH DAY
CHAIRING THE BARD
BARDIC GORSEDD
In Kensington Gardens, June 15, 17, 18
Held by ARCH-DRUID and BARDS
GRAND EVENING CONCERTS
JUNE 16, 17, 18, 1909
AT
QUEEN'S HALL
(CHAPPELL & CO · SOLE LESSEES)
ELGAR'S "CARACTACUS" 16 JUNE
EISTEDDFOD CHOIR OF 300 VOICES
PRICES of ADMISSION from 1/- to 7/6
SERIES TICKETS at CHEAPER RATES
FOR FULL PARTICULARS APPLY TO—
GENERAL SECRETARIES
63 CHANCERY LANE W.C
GARTH JONES.

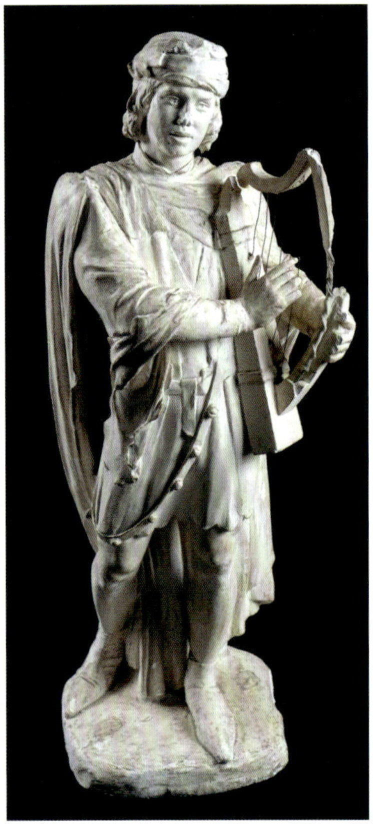

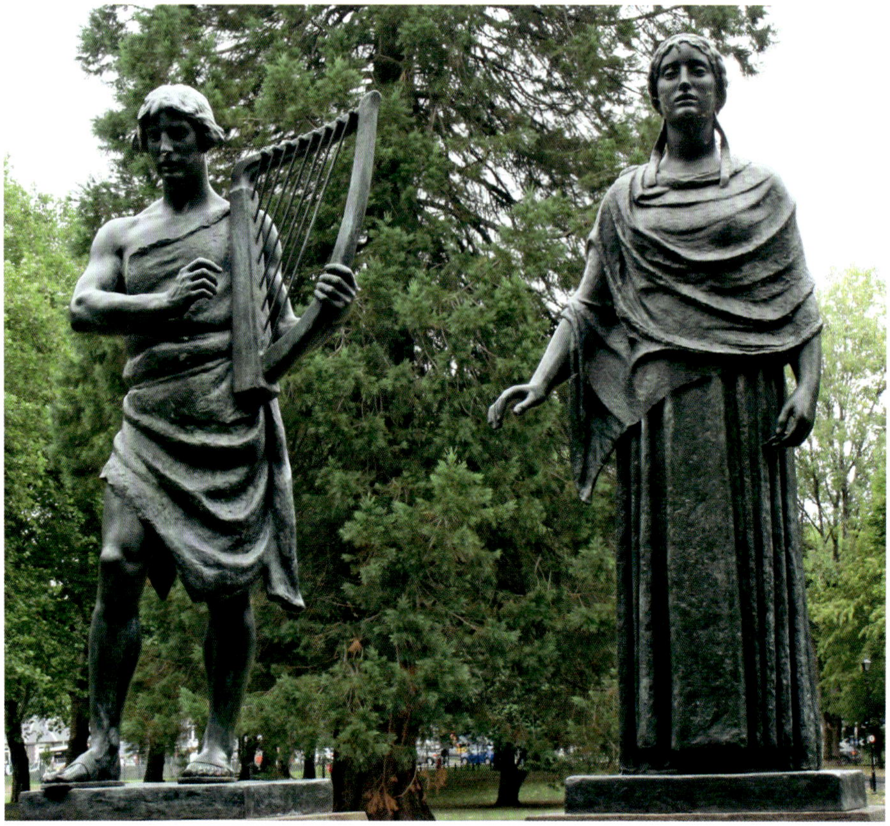

239 William Wheatley Wagstaff, *Maquette for the Statue of Dafydd ap Gwilym*, 1914–16

240 William Goscombe John, *Memorial to Evan and James James*, 1929

at Pontypridd, he chose to do so with an exceptional twist of iconography. Reflecting quite closely the form of Wagstaff's Dafydd ap Gwilym statue – the statue of a poet – John conceived a youthful male figure with a harp, and identified him as a celebration of music, rather than of poetry:

> I have shown a small model of my proposed work to the committee. The figures are of a man playing a harp, to be symbolical of music, and of a woman, who will signify poetry. The figures will be of bronze, about six feet high, fixed in blue Pennant rock, and in its finished state the whole memorial will stand about ten feet high. On the back of the statue will be engraved, in facsimile, the words and music from the original manuscript of the authors, and a medallion of each of them to perpetuate the features of these notable men.[79]

In the Welsh context, given the archaism of the loosely clad harper, suggesting a period in which poetry was largely confined within the male bardic tradition, it seems counterintuitive (unless John intended the woman as a muse and the man as an Orpheus figure) that John chose a female embodiment of poetry. This is unlikely, given that in 1931, at the Royal Academy exhibition, the sculptor exhibited the maquette for the male figure under the more specific title of *Folk Song*. Furthermore, the posture of the woman resonates strongly with the many contemporary portraits of divas, with which he would have been familiar, suggesting that it was she who ought to represent music:

> A word must be said about the heroic figure by Sir W. Goscombe John which occupies a commanding position in the lecture-room. The title is 'Folk Song' and it is described as the model of a bronze statue for the memorial to the authors of the Welsh National Anthem at Pontypridd. An alternative title might be 'The First of our Lyricists'. It is the figure of a full-blooded youth, instinct with vigour and energy, pouring out his soul in music as though by some irresistible impulse. In one hand he clasps a bardic harp, while the other is lifted in the act of playing. Despite the heroic proportions of the figure, it is so well posed that one feels no sense of undue weight.[80]

That the reviewer was unconvinced about the figure as an embodiment of folk music was an understandable point of view during a period in which, from its foundation in 1906, the Welsh Folk-Song Society – whose work was familiar to Goscombe John – had been recording material alive in the memories of older members of working-class communities across the country such as Benjamin Davies of Drefach Felindre. A scantily dressed mythic bard, clutching a medieval harp, was a strange choice to embody the music of the *gwerin*, especially given the modernist precedent that the sculptor had set in his Llansannan memorial, thirty years earlier. At that time, writing to T. E. Ellis, Goscombe John felt that 'any academic or conventional representations would have been out of place', and hoped he would understand his intention to make his work 'an embodiment of the present-day thinking.'[81]

What is clear is that the initial inspiration for Goscombe John's memorial had been the opening phrase of the second line of Evan James's words to the anthem, celebrating the nation as 'Gwlad beirdd a chantorion' – 'The land of bards and singers'. Since the beginning of the twentieth century, at least at home, the notion of Wales as the 'Land of Song' – whether embodied by the demure female harper or the male voice choir – had gone largely unchallenged and, alongside Welsh costume and the mountain landscape, had become a central visual manifestation of the national brand abroad.

79 *Western Mail & South Wales News*, 1 July 1929, p. 11.

80 Ibid., 2 May 1931, p. 9. At the Royal Academy in 1941, Goscombe John exhibited a 'Sketch model for a memorial erected at Pontypridd' under the title *Music*, presumably the same piece, though the catalogue entry does not clarify which of the two figures was shown. Since 1909, and perhaps earlier, Goscombe John had been a member of the Welsh Folk-Song Society, and from 1909 he was a member of its General Council.

81 NLW T.E. Ellis Papers 987. For the memorial and the evolution of John's public sculpture, see Lord, *Imaging the Nation*, pp. 348–52, 358–60.

241 Ruth Herbert Lewis and Annie Jane Ellis, *Benjamin Davies of Cefnllechclawdd, Drefach Felindre,* 1913

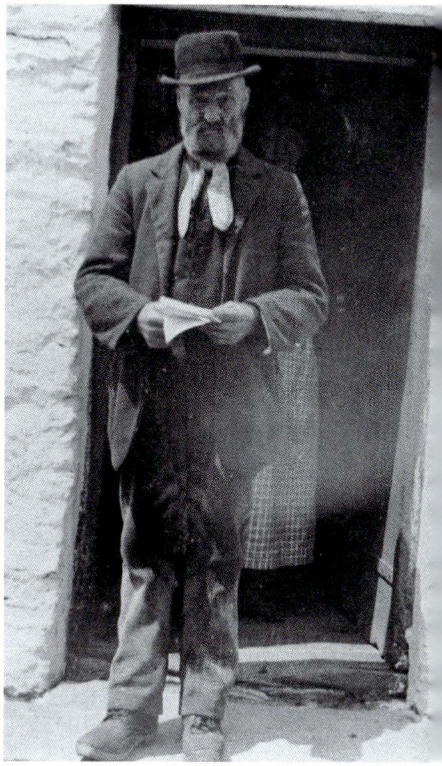

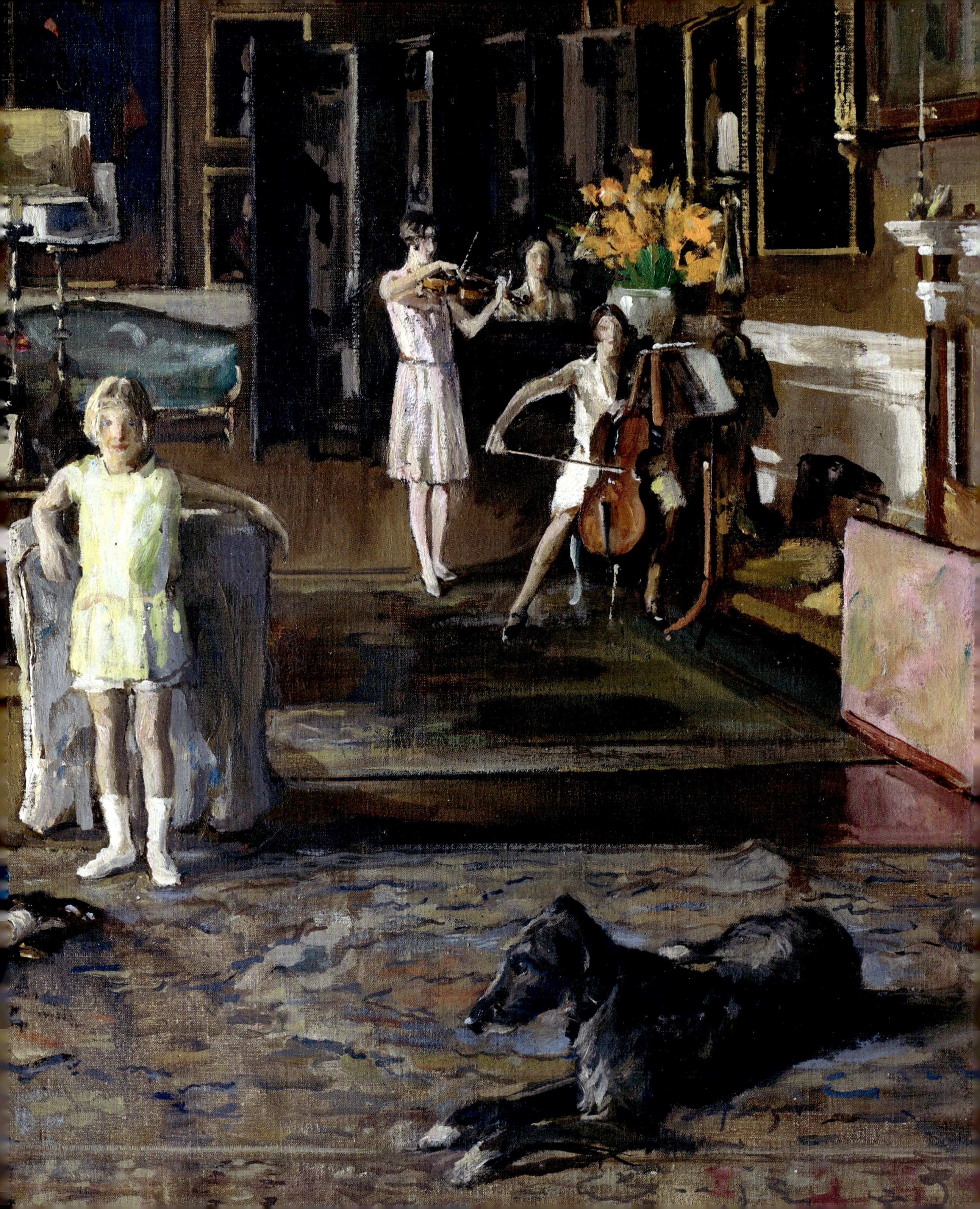

CHAPTER FIVE

CODA

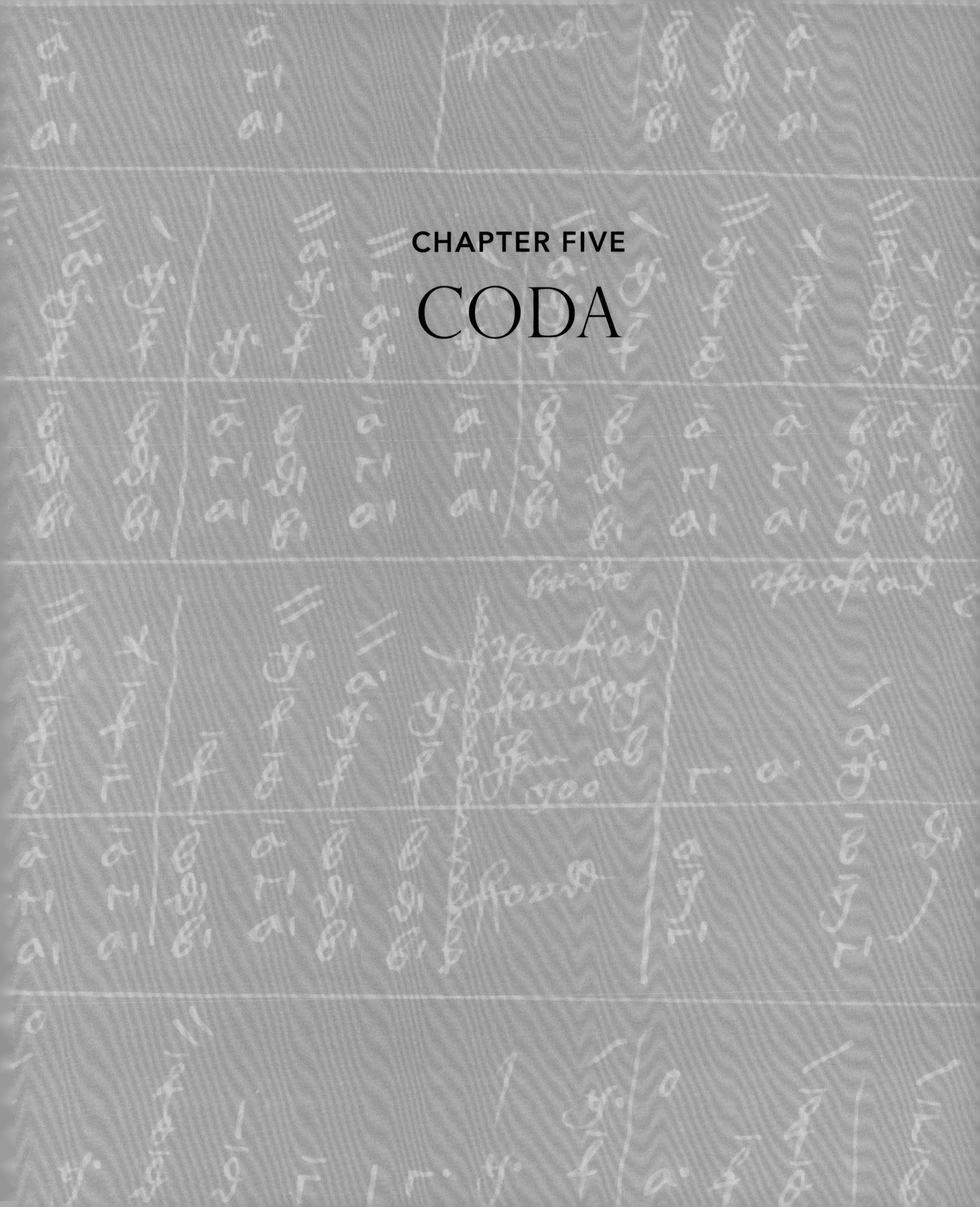

'KEEP THE HOME FIRES BURNING'

By 1914, the branding of Wales as the 'Land of Song', was firmly established, both at home and abroad. The visualisation of that brand turned from promotion to exploitation, with much of the imagery emerging in kitsch, postcards, posters and other popular art forms, and in the new media of sound recording and film. High art engagement with the brand receded among intellectuals in the interests of the waning agenda of national worthiness within Britain. The two public memorials carried out in the interwar years by William Goscombe John, celebrating Caradog and the James family, were essentially hangovers from the pre-war cultural revival that had been rooted in a pervasive sense of national inadequacy and marginalisation.

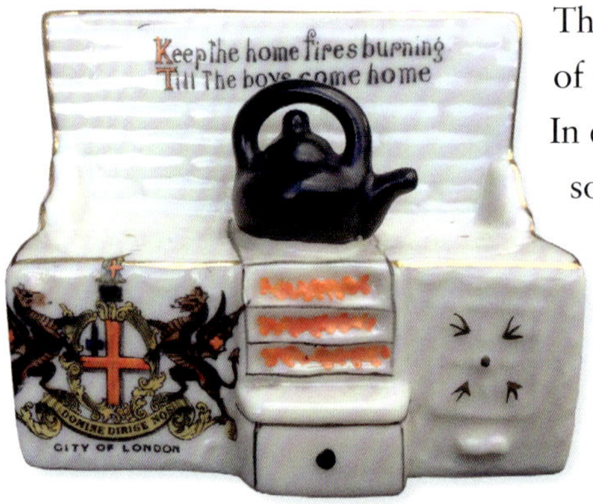

242 Carlton of Stoke-on-Trent, *Till the Boys Come Home*, *c.*1917

The promotion of the most frequently imaged of all the male Welsh musicians of the interwar years, Ivor Novello, rarely made reference to his nationality. In earlier and psychologically more needy periods, it might well have done so regularly, since his family credentials were impeccable. He was the great-great-grandson of the Revd William Evans, a Methodist minister who had become celebrated for the theatricality of his preaching. Novello's mother, Clara, remembered well the effect his sermons had upon her as a child.[1] In the years leading up to the Great War, her own celebrity as a teacher and conductor of the Royal Welsh Ladies' Choir remained high, and the development of her son's public profile had been initiated in the classic manner, on the Eisteddfod stage. At the age of about ten, he had won a national prize, awarded by Pencerdd Gwalia. The performance resulted in a poetic effusion written by one Idris and published in a newspaper:

Be yours the gift to pass along
  When voices of to-day are dumb,
That Wales may be a land of song,
  Down the years to come.[2]

During his childhood in Cardiff, Novello had come to know many leading musicians, including Adelina Patti and Clara Butt, and after moving with his mother to London just prior to the war, he became thoroughly embedded in the metropolitan world of popular music and theatre. As in the conflicts with

France, a hundred years earlier, the war brought with it – initially at least – a barrage of patriotic sentiment in pictures and music that promoted insular unity and British identity, to which Novello's song, 'Till the Boys Come Home', written in 1914, was among the most potent and long-lasting contributions, and its genesis became the stuff of legend. Challenged by his mother to write a war song, Novello at first refused, but when Clara responded with her own attempt,

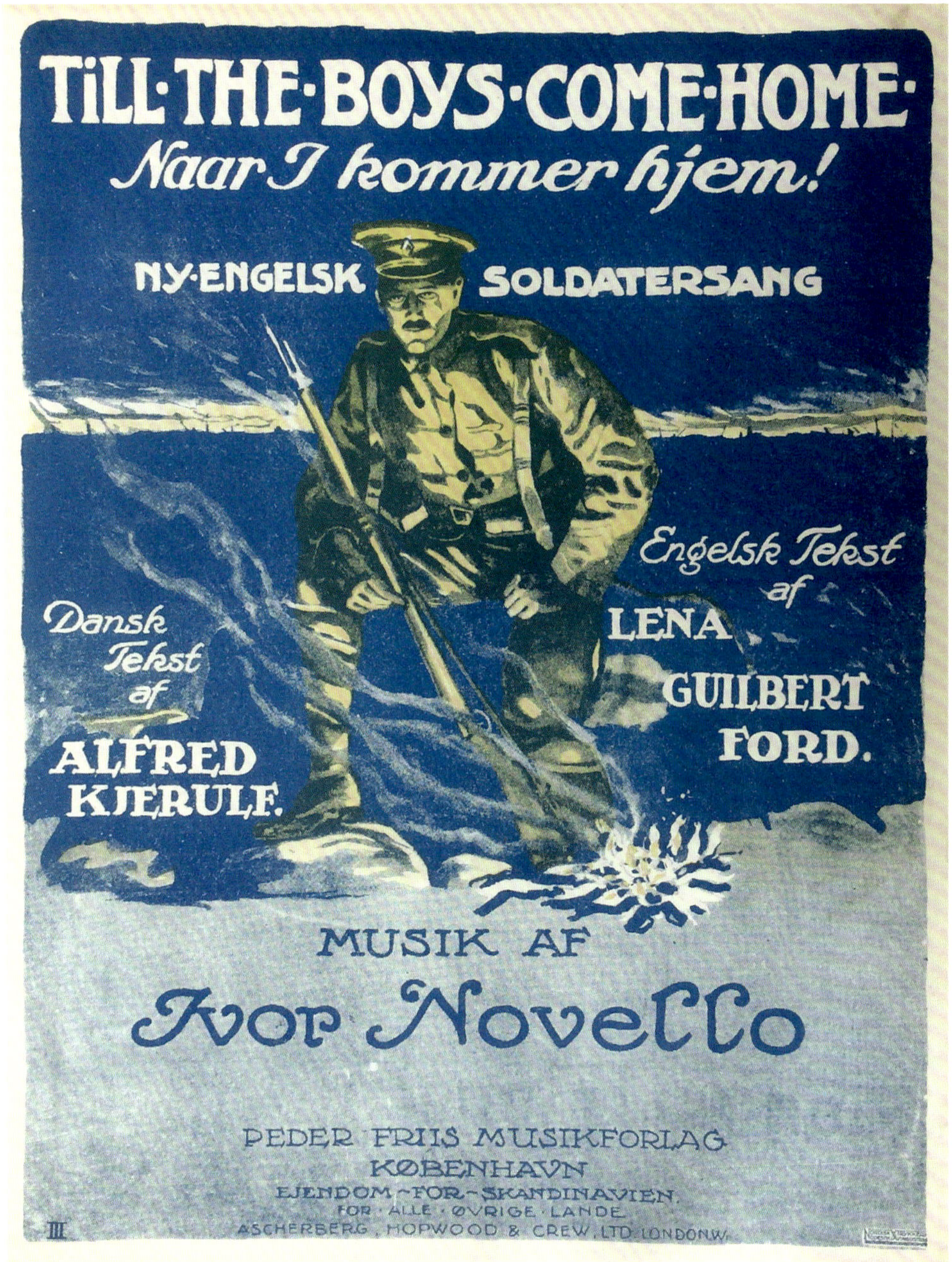

243 Unknown artist, cover for Ivor Novello, *Till the Boys Come Home*, 1914

1 Clara Novello Davies, *The Life I Have Loved* (London, 1940), pp. 2-3.

2 The story is recounted and the poem given in full in Peter Noble, *Ivor Novello* (London, 1951), p. 28. Noble knew Novello well, and had access to his cuttings book, in which this was apparently the first notice. However, Noble's account is certainly inaccurate in detail, since it states that the performance took place at the National Eisteddfod at Aberystwyth in 1903. The National Eisteddfod was held at Llanelli in that year. Presumably Noble was recalling Novello's own faulty memory of the location of the event. The published source of the poem has not been traced.

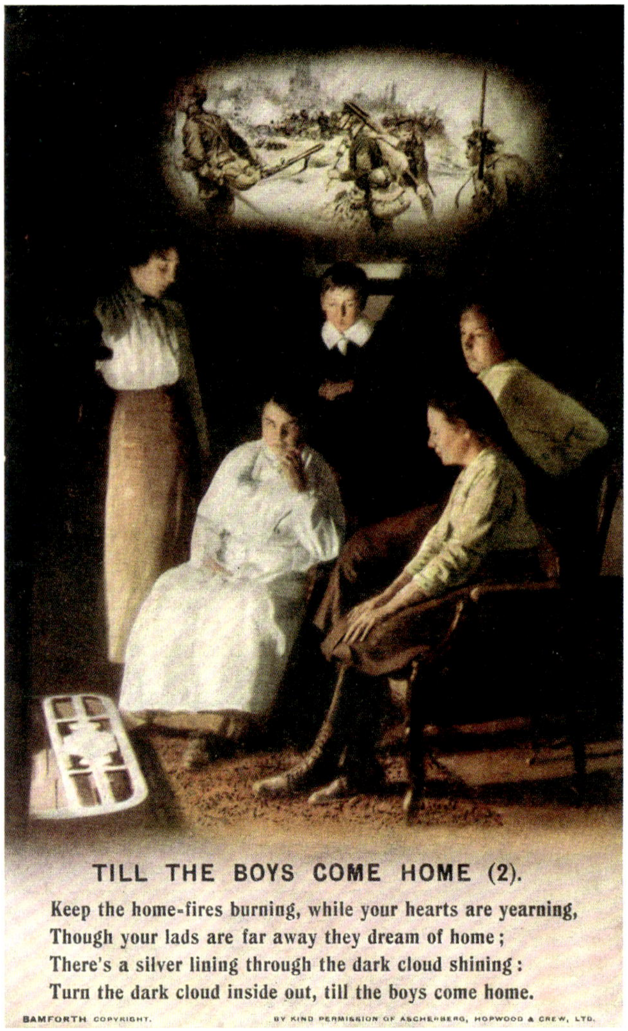

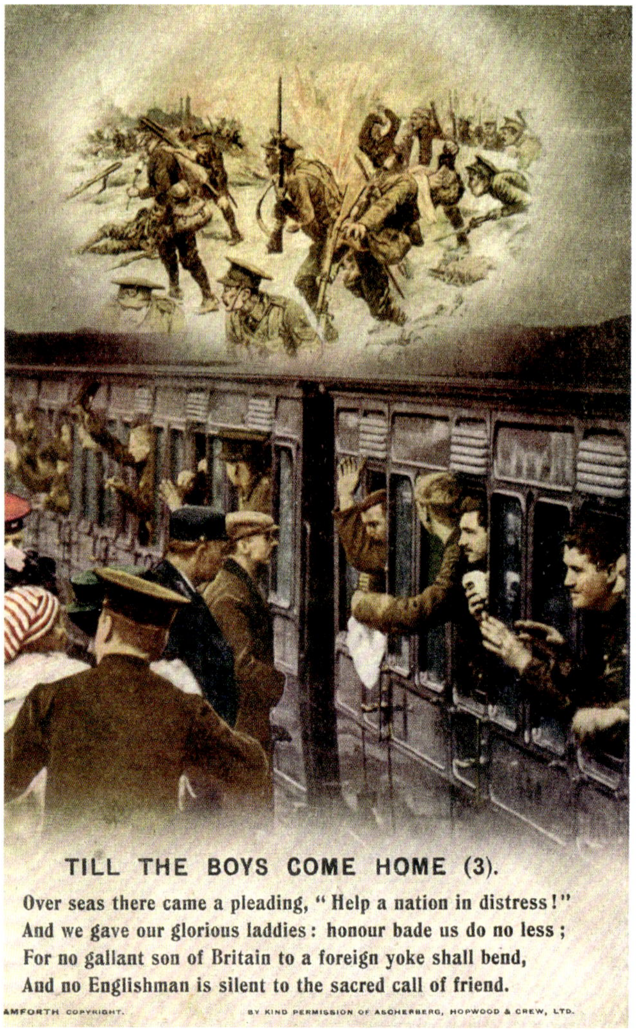

244 Unknown artist, *Till the Boys Come Home*, c.1914–18

which both agreed fell rather short of the mark, the young man rapidly came up with an alternative. The words would be attributed formally to Clara's friend, the American poet, Lena Guilbert Ford, but it seems that Ivor wrote most of them, and certainly the key phrase, 'Keep the Home Fires Burning', which soon became accepted as the unofficial title. First performed in public by Sibyl Vane,[3] one of Clara Novello Davies's protégées, it made the composer both famous and prosperous. By 1916, the sheet music had sold a million copies and the lyrics were available in at least six languages.[4] Novello sang it to the troops himself on a tour through France, while in the United States, visited several times during the conflict by Clara, it was influential in eroding isolationism and paving the way for American intervention in Europe.

The central metaphor of the song proved directly transferable into visual imagery presented on sheet music covers and in other popular art forms. In a remarkable series of composite photographs, coloured and distributed widely as postcards, the ghostly imaginings of women, children and the elderly seated around fireplaces at home were imaged in surreal fashion. Manifestations of the song in ceramic, in the tradition of figurines and fairings, focused on the kitchen range and the boiling kettle, ready to make a cup of tea for the returning soldier. First produced during the war, they would prove to have a long shelf life in the tourist market, sold as mementos of towns all over the British Isles.

More conventionally, in a wartime reversion to British inclusivity that reflected the manifestations of four-nation solidarity visualised during the French wars, a printed handkerchief featured the song surrounded by the flags of the Empire,

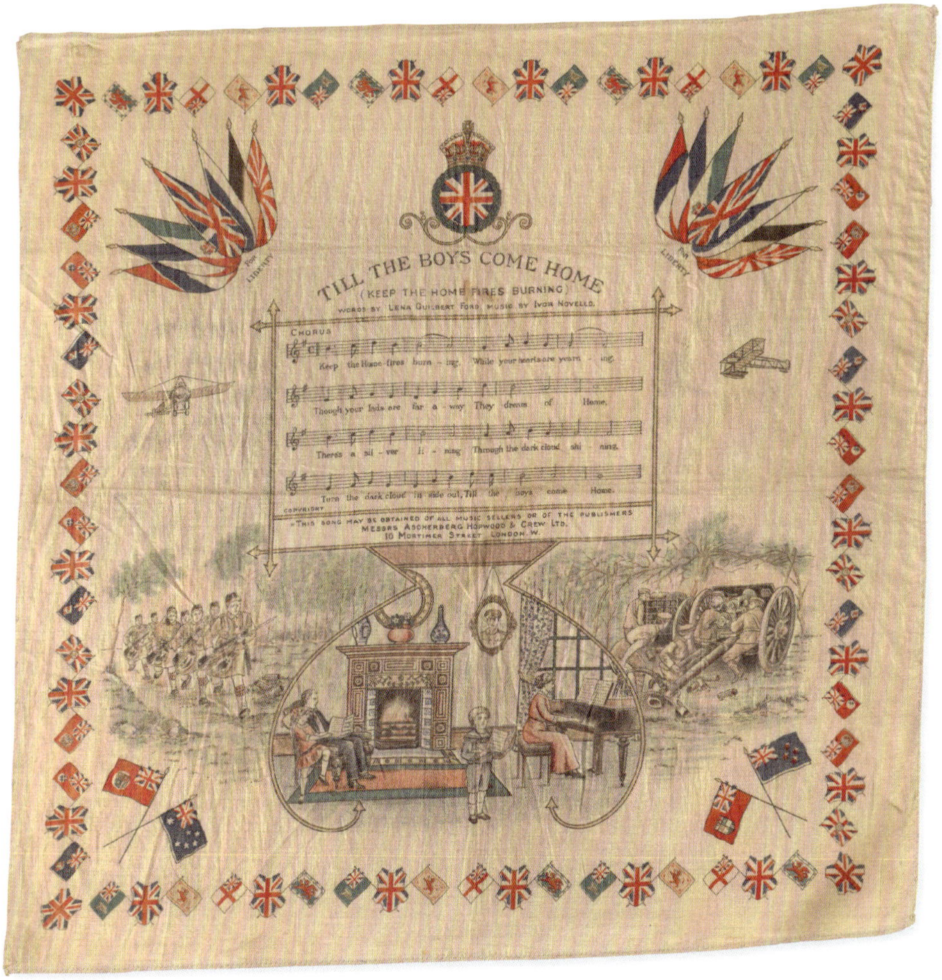

245 Unknown artist, *Till the Boys Come Home*, *c.*1914–15

3 The Cardiff soprano Elizabeth Jenkins (1887–1959) studied with Clara Novello Davies and made her professional début as Gretel at Covent Garden in 1913, borrowing her stage name Sibyl Vane from Oscar Wilde's character in *The Picture of Dorian Grey* at Ivor Novello's suggestion. Her versatile career included appearances in musical comedy and vaudeville as well as opera in Europe, America, Canada and Australia.

4 The song was advertised heavily by its publishers in the newspapers from February 1915. It was recorded later in the year by the tenor Herbert Payne for Zonophone Records, who promoted it as 'the most popular ever issued' (*Daily Mail*, 9 December 1915, p. 6).

including the Welsh dragon, and with Highland troops marching. A contemporary textile illustrating 'It's a Long Way to Tipperary' – another song popular with soldiers during the war (though it was written earlier and in a different context) – strikingly manifested the infantilisation of the Welsh stereotype. A child in national costume clings to the back of Mother England's reassuringly homely throne, while Scotland and Ireland stand independently proud.

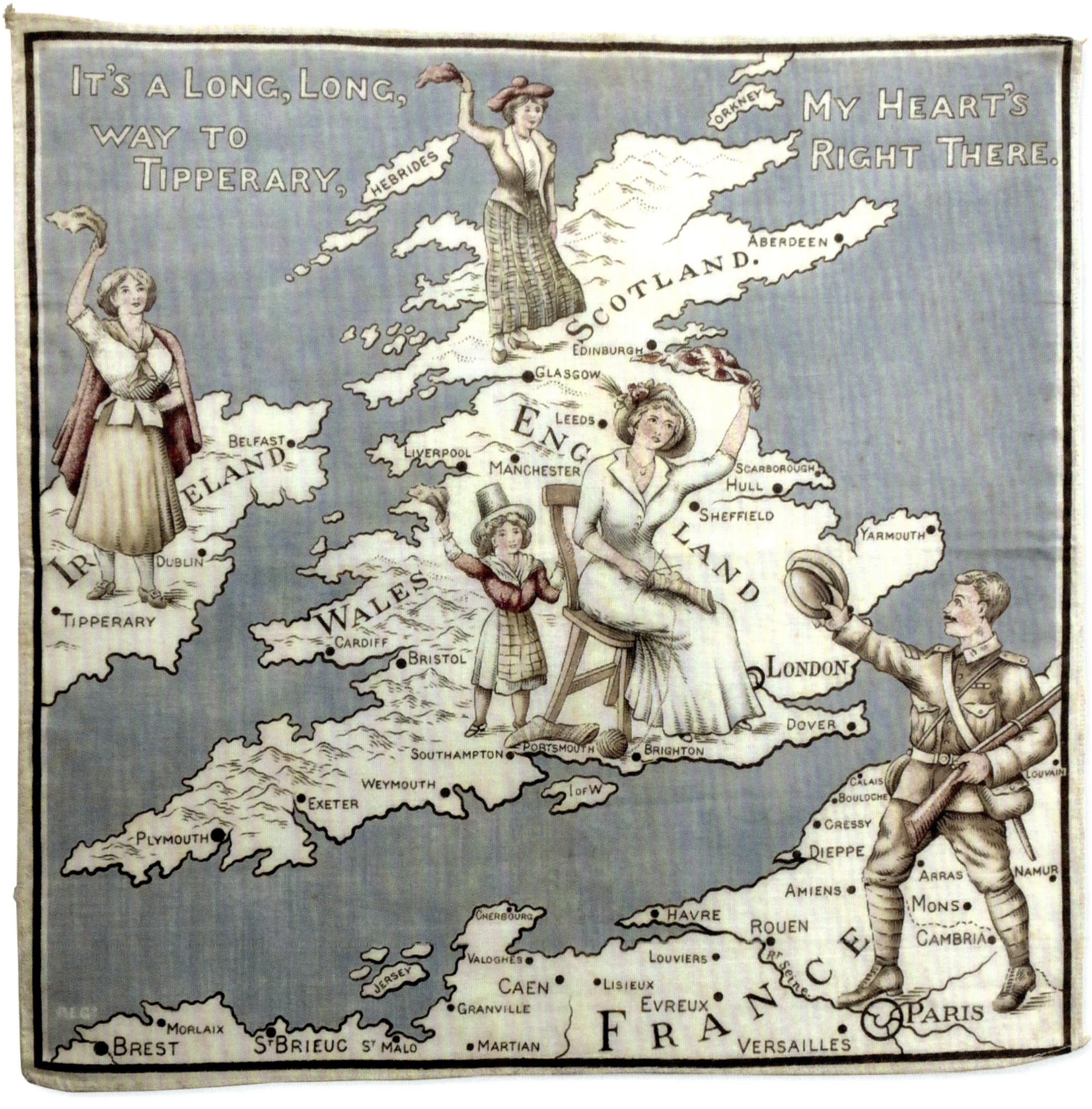

246 Unknown artist, *It's a Long Way to Tipperary*, c.1914–18

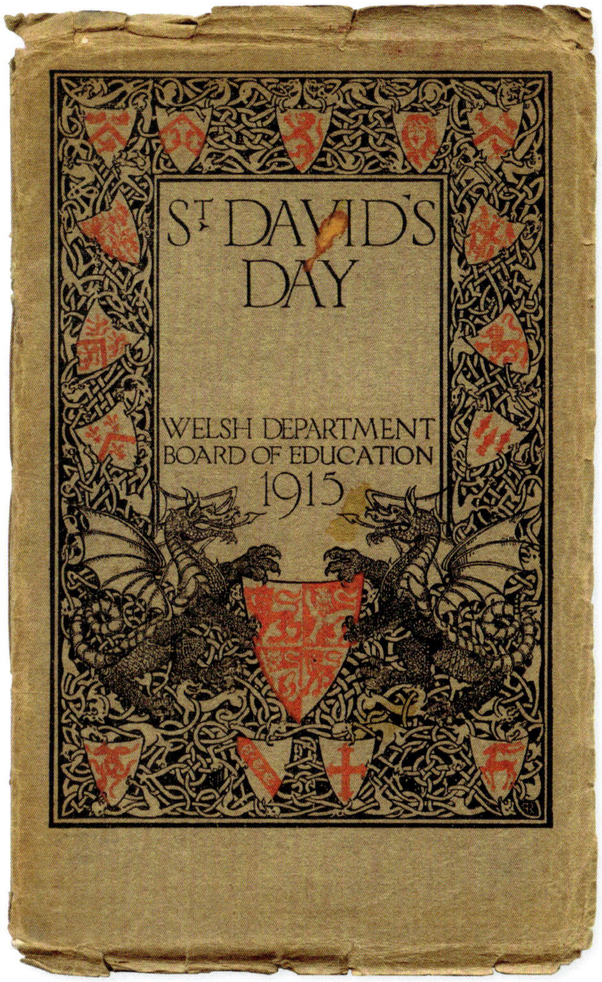

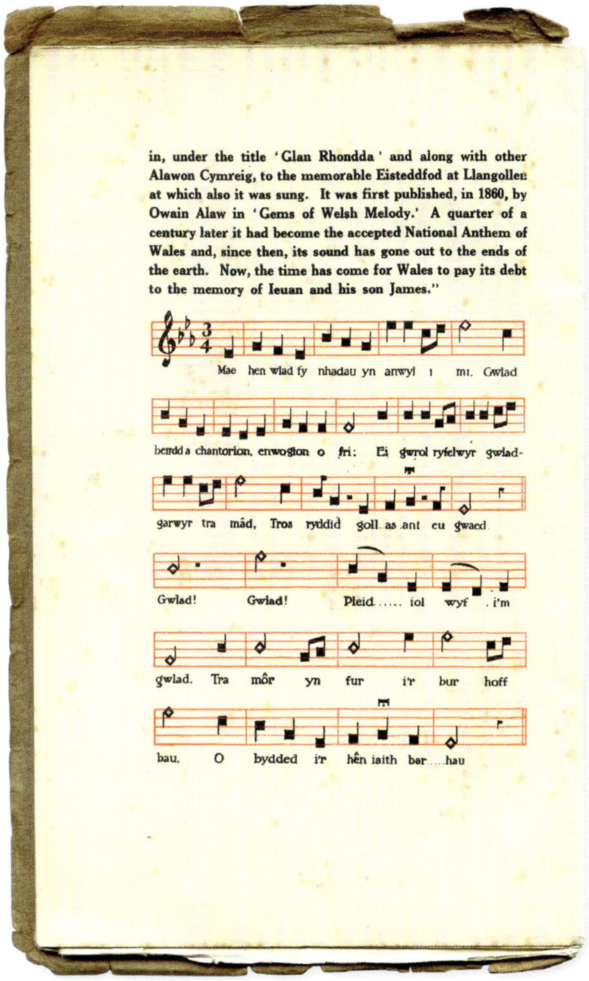
in, under the title 'Glan Rhondda' and along with other Alawon Cymreig, to the memorable Eisteddfod at Llangollen at which also it was sung. It was first published, in 1860, by Owain Alaw in 'Gems of Welsh Melody.' A quarter of a century later it had become the accepted National Anthem of Wales and, since then, its sound has gone out to the ends of the earth. Now, the time has come for Wales to pay its debt to the memory of Ieuan and his son James."

247 Fred Richards, cover for and illustration from *St David's Day*, 1915

For the Welsh audience in particular, the English words of 'Hen Wlad Fy Nhadau' ('Her fighters so fearless, her heroes so bold,/For freedom have fought from of old') and especially 'God Bless the Prince of Wales' ('Above the throne of England/ May fortune's star long shine') proved perfectly adaptable to the new cause. The anthem – 'the accepted psalm of Welsh nationalism' – appeared in two compilation books of 1915, *The Land of My Fathers* and *St David's Day*, both published to direct patriotic sentiment in support of the war. They were produced in English- and Welsh-language versions, and were notable for their visual content. *The Land of My Fathers* illustrated in colour the work of contemporary Welsh painters including Margaret Lindsay Williams and Edgar Thomas, and *St David's Day* was elaborately illuminated by the artist Fred Richards. Although he grew up in relatively humble circumstances in Newport, with the aid of scholarships Richards had been able to train at the Royal College of Art in London.[5] His Celticist designs were juxtaposed with faux medieval notation for the melody of 'Glan Rhondda' in

5 The work of Fred Richards was celebrated during the war with a substantial illustrated essay: Edgar Jones, 'A Welsh artist: The work of Mr Fred Richards, A.R.E.', *The Welsh Outlook*, 4 (1917), pp. 310–13.

248 Einar Nerman, *Ivor Novello*, illustration from *Darlings of the Gods*, 1929

St David's Day, accompanied by the familiar story of how the anthem came to be written. Mair Mynorydd acted as musical adviser for both volumes, and they were widely distributed. Indeed, the text of *St David's Day* pointed out that it was being printed in an edition of forty thousand. It was intended for children, and stressed military tradition in the music of the nation:

> What of the battle music of the Welsh?
>
> The 'March of the Men of Harlech' is considered to be one of the finest War Marches, if not actually the greatest piece of war music, in the world. To the stirring strains of that great march, or of others like it – such as 'Captain Morgan's March' and 'March of the Men of Glamorgan' – Welshmen have marched to do battle and to victory in olden times and in our own day.[6]

Notwithstanding the huge contemporary success of Ivor Novello's song, it was too early for the young composer to have made an impression on the highbrow tastes of the compilers of *The Land of My Fathers* and *St David's Day*, steeped in the historicism of the *fin de siècle* national revival that their generation had inspired. In the post-war era, Novello's career as a songwriter and screen actor would eclipse them all in the public mind, though paradoxically, in the 1920s and '30s, he became the focus of a glamorous metropolitan elite, living in a world insulated from the realities of a period scarred by extreme social and economic polarities. Novello supplied, one after another, songs, films and stage productions in which fantasy never-never lands offered an hour or two of escape from the worst of those realities for those who could afford to attend. Clearly conscious of this essentially trivial context, a decade after the composition of his most famous work, Novello reflected in an interview that 'Till the Boys Come Home' was 'the best thing that has happened in my life … It had to do with big issues, and I am proud that I had this connection with them.'[7]

Novello's stellar career was followed in the London columns of the Welsh press, though by comparison with the celebration of earlier musicians who had achieved success in the metropolis, there was hesitancy in claiming him in the promotion of a national agenda. It may be that his field of popular theatre inhibited leaders of intellectual life at home, still heavily influenced by Nonconformist Christian ethics, and he was known to be homosexual.

6 Various authors, *St David's Day* (London, 1915), no pagination. The booklet was printed by the Welsh Outlook Press in Cardiff on paper made in Wales. Among many familiar poems by Ceiriog and others, *The Land of My Fathers* republished Felicia Hemans's 'The Harp of Wales' (1824).

7 *Picture Show*, given in theconversation.com/the-story-behind-world-war-is-greatest-anthem-100-years-on-31601.

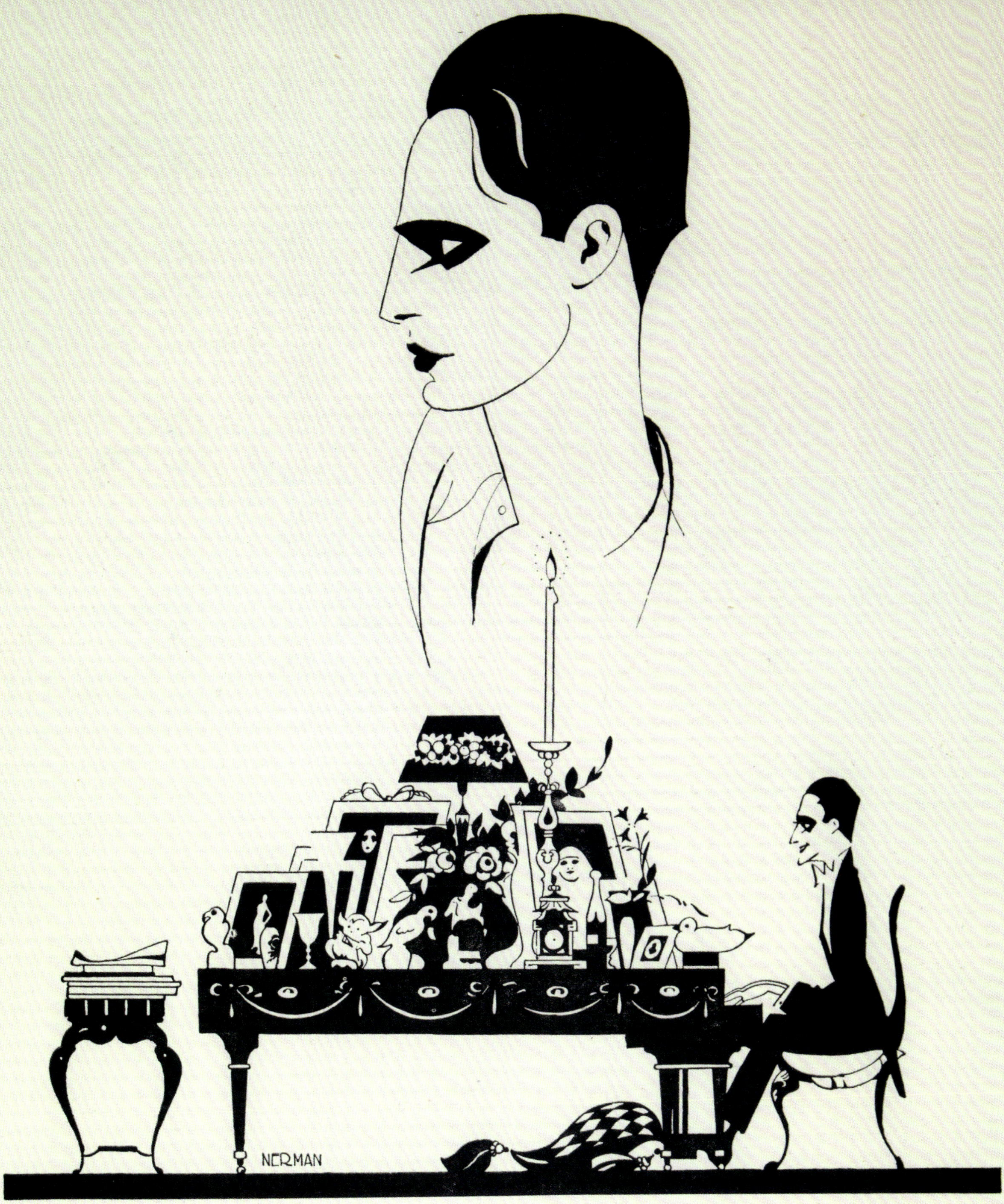
NERMAN

Certainly, Novello himself seems to have felt no need to trade on his nationality and become a stage Welshman. Like so many celebrated London performers before him, he was caricatured – notably by the Swedish artist Einar Nerman of *Tatler* – but without recourse to the familiar leeks, goats and harps of earlier years. Novello featured prominently in Nerman's mural painted to decorate the fashionable Fifty-fifty Club, opened in 1924 by the musician himself.

FANTASY LANDS

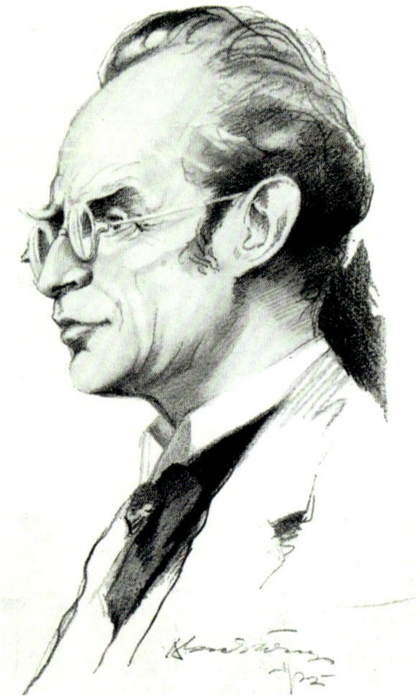

249 Alan Stern, *Josef Holbrooke*, 1922

Also producing work located in a parallel universe, remote from the increasingly harsh economic realities faced by the common people after the war, was a group of academically-trained English musicians and visual artists who established strong Welsh associations in both their private lives and in their compositions and images. However, their fantasy lands were rather different from those occupied by Novello. Emerging before the Great War, they inherited the Celtic Romanticism underlying the cultural revival of the late nineteenth century and attempted to carry its themes forward into the post-war era. Linking their association was the patronage of one of the wealthiest men in England, T.E. Scott-Ellis, 8th Baron Howard de Walden, who, in 1911, leased the medieval fortress of Chirk Castle.[8] Although he retained his London house, de Walden soon came to regard the castle as his home. He spent considerable periods of time there, bringing many prominent London-based musicians and artists to Wales, as Sir Watkin Williams Wynn had done at Wynnstay in the eighteenth century. De Walden's infatuation with Welsh mythology had first emerged in practical terms some years before he established himself at Chirk when he met the composer Josef Holbrooke. De Walden had conceived the idea of writing a drama, *The Cauldron of Annwn*, inspired by the stories of the Mabinogion and other early Welsh texts, familiar to him initially in English-language translation. However, after attending a London performance of Holbrooke's *Apollo and the Seaman*, he engaged the composer to collaborate in transforming his original conception into a three-part operatic cycle with the painter Sidney Sime as designer.

By 1910, the first part of the cycle, *Dylan, Son of the Wave*, had been published with a cover by Sime, though it was the second part, *The Children of Don*, that reached the stage first, performed at the London Opera House in 1912 and

8 See Peter Lord, 'Medieval fantasies and modern artists: Howard de Walden and visual culture at Chirk and Harlech', in *Looking Out: Welsh Painting, Social Class and International Context* (Cardigan, 2020), pp. 140–98.

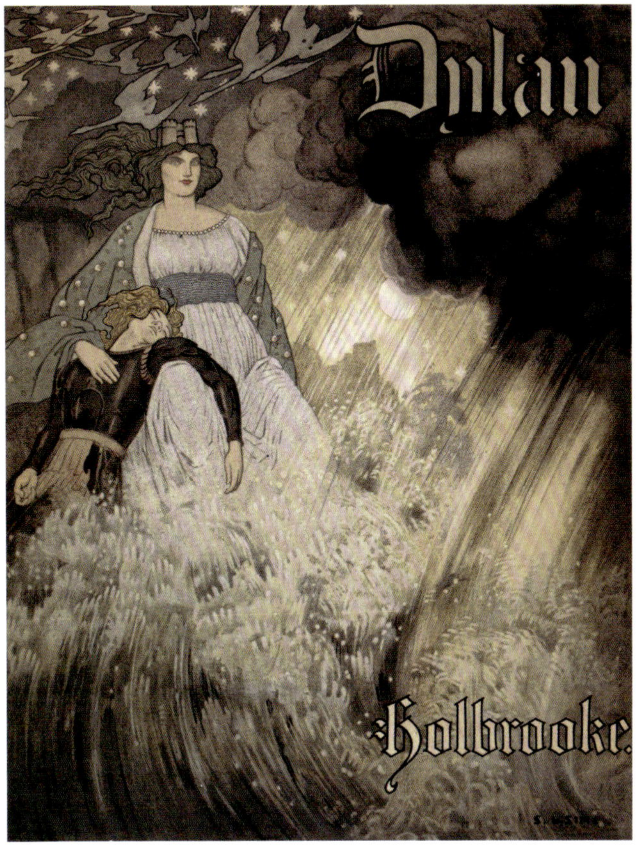

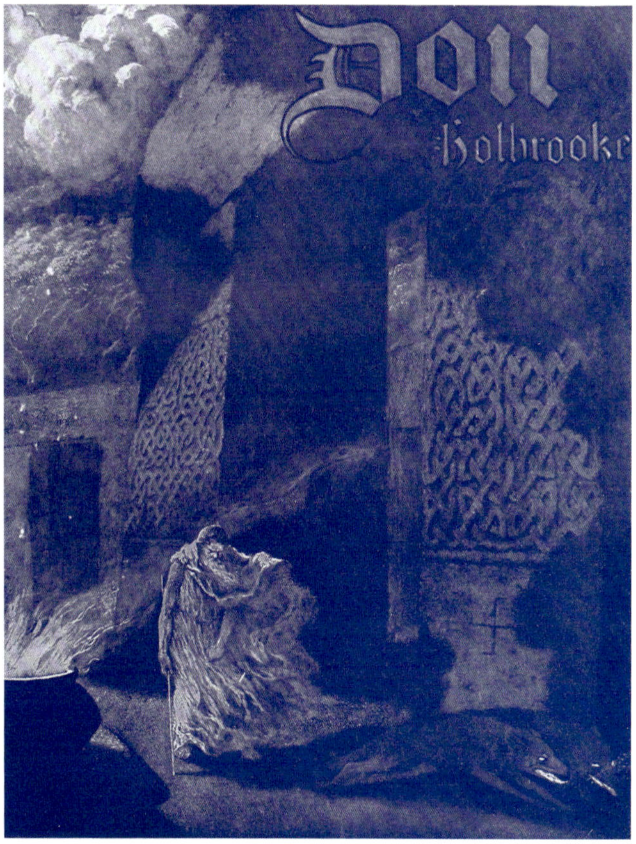

250 Sidney Sime, cover for Josef Holbrooke, *Dylan*, 1910

251 Sidney Sime, *Lord Howard de Walden's Opera 'The Children of Don'*, 1912

252 Unknown artist, *Lord Howard de Walden's Opera Produced in London*, 1912

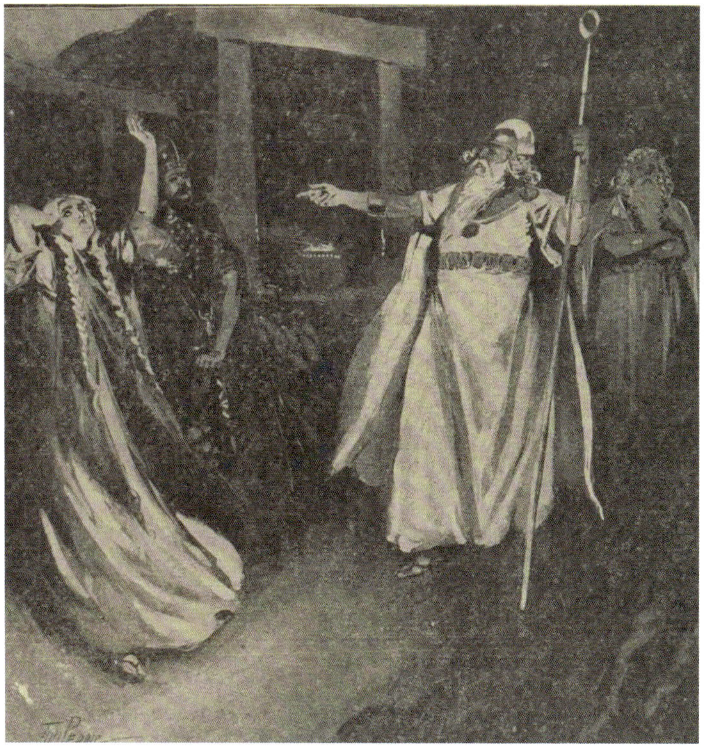

produced by Oscar Hammerstein I. De Walden and Holbrooke attempted to première *Dylan* in Wales, at the Abergavenny National Eisteddfod of 1913, but the project was defeated by cost. It was produced in London a year later, shortly before the outbreak of the war, and again with sets and graphics by Sime. De Walden influenced other aspects of Holbrooke's output, including his first Piano Concerto entitled *The Song of Gwyn ap Nudd*, and the encouragement of Holbrooke's work by Granville Bantock further reinforced his Celticist inclinations. Bantock, whose father was Scottish, was Professor of Music at

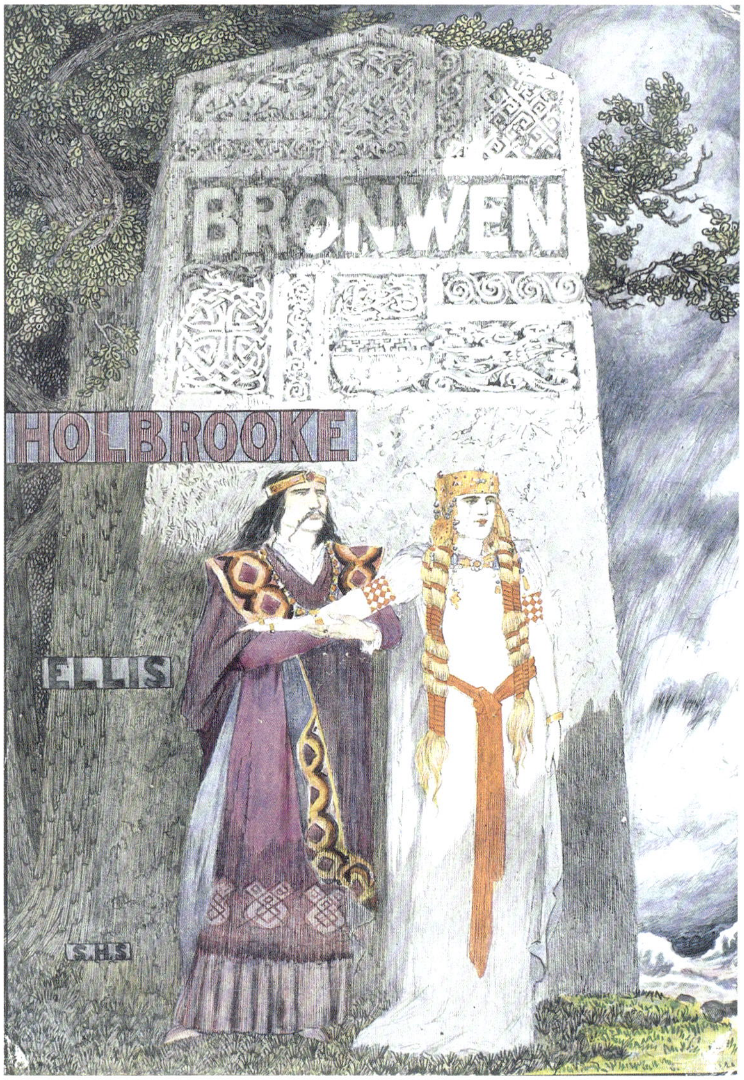

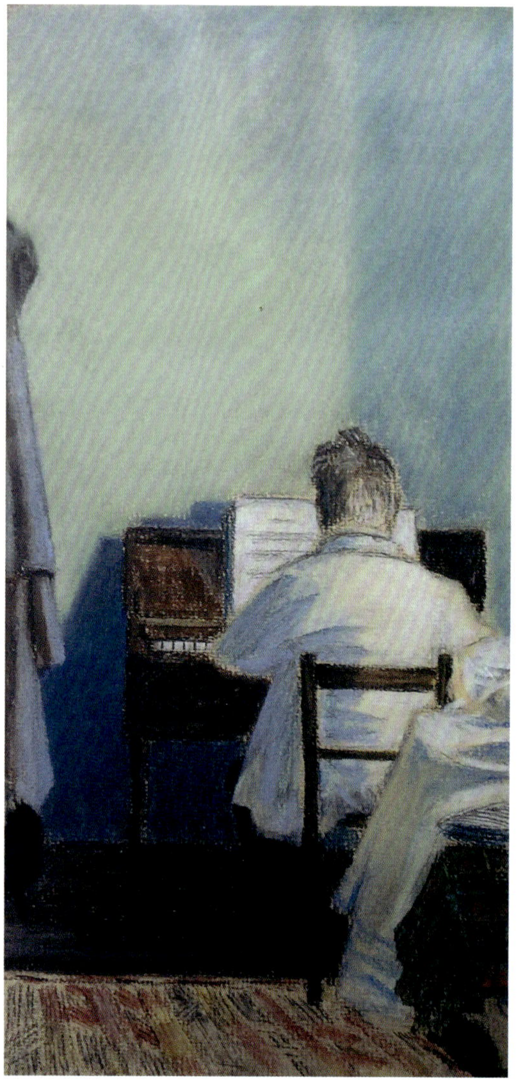

253 Sidney Sime, cover for Josef Holbrooke, *Bronwen*, 1920

254 Myrrha Bantock, *Granville Bantock at Coed-y-Bleiddiau*, early 1920s

Birmingham University but spent many summer holidays in Snowdonia in the company of Holbrooke, who had taken up residence in Harlech shortly before the war, and the pianist-composer Cyril Scott, another regular visitor.[9] Bantock's own *Celtic Poem* for 'cello and piano was composed in 1914, followed a year later by his *Hebridean Symphony*, inspired by Gaelic folk melodies.

The first two parts of the co-operation between de Walden and Holbrooke received mixed reviews. The score of the third part, *Bronwen*, was published in 1920 with another striking cover by Sidney Sime, but was not fully staged until 1929, and then by the Carl Rosa Company in Huddersfield, rather than in London.[10] Although this location might suggest that, in the post-war context, Celtic Twilight fantasy, as presented in Wagnerian style by Holbrooke, was considered passé by the

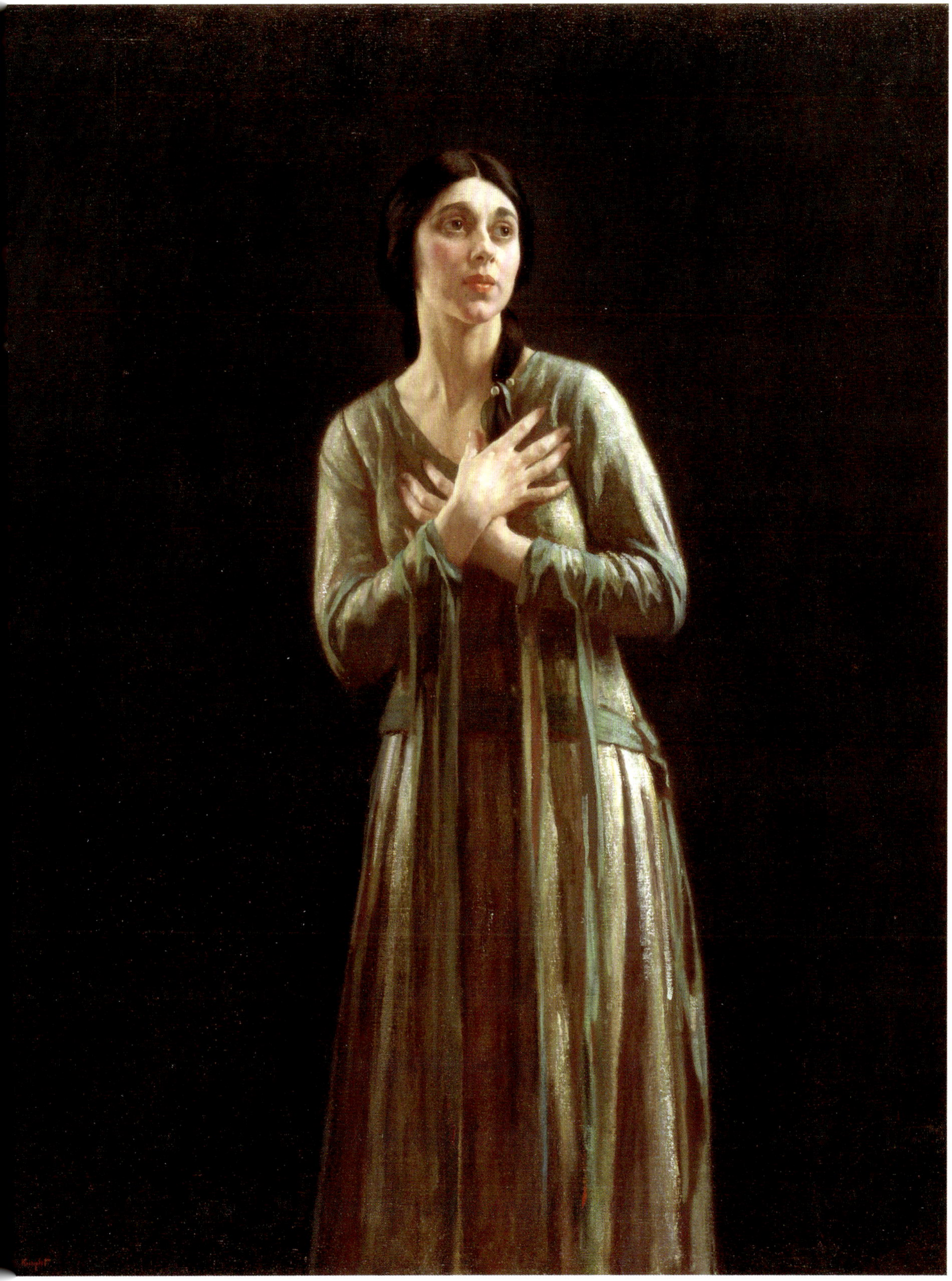

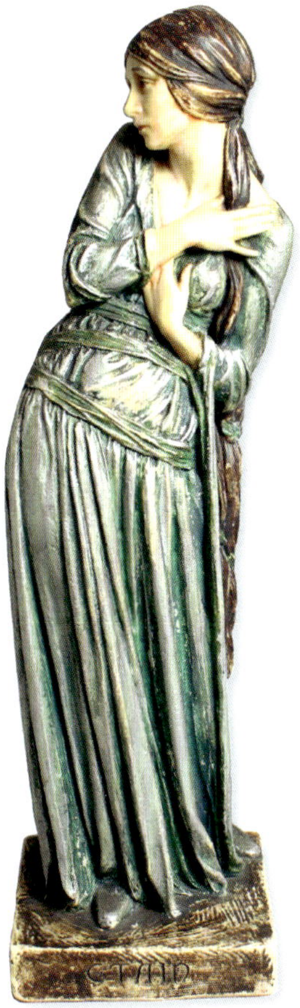

255 Agatha Walker, *Gwen Ffrangcon Davies as Etain*, 1923

256 Harold Knight, *Gwen Ffrangcon Davies as Etain*, c.1922

9 Bantock rented Coed-y-Bleiddiau, near Tanygrisiau, for his holiday visits.

10 1 February 1929. The Prelude to the opera had been given first in Liverpool, 5 February 1921, and subsequently in Munich, 24 November 1921, prior to the first staged performance.

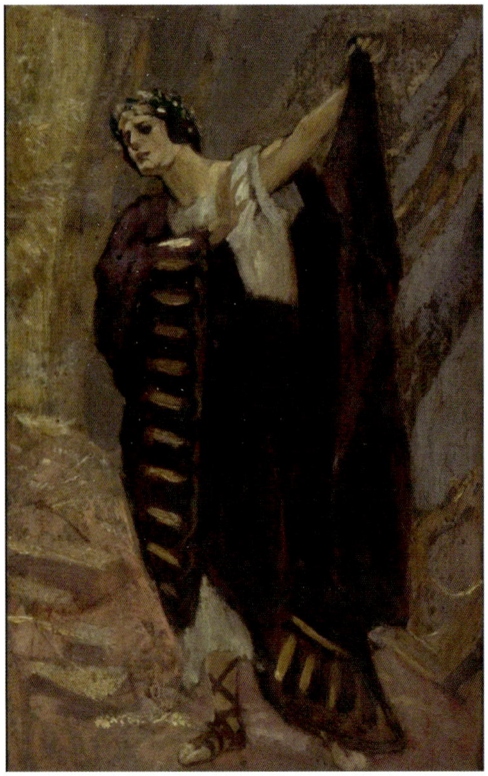

metropolitan cognoscenti, another contemporary opera, *The Immortal Hour*, certainly achieved both critical and popular success in London. It was based on the verse drama written by William Sharp, the Scottish Celticist, with a score by Rutland Boughton. Deriving from the medieval Irish mythological tale, 'Tochmarc Étaíne' (The Wooing of Etain), but also with classical resonances from the Orpheus and Eurydice legend, it was first staged in 1914 at the appropriate location of Glastonbury during the inaugural festival in the town. Revived in Birmingham in 1921, it reached London the following year where it played an unprecedented long run. In this restaging, the central female role of Etain was sung by Gwen Ffrangcon Davies. Her performance contributed substantially to *The Immortal Hour* approaching cult status and she was painted as Etain by Harold Knight. More than any other part, Etain fixed in the public mind the ethereal professional persona of Davies, though she intriguingly remarked of herself that, while she was 'ethereal from the waist up', she was 'all Welsh pony down below.'[11] The remarkable longevity of her professional career resulted in a visual iconography which equalled that of Novello, with whom she would perform on stage. In addition to the Knight portrait, Davies was depicted in the role by at least two other artists, and Walter Sickert seems to have developed something of an obsession with her, painting several portraits, most of them on the basis of her publicity photographs.

257 Frederick Samuel Beaumont, *Leila Megàne as Orphée*, c.1920

258 Gustavo Bonaventura, *Leila Megàne as Orphée*, 1916

Harold Knight's depiction of Gwen Ffrangcon Davies stands in the line of Welsh diva portraits that included Margaret Lindsay Williams's image of Clara Novello Davies and extended to that of the mezzo-soprano Leila Megàne, Davies's exact contemporary. Leila Megàne was painted by Frederick Samuel Beaumont performing in Gluck's interpretation of the Orpheus legend, *Orphée et Eurydice*, although the date of this picture is unclear. Megàne, born Margaret Jones in Bethesda, had emerged by a conventional route, winning prizes at eisteddfodau and training in London, but unusually her career had then developed on the European continent as a result of six years' study with the Polish tenor, Jean de Reszke, in Paris. In the leading role of Orphée, Leila Megàne sang excerpts from Gluck's opera in 1916 in Rome, where she was photographed in a distinguished series of romantic soft-focus images by Gustavo Bonaventura, a photographer otherwise noted for his association with Italian Futurism. Megàne did not sing Orphée in a complete staged performance until she appeared at Nantes in 1921, and it seems likely that the Beaumont portrait dates from the 1920s.[12]

11 Interview for 'Gwen Ffrangcon Davies: a Juliet Remembered', *Omnibus*, BBC2, 1998. See Helen Grimes, 'Gwen Ffrangcon Davies, "Ethereal from the Waist Up and All Welsh Pony Down Below"', *New Theatre Quarterly*, 27 (August 2011), pp. 203–14.

12 Later, at the height of a career which took her all over Europe and to the United States, Leila Megàne was drawn by the cartoonist Illingworth, the successor to J.M. Staniforth at the *Western Mail*, though by this time he was working freelance for *Punch* and other periodicals. She was also painted by Sir John Berrie, though he worked from a photograph as, according to her own account, she was too busy to sit to him.

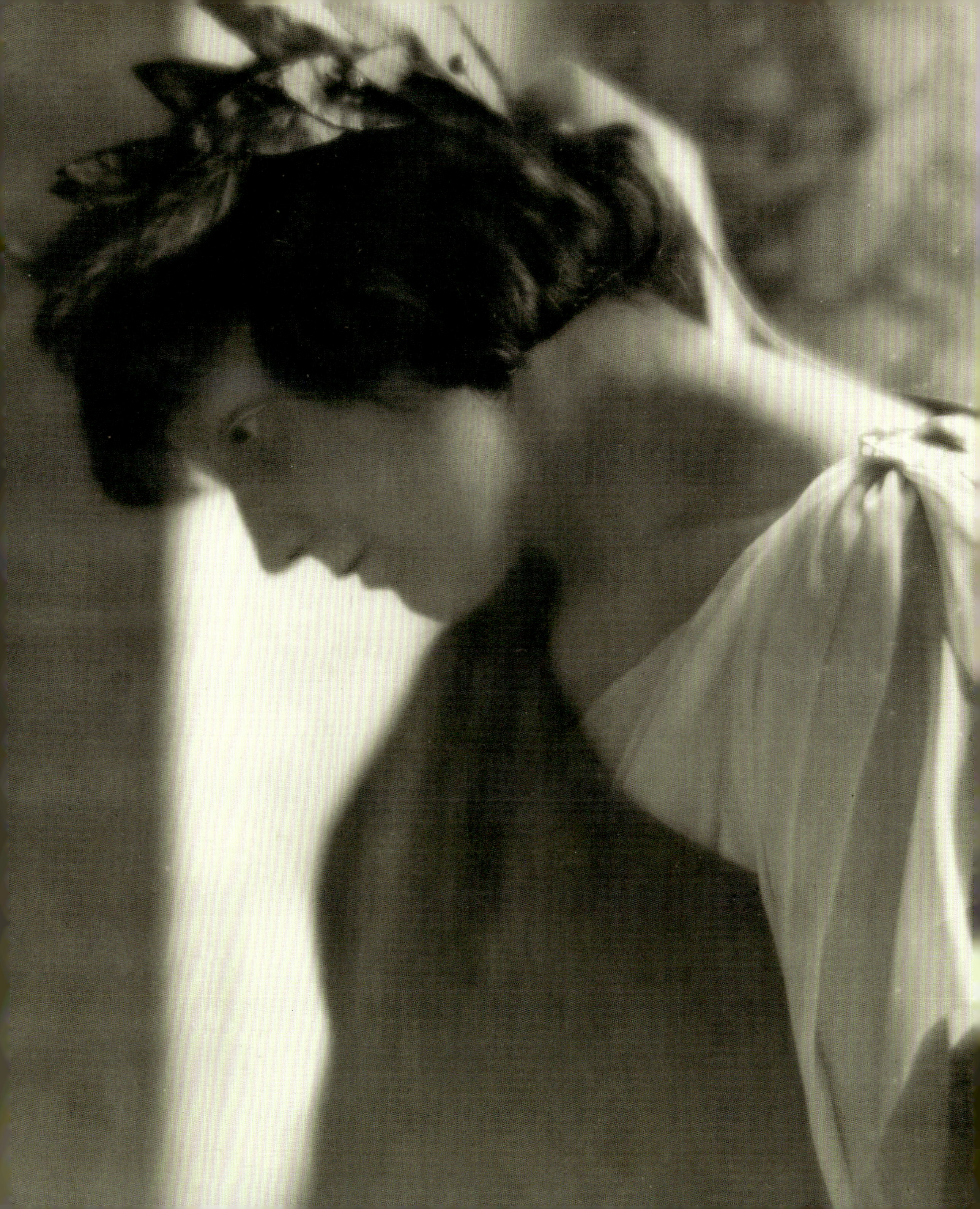

Gwen Ffrangcon Davies's role as Etain in *The Immortal Hour* had included a simple and wistful song that achieved an independent and long-lasting celebrity, 'How beautiful they are, the Lordly Ones'. By contrast, some critics had detected in Josef Holbrooke's music for *The Children of Don* a rather pretentious quality, which the final part of the cycle, *Bronwen*, appears not to have transcended.[13] In his autobiography, Augustus John would recall an incident that occurred when he was staying – at Howard de Walden's expense – near Tanygrisiau before the Great War. The party had included Holbrooke, armed with an out-of-tune piano. John noted that he 'communicated to him the air "Morfa Rhuddlan", of which a sadly dragged-out version is introduced in his opera Bronwen.'[14] Personally, de Walden's wealth insulated him from the necessity for commercial success, but the failure of *The Cauldron of Annwn* to capture the public imagination in the way that *The Immortal Hour* had done suggests that contemporary Welsh branding through music had become largely detached from its eighteenth- and nineteenth-century manifestations in druidic mysteries.

Indeed, it was suggested in the 1920s that the national brand had become entirely detached also from contemporary reality. The composer Cyril Jenkins was born in Dunvant, Swansea, and worked as a music teacher in the Rhondda before the Great War before being appointed Director of Music to the London County Council in 1921. From this elevated position, in a lecture delivered in Manchester during that year, he attacked what he regarded as the insularity and backwardness of musical practice in Wales. Jenkins had a particular contempt for the high regard in which Joseph Parry was held at home, which seemed to him emblematic of a wider problem. Jenkins's theme was taken up a few years later in an extraordinary attack on the idea of Welsh musicality by his friend C.F. Kenyon, writing under the pseudonym of Gerald Cumberland. For Kenyon, Wales was 'a cemetery for those who possess a musical talent.' On the subject of the myth itself, he was of the opinion that 'In the past, Welsh singing has been so continually and universally praised that not only singers, but composers, organists, pianists and harpists as well, have come to regard themselves as the musical salt of the earth':[15]

> I am fully persuaded that music in Wales cannot begin to develop – cannot even begin to be music, in the true sense of the word – until Welshmen

13 *New York Times*, 16 June 1912. Despite having gained an unusually favourable opinion of Holbrooke as a person, the composer Peter Warlock was of the same opinion: 'In several hundred pages I found nothing – absolutely nothing. A dreary jungle of notes, that is all. The libretti of "Dylan" and "Children of Don" are impossible to begin with. But quite apart from that, the music is a dismal failure – as bad as any fourth-rate German Kapellmeister's attempt to ape the grand manner of Strauss.' Letter to Fritz Hart, 7 February 1922 (National Library of Australia MS 2809/36).

14 Augustus John, *Autobiography* (London, 1975), p. 251. Morfydd Owen's tone poem for orchestra, also based on the air 'Morfa Rhuddlan', was composed in 1914.

15 Gerald Cumberland, *Written in Friendship* (London, 1923), p. 183.

16 Ibid., pp. 180–1. Kenyon had first written in praise of Jenkins in *Wales*, 3 (1913–14), pp. 34–8. Curiously, given their opinions about the tradition, in 1924, Jenkins wrote a setting of 'Men of Harlech' to new English words by Kenyon.

> free themselves from that intellectual slackness and spiritual fear that find expression in a narrow interpretation of religion, and in a distrust of that natural expansiveness of the soul without which there is no true life.
>
> Mentally they are indolent; spiritually they are cowards. Their cowardice stultifies their imagination. They do not even dimly sense the implications of a work of art. Music to them is notes to be sung or played; the spiritual impulse that has brought these notes to life – that has arranged and patterned them – matters nothing; one doubts if the ordinary Welsh musician is aware that spiritual impulse precedes the creation of a work of art.[16]

Though the specifics of his complaint about musicality scarcely disguised a wider animus against the Welsh people, nevertheless Cumberland – and Jenkins – were not alone in feeling that the national brand was built on shaky foundations in terms of the general musical literacy of the people. In 1919, the organist, composer and conductor Henry Walford Davies, born on the Welsh border in Oswestry, had been appointed Professor at the University College of Wales, Aberystwyth, with the ambition to improve standards. Already a figure of substance in musical education in the classical tradition (Rutland Boughton had been among his students when he taught at the Royal College of Music), with the prodigious energy and enthusiasm for which he was renowned he entered into the work of raising the quality of tuition and performance, and of bringing artists of international calibre before Welsh audiences. Gregynog, near Newtown, the home of the Davies sisters, Gwendoline and Margaret, whose patronage underpinned his appointments, provided a second focus for his activities. In addition to leading figures in the English musical world – including Elgar, Holst and Vaughan Williams – Walford Davies invited Béla Bartók to Aberystwyth to give his first public recital in Britain in 1922.

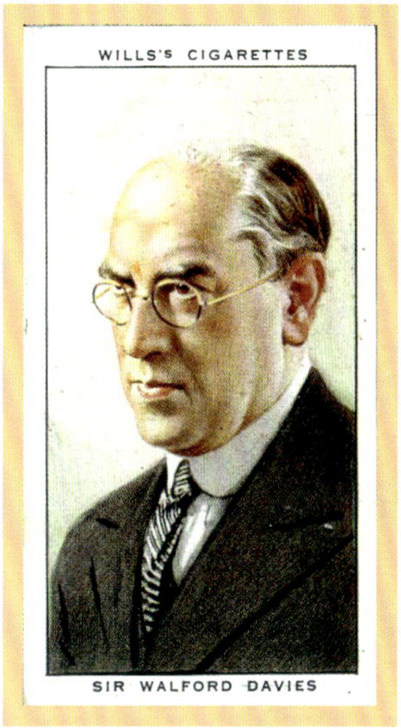

259 Unknown artist, *W.D. & H.O. Wills's Radio Celebrities, Sir Walford Davies*, 1934

Walford Davies did not make waves without encountering some opposition and jealousy among his contemporaries, but others regarded him as a visionary. Winifred Coombe Tennant, newly embarked on her career as a patron of young Welsh painters, portrayed him in messianic terms in an essay that she wrote for *The Welsh Outlook* in 1922:

> He is pure cinque-cento Florentine, lifted out of the Renaissance – for our deliverance – into this age. Before him shrivel all the ugly things of Wales –

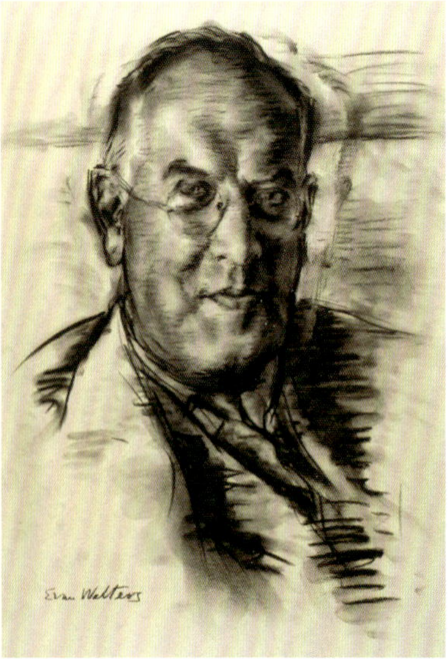

260 Evan Walters, *Walford Davies*, 1936

> the bad architecture expressed in a thousand chapels, the poor art revealed in the average picture sent in for Eisteddfod competitions, the commercial joyless furniture of its million homes, the dreadful so-called 'Music' of the 'Children's Operetta', a painful reminder that it is possible to feed them with crumbs left from the dog's platter – all these things fly from before the face of Walford Davies, and he creates for us a new Wales – by an act of faith we see it as he sees it – a Wales where the things of everyday life shall be beautiful, simple, real, sincere. He takes the common things of life and makes them holy, the humblest bush touched by him glows with the fire of God. Here is genius making its habitation among us – are we realising it, are we seeing Light in his light?[17]

The efforts of Walford Davies were rewarded in the same year with a knighthood, given by Lloyd George. Although he resigned from Aberystwyth in 1926, his involvement with Wales continued as Chairman of the National Council of Music, established in 1918 as the supreme consultative body on all matters with which the musical education of Wales was concerned. Walford Davies had been portrayed five years before his sudden death by Coombe Tennant's protégé, the painter Evan Walters. The drawing captured his sitter's ability to engage closely with an audience, a characteristic noted by many who listened to his BBC broadcasts about music that made his voice familiar in homes across the world.

In 1924, Walford Davies had taken Welsh choral music to London on a grand scale during the British Empire Exhibition. Reinforcing the tradition that dated back to at least the 1860s, and which Caradog's victories at the Crystal Palace in 1872 and 1873 had fixed in the public mind, he assembled a choir of three thousand voices at the newly built Wembley Stadium. They sang a programme which presented not only the familiar repertoire of *Messiah* and *Gerontius*, but also penillion and congregational hymn tunes with which the nation was, by then, particularly associated. The conventional publicity for the event was augmented by a poster designed by Robert Ashwin Maynard, produced at the Gregynog Press, where he had been Controller since its foundation, two years earlier. Maynard's elegant design epitomised the standards of excellence which Walford Davies was seeking to bring to musical practice in Wales, and his visual skills were also deployed in support of the festivals whose work was developed by the National Council of Music in Aberystwyth and Newtown.

17 Gwytherin [Winifred Coombe Tennant], 'The Welsh School of Social Service, 1921: An impression', *The Welsh Outlook*, 9 (1922), p. 10. In addition to directly encouraging the work of young Welsh painters, in a close parallel to Walford Davies's policy of bringing prominent figures from outside into Wales, Coombe Tennant bought contemporary French paintings that she regarded as representing high standards to show to her protégés at home. Her intention was that the collection would go to the National Museum to further that purpose, but her aspiration was not fulfilled.

18 The Council was established as a consequence of the Haldane Commission on the University of Wales (1918). See David Ian Allsobrook, *Music for Wales: Walford Davies and the National Council of Music, 1918–41* (Cardiff, 1992).

Central to the aims of the Council was 'the expression of Welsh nationality in Music',[18] and consistent with that aim, the accessibility of the tradition was increased in the 1920s by a series of collections, several of which were promoted by their publishers with commissioned covers, rejuvenating the publication conventions of the late eighteenth-century cultural revival. Two of the new publications carried the name of the seminal figure of John Lloyd Williams, who

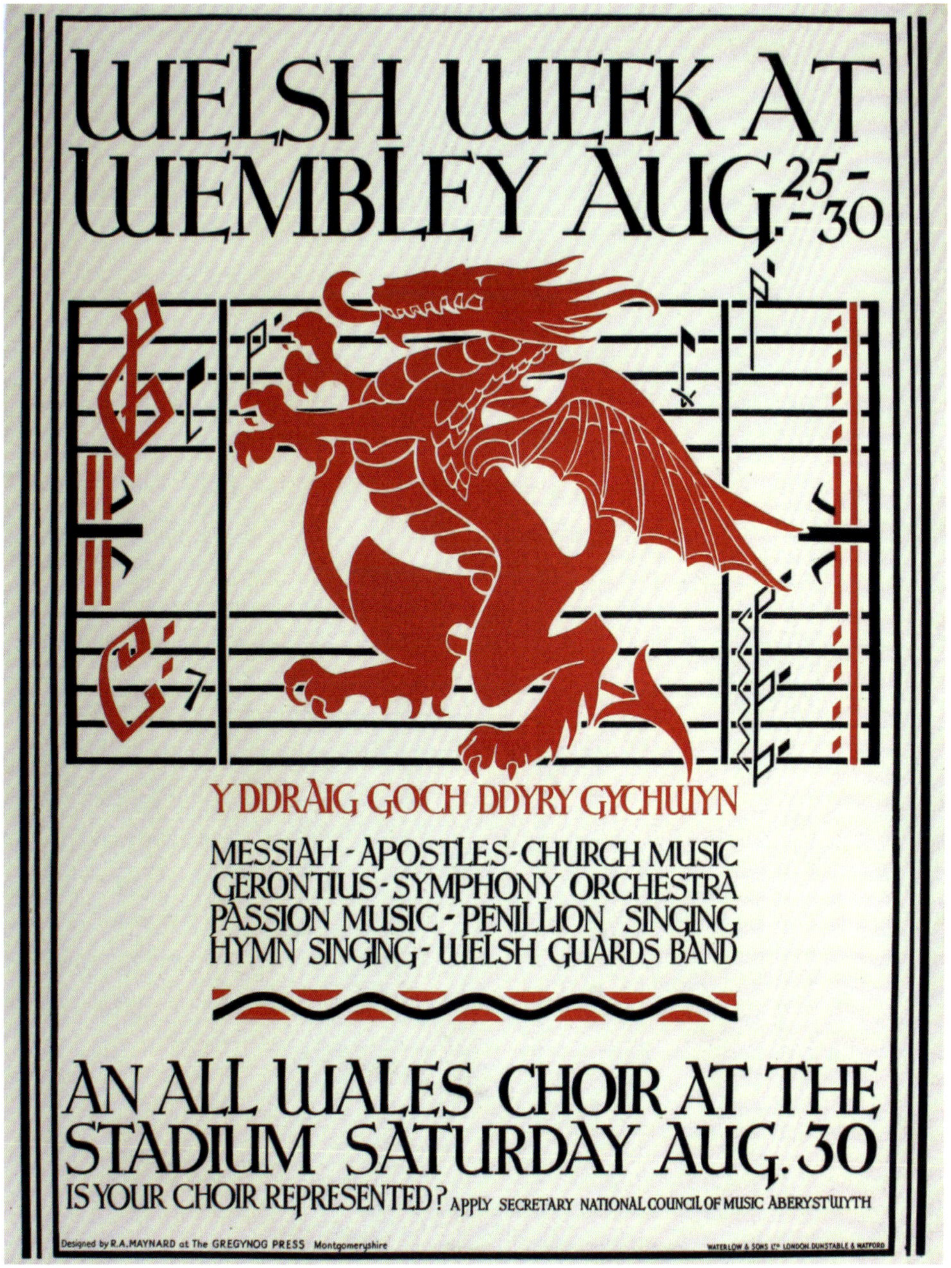

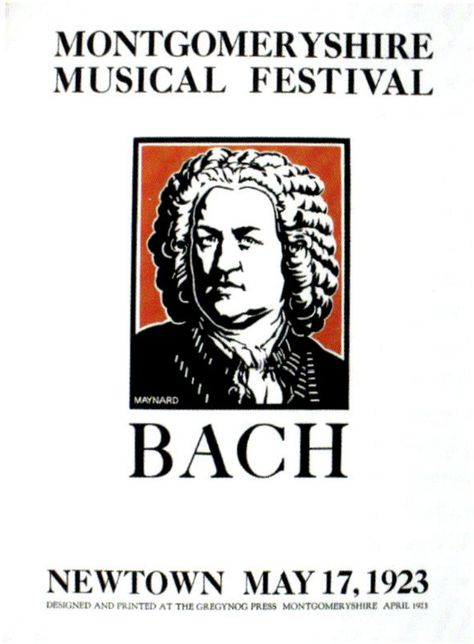

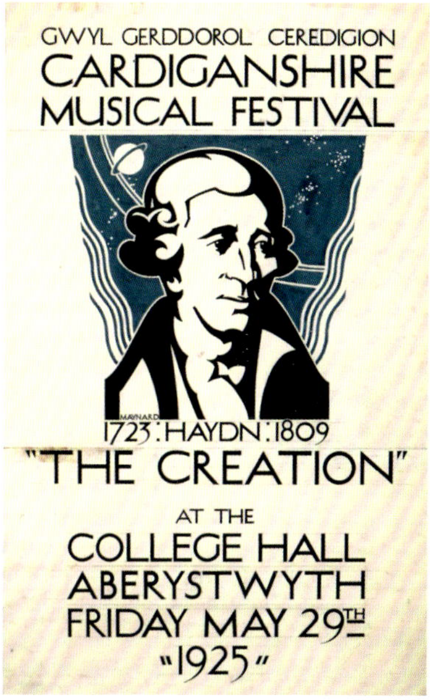

261 Robert Ashwin Maynard, poster for *Welsh Week at Wembley*, 1924

262 Robert Ashwin Maynard, poster for *Montgomeryshire Musical Festival*, 1923

263 Robert Ashwin Maynard, poster design for *Cardiganshire Musical Festival*, 1925

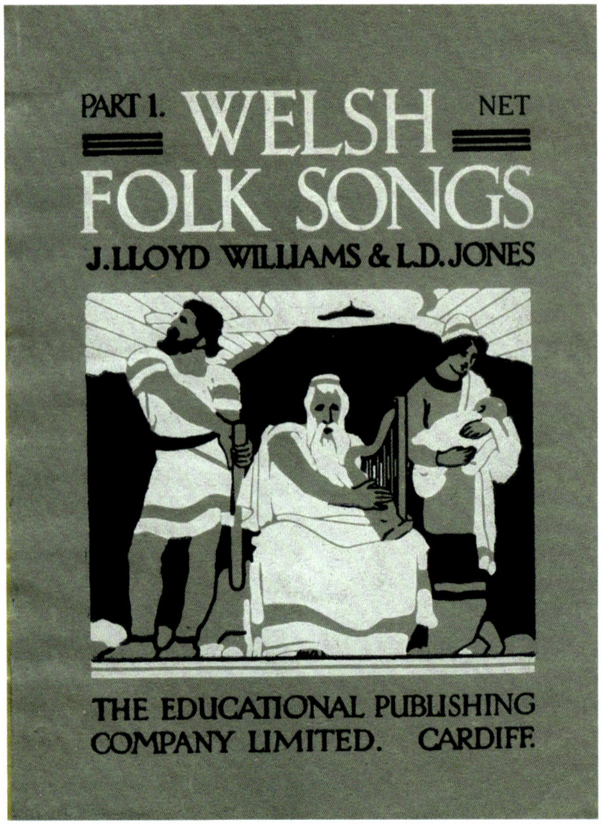

264 Unknown artist, cover for J. Lloyd Williams and L.D. Jones, *Welsh Folk Songs*, 1924

had been among the founders of the Welsh Folk-Song Society in 1906. Indeed, the series *Welsh Folk Songs*, first published in 1924, carried the endorsement of the Society. In the hands of the unidentified designer of the cover, the Bard reappeared, suggesting a medievalism that reflected both the conventions of a century earlier and the contemporary historicist sensibility of Howard de Walden, from the sets of whose operas the characters might just have walked. Though attractive in itself, the imagery of mythic courtly life was, perhaps, not altogether appropriate for the folk material that the collection presented. The airs were arranged by Williams, whose colleague L.D. Jones, 'Llew Tegid', provided both English translations and additional Welsh verses for the songs, in the tradition of Talhaiarn and Ceiriog. For a subsequent publication, *Hwiangerddi Cymraeg*, Williams wrote a forthright introduction, rooted in the experience of the pre-war nationalist generation. He was born in 1854, and so was able to recall the status of Welsh music in the nineteenth century, in a school where he had taught:

> Indeed, most of us had been so thoroughly imbued with the English spirit that we didn't think, even in a school in Caernarfonshire, that there was any such thing as Welsh song, that was consistent with the notion of 'culture'. The school Inspector could put up with 'Mary and Martha's just gone 'long'; but he baulked when 'Wele goelcerth wen yn fflamio' (Behold a white fire flaming) was sung to him. 'Now Mr Williams', he said, 'I am surprised at you! How can your pupils ever acquire a mastery of the English language when you allow them to sing Welsh in school.' And thinking about it, the thing was repugnant when it is remembered that we were expected to ensure that the poor children did not speak a word of Welsh, even at play.
>
> Now, here are Welsh National airs, yes, the simple songs of the common people, acknowledged and sung, and enjoyed in most schools; and here is at least one Welshman who rejoices that he has lived long enough to see this much freedom from English Incarceration.[19]

19 J. Lloyd Williams, *Hwiangerddi Cymraeg* (Wrexham and Cardiff, 1928), p. 5.

The publishing house Hughes and Son of Wrexham had already shown itself well disposed to illustrators and designers, and for the covers of the children's collections, *Hwiangerddi Cymraeg* and *Caneuon Gwion Bach*, the latter prepared by J. Morgan Lloyd and T. Gwynn Jones, they turned to the young Wilfred Mitford Davies. Then setting out on what proved to be an enormously productive career, especially in the illustration of children's literature, Mitford Davies provided covers that probably originated as linocuts and truly reflected the directness and simplicity of songs including 'Cysga di, fy Mhlentyn Tlws' and 'Siân Elin'.

Contemporary graphics deployed by the Eisteddfod also moved forward in their stylistic sophistication in the 1920s though, perhaps inevitably, given the visual limitations of the national brand as purveyed in the promotion of Welsh music in England, they continued to depend on the Abergavenny prototype – with the remarkable exception of the National Eisteddfod at Swansea in 1926. Evan Walters had first exhibited his paintings before the Great War, when

265 Wilfred Mitford Davies, cover for J. Morgan Lloyd, *Caneuon Gwion Bach*, c.1930

266 Unknown artist, cover for *Songs of Wales*, c.1930

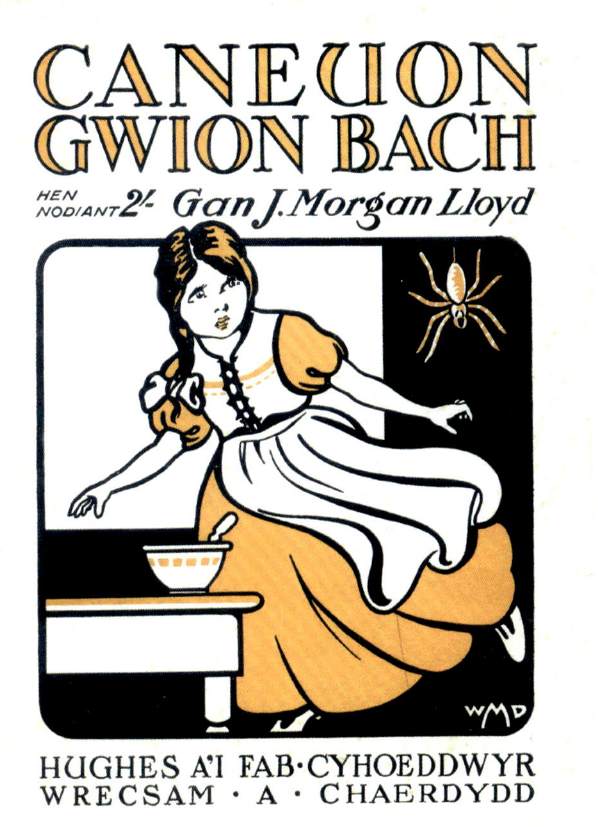

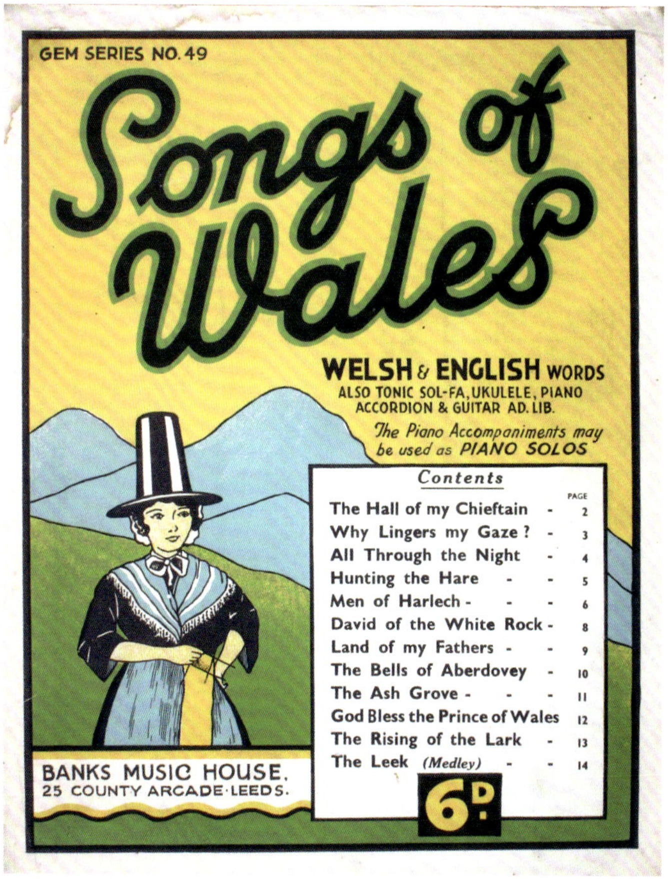

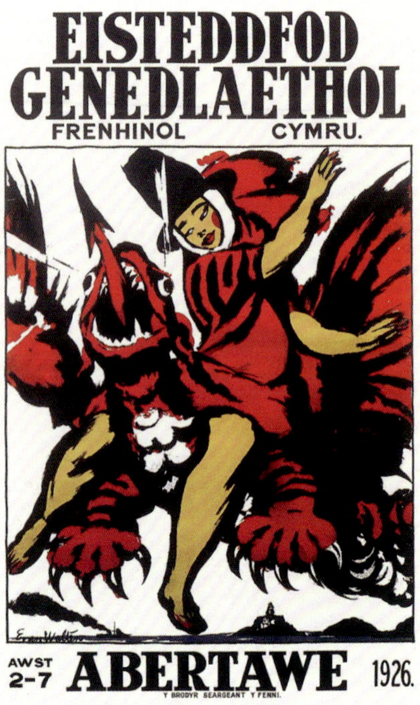

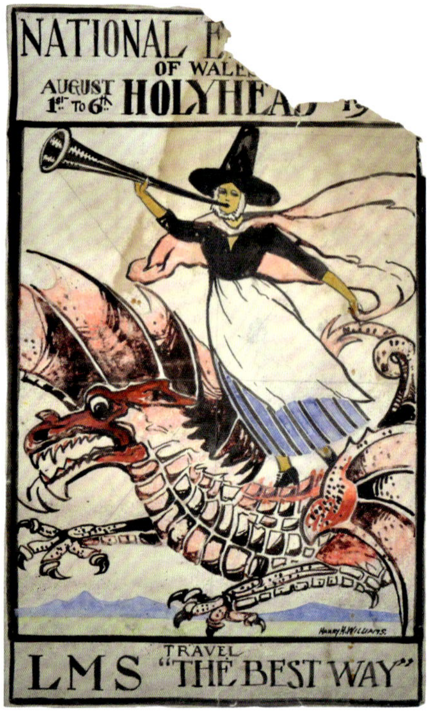

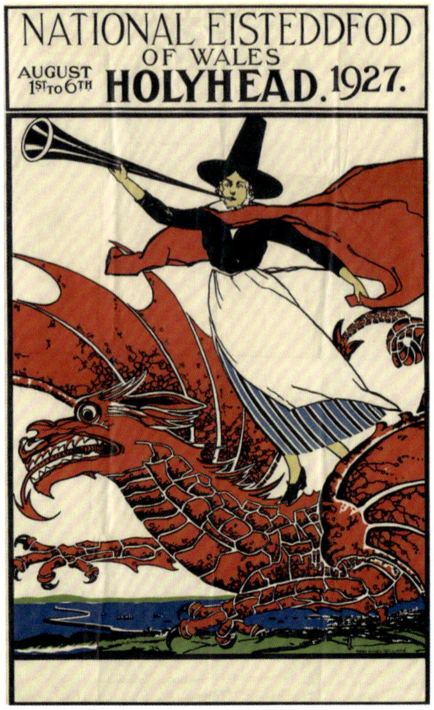

267 Evan Walters, poster for *Eisteddfod Genedlaethol Abertawe*, 1926

268 Harry Hughes Williams, poster design for *Holyhead National Eisteddfod*, 1927

269 Harry Hughes Williams, poster for *Holyhead National Eisteddfod*, 1927

still a student at Swansea School of Art. He trained subsequently at the Royal Academy in London, and spent a part of the war in New York. In 1920, he was given a show at the Glynn Vivian Art Gallery, where his work was bought for the first time by Winifred Coombe Tennant, who would become his most important patron. But it was the National Eisteddfod of 1926 that presented Walters with the platform from which his career took off in the public mind. The art adjudicators, Augustus John and George Clausen, failed to agree on the awards and so Walters – supported by John – was forced to share the prizes with less radical painters, arousing considerable debate in the press. Walters's most controversial contribution was his subversive design for the Eisteddfod poster, the explicit sexual reference of which resulted in the whole print run being pulped, with the exception of a copy preserved by Coombe Tennant. It seems unlikely that Walters's young contemporary, Harry Hughes Williams, a painter from Anglesey who had won awards at Pontypool in 1924 and Pwllheli in 1925, had not had a sight of the poster before it disappeared from view. In the following year, his design for the National Eisteddfod at Holyhead appeared to recycle the image in sanitised form, while adding also a musical reference. Two years later, at Liverpool, Williams was again responsible for the Eisteddfod poster, in which he formalised and refined his earlier design, featuring the sounding of the Gorsedd trumpet, the *corn gwlad*, over the Liverpool waterfront.

270 Harry Hughes Williams, poster for *The Royal National Eisteddfod of Wales, Liverpool*, 1929

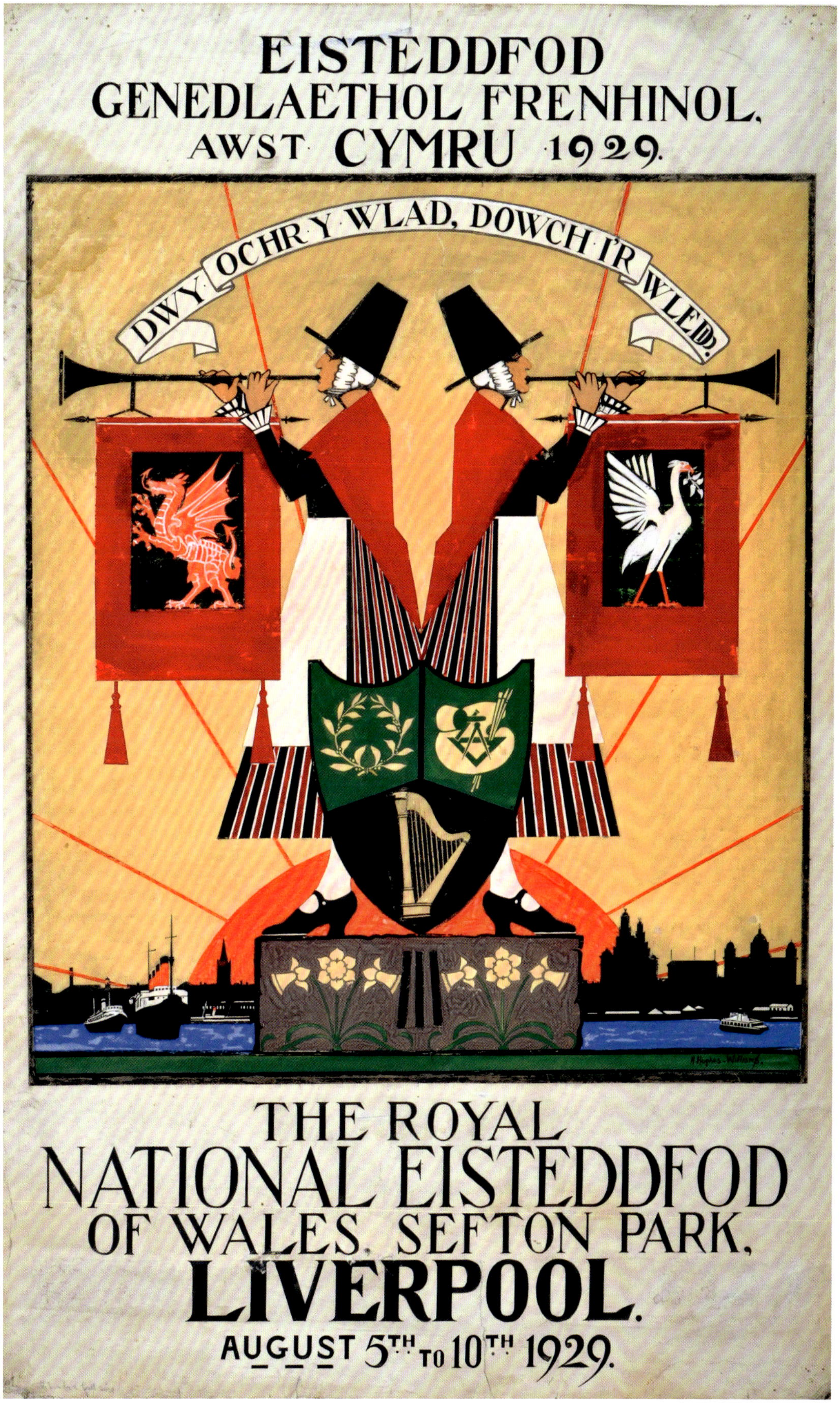
EISTEDDFOD
GENEDLAETHOL FRENHINOL.
AWST CYMRU 1929.
DWY OCHR Y WLAD, DOWCH I'R WLEDD.
THE ROYAL
NATIONAL EISTEDDFOD
OF WALES. SEFTON PARK,
LIVERPOOL.
AUGUST 5TH TO 10TH 1929.

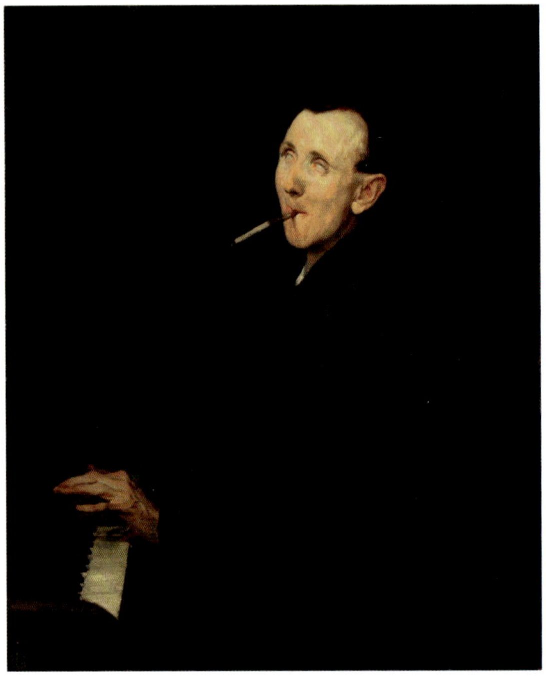

271 Evan Walters, *Blind Pianist*, 1925

In 1925, perhaps in Swansea, Evan Walters painted the portrait of an unidentified pianist at work, providing a glimpse of a Welsh musical underworld of clubs and bars, rarely recorded visually since *The Illustrated London News* had presented 'stepping' to harp accompaniment at a Merthyr pub in 1873. At this stage in his career, Walters was building a reputation by painting society portraits to commission, and it is notable that the *Blind Pianist* was never sold to a collector or a gallery, remaining in his studio until his death. A similar fate befell most of the allegorical works that he painted, which seem, in retrospect, to have greater significance than the portraits. Among his contributions to the Swansea Eisteddfod art exhibitions in 1926, Walters presented just such a picture that, uniquely, brought music into engagement with the experience of so many of those people whose lives were to become dominated for more than a decade by deepening economic depression and its social and political implications. Winifred Coombe Tennant saw *Bydd Myrdd o Ryfeddodau* in March 1926 in the painter's studio but – perceptive critic though she generally was – she failed entirely to grasp its significance, describing it prosaically as 'a weird queer thing of a funeral group near a Welsh Chapel singing hymns whilst some naked boys (having stigmata à la S. Francis) sprawl in the foreground.'[20] Walters tried to explain his thinking to her, acknowledging also that his wider Welsh audience, not accustomed to being presented in visual art with uncomfortable realities, would find the picture difficult:

> I do not think many Welsh people will approve of this. I consider it to be about my best work, but my friends in Wales will hardly think so, I'm afraid. And yet it is quite true. Here you see the dark group in the hills: below, the grave, with its young white bodies. There is no sign of happiness or resurrection in the singing. All is hopeless, dreary, dark, and it rends the hearts of the spirits as they hear it, so melancholy and mournful are the sounds.

20 NLW, Winifred Coombe Tennant Papers, Diary of Winifred Coombe Tennant, 2 March 1926.

21 'There will be a myriad of wonders/At the break of tomorrow's dawn,/When the children of the waves come/Saved from the great tribulation,/All in their white robes,/Transfigured,/Like unto their Lord/From the grave to the shore.'

22 NLW, Winifred Coombe Tennant Papers, Evan Walters to Winifred Coombe Tennant, undated. A part of this statement was published in the *South Wales Daily Post*, 16 November 1927, p. 7.

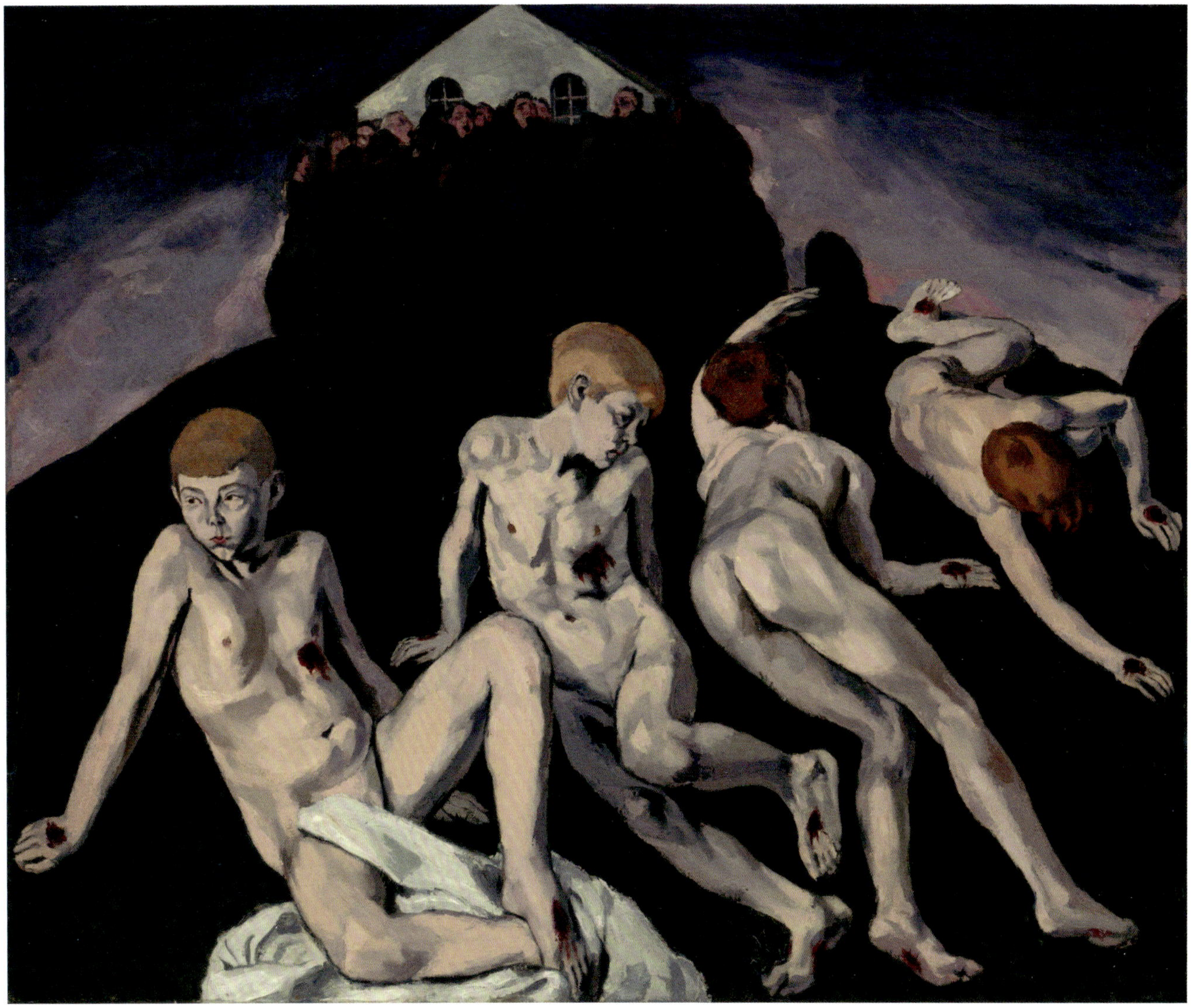

272 Evan Walters, *Bydd Myrdd o Ryfeddodau*, 1926

'Bydd Myrdd o Ryfeddodau' is an expression of my mind when looking at a group of people standing around a grave singing 'Bydd Myrdd', etc. That group of mourners is in the back ground in front of the little chapel. While the boys in the fore ground represent the expression of (and not an illustration) 'Pan ddelo plant y tonnau/Yn iach o'r cystudd mawr/Oll yn eu gynau gwynion/Ac ar eu newydd wedd/Yn debyg idd ein Harglwydd/Yn dod i'r lan o'r bedd.'[21]

The colour of the picture you will notice is rather in the minor key like the music in the hymn. The picture is an expression of the whole thing – the chapel – the graveyard – people and their voices – the tune and the words – all combined.[22]

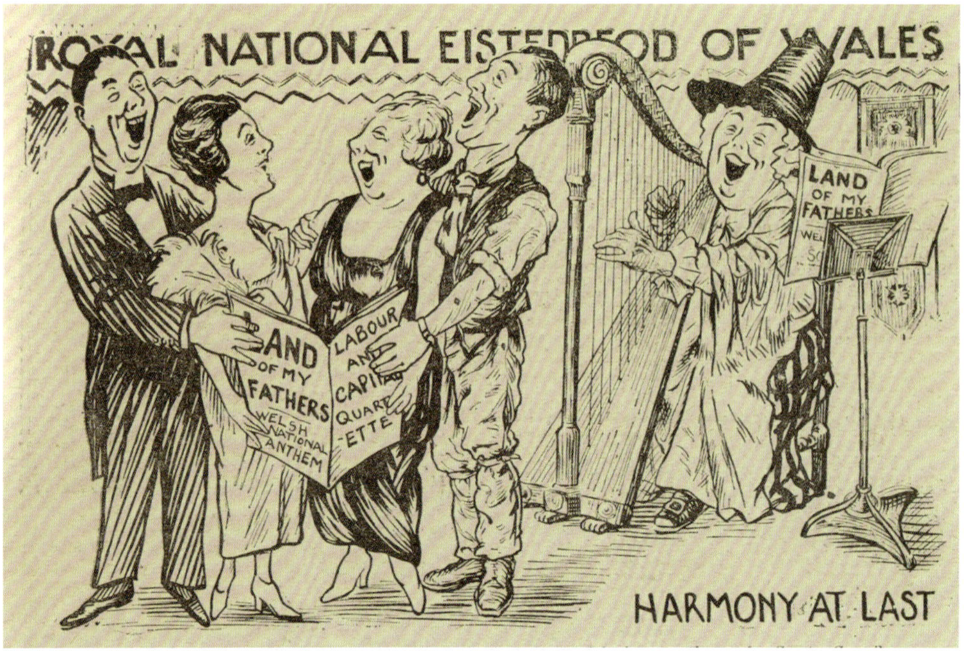

273 Trefor C. Jones, *Harmony at Last*, 1926

By the time that the picture was exhibited to the public at the Eisteddfod, just a few months later, the General Strike had come and gone, but the industrial dispute in the coalfield continued, with all its attendant hardship. Redeploying Staniforth's Dame Wales, armed with a harp, the young cartoonist Trefor C. Jones remarkably sought to present music as medicinal bromide creating an oasis of joyful harmony in these tense circumstances. It seems unlikely that his work was intended to be ironic. By contrast, not only did Evan Walters's picture confront unpleasant realities which Jones conspicuously avoided,[23] but it did so with a forthrightness and a radical aesthetic that appears to have left most of the domestic audience at best nonplussed as, indeed, Walters had predicted. *Bydd Myrdd o Ryfeddodau* was a meditation on how to respond to the increasingly traumatised state of modern industrial society. It questioned theological assumptions underlying the trope of reassuring Welsh piety, as had been purveyed characteristically to the English public on a grand scale by Walford Davies in the hymn singing at Wembley Stadium two years earlier. It questioned the adequacy of the hope of eternal life for the righteous in a world to come as a response to the waste of young lives in the terrible social conditions overwhelming the Valleys.

One wonders what the poet Gwenallt made of it. Many years later, reflecting on the period in a memoir, he recalled that 'Marxism was, to us, a much better gospel than Methodism.'[24] But in 1926 he was still escaping in his poetry – like Howard de Walden in his opera libretti – into a world of medieval fantasy under the influence of T. Gwynn Jones. It was at the Swansea Eisteddfod that Gwenallt won the chair for his ode 'Y Mynach' (The Monk). The following year, his father was killed in an industrial accident:

> Years later my father's body came home after it he had been burnt to death by molten metal, and that unnecessarily. When, in the funeral sermon, the minister said that it was God's will, I cursed his sermon with all the haulier's swear-words that I knew, and when they sang the hymn Bydd Myrdd o Ryfeddodau at the graveside, I sang in my heart the Red Flag.[25]

With the explanatory English title of *The Welsh Funeral Hymn*, it was also in 1927 that *Bydd Myrdd o Ryfeddodau* was shown in London at a one-person exhibition of Walters's work that brought him celebrity beyond Wales. Some London commentators were responsive to the picture. It was reported as 'a work of genius and extraordinary power' and 'an amazing picture that leaves the onlooker breathless', and one of the most influential of the London critics, P.G. Konody, described it as a picture of 'passionate intensity of realisation'.[26] Nevertheless, there was no published attempt to analyse the work or to assess its significance, either in terms of the theological issue it raised or its paradoxical relationship to received wisdom about the Welsh musical tradition.

In stark contrast to Walters's vision, in a eulogistic passage from his novel *The Valley, The City, The Village*, published in 1956, Glyn Jones presented a sunlit reflection on the pre-war Nonconformist musical culture in the voices of a mining community. Seen through the eyes of an aspiring painter, a day-tripping party of colliers and their families rests in fields overlooking the sea:

> In an open circle a group of people, perhaps seventy or eighty, sat spread out on the wooded rivers of beech roots pouring into the ground. Having finished their open-air meal they sat around dying fires, singing their chapel hymns under the trees with the sun and the beech-bough shadows upon them. Many of the singers were blue-marked colliers, pale and bone-faced, wearing cloth caps; many were their wives in day trip finery; many their children … To hear those sweet harmonies and the words of the saintly lyricist was for me, born in the valleys, to be overwhelmed. Hearing miners … singing with concerted passion the exultant poetry of their faith, I dared not speak … My every hail and acknowledgement to

23 He was working in a long tradition of Welsh visual artists in denial of social realities, see Lord, *Looking Out*, pp. 262–6.

24 Gwenallt, 'What I believe', *Planet*, 32 (June 1976), p. 3. For the wider context of Walters's *Bydd Myrdd o Ryfeddodau*, see Peter Lord, 'Biblical and Marxist rhetoric in the painting and literature of the Depression', in Christopher Meredith (ed.), *Moment of Earth: Poems & Essays in Honour of Jeremy Hooker* (Aberystwyth, 2007), pp. 201–17.

25 Gwenallt, 'What I believe', p. 3. For the expression of complex Welsh identities through song in the contrasting forms of congregational singing and the parlour ballad in this period, see E.G. Millward, 'Canu'r byd i'w le', *Y Traethodydd*, 136, 578 (January 1981), pp. 4–26.

26 Unnamed London correspondent for the *South Wales News*, 16 November 1927, and P.G. Konody, *Daily Mail*, 15 November 1927.

compassion, to humility, to the contrite spirit, to earth's visual radiance and to her spiritual loveliness, every salute to the multitudinous loyalties and heroisms of this world, every gratitude for tenderness, every prayer, worship, adoration, is expressed for me in the mysterious grandeur and sanctity of this singing, this eloquent, unconquerable sursum corda beneath the beech flecks and the shadow fragments of this sunlit wood. At the culmination, the unutterable fulfilment, I walk out of ecstasy filling my sea ear with the sensual loveliness of breakers sounding upon the shore ...

We are a deeply religious and musical nation.[27]

It may well be that musical activity lifted hearts and provided moments of escape from the stress of everyday life for some members of industrial communities,[28] but the tendency that would soon emerge in retrospective literature and in film to present the tradition as a transcendent panacea was misleading. In his documentary text *Grey Children*, James Hanley illustrated, through music, a case of the corrosive psychological effect of the trauma of the times on one collier:

After tea we adjourned into his parlour. This was the second time I had been taken into it and now I noticed more closely the various sticks of furniture it contained, not forgetting the somewhat desolate-looking piano that stood against the wall. When I played almost every note gave off a sort of weird, whining sound as though it resented being interfered with. Mr. Jones seemed very sad about it all. 'Waste of good money really, but then it was the missus's idea that the kids should learn. But, damn, you don't have your hopes long before something happens to wipe them out for you. Those kids never even look at the thing. Suppose I'll sell it sometime as junk. It would bring in a few bob.' I looked at the instrument again and I thought of its history, the ambition and hope that had placed it against the wall, its closed lid, its derelict and neglected condition, the struggle it must have been for them to purchase it and then the man suddenly losing his work. It was like a little drama played in secret; there were no onlookers but the actors themselves.[29]

The deployment of the trope of musicality, implying the spiritual continuity of the Welsh people in the face of material deprivation, was in essence an extension of the myth of the Last Bard, whose death by suicide metaphorically frustrated

27 Glyn Jones, *The Valley, The City, The Village* (Cardigan, 2009), pp. 294-6.

28 According to Margherita, Lady Howard de Walden, *Pages from My Life* (London, 1965), p. 151, during the 'dreadful, black, despairing time', her husband 'subsidised the whole of Beecham's orchestra and sent them touring round the distressed areas of South Wales. Those people had never heard an orchestra, and they absolutely loved it.' De Walden was herself a musician. She believed that 'all Welsh people sing and many played the fiddle, but they had then no orchestra and knew nothing of woodwind' (Ibid., p. 150).

29 James Hanley, *Grey Children* (London, 1937), p. 145.

30 Karl Marx, 'Die Religion ... ist das Opium des Volkes' (Paris, 1844).

the oppressors' genocide. Welsh musicality would be deployed by writers and filmmakers in the mid-twentieth century in the same way as Thomas Gray's poem on the subject had been deployed, as we have seen, by Bardd y Brenin in 1784, as adequate compensation for conquest and assimilation. To the extent that music-making did perform a distractive function from material deprivation during the Depression, it might be more realistic to regard it as 'the sigh of the oppressed creature, the heart of a heartless world, and the soul of soulless conditions'; indeed, as 'the opium of the people'.[30]

NEW MEDIA

Gwenallt's response to the cultural tensions of the interwar years, expressed through the metaphor of song at his father's funeral in 1927, resonated with conflicted outsider perceptions of Wales dating back a century. An ambiguity of attitudes towards the nation was expressed in the acknowledgement of the benign musical tradition, increasingly focused on the male voice choir from the mining valleys, both pious and loyal, and the simultaneous demonising of left-wing political activism, manifested in those same communities. As the Second

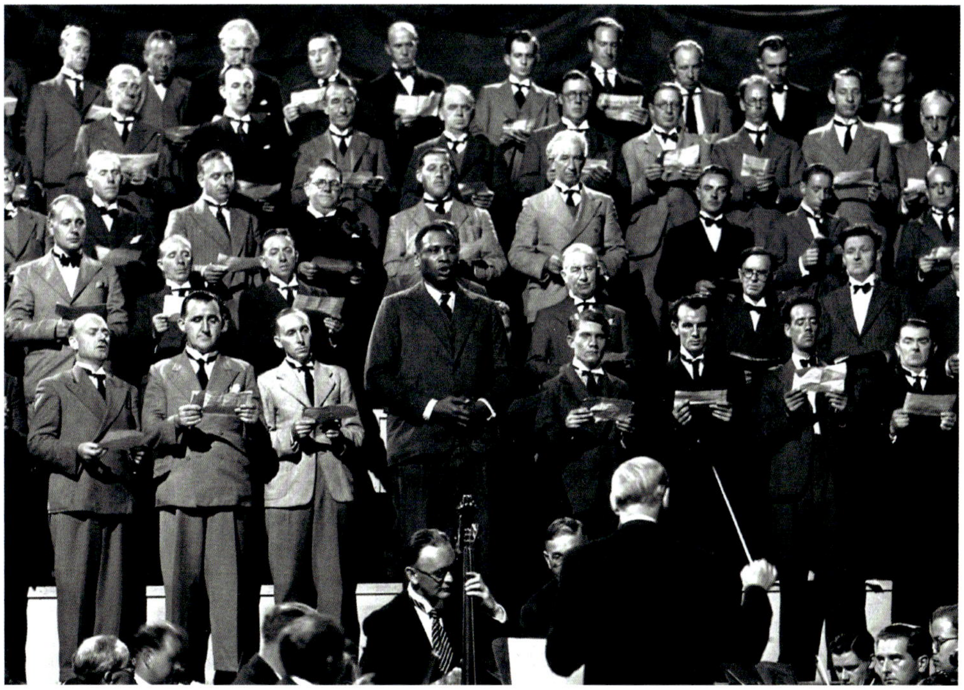

274 Paul Robeson in Pen Tennyson, *The Proud Valley*, 1940

World War approached and economic activity revived, visual images from two films about Welsh life crystallised in the public mind the centrality of the 'religious and musical nation' trope to the national brand, while avoiding a clear exposition of this paradox.[31] They did so primarily through the fetishising of the male voice choir which had not previously featured strongly in the imagery. It seems that – almost by stealth – male voices had usurped the place of the mixed choir, which had been central to the development of the choral tradition for most of the nineteenth century. Their emergence as the dominant manifestation of the brand was abetted by association with two other essentially masculine stereotypes, coal mining and rugby. Although *The Proud Valley* and *How Green Was My Valley* were profoundly different films in terms of their genesis and

275 Unknown artist, poster for Pen Tennyson, *The Proud Valley*, 1940

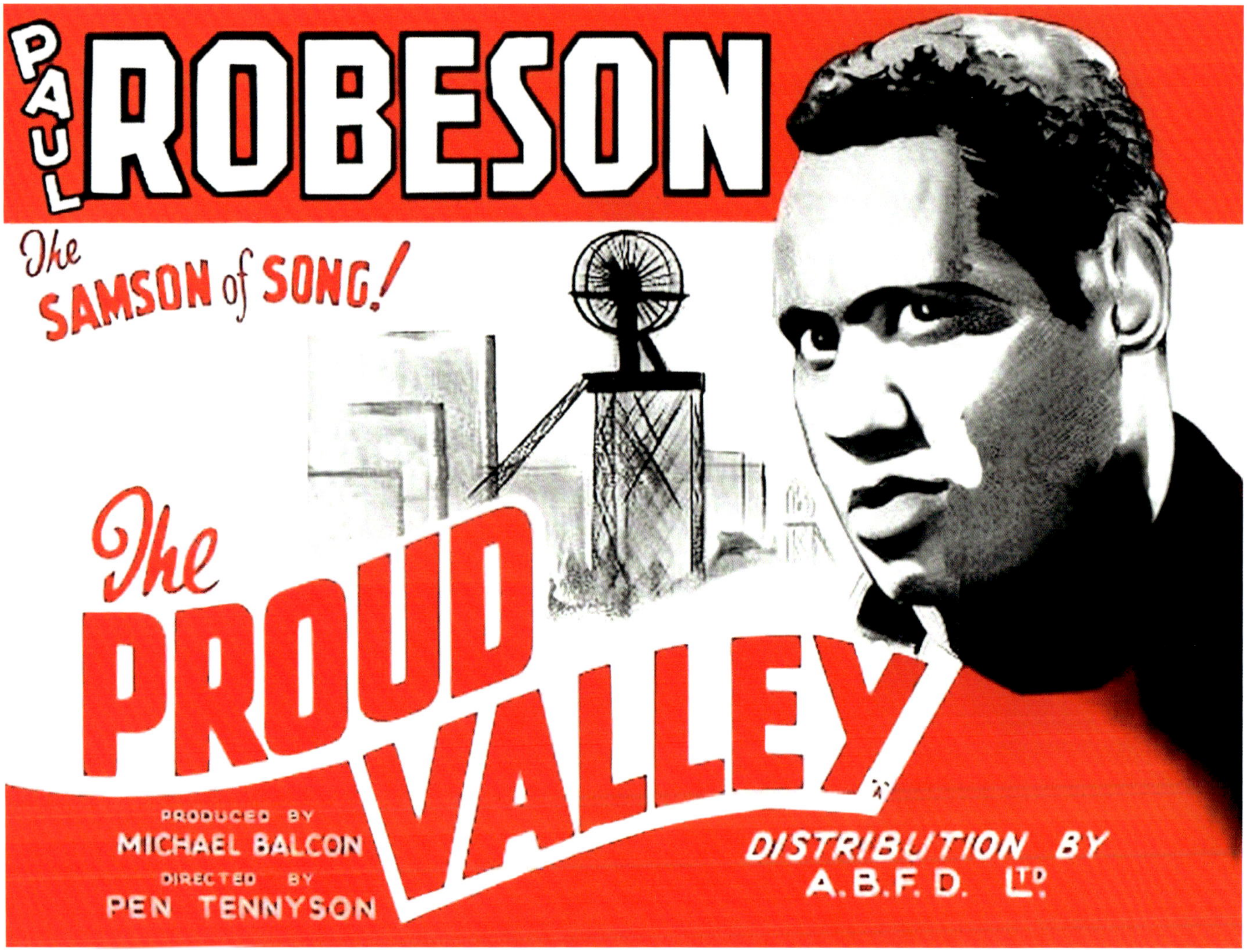

realisation, the imaging of song as central to the culture of the Welsh people was a crucial common feature, on which both depended for their emotional impact.

The Proud Valley was conceived in 1939 on the basis of an outline by two socialist intellectuals, Herbert Marshall and Fredda Brilliant, who had met while living in Moscow. Notwithstanding the performance in the central role of Paul Robeson (whose socialist politics were well known), the radical conception of the film was diluted when produced, in particular by changing the script's conclusion. Robeson's character, an itinerant former seaman who wanders into a mining valley and whose vocal talent is immediately recognised by the conductor of the local male voice choir, is largely passive in terms of leading the film's narrative. However, he comes to prominence when the choir performs 'Deep River' at the Eisteddfod.[32] The critical reception of the film was generally favourable, but its distribution and so its impact on a mass audience was limited by the hostility of the political right, manifested notably in the person of Lord Beaverbrook, whose newspaper the *Daily Express* blacklisted it. On the other hand, *How Green Was My Valley*, released in 1941, was an outstanding success both in terms of critical response and public popularity. Reflecting the first part of Richard Llewellyn's novel of 1939, this tale of community breakdown before the Great War is narrated through the childhood perceptions of Hugh, youngest son of a family whose disintegration is portrayed by the film as an exemplar of the wider disruption. But a reassuring cultural message, contradicting the social tension that is ostensibly at the heart of the story, is suggested early in the narrative, when Hugh states that 'singing is in my people as sight is in the eye.' Particularly potent in this context is the scene in which, despite the emerging generational conflict over the response to the pit owners' demand to lower the colliers' wages, the male members of the community unite to sing the English national anthem when a telegram arrives from Windsor Castle commanding the choir to appear before the Queen. Welsh loyalty is assured, even in adversity. The imaginary incident had its roots in the visit of the Treorchy Male Choir to Windsor by royal command in 1895. That performance had been imaged by J.M. Staniforth, apparently dispatched by his employers, the *Western Mail*, expressly to record the auspicious occasion for the nation.

The success of *How Green Was My Valley* was all the more remarkable for the fact that it was made in the United States with a largely Irish cast, and directed by John Ford, whose knowledge of Wales was scanty to say the least. Among

31 For detailed analysis of the films and their wider cultural context, see David Berry, *Wales and Cinema: The First Hundred Years* (Cardiff, 1996).

32 In 1940, the BBC presented a radio adaptation of the film, written by Jack Jones but using the original film soundtrack for the music.

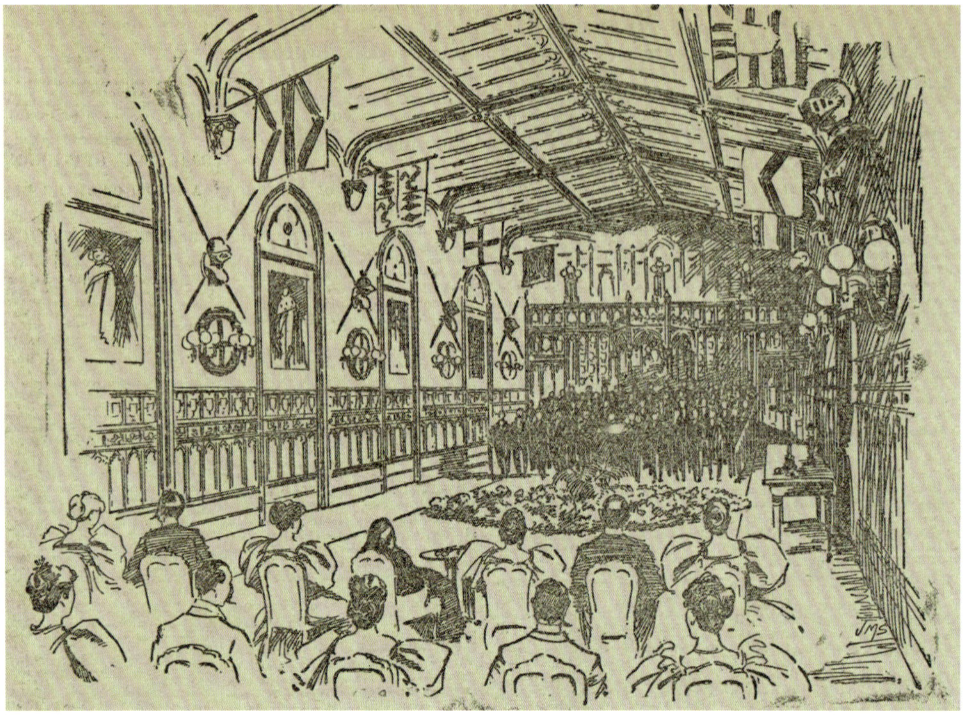

276 J.M. Staniforth, *Scene in St George's Hall, Windsor*, 1895

the five Oscars that the film accumulated in 1942 were Best Art Direction and Best Cinematography. The surreal exterior set and lighting, in which the mining village was dominated, Calvary-like, by the winding gear of the pit at the top of the mountain, was more suggestive of *The Wizard of Oz* than the Rhondda, but coupled with the frequent recourse to song (Joseph Parry and Mynyddog's 'Myfanwy', in particular), it may well have done more than any other art work of the twentieth century to fix in the minds of people beyond Wales the national brand.

After the war, in 1947 a second film that began with left-wing aspirations to deal with current social and political issues – in this case, the implications of the nationalisation of the coal industry – was compromised in production by the perceived box-office necessity for a love story. *Blue Scar*, directed by Jill Craigie, deployed music relentlessly throughout in set piece, male voice choir performances, including an improbably spontaneous outburst at the Miners' Institute and a *noson lawen* at home. Even when music-making was not imaged on screen, the score, composed by Grace Williams, reinforced the action with familiar Welsh melodies. The leading character sums up the survival strategy of the Valleys as 'Singing, football and night classes – that's how we keep ourselves alive.' Tom remains committed to his community while his girlfriend, aspiring to a career as an opera star, leaves for Cardiff, then London. Singing is deployed as an escape mechanism both in a metaphysical and a sociological sense, lifting the spirits of the community at home above the daily grind, and offering a route out of the working-class home and into a smart London flat for the aspiring diva. Ludicrous caricaturing of the inhabitants of that latter world undermines the concluding metaphor of disillusionment as Olwen, in her only metropolitan success, sings 'Home, Sweet Home' on the wireless.

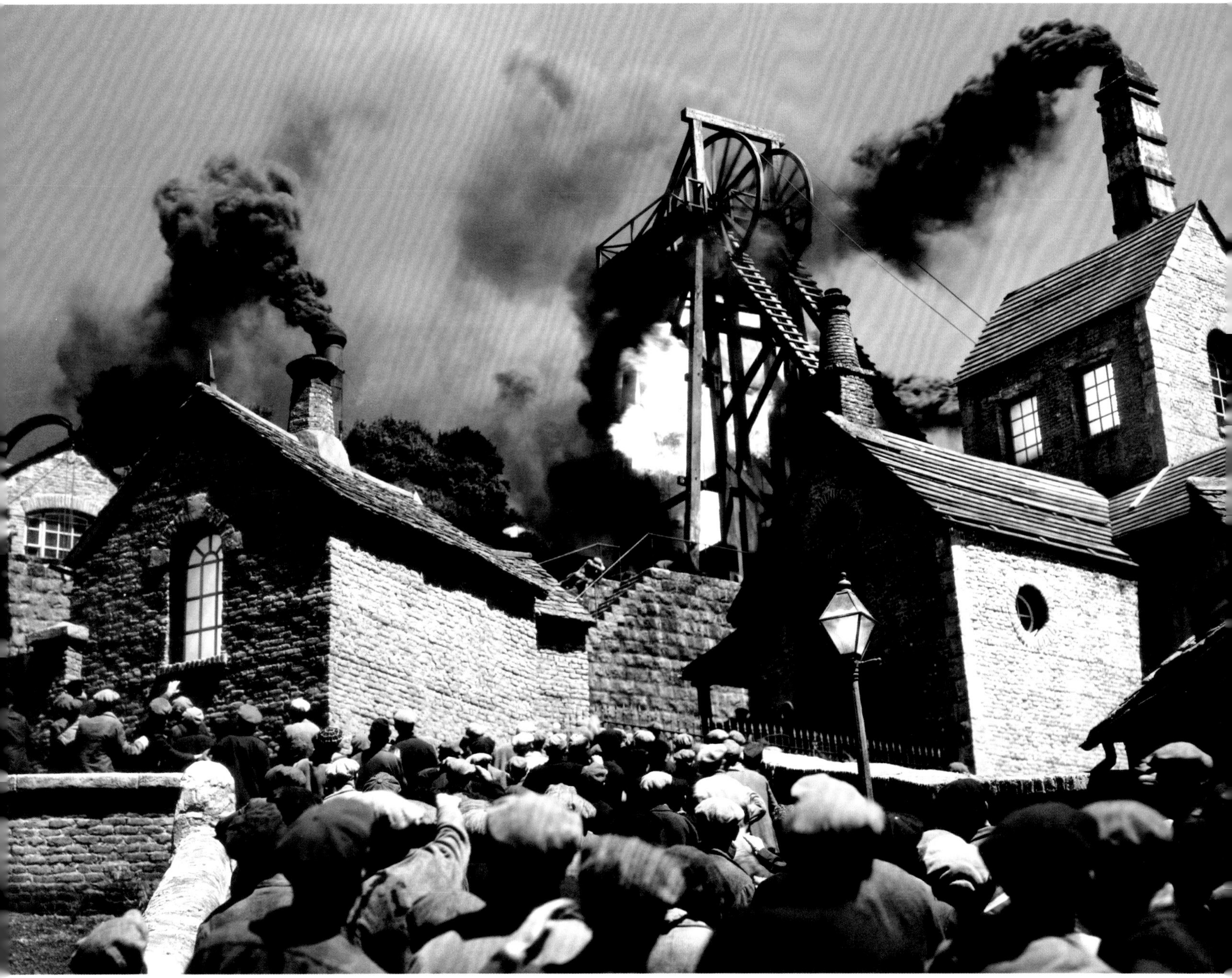

277 Scene from John Ford, *How Green Was My Valley*, 1941

278 Unknown photographer, *King Ned on the streets of Birkenhead*, c.1910

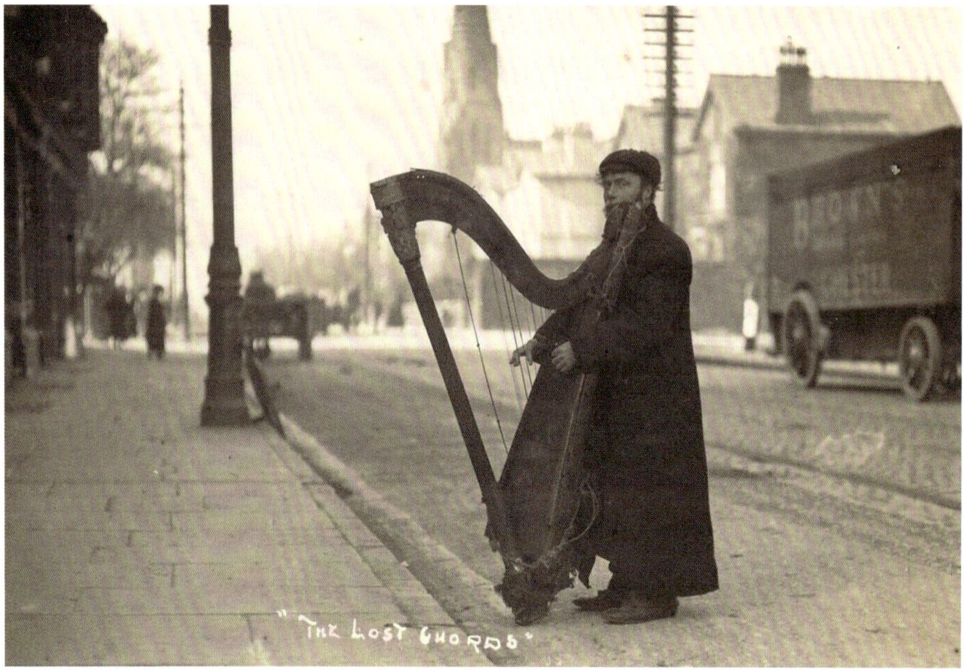

Even more than its two predecessors, the residual message presented by *Blue Scar* to the vast cinema audiences of the 1940s and '50s was the centrality of music to Welsh life – indeed, it was presented as its only 'cultured' characteristic. The idea was persistently reinforced both in cameo roles in the margins of films in which Welshness was not the core narrative,[33] and centrally in features such as the comedy *A Run for Your Money*, made in 1949 by the Ealing Studios. The historian of Welsh film, David Berry, observed that the makers of the Ealing comedies were:

> ... anxious to bury national differences within the UK. The studio sought to project images of a homogenous Britain ... Ealing had no truck with angst. They specialised in benign characters and presented a Britain more or less at ease with itself.[34]

As in the days of Bardd y Brenin, music continued the focus for Welsh collusion in this project. Depending as ever for its humour on the ancient trope of the congenital stupidity, or at best, harmless naivety, of the common people of Wales,[35] *A Run for Your Money* – perhaps unknowingly – presented historically resonant images of the actor Hugh Griffith portraying a dissolute harper, surviving by busking in London.

33 In *The Blue Lamp* (1950) Meredith Edwards played an obsessive police choirmaster.

34 Berry, *Wales and Cinema*, p. 214.

35 See Peter Lord, *Words with Pictures: Welsh Images and Images of Wales in the Popular Press, 1640-1860* (Aberystwyth, 1995), pp. 33-51.

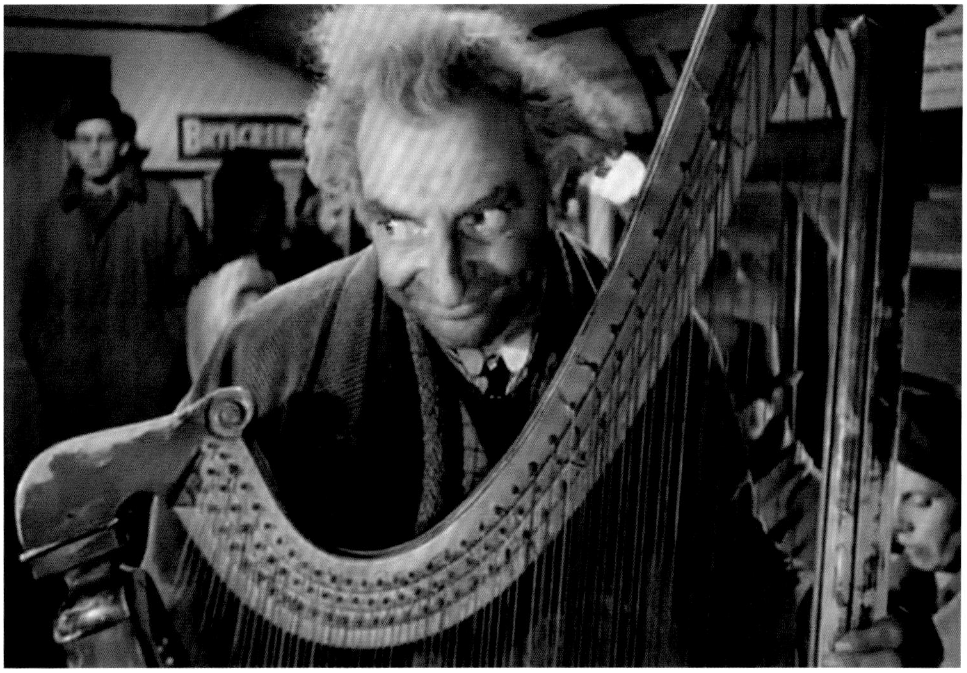

279 Hugh Griffith in Charles Frend, *A Run for Your Money*, 1949

Based on a story by Clifford Evans, the script of the film was substantially revised by the Cardiff-born actress Diana Morgan, who had made her stage début in Ivor Novello's *Cavalcade* in 1931. Wales had scarcely featured in Novello's vast creative output between the wars, but perhaps the death of his mother in 1943 and a four-week imprisonment for breaking petrol rationing laws the following year engendered in him a more reflective state of mind in the last period of his life. In a radio drama in 1947, he played the part of a choirmaster who returns from a career in London to his native valley with, at the outset, unsatisfactory consequences for community harmony. Exploiting an extensive range of Welsh stereotypes, from cheerful singing colliers to gossiping chapel women, *Choir Practice* was a popular success in which the troubled evolution of a performance of *Messiah* provided the main narrative. The story was written by Cliff Gordon but, after Novello's death in 1951, it emerged that he too had been writing a show partly set in Wales. Reversing the narrative of *Choir Practice*, Novello's *Valley of Song* shared the same essential plotline as *Blue Scar* – an ambitious young soprano who turns her back on her native valley to pursue a career in opera, leaving behind a young man caught between love for her and loyalty to his community. Set in the period of Novello's own youth, immediately before the Great War, and completed by his long-time collaborator, Christopher Hassall, the musical included a rendition of 'Keep the

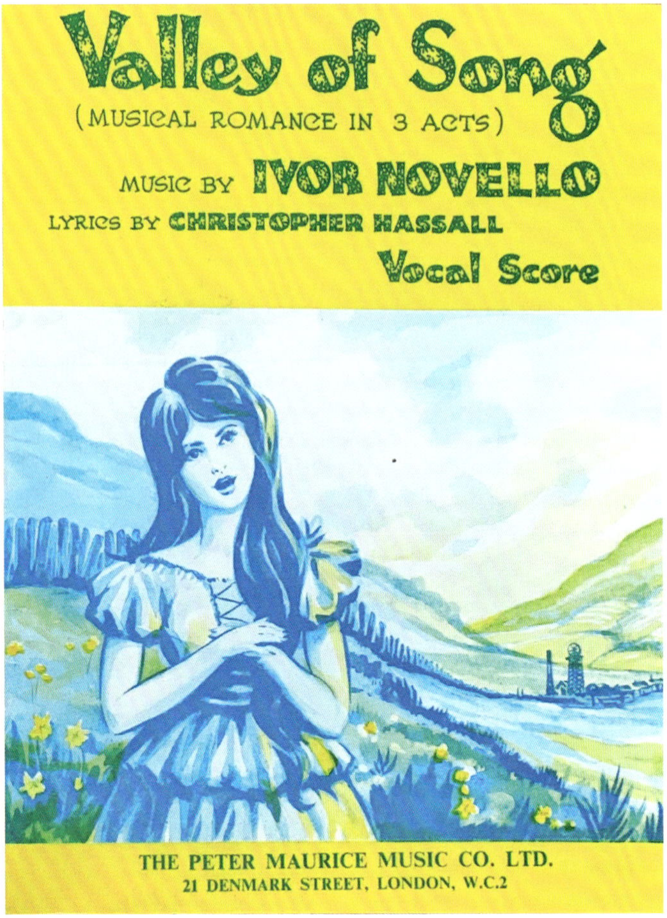

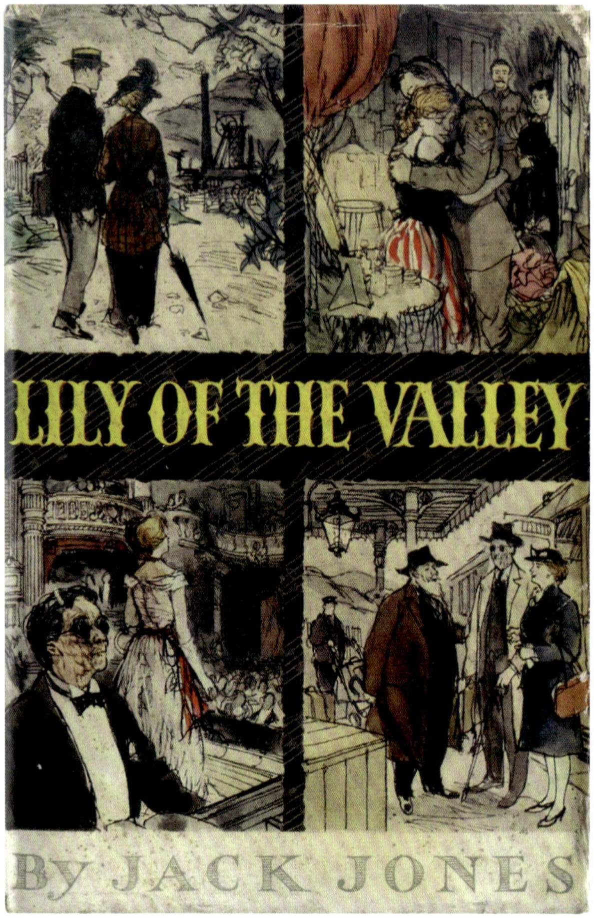

280 Unknown artist, cover for Ivor Novello, *Valley of Song*, c.1952

281 Unknown artist, cover for Jack Jones, *Lily of the Valley*, 1952

Home Fires Burning'. The cover illustration for the published score presented an eclectic assemblage of visual tropes. A coal mine nestles beneath Snowdonian mountains and a slate-slab fence, before which a Heidi-like heroine performs. The popular film version of the novel, *Heidi*, in which longing for and eventual return to a remote and beloved mountain home was also the central theme, was contemporary – released in 1952.[36]

It appears that Novello had also discussed the basic idea for what emerged as *Valley of Song* with the writer Jack Jones:

> The late Ivor Novello … had for long had in mind a musical play to be entitled *Lily of the Valley*. It was to be the story of a girl from our South Wales valleys, a singer who made a name for herself in London … In *Lily of the Valley*, he would, had he been spared, have played a leading part, probably the part of a choir conductor, a part such as he played in *Choir Practice*.[37]

36 Late in his life, Novello also wrote 'Among the Hills of Wales', a song associated subsequently with the successful career of Donald Peers.

37 Jack Jones, *Lily of the Valley* (London, 1952), p. ix.

38 Jack Jones had, earlier, been a script advisor to Louis Golding for *The Proud Valley*. He also played a small part in the film. See Berry, *Wales and Cinema*, p. 168 and note 28.

Jones explained that he had 'tried to write the story which I think he had in mind', though with unfortunate consequences, as *Lily of the Valley* proved to be the literary equivalent of painting by numbers. The first edition of the laborious text was somewhat enlivened by an unusual narrative cover.[38]

Confirming its popularity, the publicity for a film version of the radio drama *Choir Practice*, released in 1953, six years after the initial broadcast, made direct reference to the original. It was retitled *Valley of Song*, though there was no connection with Novello's musical of the same name. Return to the valley again provided the opening theme. Choirmaster Geraint, the central character, is greeted on his arrival from London by a quartet of colliers who spontaneously render 'Y Mochyn Du'. Though no doubt considered essential to confirm the

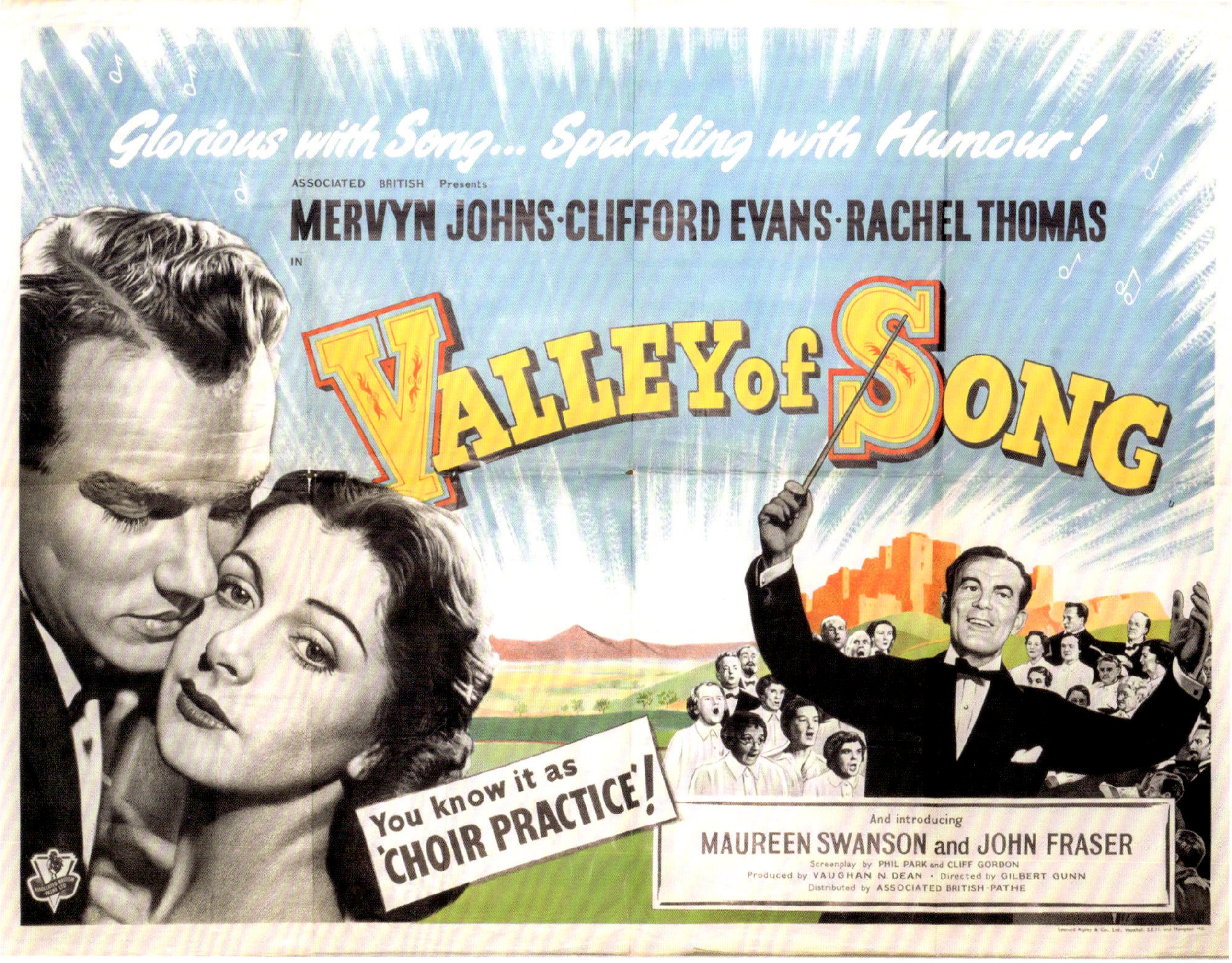

282 Unknown artist, poster for Gilbert Gunn, *Valley of Song*, 1953

stereotype, no further reference is made to their inexplicable appearance in a rural valley near Llandeilo, dominated by Carreg Cennen Castle. It would appear that audiences, certainly outside Wales, were not unduly disconcerted by this bizarre conflation of eighteenth- and nineteenth-century symbols of nationality, because the film was a popular success.[39]

The musicals, books, films and plays from this period on the theme of the aspiration for a musical career in London[40] might almost be counted a distinct genre, fictionalising migrations that – as we have seen – had been in evidence since at least the early eighteenth century. There had been conspicuous successes, but also many failures, as the journalist Glyn Roberts, himself an émigré from rural Ceredigion, noted in the 1930s. 'There are a number of able but unhappy Welsh folk in London, trying desperately to make a living from their voices and only just doing it,' he reported. 'The sense of inferiority wreaks dreadful damage among them.'[41]

283 Alfred Janes, *Daniel Jones*, 1947

284 Ceri Richards, *Thomas Richards*, 1955

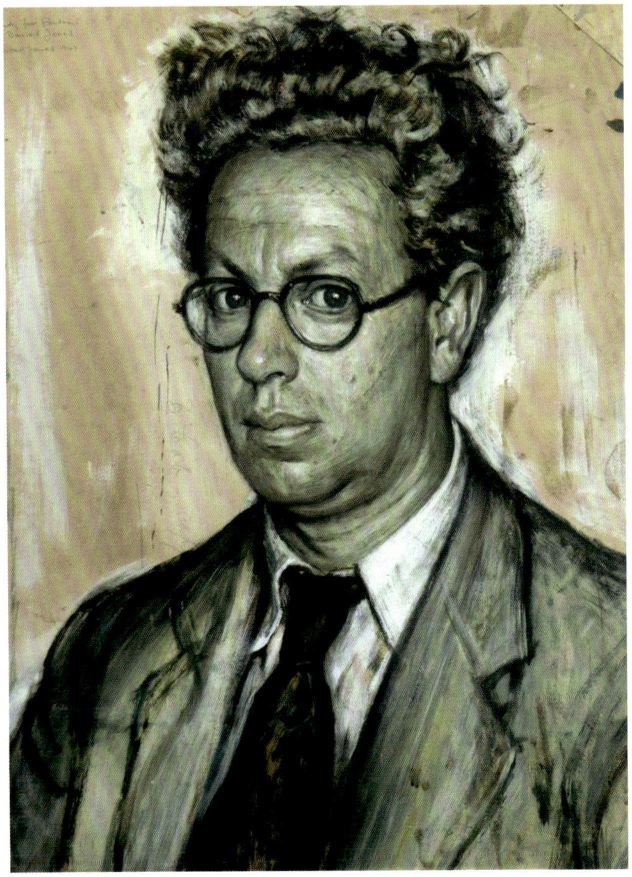

PAINTER AND PIANIST – CERI RICHARDS

The pattern of artistic migration to London was not confined to musicians. Evan Walters, after tasting success with his 1927 exhibition, established himself in the metropolis. His younger contemporaries, Archie Rhys Griffiths and Ceri Richards, also trained initially in Swansea and stayed on after finishing their courses at the Royal College. A decade later,

39 The cast included two of the most distinguished female actors of the period, Rachel Thomas (who had first appeared in *The Proud Valley*) and Rachel Roberts, in an exuberant comedy role purveying both milk and gossip around the village, that would prove unique in her career. With the exception of the closing sequence, all the singing was performed in English.

40 Though in pursual of even greater romantic fantasy, Novello took his heroine to Venice in *Valley of Song*.

41 Glyn Roberts, *I Take This City* (London, 1933), p. 268. Roberts had been informed by one 'conspicuous exception' about 'dozens of young men he had known who had come up to London's training academies, with voices of gorgeous promise, but who had quarrelled and bickered and generally behaved impossibly, and ultimately returned disillusioned to the plough or the pit whence they had started with so much hope.' Roberts also noted of the singers that 'it is true to say that if they succeed in any large degree they inevitably and quite naturally lose touch with Welsh affairs, at least until they retire.'

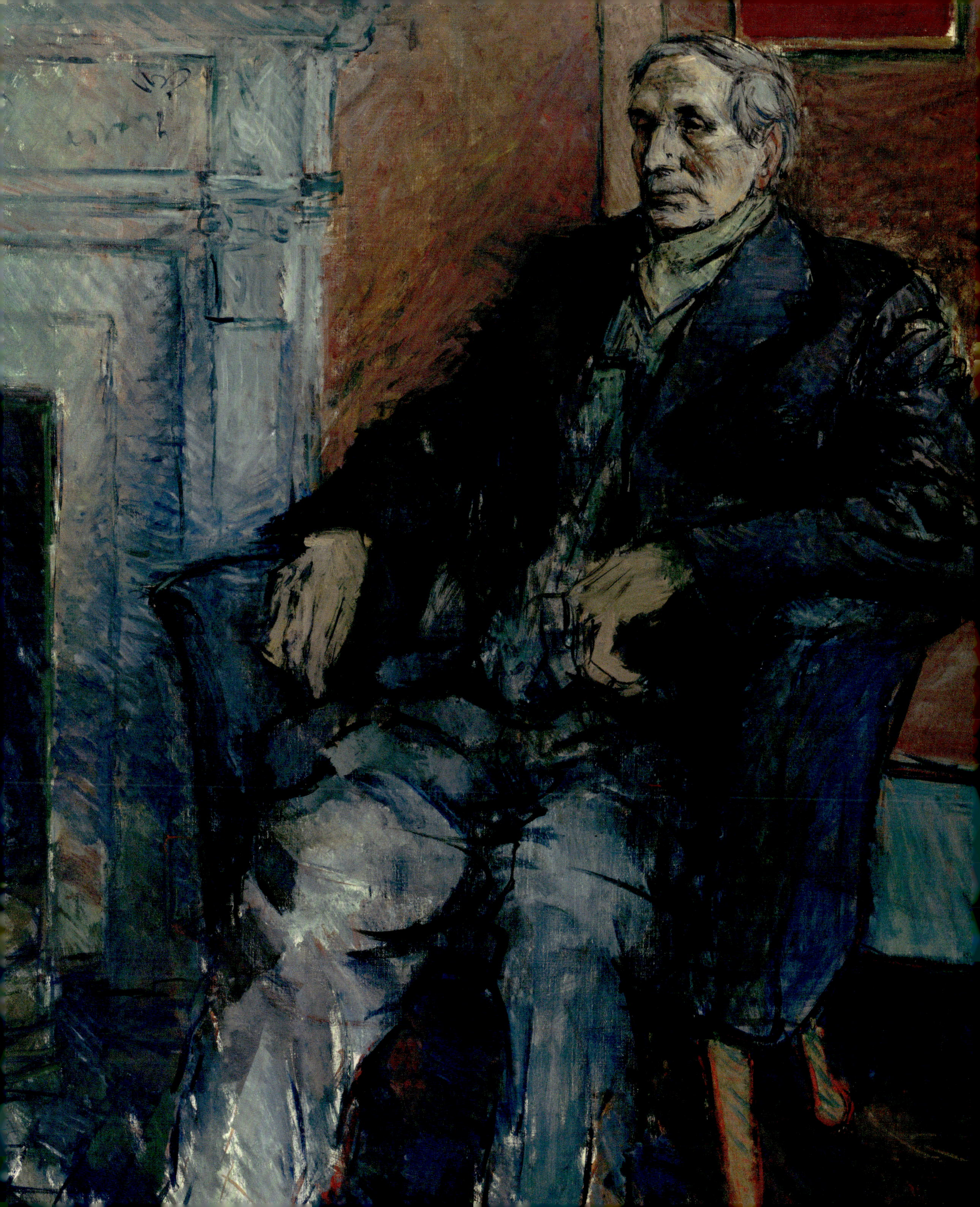

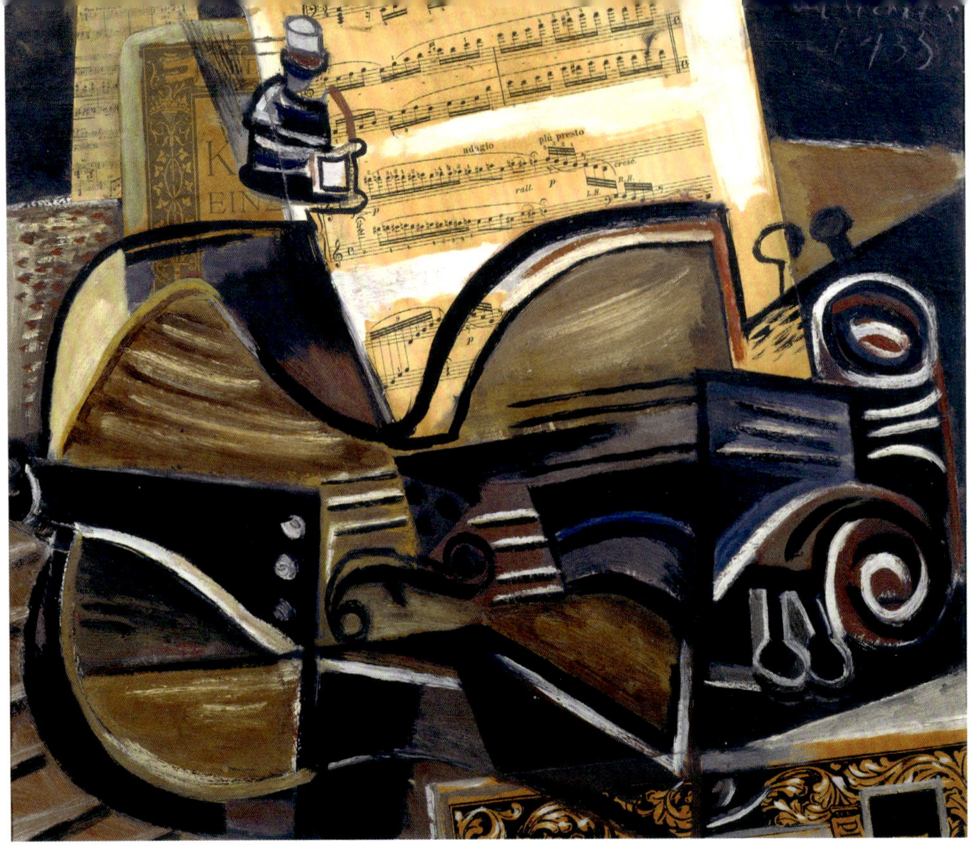

285 Ceri Richards, *Still Life with Music*, 1933

Mervyn Levy followed the same route with Dylan Thomas, Alfred Janes and the composer Daniel Jones. In old age, Levy reflected on his flight from life at home during the Depression: 'What we wanted to do was to go to London and if possible go to Paris and somehow or other to identify ourselves with the French and continental avant-garde.'[42] However, attitudes to what they left behind varied considerably. Walters and Griffiths, both from working-class backgrounds, retained the images and ideas formed in their early years and brought them to the fore in their painting.[43] On the other hand, Richards, like Levy, showed no interest in deploying images of the Depression, and turned to the continental radicals of the recent past for the direction his art would take. Nevertheless, one aspect of his early family life in Dunvant stayed with him. Richards's father, Thomas Coslett Richards, had been deeply involved in choral music in chapel, and was a founder of the Dunvant Male Choir. In 1955, two years before his father's death, Richards painted a portrait of him which, in its reversion to a realist aesthetic, untypical of his work at this time, expressed the contrast between the painter's origins and the cosmopolitan art world into which he moved.

Tom Richards had ensured that his children were taught music, and Ceri became an accomplished pianist. Music would remain a central feature of his life. In 1928 his first outing with the woman he would soon marry, Frances Clayton, was to hear Arnold Schoenberg conduct his *Gurrelieder* at Queen's

42 Peter Lord, interview with Mervyn Levy, London, 1995 (NLW Welsh Visual Culture Research Project). In a broadcast talk in 1961, in which he reviewed the history of Welsh music with an emphasis on the idea of national characteristics, Daniel Jones had almost nothing to say of the interwar years, apart from drawing attention to the work of the composer David Vaughan Thomas (Daniel Jones, *Music in Wales: An Aspect of the Relationship between Art and the People* (London, 1961), p. 27).

43 See Peter Lord, 'Biblical and Marxist rhetoric in the painting and literature of the Depression', in Meredith, Moment of Earth, pp 210-17.

Hall in London.[44] So also in his art. Developing rapidly in the 1930s as a Modernist, Richards included fragments of sheet music in his montages and relief constructions, and by 1940 his paintings had begun to present the image of a woman seated at a piano, a subject that he would develop in many mature works over the next decade. The theme, in which the piano keyboard was a constant feature, was sometimes expanded to include other musicians, producing pictures which resonated with a tradition of paintings of domestic music-making that extended back to the early eighteenth century, when it was represented by the double portrait of *Thomas and Mary Powell of Nanteos*. In the twentieth century, but still in the context of gentry patronage, much of Howard de Walden's encouragement of artists and musicians had taken place within the confines of his private life at Chirk Castle, in the company of London socialites. When the Irish painter John Lavery visited in 1929, the family group that he was commissioned to paint included the de Walden children at their music.[45]

44 Mel Gooding, *Ceri Richards* (Moffat, 2002), p. 18. Gooding noted that Frances sat next to Arnold Bennett, and that Delius was also present. Parry Jones sang Waldemar, but not to the satisfaction of the critic Kaikhosru Shapurji Sorabji: 'Mr Parry Jones worked hard at the also very difficult music of Waldemar. But imagination and sympathy with anything are not that gentleman's conspicuous qualities' (*The New Age*, 9 February 1928, p. 175).

45 For the difficulties encountered by Lavery in painting the picture, see Lady Howard de Walden, *Pages from My Life*, p. 155.

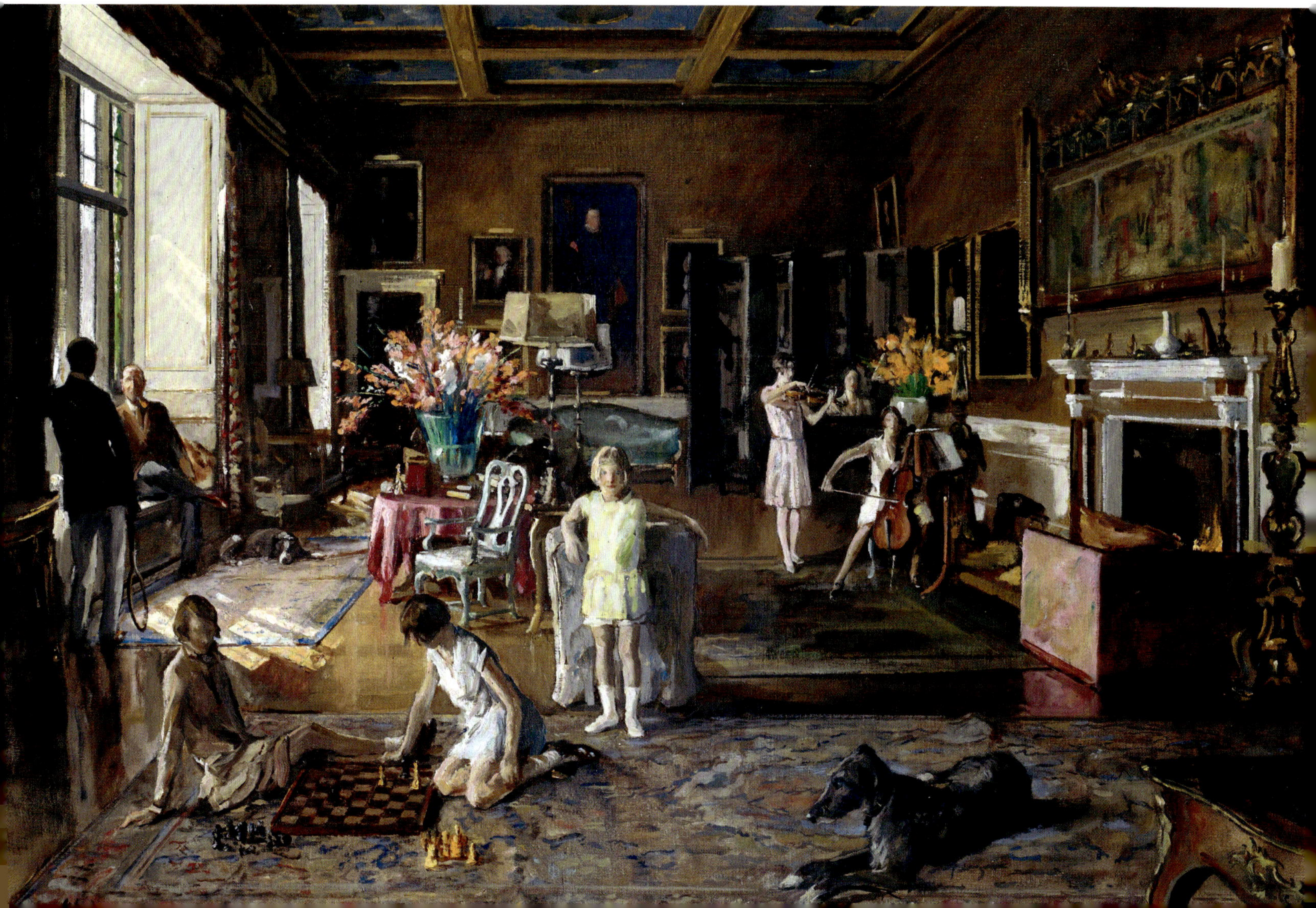

286 John Lavery, *The de Walden Family at Chirk Castle*, 1929

The theme would continue to appear in Welsh imagery through the second half of the twentieth century. Firmly rooted in the long tradition, Claudia Williams made pictures that emphasised the social interaction of chamber music. From an early age, music had been an important inspiration to Williams,[46] but the engagement of Richards with soundworlds was of a different order, since it extended well beyond the straightforward depiction of performance. Daniel Jones wrote of Richards that 'His pianos are not like the lutes strummed by Italian angels or Dutch gentlemen, ceremonial or homely adjuncts':

> The forms derived from them dominate the whole like principal actors in a play; the reference to music may be oblique, but the artist evidently means to stress it by giving these forms so much importance.

46 Robert Meyrick and Harry Hauser, *Claudia Williams. An Intimate Acquaintance* (Bristol, 2013), p. 24.

47 Daniel Jones, 'Ceri Richards', article for the catalogue of the opening exhibition of the Ceri Richards Gallery, Taliesin Arts Centre, UCW, Swansea, [1984] (NLW, Daniel Jones Archive, File CC29).

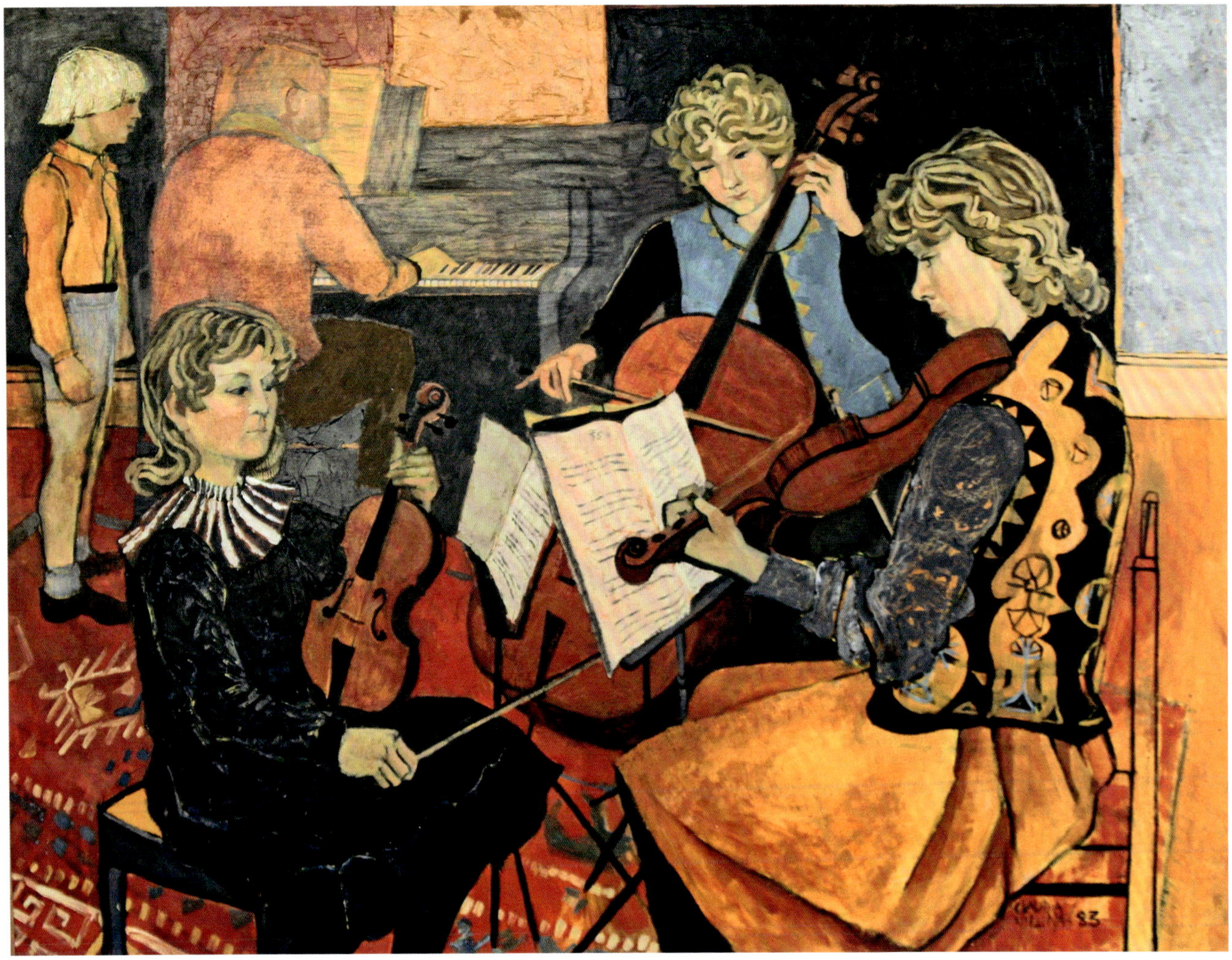

287 Claudia Williams, *The Music Lesson: Tirion, Eira, Tanwen and Ceinwen*, 1983

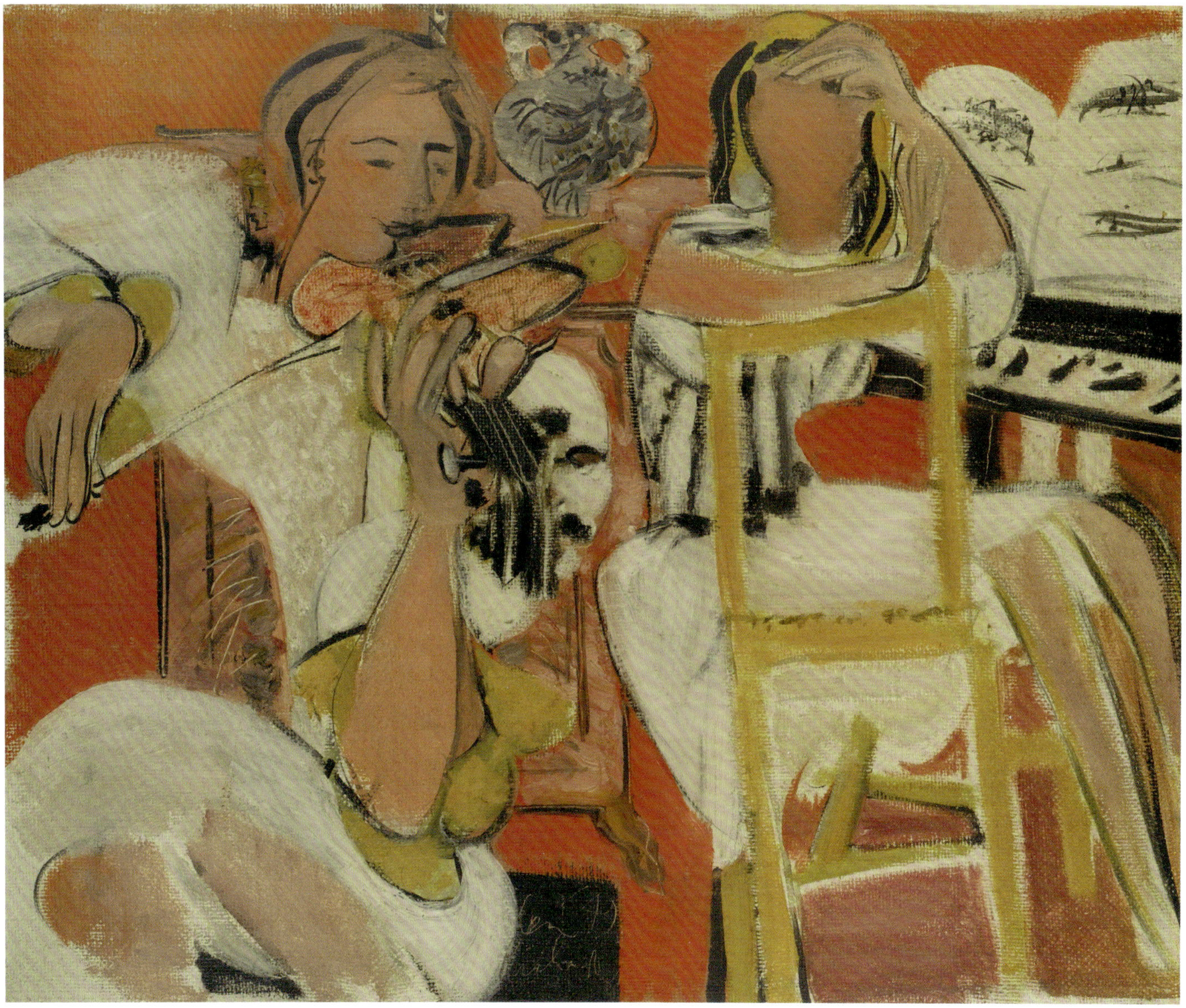

288 Ceri Richards, *Two Musicians*, 1949

> The group 'Interiors with Piano and Pianist' adds another ingredient, the forms suggested by actual performance: the rapid movement of the fingers over the keyboard, the attentive posture of the player, the pages of music, which are by no means static, but have been or are about to be turned over. The rhythm of the performance is transformed into a visual rhythm that overflows the closed area of the picture with vitality.[47]

In his later works, notably the long series on the theme of *La Cathédrale engloutie* that parallels the prelude for piano written by Debussy in 1910, Richards sought to create an experience equivalent to that of music, which he understood as having the same structural and spiritual essence as painting. The pictures, like Debussy's composition, evoke the mysterious sounds emanating from the submerged cathedral of Ys, off the coast of Brittany. Of these pictures, the critic Norbert Lynton aptly remarked that 'Here music, so often a guest in Richards's paintings, becomes the subject itself.'[48]

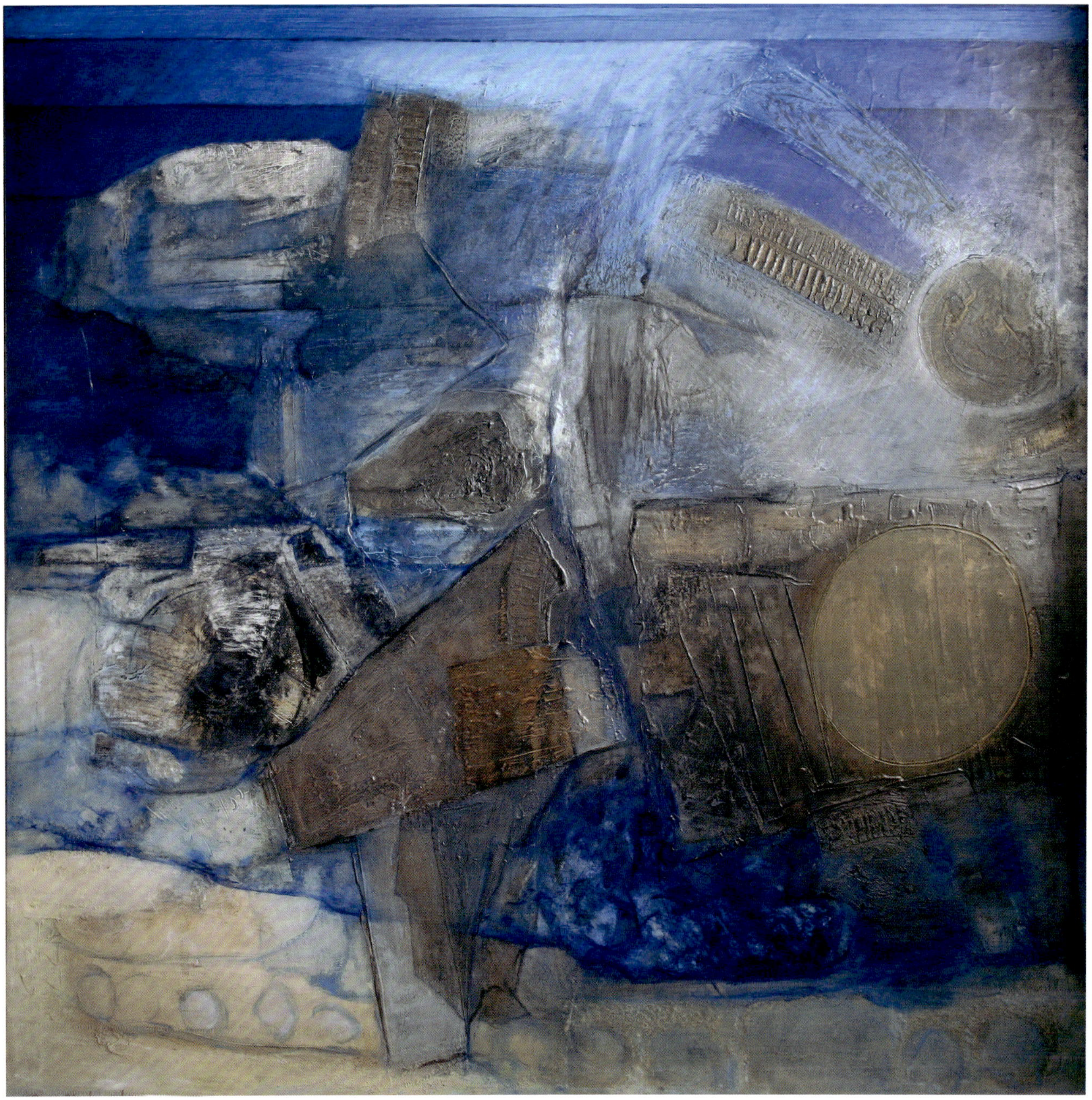

289 Ceri Richards, *La Cathédrale engloutie III*, 1960

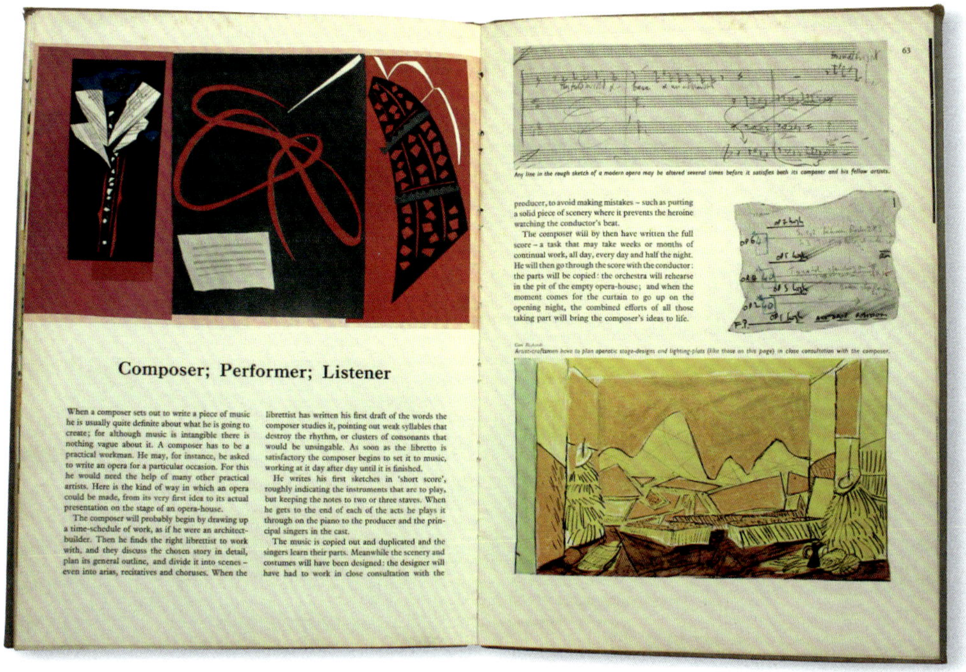

63

Composer; Performer; Listener

When a composer sets out to write a piece of music he is usually quite definite about what he is going to create; for although music is intangible there is nothing vague about it. A composer has to be a practical workman. He may, for instance, be asked to write an opera for a particular occasion. For this he would need the help of many other practical artists. Here is the kind of way in which an opera could be made, from its very first idea to its actual presentation on the stage of an opera-house.

The composer will probably begin by drawing up a time-schedule of work, as if he were an architect-builder. Then he finds the right librettist to work with, and they discuss the chosen story in detail, plan its general outline, and divide it into scenes – even into arias, recitatives and choruses. When the librettist has written his first draft of the words the composer studies it, pointing out weak syllables that destroy the rhythm, or clusters of consonants that would be unsingable. As soon as the libretto is satisfactory the composer begins to set it to music, working at it day after day until it is finished.

He writes his first sketches in 'short score', roughly indicating the instruments that are to play, but keeping the notes to two or three staves. When he gets to the end of each of the acts he plays it through on the piano to the producer and the principal singers in the cast.

The music is copied out and duplicated and the singers learn their parts. Meanwhile the scenery and costumes will have been designed: the designer will have had to work in close consultation with the

Any line in the rough sketch of a modern opera may be altered several times before it satisfies both its composer and his fellow artists.

producer, to avoid making mistakes – such as putting a solid piece of scenery where it prevents the heroine watching the conductor's beat.

The composer will by then have written the full score – a task that may take weeks or months of continual work, all day, every day and half the night. He will then go through the score with the conductor: the parts will be copied: the orchestra will rehearse in the pit of the empty opera-house; and when the moment comes for the curtain to go up on the opening night, the combined efforts of all those taking part will bring the composer's ideas to life.

Artist-craftsmen have to plan operatic stage-designs and lighting-plots (like those on this page) in close consultation with the composer.

290 Ceri Richards, illustrations for Benjamin Britten and Imogen Holst, *The Story of Music*, 1958

Richards also collaborated with musicians, notably at the Aldeburgh Festival where, in 1956, he designed Lennox Berkeley's opera *Ruth*, and in 1958, Benjamin Britten's *Noye's Fludde*. His cooperation with Britten and his assistant Imogen Holst would reach a wider audience in that year, with the publication of a book written jointly by them that was designed to introduce the subject of music to young readers. Britten wrote about his attitude to the illustration of *The Story of Music*:

> The other conclusion we have come to is to do with the visual side of the book; it is clear that this aspect is as important as the reading matter, therefore the collaboration between the artist and writers should be as close as possible. In the past I have always worked in opera, ballet, straight stage and film with artists in whom I have complete confidence … One person we have in mind is Ceri Richards, whom I gather worked for many years for an advertising firm, is an artist whom we both admire enormously, and happens to be a first-class amateur musician; he also happens to be extremely nice and easy to work with.[49]

Each chapter of the text opens with an image expressive of the subject matter, created by Richards originally as collage. As with much of the painter's output in this period, forms that evoke the observed realities of an auditorium, a keyboard,

48 *The Guardian*, 11 June 1965.

49 Letter to James Fisher, 8 February 1957, given in Philip Reed, Mervyn Cooke and Donald Mitchell (eds.), *Letters from a Life: The Selected Letters of Benjamin Britten: Volume Four 1952–1957* (Woodbridge, 2008), pp. 510–11. Britten's association with Richards lasted until the end of the painter's life. He accompanied the singing of Peter Pears at the memorial service for Richards in 1971.

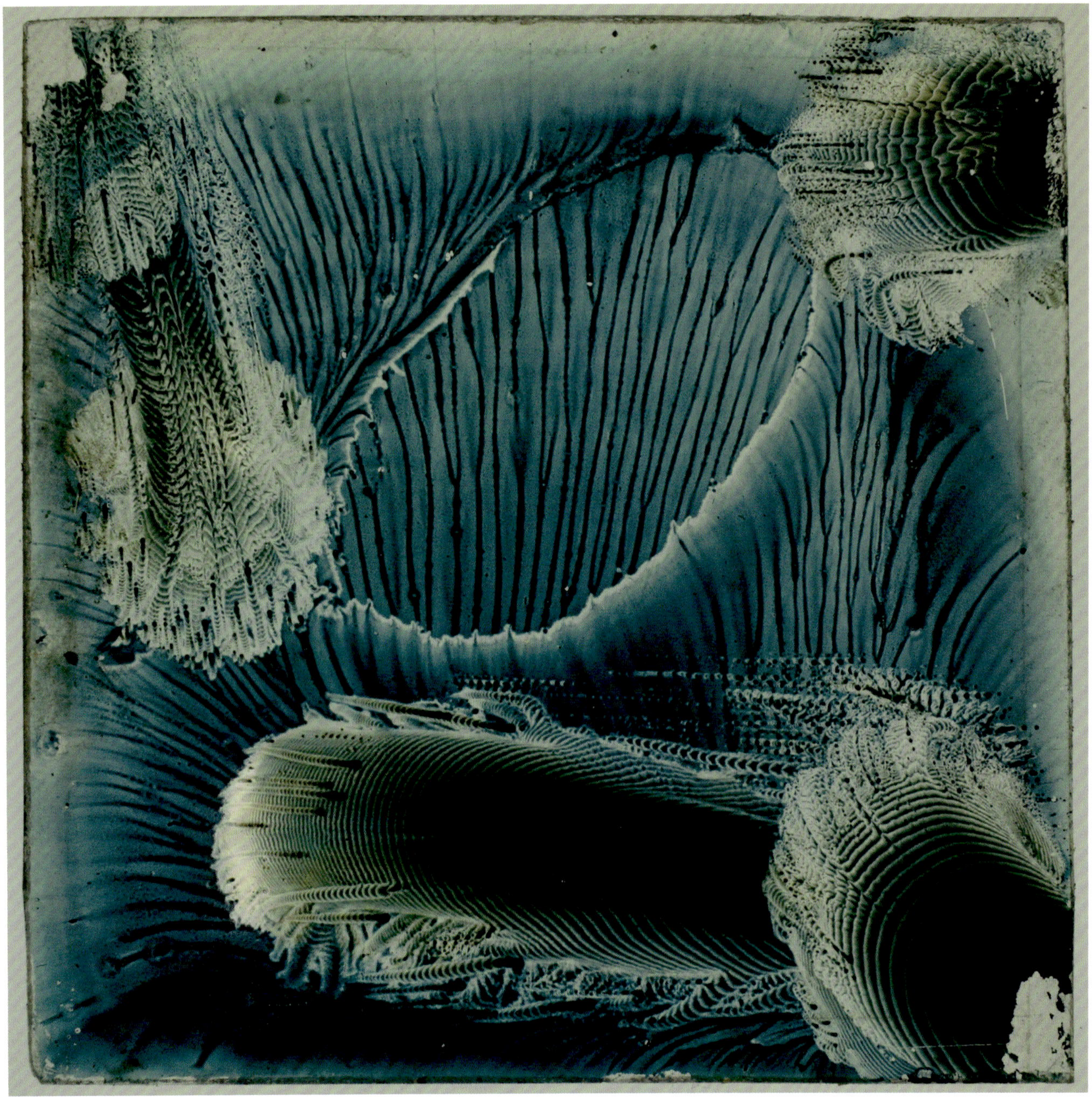

291 Margaret Watts Hughes, *Square Voice Figure*, c.1896

or sheet music, are combined with non-figurative elements that suggest rhythm or melody. Although he was probably unaware of them, Richards's images in which he was attempting to create visual resonances of the auditory experience reflected the remarkable 'voice figures' first created by Margaret Watts Hughes in experiments carried out in 1885. Watts Hughes developed an instrument that she called an Eidophone, which created visual representations of her soprano singing voice by means of a vibrating membrane.[50]

As had been the case with Ivor Novello, little critical comment linked Ceri Richards's early career interest in music to his Welsh background. He was absorbed into an internationalist art world unconcerned with issues of personal cultural identity. However, during the Second World War, when Richards returned from London to teach in Cardiff, he became involved with the work of Dylan Thomas, initially reconceiving the imagery of the poem 'The force that through the green fuse drives the flower', as he had done with Debussy's 'La Cathédrale engloutie'. Subsequently, in 1952, Richards inscribed the painting *Afal Du Brogwyr* with the words 'Gwrogaeth i Dylan Thomas' – 'Homage to Dylan Thomas'. The picture came to be regarded as among his major works, and Mel Gooding, biographer of Richards, described it as:

> … a kind of homecoming, a re-affirmation of the importance of his Welsh roots, of his affinities with the two greatest Welsh poets of his time [Thomas and Vernon Watkins], of his fidelities to the most ancient sources of inspiration, to a landscape, to a poetry of nature and myth.[51]

The engagement of Richards with the work of Thomas stimulated a reawakening among some critics of a dormant mythic notion of Welshness in visual art, and its relationship with literature and music. One of Richards's early patrons, the shipowner Colin Anderson, wrote:

> As the strange mystery of his Christian name proclaims, Ceri Richards is not English. The name Ceri … proclaims him of some other race – and, as it happens, of a race far surpassing the Anglo-Saxon in its readiness to overflow with eloquence. He is Welsh; he is a Celt; and his work shows this, once one knows where to look for the signs. In it there is a strain of exuberant, fluid self-expression that is not like the work of the other painters of his generation in this country.[52]

In 1958, in the course of writing a book about Dylan Thomas, the Italian poet and writer Roberto Sanesi visited Wales for the first time. He met Vernon Watkins, Daniel Jones and Ceri Richards, and engaged with ideas of Celticity and Welshness that he applied later in writing about the painter's graphic work. Discussing the six lithographs of the *Hammerklavier Suite with Variations*, he suggested that they marked a period when Richards was renewing his interest in relating music and visual imagery through the work of Beethoven and Debussy:

50 Mrs Watts Hughes, *Voice Figures* (London, 1891). Margaret Watts Hughes (1842–1907) is also widely referred to as Megan Watts Hughes.

51 Gooding, *Ceri Richards*, p. 116. Richards met Thomas only once, shortly before the poet's departure for the United States, where he died.

52 NLW MS 23007E, f. 15, typescript 'Foreword' to a Richards exhibition, dated 30 November 1953. Colin Anderson had known Richards for nearly twenty years. In 1935 he had commissioned him to design and illustrate the publicity brochure for his new passenger liner, RMS *Orion*. Two years later, Richards painted a mural for *Oriades II*, entitled *'Conversation Piece' – Neptune*. Frances Richards was commissioned to create a textile for a first-class cabin on the ship.

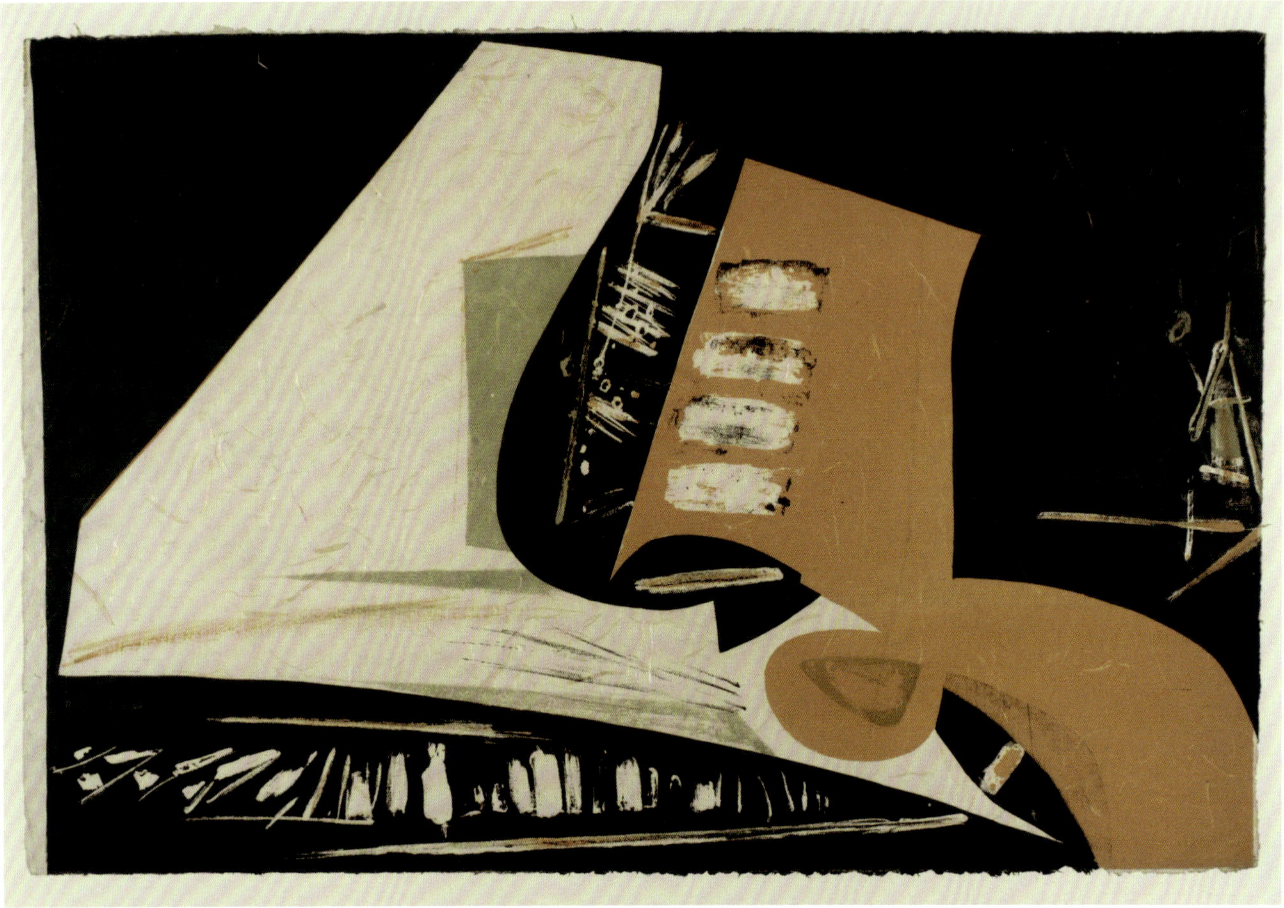

292 Ceri Richards, trial proof for *Hammerklavier*, 1959

53 Roberto Sanesi, *The Graphic Works of Ceri Richards* (Milan, 1973), p. 71.

54 Ibid., pp. 5-6. In the same vein, see also Richard Burns, *Keys to Transformation: Ceri Richards and Dylan Thomas* (London, 1981). Burns was the translator of Sanesi's volume.

55 For the evolution of the character of Polly Garter, and some observations on the role of song in the construct, see 'Conceiving Polly Garter', in David N. Thomas (ed.), *Dylan Remembered, Vol. 2, 1935-1953* (Bridgend, 2004), pp. 313-22.

> The group may therefore be considered as one of the first finalized realisations of his visual researches into the various possible associations both within the legend [of Ys] itself and its correspondences with the pervading tendency of the Welsh sensibility towards mystical metamorphosis – all of which are blended with his own personal understanding as a painter of the perennial flux of procreation, death and resurrection.[53]

Sanesi had opened his discussion of the work of Richards by quoting the opinions of Matthew Arnold on the Celtic spirit. His notions of historic visual culture in Wales now seem equally archaic, but closely reflected the received wisdom of his times about national deficiencies in the field which, clearly, he absorbed from those establishment figures that he met in the 1960s. Sanesi proposed that Richards was one of the few 'exceptions that prove the rule':

But wherever one finds the artist's perception and treatment of natural data reflected and transcended in sudden strange outbursts of spiritual or religious meditation, wherever an awareness of the mysteries of natural metamorphosis is seen to give rise to a constantly drawn out mystical tension and express itself in terms of a restless lyricism, there is bound to have been some degree of Celtic infiltration or influence. And these are the qualities that make the work of Ceri Richards stand out so sharply from that of his contemporaries.[54]

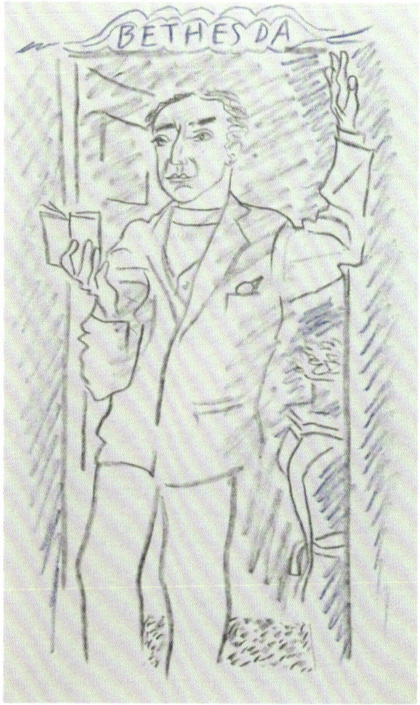

293 Ceri Richards, *The Revd Eli Jenkins*, c.1971

Much later, in 1972, but again mediated through the work of Dylan Thomas, Richards's posthumously published illustrations to *Under Milk Wood* reinforced the deep-rooted though conflicted network of associations that had created the national brand. Among the characters drawn by the artist was the Revd Eli Jenkins who, in the drama, eulogised the singing of Polly Garter with what has become the most celebrated and memorable of all its many iterations: 'Praise the Lord! We are a musical nation.'[55] The eulogy of the Revd Jenkins, delivered on the doorstep of Bethesda House, marked the high point in its evolution. The subversion of the trope of Welsh piety which lay beneath Thomas's conception of the Christian minister's celebration of the sexually promiscuous Polly Garter was lost in the deeper resonance of the phrase, towards which Talhaiarn and other precursors had edged for a hundred years.

LEGACY – LIVING KITSCH OR CREATIVE REDEPLOYMENT?

Near the end of his life, Ceri Richards had worked from the distance of voluntary exile on *Under Milk Wood*. The painter's becalmed engagement with Thomas's mildly ironic fantasy of Welshness both coincided and contrasted with a period of political reality manifested on the streets at home, for which the Investiture of the Prince of Wales at Caernarfon Castle in 1969 had recently been the focus. The official musical presence at the Investiture was provided by commissions given to Arthur Bliss, Daniel Jones, Alun Hoddinott, and Grace Williams, for whom Caernarfon had a personal resonance as the home of her ancestors.[56] However, the compositions of these four would prove ephemeral by comparison with the alternative commentary on the Investiture provided by Dafydd Iwan, who was emerging as a singer-songwriter through appearances on

56 Writing of herself in the third person for the official programme note to the event, Williams described her aspirations for the piece: 'The composer's thoughts had been concentrating on the rhythms and cadences of Welsh poetry and oratory, the medieval legends of the Mabinogion, and the atmosphere of Welsh castles – particularly that of Carnarvon (the home of her father's family). She wanted to pay tribute, as best she could, to a proud nation's ancient history, so full of contrasts; at times harsh and ruthless, at times rejoicing in spontaneous lyricism' (NLW, Grace Williams Music MS A18/6).

Welsh medium television, and among the politically conscious as a leading figure in the language protest movement.[57] In advance of the Investiture ceremony, his song 'Carlo' lampooned Charles, the prospective Prince of Wales, and the monarchy in general. Especially among the singer's contemporaries, it remains an aide-mémoire to the passionate feelings aroused by the event, and – with all the power of paradox, given its deployment of humour as a medium – to the violent deaths that were among its consequences.

'Carlo' rapidly became by far the most successful Welsh language song of its time, and aroused the indignation of loyalists. The editor of the *Caernarvon and Denbigh Herald* described it as 'a hymn of hate'.[58] Grace Williams appears to have been unaware that the Investiture would arouse such intense feelings when she accepted the commission to write her processional music, 'Castell Caernarfon'. She had been 'all for it & felt it was a marvellous opportunity to make the world familiar with our character, history, traditions.'[59] Between the completion of the work and its performance, the reality of the situation was brought home to her by the activities of the Free Wales Army, whom she thought 'not nice at all':[60]

> I feel so sad about the Free Wales Army – & even the Plaid's & the Urdd's anti-Investiture stand …
>
> It's all so petty & now when the world needs to unite more than at any time. I've often said that if we had an attack from another planet we'd unite instantaneously … It needs to be hammered home.

Clearly unaware of 'Carlo', she added: 'I almost wish someone would write a pop song about it!'[61]

In the immediate aftermath of the ceremony, Dafydd Iwan wrote a second song, 'Croeso Chwedeg Nain', though it was aimed in a significantly different direction. The title derived from the Wales Tourist Board's campaign, *Croeso '69*, to 'welcome the world' to Caernarfon for the event. The words of the song satirised the phenomenon of royalist Welsh loyalty that had been celebrated nearly thirty years earlier when the united male voices of a disintegrating community joined together to sing 'God Save the Queen' in the film of *How Green Was My Valley*:

57 E. Wyn James, 'Painting the world green: Dafydd Iwan and the Welsh protest ballad', *Folk Music Journal*, 8, 5 (2005), pp. 594-618.

58 Given in Craig Owen Jones, '"Songs of malice and spite"?: Wales, Prince Charles, and an anti-Investiture ballad of Dafydd Iwan', *Music & Politics*, 7, 2 (Summer 2013), quod.lib.umich.edu/m/mp/9460447.0007.203/--songs-of-malice-and-spite-wales-prince-charles-and-an-anti?rgn=main;view=fulltext.

59 Letter to Enid Parry, 23 May 1969, given in Graeme Cotterill, 'Music in the blood & Poetry in the Soul? National identity in the life and music of Grace Williams' (unpublished PhD thesis, Bangor University, 2012), p. 103.

60 Letter to Elizabeth Maconchy, 18 December 1968, given in Sophie Fuller and Jenny Doctor (eds.), *Music, Life, and Changing Times: Selected Correspondence between British Composers Elizabeth Maconchy and Grace Williams, 1927-77*, (London, 2019), vol. ii, p. 329.

61 Christmas card to Enid Parry, n.d. (Bangor University Archives, Enid Parry Papers, uncatalogued).

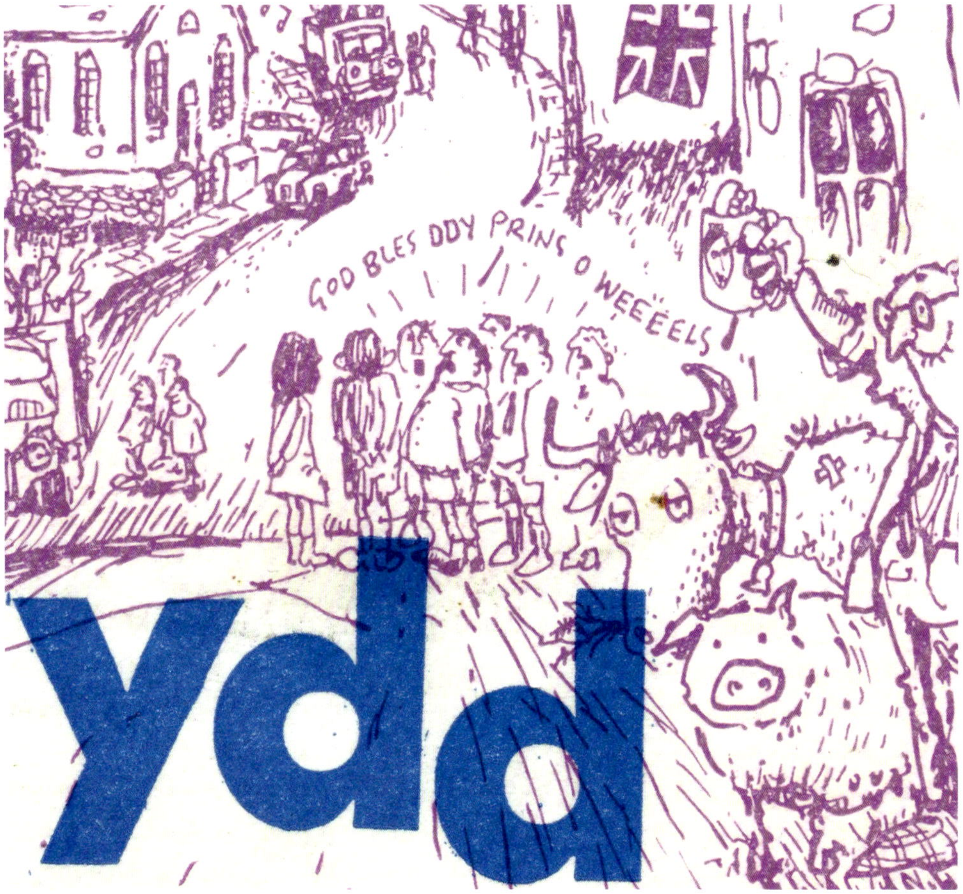

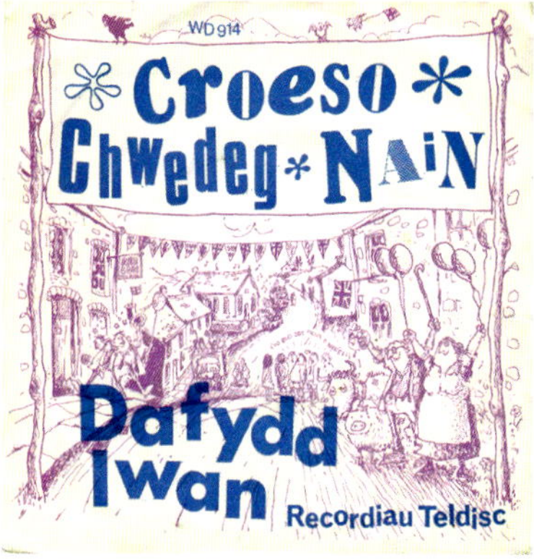

294 Elwyn Ioan, cover for Dafydd Iwan, *Croeso Chwedeg Nain*, 1969

Mae Mam wedi dysgu'r plant bach drwg sy' wedi mynd oddi ar y rêls,
I ganu mewn falsetto 'God Bless The Prince of Wales',
Mae'r ffys wedi hala Wili'n od – mae'n siarad hefo fe'i hun,
A Matilda yn y bathrwm yn dysgu 'God Save the Queen'.

[Mam's taught the bad little children who've gone off the rails,
To sing in falsetto 'God Bless the Prince of Wales',
The fuss has turned Willy odd – he's talking to himself,
And Matilda's in the bathroom learning 'God Save the Queen'.]

The record cover for 'Croeso Chwedeg Nain' was designed by the graphic artist Elwyn Ioan. Referencing many of the visual characteristics prominent in the films of the 1940s and '50s, he drew attention once again to the pervasive influence over the previous century of Brinley Richards's 'God Bless the Prince of Wales', cited by Dafydd Iwan in the song.

The period was marked not only by protest but by positive action that facilitated the work of creative artists in literature and music. Publishing in the Welsh language was stimulated by the establishment of Y Lolfa press in 1967, and in the year of the Investiture itself, Dafydd Iwan and Huw Jones established Sain, which would grow to dominate the Welsh record industry and provide opportunities for visual artists to work creatively alongside musicians in the design of covers and marketing material. The most striking common feature of the large number of covers that were produced over the succeeding three decades – the equivalent of the sheet music covers promoting the popular music of the nineteenth and earlier twentieth centuries – was the almost complete absence of conventional symbols of Welsh identity. The work of individual singers and songwriters including Meic Stevens, Geraint Jarman and Steve Eaves, and bands

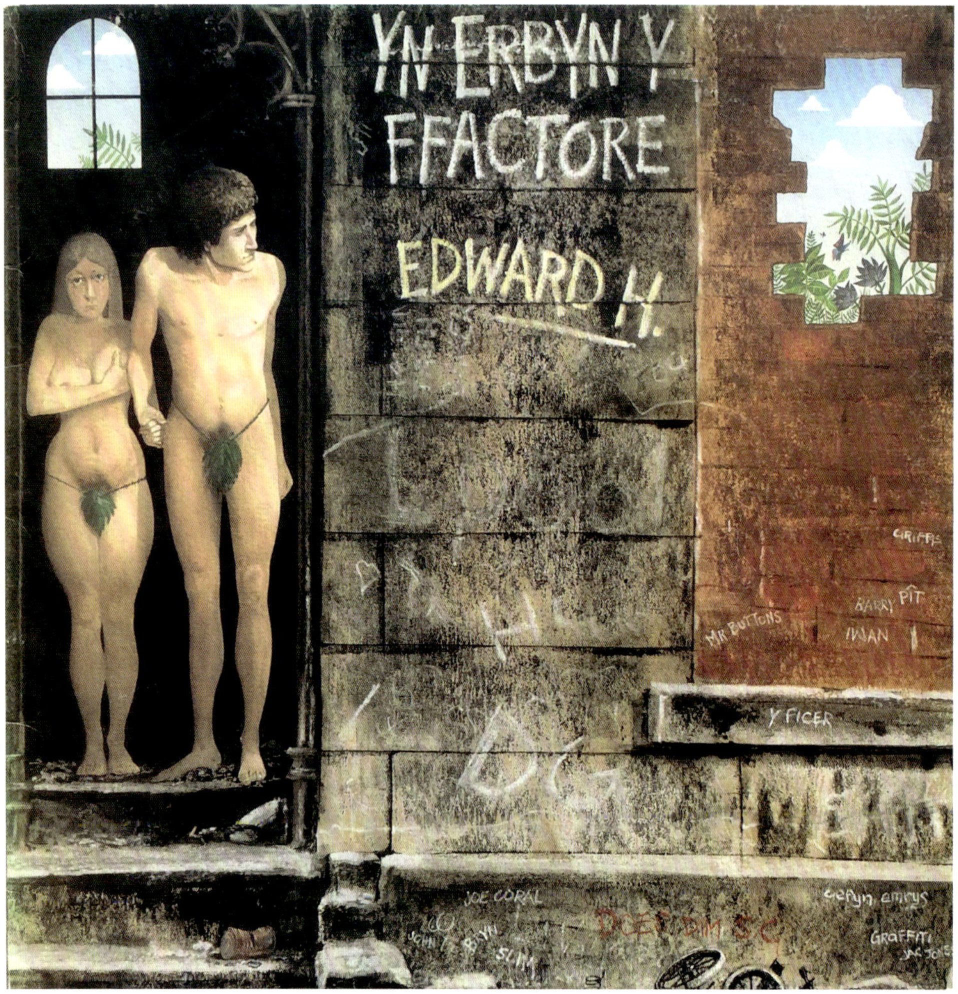

295 Jac Jones, cover for Edward H. Dafis, *Yn Erbyn y Ffactore*, 1979

62 Between 1958 and 1964, the baritone Ivor Emmanuel's television series *Gwlad y Gân* not only became popular in Wales, but also provided a springboard for a successful career in English-language film, musical theatre and recording. Among his recordings was *Land of Song*, advertised as 'Selections from the ITV network show from Wales'.

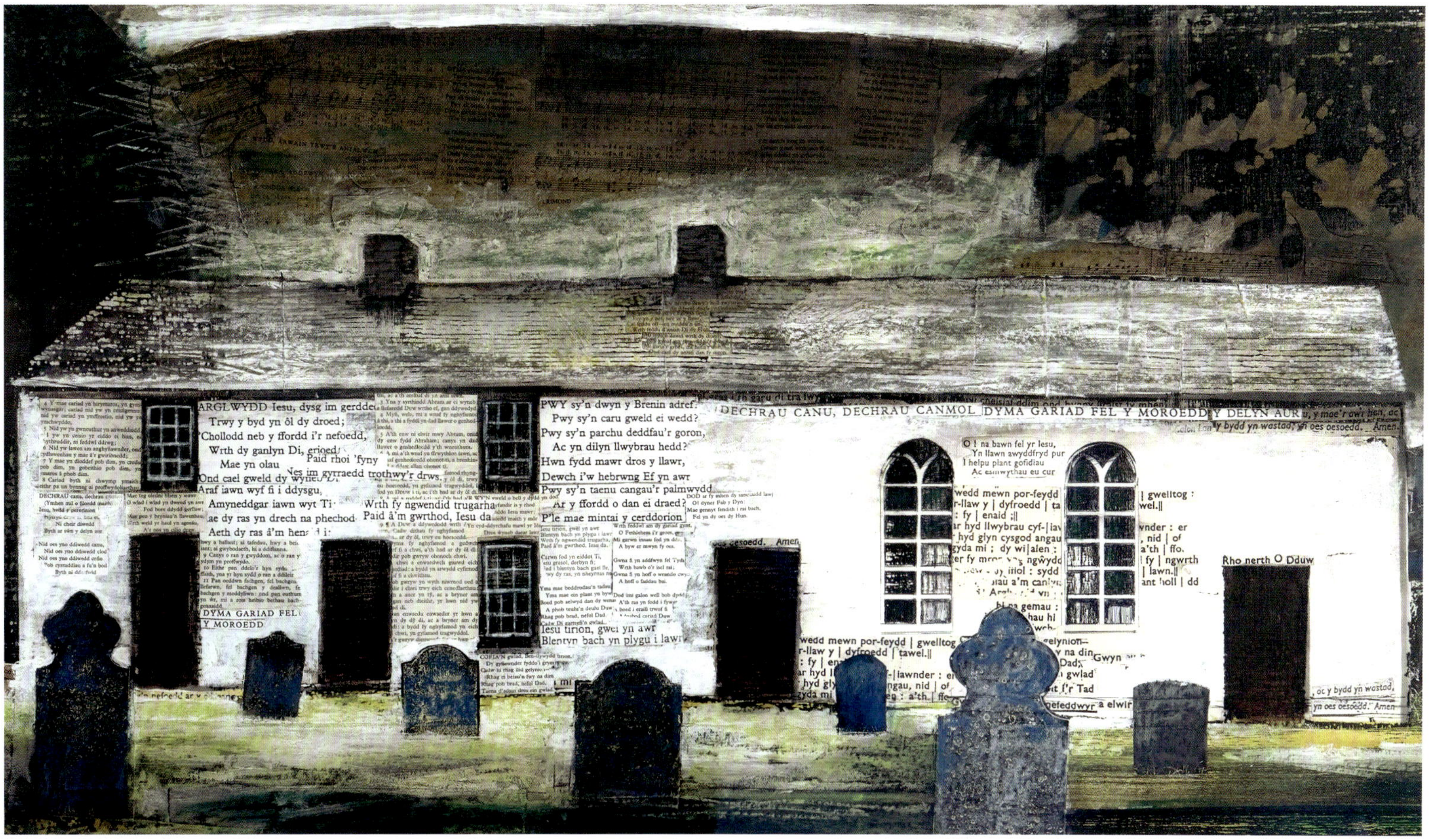

296 Ogwyn Davies, *Capel Soar y Mynydd*, 1990

such as Edward H. Dafis, ranged over many genres and expressed differing concerns, but the promotion of the myth of the 'Land of Song' was conspicuous by its absence among them. Their work addressed an audience markedly different in terms of its confidence and assertiveness from that which preceded it, and which had no use for a politically tainted brand. Although some visual artists, including Ogwyn Davies, did seek to deploy the brand positively within a politically radical oeuvre, artwork produced for musicians marketing their work beyond Wales remained locked into the conservative deployment of historical visual tropes. The most celebrated male voice choirs – including Pendyrus, Morriston and Tredegar – were particularly vulnerable to banal cover art and the repetition of 'Land of Song' branding in their promotional material.[62]

The legacy of five hundred years of imaging Welsh nationhood through music remained evident into the first decades of the twenty-first century. Presenting

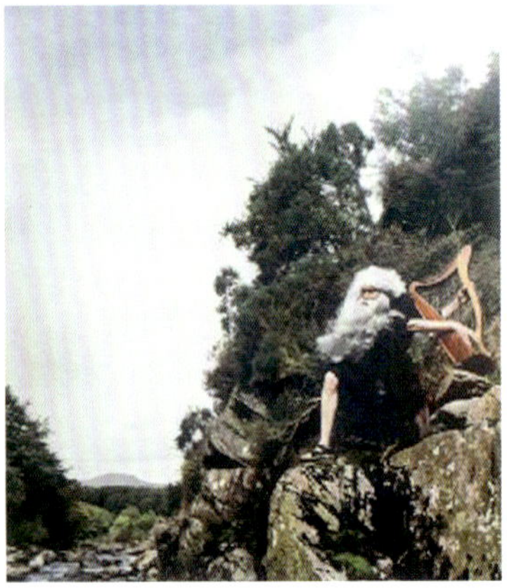

297 Bedwyr Williams, *Bard Attitude*, 2005

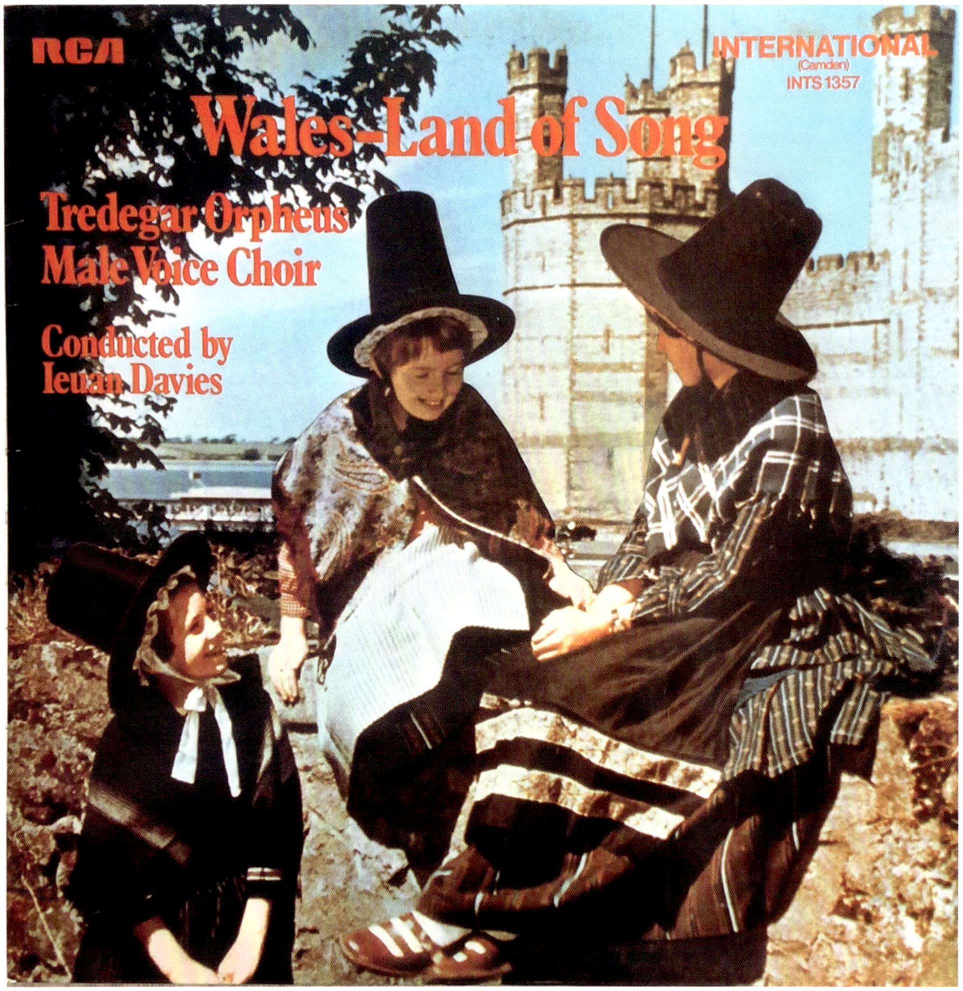

298 Unknown designer, cover for Tredegar Orpheus Male Voice Choir, *Wales - Land of Song*, 1972

themselves to the world as living kitsch, some internationally celebrated Welsh performers, aided by their marketing managers and publicists, continued to regard association with a Wales branded as the 'Land of Song' as a commercial asset. More sophisticated appreciations of the visual tropes of the tradition emerged in the form of work that engaged the conventions with irony. In 2005, Bedwyr Williams deployed Philippe de Loutherbourg's image, *The Bard*, as a vehicle for his spoken observations on contemporary society in a performance piece entitled *Bard Attitude*. Nevertheless, Williams chose to perpetuate his ephemeral performance in the form of photographic prints of himself in costume, staged in various locations. This manifestation was not without additional irony, in that the Government Art Collection was among the purchasers of what was initiated, presumably, as a critique of established societal and political norms. Williams's subversive parody thereby reverted to the status of the high-art object, treated with due reverence by the owner.

Reflecting the interest displayed by Ceri Richards in the visual exploitation of music as an aspect of a Welsh identity, artists who were able practitioners in both disciplines created historically resonant imagery. Coming from a primary training as a musician, Rhodri Davies co-operated internationally with other musicians and with visual artists especially in the field of improvisation, contributing from his particular identification with the Welsh harp tradition both as celebrant and iconoclast. In 2010, Davies created a perforated graphic score on the tercentenary of the birth of John Parry, Telynor Dall.

Approaching from the direction of a training in visual art, Christine Mills fused musical and visual tradition in a series of works. In a large-scale drawing that referenced both the pan-European high art tradition and the artist's origins in rural Wales, she sought to engage with fundamental cultural and environmental issues brought to the fore by the Coronavirus pandemic of 2020–22. *Cymerwch Sêt* – 'Take a Seat' – transposed Nicolas Poussin's painting *A Dance to the Music of Time* to a Welsh farm kitchen. Mills transformed Poussin's figure of Time, playing a lyre, into the harper of bardic tradition, derived ultimately, as we have seen, from the myth of the druids, among whose characteristic attributes were respect for nature and the gift of prophecy. However, the drawing suggests that something is amiss, because the triple harp is played by hands shielded by the protective blue gloves that became familiar during the pandemic.

299 Unknown photographer, *Shirley Bassey performing at the Welsh Assembly Concert*, 1999

300 Michael Olivers, *Owain Arwel Hughes at the Last Night of the Welsh Proms*, 2009

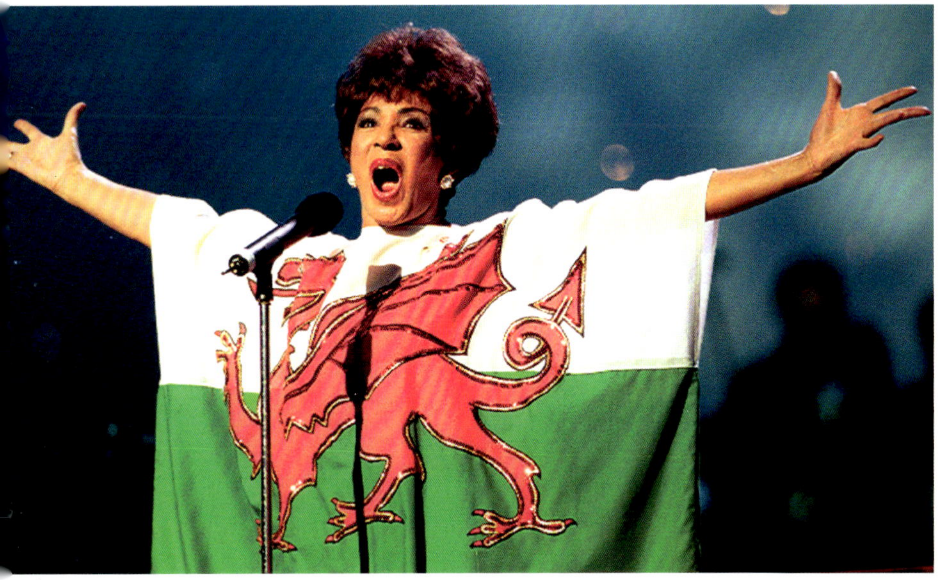

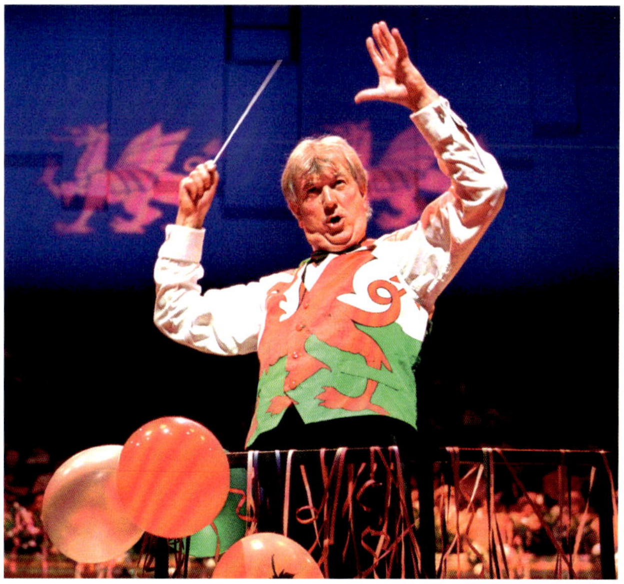

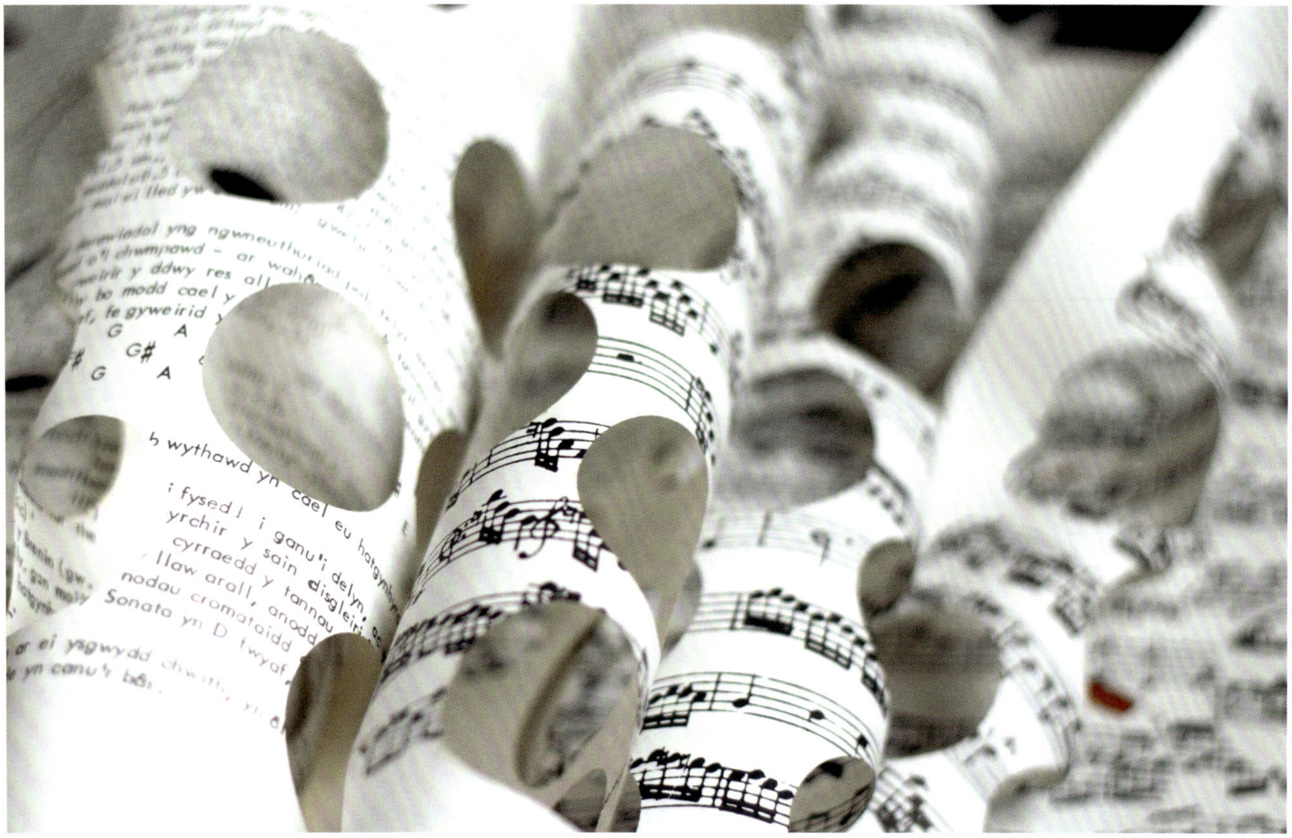

301 Rhodri Davies, *harp feedback (1710–2010)*, 2010

Poussin's dancers represent the cycle of nature through the seasons, moving from abundance to famine whilst both civilisation as a whole and individual human beings, who remain a part of nature, move from riches to poverty. Mills presents them on a plate – that is, in a way that their meaning should be perfectly obvious to the observer. What is required is simply to sit down and take notice – but the chairs are empty. The kitchen is lit by electric light bulbs, rather than by the sun god, Apollo. The arcing transfer of Apollo over the earth from dawn to dusk depicted in the Poussin painting is referenced in the drawing through the arc of the ceiling beams in the human habitation. The pandemic reveals the vulnerability of us all, and the symbols displayed by the putti – blowing bubbles and observing the sands of time – reinforce awareness of the transience of human existence.

The works of Christine Mills, Bedwyr Williams and Rhodri Davies exemplify how the potential that the visual tropes deployed over centuries to brand the Welsh nation through music, and particularly through the music of the harp, might evolve creatively, rather than ossify into vacuous stereotypes. They represent confident engagement with cultural and political issues of universal concern, emanating from within an understanding of an often conflicted national tradition. However, realising the power of images such as these is dependent on the continuing resonance of complex cultural references such as The Bard – resonances that no longer may be taken for granted. If the difficult project of pursuing cultural evolution without sacrificing historical identities is to be creatively undertaken, then understanding the construction of tradition in the key areas for Wales of music and the visual arts will remain profoundly important.

302 Christine Mills, *Cymerwch Sêt*, 2021

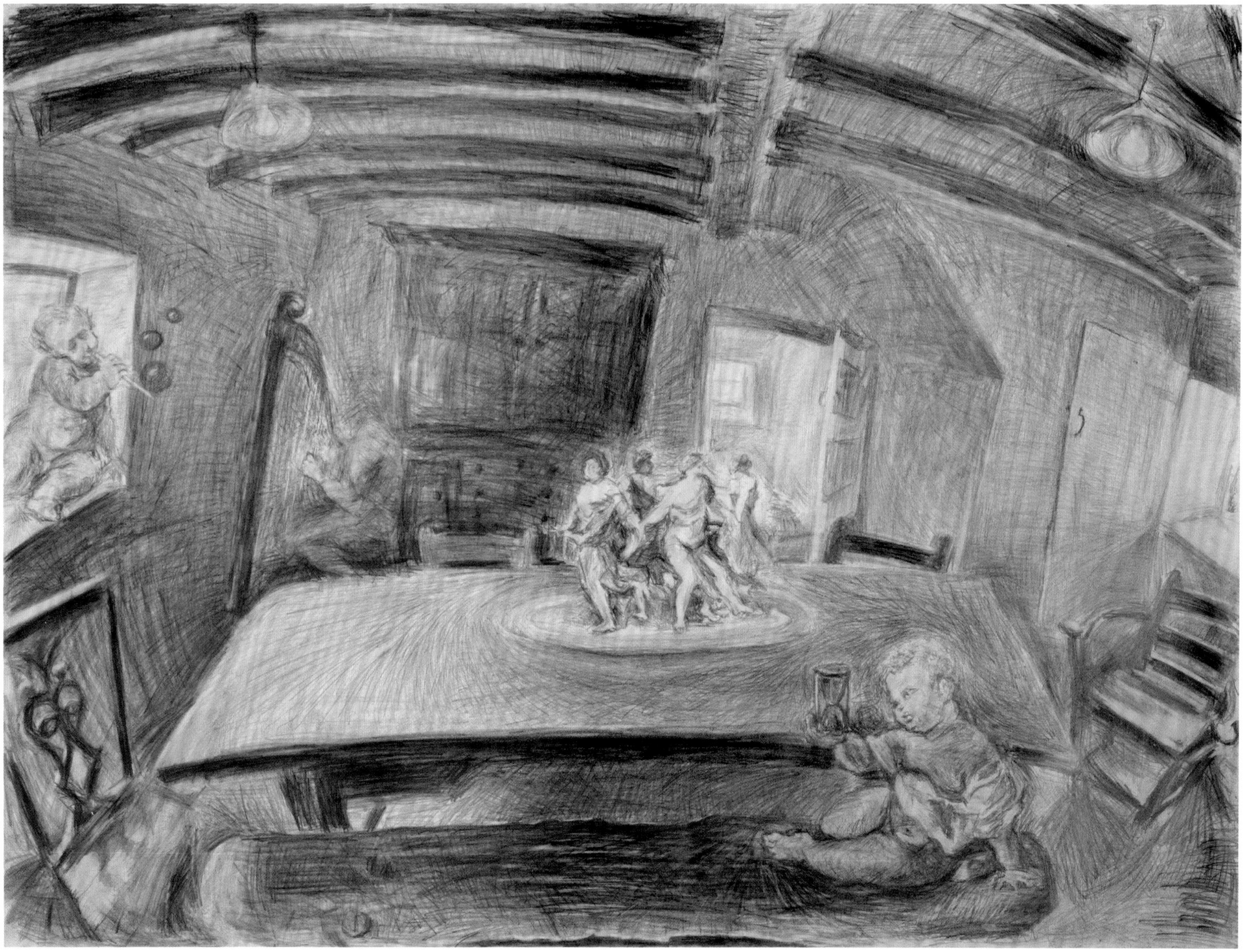

INDEX

General references are to pages, followed where appropriate by the ***number*** of each illustration in ***bold italics***.

ACKNOWLEDGEMENTS

20th Century Fox Film Corporation ©/Courtesy Everett Collection/ Alamy Stock Photo 277
Aberdeen City Council (Archives, Gallery & Museums Collection) 40
Amgueddfa Genedlaethol Cymru/National Museum of Wales 9, 22, 28, 36, 37, 38, 45, 47, 48, 50, 52, 75, 93, 105, 106, 113, 115, 121, 122, 152, 153, 154, 157, 161, 173, 228, 230, 241, 256 © The Estate of Harold Knight, 257, 260
Amoret Tanner/Alamy Stock Photo 198
Arts Council Collection, Southbank Centre, London 288 © Estate of Ceri Richards. All rights reserved, DACS/Artimage 2022
Bath in Time 107, 111
Bedwyr Williams © 297
Bibliothèque nationale de France, département Musique/ Europeana 62
Brecknock Museum 225
BTEU/AUSMUM/Alamy Stock Photo 30
Cambridge University, Faculty of Music 150
Cathedral of Saint Deiniol Bangor/Archives and Special Collections, Bangor University 4
Charles and Patricia Aithie, ffotograff 6, 7, 16, 17
Château de Versailles, Dist. RMN-Grand Palais/Christophe Fouin © 61
Chronicle/Alamy Stock Photo 55
Compton Verney/Bridgeman Images © 25
Cuillin Bantock/The Landmark Trust 254
Cyfarthfa Castle Museum & Art Gallery, Merthyr Tydfil 233, 291 UAL London College of Sound & Communications
Glynn Vivian Art Gallery, Swansea/Bridgeman Images 226, 271, 283 © Alfred Janes. All rights reserved 2022, 289 © Estate of Ceri Richards. All rights reserved DACS 2022
Gwasg Gregynog, University of Wales/Photo: © Andrew Baldwin 263
Ioan Lord © 8
Llandovery College 151, 156
Llyfrgell Genedlaethol Cymru/National Library of Wales 2, 13, 14, 19, 20, 23, 32, 42, 43, 46, 51, 56, 58, 68, 69, 71, 72, 80, 81, 82, 84, 87, 88, 89, 90, 91, 92, 94, 95, 96, 97, 100, 104, 116, 117, 118, 119, 120, 123, 125, 126, 127, 128, 129, 130, 133, 134, 135, 136, 137, 141, 142, 143, 144, 145, 146, 147, 148, 149, 155, 159, 160, 162, 163, 164, 165, 167, 168, 169, 170, 172, 174, 175, 176, 178, 179, 184, 187, 188, 189, 190, 191, 192, 193, 195, 196, 197, 204, 205, 206, 207, 208, 209, 210, 215, 222, 224, 227, 232, 238, 239, 248 © DACS 2022, 249, 250, 253, 258, 269, 272, 273, 276, 284 © Estate of Ceri Richards. All rights reserved, DACS 2022, 293 © Estate of Ceri Richards. All rights reserved, DACS 2022
Lord Mostyn/Mostyn Estates ©/Photo: © Shaun Evans 103
Mary Evans Picture Library 251
Michael Olivers/Alamy Stock Photo 300
Miles Wynn Cato Welsh Art 41
National Galleries Scotland/Creative Commons CC by NC © 26
National Portrait Gallery, London211
National Trust Images © 10, 15, 21 John Hammond, 177, 286 Private Collection
Oriel Môn Collection, reproduced by kind permission of the family of Harry Hughes Williams 268, 270
Peniarth Collection 124
Private Collections 24, 27 (descendant of the sitter, private collection, Wales), 29, 35 © NPL – DeA Picture Library/ Bridgeman Images, 49, 57, 63, 66, 70, 83, 85, 102, 110, 114, 131, 138, 139, 140, 158, 166, 180, 181, 182, 183, 185, 186, 199, 200, 201, 202, 203, 213, 214, 216, 217, 218, 219, 220, 221, 223, 236, 242, 243, 244, 246, 247, 252, 259, 261 © The Artist, 262 © The Artist, 264, 265, 266, 267, 278, 280, 281, 282, 287 © The Artist, 290 © Estate of Ceri Richards. All rights reserved, DACS, 294 © The Artist, 295 © The Artist, 296 © Estate of Ogwyn Davies, 298, 302 © The Artist/Photo: © Martin Crampin
Radnorshire Museum, Powys County Council 212
Rhodri Davies ©/Photo: © Daryl Feehely 301
Rhondda Cynon Taf Libraries 237
Royal Academy of Music, London/Bridgeman Images © 234
Royal Collection Trust/© Her Majesty Queen Elizabeth II 2022 73, 74, 109
Royal Commission on the Ancient and Historical Monuments of Wales. Crown Copyright 79
Sir John Soane's Museum, London 39 SM P42, 59 SM Adam 40/71, photograph by Ardon Bar-Hama
Storiel (Gwynedd Museum & Art Gallery), Bangor 132, 231
Tate Gallery 285 © Estate of Ceri Richards. All rights reserved, DACS 2022/Photo: Tate, 292 © Estate of Ceri Richards. All rights reserved, DACS 2022/Photo: Tate
TCD/Prod.DB/Alamy Stock Photo 274, 275
The Art Institute of Chicago/Creative Commons Zero 229 (Wirt D. Walker Collection)
The Board of Trinity College Dublin 64
The Bodleian Libraries, University of Oxford/Creative Commons Licence CC-BY-NC 4.0 101 MS M. Deneke Mendelssohn d. 8, f. 25
The British Library Board © 1 C.71.b.29, 5 Royal MS 17 F I, 12 Add MS 14905, 18 Royal MS 2 A XVI
The Devonshire Collections, Chatsworth/Reproduced by permission of Chatsworth Settlement Trustees/Bridgeman Images 11
The Lewis Walpole Library, Yale University 44
The New York Public Library 31 (Music Division), 60 (Wallach Division Picture Collection), 76 (Music Division)
The Orion Publishing Group Ltd 194
The Picture Art Collection/Alamy Stock Photo 171
The Society of Antiquaries of London 3
Trinity Mirror/Mirrorpix/Alamy Stock Photo 299
Trustees of the British Museum © 65, 77, 78, 86, 98
Victoria and Albert Museum, London © 53, 99, 255 © Agatha Walker
Victoria Art Gallery, Bath and North East Somerset Council © Victoria Art Gallery, Bath/Bridgeman Images112
Victoria University Library, Toronto 34
Yale Center for British Art 54, 67 (Paul Mellon Collection), 245 (Friends of British Art Fund)